Object-Oriented Technology

From Diagram to Code with Visual Paradigm for UML

Curtis HK Tsang
Clarence SW Lau
Ying K Leung

Singapore • Boston • Burr Ridge, IL • Dubuque, IA • Madison, WI • New York
San Francisco • St. Louis • Bangkok • Bogotá • Caracas • Kuala Lumpur
Lisbon • London • Madrid • Mexico City • Milan • Montreal • New Delhi
Santiago • Seoul • Sydney • Taipei • Toronto

The McGraw-Hill Companies

Object-Oriented Technology
From Diagram to Code with Visual Paradigm for UML

3 4 5 6 7 8 9 10 BJE 09 08 07 06 05

When ordering this title, use ISBN 007-124046-2

Printed in Singapore

Contents

Preface

Computer science and software engineering students nowadays have to take a subject such as object-oriented analysis and design or object-oriented software engineering as part of the undergraduate curriculum. However, despite the wide variety of books in the object-oriented technology area currently available in the market, there appears to be a lack of a comprehensive textbook which covers the entire software development process: from modeling and analysis to implementation, that is from theory to practice. Consequently students often have fragmented knowledge about this powerful technology, and worst still some even have very misconceived ideas about it.

This phenomenon may be attributed to a number of factors. First, the UML has a very rich set of notations; many students do not know how to use them systematically. Second, the Unified Process does not specify what models are required in different situations; indeed some models or even workflows may be optional. Third, books in the market do not provide a complete, practical coverage of the entire development life cycle, and students have difficulties in applying the theories learnt to practical situations. Fourth, there is not a universal method that can be applied to any type of problem. Students, or even practitioners, tend to blindly follow a "proven" methodology, only to be frustrated to find that it does not work well at all for their systems.

The most fundamental problem is that many students and practitioners do not know that there are three key elements in a software development method: process, notation and techniques and how they should be applied in a systematic way to reap the benefit of developing systems effectively and efficiently. Most books that discuss UML focus only on the notations and perhaps a bit about the Unified Process. A handful of books on UML cover software tools which only illustrate how the software development process can be automated. Individual software vendors typically talk about their own tools in their user manuals, and understandably they tend to be biased toward their own adopted approach. However, many products are not even compliant with the UML standards.

This book was primarily motivated by the need for a textbook that covers the entire software development life cycle to guide students and practitioners through the steps involved in building large-scale systems. By taking readers through various stages, from modeling and analysis stage to implementation, they will appreciate the power of the "from diagram to code" concept using the

Visual Paradigm for UML CASE tool. Each chapter includes a mini-case study which help readers understand how the knowledge can be applied in practice. We have also proposed the framework of view alignment techniques (VAT) which facilitates method customization for different types of applications. Based on the VAT framework, we then describe the Activity Analysis Approach, which is particularly suited for the development of interaction-intensive systems. In this book, the practical aspects of software development are illustrated through the use of VP-UML, an awarding-winning CASE tool.

This book is an important part of our dream to make the development of large-scale software systems a straightforward and easy task. We trust the proposed VAT framework would help practitioners and students create their own methodology to suit their own needs and take the frustration and fear out of system development.

This title features additional material which can be found at http://www.mcgraw-hill.com.sg/olc/tsang. Instructors will benefit from useful tools such as PowerPoint slides (password protected) and answers to exercises (password protected), while students can obtain source code and additional exercises and test questions.

Acknowledgments

This book is a result of more than two years of hard work by the authors, but without the support of the technical team of Visual Paradigm International, it would not have been possible. The encouragement of our colleagues in the Object Oriented Technology Centre at the Hong Kong Institute of Vocational Education was also crucial in seeing this project through; particularly, we are indebted to Angus Chan, Mercus Chan, Thomas Chan, Samson Fu, W.H. Kong, Martyn Leung, Maurice Leung Antony Ng, C.K. So, Andy Tsoi, Rain Wong and C.K. Wong. We would also like to thank Bruce Lo (University of Wisconsin), TH Tse (The University of Hong Kong), Edward Chan (City University of Hong Kong), Vivienne Farrell (Swinburne University of Technology), Michele Lanza (University of Bern), and Matthias Taulien (University of Karlsruhe), and Jacek Starzynski (Warsaw University of Technology) who painstakingly reviewed earlier drafts of the manuscripts and offered us a lot of valuable comments and suggestions. We appreciate the assistance of the McGraw-Hill team in speeding up the publication of this book. Finally, we dedicate this book to our families for their encouragement, emotional support and sacrifices, without which this project could not have been completed.

Curtis HK Tsang
Clarence SW Lau
Ying K Leung
Hong Kong

Chapter

1

Introduction

Overview

One of most important issues in any software project is that the system delivered is reliable and satisfies the client's requirements and expectations. Unfortunately, there are many well-documented reports that a large proportion of systems delivered simply sit on the shelf, never to be used. This problem is particularly acute for large systems or when large project teams are involved in the system development process.

Over the years, many software development methods have been proposed to alleviate this problem. However, there is a lack of appropriate techniques or heuristics to guide the designer in using them flexibly and tailoring them for different situations. Consequently, designers have tended to follow these development methods rigidly, resulting in a system which may not meet the requirements of the client.

This chapter highlights some of the common problems in software development and argues for the object-oriented approach for system analysis and design. Three components of a software development method will be described, together with the representation system, process, techniques and the CASE tool adopted in this book.

What You Will Learn

On completing the study of this chapter, you should be able to:

- describe the advantages of the object-oriented approach to software development
- discuss the roles of the three key components in software development

- describe at a high level what the Unified Modeling Language (UML), the Unified Process, View Alignment Techniques and Visual Paradigm for UML are
- understand the organization of this book

Software Engineering Approaches

Developing reliable software is a labor-intensive and expensive business. There have been countless documented reports of software project failures, so software development can be a high-risk venture. The rapid growth of the software industry over the past few decades has highlighted the need for disciplined approaches to developing large-scale software systems. Nowadays, developers adopt well-proven software engineering methodologies and sound project management practices to ensure that the software built not only meets the customer's requirements in terms of functionality but also that it is delivered on time and within budget.

Because software is invisible, it is inherently difficult to exhaustively identify bugs that exist in it. Indeed, totally bug-free, complex software systems can only be a dream of software developers, regardless of how much resource and effort they are prepared to put in. While we have to accept that such systems are highly unlikely to be totally bug-free, we must be mindful of the consequences of software failures. Nowadays, software systems are widely used to support the smooth-running of governments, commercial organizations and many aspects of our daily activities. Therefore, software system failures would invariably affect our lives and can potentially cause a lot of damage, even the loss of life. Quality is, therefore, a very important issue in the software industry. The most common way to address this quality issue is the adoption of well-proven processes for developing software systems.

Whilst quality issues are important, one of the greatest difficulties in developing large-scale software systems is the fact that, because such projects involve long development time, system requirements invariably change for a variety of reasons. Very often, at the start of the project, clients do not have a clear and concrete idea of what they want. Consequently, when the project is delivered, the client may realize that the system does not perform to expectations. Rapid technological change itself can be a problem too. If the project's development time is long, technological changes may take place many times during the development of the project. The project manager is often caught between having to change the system design to adopt the new technology with the consequence of blowing the budget and extending the development time, or building a totally irrelevant system that will end up on the shelf having never been used.

Another difficulty in developing large-scale systems is that the development typically involves a large team of professionals who are experts in their own fields, and as such, effective communication between team members is extremely important. Indeed, poor communication and human factor issues rather than technical problems have sometimes been cited as one major reason for project failure.

Software engineering is about the application of a systematic, disciplined, quantifiable approach to development, operation and maintenance of software. It is based on sound engineering concepts, and indeed many have likened the development of the software engineering discipline to that of the building construction industry where it has changed from a primarily craft-based activity to a refined industrial process.

Like other engineering disciplines, software engineers build models of the software system before carrying out the actual implementation. Modeling is a very important activity in software development since the software engineer usually spends a lot of time developing models with different levels of abstraction before the software system is finally designed and implemented. Models are an effective communication tool, especially in situations where detailed information is not required. For example, highly abstracted topological maps are commonly used to represent the train routes of a transportation system. In software systems, different stakeholders invariably need information about different aspects of the physical system. For example, a passenger needs to know the fares and the bus stop locations of a bus route. The bus driver needs information about the exact route of a particular bus service. The bus station manager needs to know the timetable of all the buses departing from and arriving at the bus terminus. To cater for the different needs of these stakeholders, different models would be created for them, as in the following:

A model for the passenger. It can be represented by a straight line with circles on it, showing the bus stop names and possibly the associated fares.

A model for the bus driver. It may be a simplified map showing the route covered by a bus service. Street names and the physical path will also be included to provide more details to the driver.

A model for the planner of bus routes. It may consist of a detailed road map with the path of the bus routes. The path of the each bus route is labeled and shown in different colors.

A model contains one or more views, with each view representing a specific aspect of the system. For example, the model for the passenger contains the fare view and the path view. The fare view provides fare information for various stops along a route, while the path view provides route information including the associated street names. Models based on different views of a system must be consistent. For example, the three-dimensional model of a building must be consistent with different elevations (models) of the same building. Furthermore, a model should be expressed using a suitable notation (language) that can be understood by the stakeholders. In the context of software development, a system can be adequately described by three orthogonal views:

- A functional view that covers the transformation of data within the software system
- A static view that covers the structure of the system, and the data associated with it
- A dynamic view that covers the sequence or procedure of a transaction in the software system

Broadly speaking, there are two general approaches to software development: the structured approach and the object-oriented approach. The former has been very fashionable since the 1970s as it was adequately supported by conventional procedural languages. With the advent of object-oriented programming languages such as C++ and Java since the 1990s, the object-oriented approach has gained increasing popularity over the years.

The two software development approaches can best be compared in terms of the way in which the various views of a system are modeled and their associated processes. The structured approach is centered on the system's functional views and uses different models at various stages of the development process. When development progresses from one stage to the next stage, the models in the current stage are transformed into the models of the next stage. There are three major weaknesses with the structured approach.

Firstly, because the structured approach centers on the system's functional views, when the functions of the system change, the analysis, the design models and the implementation of the system have to be changed substantially.

Secondly, in the structured approach, model transformation needs to take place whenever the models created in the early stages have altered as a result of changes in the requirements or the correction of previous mistakes. In the analysis stage, diagram flow diagrams (DFDs) are used to model the system as a set of functions with data flow between functions. In the design stage, the system is modeled as structure charts which consist of a hierarchy of functions. If the functions of the system have to be changed, it is necessary to go through and rework the whole analysis and design stages again, which involves significant time and effort.

Thirdly, the dynamic view is almost non-existent in the structured approach. DFDs consist of two views: the functional view and the static view. The use of graphical user interfaces and the increased complexity of the software system make the dynamic view increasingly important. The structure of the software modules is specified by the structure charts that are obtained from the transformation of the DFDs. However, many dynamic behaviors of the system cannot be deduced from data dependency between functions. Dynamic modeling is still difficult to achieve with the structured approach, even with the introduction of control flow diagrams (CFDs), because the system is not modeled properly in the dynamic view.

The above weaknesses of the structured approach have made it less cost-effective compared with the object-oriented approach. The object-oriented approach models a software system as a collection of collaborating objects. An object interacts with other objects through messages sent and received by it, manipulating the object's data in the process. The object-oriented approach makes it easier for the software engineer to develop consistent models of a software system because the same set of models are used throughout the whole development process. Hence, no effort or time will be wasted in transforming and updating models at different stages.

Furthermore, the structure of a system developed by the object-oriented approach is more stable than that by the structured approach. This is because changes to an object-oriented system are localized in the objects themselves and hence changes are easier to accomplish than in a system designed by the structured approach. Consequently, a software system developed by the object-oriented approach takes less effort to develop and maintain.

Visual Modeling

The human brain is capable of handling and processing only a limited amount of information at any one time. Models can help reduce complexity by creating an abstract hierarchical representation of the real-world system. Creating models through abstraction is a fundamental technique that is used to perceive the world, and in the context of developing a large-scale software system, it is an important first step.

When creating models, information is classified into hierarchies based upon rules that are carefully structured so that they are neither too general nor too restrictive. Despite the fact that modeling is such a natural process for humans, the development of an appropriate model for a software system is perhaps the most difficult aspect of software engineering. This is because there is often more than just one solution; different observers working independently are almost guaranteed to arrive at different models. It is, therefore, useful to develop a systematic process to determine the abstraction that should be applied at the various levels in order to derive a reasonably consistent model. If we follow a proven checklist of steps for producing a model, chances are we will not omit important features or critical requirements.

Visual modeling is about representing the system from a particular perspective using some standard graphical notations. For example, a system can be represented by a class diagram from the perspective of static structure. In a class diagram (see Figure 1.1), an object or a class (type of object) is represented by a rectangle, and relationships between the objects or classes by lines connecting objects or classes.

Figure 1.1. Examples of classes from real-life objects

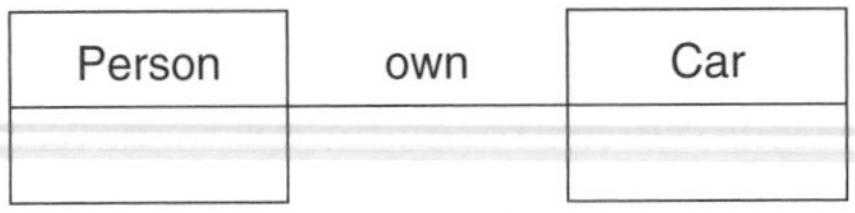

Visual modeling techniques have been widely used, especially in software development of large-scale systems. In the software development process, visual modeling can be applied to:

- capture business objects and logic
- analyze and design applications
- manage complexity
- define the software architecture
- model systems independent of the implementation language

As the object-oriented approach matured and became popular over the years, the Unified Modeling Language (UML), after much debate in the object-oriented fraternity in the early 1990s, was finally accepted as the visual modeling language to specify models of a system for software development. The UML covers all the commonly used models for developing systems using the object-oriented approach.

Software Development Methods

A software development method, according to Budgen (1994), primarily comprises three components: (i) a process, (ii) a representation system or a modeling notation and (iii) techniques, heuristics, steps or procedures (see Figure 1.2). A design process corresponds to a process of navigation from the problem space to the solution space. Throughout this process of navigation, the designer is presented with options where he or she has to make a selection or a decision. The techniques part of a development method assists the designer by providing some heuristics and guidance for the right selection. Typically, system artifacts are produced at the end of each task or activity in the process. The artifacts are represented by a recommended notation that is used to model both the structure of the initial problem (requirements) and the yet-to-be realized solution, with one or more viewpoints (models) and different levels of abstraction.

Figure 1.2. Three components of a method

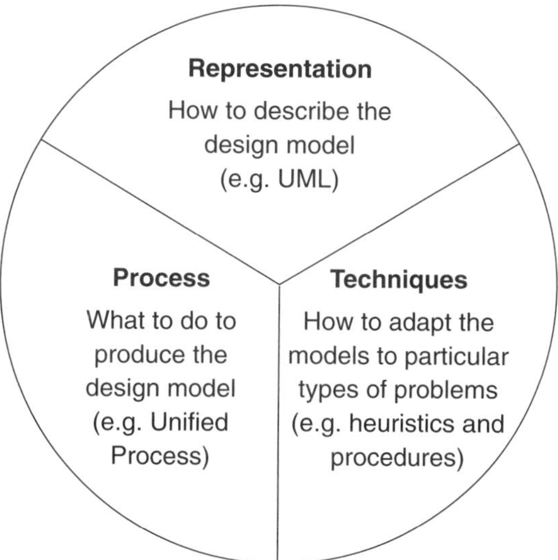

Role of Notation

A notation is used as a common language for the stakeholders of a system. In the context of software development, a notation helps the developer perform the following activities:

- capturing requirements of the system. The notation used should be understandable by the users and the developers.
- analyzing the system by developing suitable analysis models. Models are expressed in an appropriate notation so that the developer can quickly and easily extract information from them.

- developing the design of the system. Design models are developed and expressed in an appropriate notation that can be understood by the system designer and the programmer. The system designer may need to manipulate the analysis model and make design decisions in the process.
- implementing, testing and deploying of the system. Again, the artifacts of these activities are expressed in a suitable notation which can be understood by the system designer, the programmers and system testers.

In order to support the above activities, an ideal notation should:

- facilitate effective communication between team members and the client
- represent the user requirements unambiguously
- provide semantics that are rich enough to capture all important strategic and tactical decisions
- offer a logical framework for humans to reason the models
- facilitate the use of tools to automate at least part of the model building process

Role of Process

Developing a system without a well-planned procedure would result in prolonged development time, inflated cost or even incompletion of the project. Hence, it is important that developers, especially junior developers, follow some well-proven process or procedure to develop a system so that a usable system can be completed within a reasonable budget and time. However, there is no one single process suitable for all situations. Hence, the chosen process would only guide developers to apply suitable techniques in developing systems. At the same time, it should allow experienced developers to organize the development steps in their own way, thereby promoting creativity and innovation. Ideally, a process should offer the following features:

- A well-managed iterative and incremental life cycle to provide the necessary control without affecting creativity
- Embedded methods, procedures and heuristics for developers to carry out analysis, design and implementation for the whole software development life cycle (SDLC)
- A guide through the iterative and incremental development process for the solution of complex problems
- A comprehensive roadmap so that designers can walk through the flexible multiple pathways of the development process depending on the nature of the problem
- Identification of less obvious requirements based on what is already known or modeled

Role of Techniques

A software development process typically starts off with capturing the system requirements from the client and representing them using a suitable modeling notation such as the UML. As the modeling notation offers a rich set of models, one common problem encountered by many developers is that they do not know what models are required to completely specify the design and how these models can be created in the process.

The main purpose of the techniques part of a method is to provide a set of guidelines and heuristics to help the developer to systematically develop the required design models and implementation. The techniques part of a method should include the following:

- A set of guidelines to produce and verify the design against the original requirements and specifications.
- A set of heuristics for the designer to ensure consistency in the structure of a design and also among the design models. This is particularly important if the design is produced by a team of designers who will need to ensure that their models are consistent and coherent.
- A system to capture the essential features of the design so as to complement the designer's domain knowledge.

Representation, Process, Techniques and Tool

For the rest of this book, the UML is adopted as the representation system, the Unified Process as the process and the View Alignment Techniques for the techniques part of the method. The model building process will be demonstrated using a full feature UML CASE Tool called Visual Paradigm for UML. The following provides an overview of each of the elements.

Overview of UML

The late 1980s and early 1990s witnessed a plethora of object-oriented analysis and design methods proposed by various practitioners and researchers. UML was the end result of many debates and countless arguments. The UML notation is now accepted by the Object Management Group (OMG) as a standard way of representing object-oriented analysis and design models. It has quickly become the *de facto* standard for building object-oriented software. This notation combines the best of previous modeling techniques proposed by the three most respected academic in the object-oriented technology arena, J. Rumbaugh, G. Booch and, I. Jacobson, sometimes referred to as the Three Amigos.

The OMG specification states:

> *"The Unified Modeling Language (UML) is a graphical language for visualizing, specifying, constructing, and documenting the artifacts of a software-intensive system. The UML offers a standard way to write a system's blueprints, including conceptual things such as business processes and system functions as well as concrete things such as programming language statements, database schemas, and reusable software components."*

By adopting a standard notation, such as the UML, easy and effective communication can be achieved between fellow system developers and the domain experts (the users). It is much more precise to use a standard notation rather than other alternatives, such as natural language or code, to convey concepts. Natural language is too imprecise and becomes complicated when it comes to more complex concepts. Code, on the other hand, is precise but too detailed and involves a lot of effect to implement. A standard notation, such as the UML, conveys concepts with a certain amount of precision while providing important details as well.

One of the biggest challenges in system development is to build a system that meets the users' requirements at a reasonable cost (in terms of both time and money). Communication with domain experts is difficult because both domain experts and system developers use different technical jargon. UML provides models of different levels of abstraction to suit the needs of different stakeholders of the system. For example, the use case model can be used as a common language between the user and the system developer. The use case model provides a way to specify the functionality of a system by defining the observable results to the user.

Readers who are not familiar with UML should refer to Appendix B which provides a more detailed description of the UML notation.

Overview of the Unified Process

The Unified Process is a widely used software development process. In the Unified Process, a system is built incrementally through a number of iterations, in which the designer may perform requirements capturing, analysis, design, implementation and testing tasks. Feedback is sought from system users throughout the entire process. In early iterations, the designer often focuses more on requirements capturing and analysis, and in later iterations, on implementation and testing. In fact, the iterations are divided into four phases: inception, elaboration, construction and transition, each with a different focus.

The work activities of the Unified Process in the same subject area are categorized as a workflow. The design workflow, for example, includes all the activities associated with designing the system. Figure 1.3 illustrates some sample workflows and their relative efforts in different phases of the Unified Process. Since each phase has a specific emphasis or focus, the relative effort for a workflow changes over time (the horizontal axis) as system development progresses.

Figure 1.3. Sample workflows and their relative efforts over time

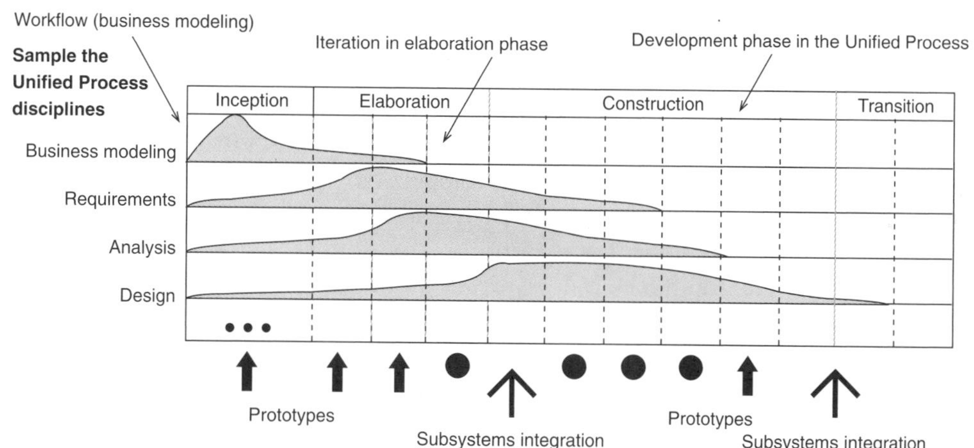

Overview of View Alignment Techniques

The key concept of the View Alignment Techniques (VATs) is based on the idea that models for different perspectives must contain some elements in common (linked elements). So we can simply start off with one model and generate a (partial) model by identifying and using the linked elements. By filling in (elaborating) the missing information in the partially completed model and identifying more linked elements, we can create other models for different perspectives. Through this incremental and iterative process, we can create all the models required. Having developed all models that describe the different perspectives of a system, we should be able to form a complete and consistent picture of the system by appropriately aligning these views (models). Therefore, not only do we ensure that the models are consistent, but we can also systematically identify the sequence in which the models should be developed. In other words, VATs can help designers to customize their method as they develop the system.

In Chapter 6, this concept will be explained in greater detail and the VATs will be applied to create a special development method that we call the Activity Analysis Approach (A^3). This approach is particularly suited for interaction-intensive systems such as typical business information systems.

Overview of Visual Paradigm for UML

CASE tools can significantly help developers to increase their productivity, particularly if they provide facilities which automate many model building procedures. Indeed, some CASE tools offer sophisticated facilities, such as diagram to code and code to diagram, maintaining real-time synchronization and consistency in both directions.

The visual modeling and CASE tool used throughout this book is called Visual Paradigm for UML (VP-UML). It is powerful and cross-platform yet easy to use, thus providing software developers with a convenient development platform to build applications efficiently and effectively. Its diagram-to-code and code-to-diagram capabilities enable developers to maintain real-time synchronization and hence reduce errors and development effort. VP-UML also facilitates excellent interoperability with other UML CASE tools and most of the leading integrated development environments (IDEs).

VP-UML, like most leading CASE tools, supports the following functions:

- Facilitate convenient model building whereby models of the system are easily developed and the editing and documentation tools provided are easy to use
- Serve as repository. Such that models can be saved and retrieved with ease
- Support navigation so that linkages between models can be maintained and traversed
- Generate documentation automatically for selected information of the software development project
- Facilitate project management so that project activities can be planned and managed with ease
- Facilitate configuration management and version control to handle documentation and components of different versions of the system
- Check model consistency
- Support model verification and validation
- Provide multi-user support so that multiple developers can work on the project simultaneously and coherently
- Generate code from models
- Reverse engineering whereby models are generated from code

- Provide integration with other tools, for example, the CASE tool can be integrated with domain specific systems or tools so as to accelerate the development process

VP-UML is not only compliant with UML and supports all UML diagrams, but it also offers numerous useful features to help the user to develop software systems throughout the complete software development life cycle. Its resource-centric user interface also provides the user with an intuitive, easy-to-learn environment, and at the same time, helps the user minimize errors when developing UML models.

Appendix A provides more information about the VP-UML CASE tool.

Organization of the Book

This book consists of seven chapters. This chapter serves to provide the reader with an overview of the contemporary software engineering approaches and identify the merits of the object-oriented approach for system development. The three key components (notation, process and techniques) for system development methods are discussed and the roles of these three components are detailed. Furthermore, an overview of the UML, the A^3 and VP-UML, which are used extensively in this book, is presented.

Chapters 2 to 4 discuss three modeling and analysis techniques (structural, use case and dynamic) and the use of UML diagrams to support them. Each of these chapters provides a systematic introduction to the fundamental concepts in UML and consists of primarily three parts: (1) a theory section, (2) a practical section that complements the theoretical concepts described in (1) highlighting the process and techniques covered, and (3) a hands-on section showing how the material in (2) can be effectively supported using the VP-UML CASE tool. A tricks and tips section is included in each of these three chapters to provide further insights into how these techniques can be applied in different situations.

Chapter 5 is concerned with implementation issues associated with transforming the UML diagrams developed for the system into code using Java. It also examines important issues in relation to the implementation of class diagrams using Java and relational database management systems.

Chapter 6 details a novel approach to software development called the View Alignment Framework (VAF). The VAF consists of a number of specific techniques, allowing the designer to explore a suitable procedure to model a system, maintain traceability between models and ensure model consistency. The VAF provides a means for the designer to customize a software development methodology to suit a particular situation. This concept is demonstrated by the proposed A^3, which provides excellent supplemental features missing in the Rational Unified Process.

Chapter 7, the final chapter, consists of a major case study illustrating how the A^3 can be applied to a real-life problem: the development of an electronic mail order system. The reader will be guided through the entire analysis and design process in order to appreciate the power of the software development method described.

The appendix at the end of the book consists of a concise User's Guide for the VP-UML CASE tool, that has been used throughout this book. This CASE tool is included in the CD-ROM accompanying this book. Users can practice on all the examples given in the book using this CASE tool.

Summary

Software developers use software development methods so that they can build reliable large-scale systems systematically and effectively.

These methods primarily consist of three key elements: a process, a representation system, and a set of techniques and heuristics.

In this book, the UML is adopted as the representation system, the Unified Process as the process and the View Alignment Techniques for the techniques part.

Modern CASE tools with sophisticated facilities are also available to assist developers to carry out analysis and visual modeling. The use of a modern CASE tool together with a development method will significantly increase the productivity of developers.

In this book, the process of system analysis and model building will be demonstrated using a powerful CASE tool, VP-UML.

Chapter

2

Structural Modeling and Analysis

Overview

Structural modeling is concerned with describing "things" in a system and how these things are related to each other. A "thing" can be an object, a class, an interface, a package or a subsystem, which is part of the system being developed. For example, a class diagram can be used to describe the objects and classes inside a system and the relationships between them. The software components of a system in a component diagram can be described by providing details as to how these software components are deployed in terms of computing resources, such as a workstation.

Structural modeling is a very important process because it is employed throughout the entire system development life cycle. At the early analysis stage, a structural model is developed to describe the objects identified from the problem domain. As time progresses, the structural model is refined and new ones created in the process. Early versions of a structural model are usually incomplete, and as such are refined iteratively and incrementally. System implementation commences only when the structural model contains sufficient details.

What You Will Learn

On completing the study of this chapter, you should be able to:

- describe and apply the fundamental object-oriented concepts
- use the standard Unified Modeling Language (UML) notation to represent classes and their properties

- model the structural aspects of problems with the class model
- perform domain analysis to develop domain class models

What Is an Object?

An object is a self-contained entity with well-defined characteristics (properties or attributes) and behaviors (operations). For example, the real-life environment consists of *objects* such as schools, students, teachers and courses which are related in one way or another. A student has a name and an address as its characteristics. Similarly, a subject has a title and a medium of instruction as its characteristics.

An object generally has many *states*, but it can only be in one state at a time. The state of an object is one of the possible conditions in which an object may exist. The state is represented by the values of the properties (attributes) of an object. In different states, an object may exhibit different *behaviors*. For example, in the awake state, a person may have behaviors such as standing, walking or running, while in the sleeping state, the person may have behaviors such as snoring or sleepwalking. For objects such as a human being or an automobile, a complete description of all the states of these objects can be very complex. Fortunately, when objects are used to model a system, we typically focus on all the possible states of the objects that are relevant only to and are within the scope of that system.

The behavior of an object relates to how an object acts and reacts. An object's behaviors are also known as *functions* or *methods*. The behavior is determined by a set of operations that the object can perform. For example, through the physical interface of the VCR system, functions like play, rewind and record can be performed, while simultaneously changing the state of the system.

Types of Objects

Physical and Conceptual Objects

Objects can be broadly classified as *physical* or *conceptual objects*, and they are things that we find around us in the real world. We interact with physical and conceptual objects all the time. In software development, real-life objects are naturally mapped onto objects of a software system.

Physical (tangible) objects are visible and touchable things such as a book, a bus, a computer or a Christmas tree. In an automated teller machine (ATM), the card reader and the receipt printer are examples of physical objects.

Conceptual objects are intangibles such as a bank account and a time schedule. Very often, conceptual objects are thought of as physical objects. For example, we would normally say we pay the mortgage (conceptual object) every month, instead of saying we pay the bankbook (where the money is deposited). We mix conceptual objects and physical objects all the time as they are well understood within the context. Some of these concepts may only be understood within a small society or even within a group of domain experts. The object designer, therefore, needs to talk to the domain experts to gain the necessary domain knowledge so that they can use the objects, concepts and terminologies that are well understood by the people working in that domain.

Domain and Implementation Objects

The beauty of object-orientation is that different software engineers are likely to identify similar sets of domain objects for the same area of application because of the natural mapping of real-world entities to objects. The objects identified from the real world are *domain objects*. Collectively, we call all objects which are not related to real-world entities as *implementation objects*. For example, bank accounts, tellers and customers are domain objects that we come across daily. On the other hand, the transaction log which provides information for error recovery is obviously an implementation object.

Domain objects tend to be more stable throughout the development life cycle as the latter is unlikely to incur a major change in the specification of the domain objects since these objects form the foundation (architecture) of a software system. On the other hand, implementation objects are more likely to change when the requirements are altered. For example, bank accounts, customers and banks are domain objects in an ATM system. Most software designers can identify a similar set of domain objects. In contrast, they have greater flexibility in choosing the implementation objects in order to satisfy the implementation constraints, such as performance and usability.

Active and Passive Objects

An object can be *active* or *passive*. It is necessary to distinguish between active objects and passive objects because they require different strategies for implementation. An active object is an object that can change its state. For example, timers and clocks can change their states without an external stimulus. Active objects are usually implemented as processes or threads, which are also referred to as "objects with life." With a passive object, the state of an object will not change unless the object receives a message. For example, the properties of a bank account will not change unless the bank account receives a message such as set balance (an operation for updating the balance of an account). Because the majority of objects are passive, sometimes it is automatically assumed that all objects are strictly passive.

What Is a Class and What Are Instances?

A *class* is a generic definition for a set of similar objects. It is an abstraction of a real-world entity that captures and specifies the properties and behaviors that are essential to the system but hides those that are irrelevant. The class also determines the structure and capabilities of its *instances* (objects). Thus, a class is a template or blueprint for a category of structurally identical items (objects). Objects are instances of a class. In other words, a class is like a mold and an instance of a class is like a molded object.

It is very important to understand the differences between classes and instances in order to get to grips with this chapter. A class has methods and attributes while object instances have behaviors and states. This concept is illustrated in Figure 2.1. In this example, *bank account* is a class. *Bank account* is a generic term that covers many different account types. John's and Robert's accounts are instances of the *bank account* class. Although their accounts are of a type of *bank account* and are not generic.

Figure 2.1. UML notation for objects and classes

Bank Account
−name −balance
+debit(in amount) +credit(in amount)

Object 1 : Bank Account
name = John Smith balance = 1,000.0

Object 2 : Bank Account
name = Robert Jones balance = −200.0

The *bank account* class specifies that a *bank account* object has *name* and *balance* as its private properties (indicated by a "−" sign) and public credit and debit operations (indicated by a "+" sign). It is noteworthy that the two instances are in different states. John's account is in the credit state (positive balance), while Robert's account is in the overdrawn state (negative balance). The state of the objects can be changed by calling the *credit* or *debit* operations, e.g. Robert's account can be changed to the credit state if a *credit* operation is invoked with a parameter of, say, 300.

Attributes

Things in the real world have *properties*. An *attribute* is a property of a class. Other words for attribute include "property," "characteristic" and "member data." For example, a book can be described in terms of its author, ISBN (International Serial Book Number), publisher, among others. More properties can be associated with the class *book* such as the number of pages, its weight, physical dimensions and so on. The abstraction of a book is limited to a specific problem domain so that the number of required properties can be reduced. For example, information on the weight and dimensions may be required for a delivery company but totally irrelevant to an information system of a bookstore.

From a human perspective, a property is a characteristic that describes an object. From a technical perspective, an attribute is a data item where an object holds its own state information. In summary, attributes have a name and a value, and attributes may also have a type, e.g. "integer," "Boolean."

Operations

Each object can perform a set of *functions* in order to provide a number of services in a software system. This is similar to the situation in a company where each member of staff provides a set of services to other members and customers. An object calls another object's service by sending it a message. A *service* is defined by one or more operations, and an *operation* is a function or a procedure which can access the object's data. An operation consists of two parts: a name and argument(s). Thus, every object must define its operations for each of its services. The collection of operations is the object's interface. Other objects only need to know the interface of an object in order to invoke the operations provided by the object.

An operation is sometimes called a *method* or a *member function*. These two terms are more widely used by programmers than designers. To a programmer, an operation is like a function (or procedure). The *return value* is the result that an operation "brings back" on completion. This is a useful way of allowing other objects to find out a piece of information about an object. In programming language, operations are similar to functions in that they have parameters and return values. For example, the savings account class in an ATM banking system may have the following operations:

- *withdraw(amount)*
- *deposit(amount)*
- *getBalance()*

Encapsulation: Information Hiding

Objects are like black boxes. Specifically, the underlying implementations of objects are hidden from those that use them. This is a powerful concept called information hiding, better known as the *encapsulation* principle. In object-oriented systems, it is only the producer (creator, designer or developer) of an object that knows the details of the internal construction of that object. The consumers (users) of an object are denied knowledge of the inner workings of the object and must deal with an object via one of its three distinct interfaces:

- Public interface which is open (visible) to everybody.
- Protected interface which is accessible only by objects that have inherited the properties and operations of the object. In class-based, object-oriented systems, only classes can provide an inheritance interface. (Inheritance and specialization will be discussed later).
- Parameter interface. In the case of parameterized classes, the parameter interface defines the parameters that must be supplied to create an instance. For example, a linked list of objects may have a parameter that specifies the type of object contained in the linked list. When the linked list is used, the actual type of object can be provided.

Structural Modeling Techniques

In UML, a class is simply represented by a rectangle divided into three compartments, containing, from top to bottom, the class name, a list of attributes and a list of operations (see Figure 2.2). Each attribute name may be followed by optional details such as a type and a default value. Each operation may be followed by optional details such as an argument list and a result type. In most cases, the bottom two compartments are omitted, and even when they are present, they typically do not show every single attribute and operation. Typically, only those attributes and operations that are relevant to the current context will be shown in a diagram. We can also specify the accessibility of an element (an attribute or an operation) by prefixing its name by a "−," "+," or "#" sign. The "−," "+," and "#" signs respectively indicate that an element is private, public or protected.

Figure 2.2. Classes providing different levels of details

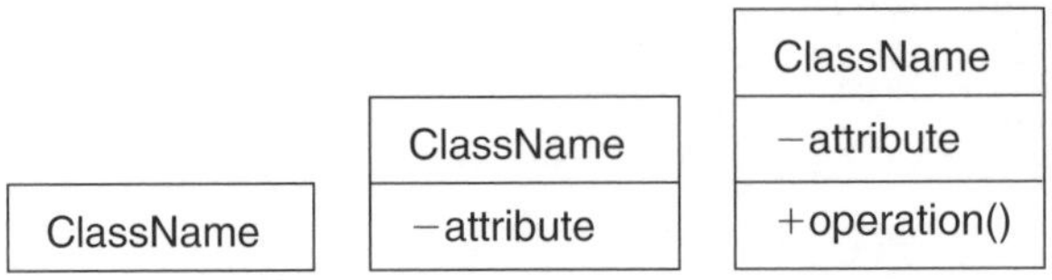

ClassName

ClassName
−attribute

ClassName
−attribute
+operation()

Figure 2.3 shows how a class is represented in the UML notation. Classes and objects are distinguished by underlining the object name and optionally followed by the class name.

Figure 2.3. UML notation for classes

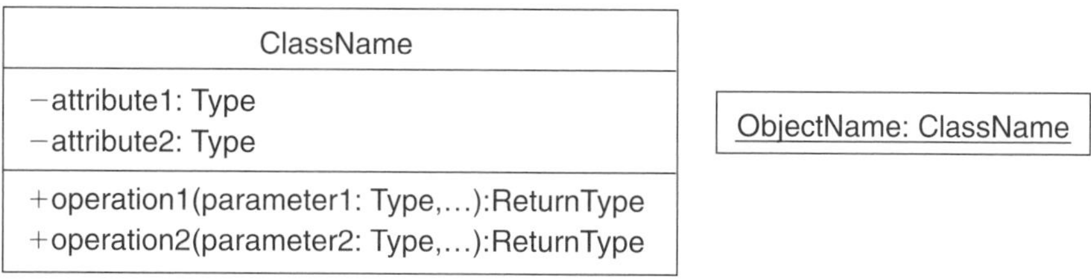

Figure 2.4 shows two examples of classes. In the first example, the *Shape* class has *origin* and *color* as attributes, with *move* and *resize* as operations. In the second example, the *bank account* class has *account number* and *customer name* as attributes and performs *get balance* and *set balance* operations.

Figure 2.4. Examples of classes in UML

Shape	Bank Account
−origin −color	−accountName −customerName
+move() +resize()	+getBalance(): float +setBalance()

Naming Classes

It is common practice to name a class with a noun or a noun phrase, but there are no firm rules on naming the elements (classes, attributes, etc.) of class models. The system development team should decide when and where upper case letters and spaces should be used, and it is important that all members of the team stick to the team's decision. When using name phrases, a widely used convention is to eliminate spaces and concatenate the words with their first letters in upper case, e.g. *SavingsAccount* and *BankAccount*.

Relationships between Classes

Relationships exist among real-life objects. For example, friendship and partnership are common examples of relationships among people. Similarly, a relationship specifies the type of *link* that exists between objects. Through the links of an object, it is possible to discover the other objects that are related to it. For example, all the friends of a person John can be determined through the links to John.

Finding relationships between classes is an important part of object-oriented modeling because relationships increase the usefulness of a model. Identifying relationships can help find new classes and eliminate bad ones. Furthermore, it may lead to the discovery of relevant attributes and operations.

There are essentially three important types of relationships between classes: *generalization/specialization* ("type-of"), *aggregation* ("part-of") and *association* relationships.

Inheritance

Object-oriented programming languages facilitate *inheritance* that allows the implementation of generalization-specialization associations in a very elegant manner. Attributes and operations common to a group of subclasses are attached to a superclass and inherited by its subclasses; each subclass may also include new features (methods or attributes) of its own. Generalization is sometimes called the "is-a" relationship. For example, *checking accounts* and *savings accounts* can be defined as specializations of *bank accounts*. Another way of saying this is that both a *checking account* and a *savings account* "is-a" kind of a *bank account*; everything that is true for a *bank account* is also true for a *savings account* and a *checking account*.

Properties of Inheritance

Generalization

The purpose of this property is to distribute the commonalities from the superclass among a group of similar subclasses. The subclass inherits all the superclass's (base class) operations and attributes. That is, whatever the superclass possesses, the derived class (subclass) does as well. Taking the *BankAccount* example from above, if *BankAccount* (superclass) has an *account_number* attribute, the *CheckingAccount* (subclass) will also have the same attribute, *account_number*, as it is a subclass of *BankAccount*. It would be unnecessary and inappropriate to show the superclass attributes in the subclasses. Similarly, suppose there is a bank application for an ATM machine. If *BankAccount* has the operation *setBalance*, then *SavingsAccount* will automatically inherit this operation as well. It would be a mistake to duplicate the attributes and operations in the superclass in its subclasses as well unless those operations have different implementations of their own. Figure 2.5 illustrates the concept of generalization, with *CheckingAccount* and

SavingsAccount inheriting their superclass's (*BankAccount*) attributes and operations.

Figure 2.5. *BankAccount* and its subclasses

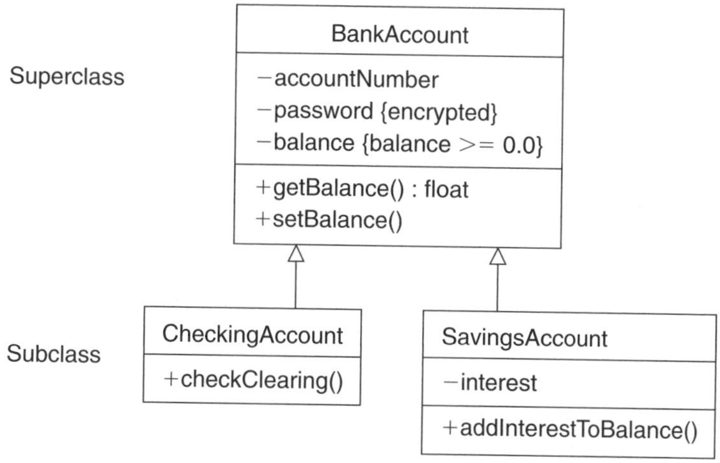

Superclass

BankAccount
−accountNumber
−password {encrypted}
−balance {balance >= 0.0}
+getBalance() : float
+setBalance()

Subclass

CheckingAccount
+checkClearing()

SavingsAccount
−interest
+addInterestToBalance()

Specialization

Specialization allows subclasses to extend the functionalities of their superclass. A subclass can introduce new operations and attributes of its own. For example, in Figure 2.5, *SavingsAccount* inherits attributes *account_number*, *password* and *balance* from *BankAccount* and extends the functionalities of *BankAccount* with an additional attribute, *interest*, and an additional operation, *addInterestToBalance*. A *SavingsAccount* has the attribute *interest* that *BankAccount* does not because not all bank accounts earn interest.

Abstract Classes

An *abstract* class is used to specify the required behaviors (operations) of a class without having to provide their actual implementation. An operation without the implementation (body) is called an *abstract operation*. A class with one or more abstract operations is an abstract class. An abstract class cannot be instantiated because it does not have the required implementation of the abstract operations. An abstract class can act as a repository of shared operation signatures (function prototypes) for its subclasses and so those methods must be implemented by subclasses according to the signatures. A class (or an operation) can be specified as abstract in the UML by writing its name in italics, such as for the class *Shape*. Here, the class *Shape* is abstract because we cannot draw a shape; we can only draw its subclasses such as rectangles, circles, etc. Figure 2.6 shows an example of the abstract class *Shape* and its subclasses. The subclasses provide the actual implementations of their draw operations since *Rectangle*, *Polygon* and *Circle* can be drawn in different ways. A subclass can override the implementation of an operation inherited from a superclass by declaring another implementation (body of the operation). In the example, the draw operation in the *Rectangle* class overrides the implementation of the draw operation inherited from the *Shape* class.

Figure 2.6. ***Shape* as an example of an abstract class**

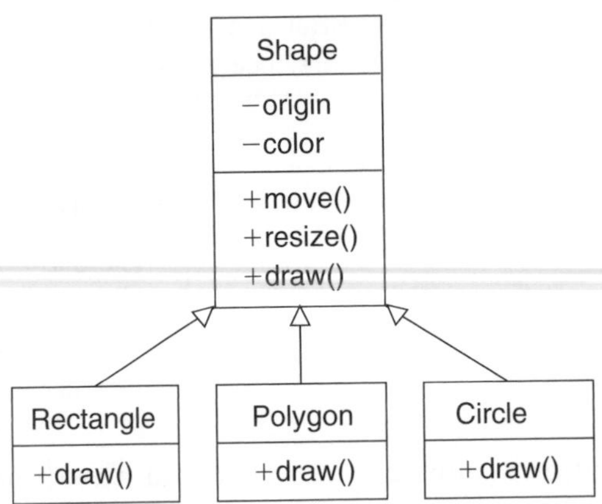

Polymorphism

Polymorphism is the ability of a variable to hold objects of its own class and subclasses at runtime. The variable can be used to invoke an operation of the object held. The actual operation being invoked depends on the actual class of the object that is referenced by the variable. For example, suppose the variable "shape" is of type *Shape*. If shape references a *Rectangle* object, then *shape.draw*() invokes the *draw*() method of the *Rectangle* class. Similarly, if shape references a *Polygon* object, the *draw*() method of the *Polygon* class is invoked by *shape.draw*().

Association

Object-oriented systems are made up of objects of many classes. Associations represent binary relationships among classes. An *association* is represented by a line drawn between the associated classes involved with an optional role name attached to either end. The role name is used to specify the role of an associated class in the association. If an association connects between two objects instead of classes, it is called a *link*. A link is an instance of an association. For example, Figure 2.7 illustrates the *WorkFor* relationship between the *Person* and *Company* classes. The relationship carries the meaning of "a person works for one company." Figure 2.7 illustrates that Bill Gates works for Microsoft and that many people can work for a company.

Figure 2.7. Association and link

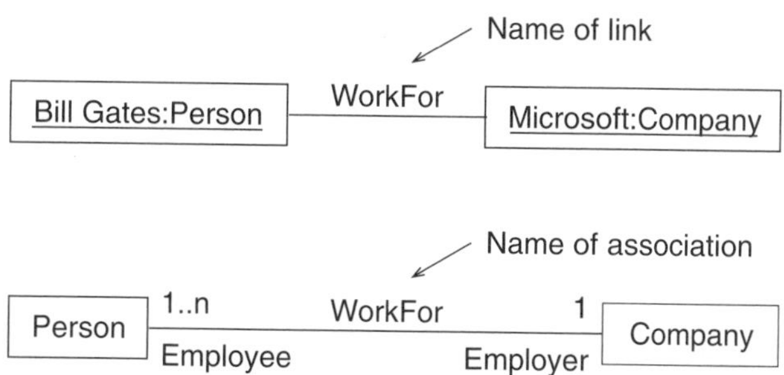

Links provide a convenient way to trace the relationship between objects. However, do not spend too much time trying to identify all possible relationships between classes, as the implementation of these association relationships adds to the overheads in your system. Only specify those relationships that are necessary for the requirements of the system, and focus on questions such as: "While you are operating on one object, do you need to know the information of another object(s)?"

Role

Each end of an association has a *role*. You may optionally attach a role name at the end of an association line. A role name uniquely identifies one end of an association. For example, the role of a person in the *WorkFor* relationship is employee and the role of a company is employer (See Figure 2.7). From the object's point of view, tracing the association is an operation that yields an object or a set of related objects at the other end of the association. For example, the employees of Microsoft can be determined by following the *WorkFor* association. During the analysis stage, an association is often considered to be bi-directional, that is, tracing can be done from either end of the association. However, during the design stage, only one direction may be needed to implement the requirements of the system.

Multiplicity

Multiplicity refers to the number of objects associated with a given object. For the *WorkFor* association in Figure 2.8, a person works for one and only one company since the multiplicity on the *Company* side is 1. On the other hand, a company may have one or more persons working in it. If the multiplicity is not explicitly specified, the default value of 1 is assumed.

Figure 2.8. Association and role

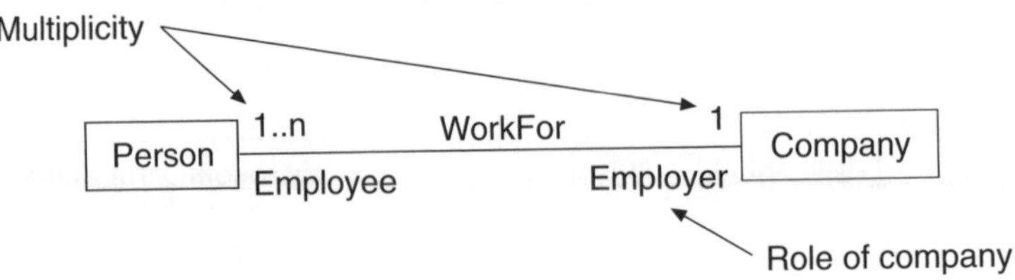

Qualification

Qualification serves as names or keys that are part of the association and are used to select objects at the other end of the association. Qualification reduces the effective multiplicity of the association from one-to-many to one-to-one. In UML, a qualifier is used to model this association semantic, that is, an association attribute whose value determines a unique object or a subset of objects at the other end of the association. For example, a bank is associated with many customers. The *account number* (qualifier) specifies a unique person of a bank (a customer) (see Figure 2.9).

Figure 2.9. (a) Many-to-many association between *Person* and *Bank* and (b) reduced to a one-to-many association

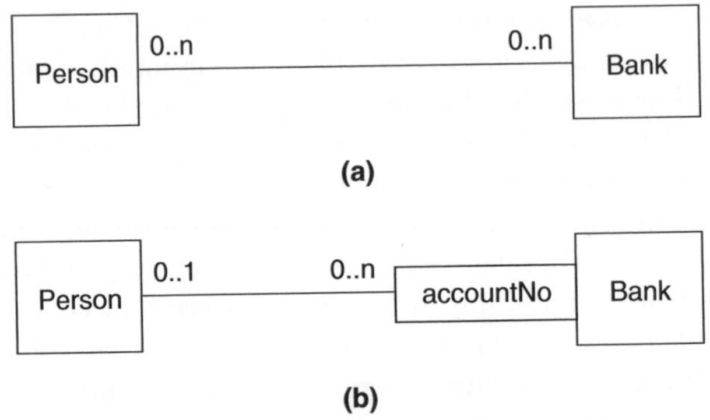

Reflexive Association and Roles

A *reflexive* association is an association that relates one object of a class to another object of the same class. In other words, a class can be associated with itself. There are two types of reflexive associations, namely, directional and bi-directional.

Figure 2.10a a shows an example of a directional reflexive association where the class *Course* is associated with itself. Here, a course may be a prerequisite for another course. Figure 2.10b shows an example of a bi-directional reflexive association where a parent directory (role: host) contains zero or more subdirectories (role: accommodated by).

Figure 2.10 (a) A directional reflexive association and (b) a bi-directional reflexive association

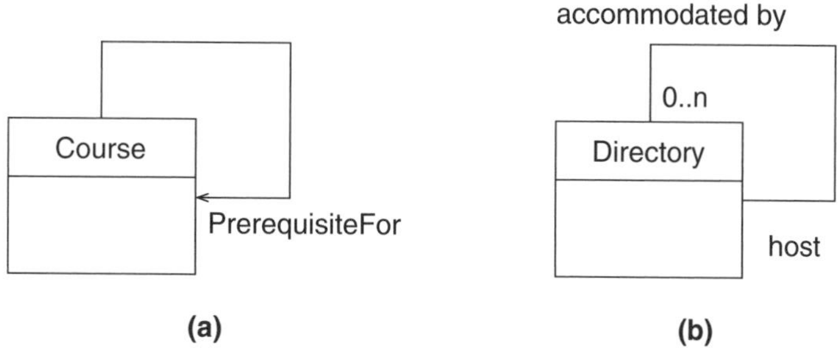

N-ary *Association*

Associations are often binary, but higher order associations are also possible. A relationship involving three classes is referred to as a *ternary* relationship, and one involving many classes is referred to as an n-ary relationship. An n-ary association is represented by a diamond connecting the associated classes. In Figure 2.11, for example, a *Student* that takes a *Course* taught by a particular *Instructor* exhibits a ternary relationship.

Figure 2.11. A ternary association

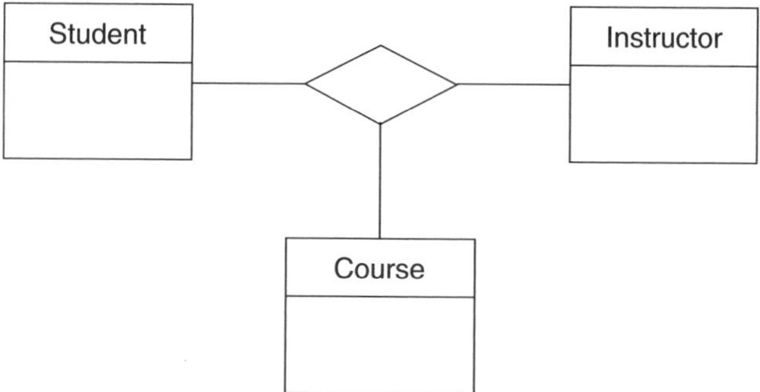

When modeling association relationships among classes, binary association is the most preferred form. A higher-order association can always be decomposed into a corresponding number of binary associations, and it is possible to convert some of the bi-directional relationships into unidirectional relationships in our class model during the design phase. For example, we can represent the ternary association in Figure 2.12 as three binary associations instead:

- a *Student* enrolls a *Course*
- an *Instructor* teaches a *Course*
- an *Instructor* trains a *Student*

Figure 2.12. Three binary associations replacing a ternary association

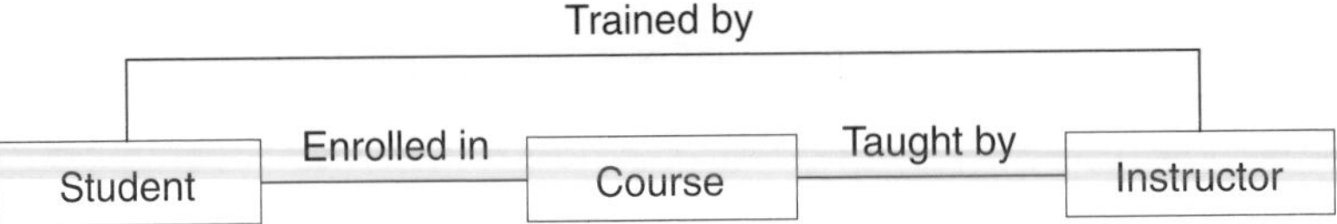

Association Classes

It is sometimes necessary to describe an *association* by including additional attributes which do not naturally belong to the objects involved in the association. In Figure 2.13, for example, the year of the enrollment of a student in a course does not belong to the *student* or *course* classes. In this case, an association class *Enrollment* is added to hold the attribute year.

There are situations where an association is complex enough to be a class in its own right. The association has its own class name and may have operations just like any other ordinary class. In the example of the association between a *Person* and a *Company* (Figure 2.14), the *Position* class contains the attributes of the association between the *Person* and the *Company*. The *Position* class has attributes of its own that do not naturally belong to *Person* or *Company*. Therefore, it is only natural or beneficial that the information belonging only to the object is contained in a separate class so as to maximize the level of module cohesion. It may sometimes be possible to transfer the attributes from the *Position* class to the *Person* or *Company* class. However, this move significantly affects the reusability of those classes, as the association attributes may be meaningful only in a specific context but not others. For example, in Figure 2.14, the *Person* class may well be suitable for other applications that do not need to know the *Position* information. Furthermore, if the *Position* class information in transferred to either the *Person* or *Company* class, it will rule out the possibility that a *Person* may have more than one *Position* with the same or another *Company*.

Figure 2.13. An association class

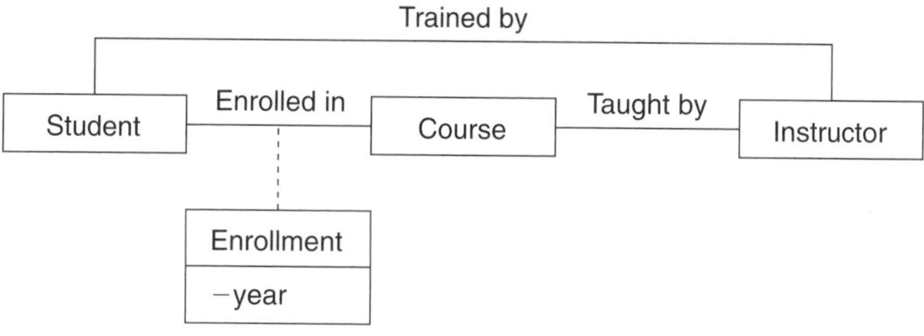

Figure 2.14. Using an association class

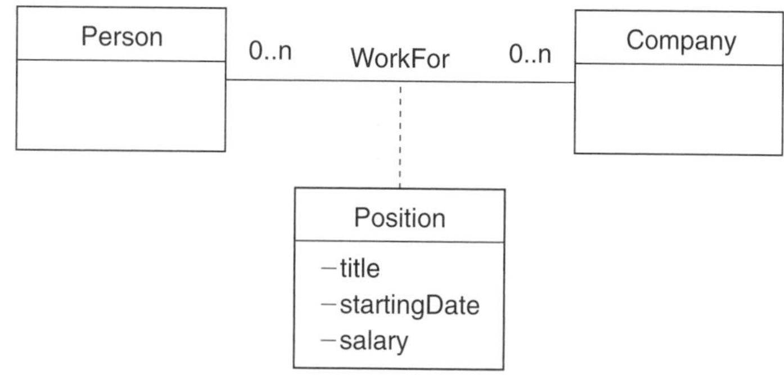

Aggregation

Aggregation is a stronger form of association. It represents the has-a or part-of relationship. In UML, a link is placed between the "whole" and "parts" classes, with a diamond head (see Figure 2.15) attached to the *whole* class to indicate that this association is an aggregation. Multiplicity can be specified at

Figure 2.15. Example of aggregation

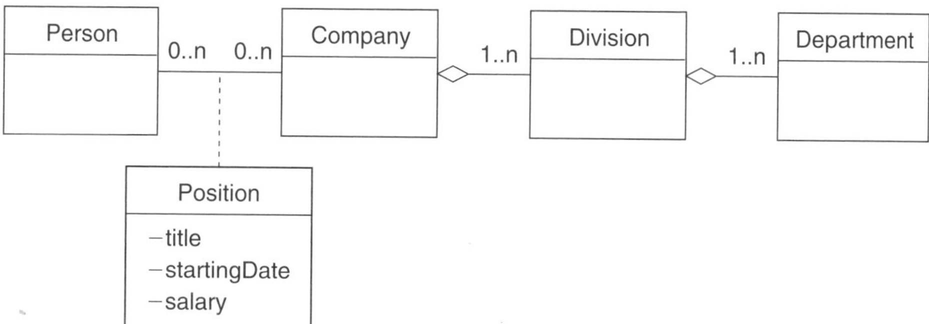

the end of the association for each of the "part-of" classes to indicate the quantity of the constituent parts. Typically, aggregations are not named, and the keywords used to identify aggregations are "consists of," "contains" or "is part of."

Composition

A stronger form of aggregation is called *composition*, which implies exclusive ownership of the "part-of" classes by the "whole" class, i.e. a composite object has exclusive ownership of the parts objects. This means that parts may be created after a composite is created, but such parts will be explicitly removed before the destruction of the composite. In UML, a filled diamond (see Figure 2.16) indicates the composition relationship. In Figure 2.15, it is more natural (closely resembling scenarios in the real world) for *Division*(s) and *Department*(s) to be created after the *Company* is set up and they will not exist if the *Company* closes down.

Figure 2.16. Example of composition

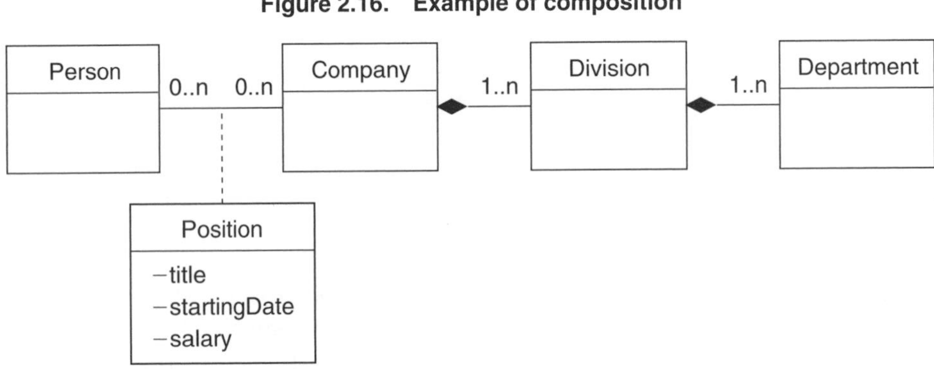

Constraints and Notes

Constraints are an extension of the semantics of a UML element that allow the inclusion of new rules or the modification of existing ones. It is sometimes helpful to present an idea about restrictions on attributes and associations for which there is no specific notation. Simply write them in braces near the class concerned. Constraints are represented by a label in curly brackets ({constraintName} or {expression}) that are attached to the constrained element. In the ATM banking example (see Figure 2.17), the *password* of a *bank account* is encrypted and the *balance* is not less than $0.

You can specify constraints for two associations such as {for}, {or}, {subset}, etc. Such constraints are called *complex constraints*. The {or} constraint indicates that only one of the associations can exist at any given time. The {subset} constraint indicates that an association is a subset of another.

Figure 2.17. Example of constraints

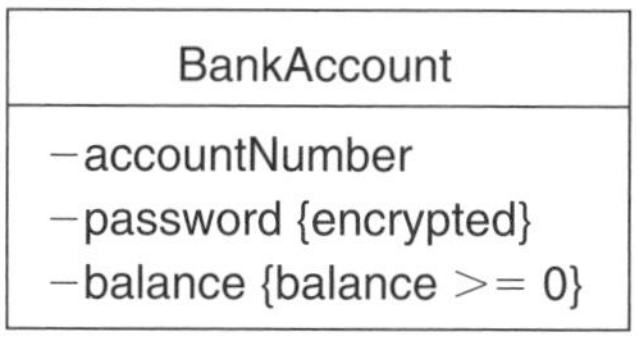

BankAccount

−accountNumber
−password {encrypted}
−balance {balance >= 0}

Figure 2.18 shows two examples of complex constraints. In the first example, the Jockey Club has two kinds of members: ordinary members and VIP members. The *VIPMemberOf* association is a subset of the *OrdinaryMemberOf* association. In other words, a VIP member is also an Ordinary member. In the second example, a *Notebook* computer has either a *CDROM* or *DVD* association but not both.

Figure 2.18. Complex constraints

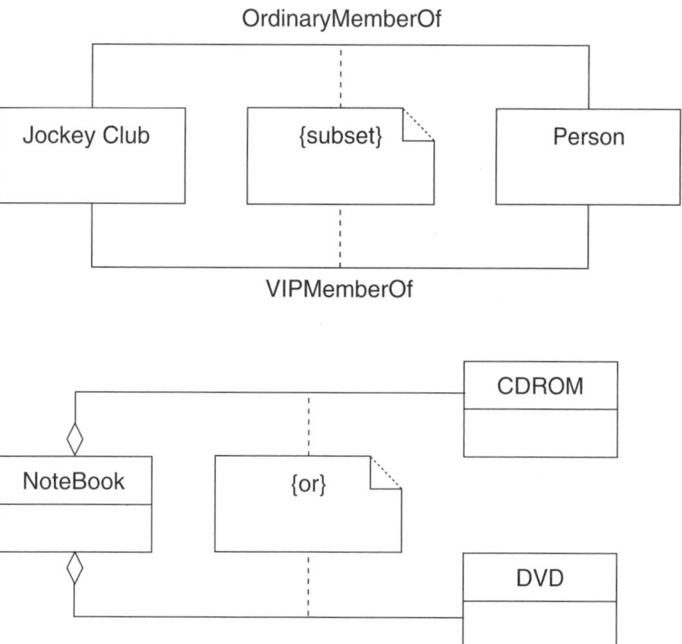

A *note*, represented by a dog-eared rectangle in UML, is a graphical symbol for holding constraints or comments attached to an element or a collection of elements. A note can also be used to link or embed other documents. It is very useful to add comments to UML models with plain text notes to provide further explanation or clarification that might not be apparent. In Figure 2.19, a note is used to provide further details about the source of information of the classes.

Figure 2.19. Note annotation

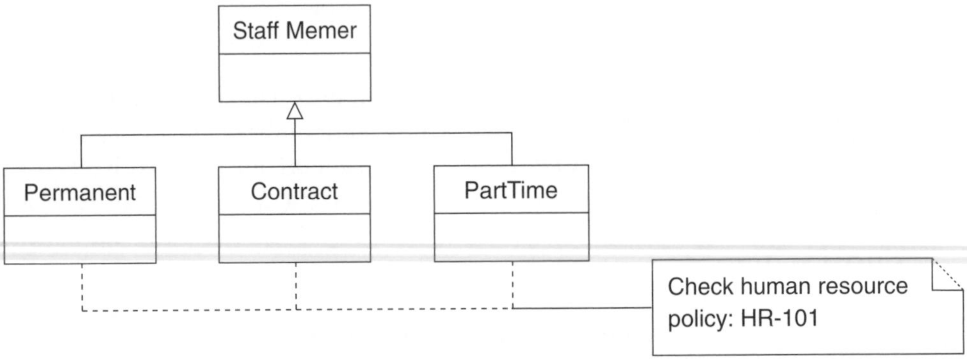

Structural Models: Examples

Example 1: A Car

A car consists of different structural components such as the engine, body, suspension, gearbox, etc. Each component in turn contains its own attributes and operations. For example, the engine has its capacity, and it can be started or stopped. Figure 2.20 shows a simplified structural model of a car in a class diagram.

Example 2: A Sales Order System

In this simple sales order system example, there are three methods of payment: cash, credit card or check. These three payment methods have the same attribute (*amount*), but they have their own individual behaviors and attributes. Figure 2.21 shows a structural model of this simple sales order system in a class diagram. The directional associations in the diagram indicate the direction of navigation from one class to another. For example, the *Order* class can access information from the *Payment* class, but not the other way round.

Figure 2.20. Structural model of a car

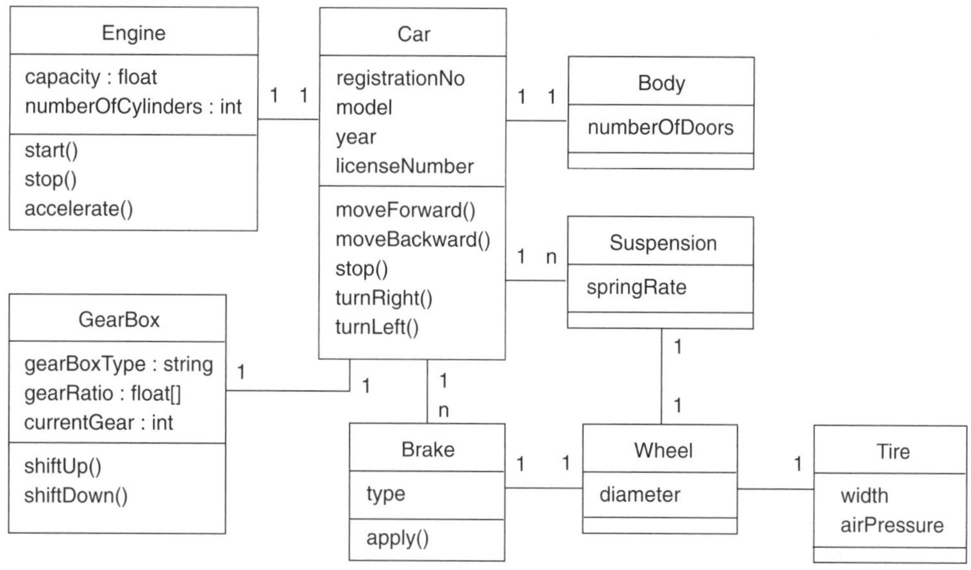

Figure 2.21. Structural model for a sales order system

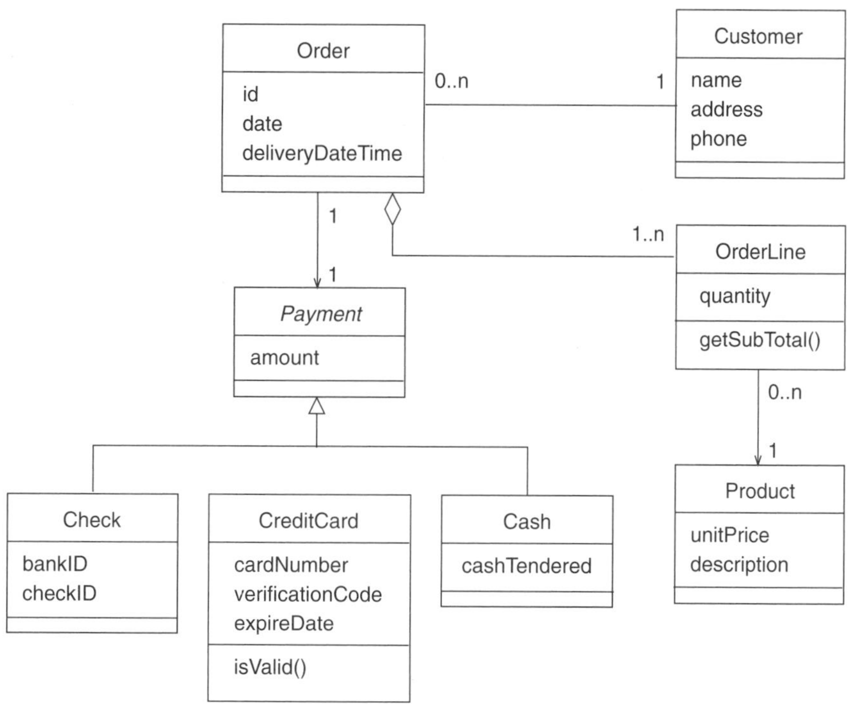

Summary of UML Notation for Structural Modeling

UML provides a comprehensive range of components for structural modeling. Table 2.1 summarizes the more common ones in the UML notation. In this chapter, we have discussed how to use the class model in structural modeling from the analysis perspective. Thus, only some of the constructs in Table 2.1 are introduced.

Table 2.1. Summary of UML notation for structural modeling

Construct	Description	Syntax
class	A set of objects that share the same attributes, operations, methods, relationships and semantics	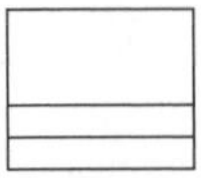
interface	A set of operations that characterize the behavior of an element	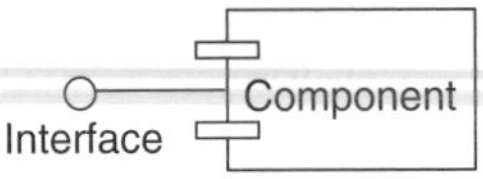 Interface Component
component	A modular, replaceable and significant part of a system that packages implementation and exposes a set of interfaces	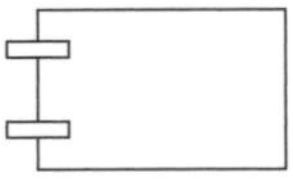
node	A runtime physical object that represents a computational resource	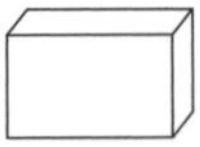
constraint	A semantic condition or restriction	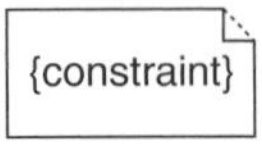 {constraint}
association	A relationship between two or more classifiers that involves connections between their instances	
aggregation	A special form of association that specifies a whole–parts relationship between the aggregate (whole) and the components (parts)	
generalization	A taxonomic relationship between a more general and a more specific element	

Table 2.1. (Cont'd)

Construct	Description	Syntax
dependency	A relationship between two modeling elements, in which a change to one modeling element (the independent element) will affect the other modeling element (the dependent element)	- - - - - - - - - - ->
realization	A relationship between a specification and its implementation	- - - - - - - - - -▷

Structural Analysis Techniques

In developing object-oriented systems, we often adopt a bottom-up approach first to develop a set of highly reusable components for assembling our system. These components should also be suitably placed in a flexible and expandable system architecture that can only be carried out through a top-down approach. To do this, a set of highly reusable components is developed first before they are assembled to form the system. In order to develop a stable system architecture that can comfortably accommodate the object components, the top-down and bottom-up approaches are often applied in an inter-play manner throughout the system development life cycle.

This section shall discuss various domain analysis techniques for object identification, after which leads you through the classical object identification process by performing a textual analysis. A set of long-established heuristics are elaborated, followed by a case study.

How Are Classes Obtained?

Practitioners and methodologists always claim that the object-oriented approach is far superior to the traditional structured approach. This may well be true. However, for those new to the object-oriented approach, they often find object identification a very difficult task, especially because a real-world object may be considered as either an attribute or an object depending on the context. For example, a city is a physical object in the real world. In the context of an *address*, *City* is only an attribute of the *Person* class. In an urban planning system, *City* would be a class itself.

How good a class model is can be judged by examining its usability, extendibility and maintainability. Furthermore, a good class model should be reusable in other object-oriented system components, so that the fruits of reusability can be harvested. Reusability is one of the key advantages of the object-oriented approach.

To tackle the object identification problem, both domain analysis and use case analysis (see Chapter 4 for details of the use case analysis) should be performed. Domain analysis starts with the problem statement to produce a class model (see Figure 2.22). Domain analysis focuses on identifying reusable objects that are common to most applications of the same problem domain. Hence, objects specific to the system can also be identified from use case descriptions. The results of both the domain analysis and use case analysis can be adopted to produce a robust and versatile class model. This will ensure that the class model can fulfill the users' requirements and be reused for other applications in the same domain.

Figure 2.22. Two ways to perform object identification

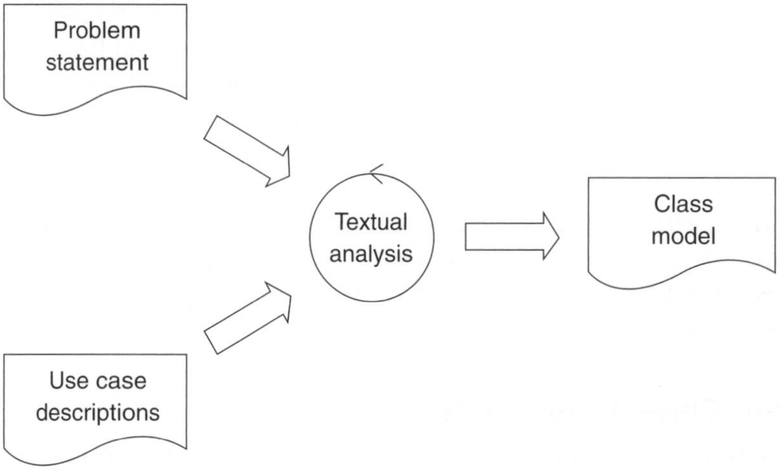

Keeping the Model Simple

Once you start modeling more than just a handful of classes, be sure that your abstractions provide a balanced set of responsibilities. What this means is that any one class should not be too big or too small. Each class should do one thing well. If the classes are too big, the models will be difficult to change and not very reusable. If the classes are too small, this will result in too many classes in the model, which may be difficult to manage or understand. The "rule of seven" is often used, which postulates that people's short-term memory can only cope with about seven chunks of information at a time.

When there are more than seven classes, draw diagrams for different contexts. For example, in a retail information system, the classes can be packaged according to different areas of activities such as sales, inventory control, purchasing, etc., which in turn are represented in different class diagrams. It is often necessary to develop the same diagram iteratively and incrementally. In other words, the initial version of the diagram tends to be conceptual and should capture the "big picture" of the model. Later iterations capture additional details and are generally more implementation-oriented. Expect to revise the model many times before you are happy with it.

Heuristics in Using Structural Analysis

The following list of heuristics can help you perform structural analysis:

- Do not attempt to develop a single giant class diagram. Choose *only* those that fit into the context. For example, a class diagram may only represent one major system functionality (use case) instead of the entire system. Remember: humans can process about seven chunks of information at one time.
- Use model management constructs such as subsystems, packages and software framework to form the system architecture through the top-down approach.
- Consider both logical and physical aspects, such as grouping by role, responsibility, deployment and/or hardware platform, when grouping classes into model management constructs.
- Use data or middleware for communication among major subsystems whenever possible. Data coupling is easier to maintain than logical coupling because a change in requirements will only result in a change in data, and not the program itself. It is, however, not possible for some real-time or time critical applications since performance may become an important issue.
- Wisely apply design patterns for those architecturally significant classifiers to make the system architecture flexible and adaptable. This will be discussed in detail in Chapter 6.
- Apply domain analysis such as textual analysis, Class-Responsibility-Collaboration (CRC) or legacy and documentation reviews to identify reusable components using a bottom-up approach, so that the concepts and terminologies are understood and well accepted by the industry.

- Inter-play what have been found in the top-down approach and the bottom-up approach to ensure that the resulting artifacts (architecture, subsystem and components) can comfortably coexist.
- Use packages to organize the domain classes incrementally as development progresses. Each system functionality (use case) developed in turn will yield a set of domain classes. The set of domain classes should then be grouped into appropriate packages so that each package contains a cohesive set of classes. Organizing the classes into packages can also make it easier to manage the domain class model as it grows.
- Conduct use case analysis to yield two artifacts: a set of use case instance scenarios to help us walk through the objects that participate (are required) in the interaction, and the responsibilities (operations) that are required to be assigned to each object through the analysis of the messages sent to and from it. These resulting artifacts (a set of objects and its operations) help us identify the missing pieces in the structural model.
- Review whether a particular class is becoming too large. If so, consider reorganizing the class into two or more classes and structure the resulting classes using relationships.

Conducting Domain Modeling and Analysis

Domain analysis seeks to identify classes and objects that are common to many applications in a domain. This is partly to avoid wasting time and effort in reinventing the wheel and to promote reusability of the system components. Domain analysis involves finding out what other people have done in implementing other systems and looking at the literature in the field. Bear in mind that the object-oriented approach is superior to the traditional structured approach because of system reusability and extendibility, and not because they are more trendy or popular.

As already stated, the goal of domain analysis is to identify a set of classes that are common to all applications when dealing with problems of the same domain. Then, according to their nature, the domain classes and the application-specific classes are grouped into different packages. In so doing, the cohesion of the class model is maximized and the coupling between classes minimized, greatly enhancing the system's maintainability and extendibility. In short, the benefit of domain analysis is that domain classes can be reused for other applications when solving problems in the same domain. Furthermore, using well-understood terminologies in the domain for naming domain classes will improve the readability of the documentation.

Unfortunately, there is no simple or straightforward way to identify a set of classes for a problem domain. The domain analysis relies heavily on the designer's knowledge of the problem domain, intuition, prior experience and skills. A common way to perform a domain analysis is to prepare a statement of the problem domain first and then perform a textual analysis to identify the candidate classes. The problem statement and textual analysis provide a good starting point for domain analysis. The candidate classes are then refined iteratively to add the associations, attributes and operations to the domain class model (see the next section for details).

Domain Modeling and Analysis Process

Overview

Before domain analysis is conducted, we need to understand the problem domain of the system. We need to find out the general requirements of the system of the domain by interviewing users and the domain experts of the system. After interviewing them, a problem statement can be prepared. The output of the domain analysis is a domain class model describing the classes and their relationships. The domain class model consists of class diagrams, a data dictionary describing the classes and their associations, and definitions of terminologies.

Developing Domain Class Models

The domain analysis starts with the preparation of a problem statement to provide a generic description of the problems of the domain. The problem statement is usually prepared after interviewing experts in the domain. Rumbaugh et al. recommend the following steps for developing a domain class model (see Figure 2.23):

1. Preparing the problem statement
2. Identifying the objects and classes using textual analysis
3. Developing a data dictionary
4. Identifying associations between classes
5. Identifying attributes of classes and association classes
6. Structuring classes using inheritance
7. Verifying access paths for likely queries
8. Iterating and refining the model

Figure 2.23. Domain analysis process

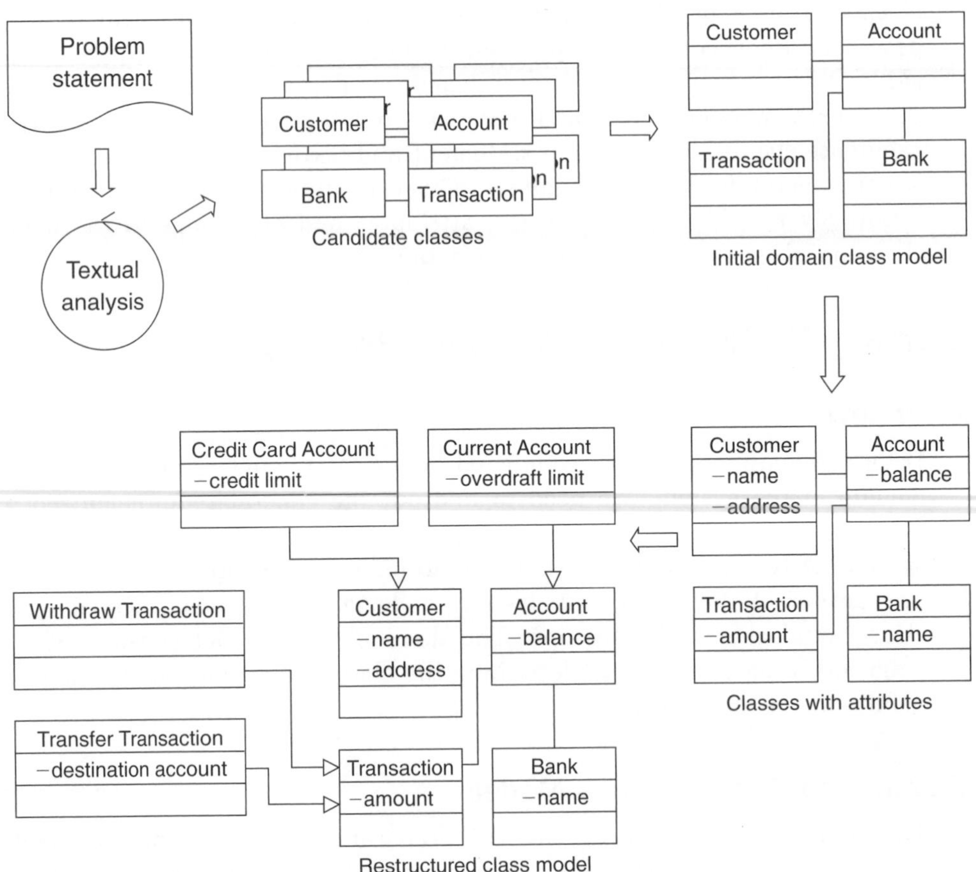

Preparing Problem Statement

Before any analysis work is carried out, it is important to clearly describe the problem in the context of the domain. A clear and detailed problem statement helps to reduce misunderstanding and the possibility of significant reworking at a later stage. Since the objective of domain analysis is to develop a class model that can be reused in other applications to solve problems in the same domain, it will be expedient that the problem statement describes the general requirements of the domain rather than the requirements of a specific application. The problem description should, therefore, focus on the description of the objects and their relationships in the domain rather than the specific procedures of the problem domain, since the procedures for carrying out tasks would not be the same for every organization. For example, in the problem statement for the banking domain, it should be described that a customer can have several accounts with a bank but avoid specifying how a person opens a bank account since each bank has its own procedure in performing the same operation. As problem statements are written in natural language, they may have ambiguities and inconsistencies. Therefore, the problem statement is just one of the many inputs to the domain analysis. Throughout the analysis process, we need to use our own judgment or that of domain experts to resolve such ambiguities and inconsistencies.

Online Stock Trading Example

The following problem statement is for an automated online stock trading system for a stock brokerage firm.

A stock brokerage firm wants to provide an online stock trading service to enable its clients to make trades via the computer. With this system, a client must first be registered before he can trade online. The registration process involves the client providing his ID number, address and telephone number. A client may open one or more accounts for stock trading. The stock brokerage firm needs to be registered with a stock exchange before its clients can trade the stocks listed on the stock exchange. A stock brokerage firm can be registered with one or more stock exchanges. The stock brokerage firm may need to pay monthly charges for using the services provided by the stock exchange. Once registered, the client can buy and sell stocks. The client can check the current price, bid price, ask price and traded volume of a stock in real time. The stock price and traded volume information is provided by the stock exchange on which the stock is listed and traded. When a client issues a buy order for an account, the client must specify the stock code, the number of shares and the maximum price (bid price) that he is willing to pay for them. A client must have sufficient funds in his account to settle the transaction when it is completed. When a client issues a sell order, the client must specify the stock code, the number of shares and the minimum price (ask price) that he is willing to sell them. The client must have sufficient number of shares of the stock in his account before he can issue the sell order.

A client can check the status of execution of his (buy or sell) orders. The client can issue a buy or sell order before the end of the trading day of the stock exchange which processed the order. All trade orders will be forwarded to the stock trading system of the stock exchange for execution. When an order is completed, the stock trading system of the stock exchange will return the transaction details of the order to the online stock trading system. The transaction details of a trade order may be a list of transactions, each transaction specifying the price and the number of shares traded. For example, the result of a buy order of 20,000 HSBC (stock code: 0005) shares at HKD 88.00 in the Hong Kong Stock Exchange may be as follows:

- 4,000 shares at HKD 87.50
- 8,000 shares at HKD 87.75
- 8,000 shares at HKD 88.00

An order will be kept on the system for execution until the order is completed or the end of a trading day. There are three possible outcomes for a trade order:

1. The trade order is completed. For a buy order, the total amount for the buy order will be deducted from the client's account and the number of shares of the stock purchased will be deposited into the account. For a sell order, the number of shares sold will be deducted from the client's account and proceeds of the sell order will be deposited into the client's account.
2. The trade order is partially completed. The number of shares actually traded (sell or buy) is less than the number of shares specified in the order. The number of shares successfully traded in the order will be used to calculate the amount of the proceeds, and the client's account is adjusted accordingly.
3. The trade order is not executed by the end of a trading day. The order will be canceled.

A stock exchange may require that the number of shares specified in an order must be in multiples of the lot size of the stock. Each stock has its own lot size. Common lot sizes are 1, 400, 500, 1,000 and 2,000 shares.

The client can deposit or withdraw cash or stock shares from his account. Upon the deposit or withdrawal of cash or stock shares, the account cash or stock balance will be updated accordingly.

Identifying Objects and Classes

To identify the objects and classes, perform textual analysis to extract all noun and noun phrases from the problem statement. The objective of this step is to identify a set of candidate objects which can be further elaborated and refined in subsequent steps. Therefore, it is not necessary (nor possible) to get it right the first time. Rather, do not be too selective in choosing classes at this stage so as to avoid the possibility of excluding some classes. For each extracted noun or noun phrase, we need to carefully evaluate whether it actually represents an object of the domain. It is necessary to stress that the object identification process is not a straightforward task. A noun or noun phrase can be an object in one domain and not so in another. We need to exercise our own judgment in the process. Amour and Miller (2001) suggest that from their past experiences, nouns or noun phrases of the following categories are more likely to represent objects:

- Tangibles (e.g. classroom, playground)
- Conceptuals (e.g. course, module)
- Events (e.g. test, examination, seminar)
- External organizations (e.g. publisher, supplier)
- Roles played (e.g. student, teacher, principal)
- Other systems (e.g. admission system, grade reporting system)

Table 2.2 shows the nouns and noun phrases extracted from the problem statement of the online stock trading example.

Table 2.2 Nouns and noun phrases extracted from the problem statement

Stock brokerage firm (concept)	Buy order (event)
Monthly charge	Stock code (simple value, attribute)
Trade (event)	Number of shares (simple value, attribute)
Trade order (event)	Maximum price (simple value, attribute)
Computer (tangible)	Transaction (event)
Client (role played)	Sell order (event)
ID (simple value, attribute)	Trading hours (simple value, attribute)
Address (simple value, attribute)	Trading day (simple value, attribute)

Table 2.2 (Cont'd)

Telephone number (simple value, attribute)	Stock trading system (other systems)
Account (concept)	Order (event)
Stock Exchange (extenal organization)	Execution result (event)
Stock (concept)	HSBC (instance of stock)
Current price (simple value, attribute)	Hong Kong Stock Exchange (instance of stock exchange)
Bid price (simple value, attribute)	Lot size (simple value, attribute)
Ask price (simple value, attribute)	Registration process (not an object)
Traded volume (simple value, attribute)	

As the purpose of this step is to identify the classes in the domain, other issues, such as inheritance and implementation, should be ignored. They will be dealt with in later steps. For each extracted noun or noun phrase, a category is assigned to it as shown in parentheses in Table 2.2. The candidate classes are then consolidated by eliminating inappropriate ones. Rumbaugh et al. (1991) suggest a set of criteria for eliminating inappropriate classes (see Table 2.3):

Table 2.3. Categories of inappropriate classes

Categories	Description
Redundant classes	Classes that mean the same thing. For example, order, trade and trade order mean the same thing. Eliminate trade and order, and retain trade order. Choose the most descriptive class.
Irrelevant classes	Classes that are not directly related to the problem. For example, monthly charge is not directly related to the system.
Vague classes	Classes that are loosely defined.
Attributes	Attributes of classes are also represented as nouns or noun phrases. Therefore, the list of nouns or noun phrases extracted by textual analysis may contain attributes of classes. For example, address and telephone number are attributes of the client.

Table 2.3. (Cont'd)

Categories	Description
Operations	The performance of actions is sometimes expressed as nouns or noun phrases. For example, the registration process is the action taken by the client to register on the system. It should be considered an operation of a class, rather than a class.
Roles	Role names help to differentiate the responsibilities of the objects in an interaction. However, they should not be considered as classes.
Implementation constructs	Implementation details of a particular solution are sometimes written in the problem statement, e.g. array, indexed sequential file, etc. Candidate classes representing the implementation details should be removed.

After following the above guidelines, a number of classes may be found to be inappropriate (see Table 2.4) in the online stock trading example.

Table 2.4. Inappropriate classes

Stock brokerage firm (irrelevant)	Stock code (attribute)
Monthly charge (irrelevant)	Number of shares (attribute)
Trade (redundant)	Maximum price (attribute)
Computer (implementation)	Trading hours (attribute)
ID (attribute)	Trading day (attribute)
Address (attribute)	Order (redundant)
Telephone number (attribute)	HSBC (instance of stock)
Current price (attribute)	Hong Kong Stock Exchange (instance of stock exchange)
Bid price (attribute)	Lot size (attribute)
Ask price (attribute)	Registration process (operation)
Traded volume (attribute)	

The revised list of candidate classes is shown in Table 2.5 after removing the inappropriate classes in Table 2.4.

Table 2.5. Revised list of candidate classes

Trade order (event)	Transaction (event)
Client (role played)	Sell order (event)
Account (concept)	Stock trading system (other systems)
Stock Exchange (external organization)	Execution result (event)
Buy order (event)	Stock (concept)

Developing Data Dictionary

After the candidate classes have been consolidated, prepare a data dictionary to record the definition of classes. For each class, write a short description to define its scope as well as details about the class such as its attributes and operations. The data dictionary also describes the associations between the classes and is continuously revised throughout the entire development life cycle of the system. Table 2.6 shows the data dictionary for the online trading system example.

Table 2.6. Data dictionary for the candidate classes

Class	Definition
Client	An individual or a company registered with the stock brokerage firm for online stock trading services. The class has attributes address, telephone number and ID. A client may have one or more accounts.
Account	A client can issue trade order on his or her accounts. An account holds details about the cash and stock balances for trading.
Stock exchange	A financial institution that provides a platform where stock trading is carried out.

Table 2.6. (Cont'd)

Class	Definition
Stock trading system	A platform for the execution of the trade orders of stock.
Trade order	A trade order specifies the price, stock code and number of shares. A trade order can be a buy order or a sell order.
Buy order	A buy order specifies the bid price, stock code and number of shares.
Sell order	A sell order specifies the ask price, stock code and number of shares.
Stock	A company listed in a stock exchange. Shares of a company can be traded only in a multiple of its lot size.
Execution result	The result of the execution of a trade order. It contains a list of transactions.
Transaction	The execution of a trade order at a particular price. It also contains the number of shares traded at that price.

Identifying Associations between Classes

An association is a relationship between objects. For example, John and Peter are instances of the class *person* and John is the father of Peter. Association can be identified by looking for verbs and verb phrases connecting two or more objects in the problem statement. In the online stock trading system example, the statement "a client may *open* one or more *accounts* for stock trading" [emphasis added] contains the verb "open" which links the client and the account. The association between the client and the *account* may be named as *has* since it is an ownership relationship. The association can also be named as *opened by* to reflect the action performed by the *client*. However, the word *has* can more accurately describe the nature of the association. Hence, the association should be named according to its nature rather than according to the verb or verb phrase linking the classes in the problem statement. Table 2.7 shows the list of verb phrases extracted from the problem statement to identify the candidate associations.

Table 2.7. Associations identified by extracting verb phrases from the problem statement

Verb phrase	Association
A client may open one or more accounts for stock trading.	has
When a client issues a buy order for an account, the client must specify the stock code, the number of shares and the maximum price that he is willing to pay for them (the bid price).	issued by, buy
When a client issues a sell order for an account, the client must specify the stock code, the number of shares and the minimum price that he is willing to sell them at (the ask price).	issued by, sell
All trade orders will be forwarded to the stock trading system of the stock exchange for execution.	executed by
When an order is completed, the stock trading system of the stock exchange will return the transaction details of the order to the online stock trading system.	returned by
The transaction details of a trade order may be a list of transactions, and each transaction specifies the price and the number of shares traded.	consists of

From the domain knowledge, we have the following associations:

- A stock is listed on a stock exchange
- A stock is traded on a stock trading system of a stock exchange
- The result of a trade order is a list of transactions
- A stock exchange has one or more stock trading systems

Based on the above information, formulate the initial domain class model for the system as illustrated in Figure 2.24.

Then refine the associations by eliminating unnecessary and inappropriate associations and by adding additional associations from the knowledge of the problem domain. Rumbaugh et al. propose the following criteria in Table 2.8 to determine whether an association should be eliminated.

Figure 2.24. Initial domain class model

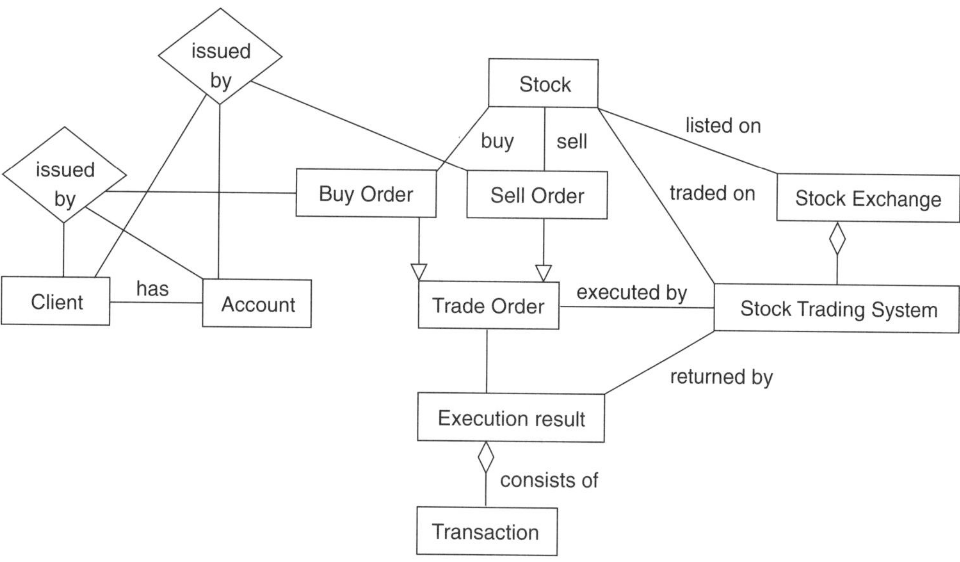

Table 2.8. Criteria to eliminate associations

Criteria	Description
Associations between eliminated classes	If a class is eliminated from the domain class model, then all associations linking to it should be removed. In some cases, the dangling links of the classes caused by the removal of a class may be joined to form a new association.
Irrelevant or implementation associations	Associations that are not directly related to the problem domain or are only related to the solution of the problem should be eliminated.
Actions	The association should define structural relationships between domain classes, not an event. For example, "the client can check the status of execution of his (buy or sell) orders" describes an action performed by the client in an interaction between the client and the system.

Table 2.8. (Cont'd)

Criteria	Description
Ternary associations	Many associations involving three or more classes can be decomposed into binary associations. For example, "a client issues a buy order for an account" can be decomposed into two binary associations: "a client issues an order" and "the order is associated with the client's account".
Derived associations	Remove associations that can be defined in terms of other associations or a condition of the attributes of the classes. For example, "the stock trading system of the stock exchange will return the execution result" can be defined in terms of "a trade order is executed by a stock trading system" or "the trade order has an execution result".

Based on these guidelines, the revised domain class model can be refined as shown in Figure 2.25.

Figure 2.25. Revised domain class model

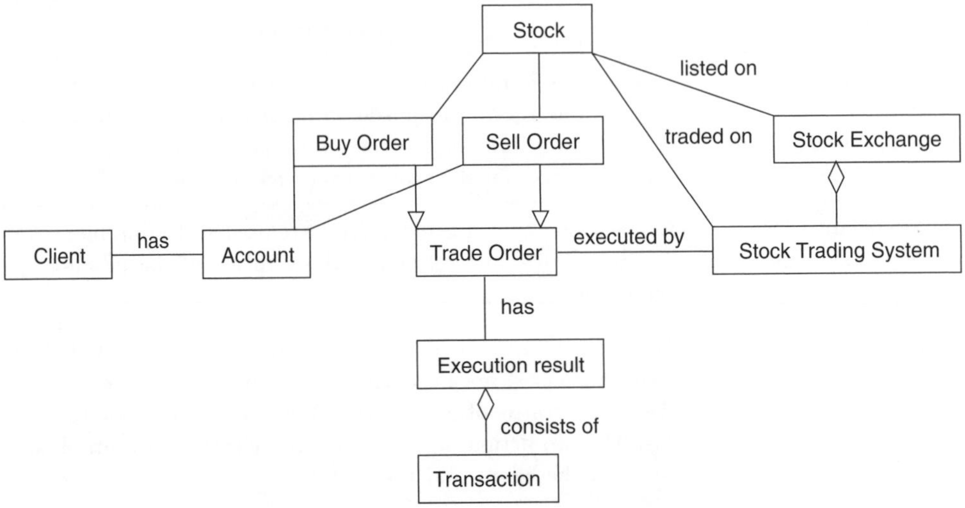

Identifying Attributes of Classes and Association Classes

Attributes are properties of a class, such as *name*, *address* and *telephone number* of the *Client* class. Look for nouns or noun phrases followed by possessive phrases, e.g. "address of the client." Adjectives that appear immediately before a noun and correspond to a class can also be an enumerated value of an attribute, e.g. "a canceled buy order." Attributes are less likely to be discovered from the problem statement. However, it is not necessary to identify all attributes in this step because the attributes do not affect the structure of the domain class model. Instead, this should only be done if they can be readily identified. At later stages of the development life cycle (e.g. detailed design phrase), the attributes can be more readily identified.

Structuring Classes Using Inheritance

At this point, most of the classes and associations have been identified, and it is possible to try to restructure the class diagram using inheritance. Inheritance provides an effective and convenient way to specify commonality between classes. Identify inheritance in two opposite directions: top down and bottom up.

Bottom-up Approach

For the bottom-up approach, we compare the properties of classes to look for commonality. Usually the names of the classes provide the first hint for the identification process. Look for classes with similar attributes, operations and associations with other classes. For example, the *Buy Order* and *Sell Order* classes both have the *price* and *number of shares* attributes and both of them are associated with the *Stock* class and *Account* class. Their names also suggest that they may share similar properties and behaviors.

Also define a *superclass* to cover classes with a common structure. For example, the *Trade Order* class can cover the common structure of the *Buy Order* and *Sell Order* classes. Add an association between the *Trade Order* class and the *Account* class, and between the *Trade Order* class and the *Stock* class. The associations between the *Buy Order*, *Sell Order*, *Account* and *Stock* classes should be eliminated as these associations can be derived from inheritance and the associations of the superclass *Trade Order*.

Top-down Approach

For the top-down approach, check whether a class has some special cases that have additional structural or behavioral requirements. Look for noun phrases consisting of adjectives and class names. For example, the *Sell Order* and *Buy Order* classes are specializations of the *Trade Order* class. Taxonomies of real-life objects can also suggest specializations of a class which may not be included in the problem statement. Think more broadly and use your domain knowledge in identifying specializations. For example, an *Account* can be categorized into two types: *Cash Account* and *Margin Account*. The revised domain class model is shown in Figure 2.26.

Figure 2.26. Revised domain class diagram after restructuring using inheritance and adding attributes

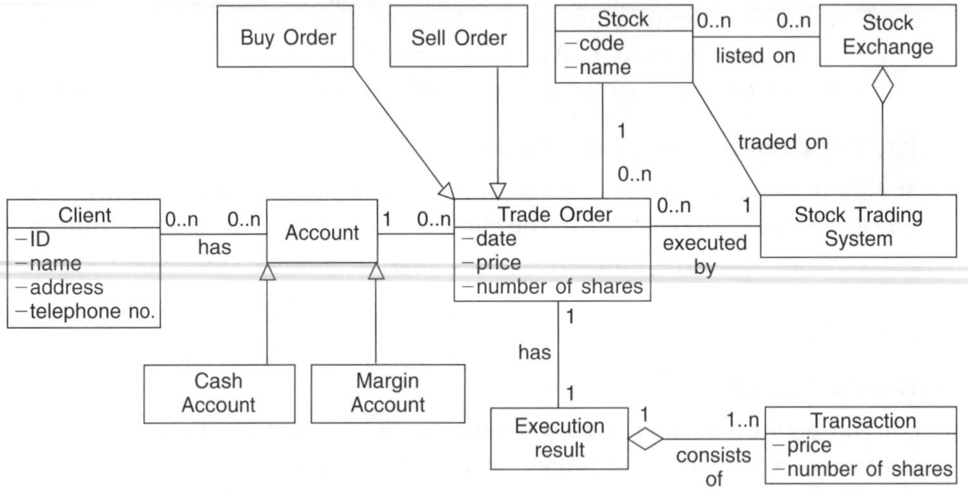

Verifying Access Paths for Likely Queries

One way to verify the correctness and usefulness of the domain class model is to check whether the domain class diagram can provide correct answers to queries that are common to other applications in the domain. In the online stock trading system example, a typical client query would be the current stock balance of his account. This requires an association between the *Account* class and the *Stock* class to provide the information on the number of shares held in the account. Although a path from the *Account* class to the *Stock* class exists in the domain class model in Figure 2.26, it would only provide the buy and sell orders information of the account but not the information on stock balances. To cope with this additional requirement, an association between the *Stock* class and the *Account* class as illustrated in Figure 2.27 needs to be added. The domain class model should always provide a correct answer to a typical query of the system.

Figure 2.27 Addition of an association between account class and stock class

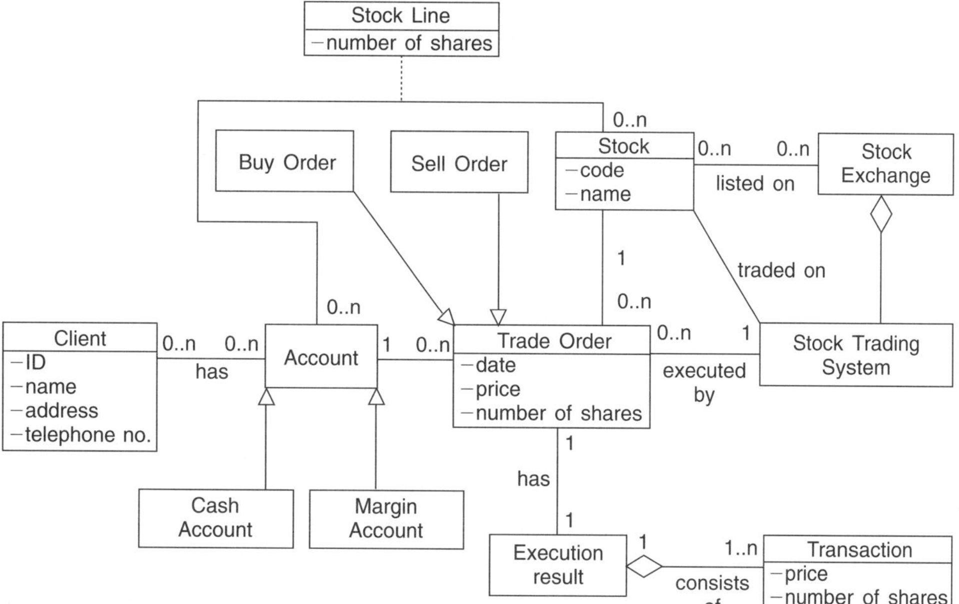

Iterating and Refining Model

It is highly unlikely that the correct domain class model can be developed in one pass. The domain class model needs to be refined several times before it becomes robust. The development of the domain class model is not a rigid process, and it is necessary to repeatedly apply the above steps until the domain class model finally becomes stable. The following checklist can help in identifying areas of improvement of the domain class model.

- Where a class is without attributes, operations and associations, consider removing the class.
- Where a class is with many attributes and operations covering a wide area of requirements, consider splitting the class into two or more classes.
- Where a query cannot be answered by tracing the domain class model, consider adding additional associations.
- Where there are asymmetries in generalizations and association, consider adding additional associations and restructuring the classes with inheritance.
- Where attributes or operations are without a hosting class, consider adding new classes to hold these attributes and operations.

Tricks and Tips in Structural Modeling and Analysis

Set Focus and Context of Diagram

Make sure the class diagram only deals with the static aspects of the system. Do not attempt to consolidate everything into one single class diagram. Before you start to develop the diagram, set the context and the purpose it is to serve and the scope of the class diagram.

Use Appropriate Names for Classes

The classes can be identified from two sources: domain analysis and use case analysis. If the classes identified from the use case analysis are similar or identical to those derived from the domain analysis, that would be a perfect situation to be in. On the other hand, where inconsistent classes are derived from these two sources, discuss them with the end users, advising them to use standard terminologies of the industry, allowing for a dominant player in the field. If they insist on using their (non-standard) terminologies, it may be necessary to put the standard ones in the libraries and use subclasses for their non-standard terminologies specifically for this application.

Organize Diagram Elements

Not only should the classes be structured with various object-oriented semantics, but also organize their elements spatially to improve readability. For example, minimize cross lines in the diagram and place the semantically similar elements close together.

Annotate Diagram Elements

Attach notes to those elements where unclear concepts need to be clarified, and where necessary, attach external files, documents or links within the notes (i.e. a http link or a directory path). Some automated CASE tools support such annotations (e.g. Visual Paradigm for UML), so that resources can be glued into a navigable visual model.

Refine Structural Model Iteratively and Incrementally

As you progress through the development stages, the structural models can be enriched from time to time. For example, dynamic models help to identify the responsibilities of the classes, or possibly even new classes, implementation classes and control classes. This concept will be discussed in more details in Chapter 4 (Dynamic Modeling and Analysis).

Show Only Relevant Associations

If a class is used by a number of use cases or even several applications, the class may have a number of associations that are related to different contexts. In the diagram, only show the associations related to the context that you are concerned with and hide the irrelevant associations. Do not attempt to consolidate all the associations and classes into a large class model as this cannot be easily managed by most people.

Domain Modeling and Analysis with VP-UML

In this section, the use of the key features of VP-UML to perform domain analysis will be demonstrated. The online stock trading system discussed earlier will be used in this chapter as an example. Simply follow the instructions on the following pages to create the sample domain class diagram. Follow the steps below to perform the domain model and analysis:

1. Prepare problem statement for the system being developed
2. Identify objects and classes
3. Develop data dictionary
4. Identify associations between classes
5. Identify attributes of classes and association classes
6. Structure object classes using inheritance
7. Verify access paths for likely queries
8. Iterate and refine the model

Step 1: Prepare Problem Statement

The problem statement is prepared through interviews with domain experts familiar with the application domain. Here, the application domain is an online stock trading system for stock brokerage firms. Alternatively, interview stakeholders of several stock brokerage firms to directly collect the requirements information. The problem statement should cover only the general requirements of an online stock trading system.

First, start up the VP-UML Integrated Development Environment and go through the following steps to enter the problem statement into VP-UML:

1.1. Click [icon] on the **application toolbar** (see Figure 2.28).

Figure 2.28. Domain analysis work area

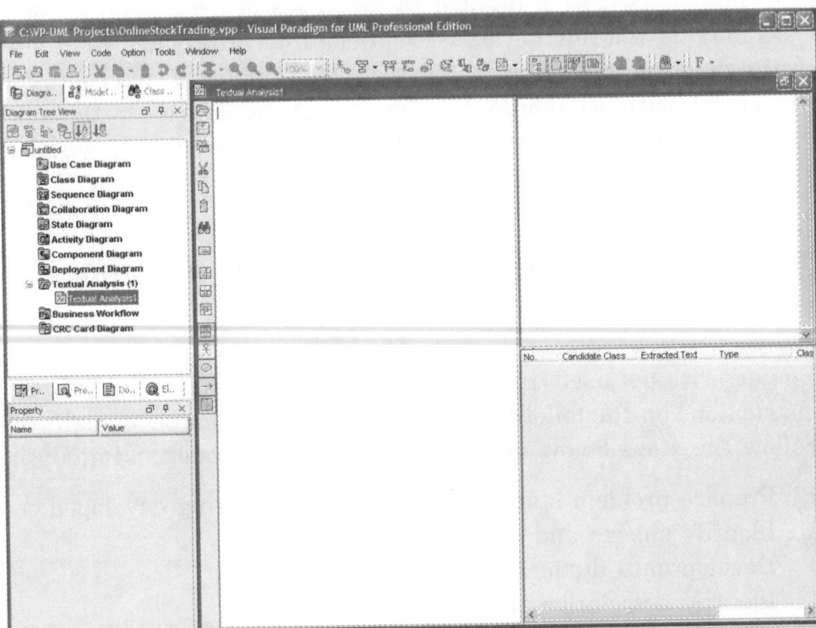

1.2. Type in the following problem statement in the **text pane**, or open it from a file (see Figure 2.29).

> For a stock brokerage firm that wants to provide an online stock trading service to enable its clients to make trades via the computer, a client must first be registered before he can trade online. The registration process involves the client providing his ID, address and telephone number. A client may open one or more accounts for stock trading.
>
> The stock brokerage firm needs to be registered with a stock exchange before its clients can trade the stocks listed on the stock exchange. A stock brokerage firm can be registered with one or

Figure 2.29. Entering problem statement

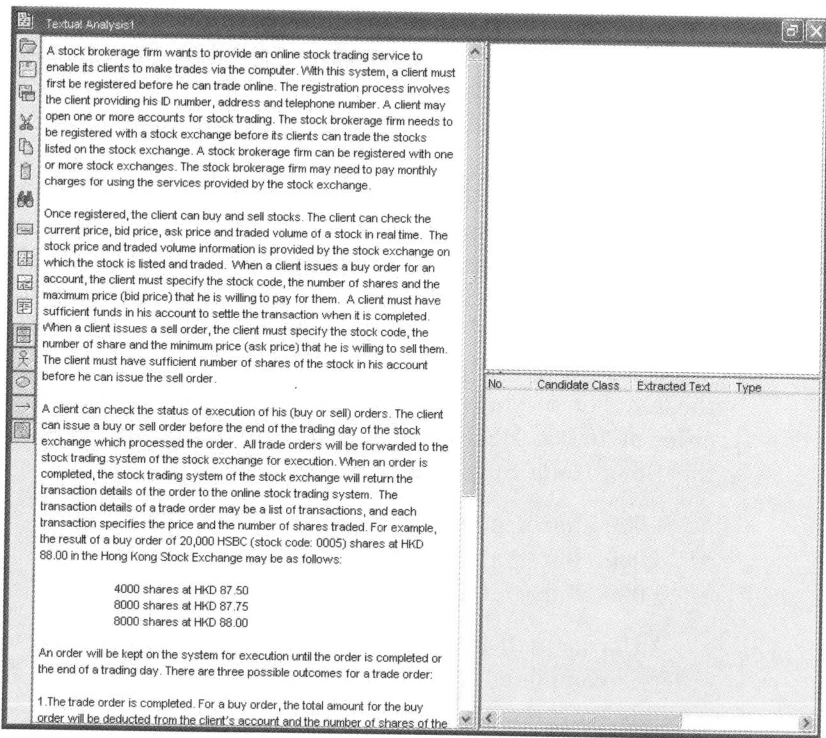

more stock exchanges. The stock brokerage firm may need to pay monthly charges for using the services provided by the stock exchange.

Once registered, the client can begin to buy and sell stocks. The client can check the current price, bid price, ask price and traded volume of a stock in real time. The stock price and traded volume information is provided by the stock exchange on which the stock is listed and traded. When a client issues a buy order for an account, the client must specify the stock code, the number of shares and the maximum price (bid price) that he is willing to pay for them. A client must have sufficient funds in his account to settle the transaction when it is completed. When a client issues a sell order, the client must specify the stock code, the number of shares and the minimum price (ask price) that he is willing to sell them. The client must have sufficient number of shares of the stock in his account before he can issue the sell order. A client can check the status of execution of his (buy or sell) orders.

The client can issue a buy or sell order before the end of the trading hours of a trading day of the stock exchange which processed the order. All trade orders will be forwarded to the stock trading system of the stock exchange for execution. When an order is completed, the stock trading system of the stock exchange will return the transaction details of the order to the online stock trading system. The transaction details of a trade order may be a list of transactions, and each transaction specifies the price and the number of shares traded. For example, the result of a buy order of 20,000 HSBC (stock code: 0005) shares at HKD 88.00 in the Hong Kong Stock Exchange may be as follows:

- 4,000 shares at HKD 87.50
- 8,000 shares at HKD 87.75
- 8,000 shares at HKD 88.00

An order will be kept on the system for execution until the order is completed or the end of a trading day. There are three possible outcomes for a trade order:

1. The trade order is completed. For a buy order, the total amount for the buy order will be deducted from the client's account and the number of shares of the stock purchased will be deposited into the account. For a sell order, the number of shares sold will be deducted from the client's account and the proceeds of the sell order will be deposited into the account.
2. The trade order is partially completed. The number of shares actually traded (sell or buy) is less than the number of shares specified in the order. The number of shares successfully traded in the order will be used to calculate the amount of the proceeds, and the client's account is adjusted accordingly.
3. The trade order is not executed by the end of a trading day. The order is canceled.

A stock exchange may require that the number of shares specified in an order must be in multiples of the lot size of the stock. Each stock has its own lot size. Commonly used lot sizes are 1, 400, 500, 1,000 and 2,000 shares.

The client can deposit or withdraw cash or stock shares from his account. Upon the deposit or withdrawal of cash or stock shares, the account cash or stock balance will be updated accordingly.

Step 2: Identify Objects and Classes

Once the problem statement is entered into the case tool, the next step is to identify objects and classes in the textual analysis working area.

2.1. Let us highlight the term *client* as a candidate class (see Figure 2.30) and drag it to the **Candidate Class Container** on the top right hand corner.

2.2. Notice that all occurrences of the same class in the problem statement is highlighted automatically (see Figure 2.31).

2.3. Repeat the above steps to identify the remaining classes:

- *Trade Order*
- *Account*
- *Stock Exchange*
- *Buy Order*
- *Transaction*
- *Sell Order*
- *Stock Trading System*
- *Execution Result*
- *Stock*

Step 3: Develop Data Dictionary

Let us define the candidate classes identified in Step 1. Select the **Class Description** cell next to the classes – *Client*. Enter the following description in the **Class Description** cell next to the class (see Figure 2.32). Adjust the size of the cell to view the whole description.

An individual or a company registered with the stock brokerage firm for the use of online stock trading services. The class has attributes address, telephone number and ID. A client can have one or more accounts.

Figure 2.30. Highlighting the word *client*

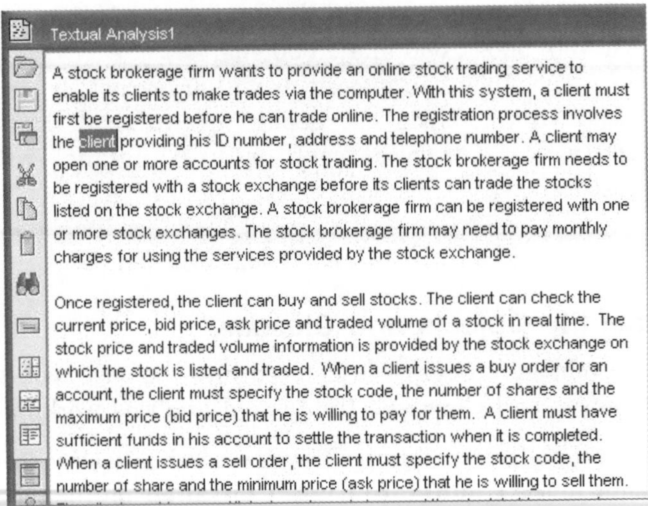

Figure 2.31. All occurrences of the word *client* are highlighted automatically

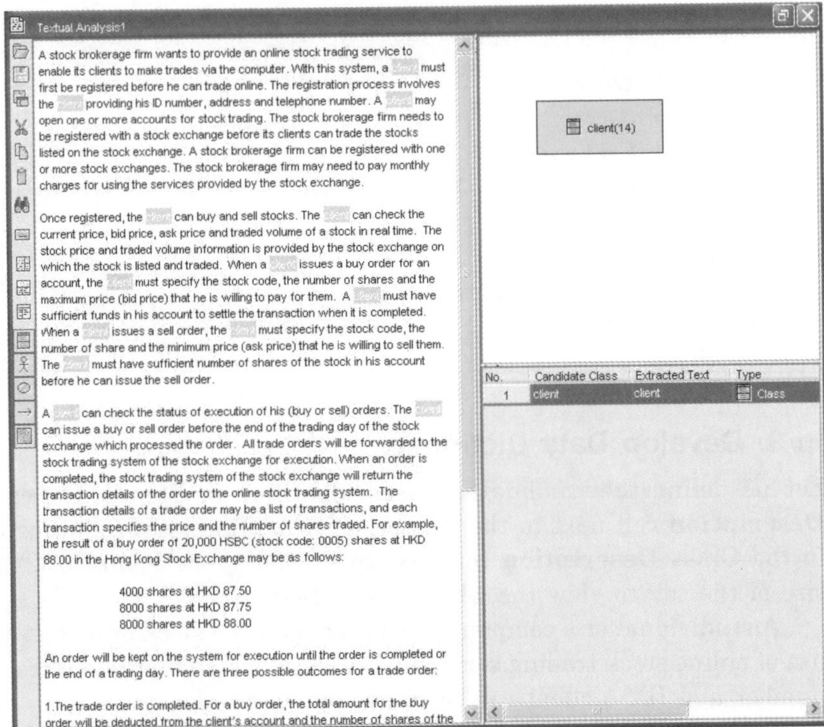

Figure 2.32. Data dictionary

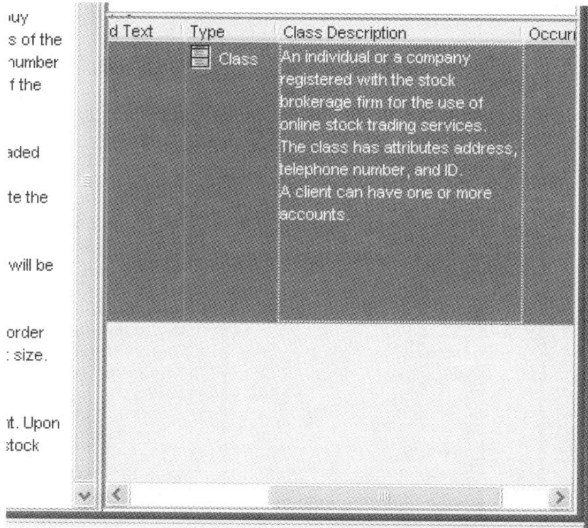

Repeat the above steps to complete the dictionary for all remaining candidate classes.

When the data dictionary has been defined, create the models from the candidate classes. To create a model, right click on the candidate class and select **Create Class Model** (see Figure 2.33). After that is done, the type of the candidate class will change to **Generated Model**, and the class model is created in the **Class Repository**.

Figure 2.33. Create model from Candidate Class

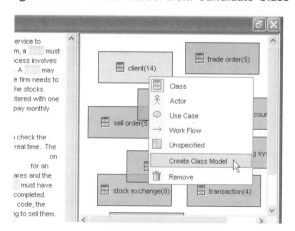

The candidate classes can be viewed by clicking the **Class Browser** tab at the bottom left corner of the screen (see Figure 2.34).

Figure 2.34. Class browser

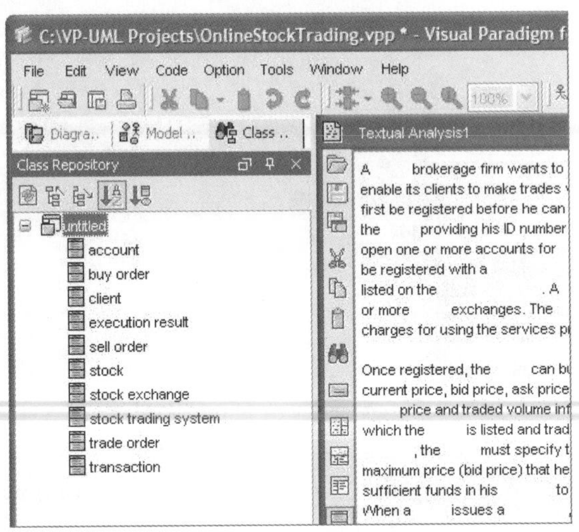

Step 4: Identify Associations between Classes

Having identified the candidate classes, the next step is to identify the associations among them. By analyzing the verb phrases in the problem statement, we find that the verb *open* connects two candidate classes in the statement "a client may open one or more accounts for stock trading." This is a "has a" relationship between *Client* and *Account*. So we can create an association between *Client* and *Account*.

4.1. Create a class diagram by right clicking the **Class Diagram** button on the toolbar and select **Create Class Diagram** (see Figure 2.35). A new class diagram will appear in the **diagram pane**.

Figure 2.35. Create a Class Diagram

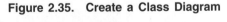

4.2. Drag the class *Client* from the **Class Browser** and drop it to the **Class Diagram** (see Figure 2.36).

Figure 2.36. Creating class using Class Browser

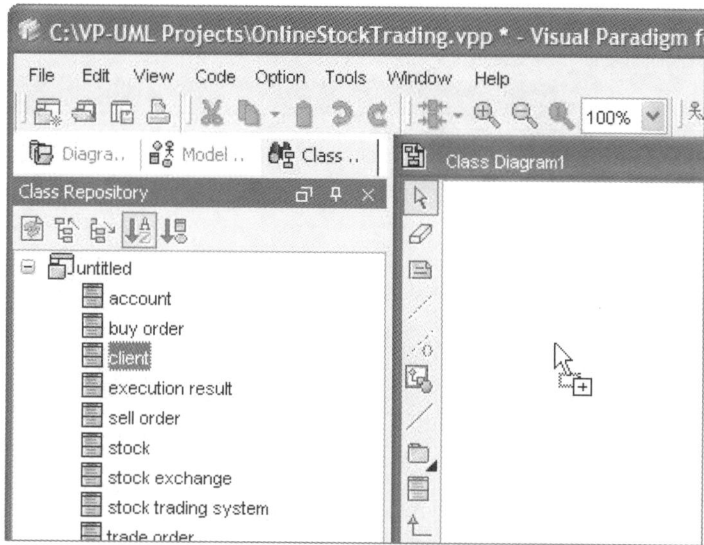

4.3 The class *Client* now appears in the **Class Diagram** (see Figure 2.37).

4.4 Repeat the previous steps to create the class *Account* in the **Class Diagram**.

Figure 2.37. Creating Class *Client*

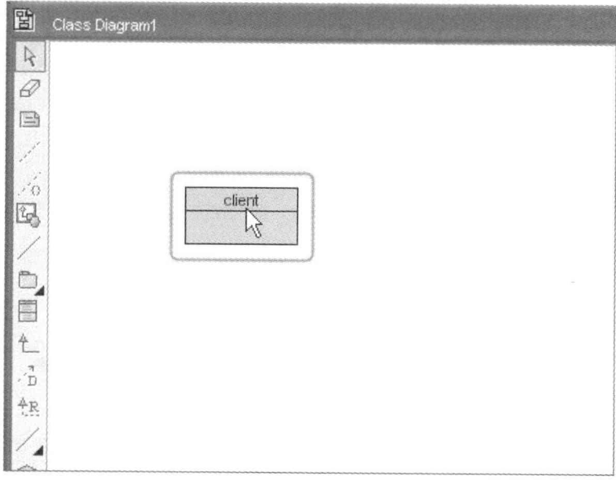

4.5 To create an association between *Client* and *Account*, select the class *Client*, then click the association icon from the resource-centric interface and drag it to the class *Account*. The association between the *Client* and *Account* classes will then be created (see Figure 2.38).

Figure 2.38. Making an association between the classes *Client* and *Account*

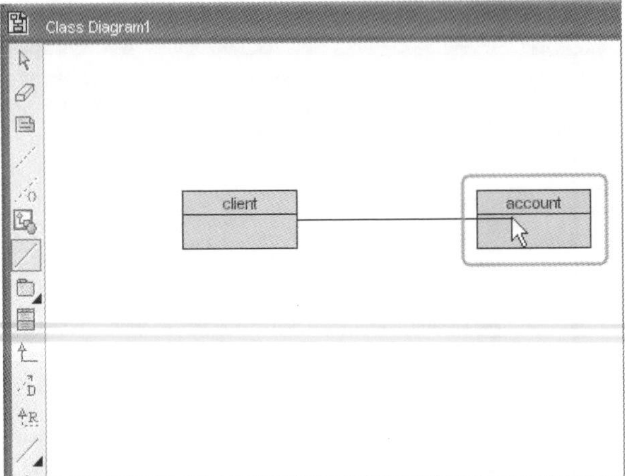

4.6 Repeat the above steps to complete all other associations. Figure 2.39 shows the initial class model for the system.

Step 5: Identify Attributes of Classes and Association Classes

At this point, the basic structure of the domain class model is up and running. The domain class model should be refined by adding attributes to individual classes. As discussed earlier, attributes can be identified by textual analysis on nouns, noun phrases or adjectives. Look for nouns or noun phrases followed by a possessive phrase and a noun and corresponding to a class, e.g. *address of the client*. Adjectives appearing immediately before a noun and corresponding to a class can also be an enumerated value of a class's attribute, e.g. *a canceled sales order*. Follow the instructions below to add attributes to individual classes.

5.1. To create attributes in VP-UML, first select a class. Right click on the class *Client*, then select **New Attribute** (Figure 2.40).

5.2. Type in the attribute in the in-line **text editing area** and then press enter (see Figure 2.41).

5.3. Repeat the above steps to enter the attributes of the other classes. The domain class diagram with attributes is shown in Figure 2.42.

Figure 2.39. The initial domain class diagram

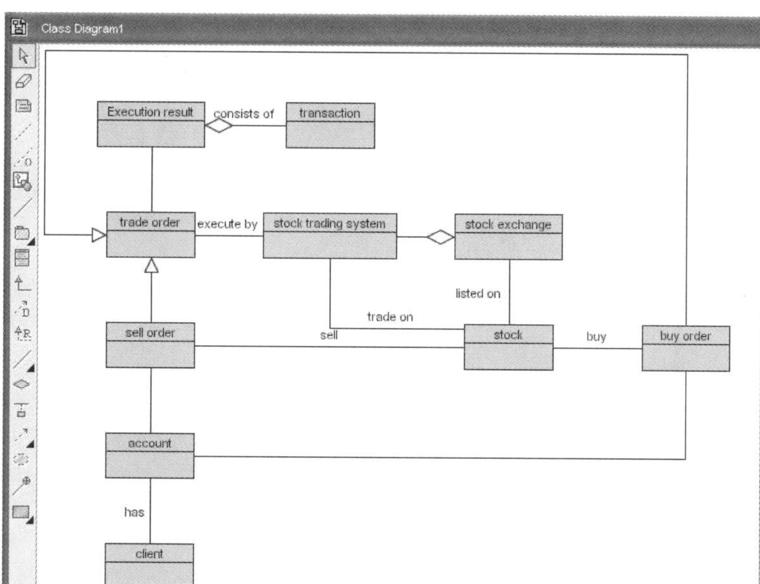

Figure 2.40. Adding an attribute

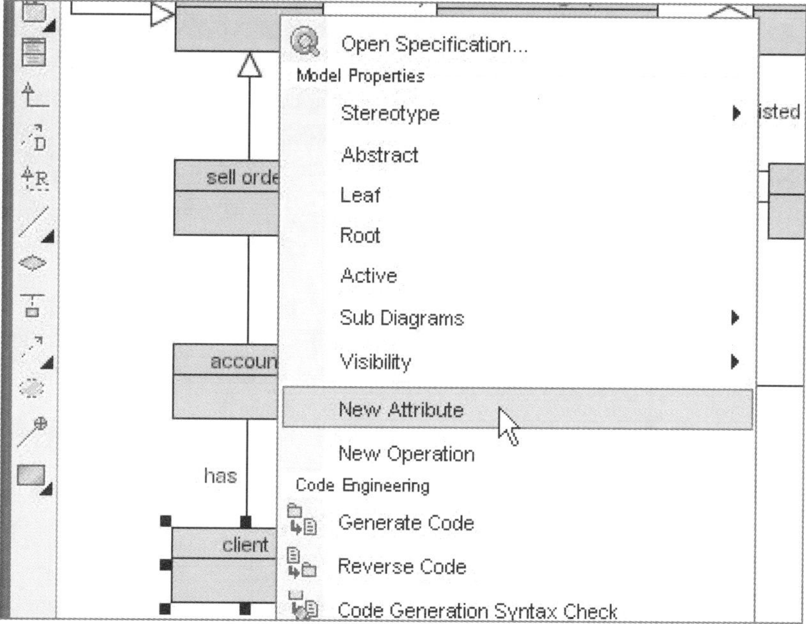

Figure 2.41. Editing an attribute name

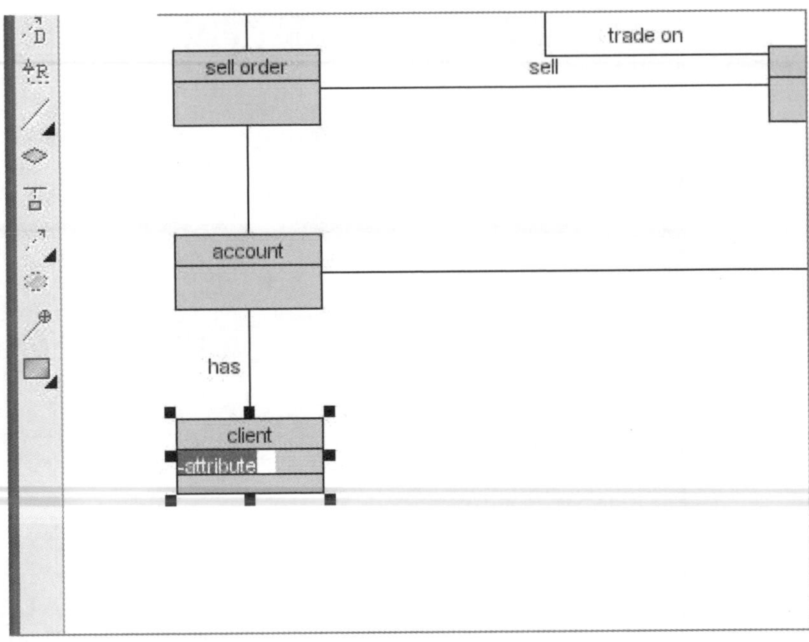

Figure 2.42. Initial domain class diagram with attributes

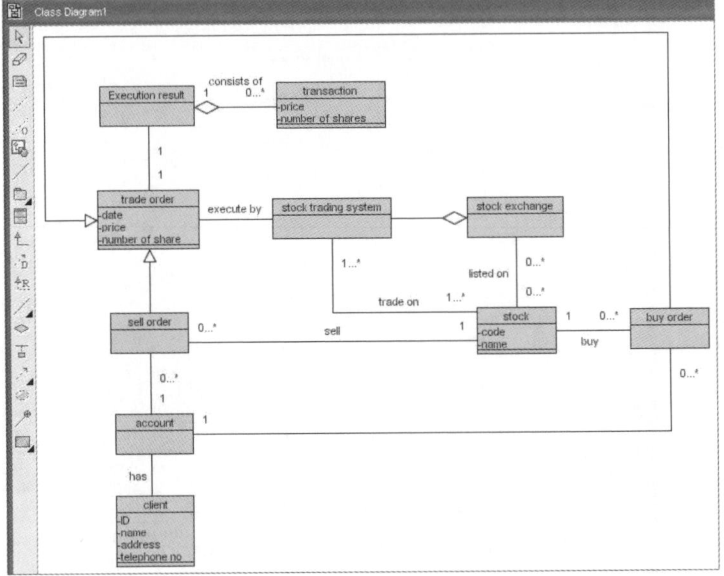

Step 6: Structure Object Classes Using Inheritance

As most classes have now been identified, start to reorganize the classes in order to further improve reusability and cohesion. We eliminate duplication of classes by singling out the common attributes and operations into superclasses. The cohesion within a class can be improved by breaking a "loosely coupled" class into two or more classes which may be related by inheritance or association.

6.1. By adopting the top-down approach, we discover that the class *Account* has two subtypes, *Cash Account* and *Margin Account*. To structure the *Cash Account* and *Account* classes using inheritance, first create the *Cash Account* and *Margin Account* subclasses.

6.2. Select the *Account* class. Then click on the icon from the resource-centric interface, and drag and place it on the *Cash Account* class. The inheritance relationship between *Account* and *Cash Account* is then specified (see Figure 2.43).

Figure 2.43. Creating inheritance relationship between *Margin Account* and *Cash Account*

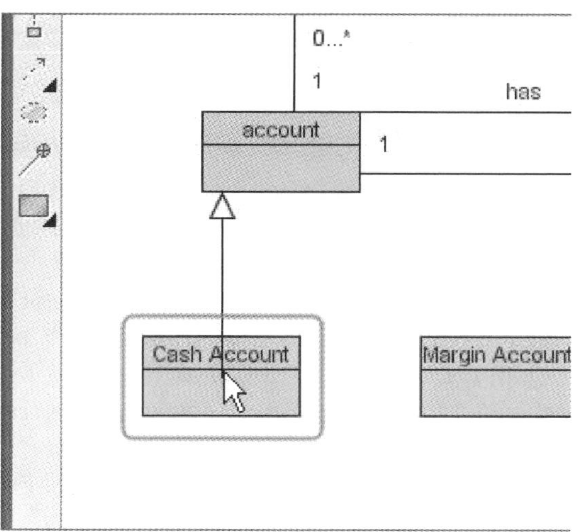

6.3. Repeat the above steps to create the inheritance relationship between the *Margin Account* and *Account* classes. The restructured domain class diagram is shown in Figure 2.44.

Figure 2.44. Restructured domain class diagram

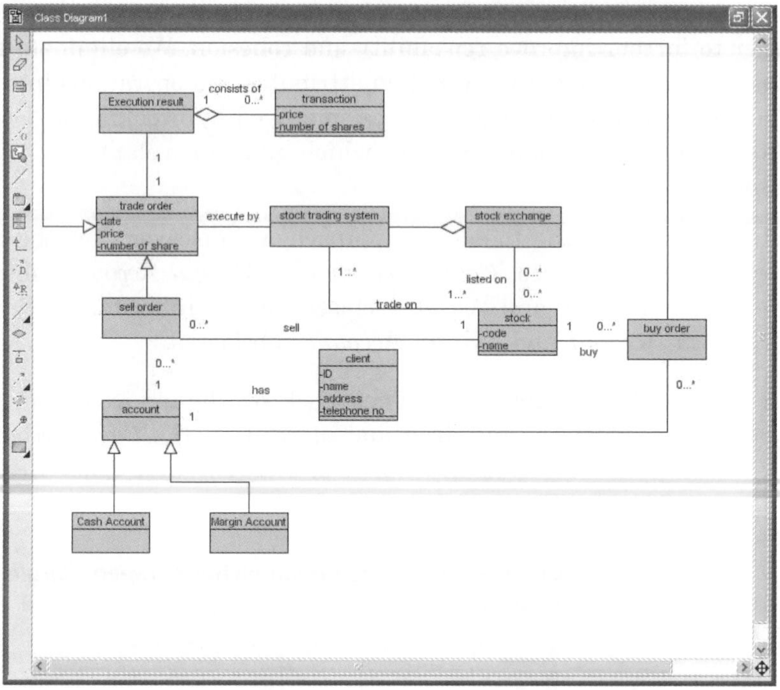

Step 7: Verify Access Paths for Likely Queries

Now verify the class diagram to see whether it can support typical queries of the application domain. Let us consider the following query: How does a client find out the stock balance of his account?

By examining the class diagram, the query cannot be answered directly as the class diagram can only show the transactions performed by the client. Of course the balance of a stock can be determined by all the transactions of the stock performed by the client. However, it is rather inconvenient and inefficient as a large number of transactions may be involved. Therefore, an association is added between *Account* and *Stock*. Follow the steps below to add the required association.

7.1. Follow the instructions given in Step 3 to create an association between *Account* and *Stock*, after which a domain class diagram like Figure 2.45 will be created.

Figure 2.45. Adding an association between *Account* and *Stock*

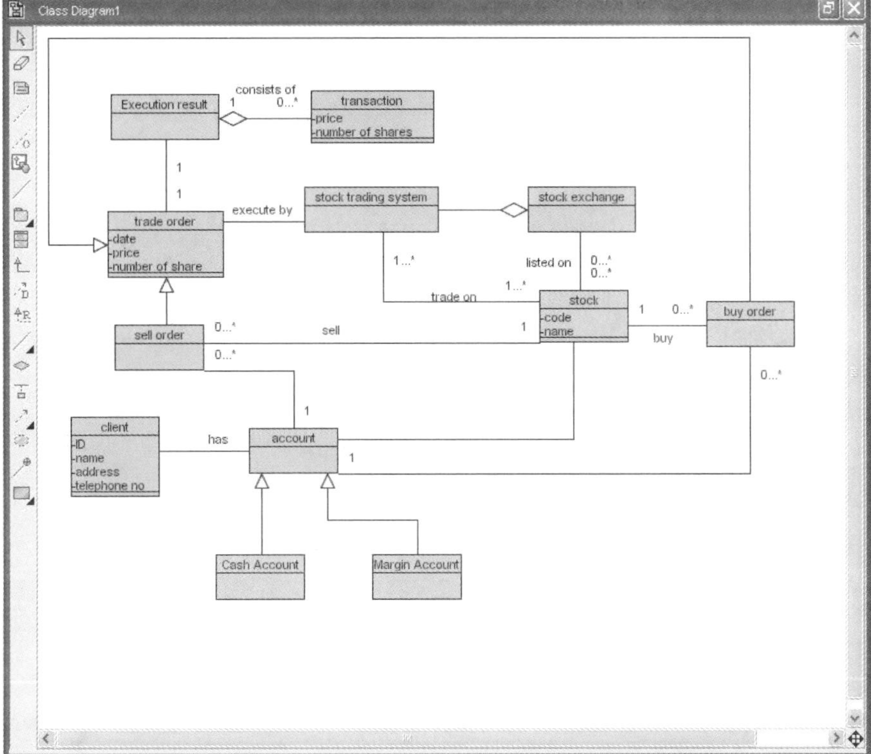

7.2. Now create an association class between *Account* and *Stock* to keep track of the balance of a stock in an account. Follow Step 6 to create the class *StockLine*. Click on the icon on the **diagram palette**, then click the *StockLine* class and drag it to the association.

7.3. Edit the name of the class in the **in-line editing area** of the class. A revised domain class diagram like Figure 2.46 will then be created.

Step 8: Iterate and Refine Model

Repeatedly apply Steps 2 to 7 to refine the domain class model until it becomes stable.

Figure 2.46. Revised domain class diagram after first iteration

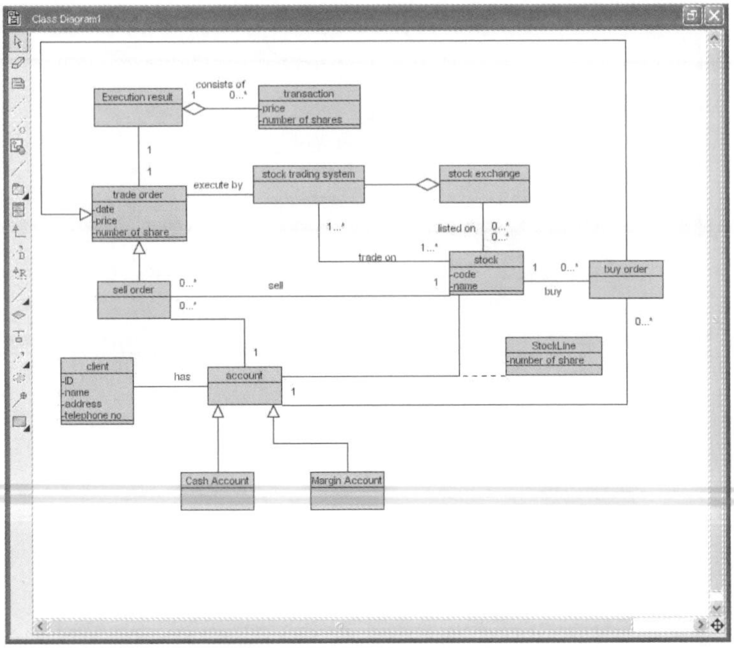

Summary

A structural model provides a static view of a system, showing its key components and their relationships. In the UML notation, a structural model is represented by a class diagram.

In performing structural modeling and analysis, we start off with the problem statement to identify the domain objects and classes, which in turn can be used to compile a data dictionary for the system. By determining the associations between the classes and by identifying the attributes of the classes, the domain's class diagram can be created. The diagram can be structured more concisely for implementation by using inheritance. Finally, access paths for likely queries are verified and the model can be further refined by repeating this modeling and analysis procedure.

To illustrate the concepts described in this chapter, the modeling and analysis of an online stock trading system has been presented, detailing the steps involved by using the powerful features of the VP-UML CASE tool.

Exercise

Consider the following problem statement:

Problem Statement of an Online Book Store

The Pearl River Book Company is developing an online book store system through which its customers can buy books and sell their used books. Public users are those who are not registered customers of the system.

Public users or registered customers can search books by entering keywords, which may appear in the title, author or book description. The system displays a list of books that matches the keywords. Each entry of the book list consists of the book title, author(s), price for a new copy and price range for used copies. The user can select a book from the list to display more detailed information about it (availability, price for new copy, prices for used copies, table of contents, author, ISBN). The user can add a copy of the book (either new or old) to the shopping cart. The user can then continue to search for another book. When the user finishes searching, the user can checkout the books in the shopping cart. The system asks the user to login to his/her account by entering the user's email address and the account password. If the user has not registered yet, the user can register for a new customer account at that point. The user enters the email address, home address and password. The system verifies that the email address has not been used by an existing customer before confirming the creation of the new customer account through an email message. The system then asks the user to select the shipping option (express, priority or ordinary). Different shipping options have different prices. The user can then select the payment method (credit card or the user account of the book store). If the user selects payment by credit card, the user enters the card number, type and expiry date. The system then sends the credit card information and the amount charged to the external payment gateway. The amount is calculated by adding the prices of the selected books and the selected shipping option. If the credit card transaction is approved, the external payment gateway sends back an approval code. Otherwise, the systems will ask the user to reselect the payment method and re-enter the payment information. If the user selects payment by his/her account with a sufficient balance, the system charges the amount to the customer account. Otherwise, the system asks the user to re-reselect the payment method. Upon completion of payment, the system arranges delivery of the ordered books. An external shipping agent is responsible for the delivery of the ordered books. If an order involves new books, the system sends a shipping request to notify the shipping agent to collect the books from the book store. New books in the same order are shipped together. If a used book has been ordered, the system sends a delivery request to notify the seller of the book and a shipping request to the shipping agent of the book store. The shipping agent collects the book from the seller and delivers the book to the buyer. Used books of the same order from the same seller are shipped together. After the book(s) has/have been delivered to the buyer, the shipping agent sends a shipping completion message to the system. Upon receipt of this message, the system updates the seller's customer account by adding the price of the used book minus the commission charge for the service.

A public user or a registered customer wanting to sell a used book can go through the above process by searching the book and displaying its information. The user can then post a used copy for sale. The system will ask the user to enter the price and the general condition of the used book. Then the system further asks the user to enter the email address and password of his/her customer account for login purposes. If the user does not have a customer account, the user can create a new customer account as described in the previous paragraph.

Incrementally and iteratively develop a domain class model for the online ticket reservation system by following the steps below:

- Identify objects and classes
- Develop a data dictionary
- Identify associations between classes
- Identify attributes of classes and association classes
- Structure object classes using inheritance
- Verify access paths for likely queries
- Iteratively refine the model

Chapter

3

Use Case Modeling and Analysis

Overview

The software development process is time-consuming and labor-intensive. The seemingly straightforward, but deceptively difficult, part of this process is to clearly understand and specify the requirements that an application must satisfy. Because of the reiterative nature of the software development process, mistakes made in early stages but are only identified at a much later stage will result in costly reworks and delays.

Use case modeling is an increasingly popular approach for identifying and defining requirements for all kinds of software applications as it is a formalized process for capturing system scenarios. While use case modeling is often associated with and used extensively in projects that utilize the object-oriented approach, it can also be applied to any project regardless of the underlying implementation technology or development approach.

This chapter provides a thorough presentation of the use case modeling approach to software requirements elicitation, including practical, proven techniques that can be immediately applied to software development projects.

What You Will Learn

On completing the study of this chapter, you should be able to:

- state the components of a use case model
- describe how use case models help address common requirements definition problems
- apply a step-by-step approach to develop use cases

- document use cases
- incorporate use case modeling into the project life cycle

Requirements Elicitation

A *requirement* describes a condition or capability to which a system must conform. Requirements are supposed to represent *what* the system should do as opposed to *how* the system should be built. They are either derived directly from user needs or stated in a contract, standard, specification or other formally imposed document.

Requirements elicitation is the process of defining your system. It involves obtaining a clear understanding of the problem space, such as business opportunities, user needs or the marketing environment, and then defining an application or system that solves that problem.

Common Problems in Defining Requirements

Numerous studies showed that over half of software development projects do not work, the major reason being that they do not do what the users actually want, suggesting that there is a breakdown in the requirements elicitation process. DeMarco and Lester (1999) observe that "ill-specified systems are as common today as they were when we first began to talk about Requirements Engineering twenty or more years ago."

Traditionally, requirements specified in software requirements specifications are simple declarative statements written in a text-based, natural-language style (e.g. "when the user logs in, the system displays a splash screen as shown in Figure X"). Developers always use typical scenarios provided in the specifications to try to understand what the requirements of a system mean and how a system is supposed to behave. Unfortunately, software requirements specifications are rarely documented in an effective manner. Use cases are a useful technique for formalizing this process of capturing scenarios.

Use Case Modeling for Requirements Elicitation

A *use case* is a sequence of transactions performed by a system that produces a measurable result for a particular actor. (An *actor* represents a role played by a person or a thing that interacts with a system.) A use case consists of a series of *actions* that a user must initiate in the system to carry out some useful work and to achieve his/her goal. Use cases reflect all of the possible events in the system in the process of achieving an actor's goal.

As mentioned before, the major difficulty in defining system requirements is that very often it is not known what the users actually want. A good use case must represent the point of view of the people who will use or interact with the system; in other words, use cases must describe the behaviors expected of a system from a user's perspective. A complete set of use cases specifies all the possible ways the system will behave, and therefore defines all the requirements (behaviors) of the system, binding the scope of the system. A use case should be considered as a unit of requirement definition or simply a user goal, such as *deposit money* or *check balance* in an automatic teller machine (ATM) system.

In the requirements elicitation process, it is important to correctly identify a set of use cases to discover the real user requirements of the system being developed.

Use Case Modeling Techniques

Use case modeling is the process of describing the behavior of the target system from an external point of view. A use case describes what a system does rather than how it does it. Therefore, use case analysis emphasizes on modeling the externally visible view and not the internal view of the system. Use case analysis allows the designer to focus on the requirements of the system, rather than on its implementation.

A use case diagram enables the system designer to discover the requirements of the target system from the user's perspective. If the designer utilizes use case diagrams in the early stages of system development, the target system is more likely to meet the needs of the user. From both the designer and user's perspectives, the system will also be easier to understand. Furthermore, use case analysis is a very useful tool for the designer to communicate with the client.

What Is Use Case Model?

A *use case model* is a diagram or set of diagrams that, together with additional documentation, show what the proposed software system is designed to do. A use case diagram consists of three main components:

- Actors
- Use cases and their communications
- Additional documentation such as use case descriptions to elaborate use cases and problem statements that are initially used for identifying use cases

In addition, a use case diagram may consist of a system boundary.

Actors

Actors are the entities that interact with the system. They include everything that needs to exchange information with the system. Actors are, therefore, the entities external to the system being designed.

An actor may be:

- people
- computer hardware and devices
- external systems

An actor represents a role that a user can play, but not a specific user. An actor, therefore, represents a group of users taking on a particular role. For example, both John and Peter may be consultants. At the same time, John may also be a project manager in the company. Thus, the same person may be an instance of more than one actor, and conversely, several people can play the same role of an actor.

The common way to identify use cases is to interview the users who will directly operate the system. This process can help design a system which suits their needs. However, other stakeholders of the system, such as the customers and the policy makers of the business process, may be missed out in the vital stages of development. Consequently, the system may not satisfy the needs of all stakeholders. For example, consider a general mail order business consisting of at least three groups of stakeholders: the customer, the staff member who operates the system and the manager of the company. These stakeholders may have different requirements of the system:

- The customer requires that the services provided by the company minimize his time and effort
- The manager wants to maximize the profits of the company
- The staff member hopes to minimize the stock level, bad debts, etc

Obviously, the stakeholders' requirements may sometimes contradict. The development team should hold meetings with all stakeholders to determine all requirements as well as to resolve those that contradict.

Representing Actors

The stick figure is most widely used to represent actors, and it is used even when the actors are not human. Another way to represent an actor in the UML notation is a class icon with the <<actor>> stereotype placed above the class name inside the upper compartment, as shown in Figure 3.1.

Figure 3.1. Equivalent UML representations of an actor: (a) a stick figure and (b) an actor icon

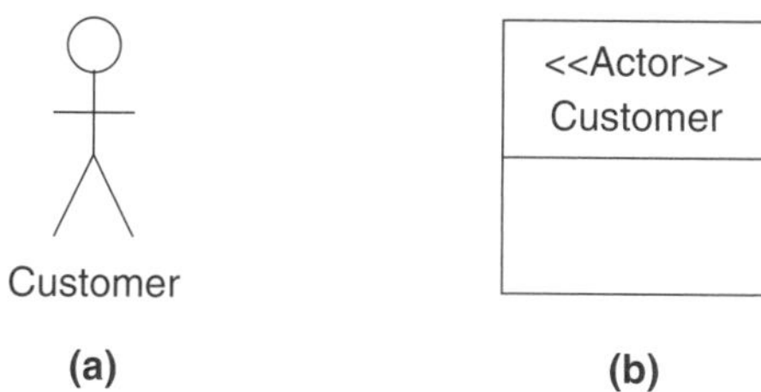

Types of Actors

Actors can be divided into two common types: primary actors and secondary actors. *Primary actors* are the main users or entities for which the system is designed, deriving benefits form it directly.

The following are some key characteristics of primary actors:

- Primary actors are completely outside the system and drive the system requirements
- Primary actors use the system to achieve an observable user goal

As such, the designer has less flexibility in specifying the roles of the primary actors in order to satisfy the requirements of the stakeholders.

Secondary actors are users or entities that supervise, operate and manage the system.

They play a supporting role to facilitate the primary actors to achieve their goals. The following are some key characteristics of secondary actors:

- Secondary actors often appear to be more inside the system than outside
- Secondary actors are usually allocated many system requirements that are not derived directly from the statement of requirements

Hence, the designer can have more freedom in specifying the roles of these actors.

For an example of the roles played by both actors, a tax return can be submitted directly by a taxpayer (the primary actor) either through the Internet or by post. If it is the latter, a data entry operator will enter the data contained in the tax return form to the system. The data entry operator can be viewed as the secondary actor, as he/she helps the taxpayer process the tax return form.

There is a less commonly used group of actors called generalization actors. Generalization is a key concept in object-orientation and object-oriented modeling, allowing models to be simplified and made more expressive. The fact that actors are classes means that actors can be generalized. Through the generalization process, similarities between different actors can be identified.

The UML icon for generalization is a small hollow arrowhead pointing at the superclass of the actor. For instance, a generic actor, such as System Designer, can be inherited by other actors, such as System Analyst and Project Manager. Figure 3.2 shows that the inheriting actors (System Analyst and Project Manager) also inherit the Use Cases associated with the inherited Actor (System Designer).

Figure 3.2. Generalization of actors

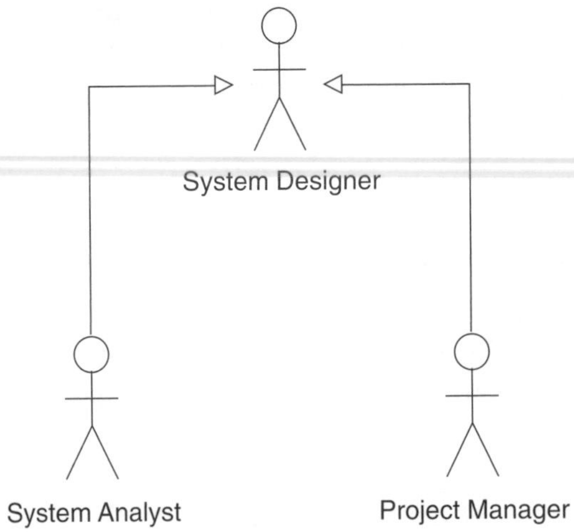

System Designer

System Analyst

Project Manager

Actors versus Roles

Cockburn (2001) suggests that the word role should be used instead of the word actor in use case modeling — the word actor could be misinterpreted leading to confusion. It may be interpreted as an individual or an official rank or a job title in an organization. None of these meanings match the required definition. In the use case model, the precise meaning of "actor" should be a set of roles that can be played by individuals or other external systems. For example, Peter is an order processing clerk and Raymond a sales manager. Both of them can process an order. Hence, Peter and Raymond can be actors of the Process Order use case. We might say that "a sales manager can perform any use case an order processing clerk can." More precisely, Order Handler is defined as the role of processing an order. As such, both Peter and Raymond can play the role

Order Handler. Hence, the same person can play different roles at different times, and staff members with the same job title may play different roles to suit the needs of the business requirements.

Use Cases

A use case describes a sequence of actions a system performs to yield an observable result or value to a particular actor. In other words, use cases are abstractions of dialog between the actors and the system; they describe potential interactions without going into the details of each scenario.

In the UML notation, a use case is represented by an oval with a label describing the actor's goal. A use case is *connected* to one or more actors using communication links represented by straight lines. For example, in interacting with an ATM system, one of the customer goals is to withdraw money from his/her account. The representation of this requirement in UML is shown in Figure 3.3.

Figure 3.3. Actor, use case and communication link

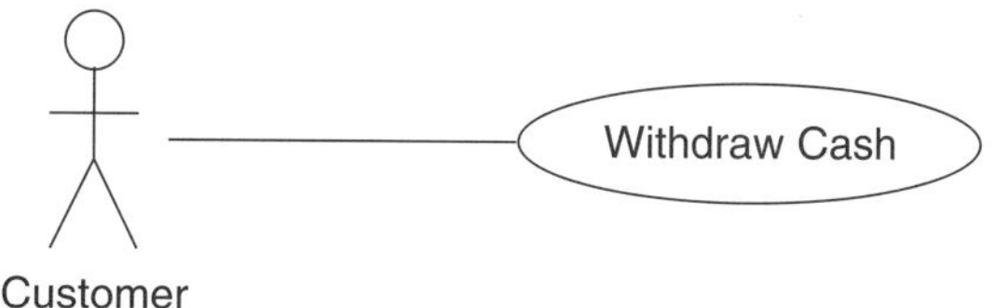

A good use case should

- describe a sequence of transactions performed by a system that produces a measurable result (goal) for a particular actor
- describe the behavior expected of a system from a user's perspective
- enable the system analyst to understand and model a system from a high-level business viewpoint
- represent the interfaces that a system makes visible to the external entities and the inter-relationships between the actors and the system

System Boundaries

System boundaries define the scope of the system being developed and are represented by rectangles in the UML notation. All use cases should reside within the system boundary. The actors are placed outside of the system boundary and all the use cases collectively make up the total requirements of the system.

Use Case Models: Examples

Example 1: An Automatic Teller Machine System

An ATM system is typically used by different types of users (actors). One type of user, the customer, operates the ATM to perform transactions with his/her account(s) through a computerized banking network. The banking network consists of a central computer connected to all ATM machines and bank computers owned by individual banks. Each bank computer is used to process the transaction requested by its customers.

In this example, Customer one is one group of actors for the ATM system. They operate the ATM to withdraw and deposit money, check the account balance, etc. We can represent these observable services as use cases. Figure 3.4 shows a use case diagram for the ATM system.

Figure 3.4. A use case model for an ATM system

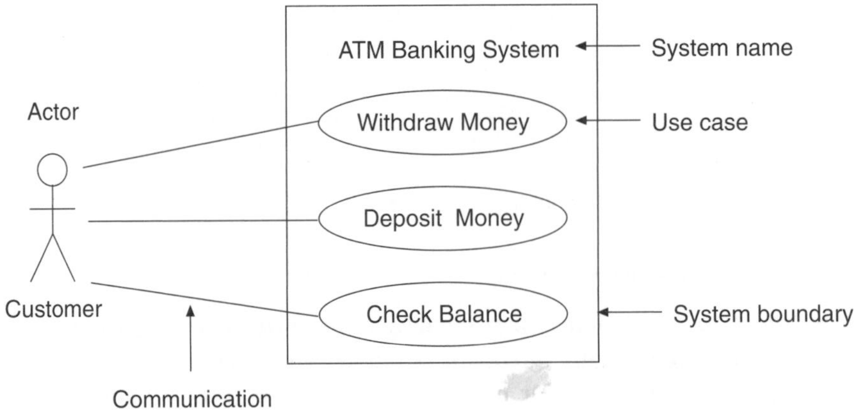

Example 2: A Hotel Information System

In this example, consider a simple hotel information system for two groups of customers: Tour Group customers and Individual customers. Tour Group customers are those who have made advanced reservations through a tour operator, while Individual customers make their reservations directly with the hotel. Both groups of customers can book, cancel, check-in and check-out of a room by phone or via the Internet.

Based on these requirements, there are four observable services as use cases: Make Booking, Cancel Booking, Check-in a Room and Check-out a Room. Figure 3.5 shows the use case model for this simple hotel information system.

Figure 3.5. A use case model for hotel information system

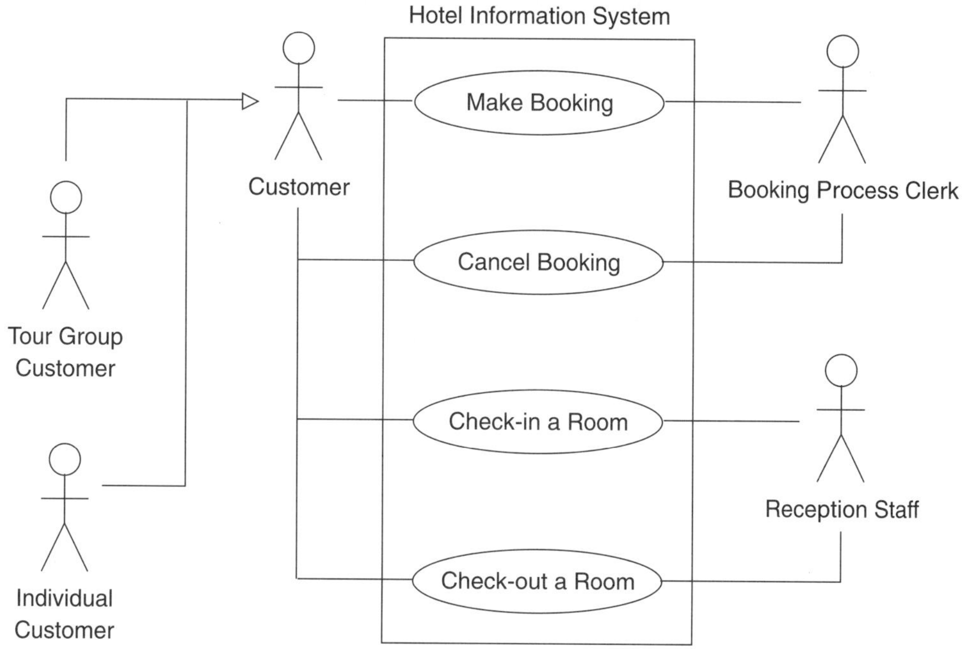

Use Case Analysis Techniques

Conducting Use Case Analysis

During the use case analysis process, the clients and/or the typical users of the system are usually interviewed. Describing a system's use case is a useful and important exercise because it helps to identify redundant or unclear functionalities. Often, clients may well assume that certain things are obvious to the interviewer and are surprised when the interviewer seeks further clarification at length. Similarly, some issues may be obvious to the designers but the end users may find them baffling, particularly in relation to technical issues. Use case analysis helps resolve these potential communication problems (use case analysis will be introduced later in this chapter).

Use case analysis may be helpful in the following areas:

- Discovering new features (requirements). New use cases often help generate new requirements as the system is analyzed and as the design takes shape.

- Communicating with clients. Their notational simplicity makes use case diagrams a mechanism for early discussions with potential users and domain experts.
- Generating test cases. The collection of scenarios for a use case may also provide a suite of test cases and a starting point from which the prototype user interface is shaped. A scenario captures a specific execution of a use case. In other words, a use case is a generalized description or template of a sequence of transactions, while a scenario is an instance of the use case which describes how the use case will be executed in a specific situation.

Summary of UML Notation for Use Case Modeling

Table 3.1. Summary of UML notation

Construct	Description	Syntax
Use case	A sequence of transactions performed by a system that produces a measurable result for a particular actor.	(UseCaseName)
Actor	A coherent set of roles that users play when interacting with these use cases.	ActorName
System boundary	The boundary between the physical system and the actors who interact with the physical system.	**ApplicationName**
Association	The participation of an actor in a use case, i.e. an instance of an actor and instances of a use case communicating with each other.	———
Generalization	A taxonomic relationship between a general use case and a more specific use case. The arrow head points to the general use case.	———▷

Table 3.1. (Cont'd)

Construct	Description	Syntax
Extend	A relationship between an *extension* use case and a *base* use case, specifying how the behavior of the extension use case can be inserted into the behavior defined for the base use case. The arrow head points to the base use case.	<<extend>> - - - - - - - - - - ->
Include	A relationship between a *base* use case and an *inclusion* use case, specifying how the behavior for the inclusion use case is inserted into the behavior defined for the base use case. The arrow head points to the inclusion use case.	<<include>> - - - - - - - - - - ->

Structuring Use Cases with Relationships

In the process of developing a use case model, it may be discovered that some use cases share common behaviors. There are also situations where some use cases are very similar but with additional behaviors. For example, in Figure 3.6, Withdraw Money and Deposit Money both require the user to login to the ATM system. In fact, the login step can also be common to other use cases as well, such as Check Balance. By identifying this common step in the descriptions of the two use cases, we can avoid duplicating efforts if a change in the login process is required. This is done by creating a separate use case called Login Account which can then be shared by other use cases. Figure 3.7 illustrates the results of factoring out the common behavior of the Withdraw Money and Deposit Money use cases.

The relationship between Login Account, Withdraw Money and Deposit Money can be expressed using the <<include>> relationship in UML, as shown in Figure 3.8.

UML supports three types of relationships for use cases: <<include>>, <<extend>> and generalization. A UML stereotype is a label written within guillemets (i.e. << >>) denoting some semantic concept which is outside the basic definition of UML. Using a UML stereotype, the semantics of UML can be extended to support specific design methods or the needs of the designer. This mechanism enriches the UML for specific applications without increasing the complexity within the basic UML notation itself. <<include>> and

<<extend>> are stereotypes for use case relationships. Each of these relationships is explained in detail below.

Figure 3.6. Two use cases with a common behavior

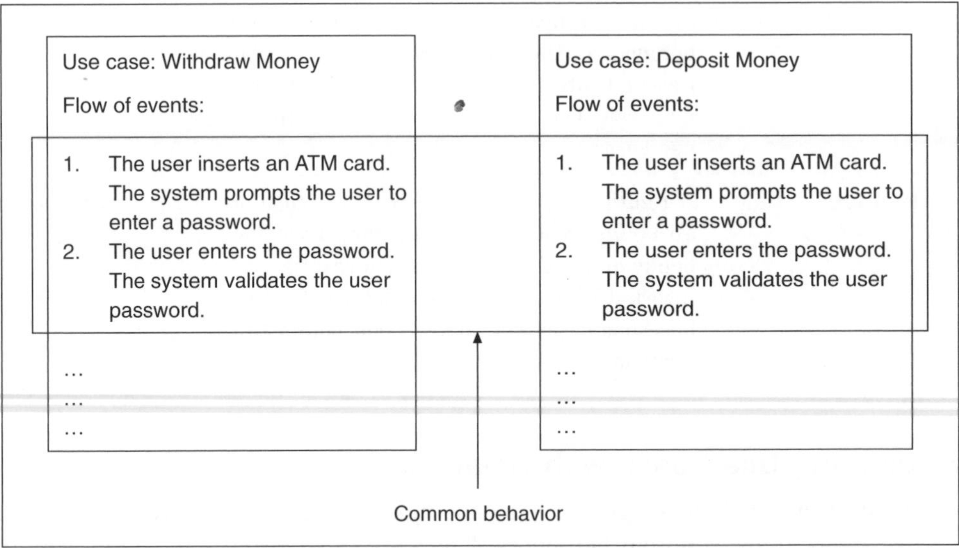

Figure 3.7. Common behavior of two use cases is extracted, named and referenced

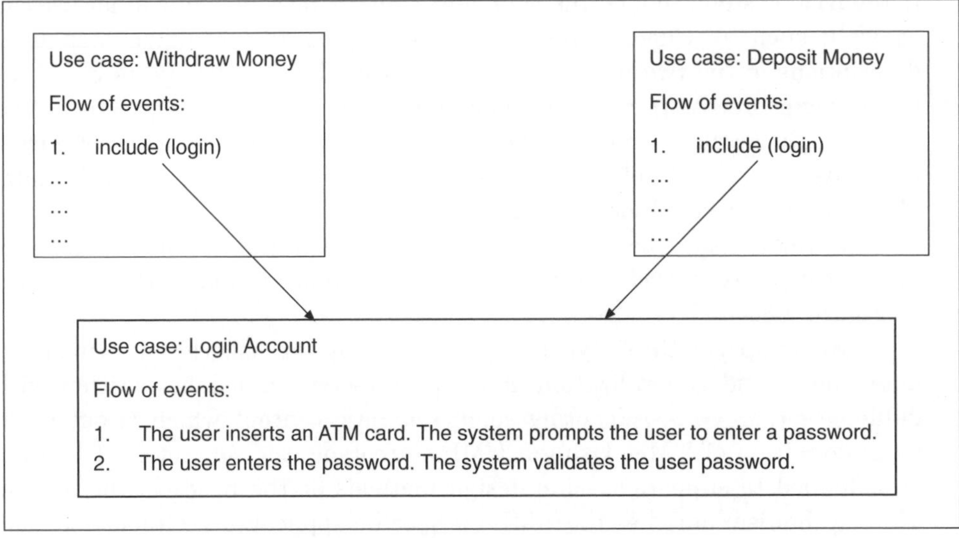

Figure 3.8. An <<include>> use case: Login Account

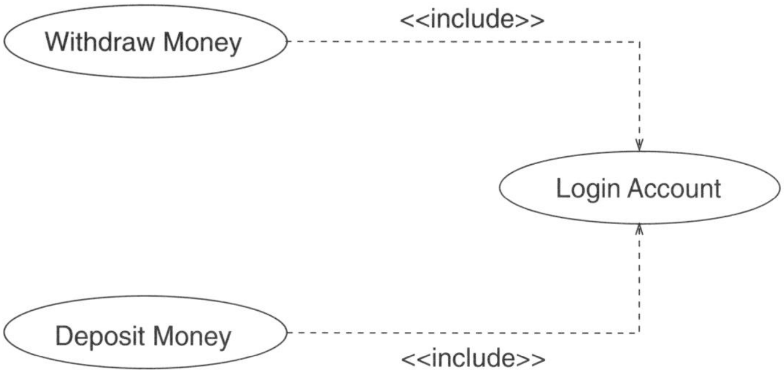

The <<include>> Relationship

<<include>> relationships are used when two or more use cases share some common portion in a flow of events. This common portion is then grouped and extracted to form an inclusion use case to be shared among two or more use cases. For example, most use cases in the ATM system example, such as Withdraw Money, Deposit Money or Check Balance, all share the inclusion use case Login Account (see Figure 3.8).

The <<extend>> Relationship

<<extend>> relationships are used when two use cases are similar, but one does a bit more than the other. For example, you may have a use case that captures the typical case (the base use case) and use extensions to describe variations. A base use case may, therefore, conditionally invoke an alternative use case. In other words, the extension use case adds an extra behavior to the base use case. For example, Withdraw Money has an optional behavior which handles withdrawal of an excess amount. We capture this optional behavior in an <<extend>> use case (see Figure 3.9).

Figure 3.9. An <<extend>> use case

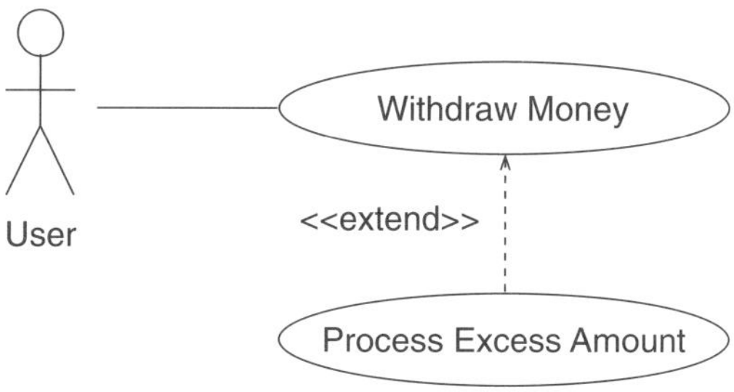

The Generalization Relationship

A child use case can inherit the behaviors, relationships and communication links of a parent use case. In other words, it is valid to put the child use case wherever a parent use case appears. The relationship between the child use case and the parent use case is the generalization relationship. For example, suppose the ATM system can be used to pay bills. Pay Bill has two child use cases: Pay Credit Card Bill and Pay Utility Bill (see Figure 3.10).

Figure 3.10. A generalization relationship

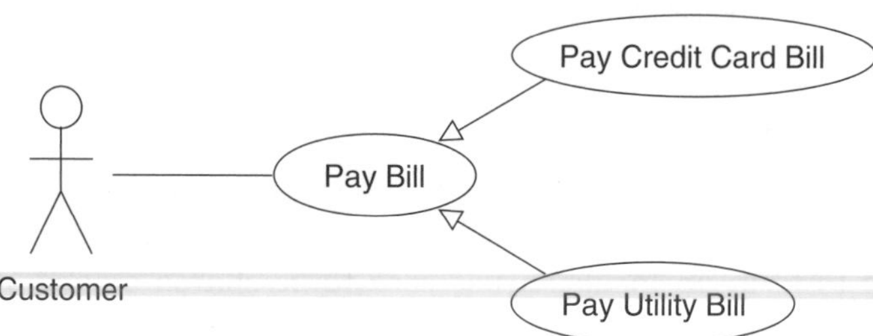

Base Use Case versus Abstract Use Case

Once a set of use cases of the system has been identified, common behaviors may be found. By extracting their common behaviors, we can form a base case (concrete use case) and an abstract use case. The former is basically the main use case which may be instantiated directly by an actor as it can achieve an observable user goal by itself. The latter can only be instantiated by a base use case as it only contains a portion of the common behaviors shared among two or more use cases. Therefore, it is not a complete goal from the user's perspective. For example, in Figure 3.8, a use case such as Login Account is not a use case but an abstract use case (or an <<include>> use case), because logging into the system does not achieve a complete user goal. A goal is not achieved if a user goes to an ATM, logs in to the system and then leaves without making a transaction. Typical operations a user may want to carry out through an ATM could be Check Balance, Request Check Book or Deposit Money, etc.

A use case may also exhibit several scenarios: the normal scenario and possible several alternative scenarios. Similarly, the base use case can be used to represent the normal scenario, while abstract use cases describe the alternative scenarios.

Figure 3.11 shows a part of a use case model for an ATM system. Withdraw Money is the base use case as it is the normal scenario for the user to successfully log in to the system, specify the transaction type and input a valid amount for withdrawal. Process Excess Amount is an abstract use case (or an <<extend>> use case) as the user may have enough money in his bank account for the amount that he wishes to withdraw.

Figure 3.11. Extension point in the base use case

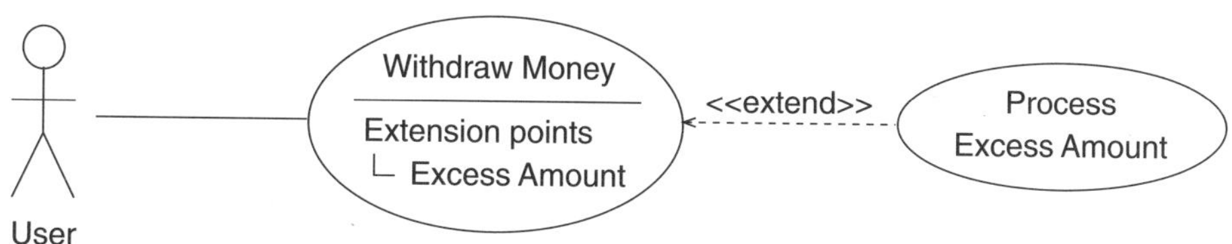

Only base use cases may be invoked directly by an actor, while abstract use cases can only be instantiated by a base use case. The instantiation of an abstract use case must return to the calling use case (the base use case) at the exact point from where the call was made. Abstract use cases are composed of portions extracted from other use cases. Abstract use cases are similar to subroutine calls, where the base use case likens to a main program. Thus, the base use case exhibits a complete behavior to achieve a user goal, while an abstract use case exhibits a partial behavior of a base use case. In the UML notation, the relationship between a base use case and an abstract use case is represented by an <<include>> or <<extend>> stereotype. Figure 3.12 illustrates the base use case, Withdraw Money with an optional behavior represented by the abstract use case, Process Excess Amount. In the figure, the base use case also includes the extension point (Excess Amount) where a call to the abstract use case Process Excess Amount can be made.

Notes: Normally similar behaviors of use cases can only be identified and extracted after they have been completely defined. A designer can then extract those parts with a similar logic into separate abstract use cases that are used by other use cases. Abstract use cases are refinements that are of more interest to the designer than the user.

It is important to note that structuring use cases is unlike developing a flow chart (deterministic sequence of flow) or a data flow diagram (functional decomposition) as it focuses on user goals. Thus, Login Account should not be considered as a base use case. This is a common mistake that some designers make because they incorrectly assume that the user needs to log in to the system first before he/she can perform tasks such as Withdraw Money or Deposit Money. Consequently, they wrongly treat Login Account as a base use case which instantiates Withdraw Money and Deposit Money as abstract use cases. In fact, the two base use cases should be Withdraw Money and Deposit Money as they share a common block in the flow of events (the Login Account inclusion use case).

Figure 3.12. Use case diagram showing <<include>> and <<extend>> relationships

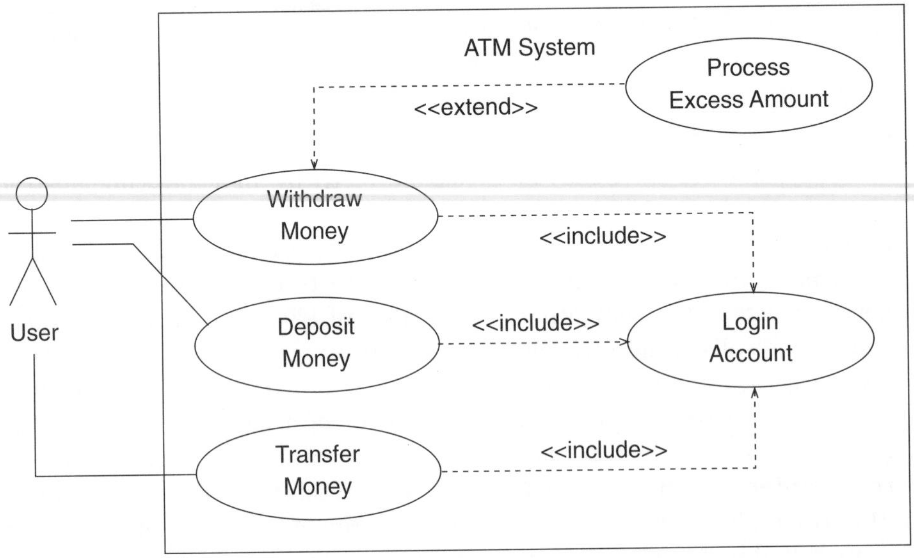

Documenting Use Cases

A use case focuses on the external aspects of a system and captures the system's functional and behavioral requirements that help users perform their tasks. It, however, does not describe how the system performs the required functional and behavioral requirements; in other words, it describes what a system is used for and who uses it without providing details of how the system performs its functions. A use case description serves as an agreed description between the user and the system designer on the flow of events when a use case is invoked. Formally, Booch (1993) defines that *"[a] use case is a description of a set of sequences of actions, including variants, that a system performs to yield an observable result of value to an actor."*

Figure 3.13 conceptualizes that a use case can be elaborated by a use case description in a more detailed form in that a use case description is explained and elaborated through scenarios (a sequence of actions). Each of these scenarios is simply an instance of the use case. In other words, a use case instance is only a particular example of a use case (a particular system service). As defined by Booch, a use case not only consists of a normal scenario, but possibly its variant scenarios. In such cases, they need to be represented in <<extend>> use cases, where each should be elaborated by a separate use case description.

Figure 3.13. Use cases and their scenarios

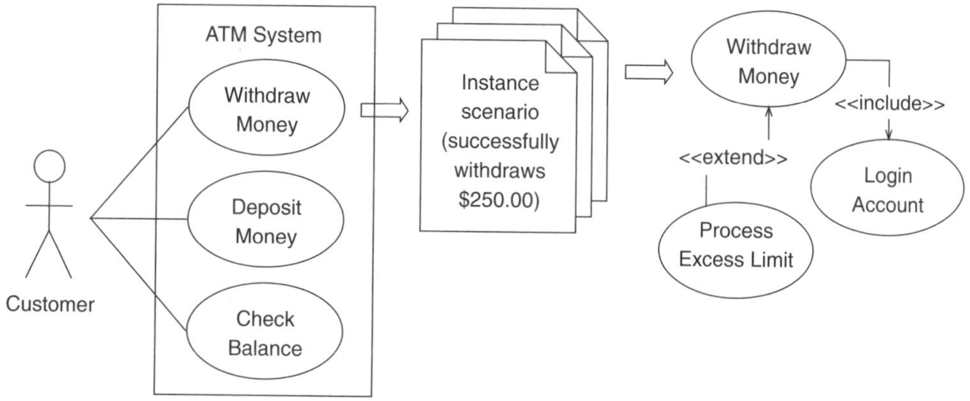

For example, the ATM system may provide the Withdraw Money service to customers in many different scenarios. A typical scenario may involve the customer withdrawing money from the machine from which he/she has requested the transaction. In another scenario, the system may report that the password keyed in by the customer is incorrect, requiring the customer to re-enter the password.

Developing Base Use Case Descriptions

As a use case diagram is a communication aid between the software designer(s) and the end user(s), it is important that descriptions are free of computing jargons and unfamiliar terminologies. Plain, simple language that the user can relate or understand should be used. Computer or technical terms that are related to the implementation of the system should be avoided. Indeed, when constructing a use case diagram, designers should not be thinking about computers at all; they should be focusing only on the users and system services.

Because the use case model has to be understood by both the users and the software developer, the base use case descriptions are written in natural language. However, most experts recommend a systematic approach by using a certain template so that useful information about the use case is not overlooked. The brief descriptions in the use case template are expanded to include details of the interactions between the actors and the use cases.

Use Case Template

A use case template captures various pieces of information, including the main path of a successful execution of a use case, as well as all of the alternative paths contained in it. Table 3.2 shows an example of a use case template. The natural language description of the behaviors and diagrammatic notations, such as flow charts or activity diagrams, can be used to complement or supplement the information contained in the template.

A use case is often described in a standard form, using a template similar to the following:

Table 3.2. Components of a use case template

Use case name	Name of the use case
Use case ID	ID of the use case
Super use case	The name of the generalized use case to which this use case belongs
Actor(s)	The name of the actor(s) who participate in the use case
Brief description	A description showing how this use case adds value to the organization; that is, what is the purpose or role of this use case in enabling the actors to do their job
Preconditions	The conditions that must be satisfied before this use case can be invoked
Post-conditions	The conditions that will be established as a result of invoking this use case
Priority	The development priority of this use case
Flow of events	A step-by-step description of the interactions between the actor(s) and the system, and the functions that must be performed in the specified sequence to achieve a user goal

Table 3.2. (Cont'd)

Alternative flows and exceptions	Major alternatives or exceptions that may occur in the flow of events
Non-behavioral requirements	The non-functional requirements of the system such as hardware and software platform requirements, performance, security, etc.
Assumptions	All the assumptions made about the use case
Issues	All outstanding issues regarding the use case
Source	Reference materials relevant to the use case

The components of a use case template written as high-level descriptions in natural language have to be agreed by both the client and the development team. Bear in mind that a use case is a high-level communication tool for both stakeholders. The following provides an explanation of each item in the template shown in Table 3.2.

- Use case name describes the goal of the actor. Typically, it is in a *verb + noun phrase or verb + noun format*, e.g. Withdraw Money.
- Use case ID is a unique identifier of the use case. It usually has a format like *UC + number*, e.g. *UC100*. The prefix generally represents the type of UML element and the number should be allocated systematically for easy reference.
- Super use case. This field can be blank. If the use case inherits a parent use case, this entry is the name of the parent use case.
- Actor(s). All the actor(s) participating in the execution of the use case are listed, such as people, systems, etc.
- Brief description. A concise description is used to define the scope of the use case and the observable value to the actor.
- Preconditions and post-conditions. Preconditions specify some constraints that must be satisfied before the use case can be invoked, while post-conditions serve to ensure that the use case has performed the task properly after invocation. Both pre- and post-conditions provide important hints for system test (at the use case level) in the subsequent software development stage. Let us consider the ATM example again. The Withdraw Money use case is a normal scenario and its preconditions may be the following: a valid ATM account, a positive balance, the maximum daily

accumulative withdrawal amount is $2,000. The post-condition may be that after processing the withdrawal transaction, the account balance must remain positive and the daily accumulative withdrawal amount must not exceed $2,000.

Well-specified pre- and post-condition elements of the use case description can significantly reduce the complexity of the use case. They can also be used as black-box test cases. Furthermore, the contents of the pre- and post-conditions can be used for deriving alternative scenarios for that use case.

- Priority. The priority in the use case template serves to indicate the priority ranking in the development schedule from the view of the development team. We usually assign a high ranking to use cases that are architecturally significant. Similarly, a high priority ranking should also be assigned to those use cases which are thought to be more difficult or have many unknown factors or risks associated with them. All high priority use cases will be analyzed and developed first in the development schedule.

  If a use case covers a wide area of the system in terms of hardware nodes or software subsystems, this use case will be considered architecturally significant. For example, the Withdraw Money use case will cover a wide area of the ATM system: card authentication, account login, account selection, amount input, etc. In terms of hardware nodes, its execution involves the collaboration of the ATM machine, the central bank computer and the individual bank's computers. On the other hand, the Check Balance use case will definitely be less significant by comparison with the Withdraw Money use case.
- Flow of events. The flow of events captures the external observable behaviors of the use case and focuses on describing the interactions between the user and the system when the use case is invoked. This component of the use case template describes the main flow of interactions. Alternative flows and exception handling are also captured in the Alternative Flows and Exceptions section of the template. Important system actions that lead to the post-conditions of the use case are also captured. Other unimportant internal logic of the system should be ignored since the purpose here is to define the specifications of the system.
- Alternative flows and exceptions describe the execution of the use case under exceptions that are not covered in the flow of events.
- Non-behavioral requirements describe the requirements other than functional or behavioral requirements: performance, user interface, etc.

- Assumptions about the use case should be recorded. For example, the password is numeric only, with not more than ten digits.
- Issues. All outstanding issues related to the use case need to be resolved. For example, should the user interface be customizable for customers of different banks?
- Source. This field includes references and materials used in developing the use case such as memos, minutes of meetings, etc.

Prioritizing Use Cases

The use case model is not only useful for requirements specification but also for planning the work process in different phases of the system development life cycle. Since the use case model should be understandable by both the system developer and the user, it is quite natural to plan the development of the system by scheduling the completion dates of the use cases in the use case model. Use cases in the use case model are normally developed at different times. Depending on the scale of the system, some architecturally significant use cases should be developed first and optional or less important functionalities of the system are developed later. In large-scale systems involving multiple software development teams, the development of several use cases are carried out *in parallel*. Optimally scheduling the development of use cases is a difficult task, and there are a number of factors that we need to consider.

Factors to Consider for Prioritizing Use Cases

The main philosophy behind prioritizing use cases is to reduce the risks and uncertainties of the project as early as possible, i.e. use cases are ranked according to their relative significance for successful completion of the system. For example, if the system involves some technologies unfamiliar to the development team, the developer should first go through the analysis of all the use cases involving these technologies to reduce uncertainty. The following factors typically increase the priority ranking of a use case:

- Architectural significance of the use case
- Use of new and untested technologies
- Problems that require substantial research effort
- Great improvement in efficiency (or revenue) of the business process
- Use cases that support major business processes

The priority ranking of a use case is determined by taking the above factors into account. Usually, a fuzzy scheme of high–medium–low would be used to rank use cases. If a more precise ranking is required, each use case can be assigned with a score for each factor and the total score will be used for ranking. For better precision in ranking, it is also possible to apply weightings to the factors in calculating the total score.

Use Case Modeling and Analysis Process

Overview

Before use case modeling and analysis can be conducted, it is necessary to carry out some background research such as interviewing users for the system requirements, and studying the business workflow or existing computer systems of the organization. Figure 3.14 illustrates the relationships between use case analysis and the other processes of the software development life cycle. The input to use case analysis can be a problem statement or business model prepared after interviewing the system users. We can also study the company's business workflows and operations associated with the system. The output is a use case model that describes the total requirements of the system from the user's point of view. The use case model consists of use case diagrams, use case descriptions and instance scenarios of the use cases. A textual analysis carried out on the use case descriptions can produce an initial class model (a domain class model) by identifying candidate classes for the system. In addition, the instance scenarios tell us how the system interacts with the actors in specific situations. The instance scenarios can be used to find out what objects will be involved and how these objects will interact in realizing the use cases. These instance scenarios can also be used as test cases of the system.

Developing Use Case Models

Before the use case analysis is carried out, it is necessary to interview the users to get a better understanding of the users' business activities. The results of the interviews are then summarized in a problem statement or a business model. The use case analysis is an iterative and incremental process consisting of the following steps:

Developing an initial use case model involves the following:

- Developing the problem statement
- Identifying the major actors and use cases

Figure 3.14. Relationship between use case analysis process and other processes

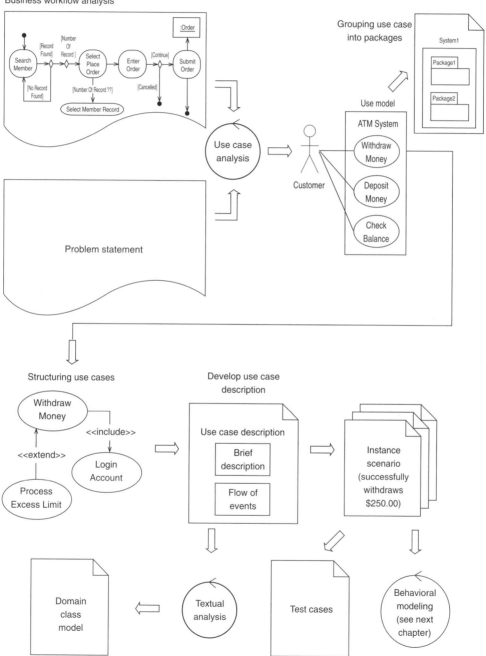

Domain analysis
Business workflow analysis

:Order
[Record Found]
[Number Of Record]
Search Member
Select Place Order
Enter Order
[Continue]
Submit Order
[No Record Found]
[Number Of Record ??]
[Cancelled]
Select Member Record

Grouping use case into packages
System1
Package1
Package2

Use model
ATM System
Withdraw Money
Deposit Money
Check Balance
Customer

Use case analysis

Problem statement

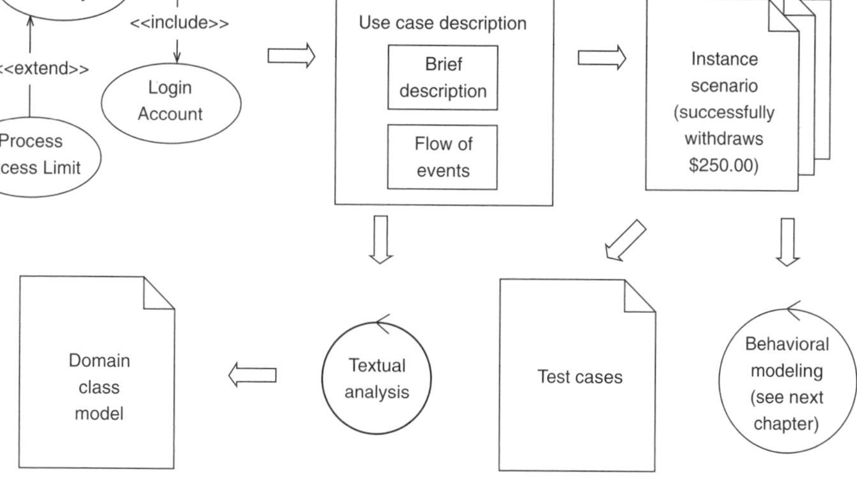

- Creating an initial use case diagram
- Describing briefly the use cases (with initial descriptions)
- Identifying/refining candidate business (domain) classes using textual analysis

Refining the use case model includes the following steps:

- Developing base use case descriptions
- Iteratively elaborating on the base use case descriptions and determining the <<extend>>, <<include>> and generalization relationships
- Developing instance scenarios
- Prioritizing use cases

The above steps need not be performed in a sequential order. Some steps may be performed *in parallel*, while others may be revisited after another step has been performed. For example, after identifying the candidate classes, the brief use case description may require revision. In addition, different use cases may be developed at a different pace. Some use cases may be fully developed, while others may just have their title designations which will be further elaborated at a later stage. Hence, the reader should treat these steps as a checklist of items to be performed to complete the use case model.

Developing Initial Use Case Model

The initial use case model provides an overview of the functionality of the system. It can serve as the agreed requirements specification of the system. The initial use case model is very useful for planning the development priorities of various use cases.

Identifying Major Actors

When identifying the actors of the system, find the answers to the following questions:

- Who will use the primary function(s) of the system?
- Who will require support from the system to accomplish their daily work?
- Who will use its results and/or supply the data?
- Who will need to maintain, administer and operate the system?
- With what hardware systems must the system interact?
- With what other computer systems must the system interact?

Use Case Modeling: Mail Order Case Study

Step 1: Develop Problem Statement

In order to improve the operational efficiency of a mail order company, the chief executive officer is interested in computerizing the company's business process. The major business activities of the company can be briefly described as follows:

A customer registers as a member by filling in the membership form and mailing it to the company. A member who has not been active (no transactions made) for a period of one year will be removed from the membership list and he/she needs to re-apply for the reinstatement of the lapsed membership.

A member should inform the company of any change in personal details such as home address, telephone numbers, etc.

A member can place an order by filling out a sales order form and faxing it to the company or by phoning the Customer Service Assistant with the order details.

The Customer Service Assistant first checks for the validity of membership and enters the sales order information into the system.

The Order Processing Clerk checks the availability of the ordered items. If they are available, he/she holds them for the order. When all the ordered items are available, he/she will schedule their delivery.

The Inventory Control Clerk controls and maintains an appropriate level of stock and is also responsible for acquiring new items.

If there is a problem with an order, the member will phone the Customer Service Assistant, who will then take appropriate action to follow up the particular sales order.

Members may return defective goods within 30 days and get their money back.

The system will record the name of the staff member who handled the transaction for future follow up action.

Step 2: Identify Major Actors

If you carefully examine the problem statement, it is not difficult to identify the Customer Service Assistant, Order Processing Clerk and Inventory Clerk as the major users of the Mail Order System. The following actors of the system are identified:

- *Customer Service Assistant*
- *Order Processing Clerk*
- *Inventory Control Clerk*

A short paragraph should then be written to describe each of the actors. Table 3.3 shows the specification of the *Order Processing Clerk*.

Table 3.3. Specification of Order Processing Clerk actor

Actor Name	Order Processing Clerk
Description	The Order Processing Clerk is responsible for processing sales orders, submitting re-order requests, requesting necessary deposits from members and scheduling the delivery of the goods to the member.

Guidelines for Identifying Use Cases

Finding use cases is an iterative process. This process normally starts with interviewing the users (actors) who directly or indirectly interact with the system. Typically, it starts from bottom up, involving the customer describing scenarios from their business activities. Each of these descriptions is a possible use case. These potential use cases can then be elaborated, modified, broken into smaller use cases or integrated into larger ones.

An important fact to remember is that people are generally not very forthcoming, and extracting useful information from the users is a skill that takes years of experience. The following questions may be useful in collecting information from users:

- What are the main tasks carried out by each actor?
- What data are manipulated and processed by the system?
- What problems is the system going to solve?
- What goals does an actor want to achieve using the system?
- What are the major problems with the current system and how can the proposed system simplify the work of the user?

Guidelines for Naming Use Cases

The name of a use case consists of a verb and a noun or noun phrase in the following format:

verb + noun or verb + noun phrase

The use case name describes an operation which achieves an observable user goal. For example, *Place Order* is a use case in an Order Process System, and *Withdraw Money* is also a use case for an ATM system (see Figure 3.15). They are in the *verb + noun* format.

Figure 3.15. Examples of use cases

As use case models serve as a communication tool between end users and system designers, it is often preferable to use high-level and non-technical naming terminology understood by the layman. Some designers prefer to use *verb + noun phase* for naming their use cases. For example, you may prefer to name a use case as "select a suitable candidate from the HR database" instead of "Select Candidate" for a human resources information system.

Step 3: Identify Use Cases

By examining the responsibilities of the actors of the Mail Order System, the following use cases are identified:

- *Check Order Status*
- *Place Order*
- *Handle Goods Return*
- *Update Membership Record*
- *Archive Membership*
- *Register New Member*
- *Process Order*
- *Schedule Delivery*
- *Order Goods*
- *Receive Goods*
- *Deliver Goods*

The complete initial use case model is shown in Figure 3.16.

Figure 3.16. An initial use case model

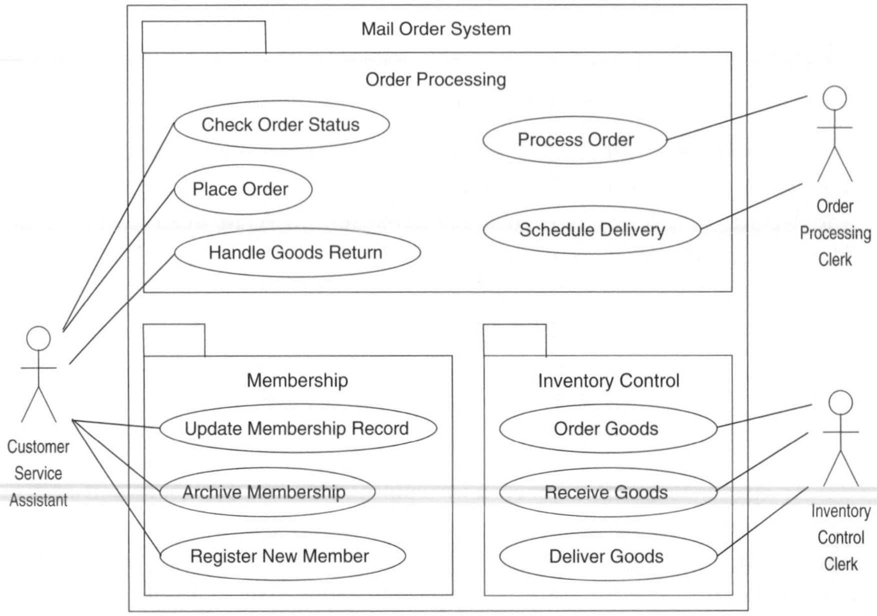

Step 4: Create Initial Use Case Diagram

In a large software project, the use cases are usually organized into packages, and sometimes a hierarchical structure of packages may be needed for very large-scale projects. A package is a place holder which can contain any UML elements, including packages themselves. By organizing the use cases into packages, the use case model can be managed more easily. In the case study, the use cases are divided into three packages. Each package contains a set of use cases for handling a certain type of business activity.

Step 5: Describe Use Case

Briefly describe each of the use cases with a short paragraph. The brief description will be further expanded and elaborated when the use case is analyzed. The following Tables 3.4 and 3.5 give a brief description of the *Schedule Delivery* use case and the *Check Order Status* use case.

Table 3.4. Initial use case description of the Schedule Delivery use case

Use Case	Schedule Delivery
Use Case ID	UC-300
Actor	Order Processing Clerk
Description	The Order Processing Clerk selects an order from the list of filled sales orders. The system displays the sales order details, together with the member's telephone number and address. The Order Processing Clerk enters the delivery date and time after talking with the member over the phone. The system records the delivery date and time in a dispatch request to the delivery team.

Table 3.5. Brief description of the Check Order Status use case

Use Case	Check Order Status
Use Case ID	UC-400
Actor	Customer Service Assistant
Description	The Customer Service Assistant enters the ID of the member. The Customer Service Assistant selects a sales order of the member. The system displays the status of the sales order.

Identify/Refine Candidate Business (Domain) Classes

Having prepared a brief description for each of the use cases, try to identify the classes of the system. The identified classes will then be used as part of the vocabulary for writing the expanded use case descriptions.

It is important to note that identification of objects and classes is a continuous process throughout the whole system development life cycle; the class model will be iteratively refined in each step of the life cycle.

During the use case analysis process, classes can be identified by performing a textual analysis on the brief use case descriptions. The nouns and noun phrases in the use case descriptions are highlighted and evaluated for possible inclusion as a candidate class. The result of the analysis is a set of candidate classes with their descriptions. An initial class diagram is drawn to show the static relationships between the classes. If a domain analysis has been performed to develop a domain class model, the results of this step will be combined with the domain class model to produce the initial class model. This was elaborated on in the previous chapter.

Step 6: Perform Textual Analysis

A textual analysis needs to be performed for each of the use cases based on their descriptions; this will yield a set of candidate classes in the process. These classes will then be considered for inclusion in the domain class model which serves as a preliminary class model for the future development of the initial class model.

A textual analysis on the *Process Order* use case is demonstrated in Table 3.6. All the nouns and noun phrases have been underlined in the brief use case description.

Table 3.6. Textual analysis on the Schedule Delivery use case

Use Case	Schedule Delivery
Use Case ID	UC-300
Actor	Order Processing Clerk
Description	The **Order Processing Clerk** selects an **order** from the list of filled **sales orders**. The **system** displays the **sales order** details, togehter with the **member's telephone number** and **address**. The **Order Processing Clerk** enters the **delivery date** and **time** after talking with the **member** over the **phone**. The **system** records the **delivery date** and **time** in a **dispatch request** to the **delivery team**.

Note: Recall that a use case model often consists of several use cases. Each of the use cases has its own corresponding use case description, including its brief description and the flow of events, providing more details. As progress is made in the development of the project, more and more use cases will be developed according to the use case schedule. Iteratively and incrementally refine and enrich the initial class model (Figure 3.17) by performing the textual analysis for each of the use cases that have been developed.

Figure 3.17. Initial class model

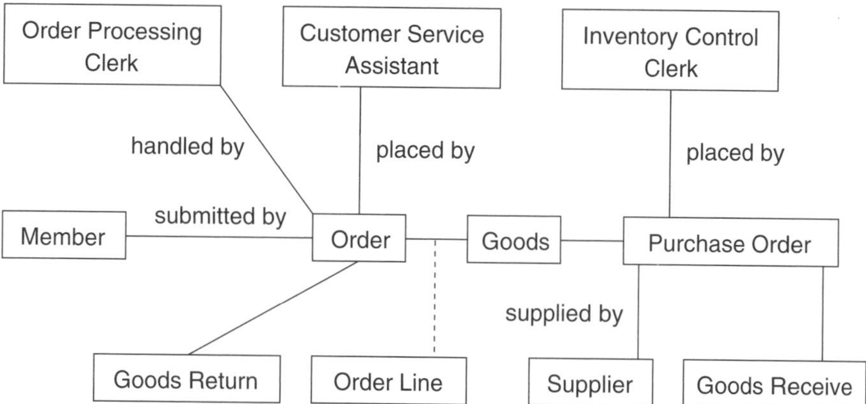

Expand Initial Use Case Model

The initial use case model is expanded incrementally in subsequent phases of the system development life cycle. In each phase, some use cases are selected and analyzed to produce detailed specifications of the necessary behavioral and functional requirements. Common behaviors and alternative behaviors of use cases are identified when the use cases are expanded and analyzed. These behaviors are extracted to become inclusion, extension and generalization use cases. These, in turn, help to make the use case model easier to maintain. The classes identified in the analysis of the use cases are used to update and refine the class model.

Step 7: Develop Base Use Case Descriptions

Table 3.7 shows a use case description for an order processing system. In this example, the use case name is *Place Order*. Along with the name, provide a brief description of each use case. The precondition can effectively reduce the complexity of the use case. For example, as a registered member, one must already have a valid account. Consequently, many alternative situations, such as invalid account, account on-hold, etc., will not be applicable to valid members.

Table 3.7. Description for the *Place Order* use case

Use case name	Place Order
Use case ID	UC-100
Super Use Case	The name of the generalized use case to which this use case belongs.
Actor(s)	Customer Service Assistant
Brief description	A Customer Service Assistant places an order and then submits it for processing.
Preconditions	The member must have registered with the system.
Post-conditions	The Customer's order will be directed to the order process department for processing.
Flow of events	1. The Customer Service Assistant finds the member's record by entering the member's ID or name. The system displays a list of members that match the information entered by the Customer Service Assistant. 2. The Customer Service Assistant selects the required member record. The system displays the details of the member. 3. The Customer Service Assistant selects "Place Order." A new order form and order ID are then generated and displayed. 4. The Customer Service Assistant selects items from the catalog and adds them to the order. 5. The Customer Service Assistant submits the order for processing. The system records the order and forwards it to the Order Processing Clerk.
Alternative flows and exceptions	At any time the Customer Service Assistant can decide to suspend the ordering process and come back to it later, or to cancel the order.
Priority	High
Non-behavioral requirements	The system should be able to handle 20,000 new orders per day.
Assumptions	
Issues	Is there any limit on the amount of an order?
Source	User Interview Memo 21, 8/9/01

Step 8: Structure Use Cases

After elaborating on the use cases, the *Place Order*, *Register New Member* and *Archive Membership* use cases have a common behavior — they all involve finding the member record from the system. Hence, the inclusion use case *Find Member Record* is created to cover this common behavior. The revised use case diagram is shown in Figure 3.18.

Figure 3.18. Revised use case model

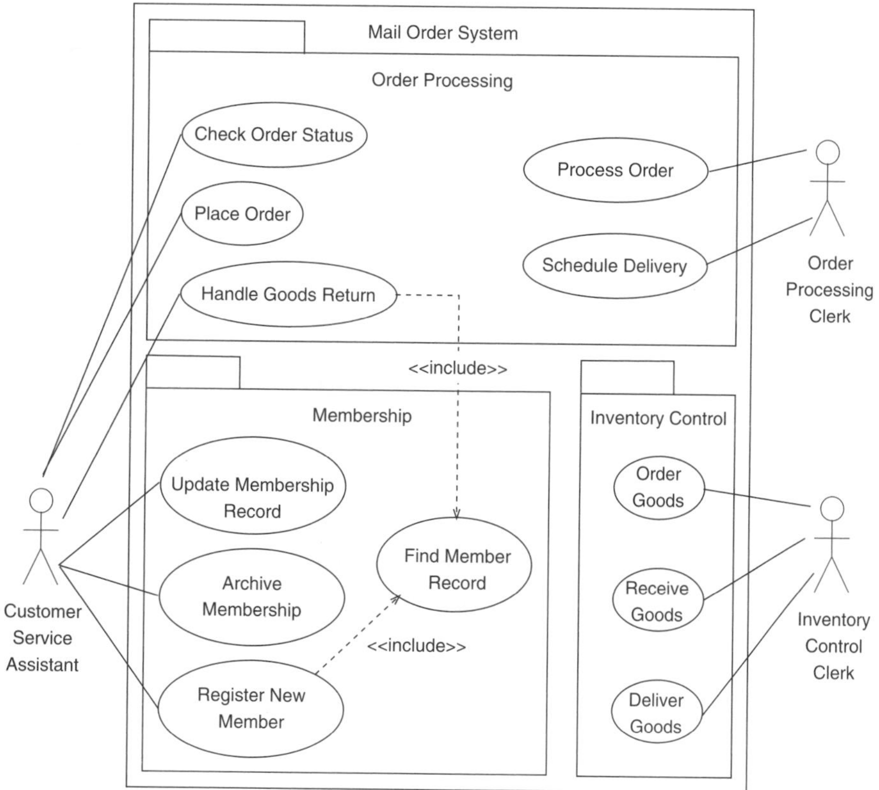

The revised descriptions of the *Place Order* and *Find Member Record* use cases are shown in Tables 3.8 and 3.9 respectively.

Table 3.8. Revised description of the *Place Order* use case

Use case name	Place Order
Use case ID	UC-100
Super Use Case	
Actor(s)	Customer Service Assistant
Brief description	A Customer Service Assistant places an order and then submits it for processing.
Preconditions	The member must have registered with the system.
Post-conditions	The Customer's order will be directed to the order processing department for processing.
Flow of events	1. Include (Find Member Record). 2. The Customer Service Assistant selects "Place Order." A new order form and order ID are then generated and displayed. 3. The Customer Service Assistant selects items from the catalog and adds them to the order. 4. The Customer Service Assistant submits the order for processing. The system records the order and forwards it to the Order Processing Clerk.
Alternative flows and exceptions	At any time the Customer Service Assistant can decide to suspend the ordering process and come back to it later, or decide to cancel the order.
Priority	High
Non-behavioral requirements	The system should be able to handle 20,000 new orders per day.
Assumptions	
Issues	Is there any limit on the amount of an order?
Source	User Interview Memo 21, 8/9/01

Table 3.9. Description of the *Find Member Record* use case

Use case name	Find Member Record
Use case ID	UC-10
Brief description	A member record is requested.
Post-conditions	A membership record is returned.
Flow of events	1. The Customer Service Assistant finds the member record by entering the member's ID or name. The system displays a list of members that match the information entered by the Customer Service Assistant. 2. The Customer Service Assistant selects the required member record. The system then displays the details of that member.
Alternative flows and exceptions	No member record is found for the customer.

Develop Instance Scenarios

A use case specifies all possible ways of using a system functionality to achieve a user goal. Sometimes, it is necessary to write some examples (instance scenarios) to illustrate the execution of a complex use case. Instance scenarios are easier for the user to understand, and they are very useful for clarifying any ambiguity in the use case description. The instance scenarios can also serve as test cases for system testing.

A sample instance scenario of the *Place Order* use case is shown in Table 3.10.

Table 3.10. Instance Scenario of *Place Order*

Parent use case name	Place order
Parent use case ID	UC-100
Instance name	A sales order form is received but the membership number is missing.
Instance ID	UCIS-100-1

Table 3.10. (Cont'd)

Environmental conditions and assumptions	The name (Peter Chan) and signature of the member are available in the system.
Inputs	A sales order form
Instance flow description	1. The Customer Service Assistant enters "Peter Chan" to find the member record. The system then displays a list of members that match the member's name. 2. The Customer Service Assistant repeatedly selects a member record. The system displays the signature of the member when a member record is selected. 3. The Customer Service Assistant selects "Place Order." A new order form and order ID are then generated and displayed. 4. The Customer Service Assistant selects items from the catalog and adds them to the order. 5. The Customer Service Assistant submits the order for processing. The system records the order and forwards it to the Order Processing Clerk.
Outputs	The sales order is placed.

Step 9: Prioritize Use Cases

Table 3.11 shows an informal ranking of some of the use cases of the Mail Order System.

Table 3.11. Priority ranking of use cases

Priority Rank	Use Case	Reason
High	Process Order	Directly improves the efficiency of the business process and affects the system architecture.
High	Place Order	Same as above

Table 3.11. (Cont'd)

High	Find Member Record	Included as part of the Place Order use case.
Medium	Order Goods	Ordering goods is less often than processing orders but still is one of the major business processes.
Medium	Deliver Goods	Can improve the control of stock level of goods.
Low	Update Membership Record	Small impact on the system architecture.
Low	Register New Member	Same as above.

Tricks and Tips in Using Use Case Analysis

Use Cases as a Communication Tool

It is important to make sure that each use case emphasizes the functions of the system as seen by the user and that they are understood by both the user and the system analyst. The use cases can then truly become an effective communication tool for the domain experts and the system analysts and designers in the early stage of the development life cycle.

Finding the Right Use Cases

Cockburn (1999) suggests that, in order to find the use cases for a given system, we must first examine the goals of the system. Use cases provide an observable value to an actor, and by focusing on how an actor can achieve the goals of a system, we can identify the correct use cases quicker. The goal of an ATM system might include *Withdraw Money*, *Deposit Money*, *Check Balance* and *Transfer Money* as shown in Figure 3.19.

Correct Focus of Base Use Case

In identifying use cases, it is easy to focus on the process, rather than the system goal. In the previous ATM example, one might have mistakenly chosen *Login Account* and *Select Transaction* as use cases. Certainly these are all

Figure 3.19. Use cases of an ATM system

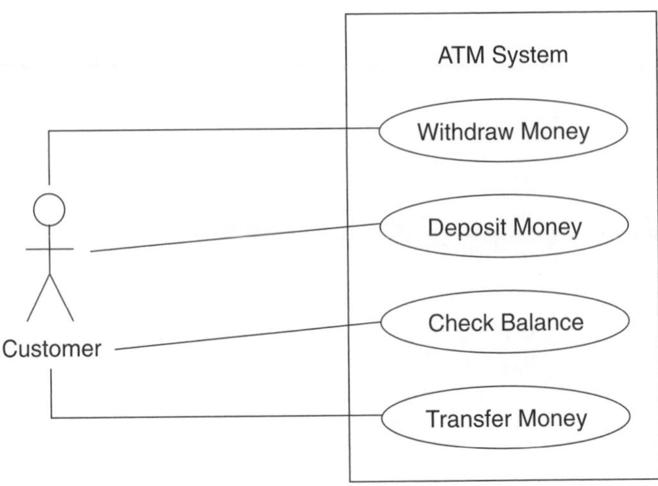

externally observable behaviors of an ATM system, but no customer would ever set his/her goal as inputting the password, selecting a transaction and then leaving the ATM. Furthermore, both *Input Password* and *Select Transaction* use cases do not yield an observable value to the user and, therefore, cannot achieve a user goal.

Good Use Cases Should be Observable

In Figure 3.20, the *Verify Password* use case is even more erroneous in that the customers cannot *Verify Password* themselves! This use case describes an internal task that the system needs to perform (hence externally unobservable) and definitely should not be included in the use case model.

Use Cases versus Process Charts

It is very easy to fall into the trap of thinking that use cases are processes and that data flows in and out along the association lines. Similarly, the <<include>> and <<extend>> arrows between use cases are often misread as directions of either data flows or control flows. Actually, nothing flows between the actors and the use cases. It should be remembered that use case diagrams are fundamentally different from flow charts, control flows or structure charts because they do not represent the order or the number of times that the system actions will be executed.

Figure 3.20. Incorrect use cases

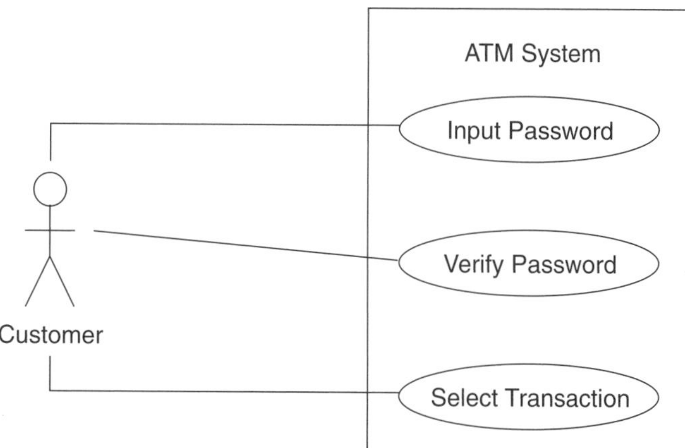

Apply Textual Analysis in Different Contexts

When defining use cases in the use case descriptions, use nouns and verbs consistently in order to identify objects using textual analysis and their interactions at a later stage. Textual analysis can also be applied to identify actors and use cases from the problem statement. To identify system actors, focus on questions such as "Who are the system users?" "What are the external entities which interact with the system?". To identify use cases ask, "What task(s) the system needs to perform to fulfill the user goals?"

When elaborating on a use case by creating the use case description, focus on what the system needs to perform in a more detailed interactive mode of description between the user and the system. This includes a brief description of the use case and the flow of events in the use case description template. The brief description clarifies what the system aims to do with the help of the use case concerned. The flow of events helps to identify the external system behaviors at this stage (use case modeling and analysis) and the internal behaviors at a later stage (behavioral modeling and analysis). See Figure 3.21.

Use Bi-directional Communication Associations

The communication association connects the actor(s) and the use case indicating the bi-directional interactions between the system and the actor(s). Even though it has been suggested that unidirectional associations can be used to represent the communications from the initiator to a use case (and most case tools do not prohibit this), use cases are still considered as a sequence of transactions (interactions), and as such, it is not necessary to show the association with an arrow (see Figure 3.22).

Figure 3.21. Application of textual analysis in different contexts

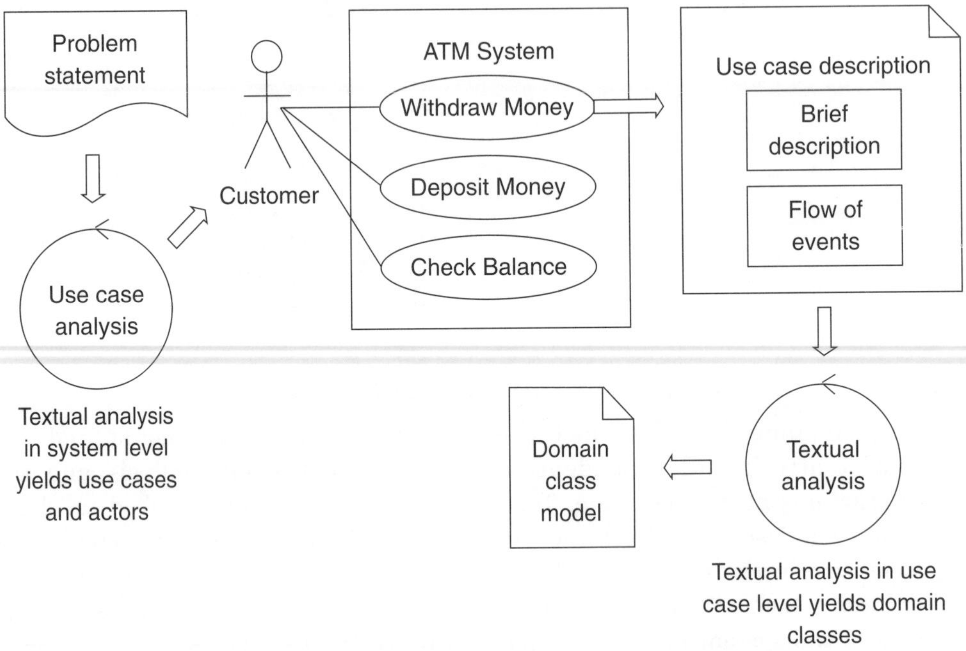

Problem statement

Use case analysis

Textual analysis in system level yields use cases and actors

Customer

ATM System

Withdraw Money

Deposit Money

Check Balance

Use case description

Brief description

Flow of events

Textual analysis

Domain class model

Textual analysis in use case level yields domain classes

Figure 3.22. Bi-directional communication association

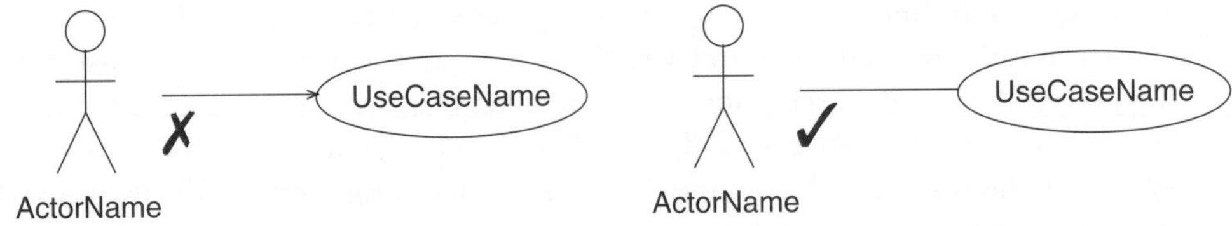

Structure Use Case Models

As the use cases are elaborated in detail, common behaviors or optional behaviors can be identified. In order to make the use case model easier to maintain, it is necessary to extract the common behaviors and the optional behaviors into inclusion use cases and extension use cases.

The use case model can be simplified by factoring out common behaviors that are required by multiple use cases and thereafter introducing the <<include>> stereotype. If the base use case is complete and the behavior is optional, consider using the <<extend>> stereotype. The use case structuring process also helps to save time and effort in analyzing the use cases. Therefore, use case structuring should be done in an iterative and incremental manner. However, remember not to put too much effort into identifying the common behaviors and optional behaviors since this may defeat the purpose of saving time and effort. The use case structuring should be carried out when it is convenient to do so.

Specify Use Cases in Detail ... but Not Too Much

When designing a use case model, it is very easy to get bogged down in excessive details. Remember that even the flow of events inside the use case description only serves to show the interaction between the actor(s) and the use case. In other words, only describe what the system is supposed to do and *not how the system does it*. Start with the most observable and general requirements first. When the users are happy that these are represented correctly, add details to the use case, where necessary. For example, you may first consider only the use case name that is the *verb + noun or verb + noun phase* pattern. Later, elaborate on the use case further by creating the use case description. When the contents are first filled in the use case template, do not try to enter everything at the same time. Instead, only fill in the information with which you feel comfortable. It is perfectly acceptable to leave some elements blank at the initial stage. As the system progresses up the development process, it will be possible to identify what the contents of these blank elements should be.

Fit Use Cases into System Architecture

Packages should be used where appropriate to make the use case diagram more easily understood. Use cases that form a natural grouping should be organized into packages. Figure 3.23 shows an example of how packages are used for a loan processing system.

Use Case Modeling and Analysis with VP-UML

The previous sections in this chapter covered the theories associated with use case analysis and modeling. Here, the practical aspects of the analysis and

Figure 3.23. Use cases grouped into packages

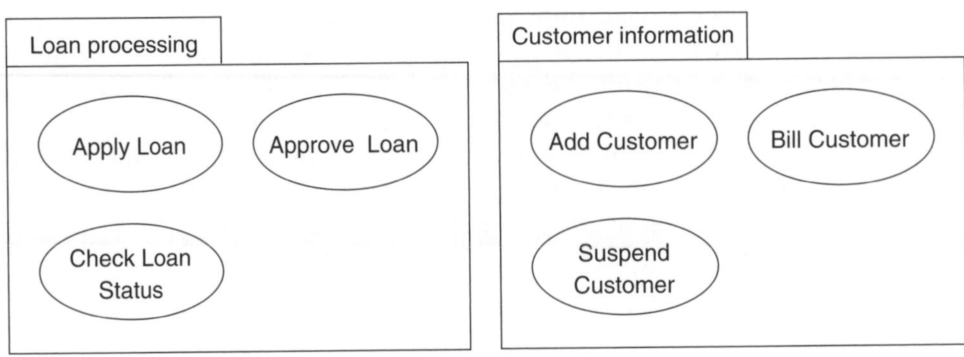

modeling process will be illustrated with the example Mail Oder System discussed earlier using the VP-UML case tool. By walking through the process step by step, you will appreciate how easy it is to perform use case analysis and modeling.

The Mail Order System example will be used to illustrate the steps in the use case analysis and modeling process. Before you begin, start the VP-UML case tool.

Step 1: Prepare the Problem Statement

The problem statement is prepared through interviews with the stakeholders of the system. Details of the problem statement for the Mail Order System have been presented earlier. The problem statement can now be entered into the VP-UML case tool for further work. Simply follow the steps below.

1.1. Enter **Textual Analysis** working area by clicking on the **application toolbar** (see Figure 3.24).

1.2. Type in the problem statement in the text pane. If the problem statement is already saved as a text file, open it from a file by clicking at the top left-hand corner of the **text pane**.

1.3. Edit the following problem statement in the text pane (see Figure 3.25).

Figure 3.24. Textual Analysis working area

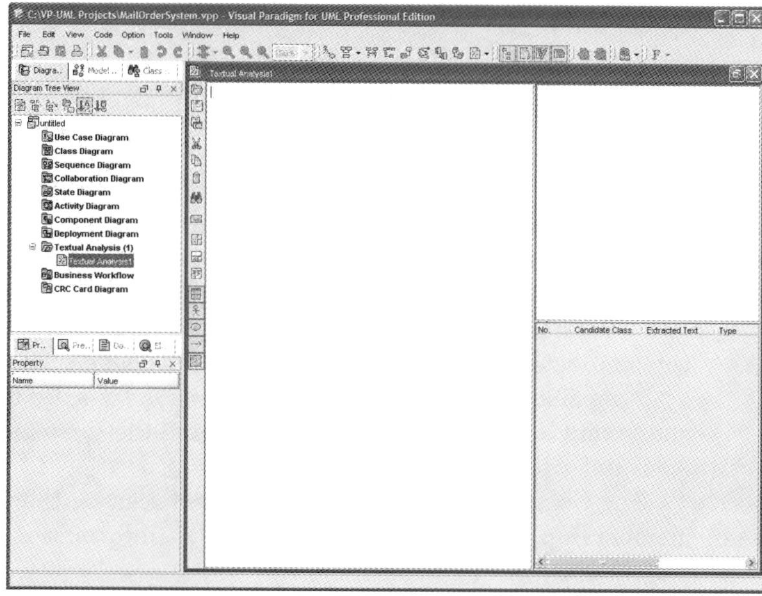

Figure 3.25. Entering problem statement for Textual Analysis

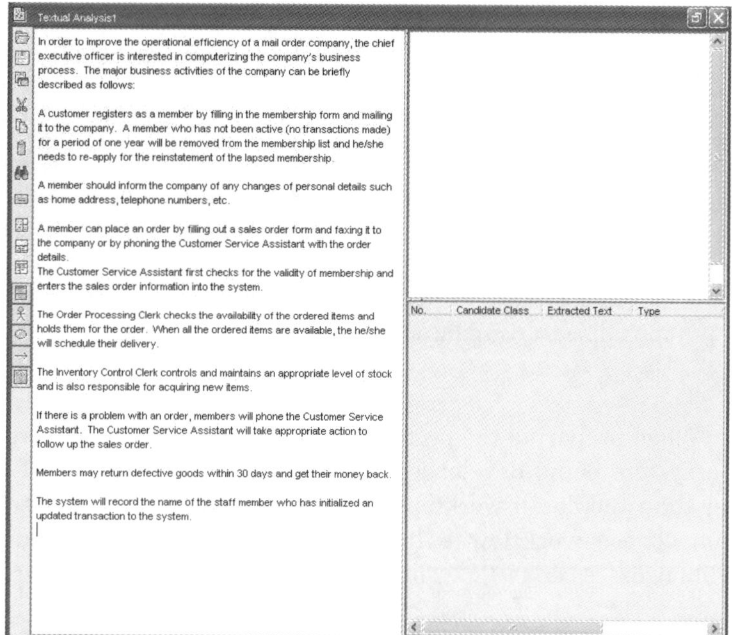

In order to improve the operational efficiency of a mail order company, the chief executive officer is interested in computerizing the company's business process. The major business activities of the company can be briefly described as follows:

A customer registers as a member by filling in the membership form and mailing it to the company. A member who has not been active (no transactions made) for a period of one year will be removed from the membership list and he/she needs to re-apply for the reinstatement of the lapsed membership.

A member should inform the company of any changes of personal details such as home address, telephone numbers, etc.

A member can place an order by filling out a sales order form and faxing it to the company or by phoning the Customer Service Assistant with the order details.

The Customer Service Assistant first checks for the validity of membership and enters the sales order information into the system.

The Order Processing Clerk checks the availability of the ordered items and holds them for the order. When all the ordered items are available, he/she will schedule their delivery.

The Inventory Control Clerk controls and maintains an appropriate level of stock and is also responsible for acquiring new items.

If there is a problem with an order, members will phone the Customer Service Assistant. The Customer Service Assistant will take appropriate action to follow up the sales order.

Members may return defective goods within 30 days and get their money back.

The system will record the name of the staff member who has initialized an updated transaction to the system.

Note: When preparing the problem statement having interviewed the key users of the system being developed, only focus on their high-level roles and goals rather than the detail workflow of the business operations associated with the system. These workflow will later be identified when you document the individual use case as flows of events in the detailed use case descriptions.

Step 2: Identify Major Actor(s)

Once the problem statement is in the case tool, the next step is to identify actors in the **Textual Analysis** working area.

2.1. Highlight the phrase *Customer Service Assistant* in the problem statement as a candidate actor and drag it to the **Candidate Class Container** at the top right-hand corner. Note that all occurrences of the same actor in the problem statement are automatically highlighted (see Figure 3.26).

Figure 3.26. Identifying major actors

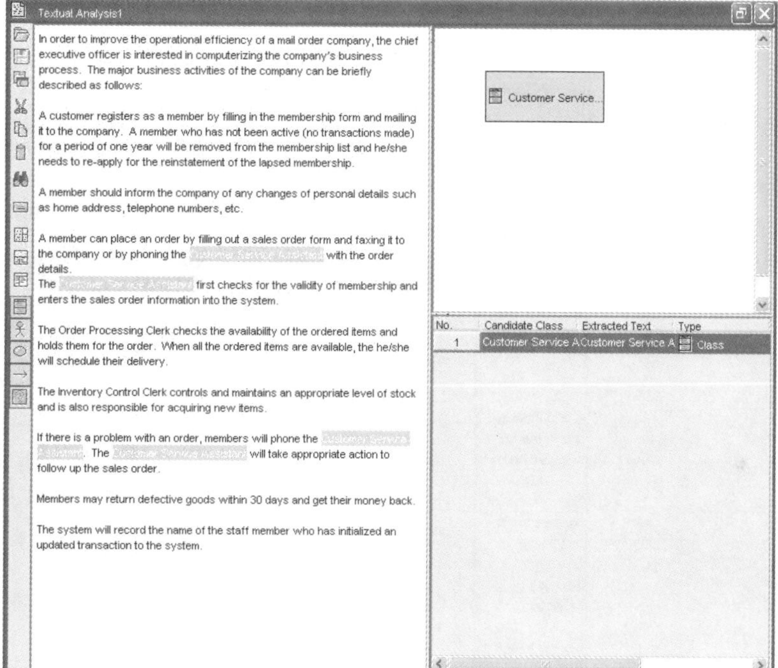

2.2. Now right click on the newly created candidate class in the **Candidate Class Container**. A pop-up menu will appear. Select the **Actor** option in the pop-up menu to declare the candidate class as an actor (see Figure 3.27).

2.3. Note that the icon of the candidate class in the **Candidate Class Container** has changed from class ⬭ to actor 웃 and the type of the candidate class has also changed to **Actor** in the table below it (see Figure 3.28).

Figure 3.27. Defining actor type

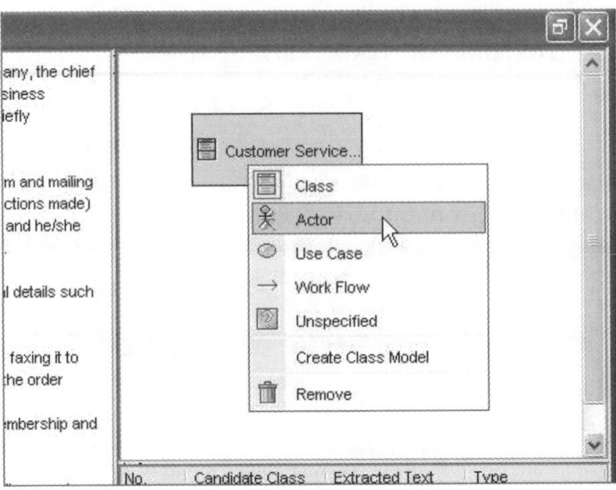

Figure 3.28. Candidate Actor in Candidate Class Container

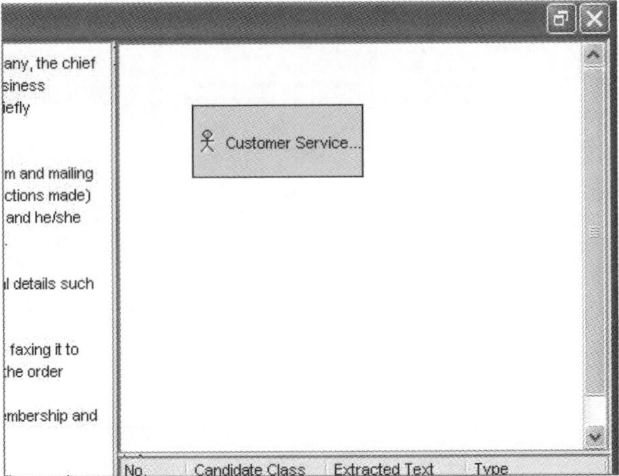

2.4. To enter the description of an actor, select the **Class Description** cell next to the actor *Customer Service Assistant* in the table in the bottom right corner. Type in a brief description such as the task(s) performed by the actor. Where necessary, adjust the size of the cell by dragging its boundary at the bottom of the cell edge to view the whole description (see Figure 3.29).

Figure 3.29. Entering actor description in Class Description

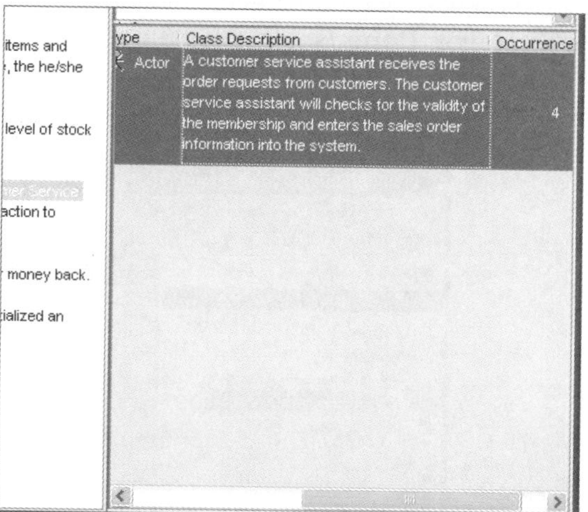

2.5. The candidate actors can be added into the model repository. Elements in the model repository can be retrieved for later use, e.g. to draw a use case diagram. To add *Customer Service Assistant* (candidate actor) into the model repository, right click on the *Customer Service Assistant*. A pop-up menu will appear. Select **Create Actor Model** in the pop-up menu (see Figure 3.30).

Figure 3.30. Creating an Actor in model repository

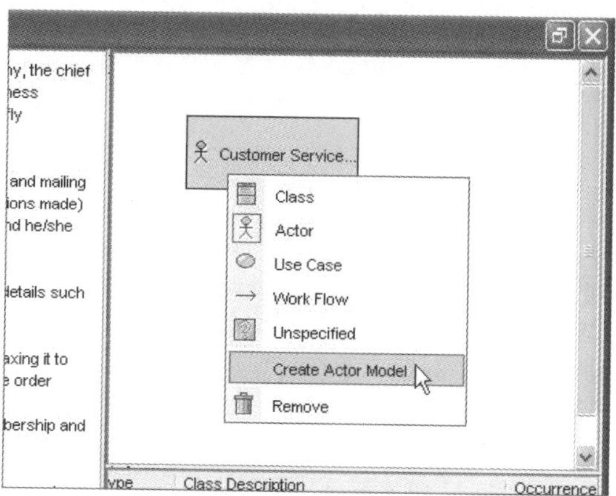

2.6. The *Customer Service Assistant* is now added to the **Model Repository Tree**. To see the newly created actor model, click on the **Model** tab in the **Project Explorer Pane** (see Figure 3.31).

Figure 3.31. Customer Service Assistant actor in Model Repository Tree

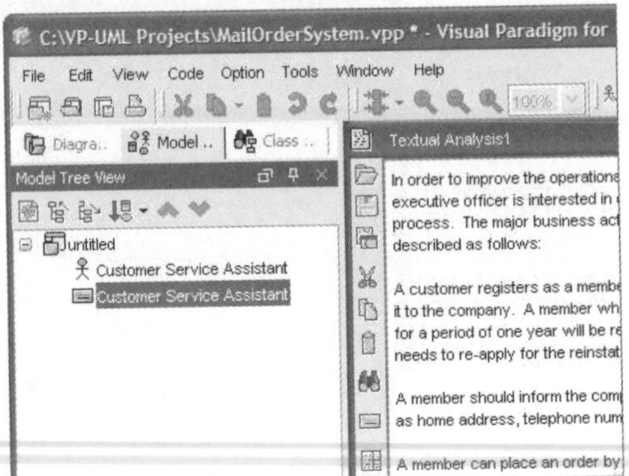

2.7. Repeat the above steps to identify and create actor models for the actors:

- *Order Processing Clerk*
- *Inventory Control Clerk*

(See Figure 3.32.)

Figure 3.32. Actor models in Model Repository Tree

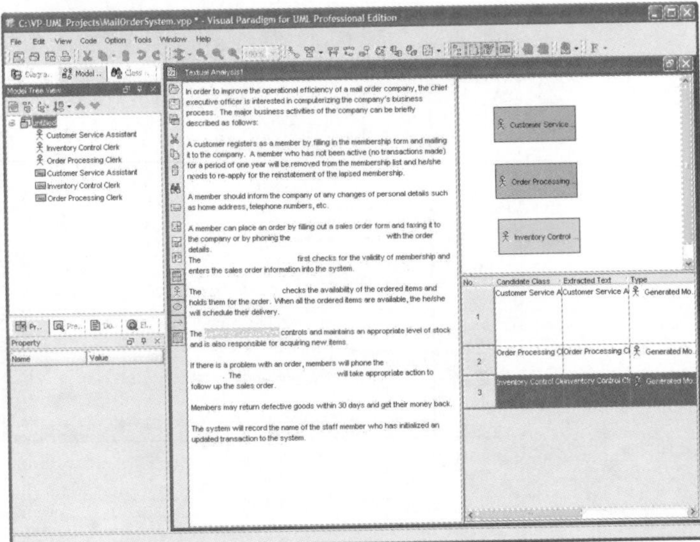

Note: When creating a candidate actor in the **Candidate Class Container**, it is not a model element until it appears in the **Model Repository Tree**. Only then can the actor be shared among various models or diagrams. To place an actor, which has been defined in the model repository, in the diagram, simply drag it from the **Model Repository Tree** to the desired location in the diagram area and release the mouse button. The actor will be created in the diagram and automatically inherit the name and the documentation that was previously defined. This operation can also be applied to create use cases and classes.

Step 3: Identify Use Cases

Let us identify a candidate use case from the problem statement. Very often we are not able to find a *verb* + *noun* pattern that directly matches the candidate use case in the problem statement. In fact, it is necessary to read through the text carefully to identify a use case. Follow the steps below to create a use case directly from the **Candidate Class Container**.

3.1. To hide the actors in the **Candidate Class Container**, click on the **Show Candidate Actors** toggle button in the **Textual Analysis toolbar**. However, note that the actor models still exist in the **Model Repository Tree** (see Figure 3.33).

Figure 3.33. Hiding Actors in Candidate Class Container

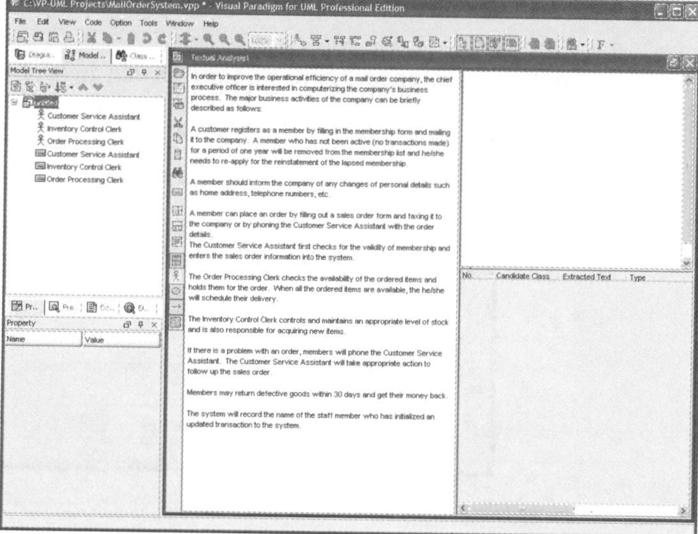

3.2. Right click on the **Candidate Class Container**. A pop-up menu will appear. Then select **Add Candidate** in the pop-up menu; a cascading menu will appear. Select **Use Case** in the cascading menu. An input dialog will appear (see Figure 3.34).

Figure 3.34. Creating a candidate use case in Candidate Class Container

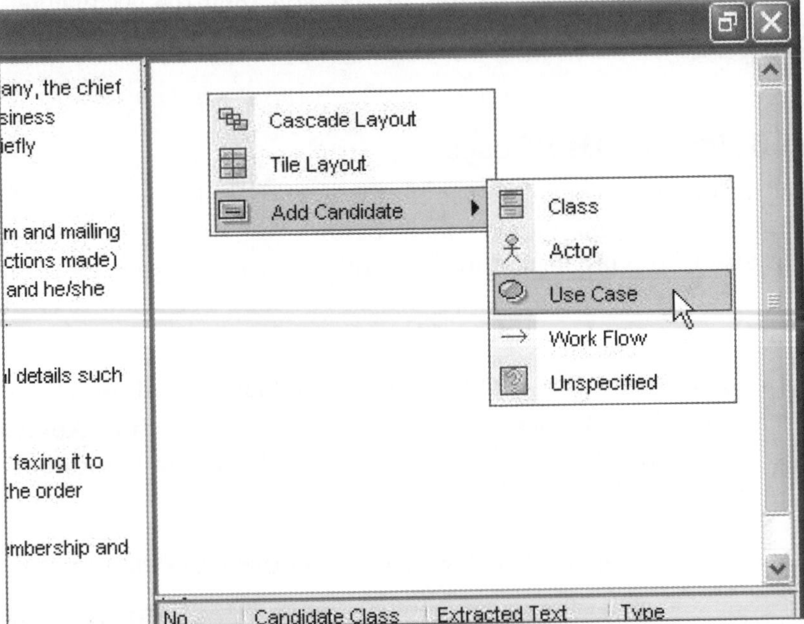

3.3. An input dialog will appear. Enter *Place Order* in the input dialog (see Figure 3.35).

Figure 3.35. Naming a new candidate use case

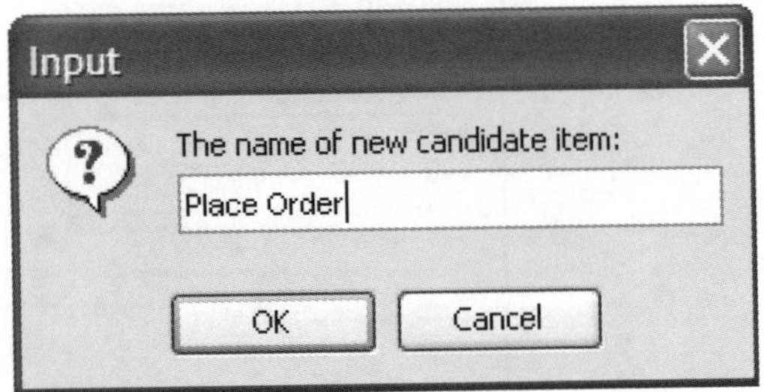

3.4. Click **OK** in the input dialog. A new candidate use case is then created in the **Candidate Class Container** (see Figure 3.36).

Figure 3.36. A new candidate use case in Candidate Class Container

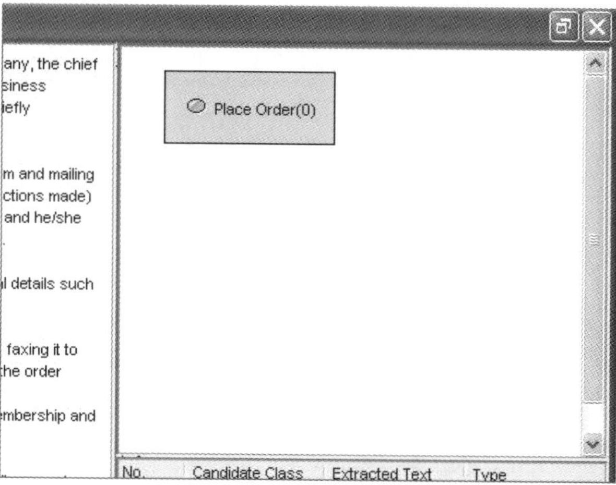

3.5. Now edit the use case brief description for the candidate use case the same way as you would edit the actor description (see Figure 3.37).

Figure 3.37. Creating a brief use case description

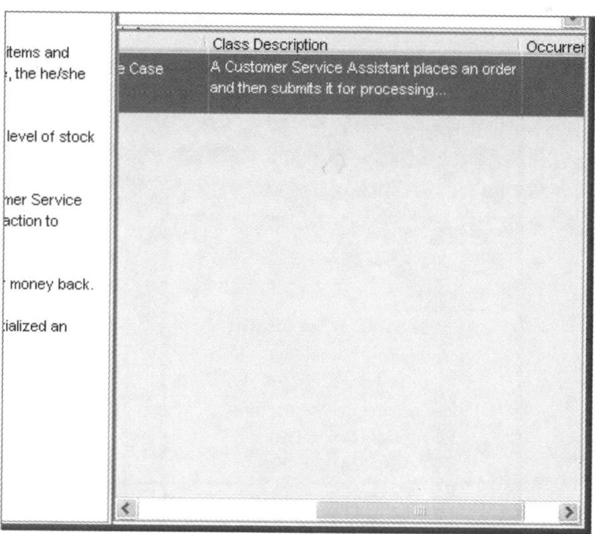

3.6. To add a candidate use case into the model repository, right click on the desired candidate use case in the **Candidate Class Container**. A pop-up menu will appear. Select **Create Use Case Model** (see Figure 3.38).

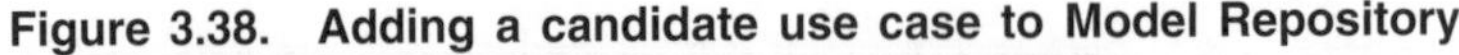

Figure 3.38. Adding a candidate use case to Model Repository

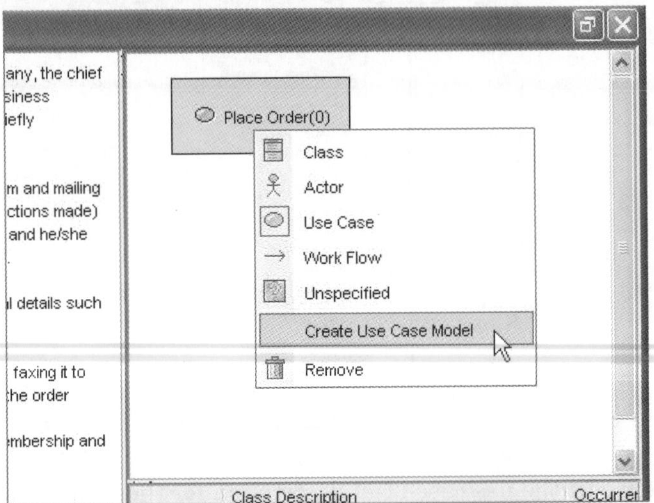

3.7. A new use case is added to the **Model Repository Tree** (see Figure 3.39).

Figure 3.39. A new use case in Model Repository Tree

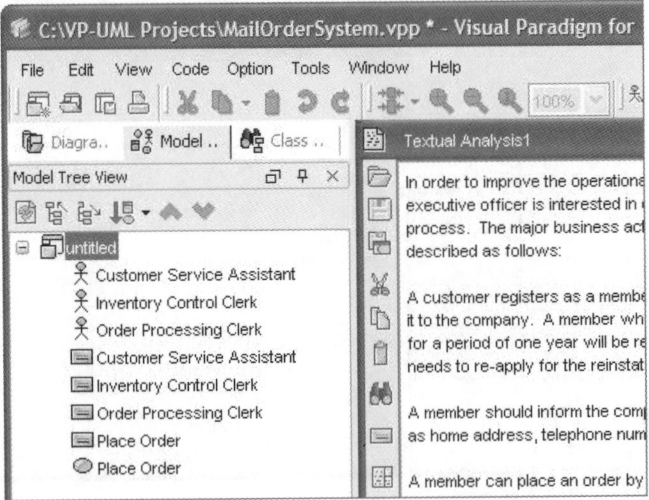

3.8. Repeat the above steps to identify all other candidate use cases below (see Figure 3.40):

- *Check Order Status*
- *Place Order*
- *Handle Goods Return*
- *Update Membership Record*
- *Archive Membership*
- *Register New Member*
- *Process Order*
- *Schedule Delivery*
- *Order Goods*
- *Receive Goods*

Figure 3.40. Use cases in Model Repository Tree

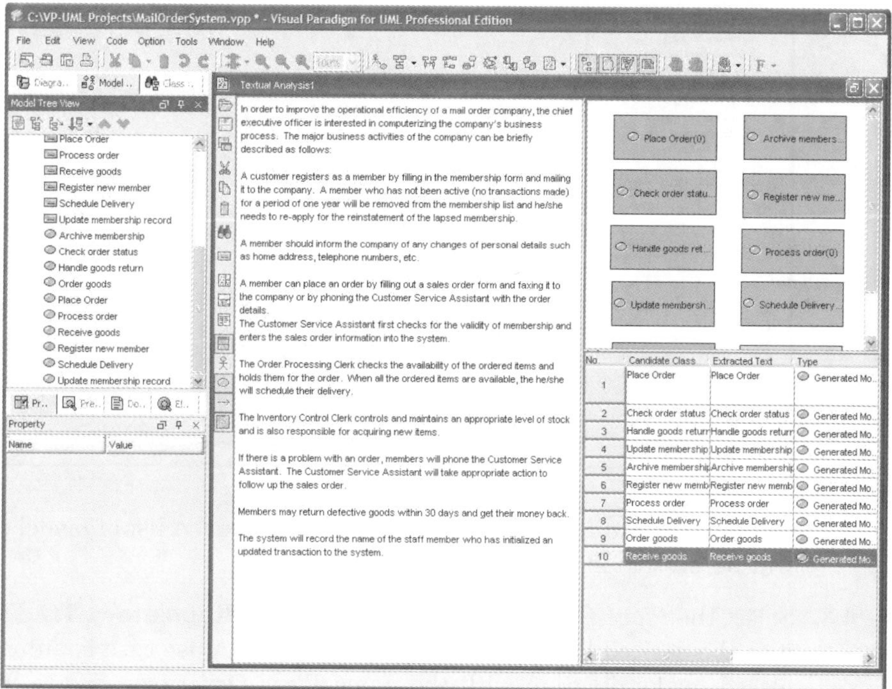

Step 4: Create Initial Use Case Diagram

Having identified all the use cases, create the use case diagrams with the case tool following the steps below:

4.1. Click on the **Create New Use Case Diagram** icon in the toolbar to create a new use case diagram (see Figure 3.41).

Figure 3.41. Creating a new use case diagram

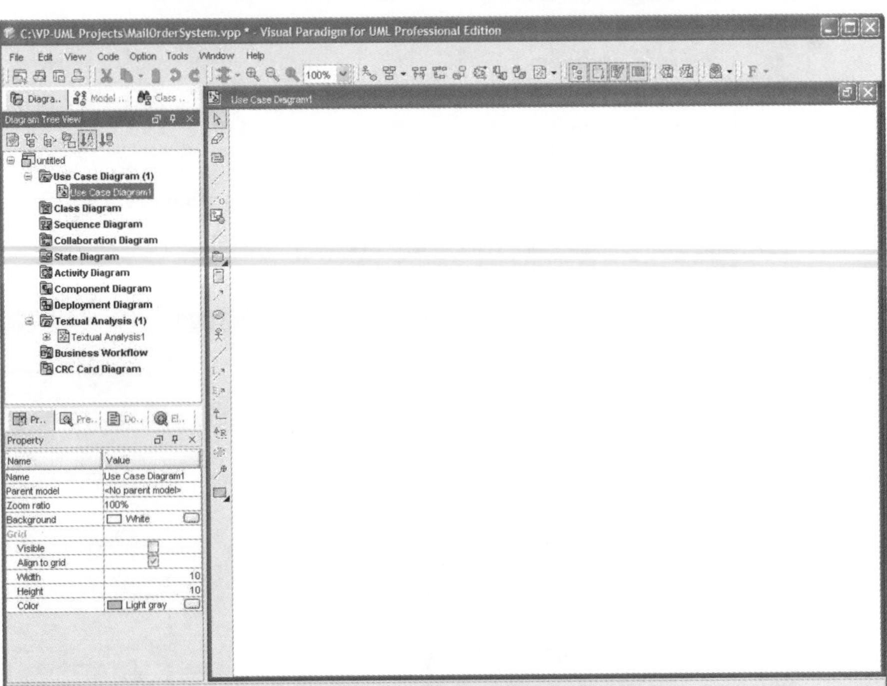

4.2. Click on the **Model** tab in the **Project Explorer**. A list of model elements will be presented (see Figure 3.42).

4.3. Select the *Place Order* model from the **Model Repository Tree** and drag it to the desired location in the diagram pane. A use case is automatically placed in the diagram with the name *Place Order* (see Figure 3.43).

Figure 3.42. Models in Model Repository Tree

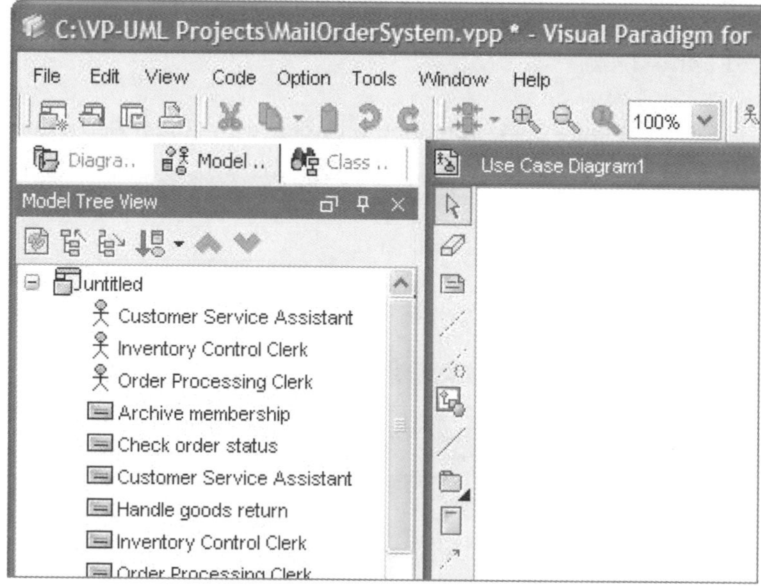

Figure 3.43. Creating a use case with Model Repository Tree

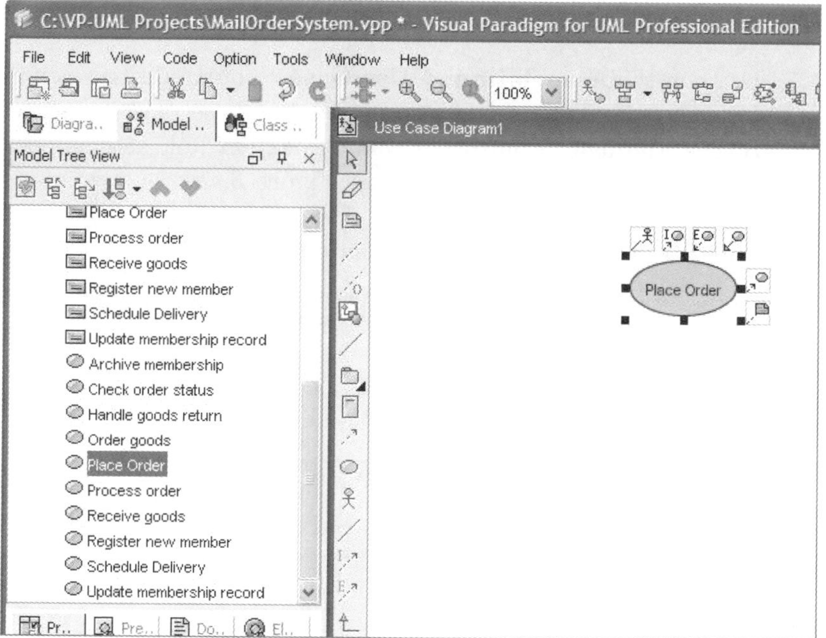

4.4. Select *Customer Service Assistant* from the **Model Repository Tree** and drag it to the desired location in the diagram pane. An actor is then placed in the diagram with the name *Customer Service Assistant* (see Figure 3.44).

Figure 3.44. Creating an Actor with Model Repository Tree

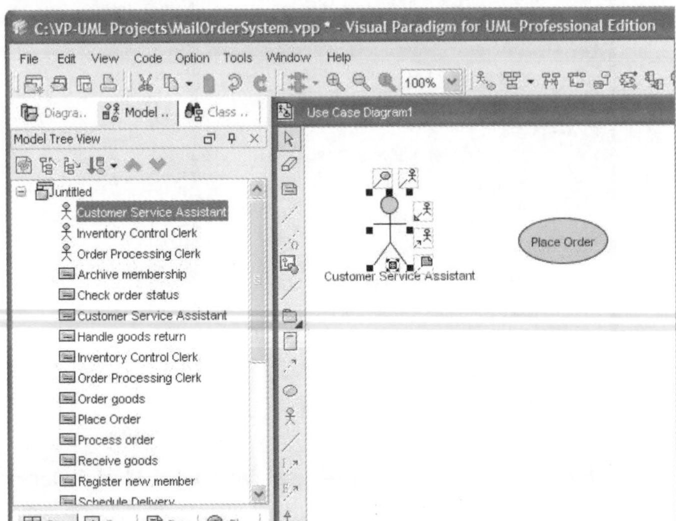

4.5. Drag on the **Association -> Use Case** resource-centric icon above the *Customer Service Assistant* actor to the *Place Order* use case and then release the mouse button. A communication link associated between the actor and use case is created (see Figure 3.45).

Figure 3.45. Creating an association relationship using resource-centric icon

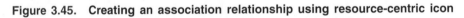

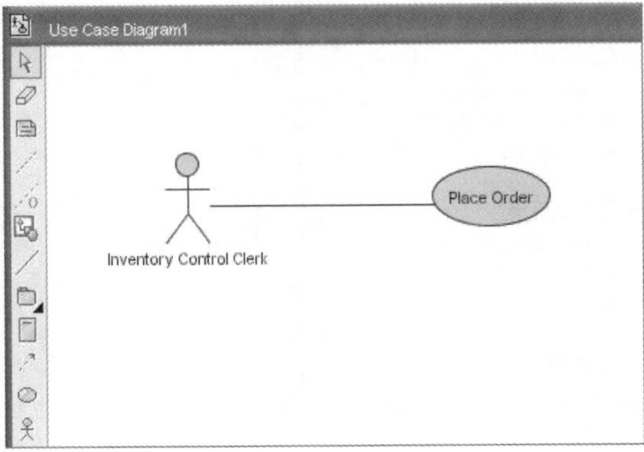

Note: The resource-centric interface saves unnecessary steps to develop the same diagram. If you do not want to use this powerful feature, click once on the **Use Case Diagram** palette, place the mouse pointer in the desired location in the diagram pane and then click the mouse button again. An actor symbol is then created in the diagram pane.

Similarly, an alternative way to connect the communication link between the use case and the actor will be to click the icon once on the **Use Case Diagram** palette, and then place the mouse pointer inside the actor icon. Then drag the communication link from the actor icon into the *Place Order* use case icon.

4.6. Repeat the above steps to create the following use cases and their association relationships with the *Customer Service Assistant* actor (see Figure 3.46):

- *Check Order Status*
- *Handle Goods Return*

Figure 3.46. Creating more use cases with Model Repository Tree

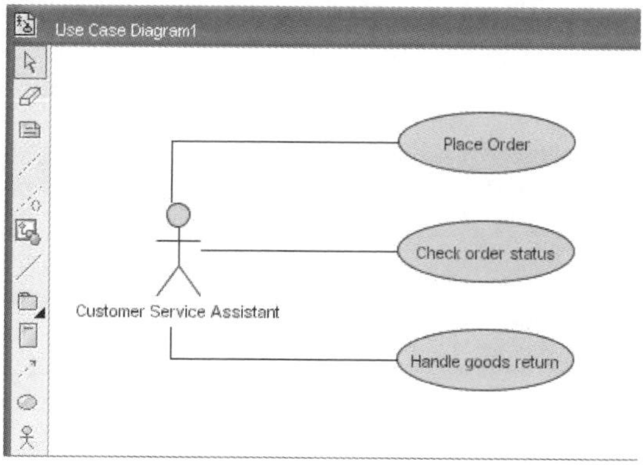

Step 5: Describe Use Cases

The use cases created require further elaboration so that the next phase of the analysis can be performed. This is carried out by providing a more detailed description for each of the use cases.

5.1. Place the mouse pointer within the *Place Order* use case, right click the use case *Place Order* and select **Open Specification** from the pop-up menu (see Figure 3.47).

Figure 3.47. Use case right click pop-up menu

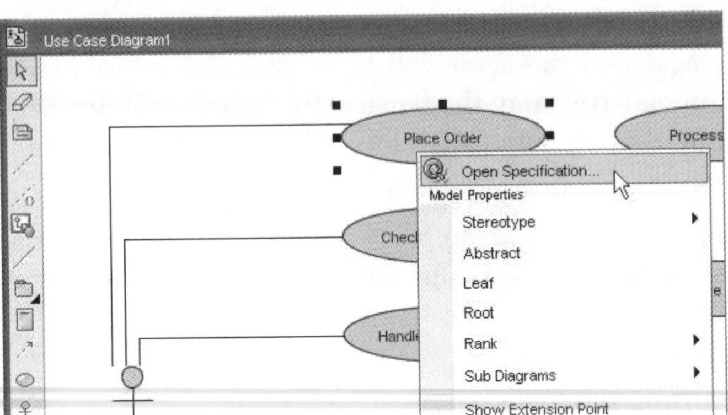

5.2. Select the **Description** tab (see Figure 3.48). A **Specification Dialog** about the files associated to the element will be displayed.

Figure 3.48. Use case specification setup

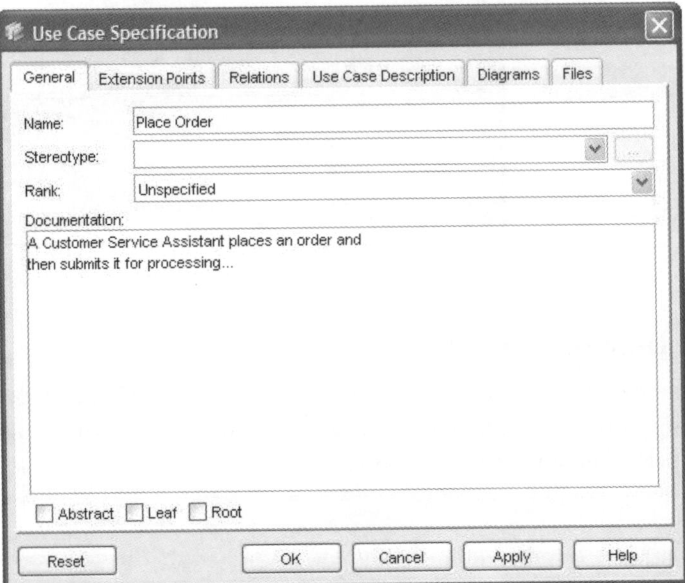

5.3. Enter the contents for each of the elements in the use case template (see Figure 3.49) and click on the **OK** button to confirm the use case description.

Figure 3.49. Use case specification and template

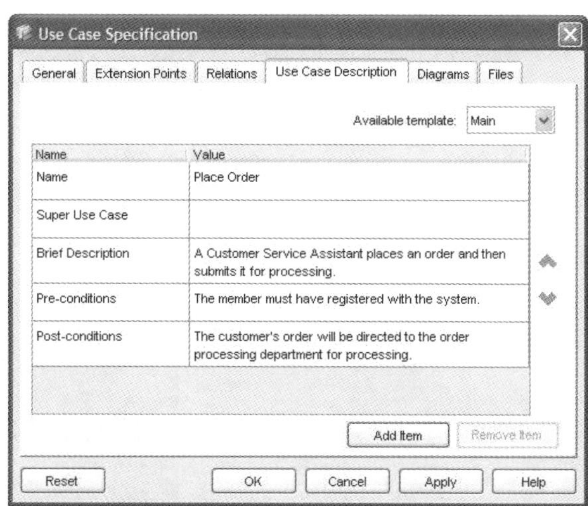

Step 6: Perform Textual Analysis

Textual analysis is a simple traditional technique for performing domain analysis (for more on domain analysis, see Chapter 2: Structural Modeling and Analysis). It is a technique to identify domain knowledge from the text description and is typically applied to requirements analysis based on the textual form of information. Many methodologists apply this technique to identify domain classes and objects as well as operations for the domain classes. However, textual analysis itself does not prevent us from applying it to identify other knowledge and concepts such as business workflow analysis or use case analysis. The only difference in applying this technique to different domains or levels in our software development process is the need to focus on the right level and analyze the right concepts that are being identified. For example, textual analysis can be applied at the beginning of the use case analysis to identify actors and use cases. In this case, focus on the set of questions that were suggested earlier: "Who will use the system?" "What is the role of the user?" Then identify the system's end users and the tasks expected to be performed by the system. Before elaborating a use case from the use case description, focus on the nouns and noun phrases or verbs and verb phrases from the use case description.

Now, let us perform a textual analysis on the *Schedule Delivery* use case.

6.1. Right click the use case *Schedule Delivery* and then select **Create Textual Analysis** from the pop-up menu (see Figure 3.50).

Figure 3.50. Launching textual analysis function with a use case

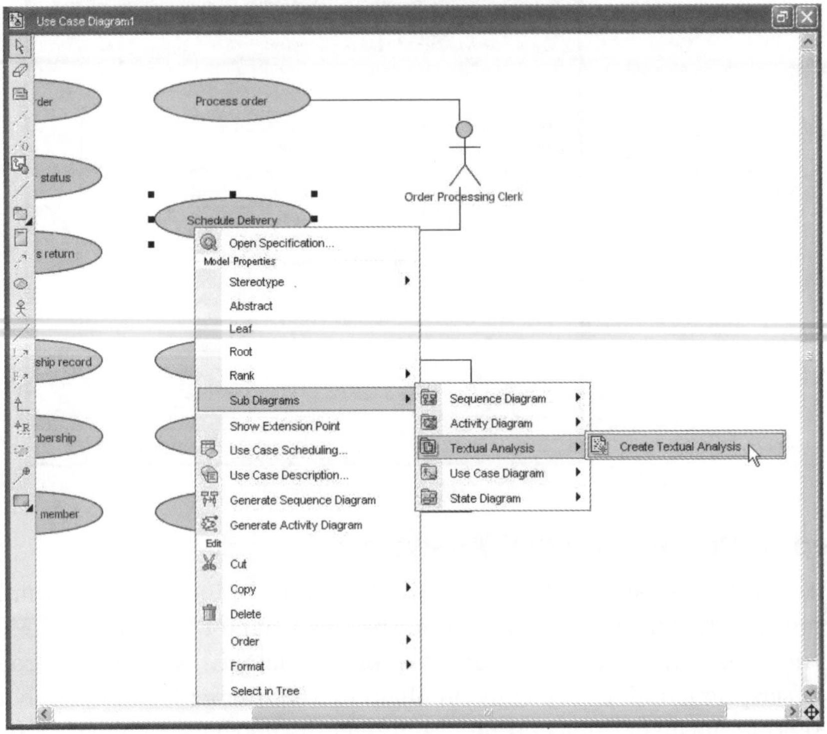

6.2. The **Textual Analysis** window will appear. Enter the following text in the text pane (see Figure 3.51).

> The Order Processing Clerk selects an order from the list of filled sales orders. The system displays the sales order details, together with the member telephone number and address. The Order Processing Clerk enters the delivery date and time after talking with the member over the phone. The system records the delivery date and time of the sales order. The system records the name of the Order Processing Clerk who has handled the sales order.

Figure 3.51. Identifying domain classes using textual analysis

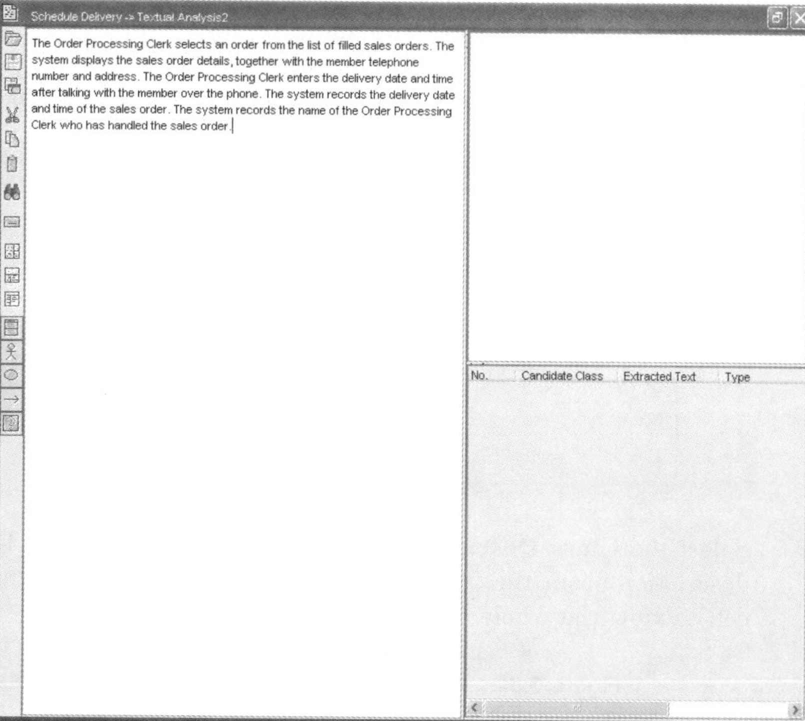

6.3. Now highlight the word *order* as a candidate class, right click on the word *order*, select **Add Text as Class** in the pop-up menu (see Figure 3.52). Note all occurrences of the same actor in the problem statement are now automatically highlighted (see Figure 3.52).

Figure 3.52. Identifying candidate classes

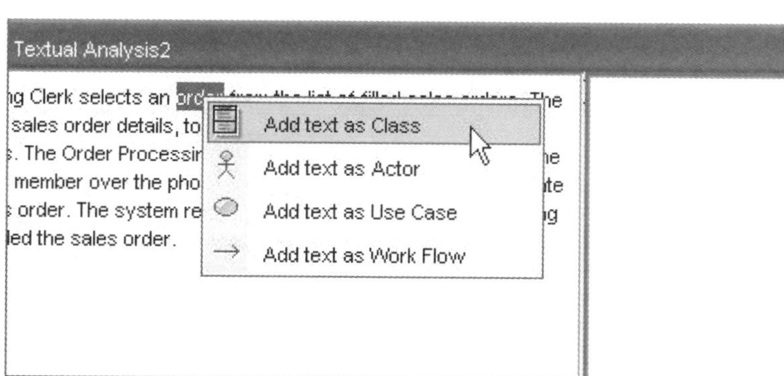

6.4. A new candidate class is automatically created in the **Candidate Class Container** on the right-hand side and all occurrences of the same class in the problem statement are automatically highlighted (see Figure 3.53).

Figure 3.53. All occurrences of candidate class are highlighted

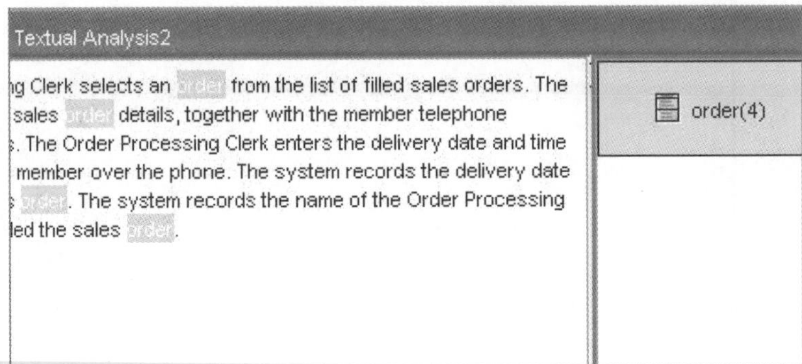

6.5. Select the **Class Description cell** next to the class *Order*. Enter a brief description about the *Order* class. Where necessary, adjust the size of the cell to view the whole description (see Figure 3.54).

Figure 3.54. Inputting class description for Order class

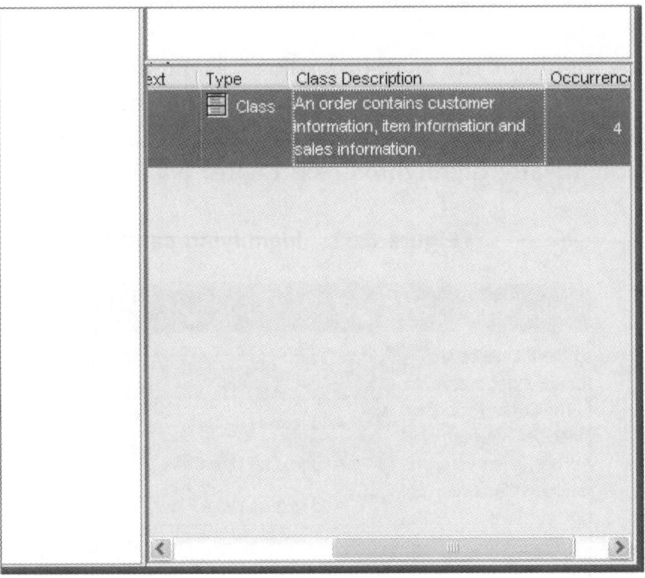

6.6. Repeat the above steps to create the following classes (see Figure 3.55):

- *Sales Order*
- *Member*
- *Delivery*

Figure 3.55. Candidate classes in Candidate Class Container

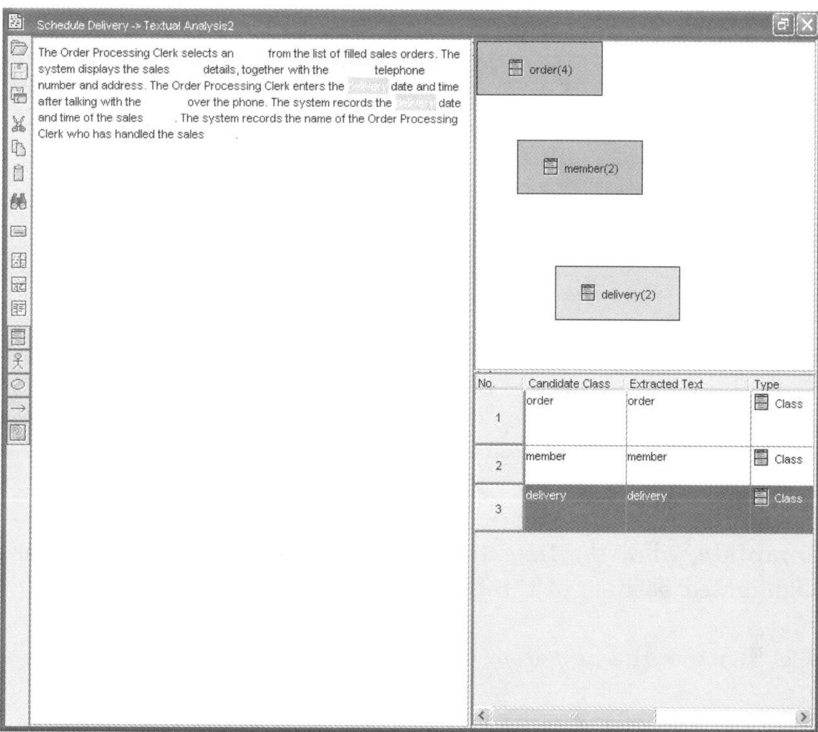

Step 7: Develop Base Use Case Descriptions

You may at times want to customize the use case template to fit the needs for use case documentations. The use case template can be modified by adding or deleting the items in the use case description template.

Follow the steps below to add or delete an item in the use case description.

7.1. Right click on the dialog box to reveal the pop-up menu, and then choose **Insert Item** or **Add Item** (see Figure 3.56).

Figure 3.56. Adding new items to Use Case Template

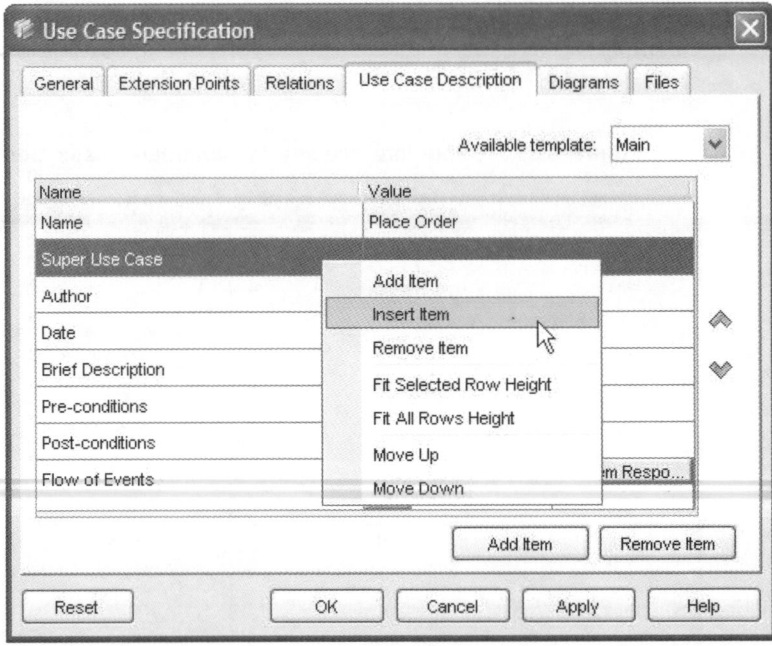

Note: The **Add Item** option appends an item at the end of the **Use Case Template**, while the **Insert Item** option creates an element after the current highlighted position of the **Use Case Description**.

7.2. Rename the new item as *Use Case ID* (see Figure 3.57).

Figure 3.57. Renaming items in Use Case Template

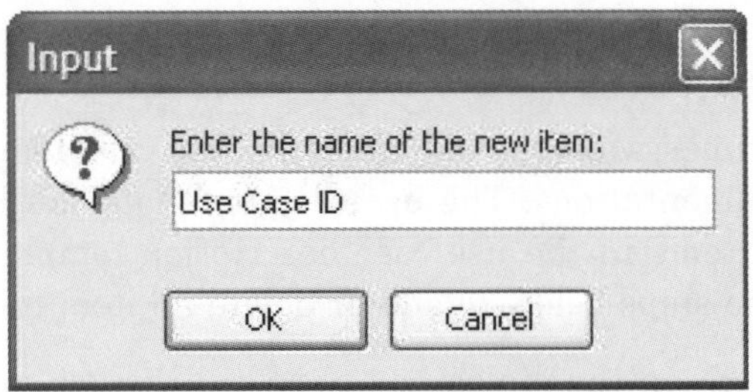

7.3. Create more items in the use case description template and fill the contents of the *Place Order* use case description template as shown in Figure 3.58.

Figure 3.58. The completed use case description

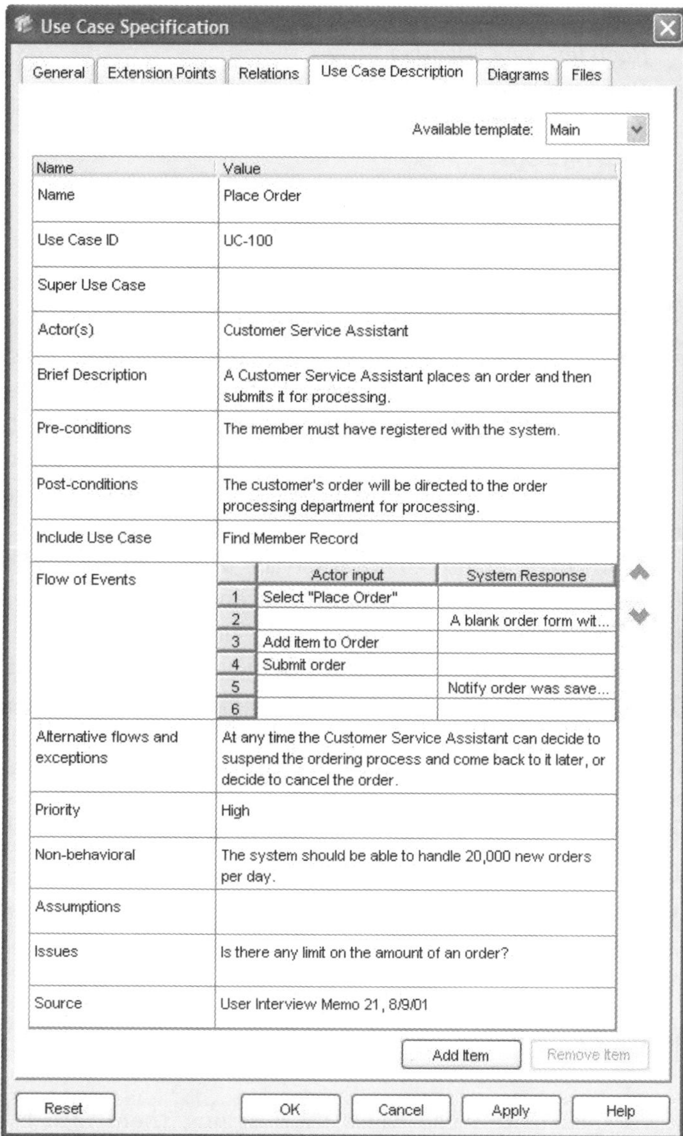

Name	Value
Name	Place Order
Use Case ID	UC-100
Super Use Case	
Actor(s)	Customer Service Assistant
Brief Description	A Customer Service Assistant places an order and then submits it for processing.
Pre-conditions	The member must have registered with the system.
Post-conditions	The customer's order will be directed to the order processing department for processing.
Include Use Case	Find Member Record
Flow of Events	(see below)
Alternative flows and exceptions	At any time the Customer Service Assistant can decide to suspend the ordering process and come back to it later, or decide to cancel the order.
Priority	High
Non-behavioral	The system should be able to handle 20,000 new orders per day.
Assumptions	
Issues	Is there any limit on the amount of an order?
Source	User Interview Memo 21, 8/9/01

Flow of Events:

	Actor input	System Response
1	Select "Place Order"	
2		A blank order form wit...
3	Add item to Order	
4	Submit order	
5		Notify order was save...
6		

7.4. Repeat the above steps to complete the use case descriptions for the following use cases:

- *Check Order Status*
- *Handle Goods Return*
- *Update Membership Record*
- *Archive Membership*
- *Register New Member*
- *Process Order*
- *Schedule Delivery*
- *Order Goods*
- *Receive Goods*
- *Deliver Goods*

Step 8: Structure Use Cases

In this step, use cases shall be grouped into packages. First, create a set of packages based on the system's logical structure; additional packages may be considered later in terms of the physical structure of the system. Consider the role of the users to structure the use cases into different packages. In the Mail Order System example, we can identify three packages, namely inventory, membership, order processing, which are associated with the major roles of the actors. The ultimate goal is to organize the use cases into packages to maximize cohesion within the individual packages and minimize coupling among these packages. The physical structure should not be considered until the system design stage. At that point, software deployment issues need to be considered as well. For example, an ATM system would have more issues to be considered in software deployment, thus the system architecture will play a much more important role to implement such a system.

8.1. Create a package by first clicking on the **Use Case Diagram** palette.

8.2. Place the mouse pointer in the design area and click once. A package symbol will then appear in the design area. Rename the new package as *Inventory Control*. Press Ctrl + Enter to finish the operation (see Figure 3.59).

8.3. Resize the package symbol so that it can accommodate the use cases (see Figure 3.60).

8.4. Move each of the use cases by dragging them into the package region where it belongs or where it is a member (see Figure 3.61).

Figure 3.59. Creating a new package

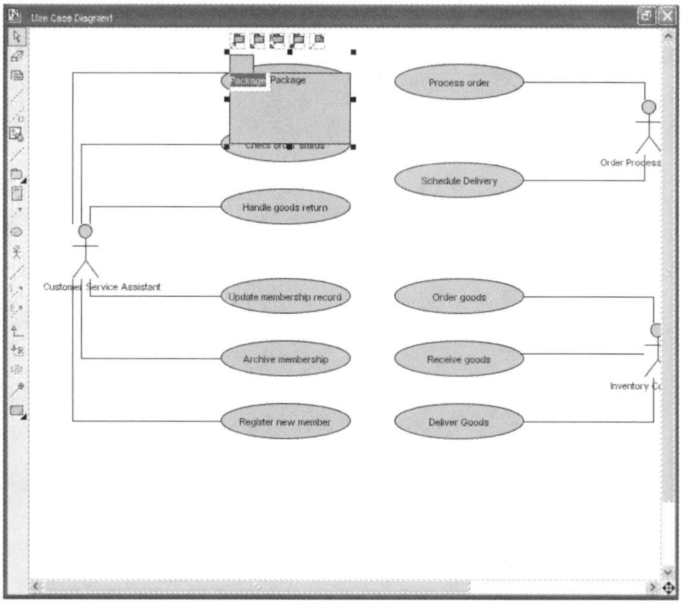

Figure 3.60. Resizing and moving the newly created package

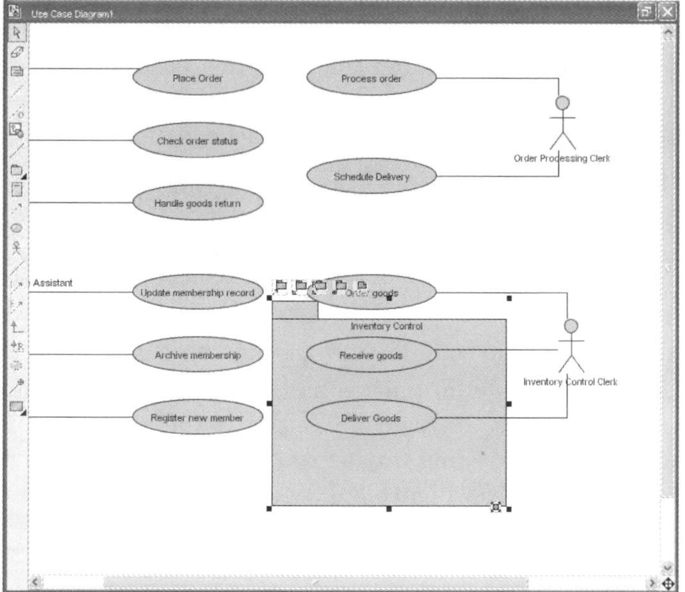

Figure 3.61. Structuring use cases into a package

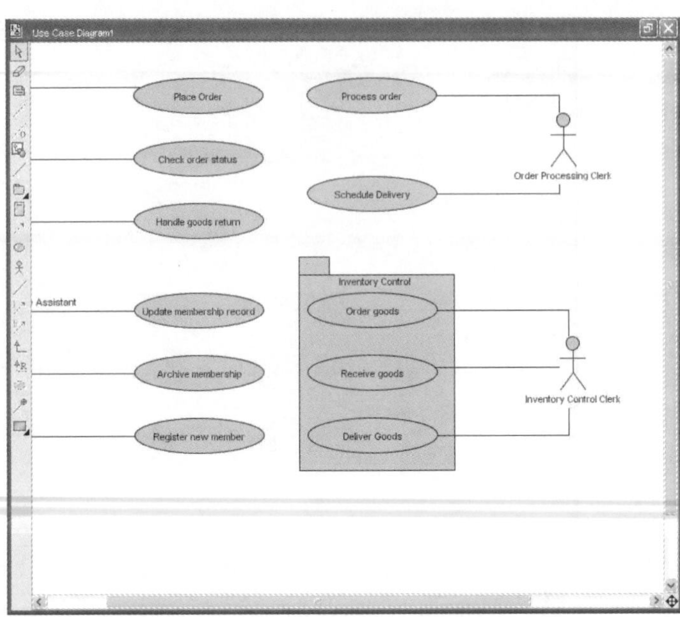

Note: A package can contain other packages, and packages can be nested within a package at multiple levels. When a package is moved around the design area, all the UML elements contained inside that package are moved accordingly, while maintaining their relative positions within the package.

8.5. Repeat the above steps to create packages for the entire use case model.

8.6. Move the elements of the use case diagram by structuring the positions of the packages, the use case within the package and communication links between use cases and actors to make the diagram tidy and easier to read (see Figure 3.62).

8.7. Add the system boundary to the use case model by clicking on the **Use Case Diagram** palette and move the mouse pointer to the desired location on the diagram pane. Move the use cases inside the system boundary in the same way as you would manipulate a package in the use case diagram (see Figure 3.63).

Figure 3.62. Structuring the use cases into packages

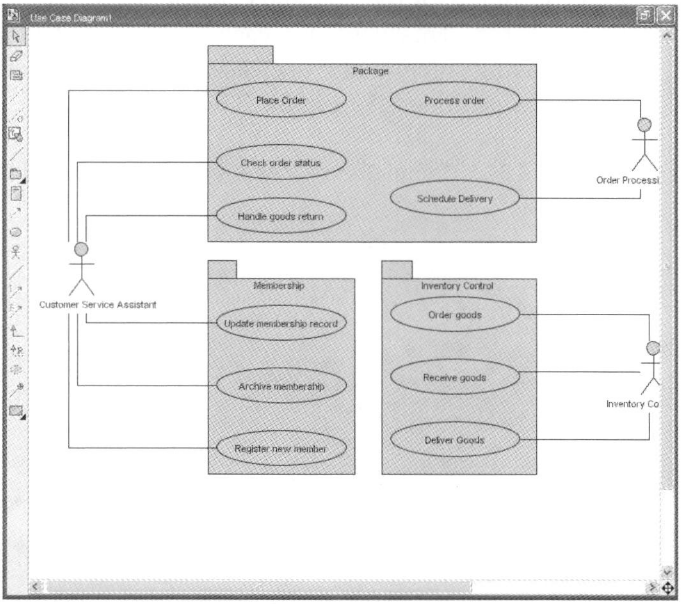

Figure 3.63. Structuring packages into system boundary

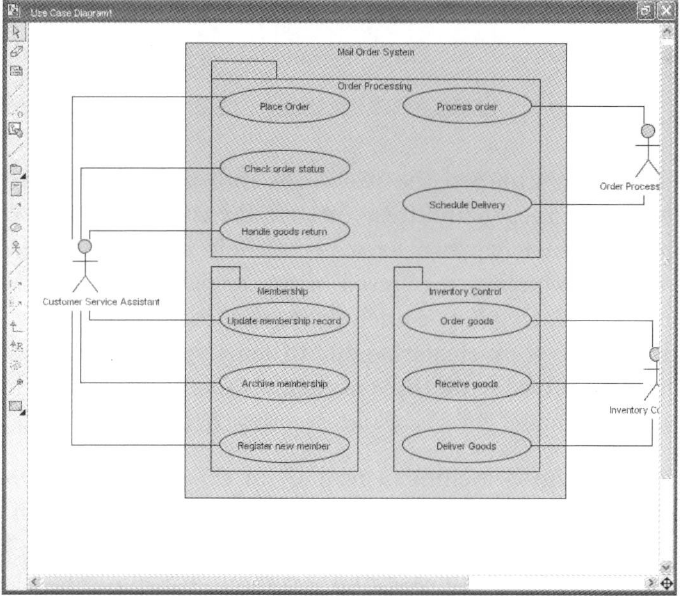

Tip: If a system boundary will eventually be placed in the use case model, it is better to create the boundary at the beginning before the first use case is created. This way, use cases are created inside the boundary without having to move the use cases and actors around to place them in the right position (see Figure 3.64).

Figure 3.64. Complete use case model structured into packages

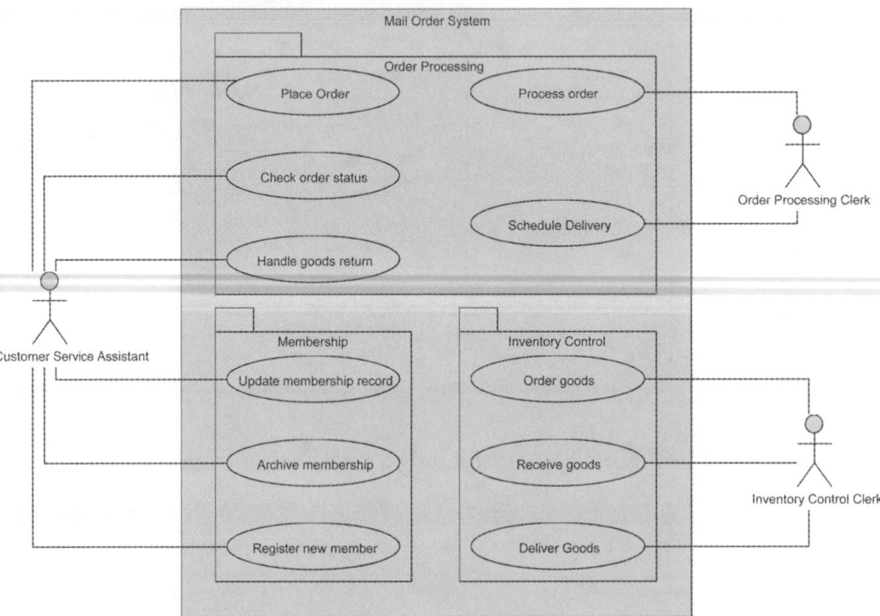

Having grouped the use cases into packages according to the actors' roles and responsibilities, further structure the use cases according to their common pattern as well as their interactive flow pattern. If some common behaviors are found in two or more use cases, we can factor them out by creating an <<include>> use case. On the other hand, if some alternative scenarios arise due to some special condition(s), we can handle these by introducing the <<extend>> use case(s). Now, let us structure the use case model for the *Find Member Record* <<include>> use case.

8.8. Click on the <<include>> icon at the top of the *Handle Goods Return* use case and drag it to a location in the diagram pane where the <<include>> use case is to be created. When releasing the mouse button, an <<include>> use case and a communication link between the base use case and the <<include>> use case will then be created (see Figure 3.65).

Figure 3.65. Creating a new <<include>> use case

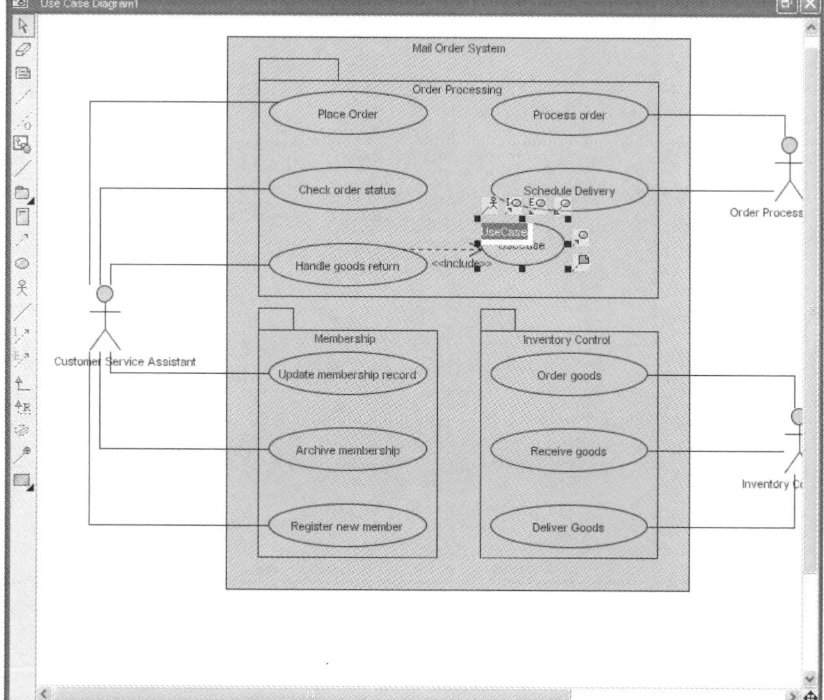

8.9. Rename the <<include>> use case by typing *Find Member Record* in the editable text field of the untitled <<include>> use case (see Figure 3.66).

8.10. Click on the <<include>> resource icon at the top of the *Register New Member* use case and drag it out to where the <<include>> use case is to be created. To create an <<include>> relationship between the *Register New Member* use case and *Find Member Record* use case, drag the <<include>> resource icon to the *Find Member Record* <<include>> use case (see Figure 3.67).

Note: If the <<include>> use case has already been created and you simply want to connect the base use case with the existing <<include>> use case, then drop the <<include>> use case into the existing *Find Member Record* <<include>> use case. A dependency link between the base use case *Register New Member* and the <<include>> *Find Member Record* use case will then be created.

Figure 3.66. Naming the new <<include>> use case

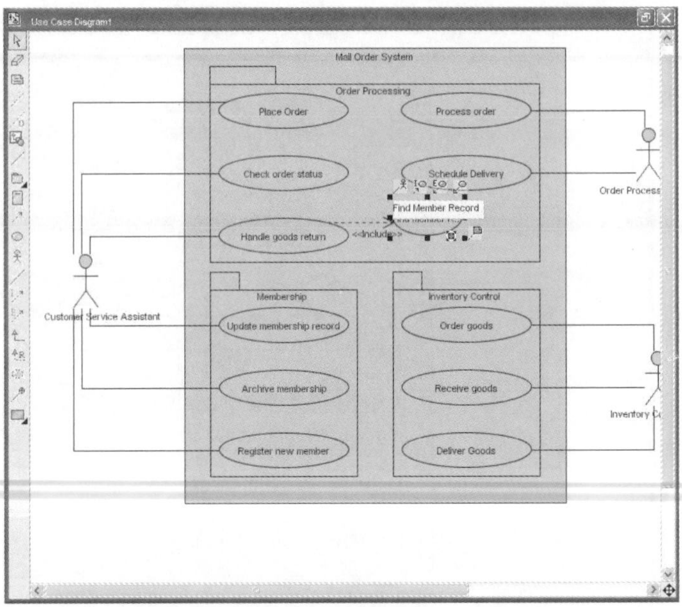

Figure 3.67. Structuring use cases with relationships

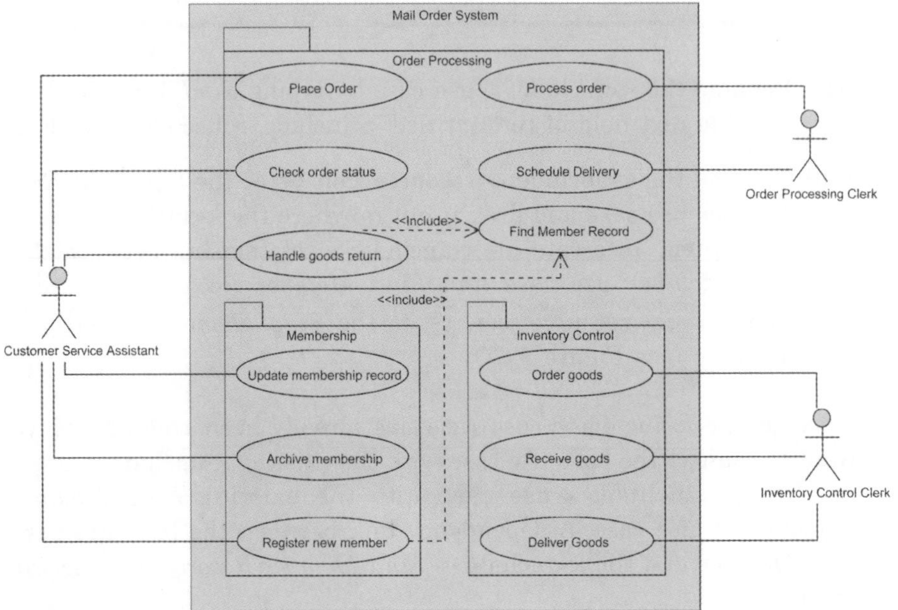

8.11. We can also add a use case description to the *Find Member Record* <<include>> use case by:

- customizing the use case description for the *Find Member Record* <<include>> use case where necessary
- filling the contents of the <<include>> use case(s) in the same way as you would edit the base use cases previously (see Figure 3.68).

Figure 3.68. Use case description for the Find Member Record use case

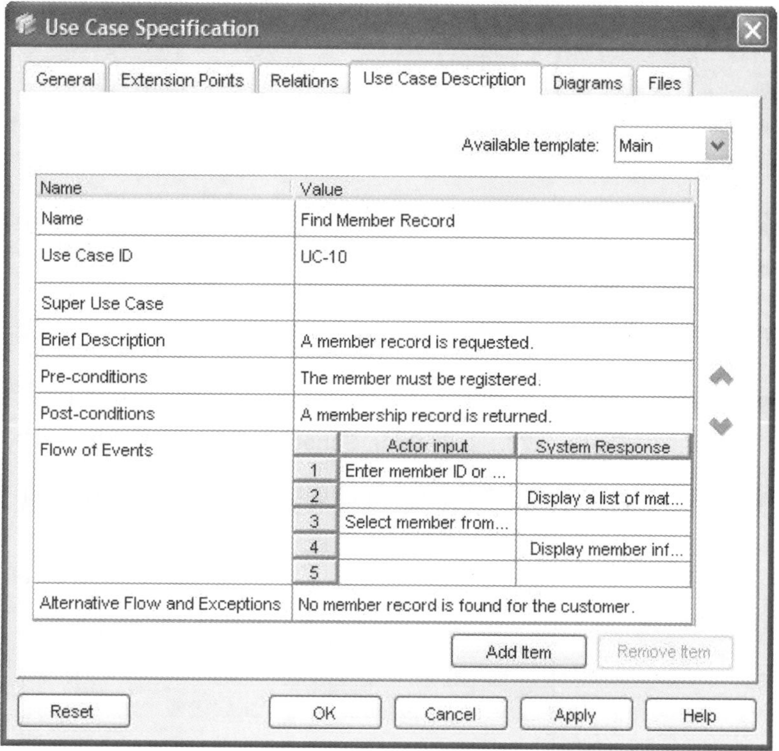

Step 9: Prioritize Use Cases

We shall prioritize the use cases using the use case schedule.

9.1. Right click on any empty space in the **Use Case diagram** and select the **open specification item**.

9.2. Select the **Schedule** tab from the pop-up menu (see Figure 3.69).

Figure 3.69. **Launching the use case schedule**

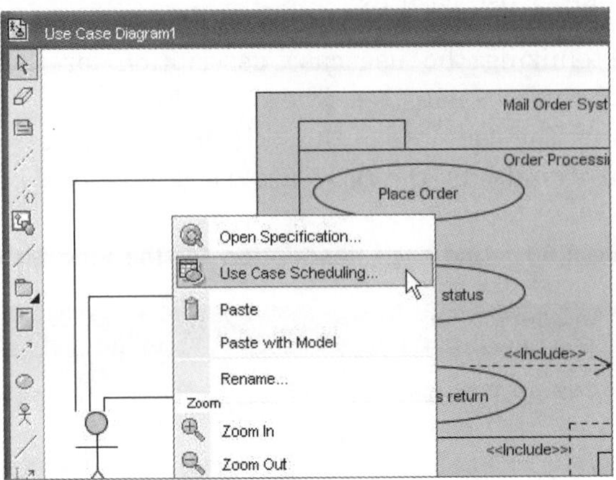

9.3. All the use cases in the **Use Case Model** are then automatically displayed in the table. Rank the use cases by choosing the appropriate option in the Combo Box.

9.4. Provide some justification for each use case in the table for future reference (see Figure 3.70).

Figure 3.70. **Use Case Schedule for the Mail Order System**

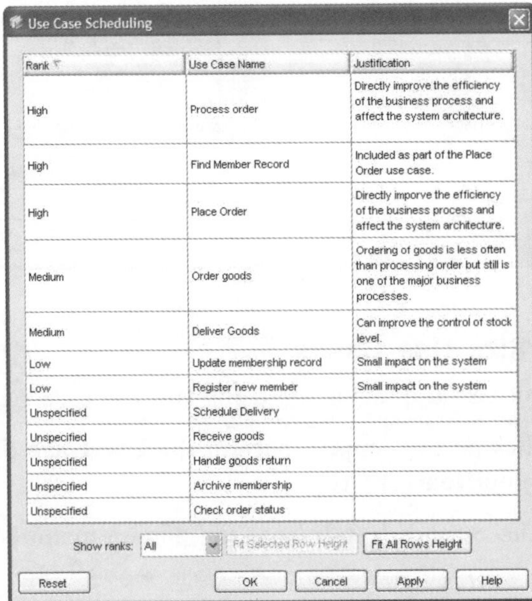

Rank	Use Case Name	Justification
High	Process order	Directly improve the efficiency of the business process and affect the system architecture.
High	Find Member Record	Included as part of the Place Order use case.
High	Place Order	Directly imporve the efficiency of the business process and affect the system architecture.
Medium	Order goods	Ordering of goods is less often than processing order but still is one of the major business processes.
Medium	Deliver Goods	Can improve the control of stock level.
Low	Update membership record	Small impact on the system
Low	Register new member	Small impact on the system
Unspecified	Schedule Delivery	
Unspecified	Receive goods	
Unspecified	Handle goods return	
Unspecified	Archive membership	
Unspecified	Check order status	

Summary

Use case modeling is the process of describing the behavior of the target system from an external point of view. Hence, use case analysis emphasizes on modeling the externally visible behavior and not the internal behavior of the system. Use case diagrams, which are artifacts of the analysis and modeling process, are used in the early stages of the system development to capture and document system requirements.

In performing use case modeling and analysis, a two-stage process is followed. We first commence with the problem statement to identify the major actors and use cases of the system so as to create an initial use case diagram. The description of the behavior of each use case can then be produced, and from which candidate business classes are identified and refined using textual analysis.

In the second stage, the use case model is further refined by developing the base use case descriptions, which are then iteratively elaborated to determine the <<extend>>, <<include>> and generalization relationships. The instance scenarios are then developed and use cases prioritized.

To illustrate the concepts described in this chapter, the modeling and analysis of an online mail order system has been described, detailing the steps involved by using the powerful features of the VP-UML CASE tool.

Exercise

Consider the problem statement of an online book store in the Exercise of Chapter 2.

Follow the steps below to develop the use case model of the system:

- Identify the major actors
- Write a description to define the roles of each actor
- Examine the roles of each actor and identify the use cases
- Draw initial use case diagrams
- Write initial descriptions for the use cases
- Perform a textual analysis to identify candidate business (domain) objects
- Develop the base use case descriptions
- Iteratively elaborate the base use case descriptions and determine the <<extend>>, <<include>> and generalization relationships. Refine the use case diagram and the use case descriptions to reflect the use case relationships.

Develop the instance scenarios. For each use case, develop the instance scenarios to cover all possible paths of execution.

Chapter

4

Dynamic Modeling and Analysis

Overview

Class diagrams are used to model the static aspects of a system by showing the classes and their relationships. However, a class diagram does not provide any information on the dynamic aspects of the system, for example, how objects interact with each other during the execution of a use case. Dynamic models can be used to describe or specify the interactions of objects when a use case is invoked or the interactions between entities such as actors and subsystems, as well as the evolution of an object during its lifetime (i.e. object states and their transitions).

In UML, there are four dynamic models, namely the sequence diagram, the collaboration diagram, the statechart diagram and the activity diagram, which represent various aspects of the dynamic behaviors of a system — a use case, a scenario of a use case (an instance of a use case), an individual object or even an operation. These four models provide different levels of abstraction of a system and also give an alternative projection of the system dynamics, highlighting some particular aspects while de-emphasizing others. In this chapter, these four dynamic models will be examined in detail. A discussion on the use of the activity diagram at different levels of abstraction will be presented in Chapter 6 (View Alignment Techniques and Method Customization).

What You Will Learn

On completing the study of this chapter, you should be able to:

- model message flows using sequence diagrams
- model message flows using collaboration diagrams
- model lifetime behaviors of an object using statechart diagrams
- model the performance of actions of a procedure or an activity using activity diagrams

Scenario Modeling Techniques: Interaction Diagram

Scenario modeling describes how the objects in a system interact with each other in a scenario. A scenario is a sequence of events that occurs during one particular execution path within a use case of a system. Each event involves the interaction of objects passing messages between them.

An interaction diagram can be used to model the collaborating objects in scenarios, showing the objects involved in the scenario and the messages sent and received by them. These objects may be external or internal of the system and the messages represent the invocation of operations of the receiving objects. There are two kinds of interaction diagrams: sequence diagrams and collaboration diagrams. Both describe the collaboration of objects in a scenario, but the former emphasizes the time sequencing of messages while the latter focuses on the structural organization of the objects and the links between collaborating objects. In essence, the sequence diagram is temporally focused, and, therefore most suitable for analyzing the order of the interactions between objects. The collaboration diagram is structurally focused and is most suitable to analyze the required structural relationship between objects to realize a scenario.

In the following two sections, the basic UML notations for sequence diagrams and collaboration diagrams will be explained. We shall also introduce some basic techniques when using them.

Common UML Interaction Diagram Notation

Object Symbol

Like the class icon, an object icon is represented by a rectangle. Within the rectangle are the object name and the object label, which is underlined to distinguish the object icon from a class icon. In Unified Modeling Language

(UML) there are minor variations of the object icon to provide more information about an object, as shown in Table 4.1.

Table 4.1. Object notations

Naming format	Notation
An object of an unspecified class	object object:
A named object of a specified class	object X: Class
An unnamed object of a specified class	: Class

Object Stereotypes

In general, stereotypes are used to provide a mechanism for extending the vocabulary of the UML. For example, in UML use case diagrams, it is common to apply stereotypes such as <<include>> and <<extend>> to the associations between use cases. There are four commonly used stereotypes for objects in sequence diagrams and collaboration diagrams, namely <<actor>>, <<boundary>>, <<control>> and <<entity>>. Sometimes, graphical stereotype icons are introduced to improve the diagram's readability. For example, a stick figure is often used to represent an actor object. Table 4.2 provides some details on these object categories and their graphical notations.

With such visual cues of these stereotypes in interaction diagrams, the interaction of objects can be visualized much more easily. The stereotypes help to identify the object that initiated the interaction (actor objects) and those that receive messages from the outside world (boundary objects). Furthermore, they can also identify how these messages are processed and coordinated (control objects) and which objects keep the data of the system (entity objects).

The classification of these three objects types (entity, boundary and control) is sometimes referred to as the Model/View/Control (MVC) software model, which is adopted by software architectures such as Java Swing. The stereotypes in Table 4.2 are quite suitable for documenting this kind of software structure.

Table 4.2. Commonly used stereotypes for objects

Object category	Description	Graphical notations
Actor object	An external entity that interacts with the system	:Object 1 <<Actor>> :Object 1
Entity object	An object that models the data in the system which often represents an object in the problem domain	<<Entity>> :Object 3 :Entity Object
Boundary object	An object that handles the communication between actor objects and the system	<<Boundary>> :Object 2 :Boundary Object
Control object	An object that models the flow of control and functionality that do not naturally belong to entity objects or boundary objects	<<Control>> :Object 4 :Control Object

Messages

Messages are a common means of communication between objects. An object can send a message to another object to invoke an operation, raise a signal, create an object or even destroy one. In an interaction diagram, a message is represented by an arrow. The different types of messages are defined in Table 4.3.

Table 4.3. Types of messages

Message	Description	Notation
Procedure call or other nested flow of control	The message sender waits for the completion of the procedure call of the message receiver.	——▶
Asynchronous communication	The sender dispatches a message and immediately continues with the next step of execution.	——>
Return message	Message returned from the procedure call.	- - - - - ->
Message with travel delay	The message will take a significant amount of time to arrive at the receiving object. (This is only used in sequence diagrams.)	↘

Sequence Diagrams

An interaction diagram models the behavior of a group of objects that work together to achieve a user goal. A sequence diagram helps to identify a set of collaborating objects involved in a scenario of a use case. A sequence diagram has two dimensions: the vertical dimension and the horizontal dimension, respectively representing the passage of time and the objects involved in the interaction. Object icons are placed horizontally at the top of the sequence diagram, and messages are passed between them. Figure 4.1 shows a sequence diagram for the login procedure of an Automatic Teller Machine (ATM) system.

By going through the scenarios of a use case, we can discover the system's objects. The object identification process typically involves a number of stages. First, perform a textual analysis on the problem statement to identify a set of domain objects (as described in Chapter 2). Then analyze the messages that are passed among these objects. By examining these messages in detail, the functionality and data associated with each of these objects, such as operations and attributes, can be discovered.

The initial version of the interaction diagram may consist of messages represented in natural language such as *Place an order*, *Retrieve product item details*, etc. (see Figure 4.2). The sequence diagram is then iteratively refined until all the messages are ultimately transformed into function prototypes, such as *placeOrder(date, company, contactPerson)*, which provide a lot more

Figure 4.1. Sequence diagram for login procedure of the ATM system

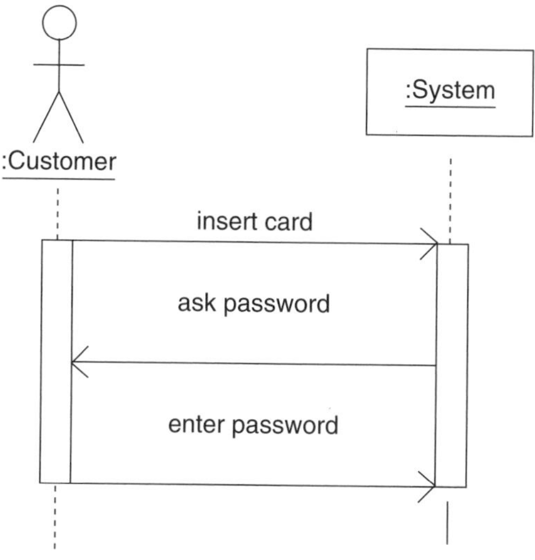

Figure 4.2. A customer placing an order

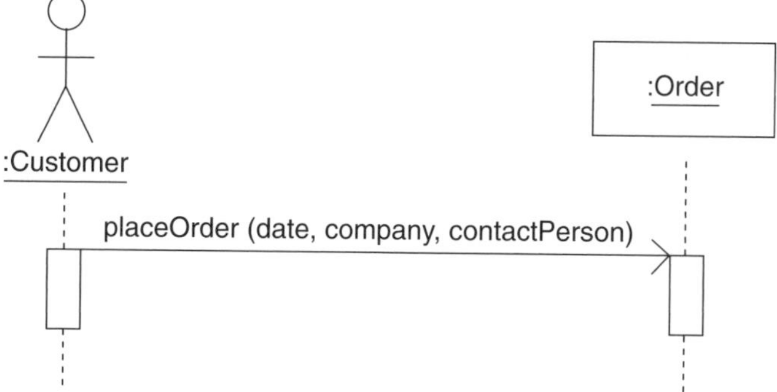

useful information for implementation. In Figure 4.2, there is an object called **customer** who places an **order** (another object) on behalf of his **company**. The **customer** performs a **placeOrder** operation with the required information. The three pieces of information (*date*, *company*, *contactPerson*) may be references for objects in the domain class model.

Lifelines

Lifelines are dashed vertical lines that indicate the object's existence over time. In other words, if the lifeline extends to the bottom of the diagram, the object will continue to exist during the entire session of interaction. If the object is positioned at the top of the diagram, it indicates that the object actually exists before the interaction.

Object Creation and Deletion

By sending a <<create>> message, an object can dynamically create a new object. In the sequence diagram, the object is created at the position where the <<create>> message is sent out. Likewise, an object can also be deleted on receiving a <<destroy>> message from another object. A large cross (X) is placed at the end of the object's lifeline to indicate that the object life has been terminated at that point. Figure 4.3 illustrates how the Receiver object is created and subsequently destroyed by the Sender object. The Receiver object is in a lower position in the diagram where the <<create>> message points at it, and the Sender object is in existence before its interaction with the Receiver.

Figure 4.3. Object creation and destruction

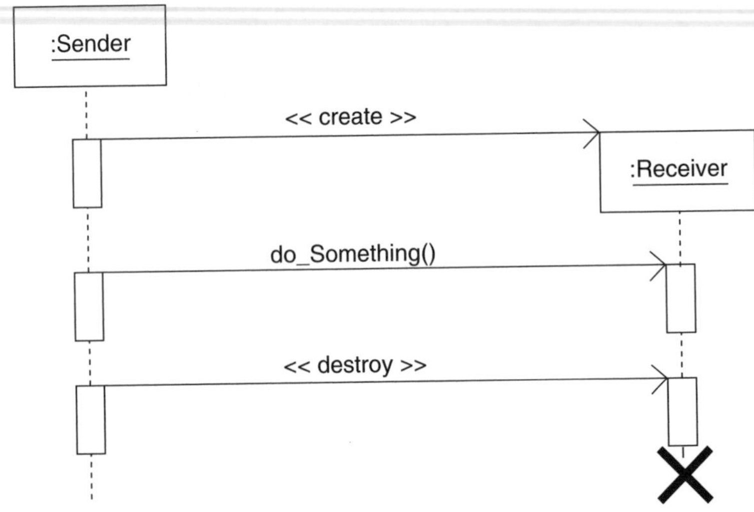

Activation

An object's lifeline gives an idea about the duration over which it exists, but it is not obvious when the object is actively performing a task or when it is inactive. A tall thin rectangle is used to represent the time during which an object is active (see Figure 4.3). The top of the rectangle signifies when the activation starts and the bottom of the rectangle its completion time. In Figure 4.3, the Receiver object is active when it receives a message from the Sender object.

Simple and Collective Iteration

Sometimes, a task may be performed repeatedly. In the sequence diagram, such a task is represented by a name preceded by an asterisk "*". In Figure 4.4, the *add an item* and *get product details* tasks may be carried out a number of times. Optionally, place the continuation condition of the iteration in brackets [ ]. Sometimes, the execution of a block of messages may be repeated, and this is represented in the sequence diagram by enclosing the group of messages within a rectangle. In Figure 4.5 the *add an item* and *get product details* tasks are grouped together in a rectangle to indicate that they will be performed repeatedly. Note that the "*" symbols preceding these two tasks have been removed.

Figure 4.4. Simple iterations in sequence diagram

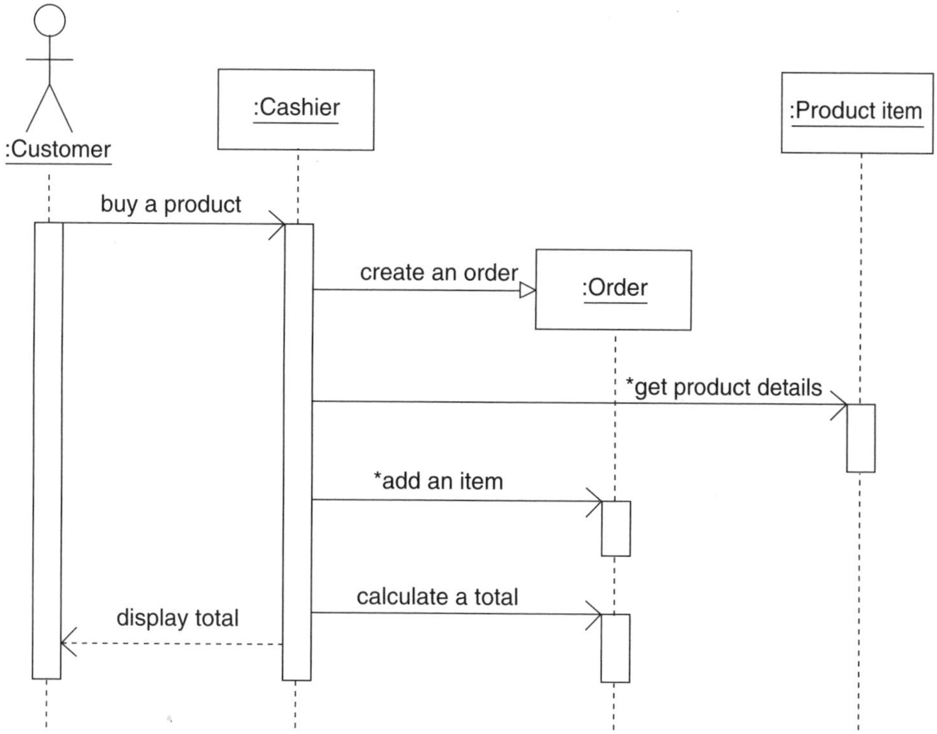

Figure 4.5. Block iterations in sequence diagram

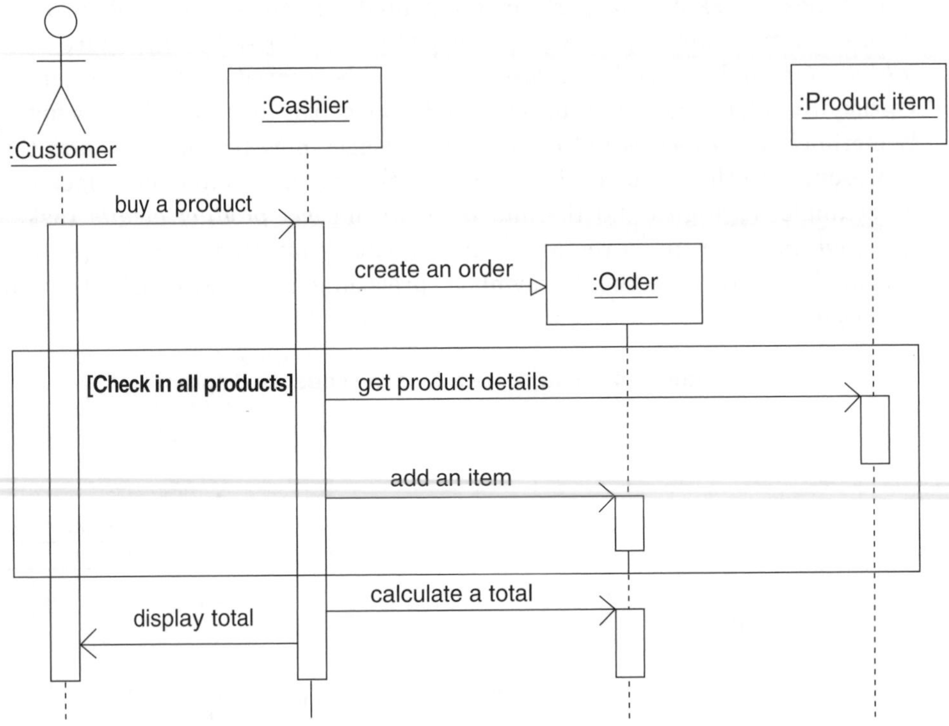

Branching

A branch is used to represent conditional action or concurrent action, and it is rendered by multiple arrows leaving the same point of the object's lifeline. Each message may be labeled with a condition. If the conditions of the messages are mutually exclusive, the branch is a conditional (see Figure 4.6); otherwise it is concurrent.

Figure 4.7 shows the same set of events as a sequence diagram that is associated with the process of making a telephone call. This example will be used to illustrate the concept of branching. Figure 4.8 shows the sequence diagram for a scenario where a call is successfully made, and the switch connects the caller and the callee at the same time when the callee lifts the receiver. This is shown by a branching at the bottom of the sequence diagram. The messages in the figure are sometimes labeled with their sequence numbers which explicitly specify their order chronologically. However, this is not a common practice because the time order of the messages is evident from the diagram. It should be noted that sequence numbers are necessary in a collaboration diagram. The use of sequence numbers in collaboration diagrams is further explained in the following sections.

Figure 4.6. Conditional case in sequence diagram

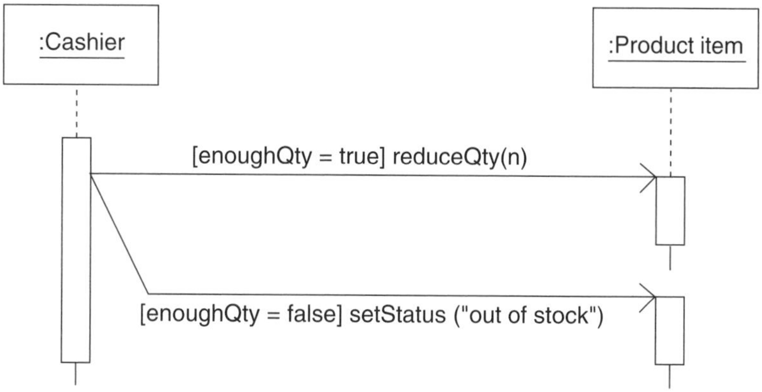

Figure 4.7. Scenario for making a phone call

- caller lifts receiver
- dial tone begins
- caller dials digits one at a time
- switch makes routing
- ringing tone on callee's receiver begins
    - phone rings on callee's receiver begins
    - callee lifts receiver
- switch makes connection between caller and callee
    - switch connects calee
    - switch connects caller

Figure 4.8. Branching in connecting caller and callee

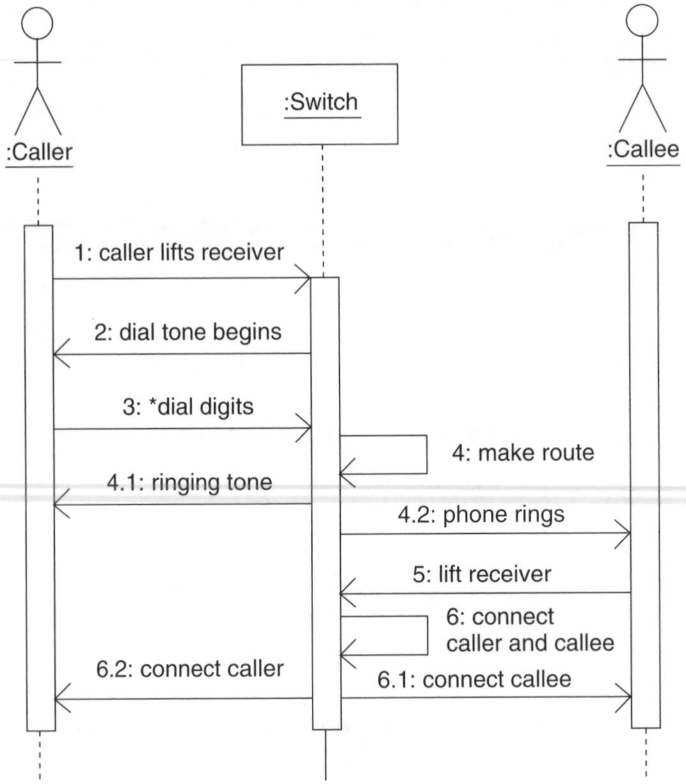

Collaboration Diagrams

Collaboration diagrams provide another way to model a scenario. In a collaboration diagram, each object is represented by an object icon, and links are used to indicate communication paths on which messages are transmitted. Messages are presented in the same way as those in a sequence diagram; in fact, sequence diagrams and collaboration diagrams are semantically equivalent.

Sequence Number

In a collaboration diagram, each message is presented with a sequence number that precedes it. The sequential numbering of messages allows us to easily trace the message in a collaboration diagram. The simplest numbering scheme is 1, 2, 3, …, etc., and for large diagrams, it is more practical and typical to use a nested numbering scheme such as 1, 1.1, 1.2, … 2, 2.1, 2.2, etc. Figure 4.9 shows a collaboration diagram for the sequence diagram in Figure 4.8.

Figure 4.9. Sequence numbers in collaboration diagram

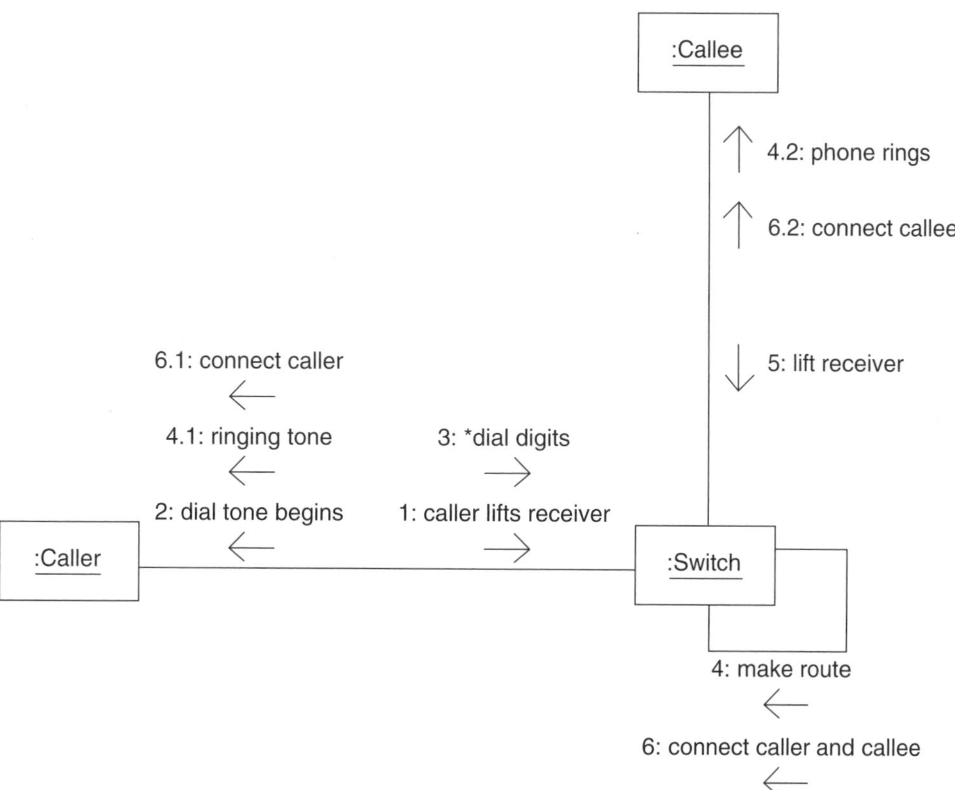

The time order of the messages in a collaboration diagram is shown explicitly by sequence numbers. It is generally harder to follow a collaboration diagram than a sequence diagram due to successive messages situated in various parts of the collaboration diagram. Furthermore, as objects in collaboration diagrams do not have a lifeline, it is not readily evident as to when an object is created or destroyed. However, collaboration diagrams facilitate the designer with a better understanding of the links between objects, and consequently, they make the task of implementing the classes easier.

Message with Duration

In many situations, especially in a network environment, a message takes a considerable amount of time to travel from one node to another. If the delays are significant, it may be necessary to provide such information in the diagram. While the vertical axis of the sequence diagram represents time, a message with duration is represented by a slanting arrow (see Figure 4.10). It is important to note that the vertical time axis is not drawn to scale in the sequence diagram and therefore it should not be used to estimate the duration of a scenario. The Object Constraint Language (OCL) is often used to specify the upper or lower bound of the delay. For example, Figure 4.11 shows the equivalent in a collaboration diagram.

Figure 4.10. Message with duration in sequence diagram

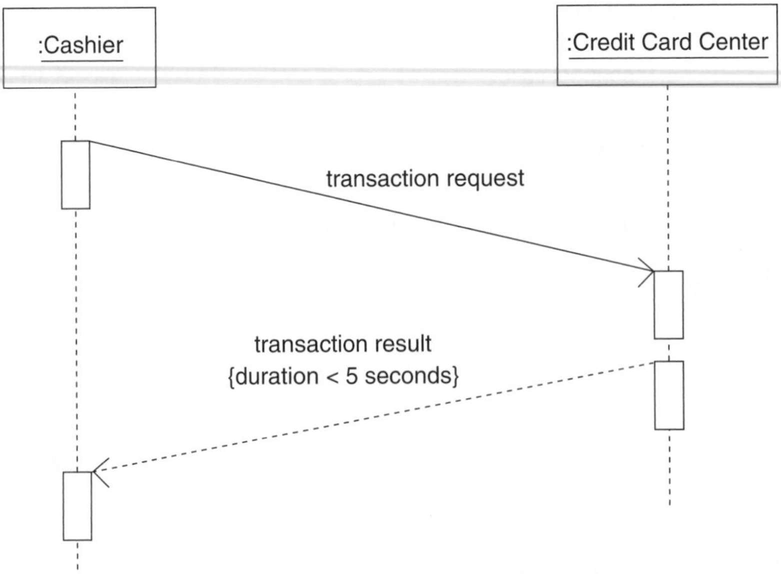

:Cashier
:Credit Card Center
transaction request
transaction result
{duration < 5 seconds}

Figure 4.11. Duration message in collaboration diagram

2: transaction result {duration < 5 seconds}
:Cashier
:Credit Card Center
1: transaction request

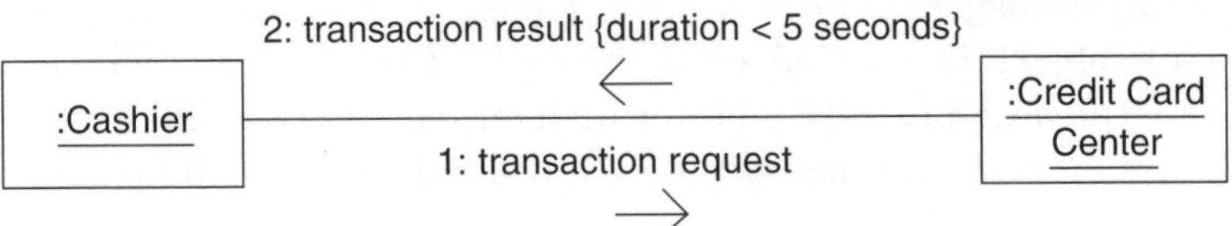

Examples of Scenario Modeling

Example 1: An Automatic Teller Machine (ATM)

An ATM allows users to perform different tasks with their bank accounts. Each task may involve a list of operations. Consider the following typical task of withdrawing cash from an ATM. Figures 4.12 and 4.13 respectively show the collaboration diagram and the sequence diagram for this (withdraw cash) scenario.

The ATM prompts the user to insert a card

The user inserts an ATM card

The ATM prompts the user to input the PIN number

The user enters the PIN number

The ATM asks the bank consortium to verify the ATM card number and PIN number

The bank consortium verifies the ATM card number and PIN number with the bank

The bank notifies the bank consortium that the PIN is correct

The bank consortium notifies the ATM the PIN is correct

The ATM prompts the user to select a service

The user selects the withdraw cash service

The ATM prompts the user to enter the amount to withdraw

The user enters the amount to withdraw

The ATM asks the bank consortium to process the request. The bank consortium forwards the request to the bank

The bank confirms the successful execution of the request to the bank consortium which in turn notifies the ATM that the request has been approved

The ATM displays the successful transaction on screen, ejects card and then dispenses cash as requested

The ATM shows the main menu to the user for selecting the next service

Figure 4.12. Sequence diagram for withdrawal of cash scenario of the ATM system

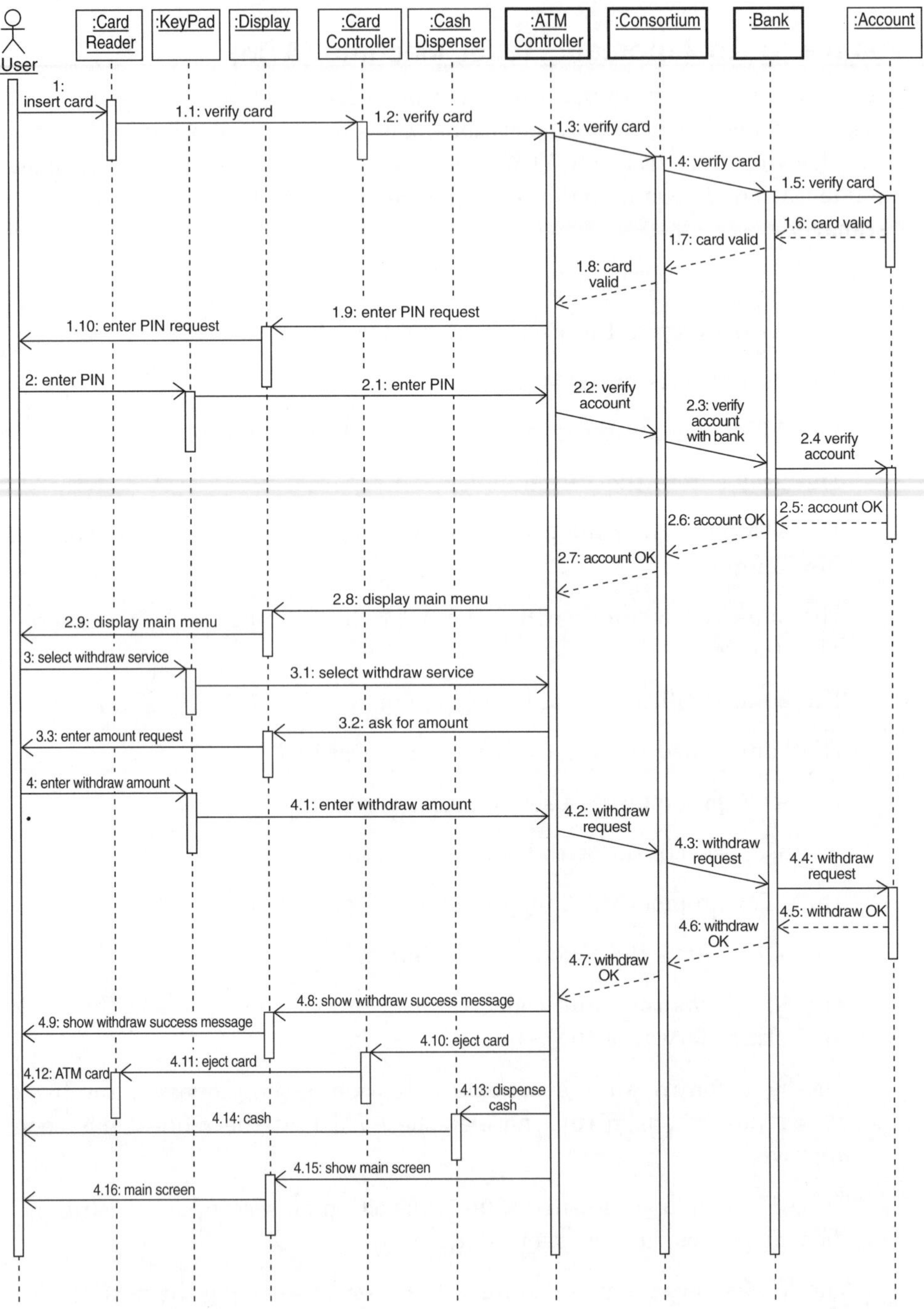

Figure 4.13. Collaboration diagram for withdrawal of cash scenario of the ATM system

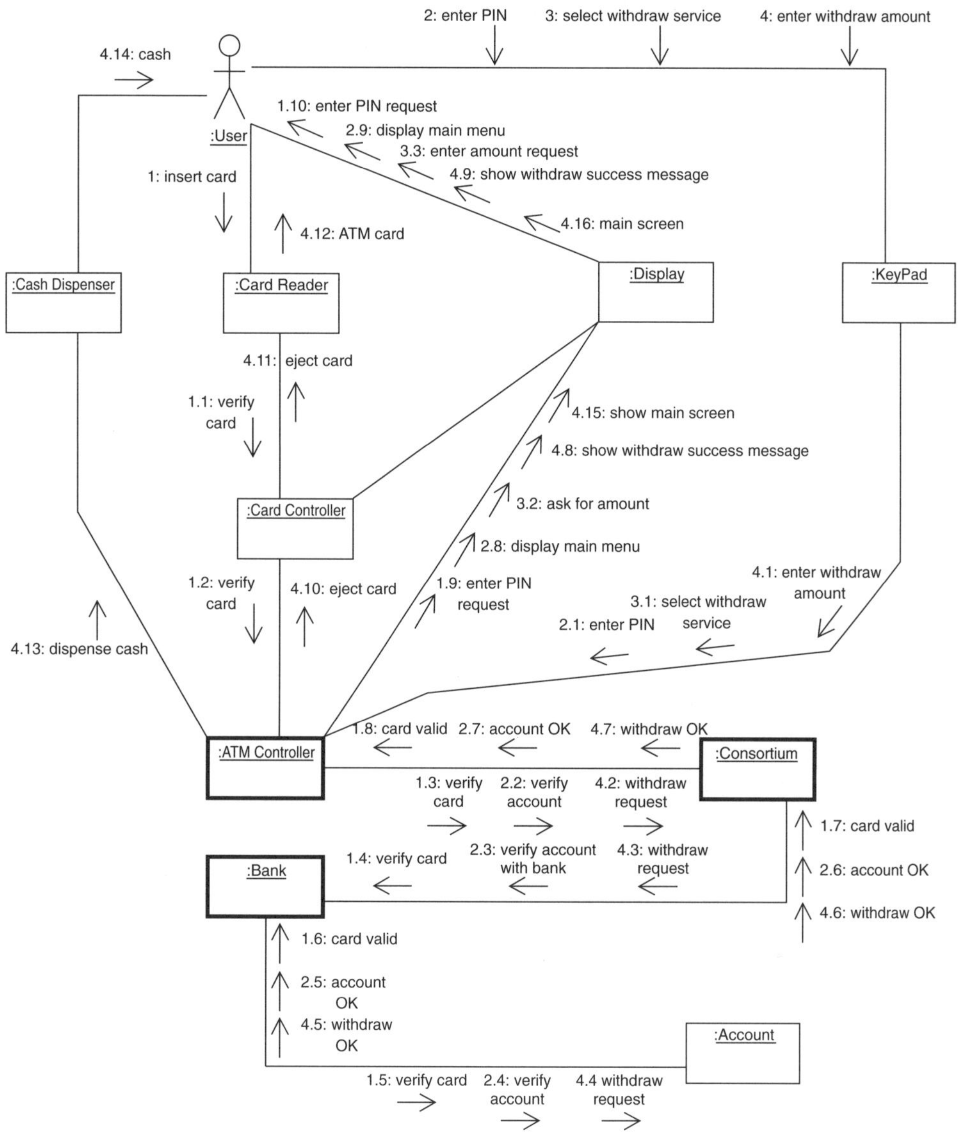

Example 2: A Soft Drink Vending Machine

A soft drink vending machine accepts coins for a variety of products. When the amount of money deposited into the machine is equal to or greater than the price of any of its available products, the respective product selection buttons will be enabled for the user to make a selection. After the user has made a valid selection, the machine will dispense the soft drink, together with the change (if applicable). Figures 4.14 and 4.15 respectively show the sequence diagram and collaboration diagram for the vending machine.

Figure 4.14. Sequence diagram for vending machine

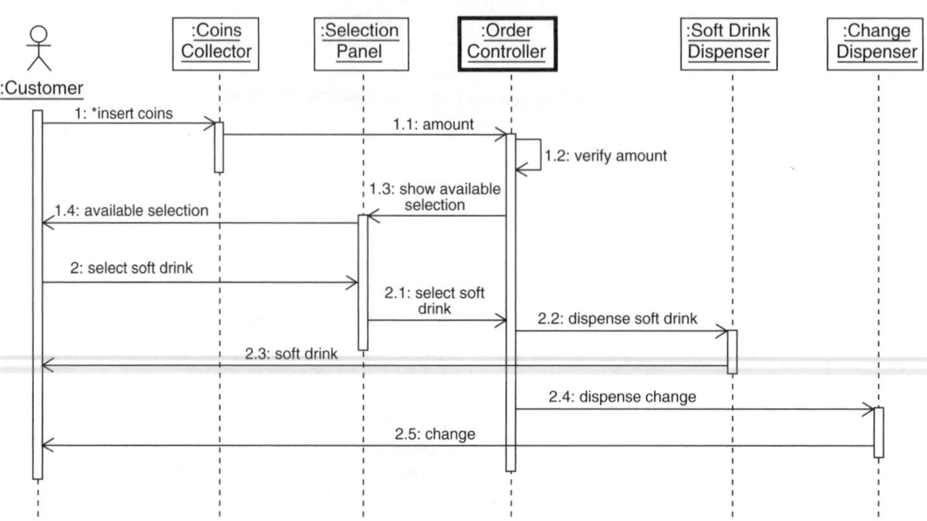

Figure 4.15. Collaboration diagram for vending machine

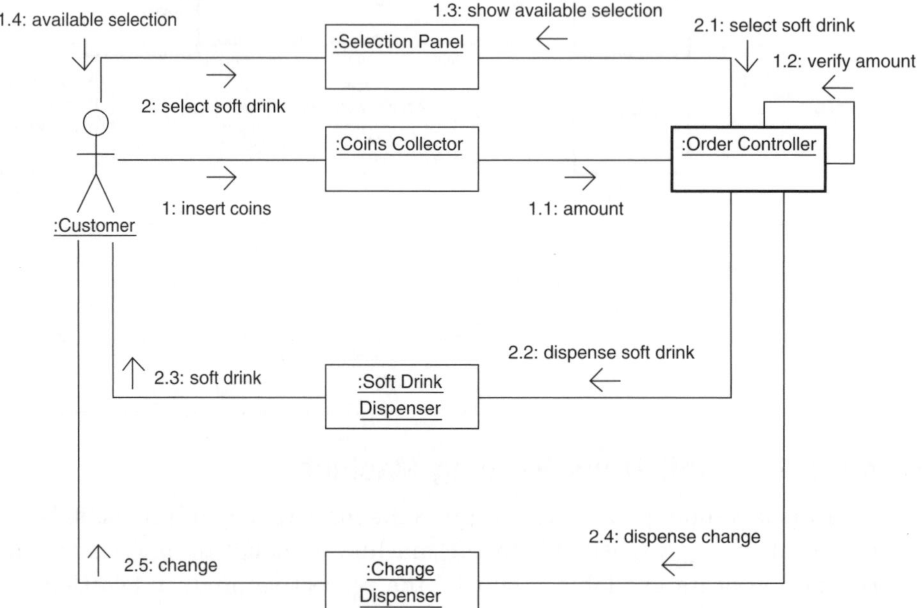

Dynamic Modeling Techniques Using Statechart Diagrams

The behavior of an entity is not only a direct consequence of its inputs, but it also depends on its preceding state. The history of an entity can best be modeled by a finite statechart diagram traditionally named *automata*. *Statechart* diagrams (or sometimes referred to as *state diagrams*) show the different states of an entity. Statechart diagrams can also show how an entity responds to various events by changing from one state to another.

What Is a State?

Rumbaugh et al. (1991) define that *"[a] state is an abstraction of the attribute values and links of an object. Sets of values are grouped together into a state according to properties that affect the gross behavior of the object."* For example, you have $100,000 in a bank account. The behavior of the withdraw function would be: balance := balance − withdrawAmount, provided that the balance after the withdrawal is not less than $0. This is true regardless of how many times you have withdrawn money from the bank. In such situations, the withdrawals do not affect the abstraction of the attribute values, and hence, the gross behavior of the object remains unchanged.

However, if the account balance becomes negative after a withdrawal, the behavior of the withdraw function would be quite different. This is because the state of the bank account is changed from positive to negative; in technical jargon, a transition from the positive state to the negative state is fired. The abstraction of the attribute value is a property of the system, rather than a globally applicable rule. For example, if the bank changes the business rule to allow the bank balance to be overdrawn by $2,000, the state of the bank account will be redefined with the condition that the balance after withdrawal must not be less than $2,000 in deficit.

There are several characteristics of states:

- A state occupies an interval of time
- A state is often associated with an abstraction of attribute values of an entity satisfying some condition(s)
- An entity changes its state not only as a direct consequence of the current input, but as a result of some past history of its inputs

In the UML notation, a state is represented by a rectangle with rounded corners. A state may have a name which is usually positioned above the rectangle. Optionally, a state may be subdivided into the name compartment and the internal transitions compartment (see Figure 4.16). The name compartment holds the state's name. The internal transitions compartment holds internal actions or activities that are performed while the entity is in that state. The actions or activities are in the format ***action label/action or activity***. Table 4.4 defines the commonly used actions and activities.

Figure 4.16. Representations of state

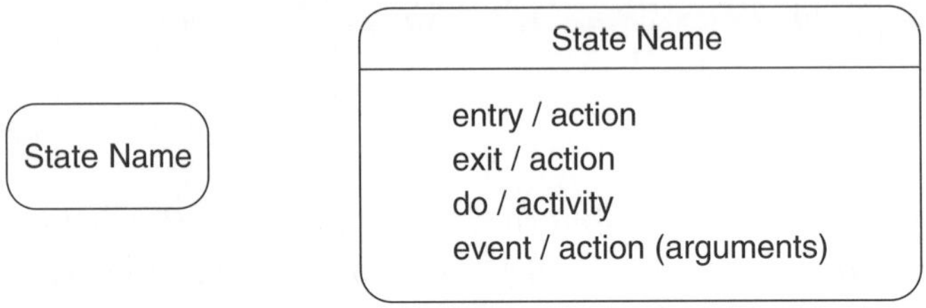

Table 4.4. Actions and activities

Action or activity	Description
entry / action 1; ...; action *n*	Upon entry into the state, the specified actions are performed
exit / action 1; ...; action *n*	Upon exit from the state, the specified actions are performed
do / activity	The specified activity is performed continuously while in this state
event-name(parameters) [guard-condition] / action 1; ...; action *n*	An internal transition is fired when the specified event occurs and the specified guard condition is true. The specified actions are performed when the transition is fired.

Transitions

A *transition* from one state to another takes place instantaneously in response to some external events or internal stimuli. A transition is represented by an arrowed line from the source state and the target state, usually with guard conditions and rules governing how and when the transition should take place. The label on the arrowed line states an event name, a guard condition and a list of actions. A guard condition is a Boolean expression, and a transition is fired when the following conditions are satisfied:

- The entity is in the state of the source state
- An event specified in the label occurs
- The guard condition specified in the label is evaluated to be true

When a transition is fired, the actions associated with it are executed.

Composite States and Nested States

Sometimes, an entity needs to be modeled at different levels of abstraction (details) so that an entity with complex dynamic behaviors can be modeled more appropriately. For example, it is often difficult to model and analyze an object with many states using a single statechart diagram. Alternatively, we may draw a high-level statechart diagram consisting of composite states and other diagrams to further elaborate the internal states inside individual composite states. For each composite state, its nested *states* (internal states or substates) and their transitions between them can be drawn. In Figure 4.17, a *composite state* (superstate) may hold a statechart diagram.

Figure 4.17. Nested statechart diagram

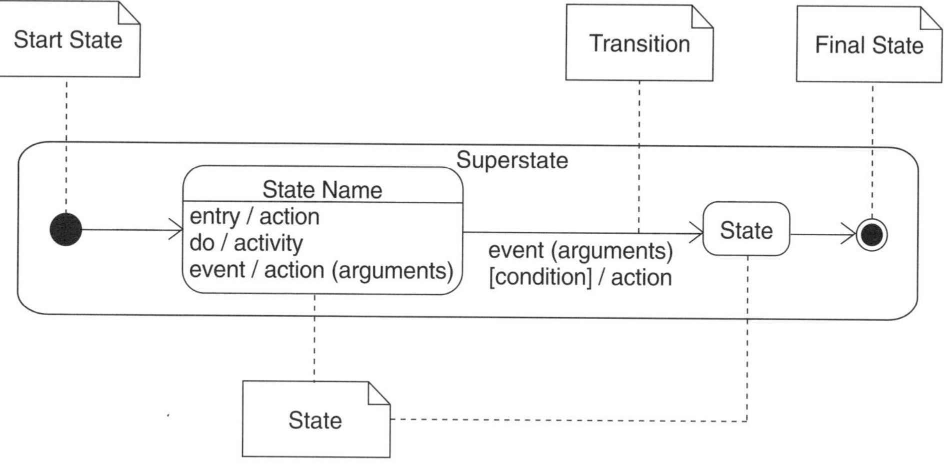

Sometimes, it is necessary to model several independent abstractions of attribute values. For example, an undergraduate student is required to complete both the final-year project and the core subjects before he can graduate. This can be represented by concurrent states as shown in Figure 4.18.

Figure 4.18. Concurrent states

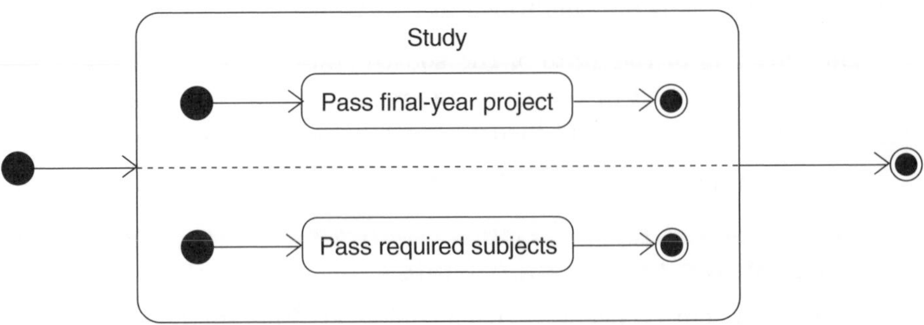

Dynamic Modeling Techniques Using Activity Diagrams

The statechart diagram is used to model entity's states and their transitions in response to events, but it is not quite suitable for modeling a procedure or an algorithm. This is because we need to translate the actions of the procedures into transitions and states. For example, it would be rather inconvenient to model the flow of events of the withdraw money use case in the ATM example using a statechart diagram.

To overcome this limitation, the activity diagram is introduced in UML. The activity diagram is specifically designed for modeling performance of actions of an activity or procedure. It is a variation of a state machine where a state corresponds to the performance of actions or sub-activities. The transitions are triggered by the completion of actions or sub-activities.

Action and Sub-activity States

The action state is used to model a single step in the execution of a procedure or a workflow process, and cannot be further decomposed. In contrast, the sub-activity state can be further decomposed as it corresponds to another activity diagram. Figure 4.19 gives examples of action and sub-activity states.

Figure 4.19. Examples of action and sub-activity states

Transition

A transition is represented by an arrow connecting two states (see Figure 4.20). A transition takes place when the actions or activities of the source state are completed. Optionally, a transition can be labeled with a guard condition for the transition to take place.

Figure 4.20. Transitions between states

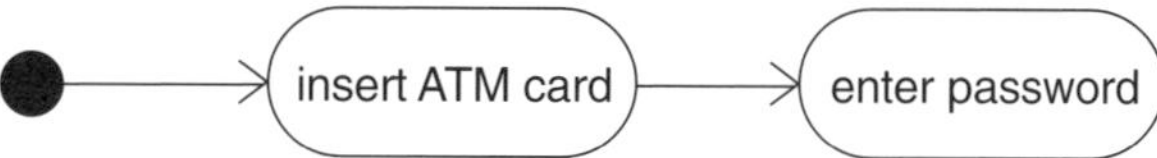

Branching

Branching is used to model conditional or optional flows in a procedure or a workflow. For example, the ATM will prompt the user to re-enter the password if an incorrect one has been entered (see Figure 4.21). A branch is represented by a diamond with an incoming transition and multiple outgoing transitions labeled with guard conditions. The guard conditions must be mutually exclusive to guarantee that there are no ambiguities.

Figure 4.21. Branching example

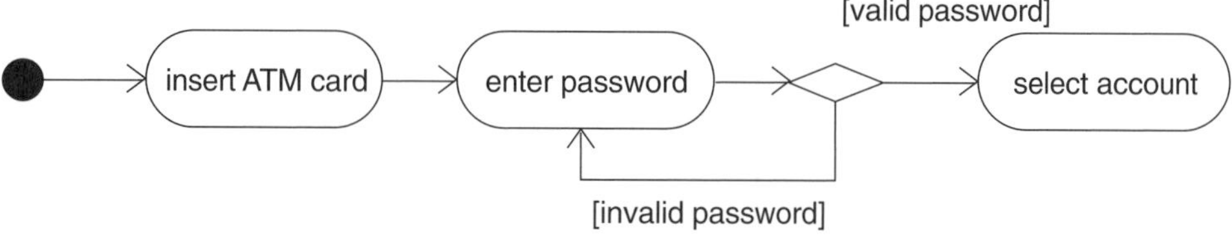

Forks and Joins

Forks and joins are used to model concurrent flows. A fork has one incoming and multiple outgoing transitions. In contrast, a join has multiple incoming and one outgoing transition (see Figure 4.22).

Figure 4.22. Example of fork and join

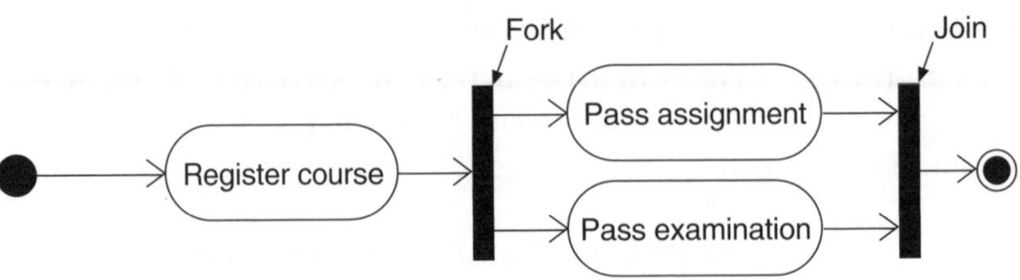

Swimlanes

A swimlane is a named partition of an activity diagram. In modeling business activities, it would be useful to group states which are performed by the same department or actor in a swimlane. Hence, each swimlane represents a set of responsibilities of an entity.

Figure 4.23 shows the procedure associated with placing and processing an order in a mail order company using swimlanes.

Figure 4.23. Activity diagram with swimlanes

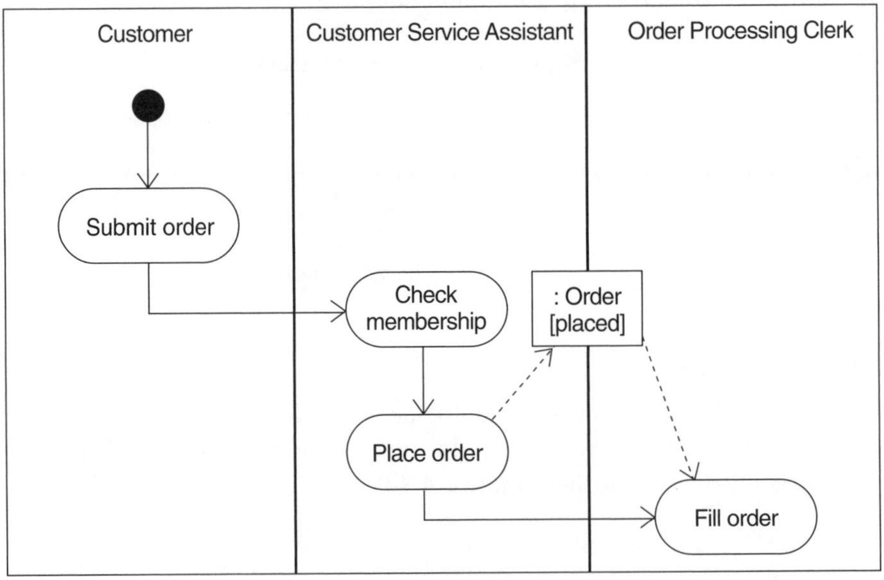

Object Flows

It is quite common that an action or sub-activity state passes some information to another state. Information-passing between states is expressed as object flows. For example, the *Place order* state in Figure 4.23 passes the *Order*, which has just been created next to the action state *Fill order*. Note that the state of the order is also indicated by the state inside the square brackets.

Dynamic Analysis Techniques

In the previous sections, the UML notations were introduced for dynamic modeling. We shall discuss how dynamic modeling and analysis can be performed using UML, starting with the use case model.

Techniques for Elaborating Use Cases

System requirements are obtained by performing use case modeling and analysis through interviewing users, reviewing the existing system and documentations, etc. Users can only express what they expect of the system. They help to provide a better understanding of what their requirements are from an external perspective, but they cannot provide the internal details of the system.

The requirements of the system are recorded in a use case model. The interactions between the users and the system are recorded in the flow of events of the use case description. The user can help confirm whether the use case descriptions match the requirements of the system. However, the process in transforming "*what the system does*" (requirements) to "*how the system is implemented*" (implementation) is not quite straightforward.

A use case consists of a main execution path (main scenario) and typically several alternative execution paths (alternative scenarios). The implementation of a scenario involves the collaboration of a set of objects. Therefore, we need to know what objects are involved in a scenario. Since the scenarios of a use case describe the external behaviors of the system, it is relatively easy to identify boundary objects that directly interact with the actor(s). However, it would be more difficult to know which internal objects are required to perform the actual computation and data manipulation. For example, we can easily determine that a form and a button are required for the user to input his/her personal particulars and to submit the data to a management information system (MIS), but it is more difficult to identify other less apparent internal objects required to implement the scenario. Therefore, it may not be a good idea to develop a fully elaborated sequence diagram directly from a use case scenario in a single step. Instead, we should first develop a high-level sequence diagram that matches a scenario as closely as possible. Then refine the sequence diagram by going through the following three steps iteratively and incrementally.

Step 1: Focus on Modeling External System Behaviors

As the flow of events in the use case description only records the external behaviors of the system and identifies the user inputs and system responses from the flow of events of a scenario, it is very straightforward to map the scenario to a system-level sequence diagram. In fact, this mapping process can be automated by a UML computer-aided software engineering (CASE) tool.

Step 2: Focus on Communication among the Subsystems

Modeling and analyzing complex systems often involves many objects, even for the realization of a single use case. To develop a detailed sequence diagram based on the system-level sequence diagram with sufficient information for a single, complete implementation generally requires a lot of effort. In order to manage the complexity associated with large and complex systems, it is advantageous to package objects into several subsystems. For example, an ATM system may be organized as a number of subsystems like the ATM, the bank consortium and the bank. Such an organization also reflects how the real world hardware and software systems are configured, since the ATM is connected to the bank consortium's system which is in turn connected to the systems of the individual banks.

The environment in which the system operates may impose certain constraints on the architecture of the system. For example, the hardware configuration of the ATM system is designed to connect the systems of the individual banks, the ATMs and the bank consortium's system. This hardware architecture suggests three subsystems: the ATM subsystem, bank subsystem and bank consortium's subsystem. Hence, the system architecture both in terms of software and hardware should be considered at an earlier stage to minimize unnecessary rework.

Being architectural centric is one of the four fundamental design principles in object-oriented modeling and analysis (the other three are: use case-driven, iterative and incremental). By architectural centric, we mean that the baseline architecture of the system should be developed at an early stage. The structure of the subsystem forms the important part of the architecture. Therefore, developing a subsystem-level sequence diagram can realize this important design principle. Figure 4.24 depicts the process of developing subsystem-level sequence diagrams and lower-level sequence diagrams for individual subsystems.

Figure 4.24. Decomposing a complex system using a subsystem approach

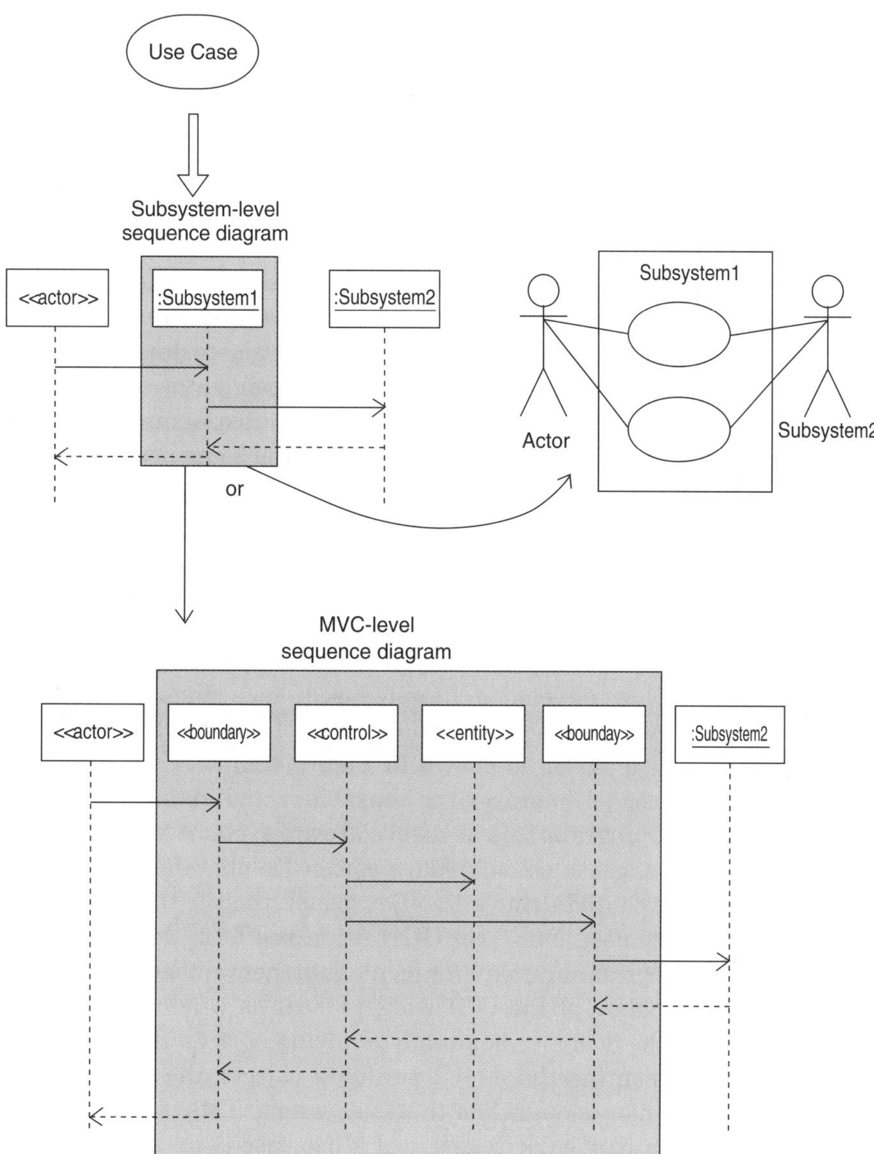

To identify subsystems effectively, consider both the logical and physical structures of the system. For example, it is obvious that the ATM system has considerable physical structure issues to be taken into account. The ATM system can be decomposed into near-independent subsystems as the previous example shows, such as the ATM, the bank consortium and the individual bank. Each of these subsystems forms a physically cohesive software structure. However, these subsystems collectively provide a complete set of behaviors of the entire system. The subsystem-level sequence diagram shows the high-level interactions among the subsystems and hides the low-level details of interactions among the internal objects inside the subsystems. Thus, if we are focusing on this level of detail of the interactions between actors and subsystems, it is possible to quickly identify the responsibilities of the subsystems rather than the detailed logic that resides in each individual object.

After having determined the individual subsystems and their responsibilities, further analyze the behavior of the individual subsystems by applying use case modeling and scenario analysis techniques recursively. In doing so, each subsystem is treated as an independent system and all other subsystems or actor(s) as external entities of the subsystem. We can develop a use case model for each subsystem and system-level sequence diagrams for the scenarios of each use case of the use case model.

Step 3: Develop Reusable Model/View/Control (MVC) Software Framework

By now, the system-level and the subsystem-level sequence diagram would have been developed. Now develop a detailed sequence diagram in three tiers involving three types of objects: boundary, control and entity objects. A typical three-tier sequence diagram is shown in Figure 4.25.

The three-tier model improves the reusability and maintainability of a use case. Traditionally, programmers develop software systems using popular visual programming languages such as Visual Basic or Delphi. Many of these systems are typically implemented using a two-tier model, that is, the programmer first designs the graphic user interface (GUI) using the form designer provided by the interactive programming environment and then embeds the control logic into the event handlers of the GUI widgets such as windows, forms, buttons, etc. Even though the designer is already applying *object-oriented programming* concepts in implementing these GUI and data objects, the system is still very difficult to maintain or debug when things go wrong. This is because the control logic belonging to a particular scenario of a use case is invariably scattered all over the event handlers of the GUI widgets. To locate a bug or modify the

Figure 4.25. Three-tier sequence diagram

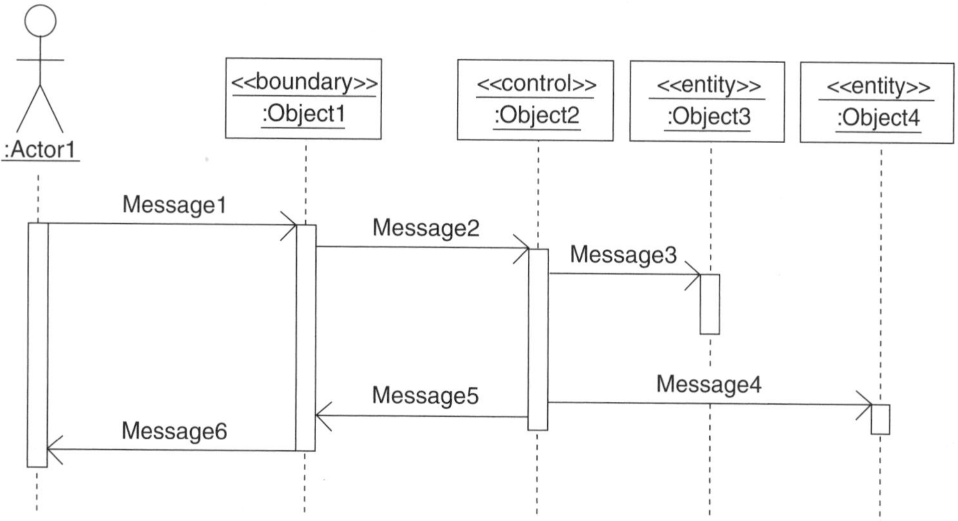

implementation of a use case, it is often necessary to go over all the code inside the event handlers of the GUI widgets. The situation sometimes can be even more complicated when several use cases share a set of GUI objects. The event handlers of these shared GUI objects will contain the control logic of these use cases. If the size of the system is large, much effort will have to be expanded to maintain such a system.

Representing Use Case Scenarios Using Path Diagrams

In this section, the path diagram is introduced as a visual representation of a use case scenario, which is usually represented by a textual description. The path diagram can help us better understand the differences between several scenarios of the same use case. Consider the use case diagram shown in Figure 4.26. Since the base use case only has one extend use case, the base use case has two scenarios: the main scenario and the alternative scenario as shown in Figure 4.27.

For the use case in Figure 4.27, there is a need to use two separate sequence diagrams to represent the two scenarios. Always include the common behaviors of the <<include>> use case in the flow of events of the base use case, as these common behaviors are essential for the base use case to achieve the task. The main scenario includes only the logic of the base use case while the

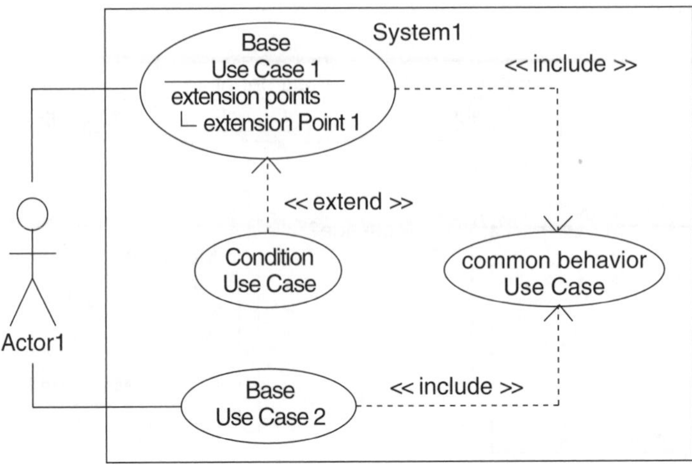

Figure 4.26. A simple use case model

Figure 4.27. Main scenario and alternative scenario of the base use case

Main Scenario of Base Use Case 1
......

Flow of events
1. Event 1 ......
2. Event 2 ......
3. ......
4. ......
5. perform Common_Behavior_Use_Case
6. .....
7. .....
8. ......
9. ....
10. ......

Alternative Scenario of Base Use Case 1
......

Flow of events
1. Event 1 ......
2. Event 2 ......
3. ....
4. ......
5. perform Common_Behavior_Use_Case
6. .....
7. .....
8. perform Condition_Use_Case
9. ......
10. ....
11. ......

alternative scenarios include both the behaviors of the main use case and the <<extend>> use case. In representing the scenarios, use a path diagram. A path without branching is represented by a straight line. Hence, the main scenario is represented as such (see Figure 4.28). A conditional branching to an <<extend>> use case is represented by a loop in the path for the alternative scenario of the base use case as shown in Figure 4.29. Note that the return point of the <<extend>> use case is where the branching takes place. Therefore, it is incorrect to interpret the <<extend>> use case as if it is a conditional flow in a flowchart (see Figure 4.29). For the <<include>> use case, the branching is unconditional and hence is still modeled by a straight line.

In summary, to develop a path diagram for a base use case, represent the main scenario by a straight line and an <<extend>> use case by a loop. Then attach the loops to the main path (see Figure 4.30). Tracing the path of the base use case, develop the paths for different diagrams as illustrated in the lower part of Figure 4.30. Since there are three extended use cases, there are three alternative scenarios and one main scenario. Each path corresponds to the branching to one of the extending use cases.

Figure 4.28. Representation of main scenario in path diagram

Figure 4.29. Execution path of an <<extend>> use case

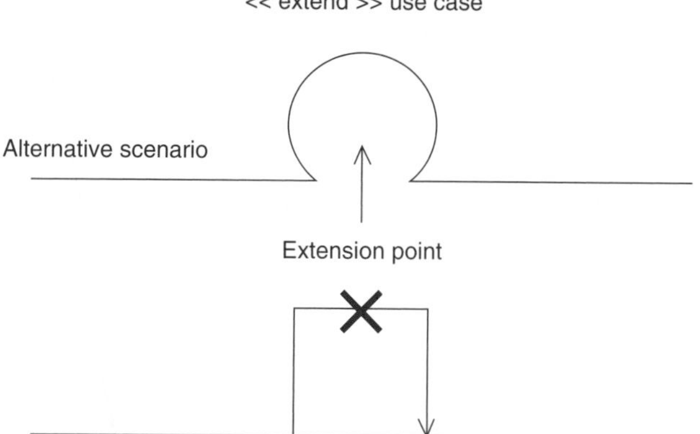

Figure 4.30. Path diagrams for elaborating a use case

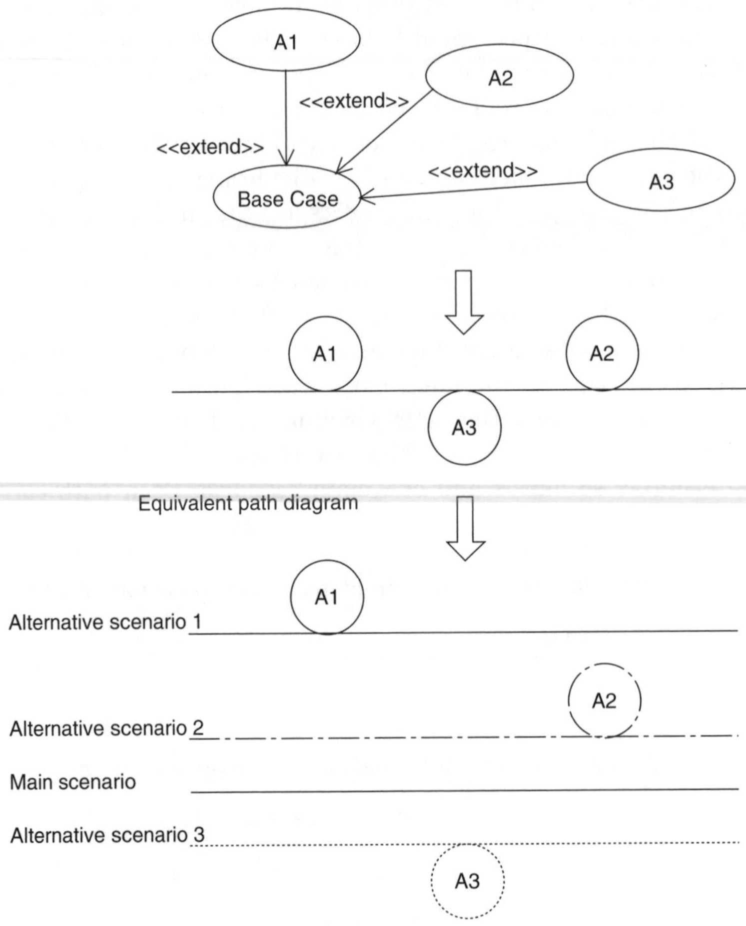

Dynamic Modeling and Analysis Process

Overview

Dynamic modeling and analysis are concerned with understanding the behavior of the system in actual scenarios when using the system. Dynamic modeling begins with expressing the use case scenarios (use case instances) and elaborating using sequence diagrams. The sequence diagrams are then refined and further developed iteratively and incrementally until they contain enough details for implementation. During the process, it is also possible to develop statechart diagrams for objects that have complex internal state transitions.

Steps in Developing Dynamic Models

The following steps are recommended for developing dynamic models of a system (see Figure 4.31):

1. Develop use case scenarios
2. Develop system-level sequence diagrams
3. Develop subsystem-level sequence diagrams (optional for simple systems)
4. Develop subsystem-level statechart diagrams (optional for simple systems)
5. Develop three-tier sequence diagrams
6. Develop three-tier collaboration diagrams (optional)
7. Develop a statechart diagram for each of these active (control) objects

Figure 4.31. Dynamic modeling and analysis process

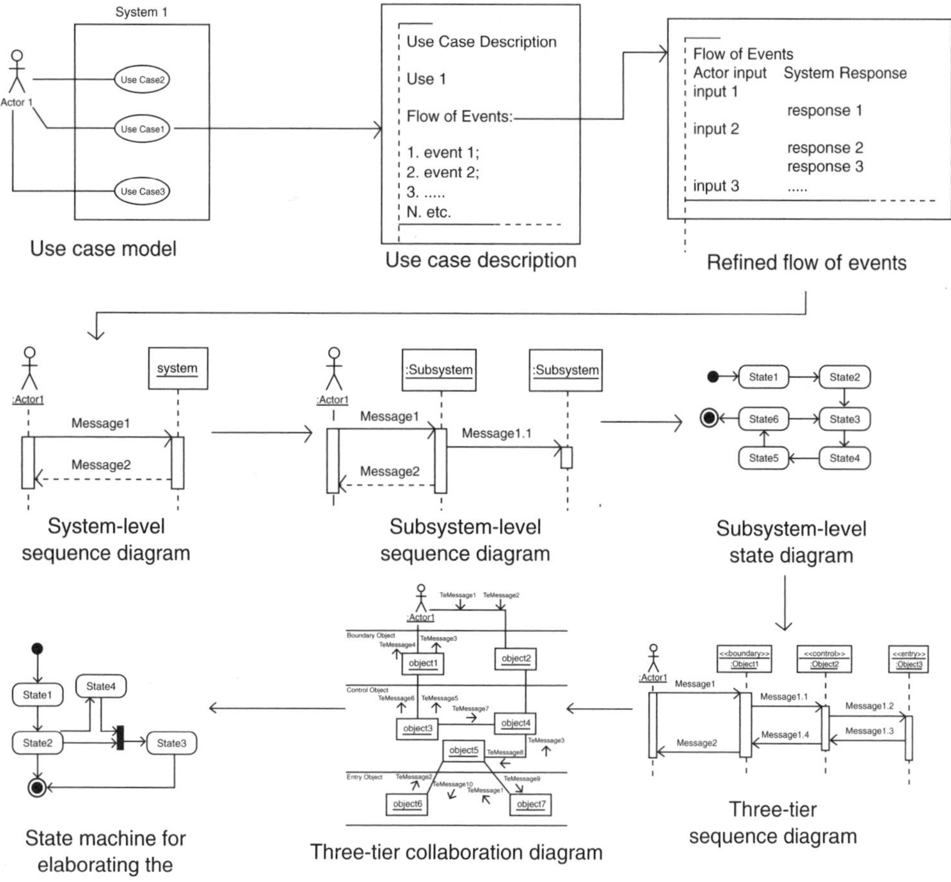

Step 1: Develop Use Case Scenarios

For each execution path of a use case, write a textual description for the flow of events of the scenario. Try using path diagrams to identify the representative scenarios of a use case. For example, the main scenario of the *Withdraw Money* use case of the ATM example is shown in Figure 4.32.

Figure 4.32. Flow of events for normal scenario of Withdraw Money use case

Flow of events

1. User inserts card
2. System prompts user to enter PIN
3. User enters PIN
4. System prompts user to select services
5. User selects service — withdraw money
6. System prompts user to enter withdrawal amount
7. User enters withdrawal amount
8. System displays *withdrawal successful* message, ejects card and dispenses money
9. User collects card and money

Step 2: Develop System-level Sequence Diagrams

When documenting the use case of a use case model, first elaborate it by filling all the sections in the use case template, including the use case name, the use case description and the flow of events. In the flow of events section, briefly describe the steps for the actor to interact with the use case, which include only its externally observable behaviors. For example, describe the flow of events like "insert the ATM card" or "input the PIN number," but do not include "verify ATM card type" or "verify password" as part of the flow of events as they cannot be observed by an actor outside the system. Some people suggest that a detailed sequence diagram can be developed simply from the flow of events. But this is not easily achievable, especially for large systems, as the designer needs to deal with too many different issues simultaneously. In this section, it will be shown how a use case can be elaborated using an iterative and incremental approach.

Separating Actor Inputs and System Responses

Based on the actor inputs and system responses of the scenario in Figure 4.32, we can separate them into two columns, clearly showing the initiators of these events, as illustrated in Figure 4.33.

Figure 4.33. Actor inputs and system responses

Flow of events	
Actor input	**System response**
User inserts card	
	System prompts user to enter PIN
User enters PIN	
	System prompts user to select services
User selects "withdraw money" service	
	System prompts user to enter the amount
User enters the withdrawal amount	
	System displays *withdrawal successful* message, ejects card and dispenses money
User collects the card and money	

Creating System-level Sequence Diagrams

The information in Figure 4.32 can readily be mapped onto a system-level sequence diagram as shown in Figure 4.34.

Figure 4.34. System-level sequence diagram

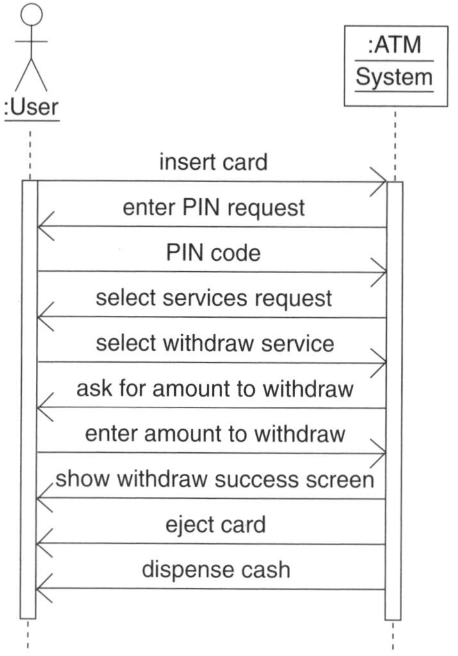

Step 3: Develop Subsystem-level Sequence Diagrams (Optional)

Identifying Subsystems

Having developed the system-level sequence diagram for a use case, create a clear picture of the detailed interactions between the actor(s) and the system. Up to this point, everything described in the diagram should be observable by the actor(s) and should not yet include any information on how the problem is to be solved. For complex systems, it may be expedient to develop subsystem-level sequence diagrams. Otherwise, it may be possible to work on the three-tier level sequence diagrams straightaway. However, those new to the object-oriented technology area should develop the models step-by-step, iteratively and incrementally. There are good automated tools that can significantly speed up this process.

The advantage of developing a subsystem-level sequence diagram is that the overall architectural issues at this development stage can be dealt with by omitting details such as identifying GUI widgets or entity objects. For the ATM system example, the problem becomes very simple if the whole system is deployed in a single piece of computer hardware. However, if deployment issues are to be accounted for, the system becomes considerably more complicated.

As ATMs are installed in many locations all over the world, issues such as networking, security and communications protocols between subsystems, etc., will have to be addressed. There is a need to consider that ATM card services may be managed by a bank consortium of which your bank is a member. Thus, the deployment of the ATM system will be clustered in three major subsystems: (1) an ATM installed in a large network of ATM machines, (2) a bank that performs the actual transactions on your account and (3) the bank consortium then routes your account details to your bank for processing the transaction.

Creating Subsystem-level Sequence Diagrams

Further elaborate the system-level sequence diagram by providing internal messages among the subsystems. For each pair of actor inputs and system responses, decide which message(s) should be sent between the subsystems in order to achieve the required functionality, by asking the following questions:

- Which subsystem is responsible for providing the interface to the actor?
- What reply is expected from the subsystem that receives a message?
- Can the subsystem handle the message with its own information? or
- Does the subsystem require help from other subsystems?

In the ATM system example, the first pair of messages are "user inserts card" and "the system prompts user to enter PIN." We know that the ATM provides an interface from which the user selects the required service. Therefore, the *insert card* message is sent from the user to the ATM. Since the ATM does not have the required information to validate the card, it sends out a message to the bank that issued the card through the bank consortium. The bank sends a reply to the ATM through the bank consortium confirming that the card is valid. Similarly, we can determine the messages between the subsystems for other pairs of actor inputs and system responses. The complete subsystem-level sequence diagram is shown in Figure 4.35.

Figure 4.35. Subsystem-level sequence diagram

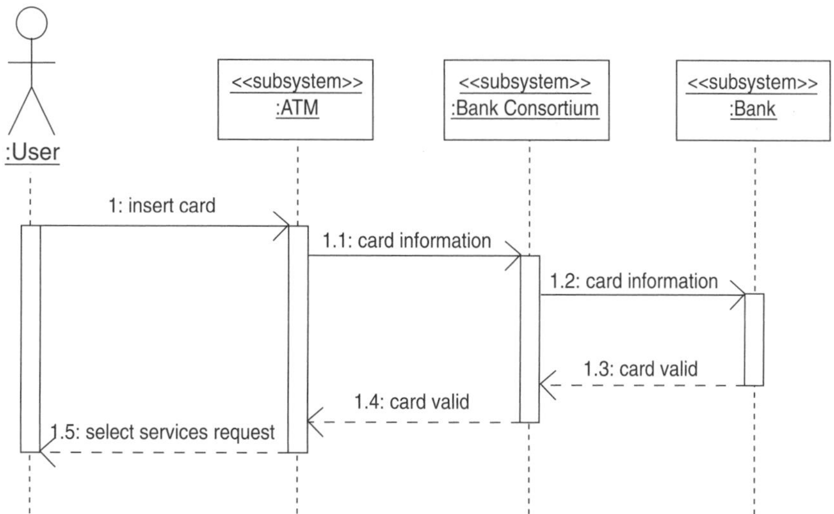

Step 4: Develop Subsystem-level Statechart Diagram

With the subsystem-level sequence diagram created in Step 2, develop the subsystem-level statechart diagram for the scenario. Let us use the ATM as an example again. When the ATM is idle, it shows the main screen, for example, the welcome screen. If the user inserts a valid ATM card, it will display a "wait for input PIN" screen. Figure 4.36 shows the scenario-based statechart diagram of the ATM system.

Figure 4.36. Scenario-based statechart diagram for ATM

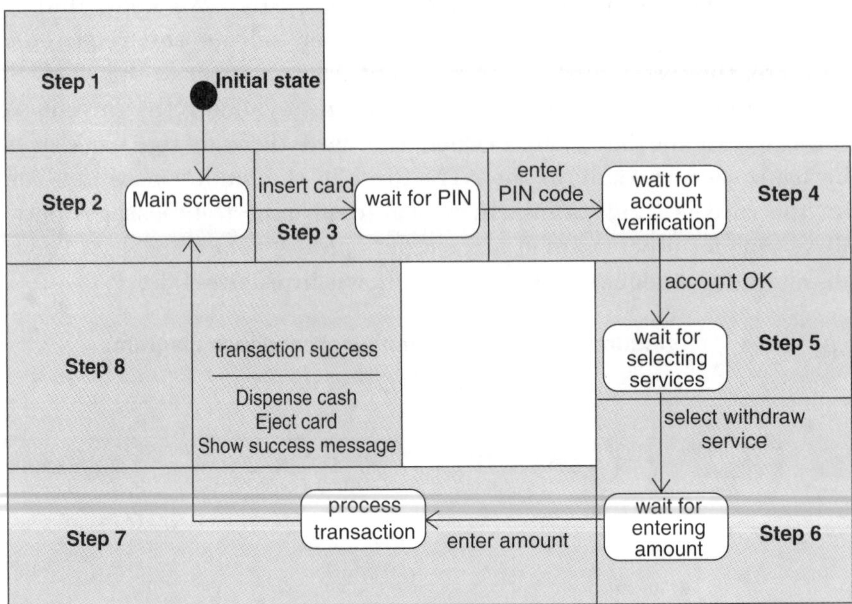

Step 5: Develop Three-tier Sequence Diagrams

Identifying Boundary, Control and Entity Objects

Having developed the subsystem-level sequence diagram, identify the boundary, control and entity objects by analyzing the messages sent between them. For example, the message *insert card* sent from the user to the ATM implies that there should be *something* to hold the card. So there must be a card reader object in the ATM, and it must be a boundary object because it communicates with the user directly.

Let us take this example further. After the user inserts the ATM card, how will the system know that the card is a valid ATM card and not just a dummy plastic card? It is reasonable to expect that the system will verify whether the card is valid or not. So create a *Card Controller* object inside the ATM which has the function of verifying the ATM card. The Card Controller must therefore be a control object, as it processes requests by forwarding them to the relevant object. The verification of an ATM card is actually done by the card-issuing bank, and not the Card Controller itself. The Card Controller, therefore, should not carry much intelligence. Furthermore, this object can be reused in other types of card-operated systems.

Furthermore, from the *withdrawal request* message between the bank consortium and the bank, we know that there should be something for the bank's subsystem to store the user account information and perform the requested transaction. An *Account* object should therefore be created. This should be an entity object because it is domain-specific as it implements the business rule of the bank. This object actually carries out the required task and is not an agent or a broker.

Once the three types of objects are identified, develop the *three-tier sequence diagram*. The three-tier sequence diagram should record the detail interactions between different types of objects. For example, in Figure 4.37, the *insert card* message is sent to the card reader which in turn sends the *verify card* message to the Card Controller, and so on.

Figure 4.37. Fragments of three-tier sequence diagram

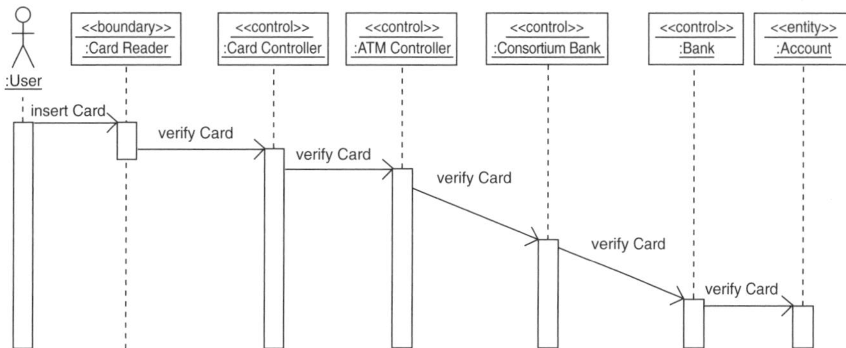

Walking through and Refining Three-tier Sequence Diagrams

By walking through and refining the three-tier diagrams for different scenarios, we may discover more objects and functions to make the system more complete.

Step 6: Develop Three-tier Collaboration Diagram

Having developed the three-tier sequence diagram, proceed to creating a three-tier collaboration diagram. The three-tier collaboration diagram shows the linkages between different objects that are useful in the implementation stage for identifying packages and defining the interfaces between objects. The three types of objects can be grouped into different packages. Objects of the same types are grouped and contained in the same package, e.g. a GUI package may be created to contain all the GUI objects. In some CASE tools, such as VP-UML, this step is automated, and the sequence diagram can be automatically converted into a collaboration diagram (see Figure 4.38).

Figure 4.38. Three-tier collaboration diagram

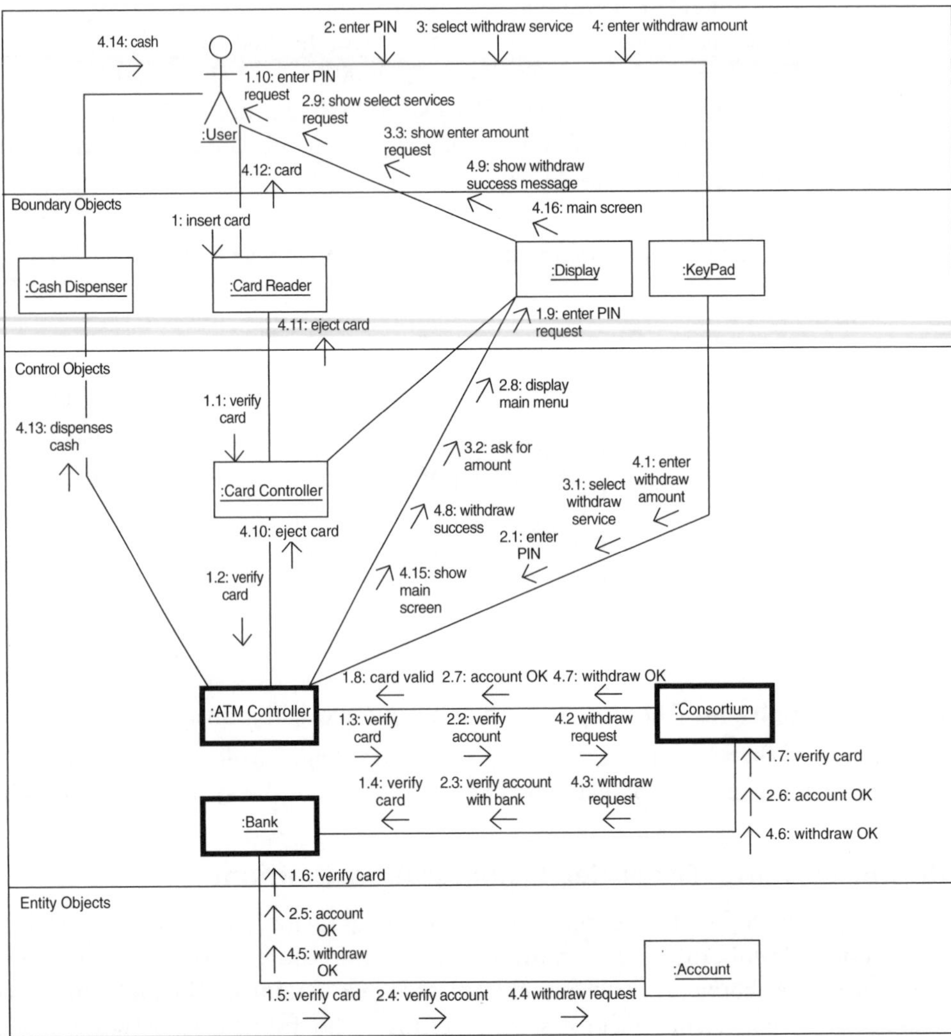

Step 7: Develop Statechart Diagrams for Control Objects

It is very important to identify the state change of control objects; it helps to implement the system more easily as the statechart diagram can be readily translated into programming code. With the complete set of three-tier sequence diagrams, we can develop the statechart diagram for each control object previously identified. Based on the messages between the boundary, entity and control objects, the internal states of the control objects and their state transitions can be identified. Figure 4.39 shows a statechart diagram for the Card Controller object of the ATM system.

Figure 4.39. Statechart diagram of card controller

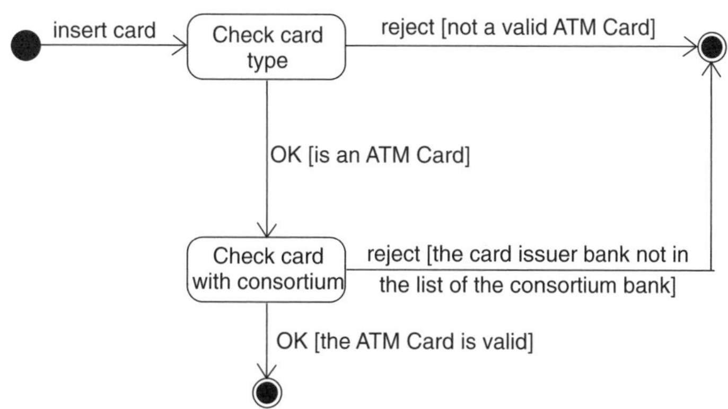

Tricks and Tips in Dynamic Modeling and Analysis

Creating Cohesive and Self-sufficient Subsystems

Subsystems may be considered as the next level of abstraction down from the entire system. Ideally, a subsystem should be a cohesive and independent part of the complex system so as to benefit from portability, reusability and ease of maintenance. A cohesive and independent subsystem is loosely coupled with other subsystems, and data coupling is the most loosely coupled communication method between entities. The following are some heuristics to achieve loose coupling between entities and strong cohesion within an individual entity:

- Use a well-defined data format to communicate between subsystems, for example, data stores such as XML, commonly used data files or configuration file.

- Use messaging server or subsystem communication protocols to communicate between subsystems such as Java Messaging Server (JMS) or SOAP.
- Use design patterns to reduce coupling and increase cohesion if tighter coupling between subsystems for efficiency is unavoidable.

Refining Class Diagrams Using MVC-level Scenario Analysis

By putting an instance of a use case through scenario analysis, we may discover more objects that are necessary to support the execution path to achieve the user goal. Contrast the object identified in the scenario with those in the domain class diagram to ensure proper use of terminology. For those newly identified objects in the sequence diagram, update missing components in the data dictionary and refine the class model accordingly.

Here is an example of how the results of the sequence diagram can be used to refine the domain class diagram. Consider the objN in the sequence diagram in Figure 4.40. There are two incoming messages (message A and message B) associated with objN. Hence, it is necessary to add two operations (operation A and operation B) to the class of objN, i.e. Class X.

Note: The high-level messages may be directly translated into a method (operation) name of the class. Later, these methods will be defined with function prototypes at the implementation stage. Figure 4.41 shows this in detail.

Understanding System Reusability for Different Types of Objects

To model the well-known MVC software framework, classify the objects into three different types called entity, boundary and control which respectively correspond to the model, view and control of the framework. Entity objects are concerned with the lower-level basic building blocks of the system. They are akin to an object library that comes with a development environment. They perform the most fundamental tasks and usually account for the highest percentage of the system. Well-designed entity objects should be highly reusable and not application-specific. Table 4.5 categorizes the reusability of different types of objects from the general to the application-specific. Obviously, the more reusable the objects are in the system, the more benefit will be derived from them in terms of reusability and maintainability. However, boundary objects (e.g. the GUI) are generally less so reusable, but most of the development tools provide a GUI builder or a screen painter which significantly reduces the amount of effort required to create them.

Figure 4.40. Refining class model with scenario analysis

Class diagram

Class name — *Association* — Class name — *Association* — Class name — *Association* — ClassX

Association

Class name

Class name

Class name

MVC level sequence diagram

<<actor>>
<<boundary>>
<<control>>
<<entity>> objN : ClassX
<<control>>
<<entity>>

message A

message B

Identify class and operations

<<entity>> objN : ClassX

message A

message B

ClassX

Attribute:

Operation:
operation A
operation B

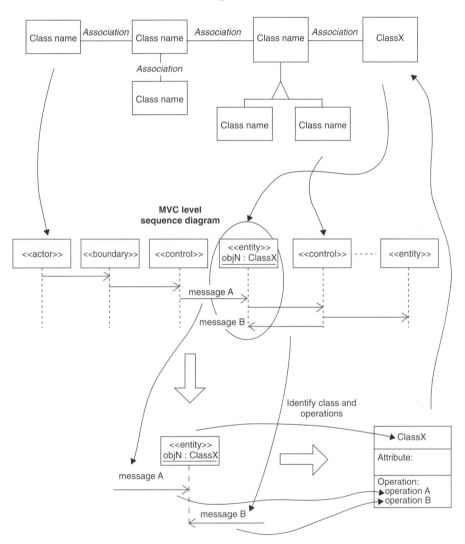

Figure 4.41. Message refinement in scenario analysis

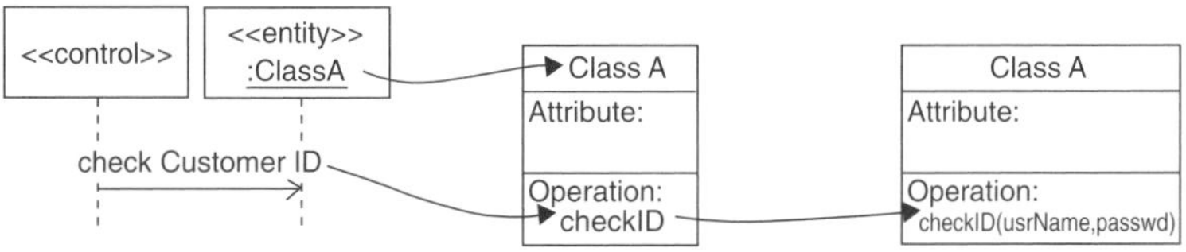

Table 4.5. Reusability of different types of objects

Type of object	Application scope	Reusability
Object library	General purpose	Any application
Entity class	Domain specific	Within the domain
Control class	Application specific	Within the application
Boundary class	Application specific	Within the application

Do Not Create Giant Control Objects

Because control objects are application specific, if they are given too much intelligence or logic, they will not be reusable for other applications. Bear in mind that control objects should be treated as a kind of coordinator or broker which do not actually perform the task themselves. Wherever possible, entity objects should carry all the intelligence. In short, we should adopt a thin-control and intelligent-entity approach when designing systems. The following heuristics provide some guidance in determining the responsibilities to be assigned to a control object:

- The control sequence of messages in the scenario
- Information about the sessions in relation to the use case scenario, e.g. session ID, session status, etc.
- Control logic of the runtime session, e.g. transaction management, error recovery, etc.

Checking Consistency between Use Case and Sequence Diagrams

As each use case is elaborated by a use case description containing the flow of events element, transform it into a system-level sequence diagram by determining the actor inputs and system responses. Each of the flow of events may be optionally placed in the left-hand side of the sequence diagrams for tracing consistency between the different levels of the sequence diagram. Figure 4.42 depicts the consistency relationships between these models.

Identifying Objects and Operations through Scenario Analysis

Boundary and control objects can be identified by walking through the flow of events of a use case scenario. Typically, each entry of the flow of events

Figure 4.42. Model consistency between a use case and its sequence diagrams

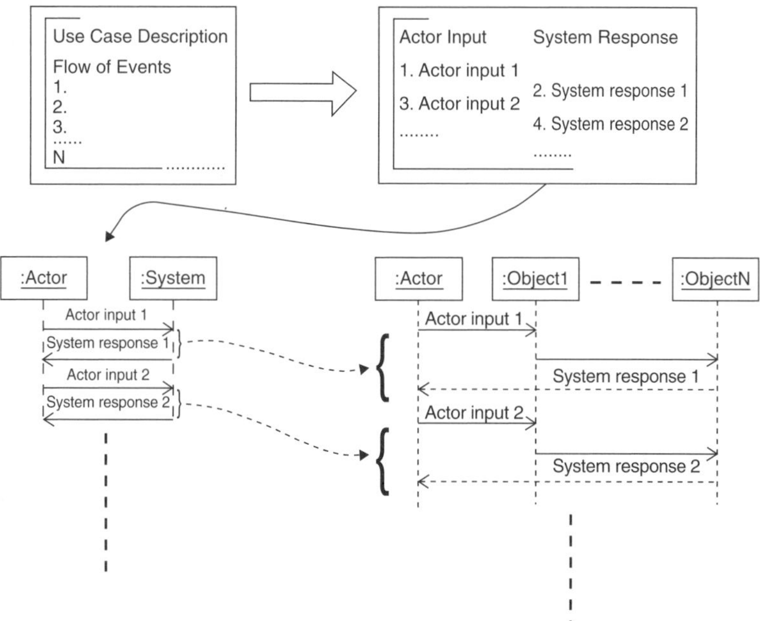

involves three steps: (1) the actor inputs some information into the system, (2) the system performs some action(s) and (3) the system responds to the actor's input. The following guidelines can help quickly identify the boundary and entity objects in a use case scenario:

- Identify boundary objects by asking questions such as
  "What input device(s) would be required for the actor(s) to enter the information?"
  "What output device(s) would be required for the system to give a response to the actor(s)?"
- Identify entity objects by asking questions such as
  "What information is required to respond to the actor's input?"

After the boundary object(s) and entity object(s) have been identified, add control object(s) to handle requirements that do not naturally belong to the boundary and entity object(s), e.g. control flow of the use case, exception handling, etc. For example, earlier in this chapter, Figure 4.32 shows the flow of events of the normal scenario of the *Withdraw Money* use case of the ATM system example. The flow of events indicates that the actor needs to insert an ATM card, enter a password, select a transaction, select an account, enter an amount, collect the cash and get a receipt. The system needs to respond to the actor by displaying messages on a screen. Hence, the boundary objects can be identified: card reader, keypad, receipt printer, cash dispenser and screen. On the other hand, from the messages displayed by the system, we know that the system needs to verify an ATM card when the actor inserts the card. To verify the card, the account information is required from the card-issuing bank. Between the account and the card reader, it is necessary to add control objects to handle the control logic in the ATM, bank consortium and the bank system since the ATM can only communicate with the bank via the bank consortium (see Figure 4.37).

Using Complementary Dynamic Models

Before we can develop the interaction diagrams of the system, we need to elaborate the use case with scenarios, and to keep track of the connections between these scenarios since the interaction diagrams for different scenarios form the complete model for implementation. When the number of scenarios of a use case increases, it would be rather difficult to keep track of the relationships between the scenarios. In this case, use an activity diagram to model the flow of events of a use case. The scenarios should correspond to the paths in the activity diagram. In other words, all the representative scenarios can be easily determined by tracing all the possible paths in the activity diagram. Hence, the activity diagram becomes a placeholder to accommodate all these scenarios of a use case together consistently. Thus, we can treat the activity diagram as a steward of a use case by modeling the extension points of a use case, glueing all its scenarios together.

Figure 4.43 shows that a use case can be elaborated by an activity diagram together with its abstract use cases (<<include>> and <<extend>>). Bear in mind that, when using an activity diagram to model a use case with abstract use cases, it is vital to adhere to the principle of extension points: the abstract use case will return to the point where it exited from. By zooming into the logic of the activity diagram, it is evident that the activity diagram is traceable through the corresponding base and abstract use cases. Each of the paths of an activity diagram should be further elaborated by a system-level sequence diagram. In addition to modeling the branching of the base use case to abstract use cases, we can model other conditional branching, such as *cancel operation*

Figure 4.43. Various complementary dynamic models

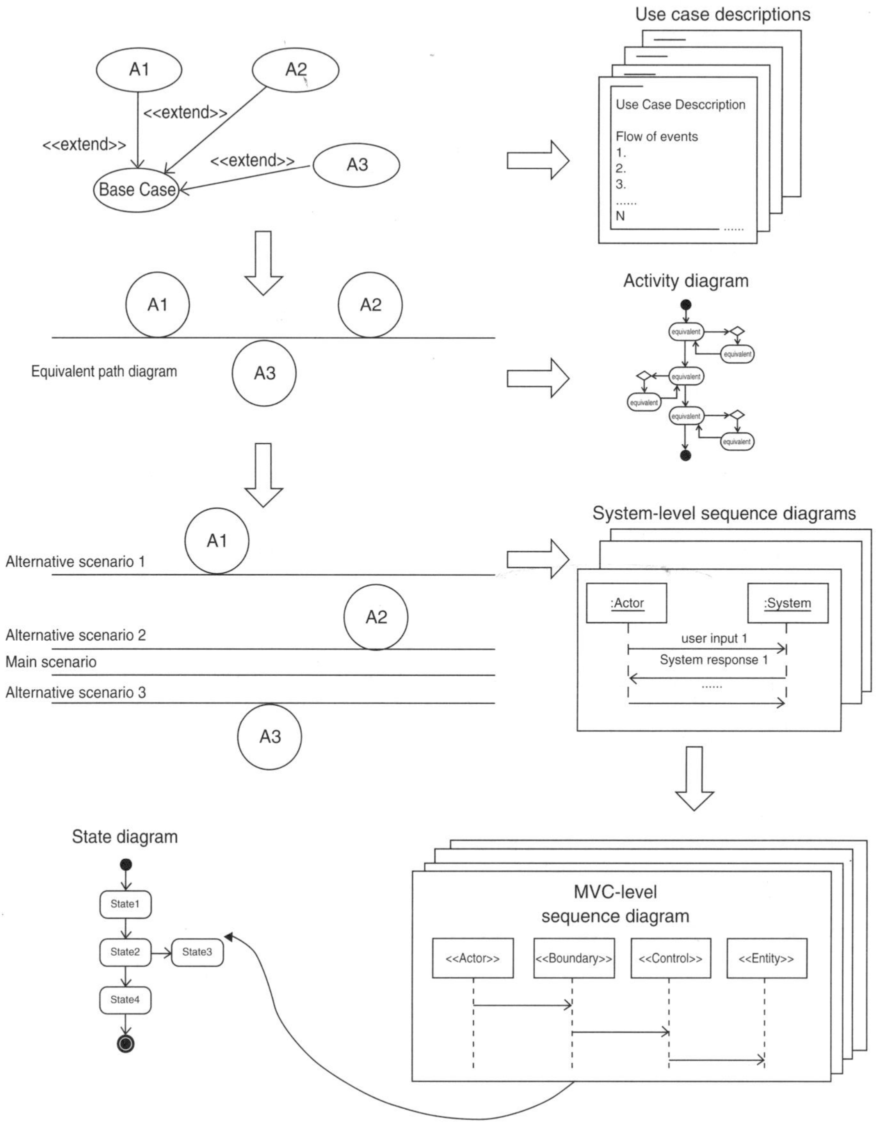

or *exceptional handling*, in an activity diagram. For example, it is useful to be able to specify that if the Cancel Button of the ATM is pressed at any time, all the preceding operations will be discarded and the ATM card ejected.

Note: Activity diagrams are not limited to being a steward of a use case, but they can also be adopted as an approach that drives the whole software development process at different levels and stages. We have developed a novel approach called the activity analysis approach, which is a major enhancement of the use case driven approach. This approach will be discussed in detail in Chapter 6.

When we go into the details of the subsystem-level sequence diagram, a statechart diagram is useful to express the complex logic and branching. By effectively using these dynamic models in such a combination, we can model the subsystem with sufficient details for implementation.

Dynamic Modeling and Analysis with VP-UML

In this section, the application of the key features of VP-UML to perform dynamic modeling and analysis will be demonstrated. We shall use the ATM system discussed earlier in this chapter as an example. Simply start up VP-UML and follow the instructions in the following pages to create various diagrams to perform dynamic modeling and analysis.

1. Develop system-level sequence diagrams
2. Develop subsystem-level sequence diagrams (optional for simple systems)
3. Develop subsystem-level statechart diagrams (optional for simple systems)
4. Create a scenario-based statechart diagram
5. Develop three-tier sequence diagrams
6. Develop three-tier collaboration diagrams (optional)
7. Develop a statechart diagram for each control object

Step 1: Develop System-level Sequence Diagrams

By tracing the path of the normal scenario of the *Withdraw Money* use case of the ATM system, we can identify the following messages between the user and the ATM:

- User inserts card
- System prompts user to enter PIN
- User enters PIN
- System prompts user to select services
- User selects *withdraw money*
- System prompts user to enter the amount
- User enters the amount

- System displays the "withdrawal success" message, ejects card and dispenses money
- User collects the card and money

Based on these messages, build a system-level sequence diagram for the scenario by following the instructions below:

1.1. Enter the sequence diagram working area, by clicking on the **application toolbar**. A new sequence diagram will be presented in the **diagram pane** (see Figure 4.44).

Figure 4.44. Sequence diagram work area

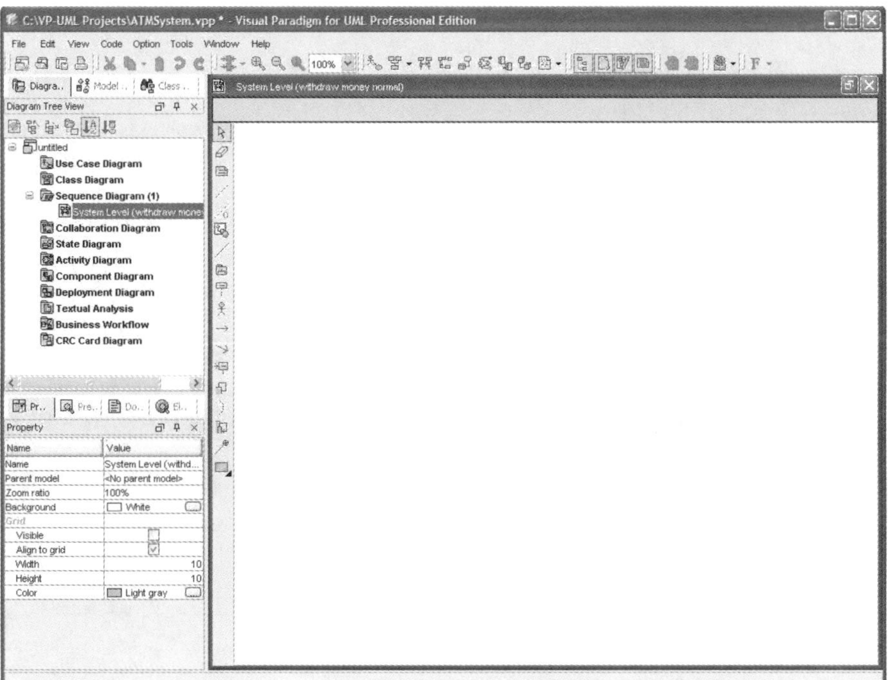

1.2. To create an actor, click on the **sequence diagram toolbar**. Move the mouse pointer to the desired location in the work area and click the left button again. An actor will then be created in the diagram and an inline editable text box is automatically opened. To rename the actor label, enter *User* and click anywhere outside the text box (see Figure 4.45).

Figure 4.45. Creating an actor

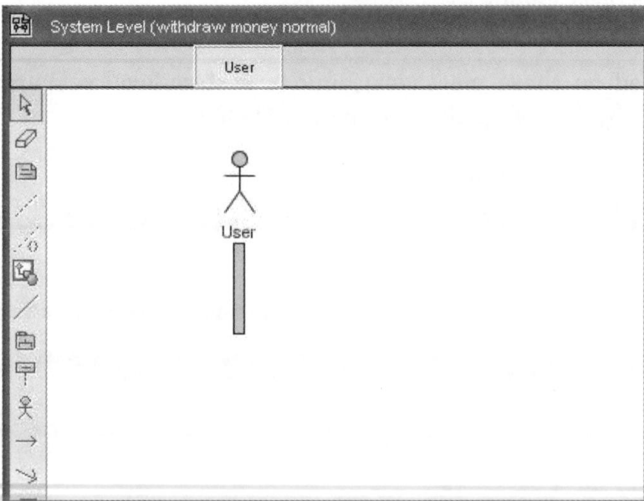

1.3. Now, click the icon on the diagram toolbar and follow the steps in creating the actor *User* to create the object. Name the object as *ATM System* using the ready-to-edit inline editable text box (see Figure 4.46).

Figure 4.46. Creating *ATM System*

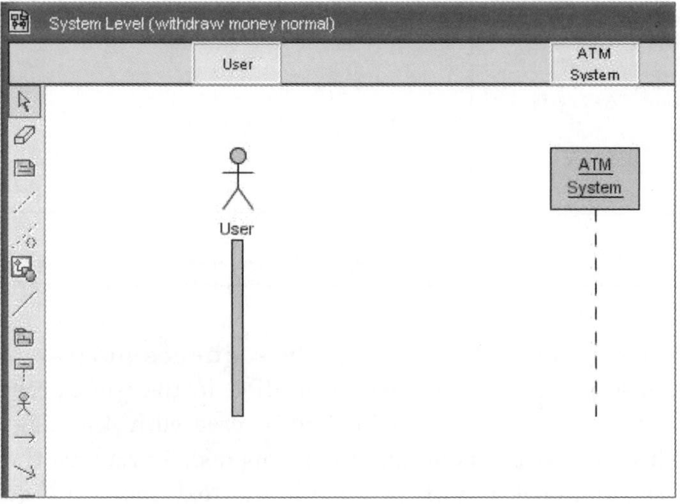

1.4. Then create the messages between *User* and *ATM System* by selecting the → icon on the **sequence diagram toolbar**, click on the lifeline (dotted line) under *User*, and then drag it to the lifeline under *ATM System*. Enter *insert card* in the inline editing area of the message and then press Ctrl-Enter or simply click on the empty area of the diagram pane to complete this operation (see Figure 4.47).

Figure 4.47. Creating a message

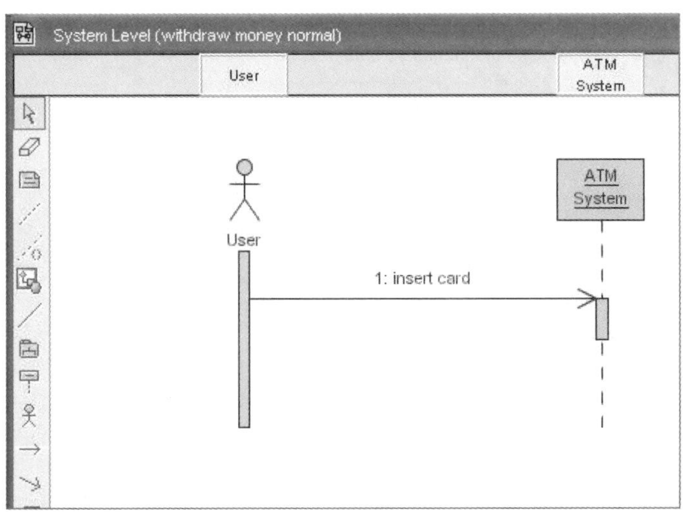

1.5. Repeat the above steps (1.1–1.4) to create the following messages (see Figure 4.48):
- System prompts user to enter PIN
- User enters PIN
- System prompts user to select services
- User selects "withdraw money"
- System prompts user to enter the amount
- User enters the amount
- System displays "withdrawal successful" message, ejects card and dispenses money
- User collects the card and money

Figure 4.48. System-level sequence diagram for normal scenario of the *Withdraw Money* use case

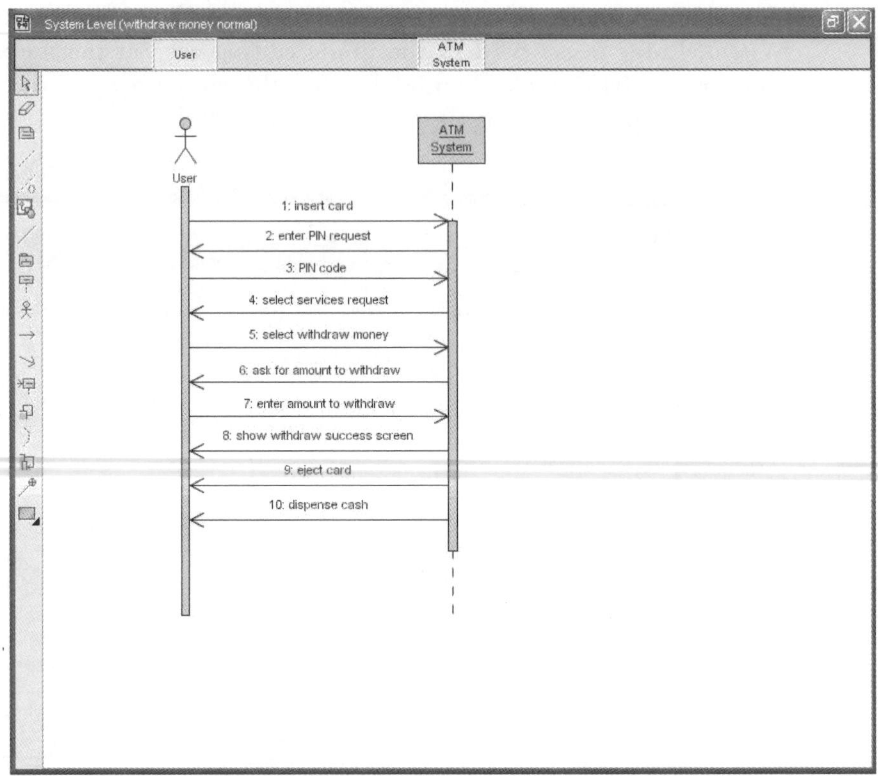

Step 2: Develop Subsystem-level Sequence Diagrams

The subsystem-level sequence diagram is developed from the system-level sequence diagram.

2.1. First of all, copy the system-level sequence diagram created in Step 1. Press Ctrl-A to select all the components in that diagram, then select **Copy** from the Edit menu or press Ctrl-C (see Figure 4.49 and Figure 4.50).

Figure 4.49. Selecting all elements in diagram

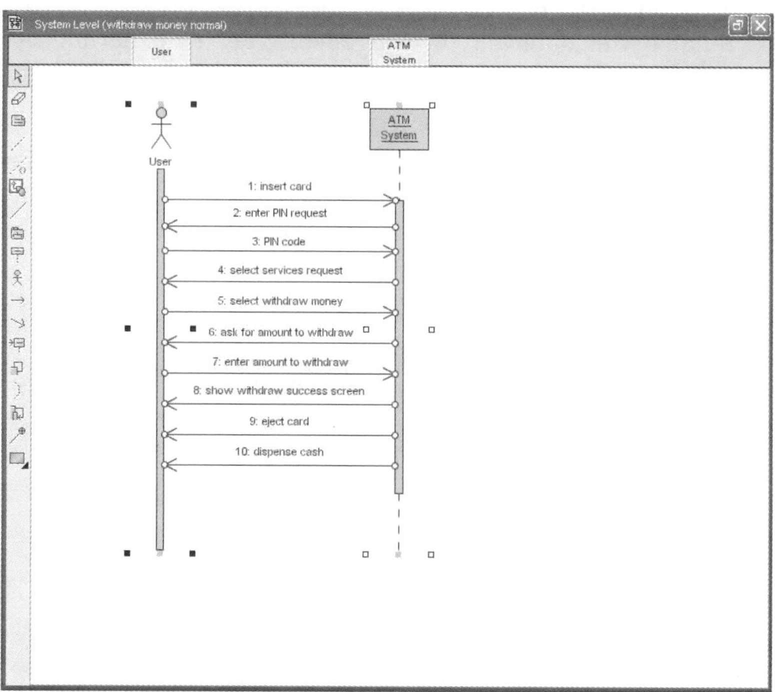

Figure 4.50. Copying diagram content

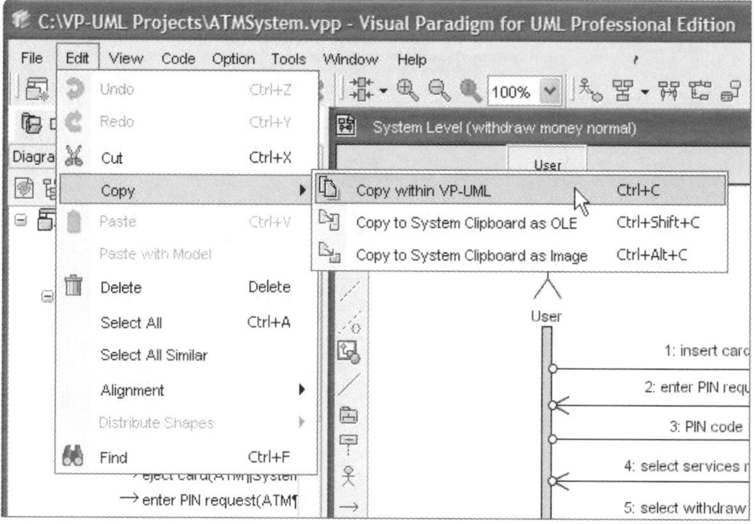

2.2. Create a new sequence diagram as in Step 1.1. Click the newly created diagram in the **project tree** on the top left corner of the screen, and then rename the diagram to *Subsystem level* (the normal scenario of the *Withdraw Money* use case) using the inline editing facility.

2.3. In the **blank sequence diagram**, right click and select **Paste** (see Figure 4.51) the copied contents in it (see Figure 4.52). Now, it is possible to develop the subsystem-level sequence diagram by modifying this diagram.

Figure 4.51. Pasting copied contents to the newly created diagram

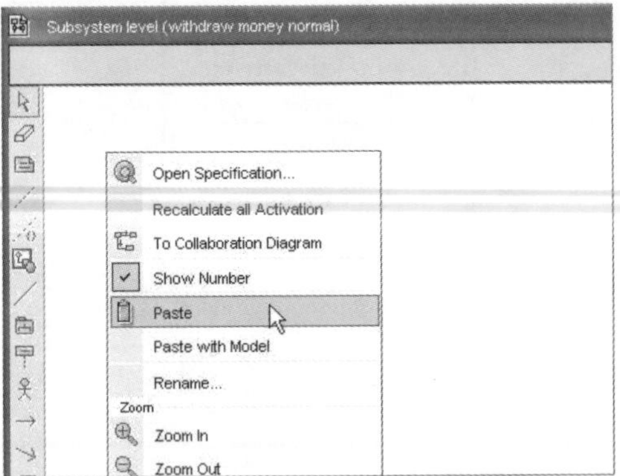

Figure 4.52. Subsystem-level sequence diagram with contents from system-level sequence diagram

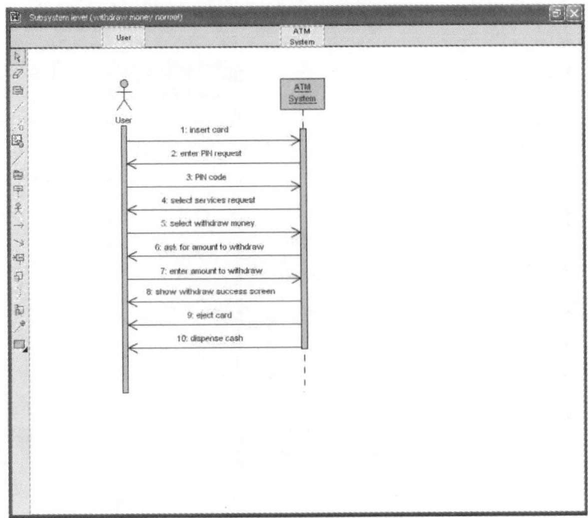

2.4. From the problem statement of the ATM system example, we found that there are three subsystems: *ATM*, *bank consortium* and *bank*. Messages are sent between *ATM* and *bank consortium* and also *bank consortium* and *bank*.

The following are typical messages between *ATM* and *bank consortium*:

- *ATM* asks *bank consortium* to verify account and password
- *Bank consortium* returns verified result
- *ATM* asks *bank consortium* to process withdrawal request
- *Bank consortium* returns result of withdrawal request

Typical messages between *bank consortium* and *bank* include:

- *Bank consortium* asks *bank* to verify the account
- *Bank* returns verified result to *bank consortium*
- *Bank consortium* forwards the withdrawal request to *bank*
- *Bank* returns result of the withdrawal request

2.5. Follow Step 1.3 to create the *bank consortium* and the *bank* objects (see Figure 4.53).

Figure 4.53. Creating *Bank Consortium* and *Bank* objects

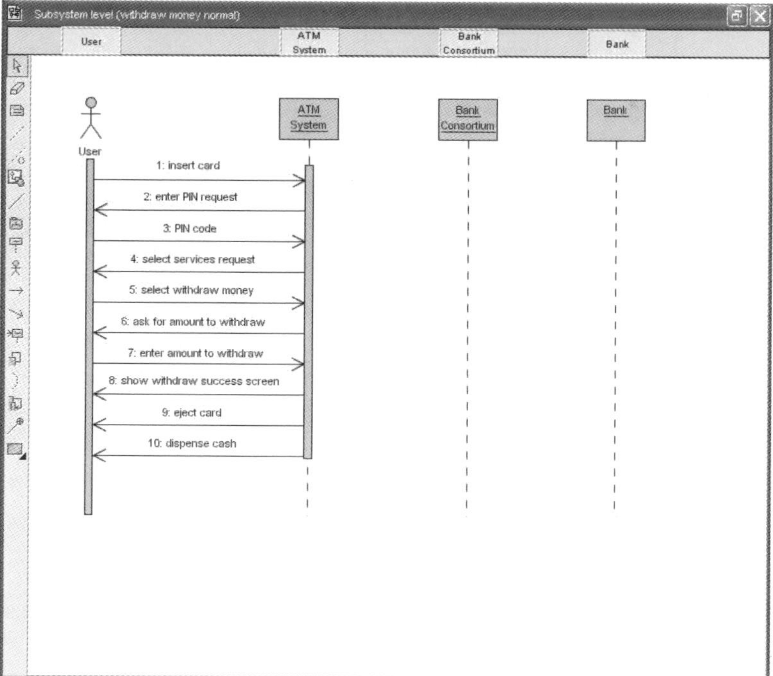

2.6. We find that the message between subsystems may have durations associated with end-to-end delays between the sender and the receiver. To create a message with a duration, simply select ↘ from the **sequence diagram toolbar** instead of the normal message icon (see Figure 4.54 and Figure 4.55).

Figure 4.54. Creating messages with duration

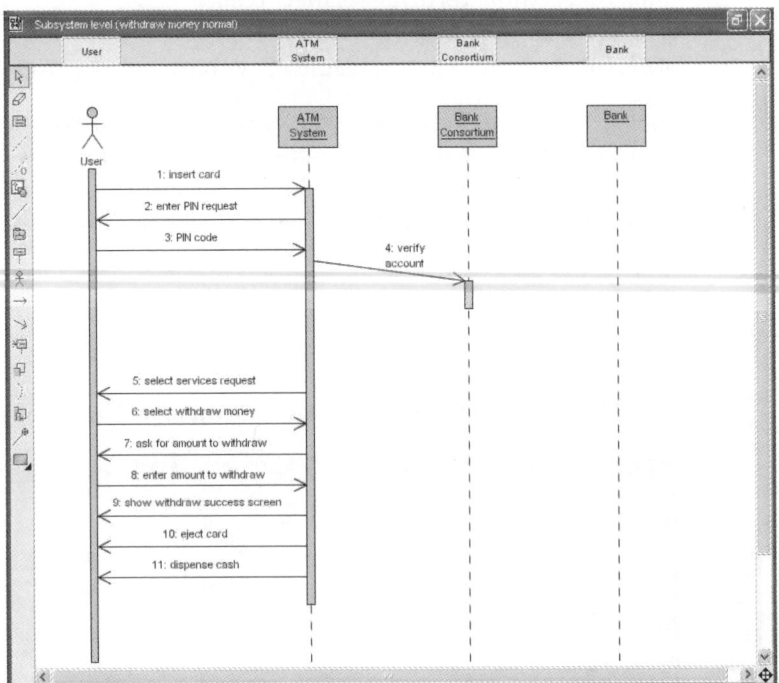

Figure 4.55. Subsystem-level sequence diagram

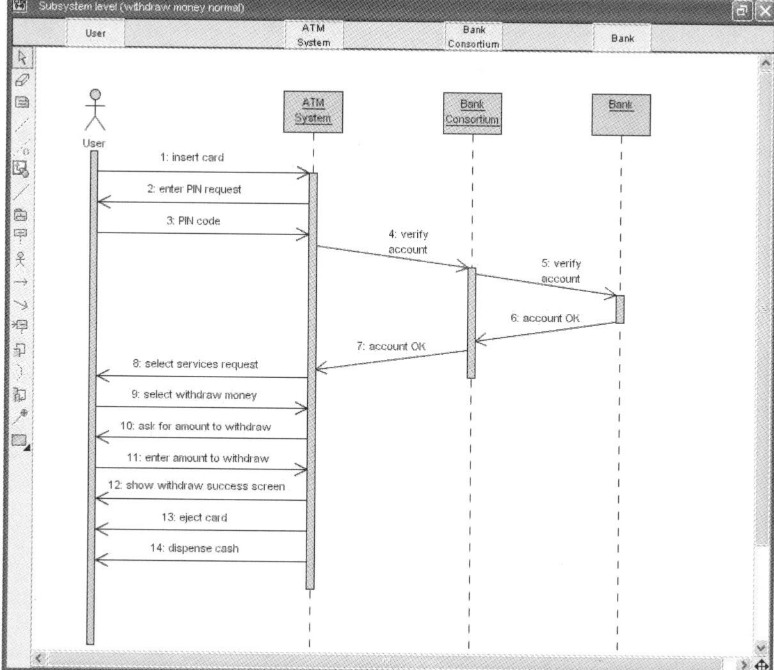

Step 3: Develop Subsystem-level Statechart Diagrams

With the above normal scenario for the ATM system example, we can develop a scenario-based statechart diagram with the following states:

- Before user inserts the ATM card
- Waiting for user to enter the PIN code after inserting ATM card
- Waiting for verification of user account
- Waiting for user to select a service
- Waiting for user to enter the amount to withdraw
- Waiting for transaction processing

Let us create the statechart diagram of the ATM.

3.1. First select [icon] from the **application toolbar**. A new statechart diagram appears (see Figure 4.56).

Figure 4.56. Statechart diagram work area

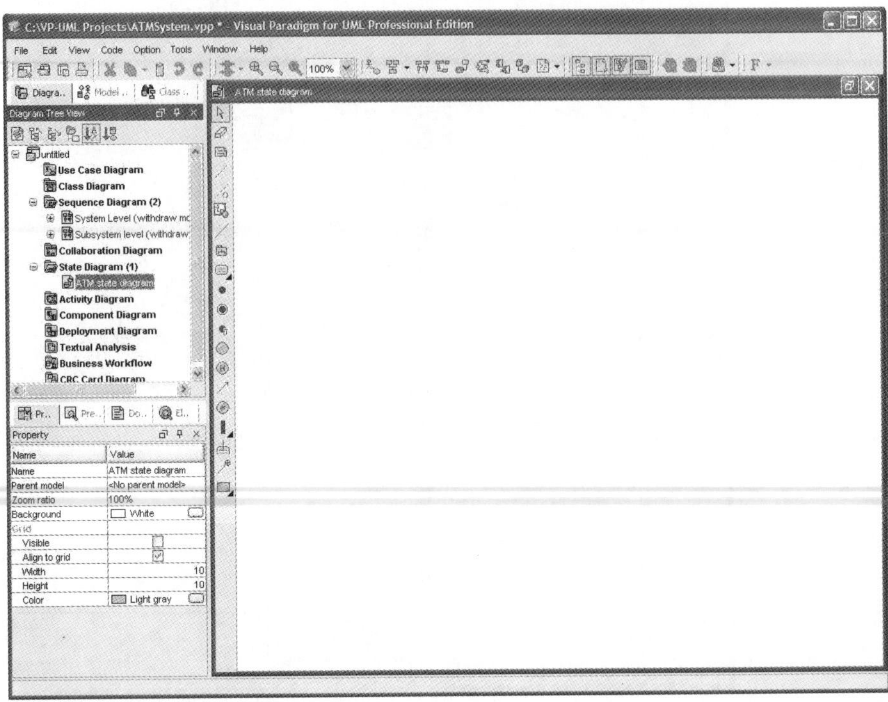

3.2. To create an initial state, click on the **statechart diagram toolbar**, move the mouse pointer to the desired location in the diagram area for the initial state and then click once (see Figure 4.57).

Figure 4.57. Creating an initial state

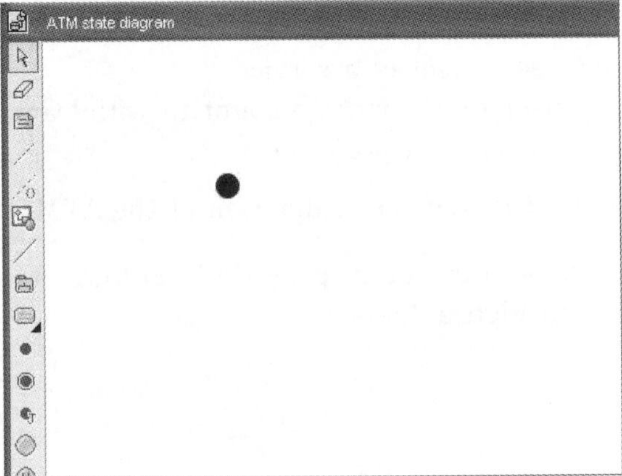

3.3. To create other states, select the icon from the resource-centric interface surrounding the initial state icon. Click and drag the icon to the desired location and release the mouse button. You can name the newly created state by typing *Main screen* in the ready-to-edit inline editable text box (see Figure 4.58).

Figure 4.58. Creating a state

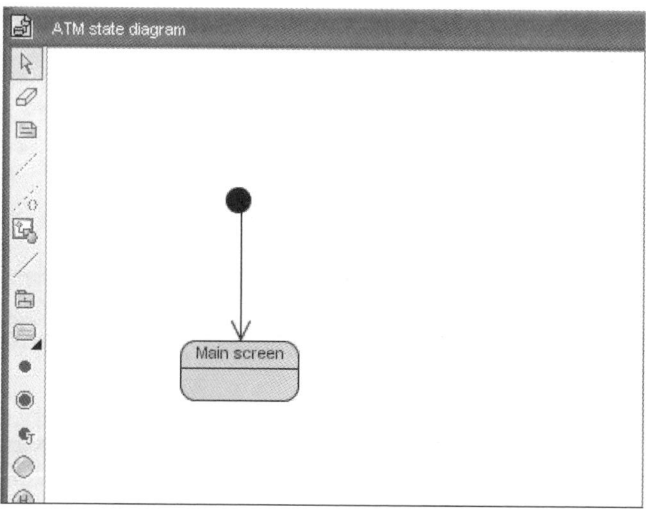

3.4. Repeat the above steps to create the following state:

- Wait for PIN
- Wait for account verification
- Wait for service selection
- Wait for withdraw amount information
- Process transaction

The statechart diagram for the ATM subsystem can be created by refining the statechart diagram shown in Figure 4.59. As mentioned before, there are other possible alternatives for the normal invocation of the *Withdraw Money* use case, for example,

- Invalid ATM card
- Incorrect PIN number entered
- Account overdrawn
- Customer canceling the action

To create the full statechart diagram of the ATM system, simply enrich the statechart diagram by including the alternative paths listed earlier. Follow the steps below to create the statechart diagram for the ATM subsystem.

3.5. Copy and paste the statechart diagram shown in Figure 4.59 into the new statechart diagram.

Figure 4.59. Statechart diagram for the normal scenario of the ATM

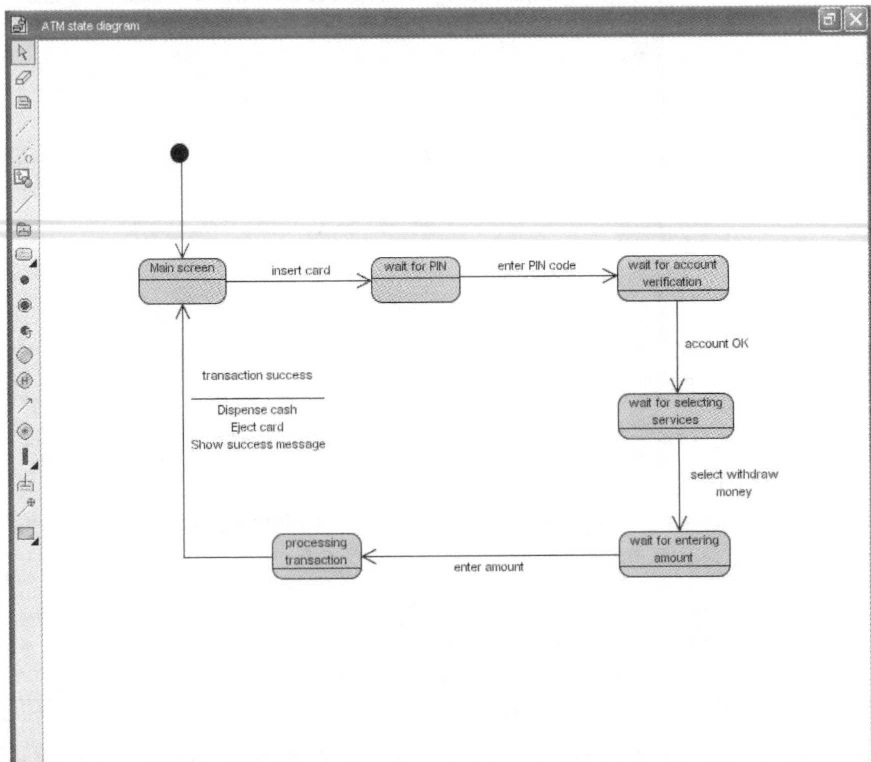

3.6. Add additional states and transitions for the alternative scenarios. Figure 4.60 shows a more complete statechart diagram of the system.

Figure 4.60. Complete statement diagram of the ATM system

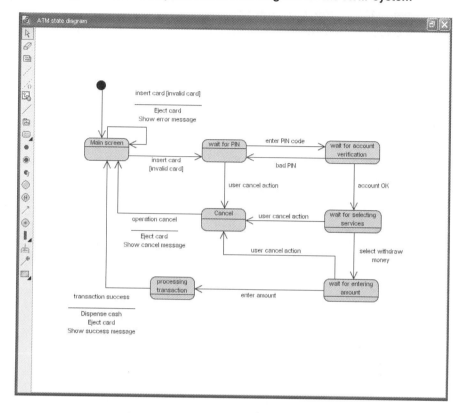

Step 4: Develop Three-tier Sequence Diagrams

Follow the procedures in Step 1 to create a new three-tier sequence diagram based on the subsystem-level sequence diagram.

From the message flow between *User* and *ATM System*, we can identify some user interface objects of the system. The "insert card" message implies that there must be a card reader and perhaps a card controller. The following are some user interface objects for the system:

- Card reader and card controller
- ATM controller
- Display
- Keypad
- Cash dispenser

Also we have identified entity objects like account from the message flow between *bank consortium* and *bank*.

Having created these objects, modify the message accordingly. Below is the revised message flow of the system.

- User *inserts ATM card* to *card reader*
- Card reader sends *ATM card information* to *card controller*
- *Card controller* sends card information to *ATM controller*
- *Card controller* asks the *Display* to show "enter PIN" message
- *Display* shows "enter PIN" message to user
- User *enters PIN* via *keypad*
- *Keypad* sends entered PIN to *ATM controller*
- *ATM controller* asks *bank consortium* to verify *account*
- *Bank consortium* forwards request to *bank*
- *Bank* verifies *account* and then confirms *account* is valid
- *Bank consortium* notifies *ATM controller* that account is valid
- *ATM controller* asks *display* to show "select service" message
- *Display* shows "select service" message to user
- User *selects withdrawal service* via *keypad*
- *Keypad* sends withdrawal service code to *ATM controller*
- *ATM controller* asks *display* to *show withdrawal dialog*
- *Display* shows "enter withdrawal amount" *dialog* to user
- User *enters withdrawal amount* via *keypad*
- *Keypad* sends *withdrawal amount* to *ATM controller*
- *ATM controller* sends a *withdrawal request* to *bank consortium*
- *Bank consortium* forwards request to *bank*
- *Bank* processes *withdrawal request* with *account* and confirms the *request is valid*
- *Bank consortium* notifies *ATM controller* that *request is valid*
- *ATM controller* asks *display* to *show* "withdrawal successful" message
- *Display shows* "withdrawal successful" message
- *ATM controller* asks *card controller* to *eject card*, and *card controller* asks *card reader* to *eject card*
- *Card reader ejects card* to user
- *ATM controller* asks *cash dispenser* to *dispense cash* to user, and *cash dispenser dispenses cash* to user

Follow the instructions below to develop the three-tier sequence diagram:

4.1. Follow instructions in Steps 1.3 to 1.4 to create the boundary, entity and control objects and the messages between them.

4.2. To indicate that an object is an active object, right click on the object and select the Active (see Figure 4.61 and Figure 4.62).

4.3. To include more details, the return message should be defined in the **Return Message** type. To change the message type of the "show PIN request" message, simply right click on the message, and then select **Return** (see Figure 4.63). The message will then be changed into a **Return Type** message (see Figure 4.64).

4.4. Repeat the above Step 4.3 to change the following messages to become a return message:
- *Account OK* from *account* to *bank*
- *Account OK* from *bank* to *bank consortium*
- *Account OK* from *bank consortium* to *ATM controller*
- *Withdraw OK* from *account* to *bank*
- *Withdraw OK* from *bank* to *bank consortium*
- *Withdraw OK* from *bank consortium* to *ATM controller*

The complete three-tier sequence diagram is shown in Figure 4.65.

Step 5: Develop Three-tier Collaboration Diagram

Based on the sequence diagram developed in Step 5, we can now develop a three-tier collaboration diagram for the corresponding scenario:

5.1. To create the collaboration diagram, click on the **application toolbar** (see Figure 4.66).

5.2. To create the layers for different types of objects, click on the **Collaboration Diagram toolbar** and place the mouse pointer in the desired area and then click once. A **horizontal swimlane box** is then created and an inline editable text box is automatically opened. Rename *Swimlane*, by entering *Boundary Objects* and then click anywhere outside the text box to complete the operation (see Figure 4.67).

5.3. Click the button next to the **Fill** row at the **property pane** (see Figure 4.68) to open the **Format Fill Color dialog** (see Figure 4.69) and change the color of the swimlane into white (see Figure 4.70).

5.4. Repeat the above steps to create the swimlanes for the *control* and *entity* objects and also an empty swimlane for the actor that does not belong to the system (see Figure 4.71).

Figure 4.61. Changing object type

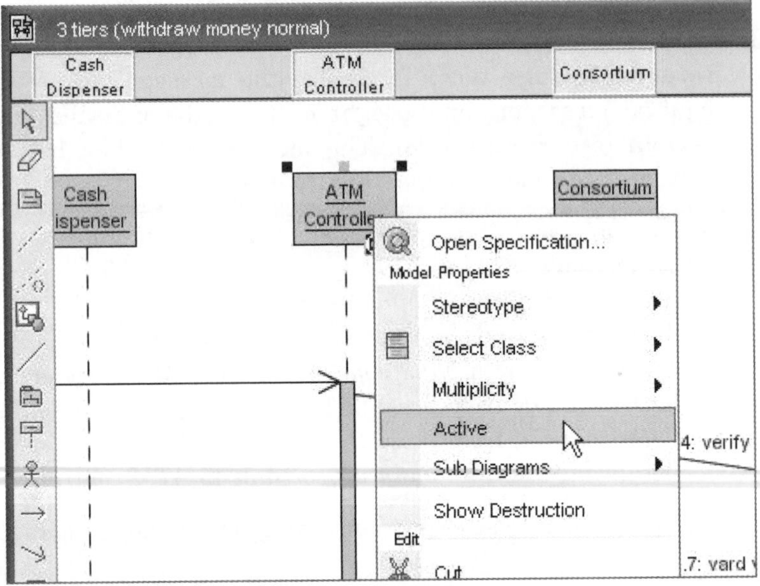

Figure 4.62. ATM controller becoming active object

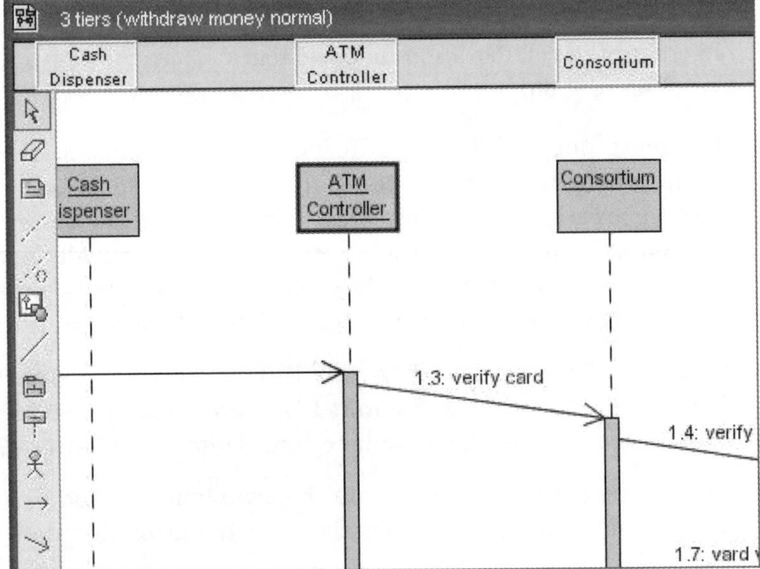

Figure 4.63. Changing message type

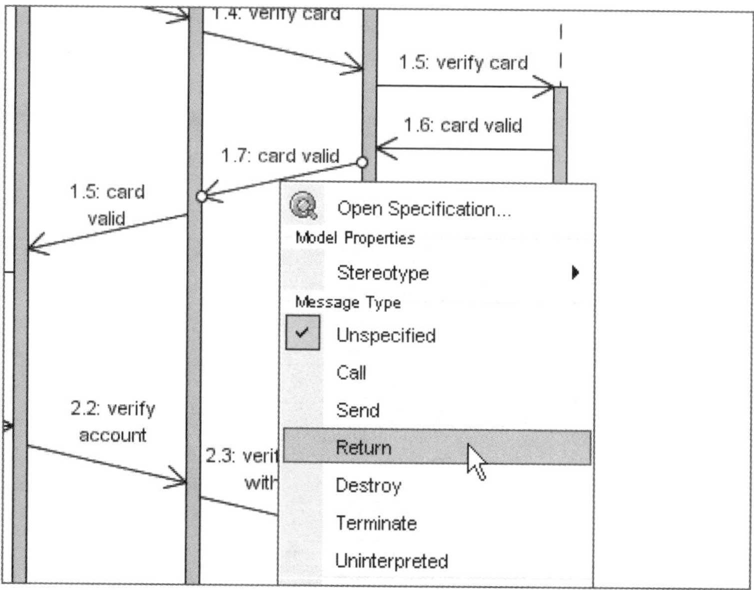

Figure 4.64. Changing message type to return

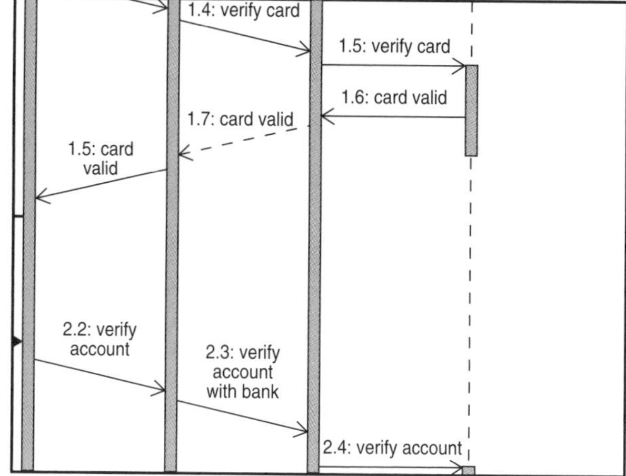

Figure 4.65. Three-tier sequence diagram

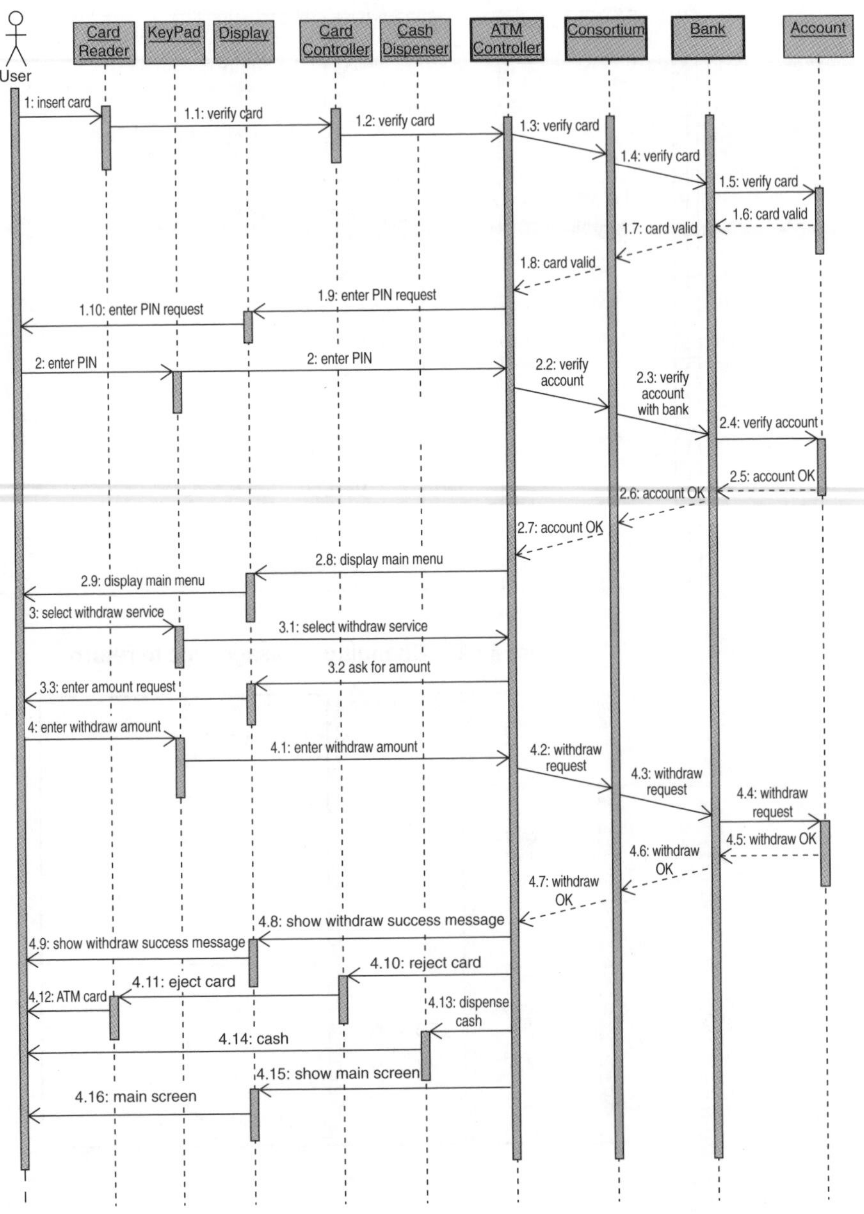

Figure 4.66. Collaboration diagram working area

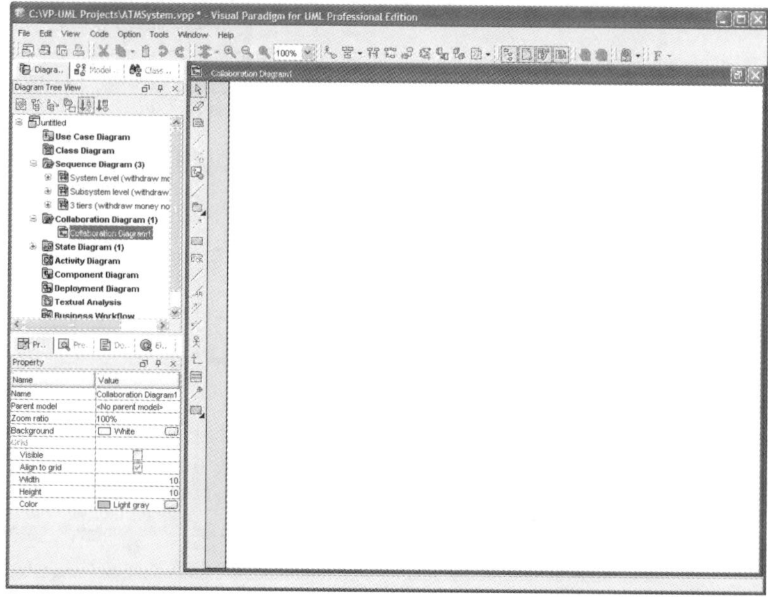

Figure 4.67. Boundary object swimlane

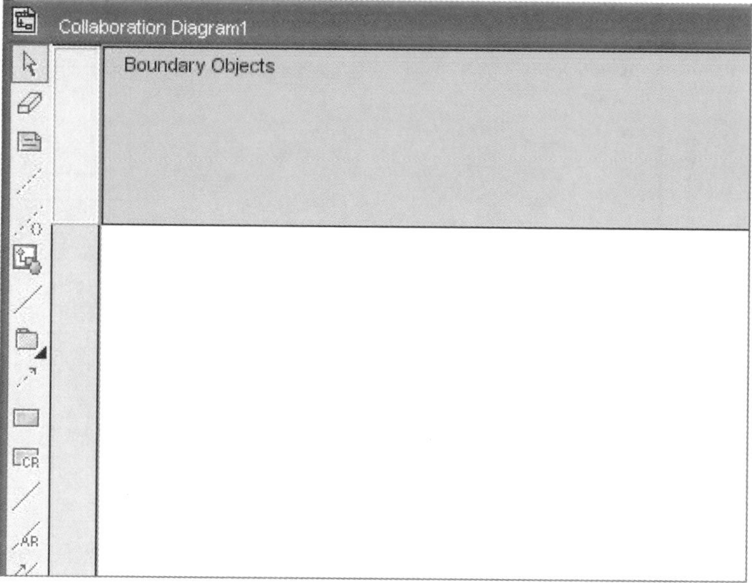

Figure 4.68. Open format Fill Color dialog

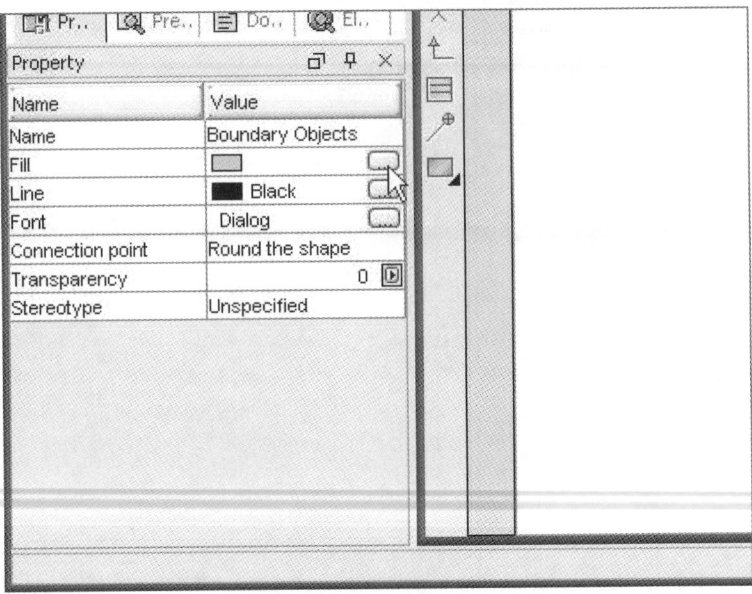

Figure 4.69. Format Fill Color dialog

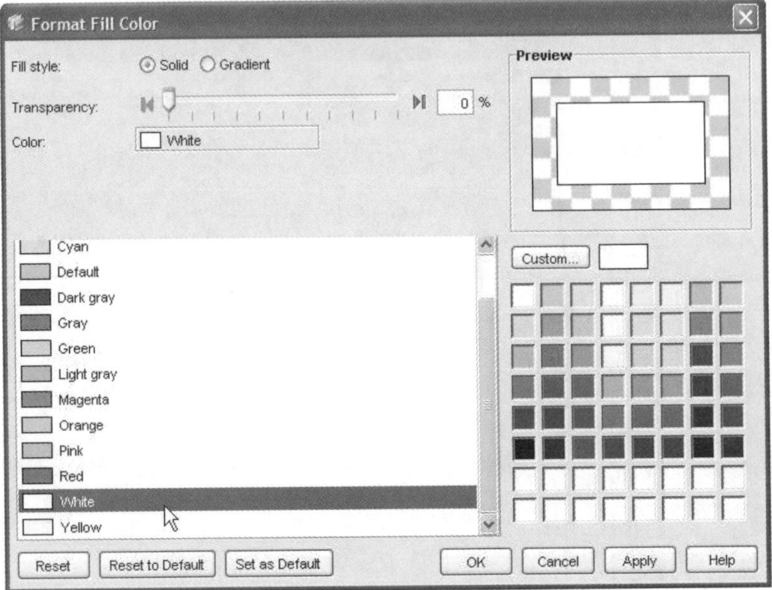

Figure 4.70. Changing Color of swimlane white

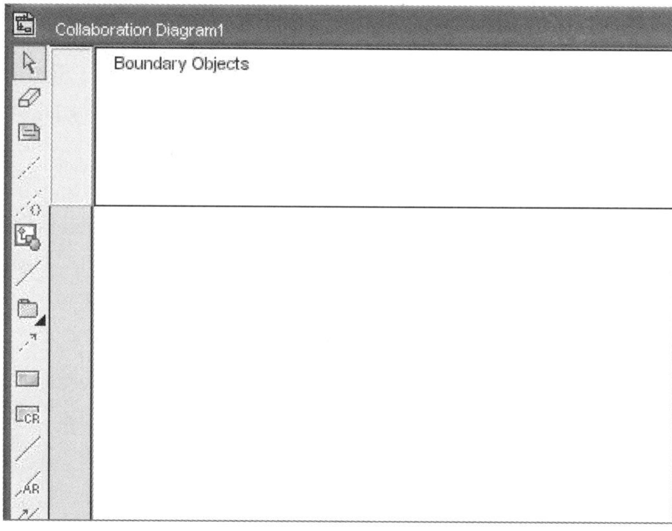

Figure 4.71. Collaboration diagram with swimlanes

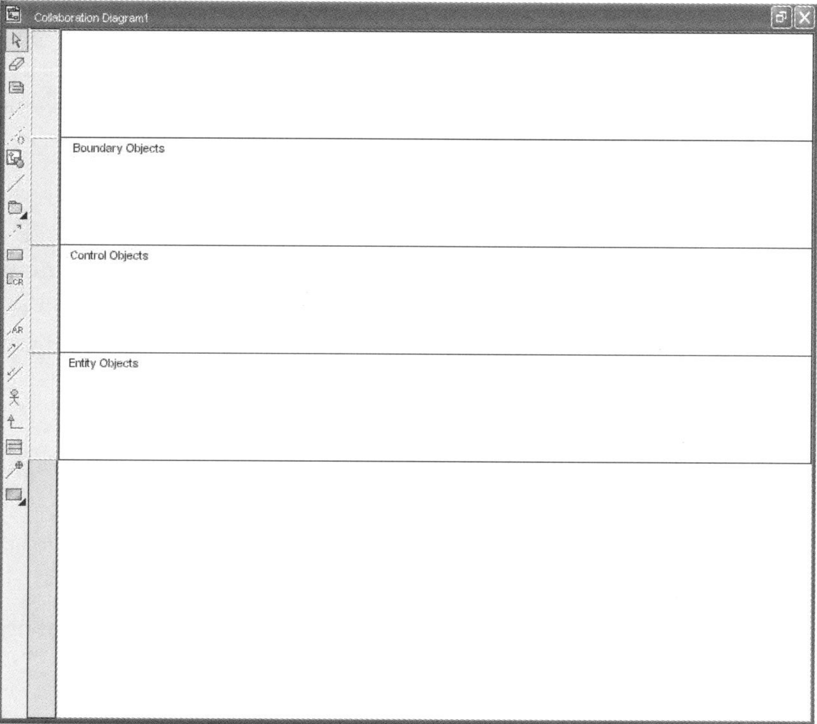

5.5. To create an actor object, click on the **Collaboration Diagram toolbar** click once in the top-most swimlane. An actor symbol is then placed in that swimlane. To create an actor in the design area rather than inside a swimlane, click once in the design area. Similar to creating the swimlane, an inline editable text box is automatically opened, which allows the renaming of the actor by editing the text box (see Figure 4.72).

5.6. Click on and drag the icon surrounding the actor's resource-centric interface and release the mouse button next to the actor in the desired location within the diagram area. The object is then created with a collaboration link attached to the actor. Type the name of the object in the inline text area (see Figure 4.73).

5.7. Repeat the above steps to create the following objects (see Figure 4.74):
- Boundary objects:
  - *Display*
  - *Keypad*
  - *Cash dispenser*
  - *Card reader*
- Control objects:
  - *Card controller*
  - *ATM controller*
  - *Consortium*
  - *Bank*
- Entity object:
  - *Account*

5.8. Now create the messages between the objects. Click on the **Collaboration Diagram toolbar** and click once on the collaboration link in which the message is to be created. A *Message to* symbol is placed next to the collaboration link. Type in the name of the message in the inline text area (see Figure 4.75).

5.9. To specify an incoming message from an object (*Message from*), click on the **Collaboration Diagram toolbar**, and repeat the steps similar to the previous instruction. If the diagram is too large to be displayed on one screen, use the button to zoom out so that the entire diagram can be displayed.

5.10. To change the object type to Active, right click on the collaboration object, then select the **Active** (see Figures 4.76 and 4.77).

Figure 4.72. Creating an actor

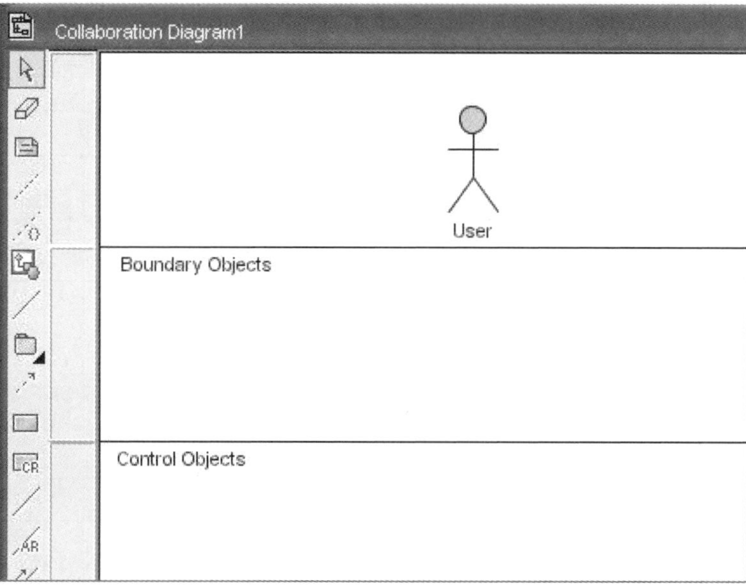

Figure 4.73. Creating objects

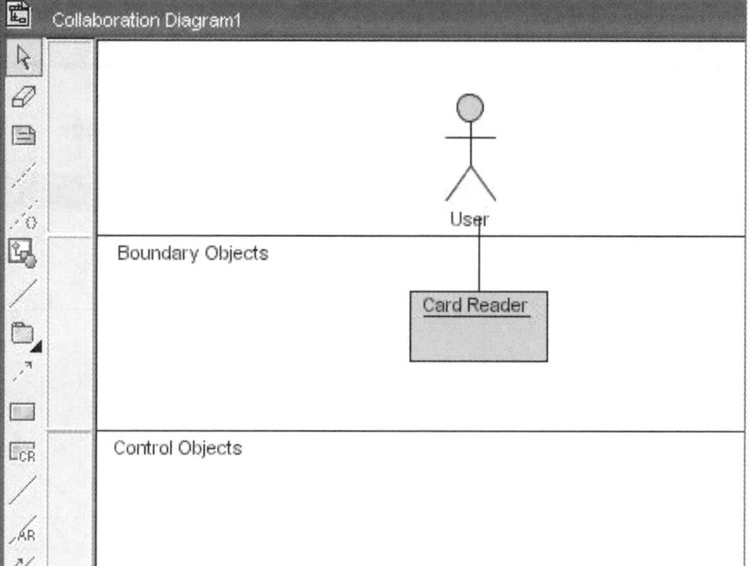

Figure 4.74. Three-tier collaboration diagram

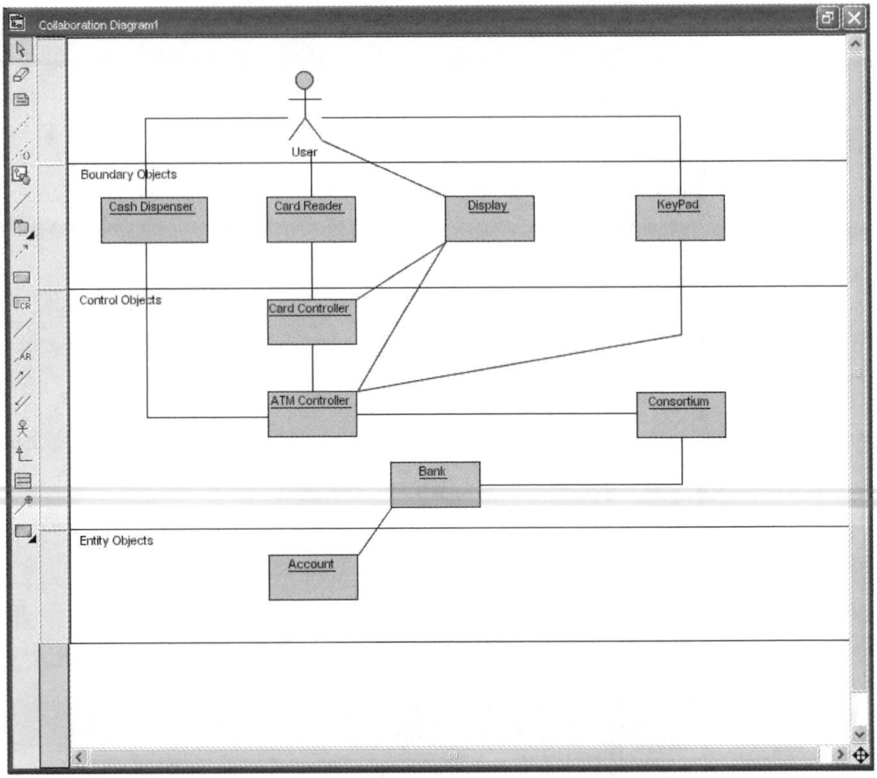

Figure 4.75. Creating a To Message

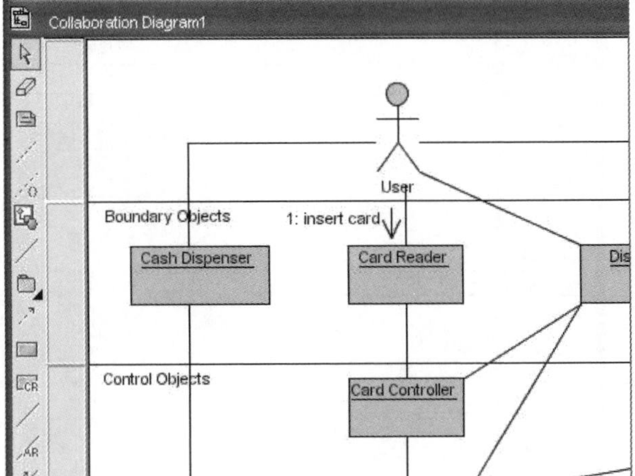

Figure 4.76. Changing object type to Active

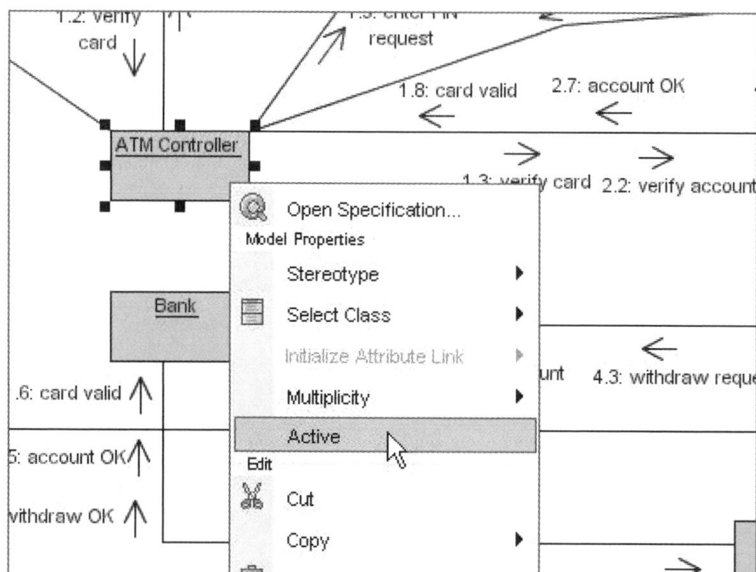

Figure 4.77. Changing object type

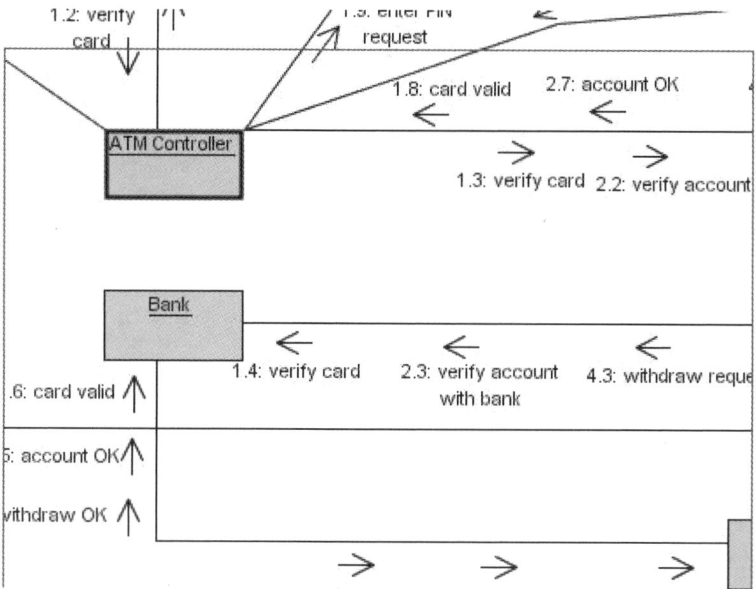

5.11. Repeat the above steps to create all the other messages shown in the three-tier sequence diagram. The complete three-tier collaboration diagram is shown in Figure 4.78.

Figure 4.78. Three-tier collaboration diagram

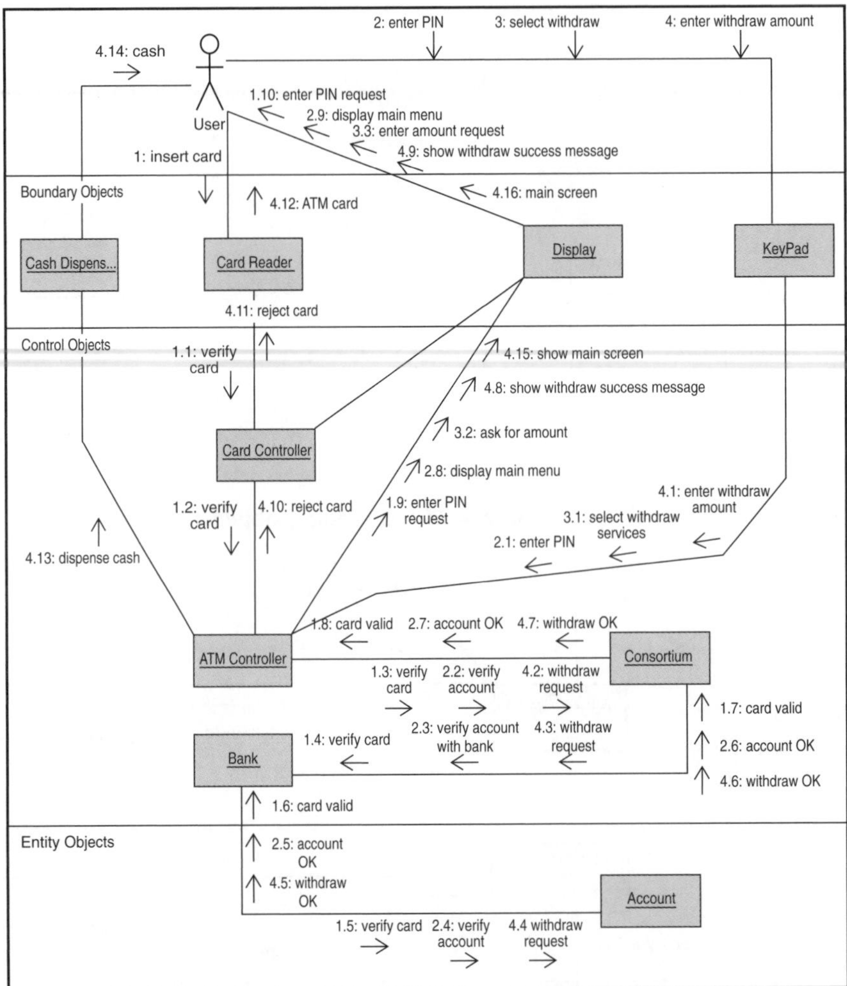

Step 6: Develop a Statechart Diagram for Each Control Object

By analyzing the incoming and outgoing messages of the *Card Controller* objects, the following states have been identified:

- Check the validity of the ATM card
- Verify the ATM card with *bank consortium* that the card issuer bank is in the service list of the ATM system

Now, create the statechart diagram for the *Card Controller* objects by following the procedure in Step 3 to create a statechart diagram as shown in Figure 4.79.

Figure 4.79. Statechart Diagram of *Card Controller*

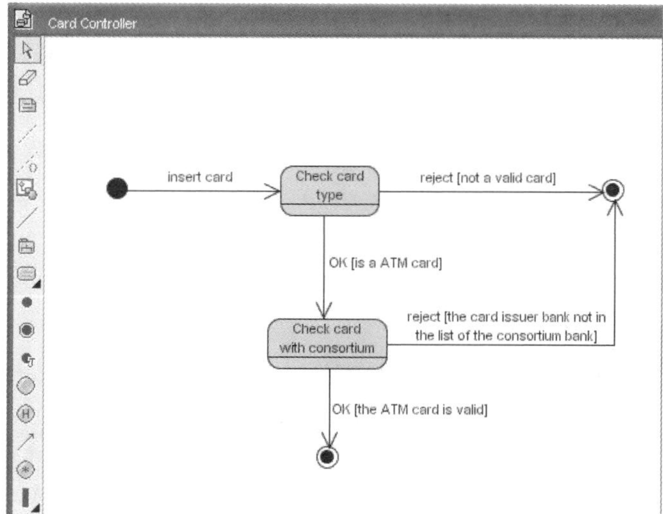

Repeat the above step to create the statechart diagrams for the following control objects:

- *ATM controller*
- *Bank consortium*

Summary

A dynamic model represents the external dynamic behaviors of a system. In UML a dynamic model can be represented by the sequence diagram, the collaboration diagram, the statechart diagram or the activity diagram, each of which exhibits a different aspect of the dynamic behaviors. Sequence diagrams are temporally focused and suitable for analyzing the order of the interactions between objects while collaboration diagrams are structurally focused and suitable for modeling the required structural relationship between objects to realize a scenario. Statechart diagrams are used to model entity states and their transitions in response to events, while activity diagrams model performance of actions of an activity or procedure.

In carrying out dynamic modeling and analysis, a system-level sequence diagram is constructed by first performing textual analysis on the textual description for the flow of events of the scenario. The creation of subsystem-level sequence diagrams may sometimes be necessary for large systems, and subsystem-level statechart diagrams can then be created. By identifying boundary, control and entity objects, the three-tier sequence diagram can be developed. Based upon the three-tier sequence diagram, a three-tier collaboration diagram is constructed by grouping these objects into different packages according to their types. Finally, the statechart diagram can be created for each of the active control objects.

To illustrate the concepts described in this chapter, the modeling and analysis of an ATM system has been presented, detailing the steps involved by using the powerful features of the VP-UML CASE tool.

Exercise

You are asked to continue the analysis of the online bookstore system described in Exercise of Chapter 3.

Follow the steps below to perform dynamic analysis and modeling of the system by:

1. Developing system-level sequence diagrams for the use case scenarios
2. Developing three-tier sequence diagrams for the use case scenarios
3. Developing three-tier collaboration diagrams (optional) for the use case scenarios
4. Developing a state chart diagram for each of the control objects.
5. Refining the class diagram that you have developed in Exercise of Chapter 2 by using the results of Steps 2 to 4 above.

Chapter

5

Implementing UML Specification

Overview

The Unified Modeling Language (UML) is the *de facto* standard for specifying the high-level structure of a software system. However, the specifications contained in the UML diagrams generally do not provide sufficient details for implementation and they have to be manually translated into code. With the aid of modern CASE tools, it is now possible to generate a framework of partially complete programming code from these diagrams. The programmer is required to fill in the necessary details to the framework to complete the coding process. UML specifications can be conveniently implemented using modern object-oriented programming languages such as Java.

In this chapter, we will focus on implementation issues for five UML diagrams, namely, class, state, activity, sequence and collaboration diagrams, as they encapsulate most of the specification information for system implementation.

What You Will Learn

On completing the study of this chapter, you should be able to:

- implement a class diagram
- implement a state diagram
- implement an activity diagram
- implement sequence and collaboration diagrams

Introduction

In the Unified Process, the system being developed is analyzed, designed and implemented incrementally in the inception, elaboration, construction and transition phases, each serving a specific purpose. In the early phases (inception or elaboration phase), the developer may want to verify the requirements or test the core technologies used for development. Therefore, at such a stage, the design of the system is usually incomplete, and the developer will only be able to implement some initial partially complete prototypes. In later phases, as more information about the requirements is available, the developer can pursue the implementation process more smoothly.

The priority of the use cases may be a helpful guide as far as the order in which they are implemented is concerned. Consequently, classes required for realizing higher priority use cases should be designed and implemented first. A class can be implemented when the attributes and the methods have been specified, typically by class, interaction, activity and state diagrams. Generally, entity classes can be specified by class and interaction diagrams. This is because entity classes are used to maintain data in the problem domain, and their methods manipulate the data or maintain the association between other entities. The logic associated with such entity classes is relatively straightforward.

For complex control classes, state or activity diagrams are usually used in addition to class and interaction diagrams to manage the control flows of use cases. For boundary classes that interact with human actors, the user interface design should be completed first before the boundary classes can be fully implemented.

Given a use case and the specifications of the required classes, the developer can then prioritize the implementation of the classes according to their architectural significance in the system. This is to reduce risks in the implementation process. For example, if the usability of the system is a high risk item, it may be necessary to design and first implement the user interface involving the boundary classes that interact with the human actor.

In this chapter, we will explain in detail the general approach to implementing the five diagrams. We then present a case study showing how the complete UML specification of a simplified lift control system is implemented in Java.

Implementing Class Diagrams

A class diagram shows the objects that are required and the relationships between them. Since the class diagram provides detailed information about the properties and interfaces of the classes, the class diagram can be considered as the main model and treat the other diagrams as supplementary models. The supplementary models provide additional information about their implementation which is specified in the class diagram. For example, the sequence diagram can be used to describe the sequence of actions performed when a method of a class is invoked.

A Single Class

A class is a collection of attributes and methods. The members (attribute or method) of a class can have different levels of visibility (public, protected, package, private). A sample class is shown in Figure 5.1.

The translation of a single class in a class diagram is carried out in a number of ways:

- Each attribute of the class is translated into a declaration of data variables in Java
- Each operation or method is translated into a declaration of a method in Java
- The levels of visibility of a class member can be specified by the Java keywords: public, protected and private. No specifier is needed if the visibility of the class member is a package

For example, the class in Figure 5.1 can be translated into the code in Figure 5.2. Note that the bodies of the methods are empty. The programmer needs to fill in the code required for implementing the methods. Very often, the programmer may need to refer to other models, such as sequence diagrams, which provide more information about the specification of the methods.

Package

Classes may be organized and grouped as a package for ease of modeling and maintenance. In Java, classes of the same package are placed in one directory and the Java keyword *package* is used to declare its name (see Figure 5.3). The package name is the path of the directory that contains the classes of the package. Hence, *ClassA* in Figure 5.3 is placed in the directory com/abc/library. In order to use the classes in the package, the developer needs to add the path of the root directory of the package in the CLASSPATH, which is an environment variable of the Java runtime and development tool.

Figure 5.1. A sample class with members of different levels of visibility

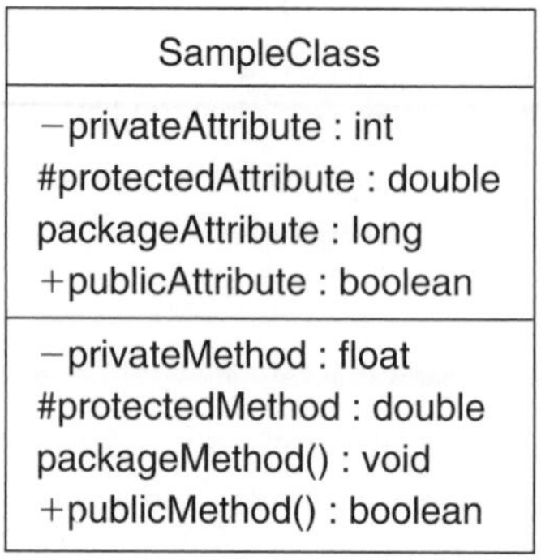

SampleClass
−privateAttribute : int #protectedAttribute : double packageAttribute : long +publicAttribute : boolean
−privateMethod : float #protectedMethod : double packageMethod() : void +publicMethod() : boolean

Figure 5.2. Java code for SampleClass

```
class SampleClass {
    private int privateAttribute;
    protected double protectedAttribute;
    long packageAttribute;
    public boolean publicAttribute;
    public boolean publicMethod(int parameter1) {
        ...
        ...
    }
    private float  privateMethod(byte parameter1, float parameter2) {
        ...
        ...
    }
    protected double protectedMethod() {
        ...
        ...
    }
    void packageMethod(short parameter1) {
        ...
        ...
    }
}  Sample Class
```

Figure 5.3. Implementation of package

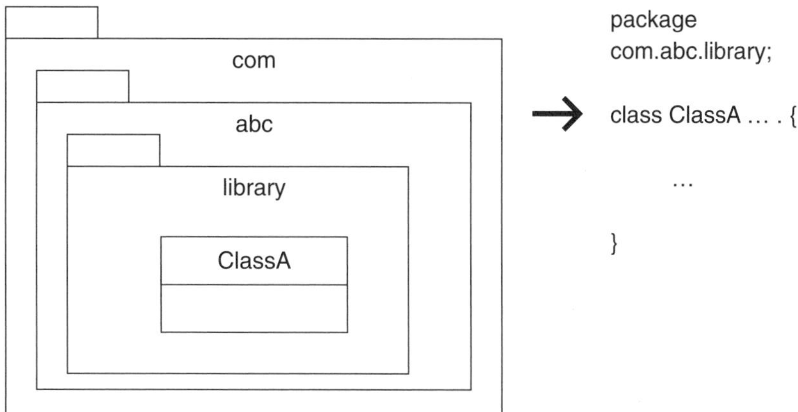
com
abc
library
ClassA
package
com.abc.library;
class ClassA .... {
...
}

Inheritance

Inheritance is useful for modeling situations where common attributes and operations are specified and shared in a base class. The shared attributes and operations can then be modeled by defining inheritance relationships between the individual classes (subclasses) and the base class. Inheritance also provides extensibility of the software system. We can build a software system as a collection of connected software components. Each component only knows the interfaces of its partner components. In so doing, we can replace any component with another which has the same interface. With this modular approach to software development, the software system can be upgraded with new functionalities by simply adding new components or replacing old ones, without major modification of existing components of the system.
In UML, there are two forms of inheritance:

- A class inherits an abstract class or a concrete class. The inheritance relationship is translated into the Java keyword *extends* (see Figure 5.4)
- A class inherits an interface. In other words, a class declares that it implements all the methods specified in the interface. The inheritance relationship is translated into the Java keyword *implements* (see Figure 5.5). In the UML notation, inheritance of an interface is represented by an arrow with a dashed-line and a stereotype <<realize>>.

Figure 5.4. Implementation of inheritance between classes

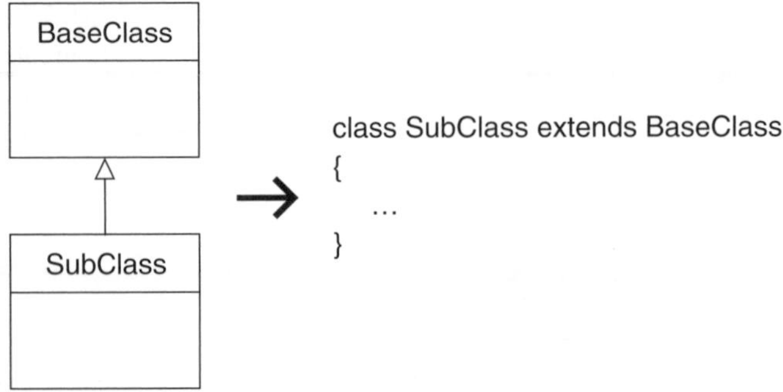

Figure 5.5. Implementation of inheritance between an interface and a class

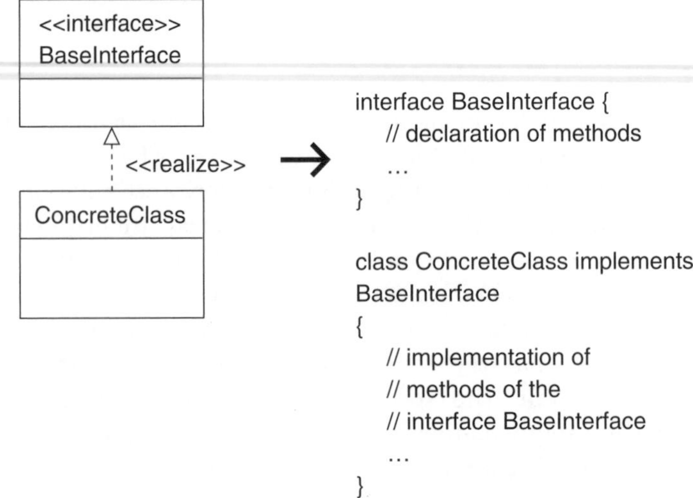

Associations

There are several ways to implement an association between classes:

- A private attribute to link one object with another
- A vector to link one object to many objects
- A hashtable to link one object to many objects, while simultaneously providing search capability

We will discuss the different types of associations next.

One-to-one Association

A one-to-one association between classes can be easily implemented as an attribute in each of the associated classes. For example, *ClassA* and *ClassB* are associated classes in Figure 5.6. In runtime, the attribute contains the reference of the associated object. If the association has additional attributes, put the association attributes to either class of the association. Figure 5.6 illustrates how a binary one-to-one association is implemented. The attributes of the association class are declared in *ClassA*, which is one of the associated classes.

Figure 5.6. Implementation of one-to-one association

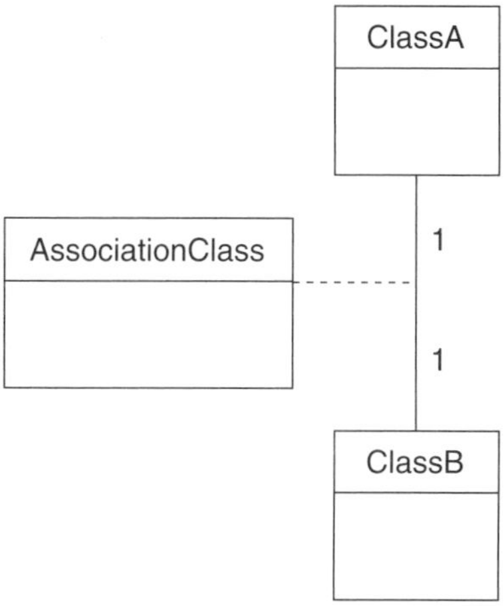

```
class ClassA {
    ClassB _b;
    // declare attributes
    // for the
    // association class
    ...
}
class ClassB {
    ClassA  _a;
    ...
}
```

One-to-many Association

A one-to-many association can be implemented by an attribute on the *many* side and by a vector on the *one* side (see Figure 5.7). A vector is an expandable array of objects where each can be accessed by an index. If the association has additional attributes, the association attributes can be stored on the *many* side of the association (see Figure 5.7). In addition to variables for implementing the association, we also need methods for maintaining the links between the objects in runtime. Since the class on the *one* side has a vector to keep all the references of the associated objects, methods for adding, removing or searching objects in the vector are needed (see Figure 5.8). Alternatively, the vector can be replaced by a hashtable or other types of data structures to facilitate faster object searches. In the class on the *many* side, an attribute is declared to hold the reference of an object of the class on the *one* side (see Figure 5.7).

Figure 5.7. Implementation of a one-to-many association

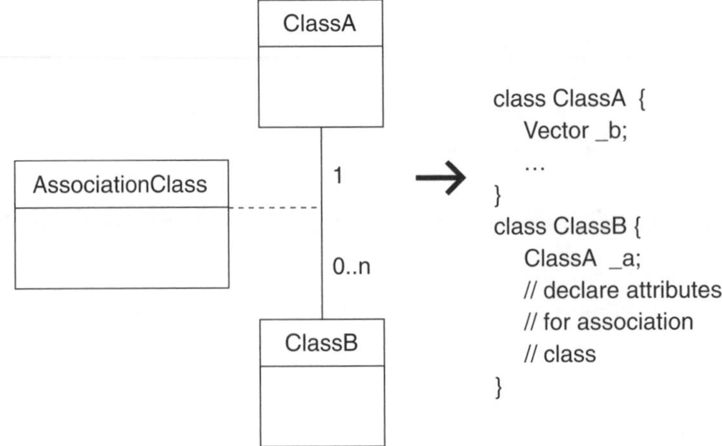

Figure 5.8. Implementation of the class on the *one* side

```
import java.util.Vector;
class ClassA {
    Vector _Bs;
    public ClassA() {
        _Bs = new Vector();
        ...
    }
    public Enumeration getBs() {
        return (_Bs.elements() );
    }
    // link a ClassB object to this object
    public void addB(ClassB b) {
        _Bs.add(b);
    }
    // remove the link between ClassB object to this
    // object
    public void removeB(ClassB b) {
        _Bs.remove(b);
    }
    // other functions for searching objects in the
    // vector
    ...
} // ClassA
```

Qualified Associations

A qualified association can be implemented by a hashtable or other types of data structures which support searching by key values. The hashtable is declared on the same side as the qualifier, which is used as the key of the hashtable (see Figure 5.9).

Figure 5.9. Implementation of a one-to-many qualified association

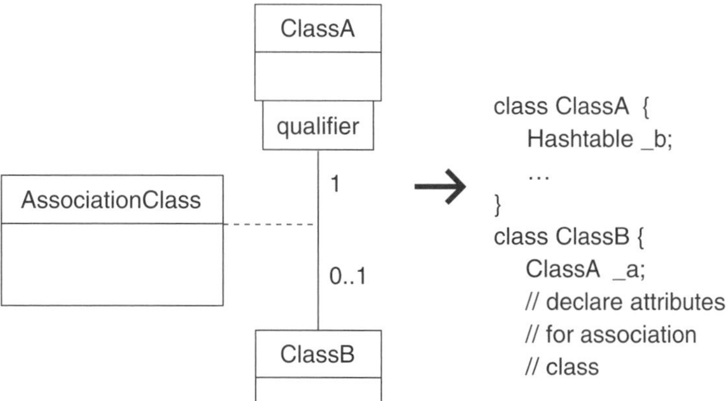
ClassA
qualifier
1
AssociationClass
0..1
ClassB
class ClassA {
Hashtable _b;
...
}
class ClassB {
ClassA _a;
// declare attributes
// for association
// class
...
}

The Java class java.util.Hashtable implements the hashtable. The hashtable is used to store a collection of objects which are accessible by keys. To store and retrieve an object by a key, a key object is required. The key object needs to provide two methods: the *hashCode* method and the *equals* method. A sample implementation of the methods for adding, removing and searching objects in the hashtable are shown in Figure 5.10. Figure 5.11 shows the code for the implementation of the key object.

Many-to-many Association

A many-to-many association can be implemented in one of the following ways:

- If the association does not have additional attributes, we can use a vector or a hashtable on each side
- If the association has attributes, each link between associated objects will have a separate value for each attribute of the association. An object on one side may have associations with many objects on the other. Therefore, it is not possible to embed the association attributes on either side of the association. A distinct association class for holding the links between the objects is therefore needed. The association class can also be used to store additional attributes of the association

Figure 5.10. Sample implementation of qualified association

```
import java.util.Hashtable;
class ClassA {
    private Hashtable _Bs;
    public ClassA() {
        _Bs = new Hashtable();
    }
    public Enumeration getBs() {
        return (_Bs.elements() );
    }
    public void addB(ClassB b, int key) {
        _ClassBs.put(new Key (key), b);
    }
    public void removeClassB(ClassB b) {
        _ClassBs.remove(b);
    }
    public ClassB getClassB(int key) {
        return((ClassB) _Bs.get(new Key (key)));
    }
} // ClassA
```

Figure 5.11. Implementation of the Key class

```
class Key {
    int _key;
    public ClassB(int key) {
        _key = key
    }
    public boolean equals(Object obj) {
        if (obj instanceof Key)
            return (((Key) obj)._key == _key);
        else
            return(false);
    }
    public int hashCode() {
            return (_key);
    }
} // Key
```

The first method has already been covered in previous sections, so we shall illustrate the application of the second with the help of an example (see Figure 5.12). The example models the relationship between the *Person* and *School* classes. A person can enroll in many schools and a school can have many students.

Figure 5.12. A many-to-many association

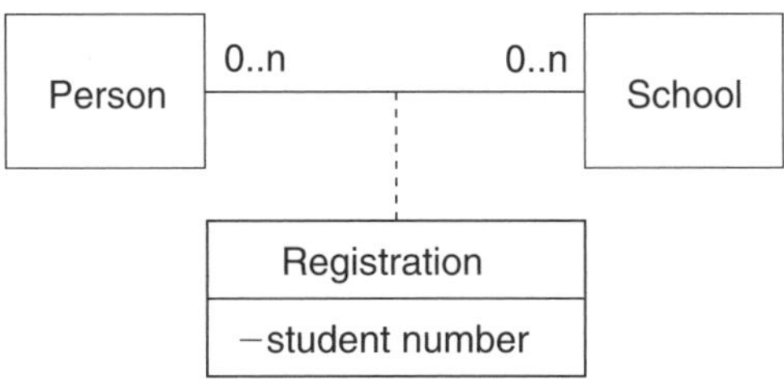

The association class keeps the links between the objects of the *Person* class and the objects of the *School* class. Each association object has three attributes: one attribute for the reference to the object of the *Person* class, one for the object of the *School* class and one for the *student number*. This is illustrated in Figure 5.13. The implementation of the association class is shown in Figure 5.14. Each school object or student object keeps links to its associated objects. The implementation of the *School* and *Student* classes are shown in Figures 5.15 and 5.16 respectively.

Figure 5.13. Association object of the Registration class

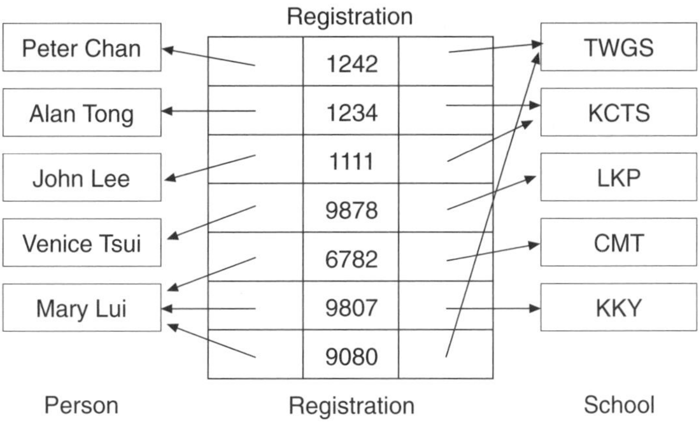

Registration

Peter Chan | 1242 | TWGS
Alan Tong | 1234 | KCTS
John Lee | 1111 | LKP
Venice Tsui | 9878 | CMT
Mary Lui | 6782 | KKY
9807
9080

Person | Registration | School

Figure 5.14. Implementation of many-to-many association with Registration class

```
Class Registration {
    private Person _student;
    private School _school;
    private int _studentNo;

    private Registration(Person student, School school, int studentNo) {
        _school = school;
        _student = student;
        _studentNo = studentNo;
    }

    static public void register(Person student, School school, int studentNo) {
        Registration reg = new Registration(student, school, studentNo);
        school.addRegistration(reg);
        student.addRegistration(reg);
    }

    public void deregister() {
        this._school.removeRegistration(this);
        this._student.removeRegistration(this);
    }

    public School getSchool() {
        return(_school);
    }

    public Person getStudent() {
        return(_student);
    }
} // Registration
```

Aggregation and Composition

Aggregation is a strong form of an association. It is used to model the relationship between a whole object and its parts. Aggregation can be implemented as a plain association.

Composition is a special case of aggregation where a whole object owns its parts for its lifetime, and a part object can exist only when the whole object exists. Hence, a composition requires that the parts of the whole object are

Figure 5.15. Implementation of *School* class

```
class School {
    private String _name;
    private Vector _registrations;

    public School(String name) {
        _name = name;
        _registrations = new Vector();
    }

    public void setName(String name) {
        _name = name;
    }

    public String getName() {
        return (_name);
    }

    public void addRegistration(Registration reg) {
        _registrations.add(reg);
    }

    public void removeRegistration(Registration reg) {
        _registrations.remove(reg);
    }

    public Enumeration getStudents() {
        int i;
        Vector students = new Vector();

        for (i = 0; i < _registrations.size(); i++)
            students.add (((Registration)
_registrations.elementAt(i)).getStudent());
        return (students.elements());
    }
} // School
```

deleted before the whole object can be deleted. We can implement this destruction behavior in the destructor of the whole object class. Such techniques can be applied to one-to-many associations to implement aggregation and composition relationships.

Figure 5.16. Implementation of *Person* class

```
class Person {
   private String _name;
   private Vector _registrations;

   public Person (String name) {
      _name = name;
      _registrations = new Vector();
   }

   String getName() {
      return (_name);
   }

   void setName(String name) {
      _name = name;
   }

   public void addRegistration(Registration reg) {
      _registrations.add(reg);
   }

   public void removeRegistration(Registration reg) {
      _registrations.remove(reg);
   }

   public Enumeration getSchools() {
      int i;
      Vector schools = new Vector();

      for (i = 0; i < _registrations.size(); i++)
         schools.add (((Registration)
_registrations.elementAt(i)).getSchool());
      return (schools.elements());
   }
}  // Person
```

Implementing Persistent Classes Using Relational Databases

Some objects have a long life span, longer than the invocation of one or more use cases. Such objects are known as persistent objects. For example, *customers* and *orders* are persistent objects in a mail order system. They need to be stored in permanent storage media such as a hard disk. Usually, a database system is used to implement persistent objects, and there are two choices of database technologies: object-oriented and relational databases. Nowadays, relational databases are more mature and very popular. If a relational database is used, the persistent classes need to be mapped onto database tables. We will illustrate this concept by implementing persistent classes using a relational database.

A Single Class

A class is mapped onto one or more database tables (see Figures 5.17 and 5.18). In object-oriented programming languages, objects are identified by reference, an internal pointer for locating the object in the memory space. When a class is mapped onto database tables, it is important to be able to uniquely identify an object in the database. Hence, we need to add an ID attribute to the database table for implementing an object reference. Normalization of database tables can be applied after the classes have been mapped onto database tables.

Figure 5.17. Mapping a persistent class onto a database table

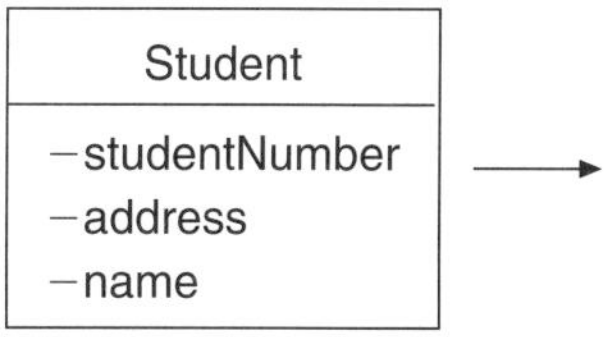

Student
−studentNumber −address −name

→

Student table		
Attribute name	Nulls?	Domain
student-number	N	ID
name	N	name
address	Y	address

Figure 5.18. SQL statement to create student table

```
CREATE TABLE Student (
        student_number        char (30)        not null,
        name                  char (30)        not null,
        address               char (30),
        PRIMARY KEY (student_number));
CREATE INDEX student_index_name ON Student (name);
```

One-to-many Association

A one-to-many association can be implemented in the following two ways:

- Embedding the attributes of the association in the table for the class on the *many* side. The table for the *many* side contains a key of the table for *one* side
- Creating a separate table for the association class

The former has the advantage of faster access time for the attributes of the association and fewer storage overheads. However, it is not applicable to a many-to-many association with an association class, as each link between associated objects has a separate pair of key values. An object on one side may associate with many objects on the other. Therefore, it is not possible to embed the pairs of key values in the tables for the associated classes. In this case, we need to implement the association as a separate table. Since it is not uncommon that the multiplicity of an association changes after the system has been developed, the first approach should be applied with care.

The latter is a more general approach and can support many-to-many associations. Hence, it is more applicable if there is a possibility that the one-to-many association may change to a many-to-many association in the future. We will discuss this approach below.

Consider a sample association shown in Figure 5.19. The association class is embedded in the person table as shown in Figure 5.20. Figure 5.21 shows the SQL statements for the declaration of the *Person* table.

Many-to-many Association

A many-to-many association can be implemented by creating a separate table for the association. For example, consider the many-to-many association shown in Figure 5.22. The association class is mapped onto a table, which has two attributes (keys) for linking the *Person* and *School* objects (see Figure 5.23). The registration table contains the keys of the *Person* table and the *School* table: *person_ID* and *school_ID*. These keys also form the key of the *Registration* table.

Qualified Many-to-many Association

A qualified many-to-many association can be implemented by creating a separate table. The table contains the primary keys of the associated classes and the qualifier. For example, consider the qualified many-to-many association shown in Figure 5.24. The association class is mapped onto a table, which has two attributes for linking the *Person* and *School* objects, with the qualifier as the attribute.

Figure 5.19. A sample one-to-many association

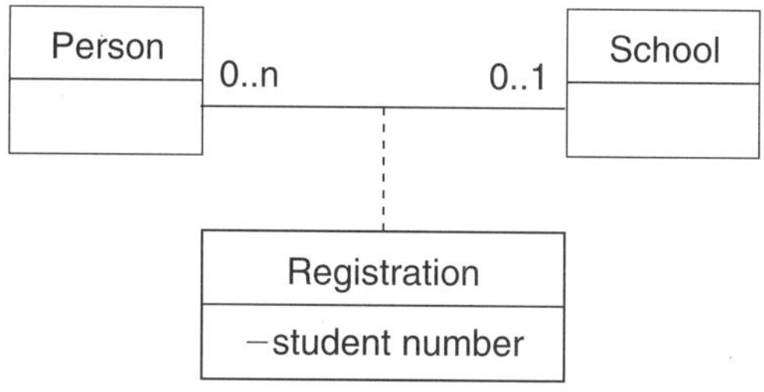

Figure 5.20. Merging the *Person* and the *Registration* tables

Person table		
Attribute name	Nulls?	Domain
person-ID	N	ID
school-ID	Y	ID
student-number	Y	String
student-name	N	name

Figure 5.21. Implementation of one-to-many association using SQL

```
CREATE TABLE Person (
        person_ID           char (30)     not null,
        school_ID           char (30)     not null,
        person_name         char (30)     not null,
        student_number      char (30),
        PRIMARY KEY         (person_ID),
        FOREIGN KEY         (school_ID) REFERENCES
                            School (school_ID));

CREATE INDEX Registration_index_person ON Person (person_name);
CREATE INDEX Registration_index_school ON Person (school_ID);
```

Figure 5.22. A sample many-to-many association

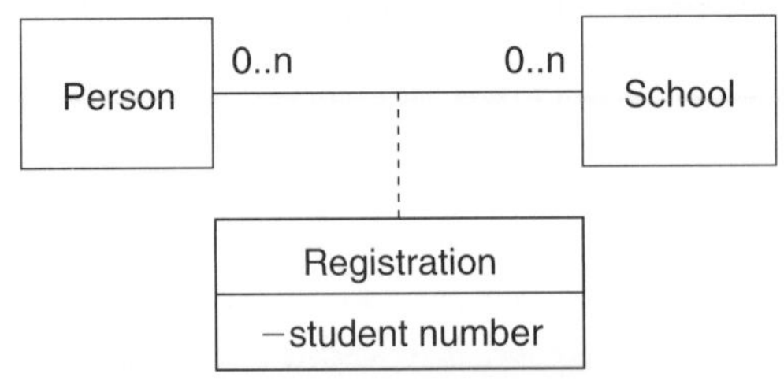

Figure 5.23. Implementation of sample many-to-many association

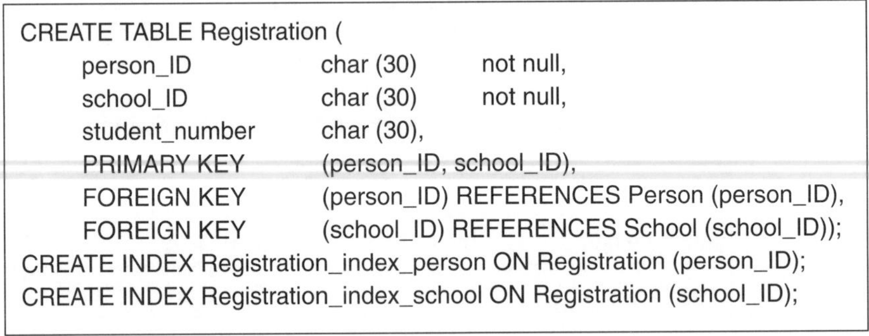

```
CREATE TABLE Registration (
      person_ID             char (30)      not null,
      school_ID             char (30)      not null,
      student_number        char (30),
      PRIMARY KEY           (person_ID, school_ID),
      FOREIGN KEY           (person_ID) REFERENCES Person (person_ID),
      FOREIGN KEY           (school_ID) REFERENCES School (school_ID));
CREATE INDEX Registration_index_person ON Registration (person_ID);
CREATE INDEX Registration_index_school ON Registration (school_ID);
```

Figure 5.24. Qualified many-to-many association

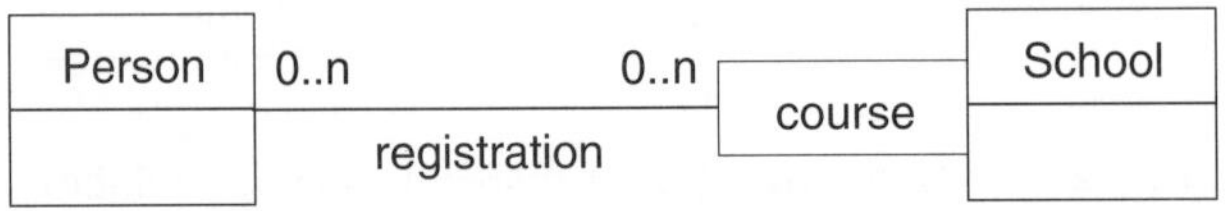

Figure 5.25 Table model of qualified association

Registration table		
Attribute name	Nulls?	Domain
person-ID	N	ID
school-ID	N	ID
course	N	course name

Figure 5.26. SQL implementation of qualified association

```
CREATE TABLE Registration (
        person_ID           char (30)       not null,
        school_ID           char (30)       not null,
        course              char (30),
        PRIMARY KEY         (person_ID, school_ID, course),
        FOREIGN KEY         (person_ID) REFERENCES Person,
        FOREIGN KEY         (school_ID) REFERENCES School);
CREATE INDEX Registration_index_person ON Registration (person_ID);
CREATE INDEX Registration_index_school_course ON Registration (school_ID, course);
```

N-ary Associations

Like a many-to-many association, an *N*-ary association can be implemented as a separate table with the primary keys of the associated classes as attributes. For example, the *N*-ary association in Figure 5.27 is mapped onto the table model in Figure 5.28. The *Timetable* table contains the keys of the *Class*, *Room*, *Teacher* and *Subject* tables. These keys also form the key of the *Timetable* table.

Generalization

There are several methods for mapping a generalization hierarchy of classes:

- Mapping one class to one table
- Replicating attributes in subclasses
- Replicating attributes of all subclasses in the root superclass

We shall illustrate these methods using an example. Figure 5.29 shows a simple inheritance hierarchy with one superclass and two subclasses. Both the student and teacher have *name* as their attribute. The student class has *year* as additional attribute, while the teacher has *position* and *expertise* as its additional attributes.

Mapping One Class to One Table

This method directly maps a class in the hierarchy onto a separate table. The tables of the hierarchy have a common ID (key) as attribute, which is used to identify an object's data. An object's data may be stored in more than one table. This method is fully extensible for adding new subclasses to the hierarchy. Furthermore, this method can also support multiple inheritance.

Figure 5.27. An *N*-ary association

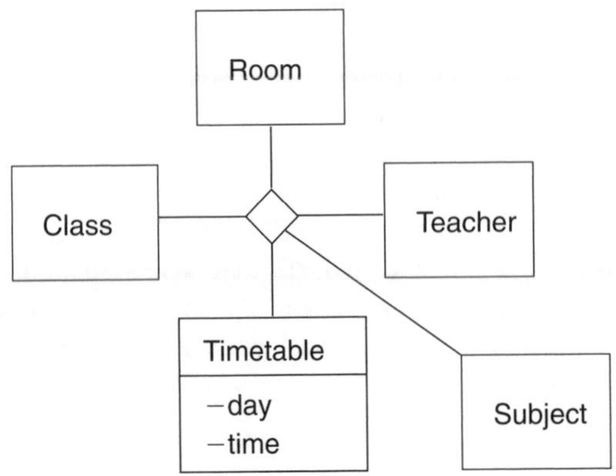

Figure 5.28. Table model of the *N*-ary association

Timetable table		
Attribute name	Nulls?	Domain
class-ID	N	ID
teacher-ID	N	ID
Room-ID	N	ID
Subject-ID	N	ID
Day	Y	Day
Time	Y	Time

Figure 5.29. A generalization hierarchy

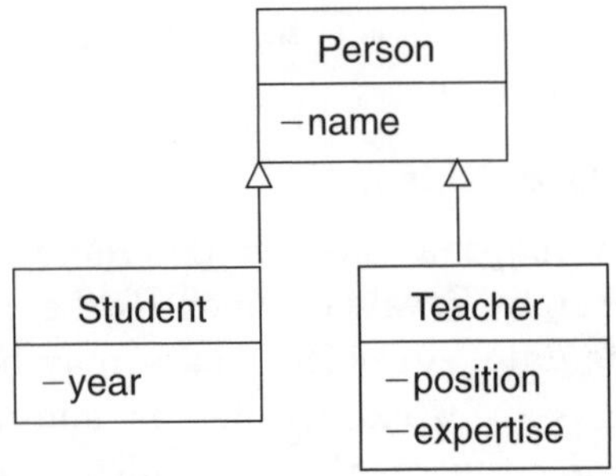

However, its disadvantage is that access to an object's data is relatively slow. The example generalization hierarchy (see Figure 5.29) is mapped onto three separate tables: *Person*, *Student* and *Teacher* (see Figures 5.30 to Figure 5.32). Each table contains the primary key *person-ID* as the attribute for identifying the object's data. Note that the *Student* (or *Teacher*) object is stored in two records: one in the *Person* table and the other in the *Student* (or *Teacher*) table. To allow easy access to the individual subclasses, we will also create views for the *Student* and *Teacher* classes (see Figure 5.33).

Figure 5.30. Table model for *Person* class

Person table		
Attribute name	Nulls?	Domain
person-ID	N	ID
person-name	N	name
person-type	N	person-type

Figure 5.31. Table model for *Student* class

Student table		
Attribute name	Nulls?	Domain
person-ID	N	ID
year	Y	year

Figure 5.32. Table model for *Teacher* class

Teacher table		
Attribute name	Nulls?	Domain
person-ID	N	ID
position	Y	job-position
expertise	Y	subject-expertise

Figure 5.33. SQL implementation of views for *Teacher* and *Student* classes

```
Create view TeacherView
as select Person.*, Teacher.*,
from Person, Teacher,
where (Person.person-ID = Teacher.person-ID);

Create view StudentView
as select Person.*, Student.*,
from Person, Student,
where (Person.person-ID = Student.person-ID);
```

Replicating Attributes in Subclasses

In this method, we eliminate all superclasses and replicate the superclass attributes in subclasses. We then map the subclasses onto tables. This method is useful if we frequently search or access individual subclasses. For example, the *Teacher* and *Student* classes in Figure 5.29 are mapped onto two separate table models, with the attributes of the *Person* class replicated in them (see Figures 5.34 and 5.35). The superclass *Person* is implemented as a view (see Figure 5.36).

Figure 5.34. Table model for *Teacher* class

Teacher table		
Attribute name	Nulls?	Domain
person-ID	N	ID
person-name	N	name
person-type	N	person-type
position	Y	job-position
expertise	Y	subject-expertise

Replicating Attributes in the Root Superclass

The whole class hierarchy is mapped onto a single table which contains the attributes of all the classes under the hierarchy. In other words, the root superclass contains the attributes of all its subclasses. The advantage of this method is the fast access time. However, a lot of storage resources are wasted if the subclasses contain many additional attributes. For example, the whole

Figure 5.35. Table model for *Student* class

Student table		
Attribute name	Nulls?	Domain
person-ID	N	ID
person-name	N	name
person-type	N	person-type
year	Y	year

Figure 5.36. *Person* class implemented as a view

```
create view person as
   select person-ID, person-name, person-type from Student
union
   select person-ID, person-name, person-type from Teacher
```

class hierarchy in Figure 5.29 is mapped onto a single table in Figure 5.37. The *Person* table contains all the attributes that can be found in every class in the hierarchy. In this case, the attributes of the *Person*, *Student* and *Teacher* classes.

Figure 5.37 Table model of a single class representing the whole class hierarchy

Person table		
Attribute name	Nulls?	Domain
person-ID	N	ID
person-name	N	name
person-type	N	person-type
position	Y	job-position
expertise	Y	subject-expertise
year	Y	year

Implementing Activity Diagrams

An activity diagram is used to represent a sequence of actions performed in a use case or procedure. It can also be used to model an algorithm, the computation flow of a control object or a subsystem. In this case, an activity diagram may be translated as executable program code if the diagram contains sufficient details. In general, there are two approaches for implementing an activity diagram:

- Implementing the control flow using the location within a program to hold the state of an object. Control statements, such as if-then-else and while statements, are used to implement the necessary branching and looping of the control flow of the activity diagram
- Implementing the control flow as a state machine

We shall illustrate the application of the former approach in this section and the latter in the next. The following are the general rules to translate the elements of an activity diagram into program code:

- Action state. It is translated to statements of actions, such as method calls, and computational statements.
- Conditional branch. It is translated to an if-then-else statement.
- Concurrent branch. It is translated to threads for each additional control flow.
- Loop. A loop in the activity diagram is translated to a while-loop statement.

Given an activity diagram, first identify the main execution path for the normal scenario. Starting from the initial state, identify and record the path through the activity diagram that corresponds to the expected sequence of actions. Then identify the alternative execution paths, which branch off from the main execution path and rejoin the main path at the next action state (see Figure 5.38). These paths will become the if statements.

Note: If the activity diagram is modeling the control object of a use case, such execution paths usually correspond to the extension use cases.

Next, identify the alternative paths (the paths that branch off from the main path). These paths will become if-then-else statements (see Figure 5.38). Finally, identify loop-back paths that branch off from the main path and rejoin it at an earlier location (see Figure 5.38). These loop-back paths will become loop statements.

Figure 5.38. Translating activity diagram to implementation

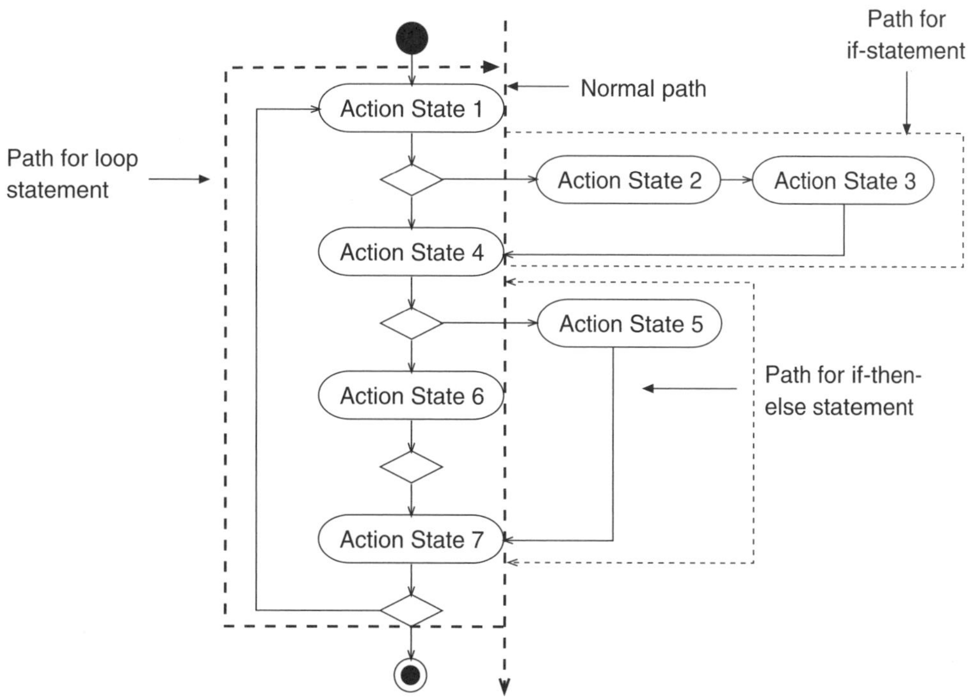

To illustrate the translation, consider the activity diagram in Figure 5.39 which models the behavior of the control object of a vending machine. In this figure, the normal execution path includes the action states *wait for coin*, *wait for selection*, *dispense soft drink* (concurrent action) and *dispense change* (concurrent). There are several loop-back paths: path A which is from the conditional branch to the *wait for coin* action state, path B from the conditional branch to the *wait for selection* action state, path C from the *dispense coins* to the *wait for coin* action state, and path D from the concurrent action state to the *wait for coin* action state.

The activity diagram is translated to program code as shown in Figure 5.40.

Implementing State Diagrams

A state diagram is typically used to model the dynamic behavior of a subsystem, a control object or an entity object. There are two approaches to implement a state diagram:

Figure 5.39. Activity diagram of controller of simplified vending machine

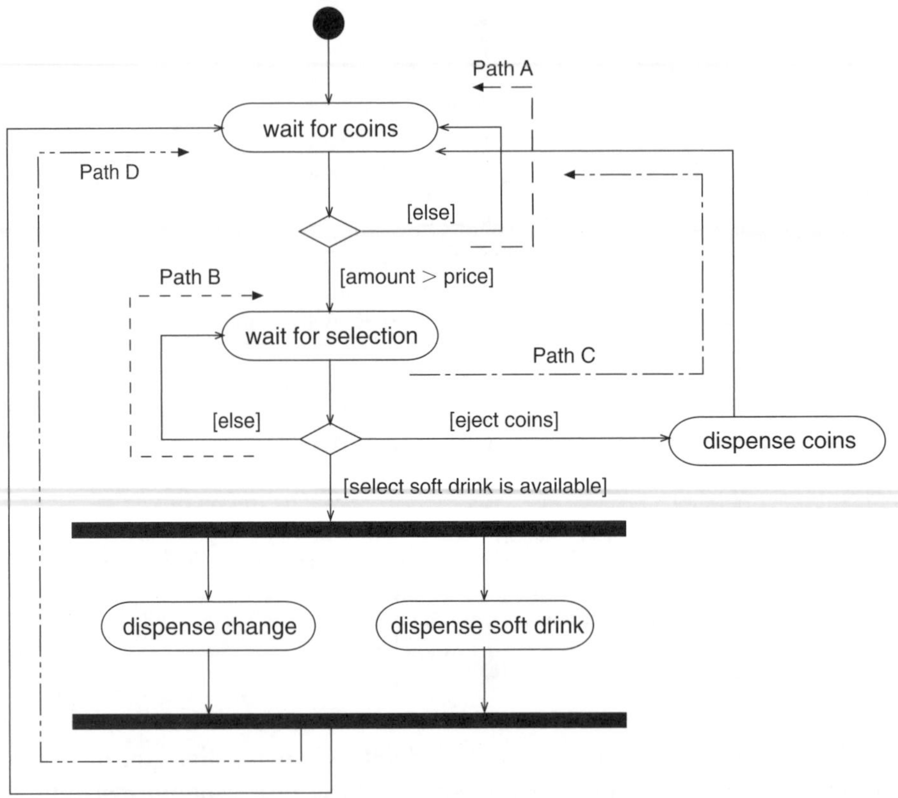

- Using the location within a program to hold the state
- Using an explicit attribute to hold the state

The first approach is suitable for implementing the state diagram of an active entity such as an active object or a subsystem. It is because the active entity already has its own control flow logic through the use of control statements such as if-then-else and while statements. This approach is similar to activity diagram implementation that has been described previously.

The second approach is suitable for implementing the state diagram of an inactive entity. We can implement the state diagram by applying the techniques below:

- Map the state diagram onto a class
- Add a state attribute for storing the state information

Figure 5.40. Pseudocode for implementing activity diagram of vending machine

```
while (true) {
    amount = 0.0;
    while (amount < price) {
        wait for a coin;
        add coin value to amount;
    }
    show all available soft drink;
    while (selection  is not done) {
        wait for selection from user;
        if selection is "eject coins" {
            dispense coins;
            set selection to "done";
        }
        else if selection is a valid soft drink {
            dispense change and dispense soft drink concurrently;
            set selection to "done";
        }
    }
}
```

- Map an event to a method and embed all required state transitions and actions of the event in the method
- For a composite state with sequential substates, it may be necessary to create a nested (inner) class for implementing the sequential substates. The parent state machine can then invoke the method of the nested class to handle transitions within the nested state diagram. Another way to implement the composite state is to transform the parent state diagram to eliminate the composite state so that it becomes a flat level state diagram.
- For a composite state with concurrent substates, create a nested class for implementing each substate. The implementation is similar to that for nested state diagrams. The composite state is exited when all the concurrent substates reach their final states.

In other words, the state diagram is implemented by a set of methods to handle an event. The methods will update the state attributes and perform appropriate actions when a transition is fired. For each transition, map the event to become a method, containing the logic for checking the guard conditions and the associated actions (see Figure 5.41). If an event appears in several transitions from different states, a switch statement is usually required to determine which transition should take place.

Figure 5.41. From a transition to its implementation

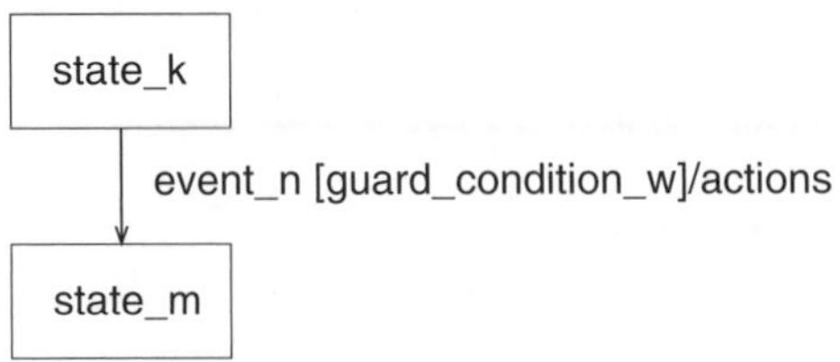


```
public void event_n(... .) {
    switch (state) {
        case state_k: // transit from state_k to state_m
            if (guard_condition_w) { // evaluate the guard condition state = state_m;
                perform the required actions of the transition;
            }
            break;
        case state_v:
            ...
            ...
    }
}
```

Example: Implementing a Simple State Diagram

Suppose we want to implement the state diagram of the control object of a vending machine as a passive object (an object without its own thread). In fact, we develop the state diagram by translating the activity diagram shown in Figure 5.39 to an equivalent state diagram (see Figure 5.42) and then simplify it by eliminating the concurrent substates for dispensing soft drinks and change. Figure 5.43 shows the implementation of the vending machine's control object.

Example: Implementing a State Diagram with Sequential Substates

To illustrate the implementation of sequential substates, modify the previous example by grouping the dispensing soft drink state and dispensing change state to a substate as shown in Figure 5.44. Consider the dispensing substate as another state machine and implement it as an inner class within the parent state machine (see Figures 5.45 and 5.46).

Figure 5.42. State diagram for control object of vending machine

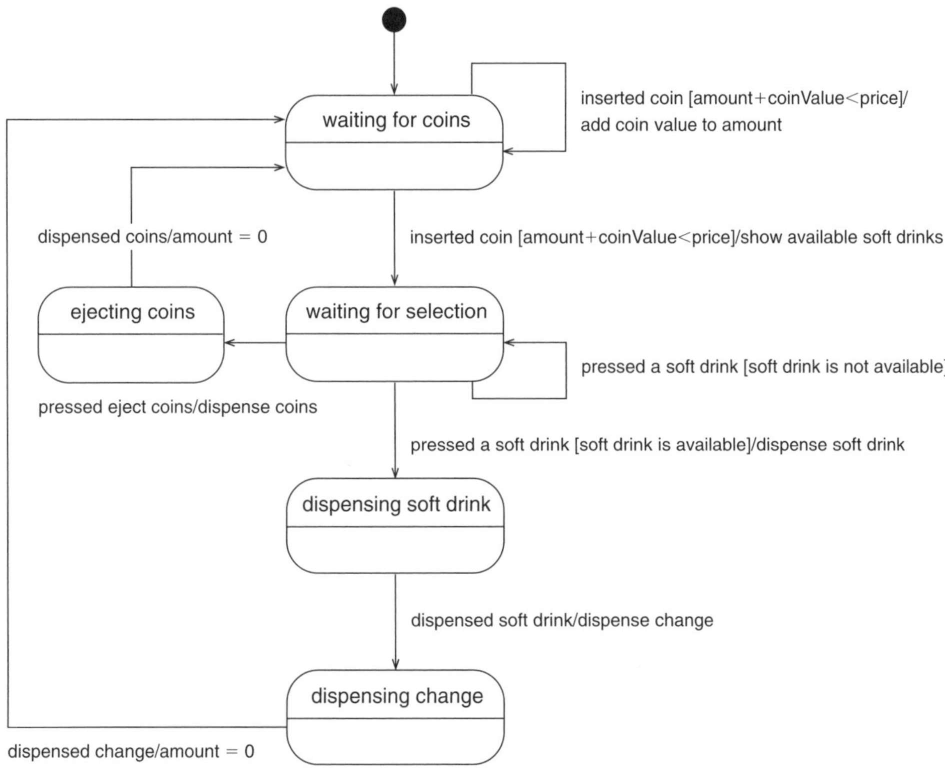

Figure 5.43. Mapping an event on to a method of state machine

```
class VendingMachineControl {

    int _state;
    float _amount, _price;
    static final int WaitingCoin = 1;
    static final int WaitingSelection = 2;
    static final int DispensingSoftDrink = 3;
    static final int DispensingChange = 4;
    static final int EjectingCoins = 5;

    public VendingMachineControl(float price) {
        _amount = 0;
        _state = WaitingCoin;
        _price = price;
    }

    public void insertedCoin(float coinValue) {

        if (_state == WaitingCoin)
        {
            _amount += coinValue;
            if (amount >= price) { // fire transition
                _state = WaitingSelection;
                show available soft drinks;
            }
        }
    } // insertedCoin
    // Declarations of methods for other events
    ...
    ...
} // VendingMachineControl
```

Figure 5.44 A state diagram with sequential substates

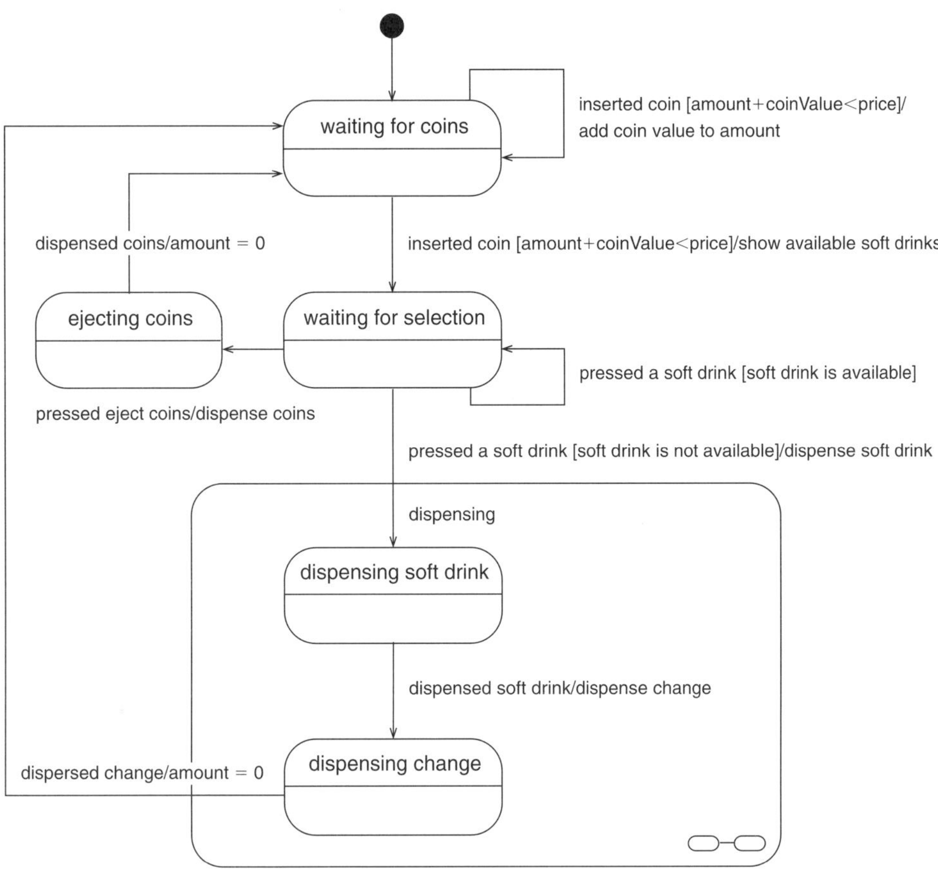

Figure 5.45. Implementation of *dispensing* substate

```
class dispenseControl {
    int _state;
    static final int DispensingSoftDrink = 1;
    static final int DispensingChange = 2;
    static final int Complete = 3;
    public dispenseControl() {

        _state = DispensingSoftDrink;
    }
    public boolean dispensedSoftDrink() {

        if (_static == DispensingSoftDrink) {
            _state = DispensingChange;
            dispense change;
        }

        return false;
    }
    public boolean dispensedChange() {
        if (_state == DispensingChange) {
            _state = Complete;
            return true;
        }
        return false;
    }
} // class dispenseControl
```

Figure 5.46. Implementation of control object of vending machine

```
class VendingMachineControl {

    declaration of state attribute, constants, other attributes;
    declaration of inner class dispenseControl;
    public VendingMachineControl(float price) {

        _amount = 0;
        _state = WaitingCoin;
        _price = price;
        _substate = new DispenseControl();
    }
    public void dispensedSoftDrink() {

        if (_state == Dispensing) {
            boolean isComplete = _substate.dispensedSoftDrink();
        }
    }
    public boolean dispensedChange() {

        if (_state == Dispensing) {
            boolean isComplete = _substate.dispensedChange();
            if (isComplete) {
                amount = 0;
                _state = WaitingCoin;
            }
        }
    }
    declaration of other methods;
} // VendingMachineControl
```

Implementing Interaction Diagrams

An interaction diagram models the behavior of a group of objects that work together to achieve a user goal. There are two kinds of interaction diagrams: sequence and collaboration diagrams. Both diagrams are commonly used to model a set of collaborating objects involved in a scenario. Sequence diagrams are most suitable for modeling the sequence of actions performed by the collaborating objects, while collaboration diagrams are useful for modeling the structural relationships between the collaborating objects. In fact, sequence and collaboration diagrams are semantically equivalent. Hence, we will only discuss the implementation of the sequence diagram here as the implementation techniques discussed can also be applied to collaboration diagrams.

Sequence Diagrams

In a sequence diagram, the collaborating objects communicate with each other through messages. A message is an invocation of a method or an actual message sent from the originating object to the target object. When an object receives a message, it may in turn send one or more messages to other objects.

We can translate a sequence diagram into code by using the following techniques:

- Translate a message to an appropriate method call. For example, a creation message is translated to a call to the constructor of the target object's class, i.e. a new statement in Java
- Implement methods for handling incoming messages in the target object's class (see Figure 5.47)

Figure 5.47. Mapping messages in sequence diagram to implementation

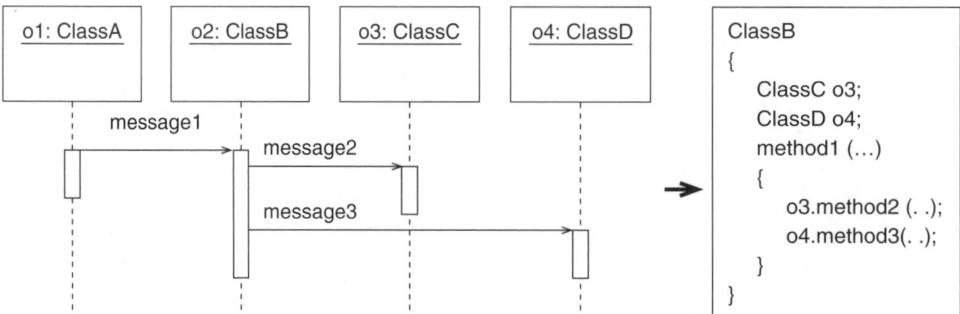

- Map conditional branchings to conditional statements such as if-else statements
- Implement active objects using threads
- Map concurrent branching using concurrent threads

Case Study: A Lift Control System

In previous sections, the basic techniques for implementing individual UML diagrams were discussed. Now, we will illustrate how all these techniques can be applied to a real-life problem. The following is a description of a simplified lift control system.

A lift consists of a door, a motor and a lift controller. The lift controller is responsible for controlling the lift system (see the class diagram in Figure 5.48). Passengers interact with the lift system by pressing buttons on individual floors or on the control panel inside the lift. Normally, the lift stays on the ground floor (*0*-th floor) of a building. If a passenger enters the lift and presses the button for the k-th floor, the lift will rise to the k-th floor. When the lift arrives at requested floor (say k-th floor), it opens the door for M seconds and then closes it. The lift then becomes idle.

Figure 5.48. Analysis class diagram of lift control system

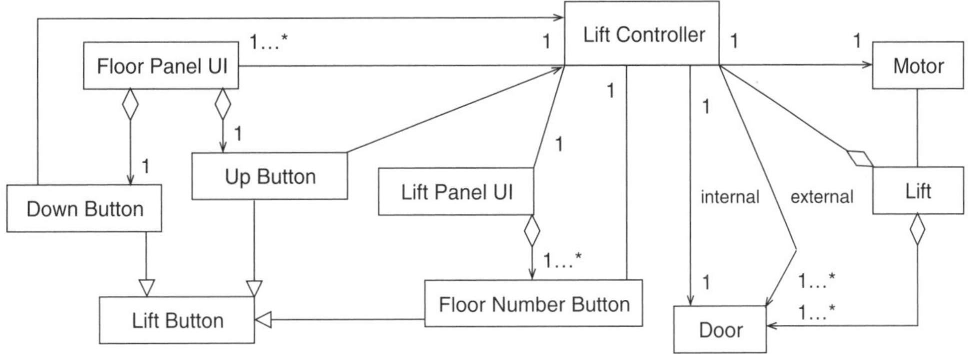

A passenger on m-th floor calls a lift by pressing the *up* or *down* button. The lift will move to the m-th floor and open the door on arrival. The passenger requests to go to a particular floor by pressing the corresponding button on the control panel inside the lift. If there is no passenger interaction on the control panel within M seconds, then the lift will return to the ground floor.

With the analysis class diagram and the problem statement, we will be able to develop sequence diagrams to further elaborate the dynamic behaviors of the system in different scenarios. The sequence diagrams can then be used to develop the state diagram of the lift controller, which is the control object of the whole system.

The following is the first scenario of the lift control system.

Scenario 1

A passenger, Peter, walks into the lift lobby on the ground floor of the building. He presses the UP button and waits for the lift's arrival. On arrival, the lift opens, he enters and presses the sixth floor button on the control panel inside the lift. The lift closes and goes up until it arrives on the sixth floor. The lift opens and Peter walks out of the lift. The lift waits for a short while (ten seconds), closes and then goes down to the ground floor. The lift will stay at the ground floor until further user interaction.

The sequence diagram for the first scenario is shown in Figure 5.49. It is developed by going through each step of the sequence of transactions of the scenario. For each step, the actor performs an action and the system responds accordingly. The actor's input and system's response will help to determine what internal actions are required inside the system. The actor's input is received by the boundary object(s). The boundary object will then send a message to the control object to handle the actor's input. Then the control object needs to send one or more messages to the entity object(s) to perform the actual required actions. Finally, the control object will send message(s) to the boundary object(s) to respond to the actor. The following is the sequence of actions for the scenario:

- Peter presses the UP button on the ground floor of the building. The press button event is sent to the lift controller. Now, consider what the lift system would do. Since the lift is on the ground floor, the lift controller should open the door.
- Peter presses the sixth floor button. The press button event is sent to the lift controller. The lift controller will then wait for timeout, close the door, controls the motor to go up and wait for the arrival event. When the lift arrives at the sixth floor, the lift controller will open the door. In the sequence of actions, the lift controller interacts with the door and the motor objects.

Figure 5.49. Sequence diagram for scenario 1

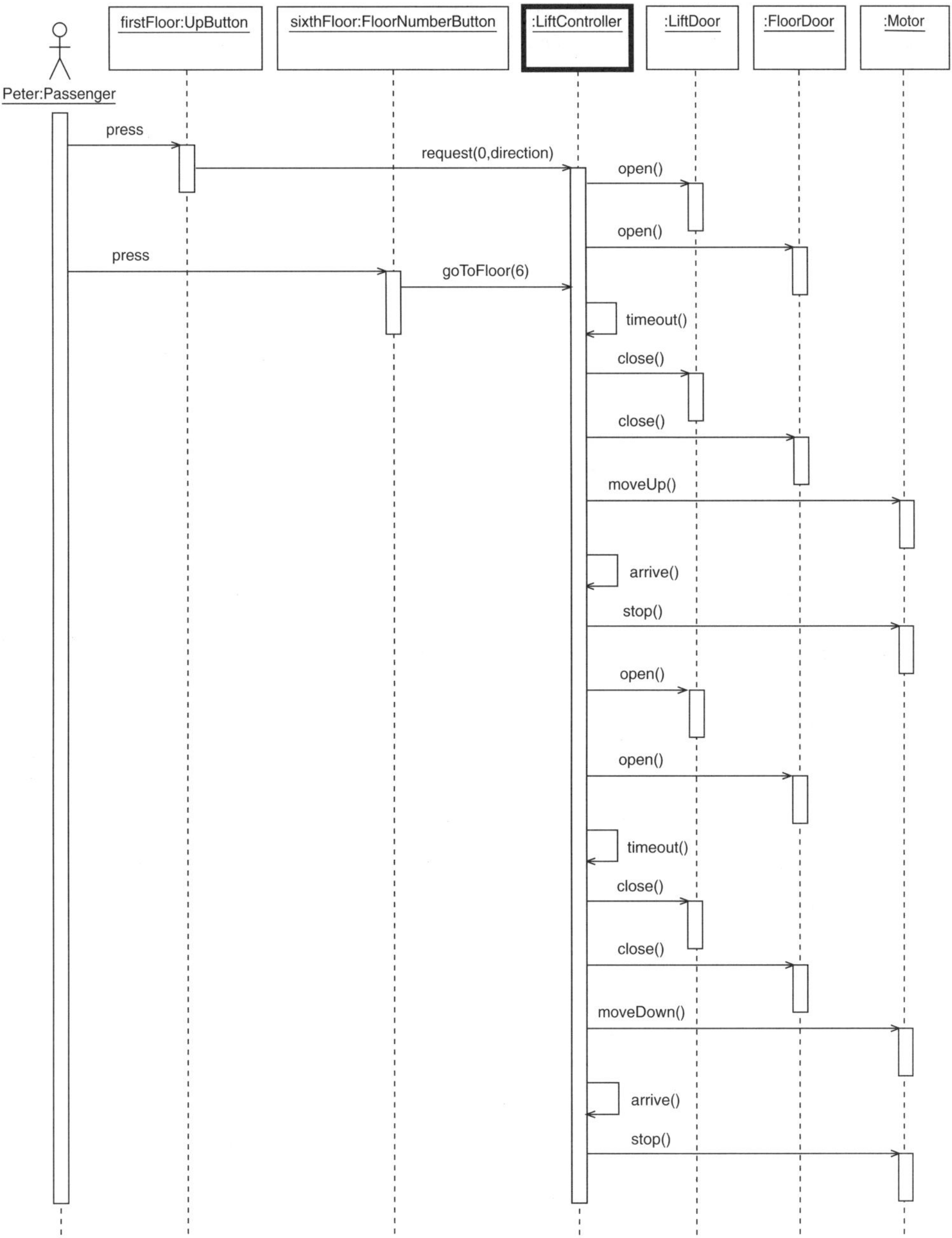

Based on the sequence diagram in Figure 5.49, develop a partial state diagram for the lift controller (Figure 5.50). Figure 5.51 illustrates a partial state diagram for the lift controller from the sequence diagram (Figure 5.49). Develop the state diagram of the lift controller or other control object by adopting the following process:

- Since a state represents a duration in time, treat the time between two consecutive incoming messages to the lift controller as a state.
- If an action takes a significant length of time to complete treat this period of time as a state. For example, the lift will take a significant length of time to go up or down. The time spent going up or down can be considered as a state.
- The controller should be in the state before the scenario takes place.
- The lift controller may transit from one state to another when it receives incoming messages or events. If the transition is not unconditional, we can determine the guard condition for the transition from the conditions of the scenario.

Figure 5.50. A partial state diagram for lift controller

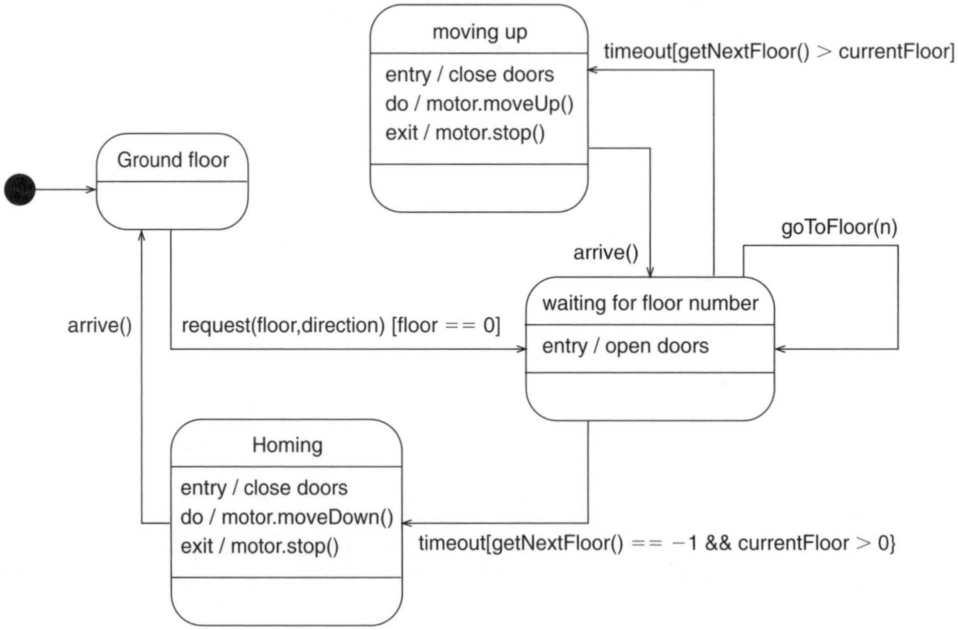

Figure 5.51. Partial state diagram from sequence diagram for lift controller

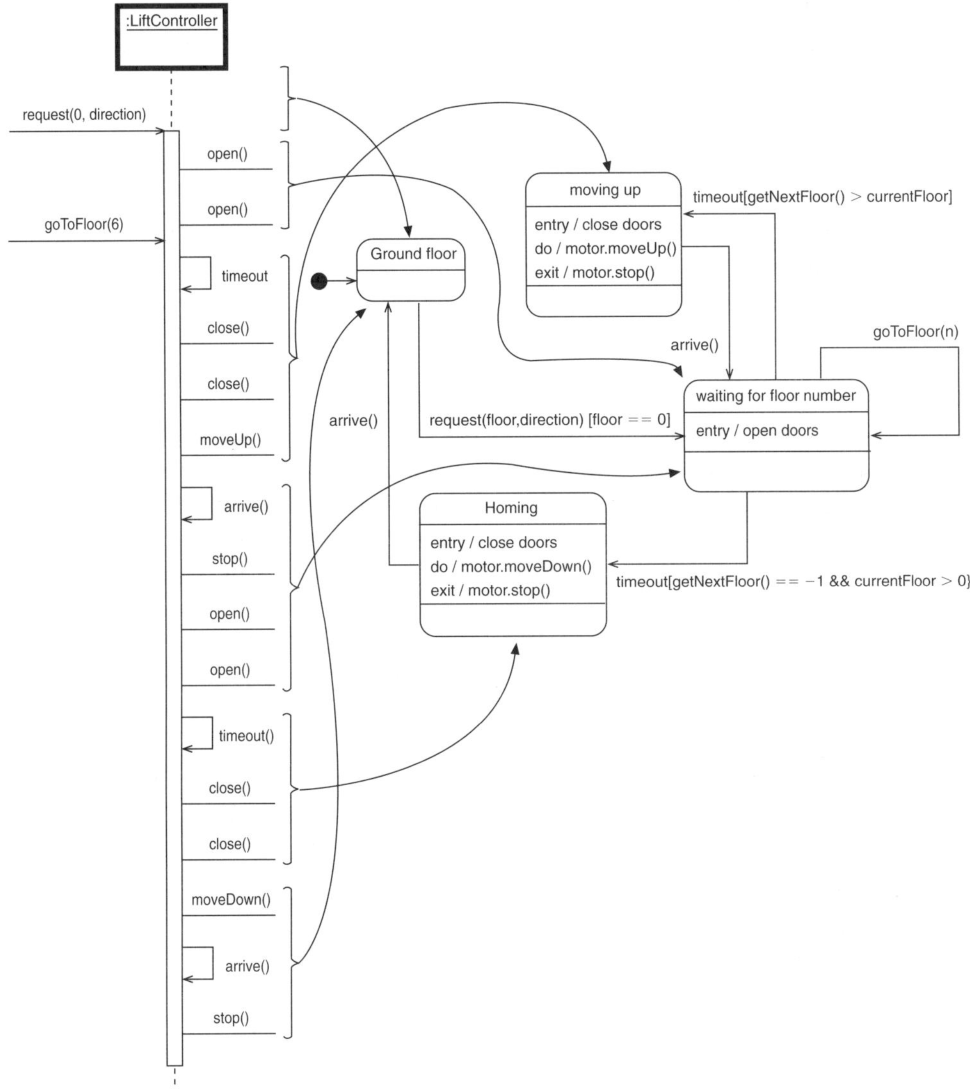

For example, the state diagram of the lift controller for Scenario 1 can be developed accordingly:

- Before any interaction occurs, the lift is on the ground floor with its doors closed; the lift controller is in the *ground floor* state before receiving any messages or events.
- When the lift controller receives the request message from the UP button on the ground floor, the lift controller opens the door and changes its state to *waiting for floor number*, where it waits for the passenger to press the target floor number. Note that the lift passenger may press the floor number which he/she is currently on.
- The passenger presses the sixth floor button and the lift controller will not do anything until the timeout event is received. Here, the lift controller's state does not change.
- When the lift controller receives the timeout event, the lift controller closes the door, moves the motor to the UP direction because the destination floor is higher then the current floor and then changes its state. Since the action of going up takes a significant length of time, we name this state as *moving up*. The guard condition is that the destination floor number is greater than the current floor.
- When the lift controller receives the arrival event, the lift stops the motor, opens the doors and waits for the passenger to press the destination floor again. Hence, the lift controller changes back to the *waiting for floor number* state.
- When there is no request (no passenger), the lift controller receives the timeout event and the lift controller will move the lift back to the ground floor. We name this state as *homing*.

Scenario 2

A passenger, Mary, is on the sixth floor of the building. She presses the DOWN button at the lift lobby to call for a lift and waits. The lift, which is on the ground floor, then goes up to the sixth floor. The lift stops at the sixth floor and opens. Mary walks into the lift and presses the ground floor button on the control panel in the lift. The lift closes, goes down and stops at the ground floor. The lift opens. It waits for a short while (ten seconds) and then closes the door.

The sequence diagram for Scenario 2 is shown in Figure 5.52. Based on the sequence diagram, develop a partial state diagram for the lift controller as shown in Figure 5.53. Figure 5.54 illustrates how to develop a partial state diagram for the lift controller from the sequence diagram Figure 5.52.

Figure 5.52. Sequence diagram for Scenario 2

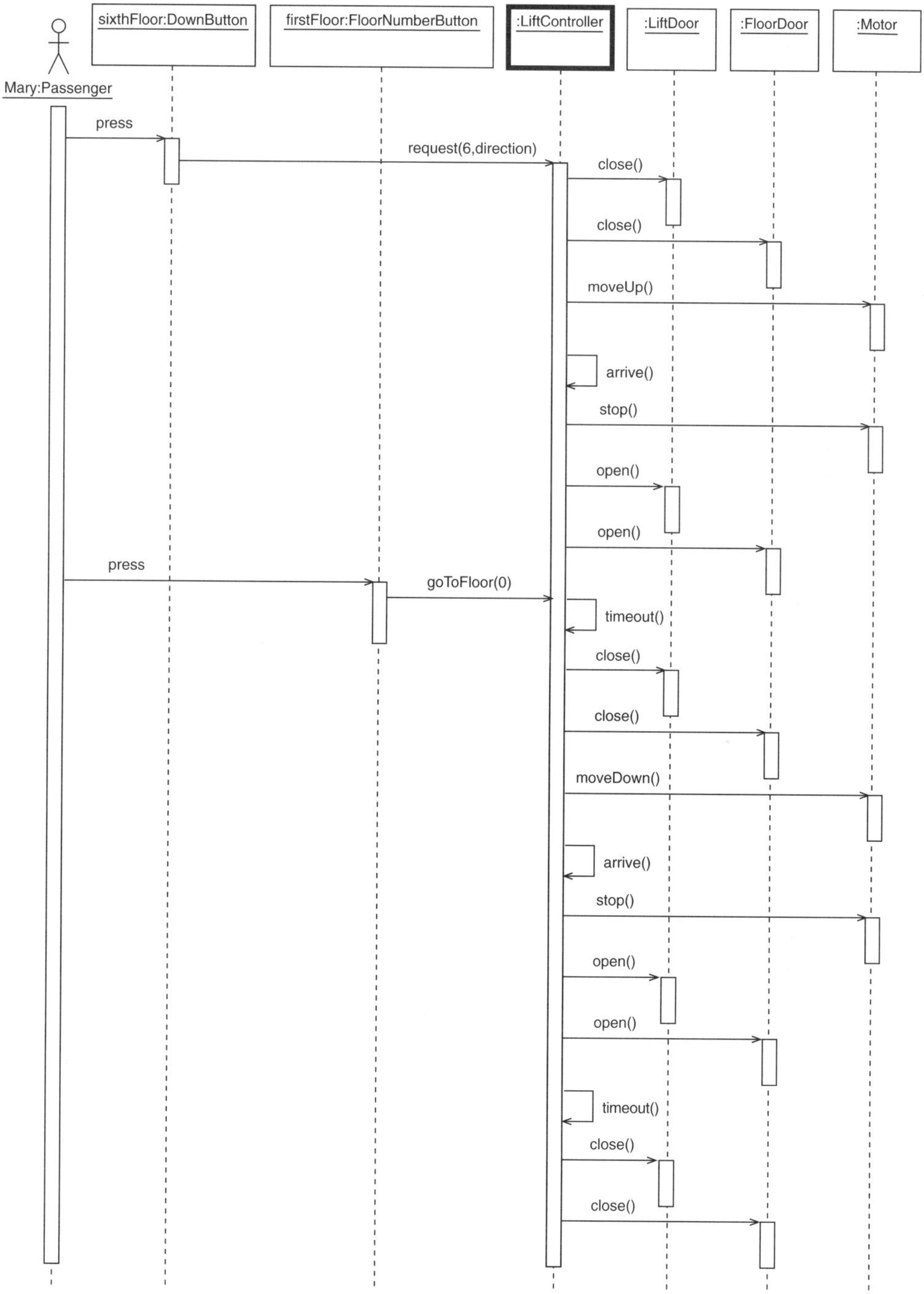

Mary:Passenger
sixthFloor:DownButton
firstFloor:FloorNumberButton
:LiftController
:LiftDoor
:FloorDoor
:Motor

press
request(6,direction)
close()
close()
moveUp()
arrive()
stop()
open()
open()
press
goToFloor(0)
timeout()
close()
close()
moveDown()
arrive()
stop()
open()
open()
timeout()
close()
close()

Figure 5.53. Partial state diagram for Scenario 2

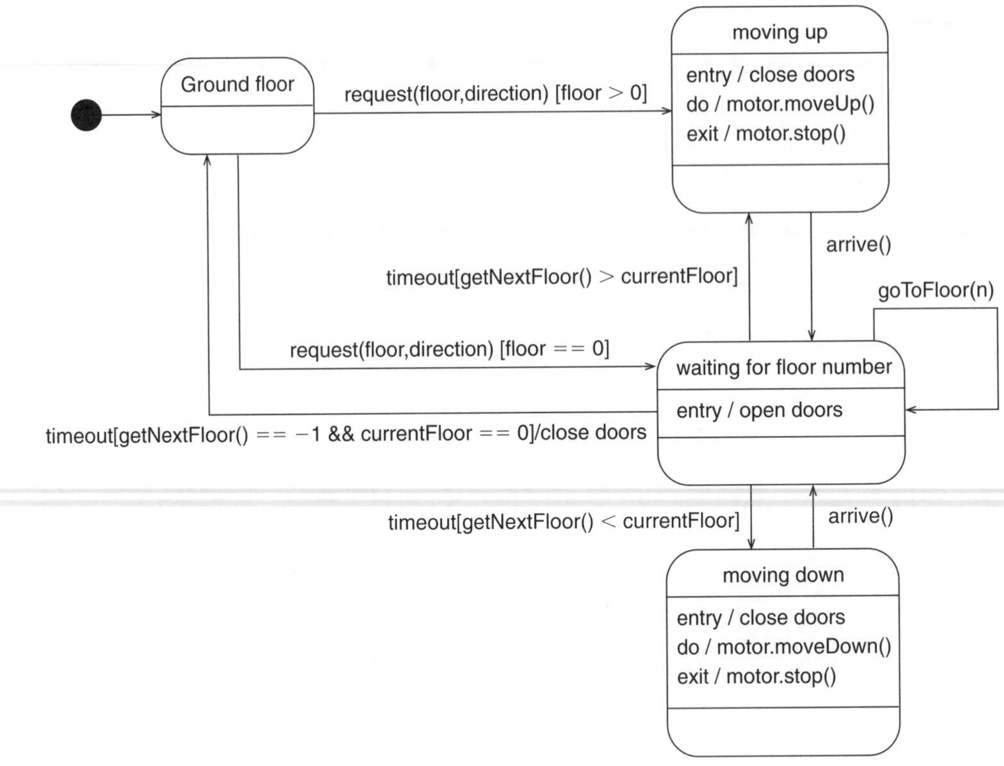

Figure 5.54. Developing a state diagram from sequence diagram for lift controller

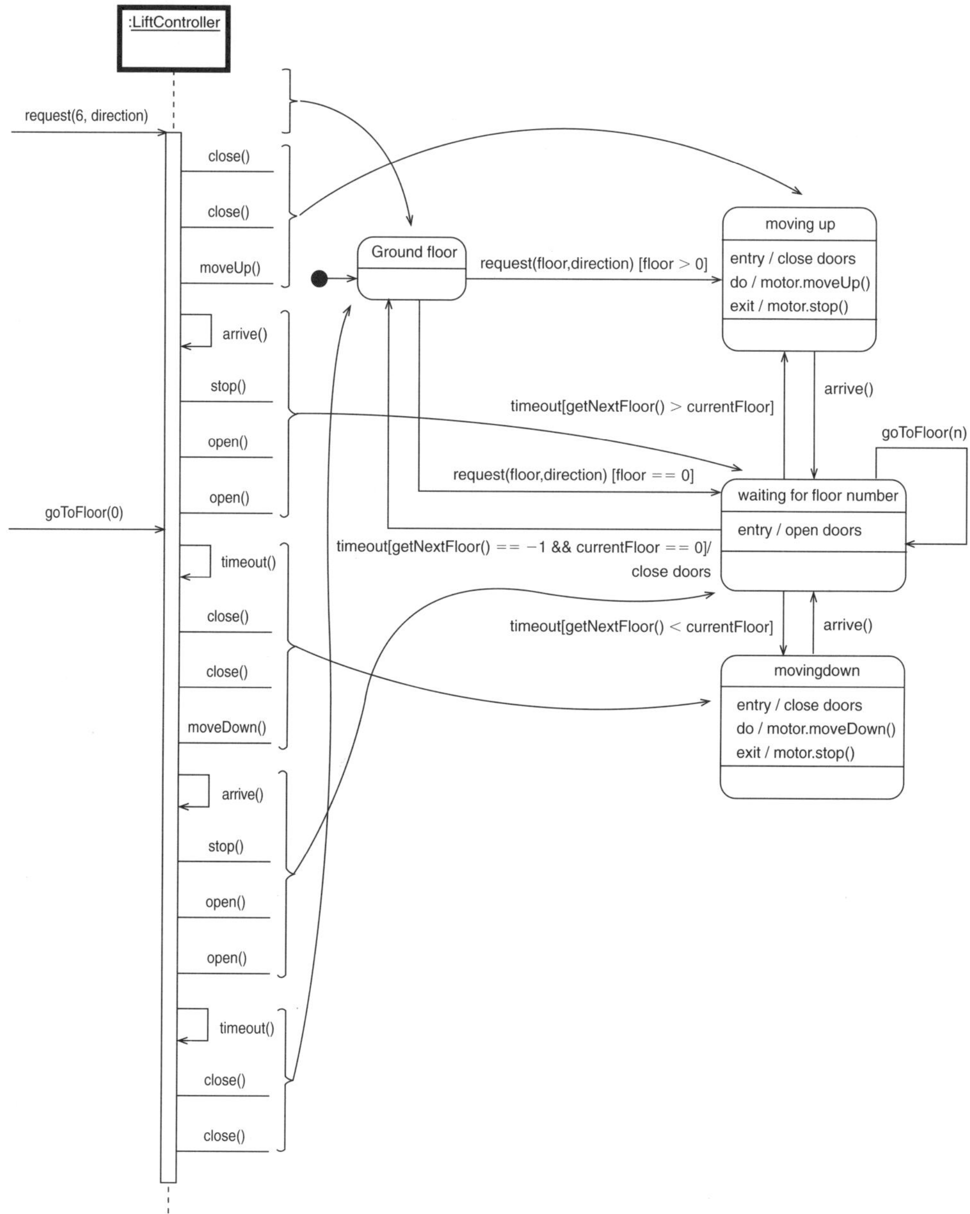

It is possible to develop the complete state diagram of the lift controller by combining all the state diagrams of different scenarios via the union of their states and transitions. If there are two transitions with the same source state, target state and event, combine these transitions to become a single transition with a guard condition which is the union of guard conditions of the original transitions. By combining Figures 5.50 and 5.53, we can develop the complete state diagram of the lift controller (see Figure 5.55).

Based on the sequence diagrams for the scenarios and the state diagram of the lift controller, the class diagram is refined to provide more information about the dynamic behavior of the system (see Figure 5.56). Methods are declared in individual classes to implement the messages received by individual classes in the sequence diagrams or state diagrams.

The complete source code of the lift control system in Java can be found in the Appendix.

Figure 5.55. State diagram of lift controller

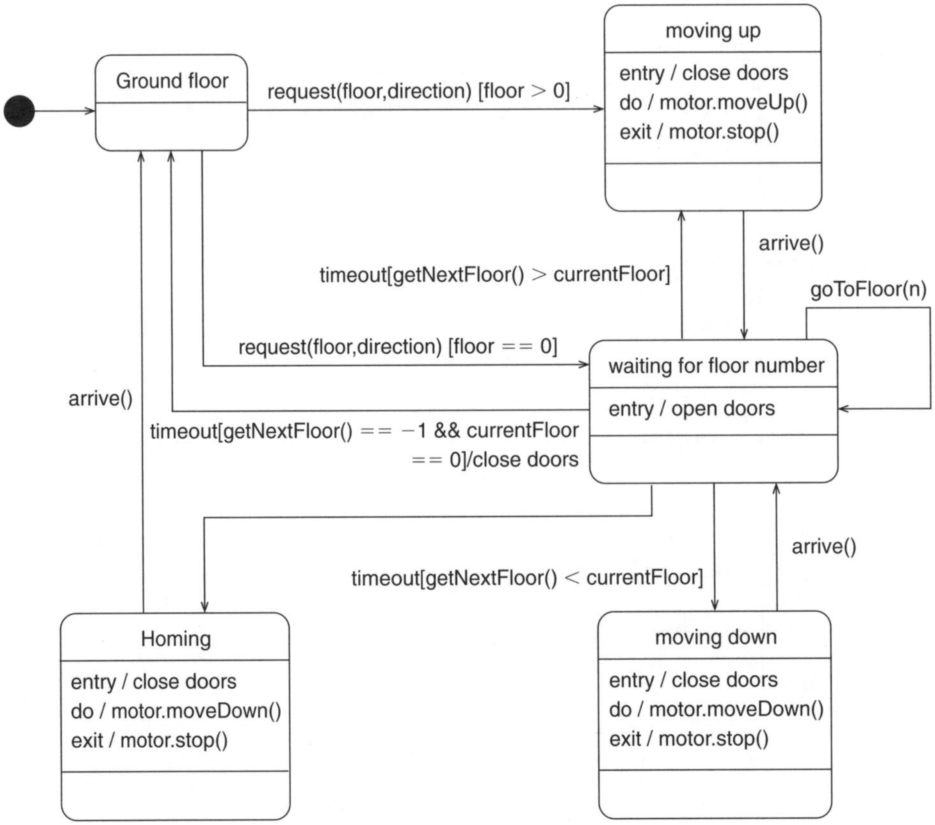

Ground floor

request(floor,direction) [floor > 0]

moving up

entry / close doors
do / motor.moveUp()
exit / motor.stop()

arrive()

timeout[getNextFloor() > currentFloor]

goToFloor(n)

request(floor,direction) [floor == 0]

waiting for floor number

entry / open doors

arrive()

timeout[getNextFloor() == −1 && currentFloor == 0]/close doors

arrive()

timeout[getNextFloor() < currentFloor]

Homing

entry / close doors
do / motor.moveDown()
exit / motor.stop()

moving down

entry / close doors
do / motor.moveDown()
exit / motor.stop()

Figure 5.56. Designing class diagram of lift control system

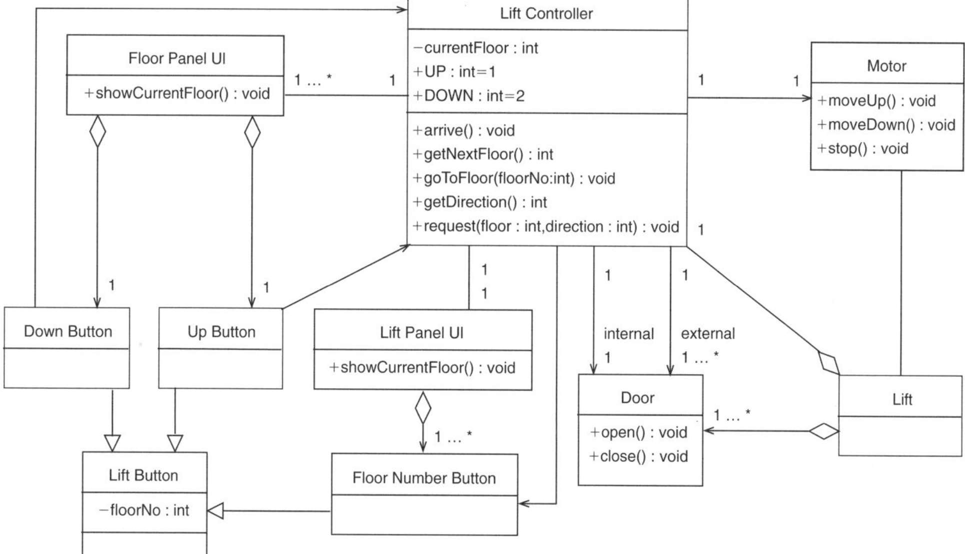

Summary

In this chapter, a number of techniques for the implementation of the more commonly used UML diagrams in Java were presented. We have described how to implement an individual class and the different kinds of associations between classes. Then we illustrated how to implement activity diagrams, state diagrams, sequence diagrams and collaboration diagrams. We have also shown how we can develop the state diagram of a control object from the sequence diagrams using the lift control system case study.

Exercises

Q1. Describe two ways to implement a one-to-many association between two classes. Discuss their pros and cons.

Q2. Using only two Java classes, write a Java program fragment for the implementation of the class diagram below. Include all the methods required for the implementation of the association.

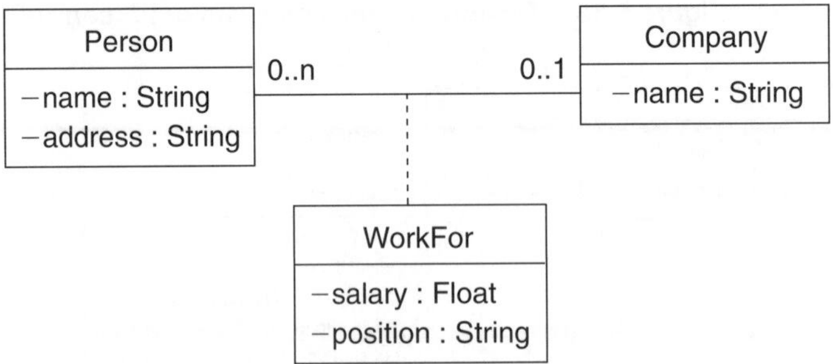

Q3. Complete the implementation of the control class for the vending machine example as described in this chapter (Figure 5.40). Write a driver program to test the control class.

Q4. Implement the design the class diagram for the vending machine as shown below.

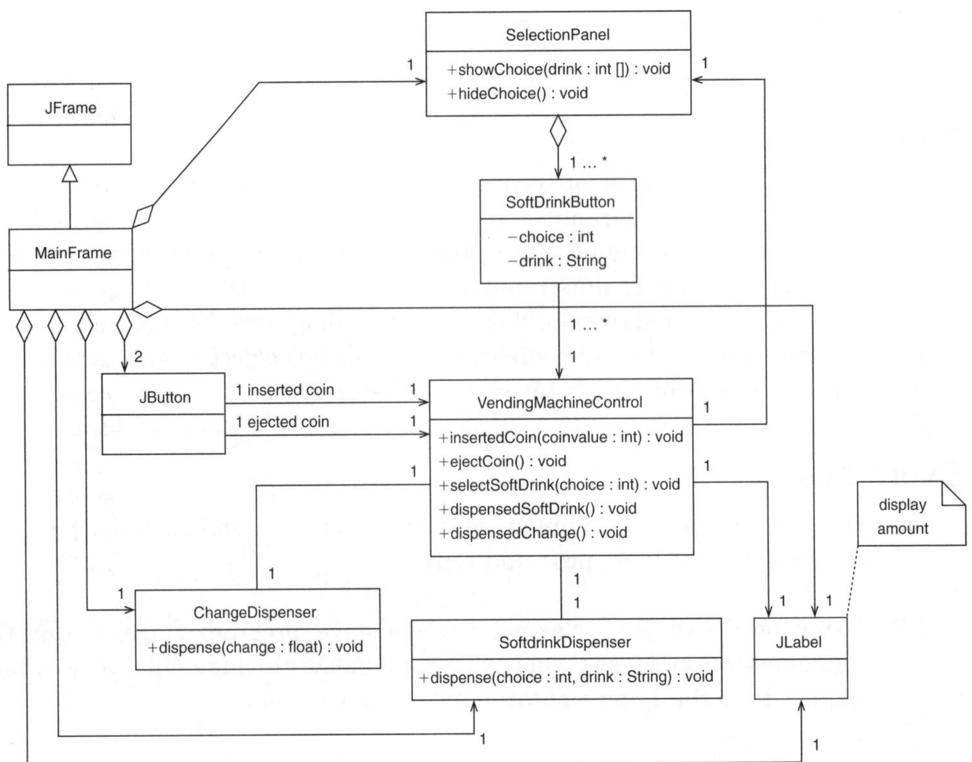

Chapter

6

View Alignment Techniques and Method Customization

Overview

Over the years, a variety of software development methods have been proposed to speed up the process of producing quality software on time and within budget. While the Unified Process and the UML are now very mature and widely used for software development, it appears that the missing link in the entire process is a set of effective heuristics and techniques guide and assist the designer throughout the software development life cycle. Consequently, there is a prevailing view that there is no one single universal method for software development.

This chapter introduces a framework of view alignment techniques that serve to methodically guide the developer through the software development life cycle. The view alignment techniques are flexible in that they focus on the amount of information available to the developer. It will be illustrated how these techniques can be applied so that the developer using a set of manipulators can design and customize their own software development methods. These manipulators will help the designer to elaborate the main model within the workflow, discover requirements for the next workflow and ensure model consistency among the workflows.

Based on the view alignment techniques, is then presented a software development approach called *Activity Analysis Approach* (A^3), which is particularly suitable for user interaction intensive systems.

What You Will Learn

On completing the study of this chapter, you should be able to:

- appreciate the benefits of using a method for software development
- understand the limitations of current software development methods
- understand the framework of view alignment techniques
- know how to apply the view alignment techniques to customize and create a method
- use the Activity Analysis Approach effectively to develop workflow-oriented and activity-intensive software systems

Software Development Methods

Software engineering is concerned with the application of a systematic, disciplined, quantifiable approach to the development, operation and maintenance of software, with the aim of producing reliable software systems on time and within cost estimates. Software engineering is therefore, particularly applicable to the development of large-scale systems; it covers not only the technical aspects of building software systems, but also management issues such as the directing of programming teams, scheduling and budgeting.

Generally speaking, the most important benefit in applying engineering concepts to building large-scale software systems is that developers can systematically and predictably arrive at pragmatic, cost-effective and timely solutions to real-world problems. Berard (1998) suggests that the most valuable engineering techniques are those that can be:

- described quantitatively as well as qualitatively
- used repeatedly, each time achieving similar results
- taught to others within a reasonable timeframe
- applied by others with a reasonable level of success
- achieving significantly and consistently better results than adopting other techniques or an *ad hoc* approach
- applicable to a relatively large percentage of cases

Before software methods came into being, development of new systems relied on the experience and intuition of the management and technical personnel. However, the complexity and the scale of modern systems and computer products have heightened the need for some kind of orderly development process. Over subsequent years, a variety of software development methods using specific software production techniques have been proposed to speed up the time it takes to develop reliable software.

Such software development methods consist of a complete set of activities needed to transform users' requirements into a consistent set of artifacts that represent a software product. Typically, a software development method specifies a series of stages that encompass requirements gathering, design, development, testing, delivery, maintenance and enhancement of a system, and helps the developer build software systems in a reliable and consistent way. In general, software development methods allow the building of models from model elements that constitute the fundamental concepts for representing systems or phenomena.

Components of Software Development Methods

The term software development method seems to confuse many people, even the practitioners. For example, some practitioners incorrectly think that the UML is a software development method, rather than just a standard notation for representing systems. The UML does not describe the process and heuristics practitioners use to build software.

Budgen (1994) considers that a software development method primarily comprises three components: (1) a process, (2) a representation system or a modeling notation and (3) techniques, heuristics, steps or procedures (see Figure 6.1).

Figure 6.1. The three components of a method

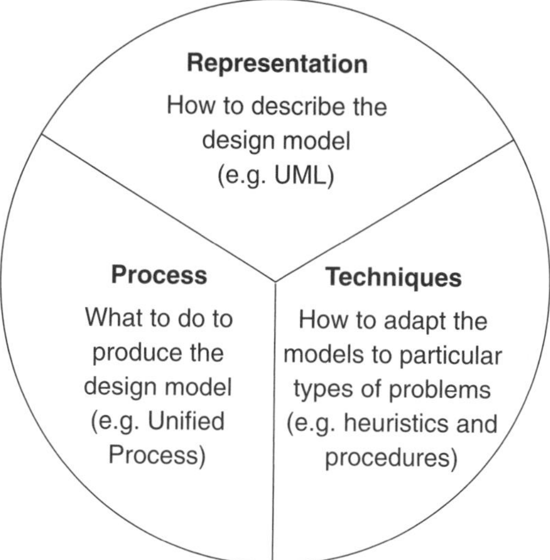

A design process corresponds to a process of navigation from the problem space to the solution space. Throughout this process of navigation, the designer is presented with options and choices, where he/she has to make a selection or a decision. The question of techniques of a development method provides some heuristics and guidance to assist the designer in making the right selection. Typically, system artifacts are produced at the end of each of the tasks or activities in the process, represented by a recommended notation.

As such the three components of software development can be more specifically described as follows:

- Representation. A set of recommended representation (notation) (e.g. UML) consisting of one or more forms of a notation that can be used to model both the structure of the initial problem (requirements) and the intended solution, using one or more viewpoints (models) and different levels of abstraction.
- Process. A framework from which a comprehensive plan for software development can be established. This development plan consists of a specific ordered set of tasks aimed at producing software solutions. Thus, a process needs to be instantiated or customized (a development plan) for individual projects, and it should cover the activities of the entire software development life cycle.
- Techniques. They are heuristics, guidelines and procedures that help designers develop the software development plan for their project. In other words, they help customize the process framework for the system being developed such as defining the order of tasks to be carried out within the process and selecting the models and their perspectives which are to be focused on at the optimum level of abstraction. Furthermore, they help the project manager allocate responsibilities for the members of the development team.

A typical development plan for a software project includes:

- a list of tasks that need to be carried out
- the order in which these tasks should be carried out
- the deliverables to be produced
- the skills required for each task

In developing a software method, the notation part is the easiest part as there are *de facto* standards one example being the UML, which is now widely used for object-oriented systems. The process part is a little more complex as it involves the balancing of multiple dimensions of parameters and constraints such as timeline, people, deliverables, quality, cost, etc., that need to be compromised. Finally, the techniques element is the most difficult part as the actual techniques largely involve experience and domain knowledge, that can only be built up over a long period of time. Users of a particular method develop certain know-how so that the method can be used optimally. Furthermore, very often such know-how or experience is situation-dependent and may not be clearly formulated and, therefore, cannot be passed on easily or readily.

Benefits of Using Software Development Methods

Why should anyone use software development methods when many software systems in the past have so far been produced without following any explicit methods? The answer to this pertinent question is that over the past three decades, the scale of a typical software system has dramatically increased in terms of size and complexity. Consequently, software development has become a labor-intensive, expensive and risky venture. Nowadays, complex projects are often developed in multiple teams working in parallel, and such teams need mutual understanding of their roles, responsibilities, and interdependence, as well as effective communication and coordination among the team and between the developers and their clients. Without a systematic process to guide the development, the likelihood of failure will be high. Furthermore, there is also a need to improve productivity to ensure that the software can be developed on time and within budget while meeting the expectations of our clients. Budgen (1994) describes some of the benefits of using the three different components of a software method:

Representation:

- Modeling notations are typically graphical, allowing both easy manipulation of models, and effective communication and exchange of information between the various parties involved in the project. A good representation strikes a balance between information density and readability.
- Notations and models help others capture and understand the intentions of the original designer.

Process:

- A framework helps identify important progress milestones and checkpoints for conducting design methods, helps record the reasons for *decisions* and consequently helps produce the various requirements specification artifacts and deliverables.

Techniques:

- The use of a method provides the designer with a set of guidelines to produce the design and to verify it against the original requirements.
- The use of a design method may assist with the formulation and exploration of the mental models used to capture the essential features of the design. Method knowledge may, therefore, provide a substitute for domain knowledge when the latter is inadequate or lacking.
- The techniques offer a set of procedures that should enable the designer to ensure consistency in the structure of a design and view alignment among design models. This is particularly important if the design is being produced by a team of designers who need to ensure that their contributions fit coherently.

Why Traditional Software Methods Didn't Work Miracles

In recent years, more and more people have realized that there is no *universal* method that can be readily applied to all problems in any circumstances without the need for customization. DeMarco and Lister coined the term *capital-M Methodology* (the universal method) as opposed to *methodology*. He points out that to ensure success, the project team should tailor the method to needs of the individual project rather than attempt to force-fit the project into the *methodology*. He is of the view that the designer should use his/her judgment and commonsense when pursuing a software development method. Others further suggest that software systems cannot be developed on autopilot as much thought and careful planning is required. Indeed, Jacobson et al. (1998) also believe that "*there is NO Universal Process! The Unified Process is designed for flexibility and extensibility*." However, Budgen (1994) highlights the unfortunate situation that purveyors of some training courses and textbooks on methods are sometimes guilty of promoting exaggerated expectations about their courseware. Consequently, many methods are made as prescriptive as possible and consist of a set of carefully itemized sequences of actions that should be performed by a designer. This type of *universal* software method is an inadequate approximation of the software development process that is seen time and time again in the IT industry. Indeed, in an article published on his website http://www.joelsoftware.com/printerfriendly/articles/fog0000000024.html and entitled "Big Mac vs. The Naked Chef," Spolsky tried to explain why some of the biggest IT consulting companies in the world do the worst development work. He depicts the following "fictitious" story that we have come across at least once.

An excerpt from Spolsky's article

Mike was unhappy. He had hired a huge company of IT consultants to build The System. The IT consultants he hired were incompetents who kept talking about The Methodology, and spent millions of dollars and had failed to produce a single thing.

Luckily, Mike found a Youthful Programmer who was really smart and talented. The Youthful Programmer built his whole system in one day for $20 and pizza. Mike was overjoyed. He recommended the Youthful Programmer to all his friends.

Youthful Programmer starts raking in the money. Soon, he has more work than he can handle, so he hires a bunch of people to help him. The good people want too many stock options, so he decides to hire even younger programmers right out of college and "train them" with a six-week course.

The trouble is that the "training" doesn't really produce consistent results, so Youthful Programmer starts creating rules and procedures that are meant to make more consistent results. Over the years, the rule book grows and grows. Soon it's a six-volume manual called The Methodology.

After a few dozen years, Youthful Programmer is now a Huge Incompetent IT Consultant with a capital-M-methodology and a lot of people who blindly obey the Methodology, even when it doesn't seem to be working, because they have no bloody idea whatsoever what else to do, and they're not really talented programmers – they're just well-meaning Poli Sci majors who attended the six-week course.

And Newly Huge Incompetent IT Consultant starts messing up. Their customers are unhappy. And another upstart talented programmer comes and takes away all their business, and the cycle begins anew ...

Spolsky's story has brought up a number of interesting points which he sums up as follows:

- You need talent to perform certain tasks really well
- It is hard to scale talent
- One way in which people try to scale talent is by having the talent create rules for the untalented to follow
- The quality of the resulting product will then become very poor

According to Budgen (1994), a software design process should provide a form of process that is used to design another process. Thus, the heuristics part of a development method should provide practical advice on the criteria that should be considered when making design choices. However, such heuristics can never be universally applied to all problems. For actual design tasks, the designer's choices and decisions will need to be resolved solely on the basis of the needs of the particular problem at hand. It is often too easy for the designer to fall into the trap of believing that a design process is itself a recipe.

We are not promoting that development methods should not be used, rather we are pointing out that they have limitations and that these need to be recognized.

Unified Modeling Language versus Software Methods

While there is no one universal method that can be used for all problems, recent literature on methods has tended to focus on the process and representation parts of the design method, for example, the Unified Modeling Language (UML) notation and the Unified Process. As mentioned previously, we need all three key components to constitute the complete software development method. Many books and courses on object-orientation (OO) only focus on one of the three components, with very few (or, more often than not, none) covering all three. The techniques part is either completely missed out or dealt with rather casually. Some attempt to cover this area under a different guise. For example, Jacobson (1998) describes "Team-Based Development" as one of the three major components of a design method (see Figure 6.2(a)). In other words, it is expected that a team of software engineers would choose and customize a method for the project concerned. Quatrani (2002) suggests that the "tool" as the third major component of a method (see Figure 6.2(b)), that is, the (CASE) tool, will provide sufficient support so that the designer can customize or create his/her own method.

It is inappropriate to substitute the techniques part by either a tool or team-based development. Although CASE tools generally provide limited support for model consistency checking, the decision to select the right model for a workflow still rests with the designer. Furthermore, beginners in the field may not be aware of the techniques part of the development process and they misconceive UML or the Rational Unified Process (RUP) as a development method. Consequently, they usually find it difficult to apply these particular concepts.

Figure 6.2. **Three components of a software development method: (a) Jacobson's view and (b) Quatrani's view**

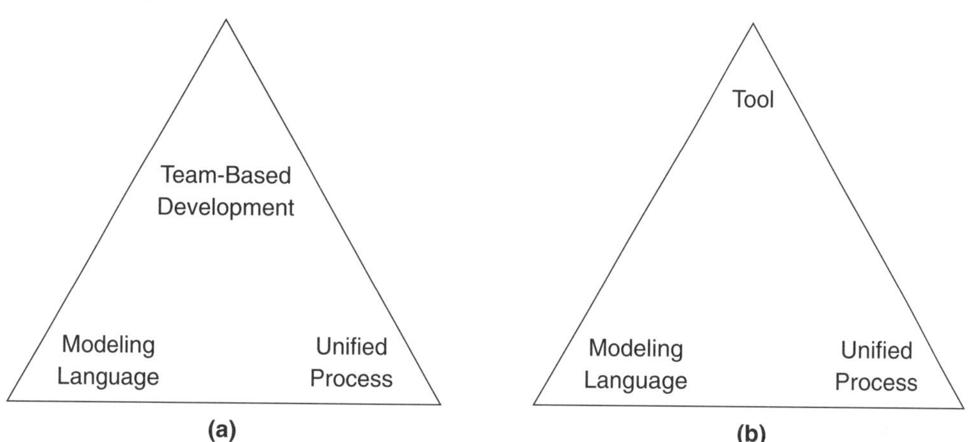

Hurdles in Applying the Object-oriented Approach

As mentioned before, a process is a framework or a template, and we need to be mindful that it is not universal for all problems. Very often, it is necessary to work out a software development plan by applying techniques at the very beginning of the project development process. A process should not be followed blindly, as this will generate useless work and artifacts that are of little added value. A process, therefore, needs to be adapted to a particular problem domain, together with the process elements that are likely to be modified, customized, added or suppressed. These process elements include artifacts, activities, workers and workflows as well as guidelines and artifact templates.

The UML provides an extremely rich set of notations to represent systems (see Figure 6.3). Booch et al. (1998) suggest that 80% of software projects use only about 20% of the UML notations. To the designer, it would be rather difficult to decide which subset of UML notations should be used for the project at hand. It is typical for designers to be confronted with many questions throughout the development life cycle:

- What models are required to represent the system?
- How should the selected models be applied to perform the development work?
- Which model should be used first, and which model(s) should follow next?
- How can the models of the system be consistent?

Figure 6.3. UML models

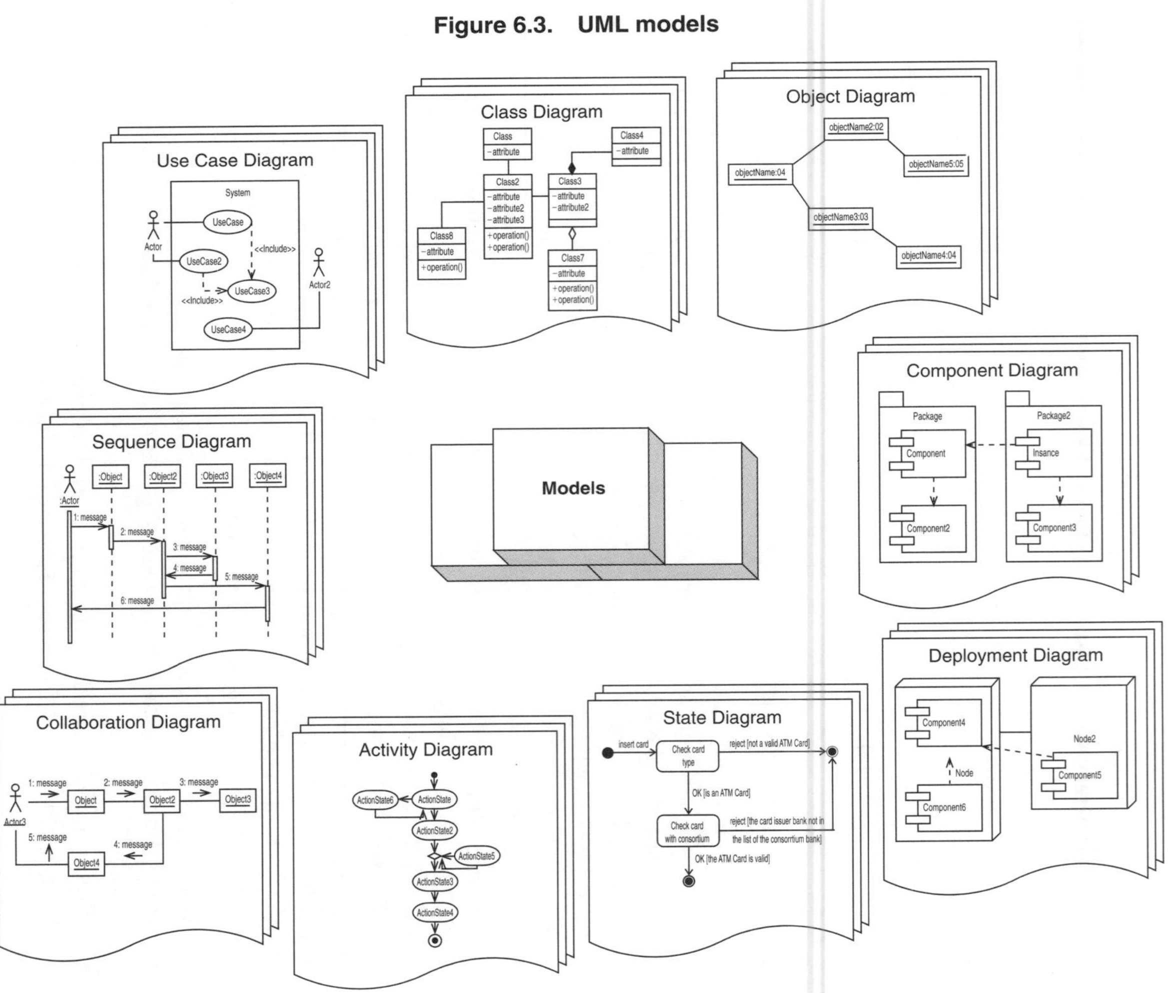

Scenarios in Learning and Using UML

Because of the misconception about software development methods and the lack of available materials on the techniques part, designers are often confused and newcomers will find it extremely difficult to adopt the object-oriented approach for their projects. Furthermore, with the absence of this key component (techniques) to guide the designer in making the right design decisions, many find it quite difficult to learn UML and apply it to their projects. We have often come across the following typical scenarios when designers start out applying UML to object-oriented projects:

Scenario I

I went to the book store and bought a copy of "UML Distilled." Having gone through the whole text, I seem to understand the contents and the examples, but I still do not know how to apply UML to my project! But when I learned Java, at least I could use it straightaway, even as a beginner!

Scenario II

The UML books that I have studied tended to give me fragmented knowledge about UML. There are so many diagrams and models in UML. I cannot see how they are related to each other.

Scenario III

Although methodologies like SSADM, SA/D and OMT are not that great, at least I can follow the steps and apply them to my projects straightaway. Having read some books and attended a training course in OOT, I still don't know how to start my small OO pilot project.

These scenarios have highlighted the problem in which current methods do not allow the designer to customize or create a method for the problem at hand. The missing link is the availability of effective techniques that can guide the designer throughout the software development life cycle.

In the rest of this chapter, there will be an overview of the widely used Rational approach, highlighting its deficiencies, after which we will outline the

View Alignment Techniques that supplement the techniques part of the method. A framework of view alignment techniques will be presented to help the designer to design or customize their own methods. Finally, we will illustrate the application of the View Alignment Techniques to create a design method called the Activity Analysis Approach (A^3). This approach is specifically designed for systems whose requirements are workflow-oriented or interaction-intensive, such as those found in many business systems.

Current Object-oriented Development Approaches

Current object-oriented development approaches do not overcome the hurdles described in the previous section. As the three major components in software development methods are representation, process and techniques, we shall examine these aspects in turn to identify the shortcomings of the current object-oriented development approaches.

Representation

It is without a doubt that the UML is now the *de facto* standard graphical language for representing systems in the software industry. The UML enables us to specify, visualize and document the artifacts of software-intensive systems, and it represents a collection of best engineering practices and model notations that have proven successful for large and complex systems. Developing a model for a software system prior to its construction is as essential as having a blueprint for erecting a large building. Good model notations are crucial for open communication among project teams, ensuring architectural soundness. As the complexity of systems increases, so does the importance of a good representation language. There are many factors to ensure the success of a project and having a rigorous unified modeling language is one of them. UML is quite easy to learn and well covered in books. There are also a wide range of learning resources, such as training courses and seminars, in the market.

The UML defines nine types of diagrams: class (package) diagrams, object diagrams, use case diagrams, sequence diagrams, collaboration diagrams, statechart diagrams, activity diagrams, component diagrams and deployment diagrams. UML notations and diagrams have been dealt with in detail in previous chapters, thus, this overview will only focus on the other two components: the process and techniques parts of a software method.

Unified Process

A software development process describes the activities for developing a system according to the users' requirements. The Unified Process is a widely used software development process, whereby a system is built incrementally through a number of iterations during which the designer may perform tasks such as requirements capture, analysis, design, implementation and testing. Feedback is sought from system users throughout the entire process.

In early iterations, the designer often focuses more on requirements capturing and analysis. In later iterations, the designer tends to emphasize on implementation and testing. In fact, the iterations are divided into four phases: inception, elaboration, construction and transition (see Figure 6.4). Each phase has a different focus:

- Inception phase. This phase focuses on establishing the business case, defining the scope of the system and estimating the amount of resources, including time, required to complete the project.
- Elaboration phase. In this phase, the core architecture of the system is incrementally developed. Risks are resolved according to priorities and the scope of the system is refined.
- Construction phase. In this phase, low-risk elements of the system are incrementally implemented and tested. The system is prepared for deployment.
- Transition phase. Beta release of the system is deployed to the end users. Bug fixes and other tasks, such as refining the system, are performed.

Figure 6.4. Four phases of unified process

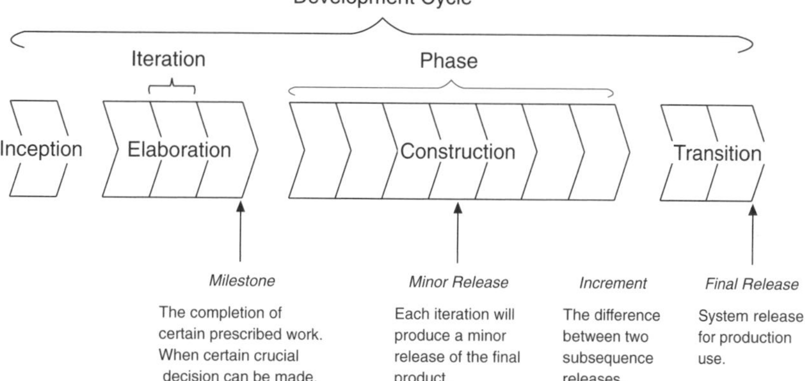

The work activities of the Unified Process in the same subject area are categorized as a workflow (some authors call it a discipline). The design workflow, for example, includes all the activities associated with designing the system. Figure 6.5 illustrates some sample workflows and their relative levels of effort in different phases of the Unified Process. Since different phases have different emphasis or focus, the relative effort for a workflow changes over time (the horizontal axis) as system development progresses.

Figure 6.5. Sample workflows and their relative efforts over time

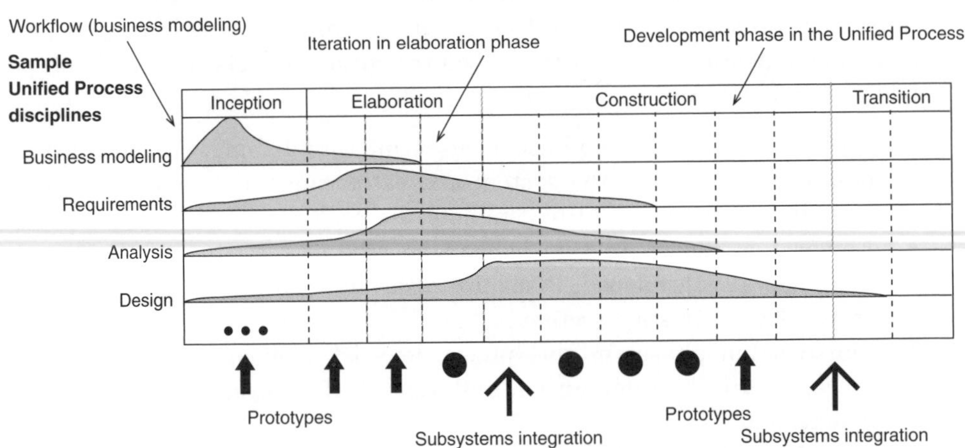

In the Unified Process, the concepts of use case-driven, architecture-centric, iterative and incremental development are equally important. Architecture-centric development provides a structure to guide the activities in the various development phases and iterations, whereas use cases define the users' goals and drive the work of each iteration. Removing one of the four key design principles would severely reduce the value of the Unified Process. They are like the legs of a stool; without one of the legs, the stool will not be stable or may even fall over.

Techniques

As mentioned earlier, the techniques part is the most difficult component of the entire software development method. Jacobson (1998) consider that teamwork is the element that glues the representation and process components together but offers very little details as to how a method can be customized or created to solve the problem. Nonetheless, he does provide some hints on which model(s) should be used in each workflow (see Figure 6.6). Each of these models associated with a workflow is elaborated by a sub-figure indicating the types of diagrams that are likely to be used (see Figures 6.7 and 6.8).

Figure 6.6. Workflow and model association

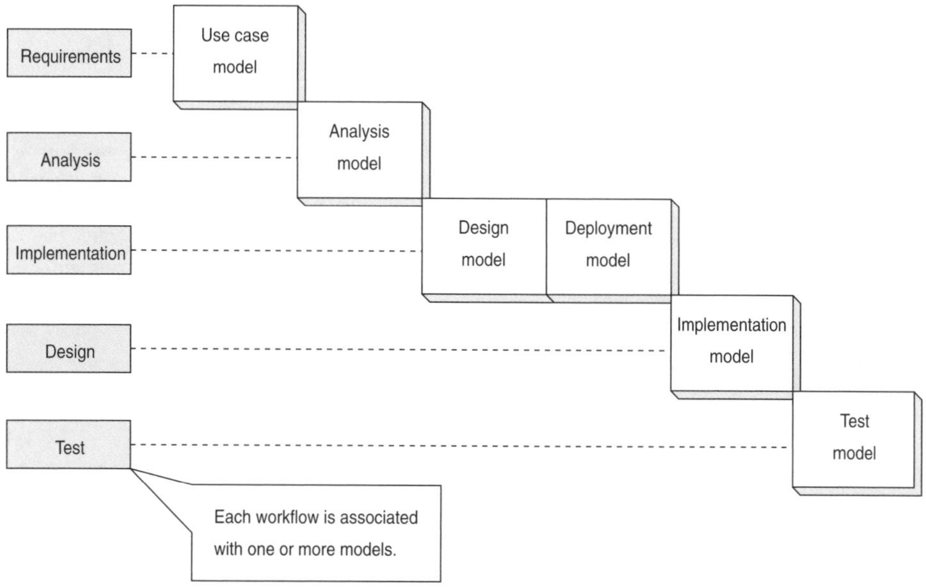

The solid lines in Figures 6.7 to 6.9 show the diagrams that are required for different models, while the dotted-lines indicate optional diagrams, depending on the type of problem at hand.

Despite these hints, little clue is provided on the selection of the right model (UML diagram) to start with and the order in which these models (UML diagrams) should be developed. For example, adopting Figure 6.6, we can start off with the requirements workflow, followed by the use case model. We will then develop the use case and sequence diagrams as shown in Figure 6.7. Depending on the type of problem, some other models (statechart diagram and activity diagram) may also be required, but the order in which these models should be developed has not been clearly spelt out. While opponents of the capital "M" methodology propose a flexible and extensible method (such as the RUP), developers have not been provided with sufficient guidelines or heuristics to systematically carry out system analysis and design. As a result, some developers may have to spend much time working on models which are not necessary or, worst still, they may miss something important in the analysis stage, yielding inconsistent or incomplete models.

Figure 6.7. Possible diagams for representing use case models

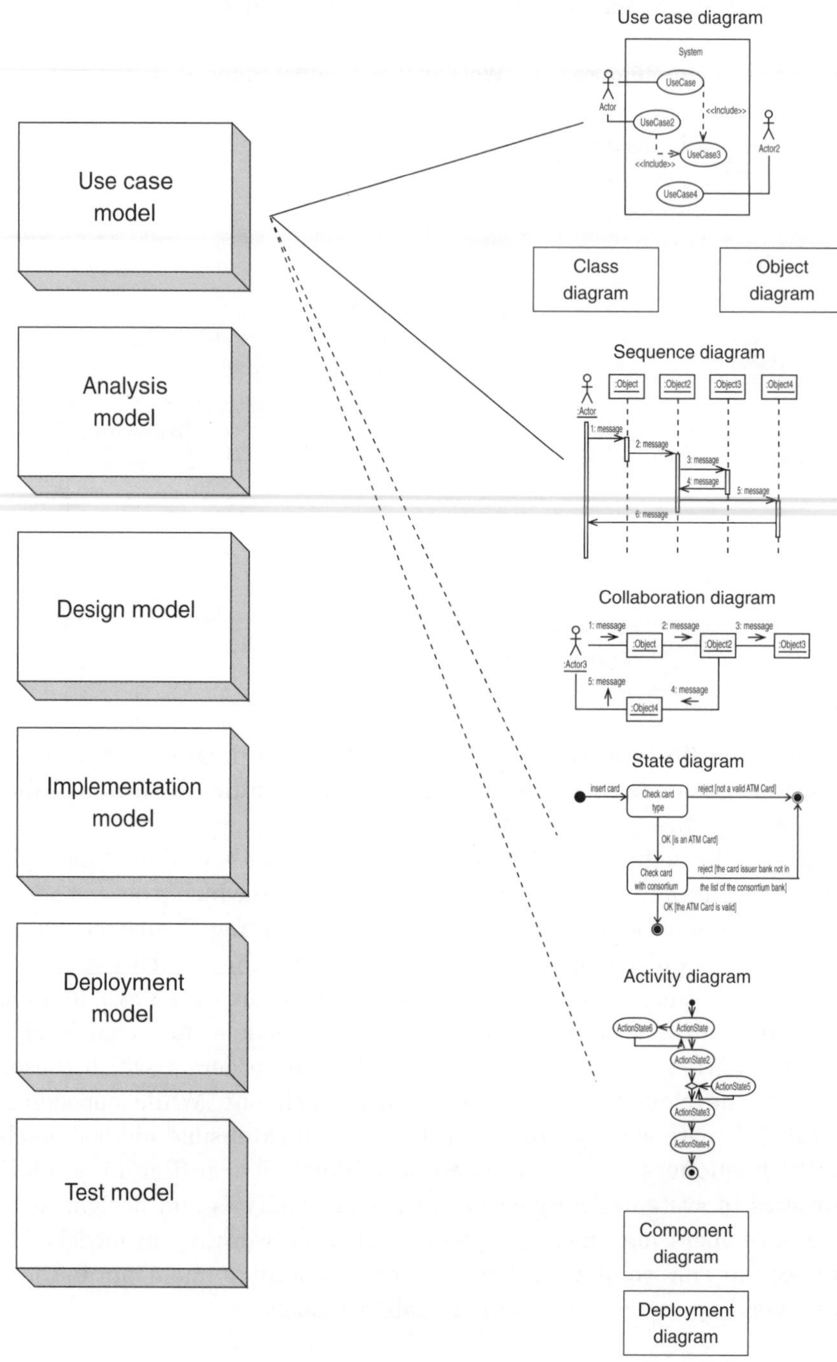

Figure 6.8. Possible diagams for representing analysis and design models

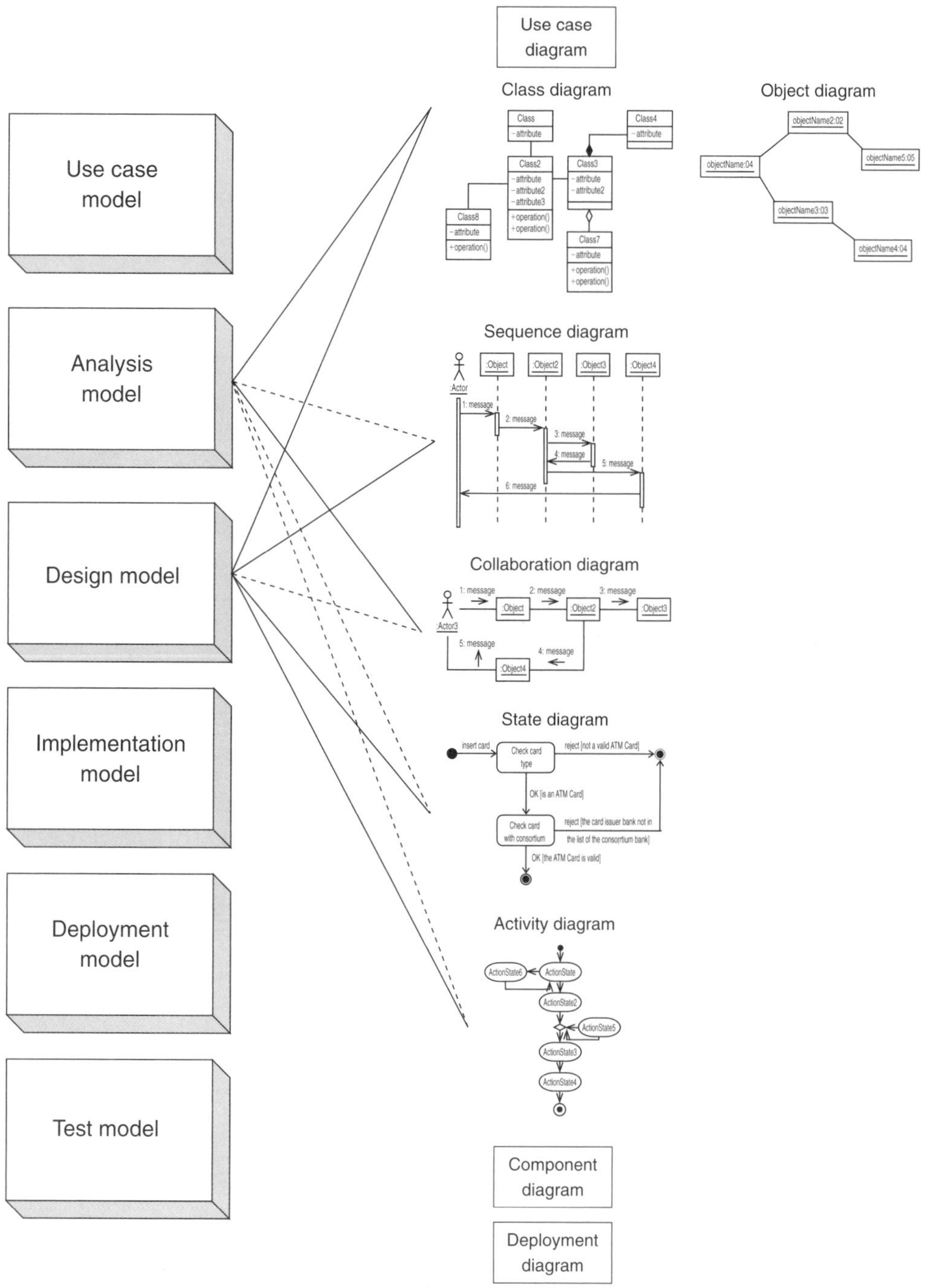

Figure 6.9. Possible diagams for representing deployment and implementation models

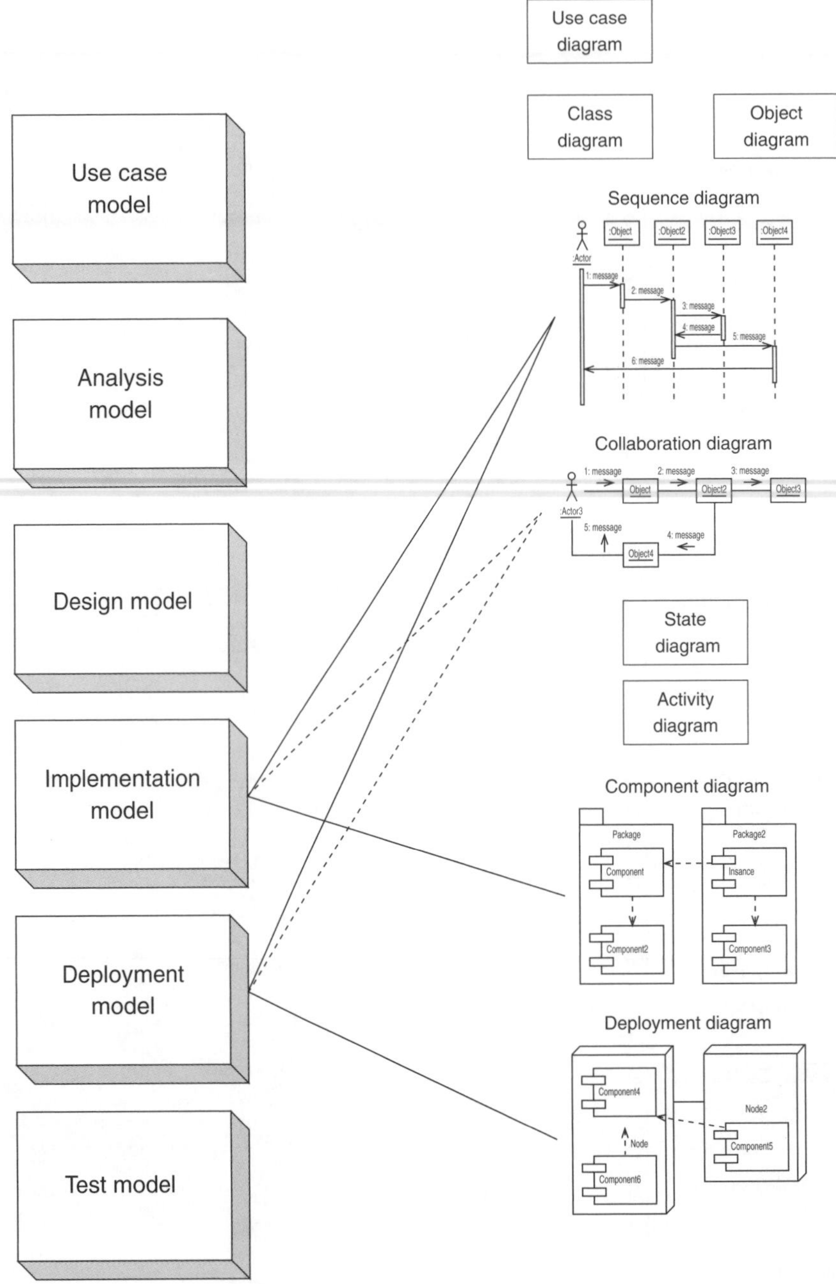

Traceability and Models Consistency

Another frequently asked question in developing models is "How do we ensure that the models we have created are consistent?" <<trace>> is one of the often-used stereotypes in Rambaugh, Booch and Jacobson's *The Unified Software Development Process*. (The three are often referred to as the Three Amigos). The <<trace>> concept may be the answer to the broad question of models consistency. Here, Jacobson regularly emphasizes the traceability between a model and its subsequent realization models (see Figure 6.10), but there is little hint as to how to ensure the traceability among the models. So it seems that it is entirely up to the designer's own imagination, and of course, it always helps if he/she is experienced. The RUP, therefore, has provided no heuristics for adopting the UML models and very little assistance to create or customize development methods.

Figure 6.10. Use case realizations in different models

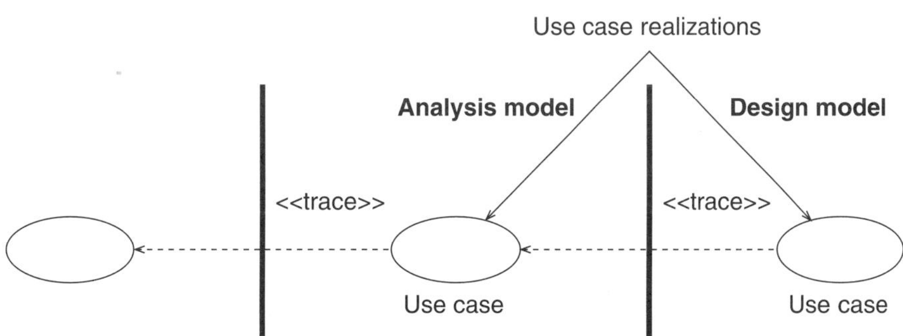

Need for Method Customization

There is no universally applicable development method because there is no single method that caters for different organizational factors. There are many different factors that would affect design decisions, thus, resulting in the need for customization of a design method to fit a specific type of problem. The human factors and cultural differences include the structure and culture of the organization, the competence, skill and prior experience of each individual in the software development team. Systems in different application domains also require different focuses or impose special constraints. For example, the emphases associated with developing mission critical systems are quite different from those that build word processors. Likewise, a real-time system imposes a lot more special requirements than those of batch processing systems. All these factors may result in the need for customizing or creating different development methods. Other factors such as life cycle — time to market, expected life span, planned future releases, etc. — and technological factors — programing languages, development tools, databases, middleware, communication and distribution, etc. — augment the need for the designer to be able to tailor development methods to suit their own needs.

Because the UML has a rich set of models and notations, we should avoid generating useless models and artifacts that are of little added value to the project. Furthermore, the consistency and traceability of the models and artifacts produced must be maintained to minimize errors.

It is quite possible to create a generic software development method that can be adapted or extended to suit the needs of an organization. The method could be general and comprehensive enough to be used "as is," i.e. out-of-the-box for a similar type of problem. This is quite often the case for those small-to-medium software development organizations, especially those that do not have a very strong process culture. However, Kruchten (1998) suggests that such an organization should be able to modify, adjust, and expand the software development method to accommodate the specific needs, characteristics, constraints, history, culture and domain of the organization.

In the next section, the View Alignment Techniques (VATs) are proposed to enable the designer to customize a software method or, in other words, create and customize (create an instance of the process) a process (method template) using the UML standard diagrams for different problems affected by one or more factors just mentioned. A generic software development method for interaction-intensive applications A^3, which are typical of most business applications, will also be introduced.

View Alignment Techniques

Humans possess limited, short-term memory and it is well-known that we can handle only "7 ± 2" chunks of information at a time. We can tackle a complex problem or system by dividing it into smaller manageable pieces through modeling and analysis techniques. A model is a simplification of reality, which is simplified by providing blueprints (models) of a system. Usually, it is necessary to develop different models in order to completely understand, design and build a system.

Every system can be described in different ways by different models. Thus, a good model includes those elements that have a broad effect on the selected perspective and omits those minor elements that are not relevant to it. Furthermore, as suggested by Booch et al. (1998), models may encompass a detailed as well as a more general view of a system from the same perspective.

In the former case, a model concentrates on a particular perspective of the system while de-emphasizing other system aspects; the latter case provides different levels of details from a particular perspective. We can summarize the characteristics of software models as follows:

- Models can have different levels of abstraction
- A model focuses on one aspect of a problem that the designer is interested in.
- Elements of a model are often represented in different ways as parts of other models

The most basic and extremely important principles of software engineering are *composibility* and *decomposability*. We *decompose* in order to understand (a problem) and *compose* in order to build (a system). When we have developed models that describe the different perspectives of the system, we should ultimately be able to form a complete and consistent picture of the system. This is the basic idea of the VATs.

In fact, the basic principles of view alignment techniques are applied in reality. When we see a physical object from a particular perspective, we project or imagine what the other views (which may be partially revealed) could be. For example, given the different elevations of a building's floor plan, we mentally create a 3D model of the building. If we extend our imagination further, we might even picture what the building would look like viewing it from a particular angle.

VATs are particularly applicable to software modeling and analysis because they can help discover what models are required to methodically develop life cycle. The designer can start with a model depending on the readily available information, and then develop other related models by applying the VATs. A software model usually emphasizes on a particular aspect (strong view) of the system, together with one or more aspects (weak views) of the system. Two models can be linked when a weak view of one model is the strong view of another. For example, an element may form a part of two or more models and thus would provide the common view (i.e. static or dynamic) of the system. In our terminology, such an element is called a *linked element*. In other words, elements in one model are often linked to elements in other models. So, instead of developing the entire model from scratch, we can start with a partial model generated or derived from the linked elements of other models. In so doing, not only will the models be consistent but the sequence can be systematically identified in which the models should be developed. In other words, VATs can help designers customize their method as they develop the system. We shall use two examples to illustrate this concept, the first using the structured approach and the second the object-oriented approach.

Example 1: Linked Elements between Data Flow Diagrams and Entity Relationship Diagrams

The data flow diagram (DFD) and the entity relationship diagram (ERD) are the two commonly used models for the structured analysis and design approach. The DFD has a strong view of functions and a weak view of data stores (entity), while the ERD has a strong view of data stores. We can start with the DFD to model the functional requirements of the system and then develop the ERD from the results of the DFD (see Figure 6.11) or vice versa. Consequently, we are not bound by the prescribed steps of a particular method. There is the freedom to choose the most suitable and convenient model to start the analysis process and then develop other models as a deeper understanding of the system is achieved. Indeed, Yourdon (1998) described the heuristics to ensure the consistency between the ERD and DFD as follows:

> *"As the ERD and DFD are being developed in parallel, they can be used to cross-check each other. Thus, stores that have been tentatively defined in the preliminary DFD can be used to suggest objects in the preliminary ERD; and objects that have been tentatively identified in the preliminary ERD can be used to help choose appropriate stores in the preliminary DFD. Neither model should be considered the dominant model that controls the other; each is on an equal footing and can provide invaluable assistance to the other."*

Figure 6.11. Models consistency between ERD and DFD

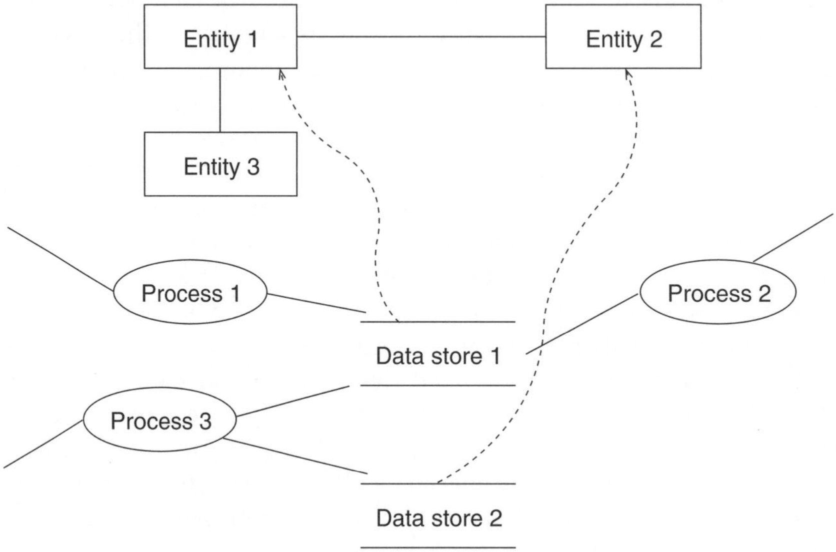

Example 2: Linked Elements between Sequence and Class Diagrams

Consider an object O in a sequence diagram that can be linked to a class C in a class diagram. If O has an incoming message, there will be a corresponding operation in C (see Figure 6.12). By aligning the linked elements associated with the models, traceability and consistency can be facilitated among the models. More importantly we can discover new system components by exploring the linked elements between models. *Aligning the linked elements in different models is a fundamental principle of the VATs.*

Figure 6.12. Linked elements between the sequence and class diagrams

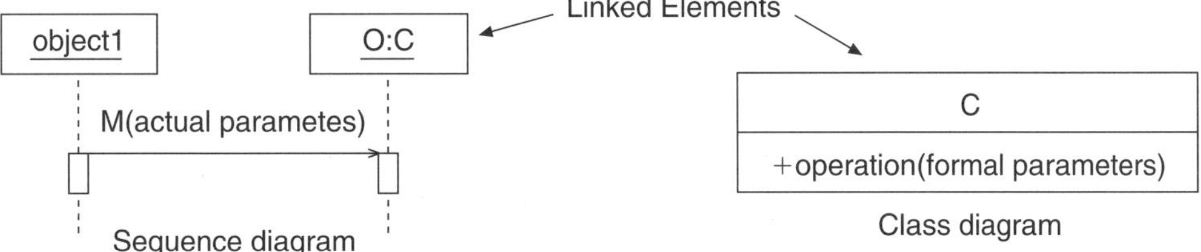

Principles of View Alignment Techniques

The underlying principles of the VATs are based on the identification of linkages among models by applying three model manipulators at three different levels of the development workflow. The three model manipulators are called Model Elaborator, Model Transitor and View Aligner. The manipulators can be used to help conduct modeling and analysis throughout the entire development process. Each of these manipulators can be applied to three different levels which are *within*, *between* and *among* the workflows, such as business modeling, requirements, analysis, design and so on. For example, a model elaborator is usually applied within one of the above workflows and a model transitor to derive the requirements workflow that is based on the business modeling workflow. Finally, a view aligner manipulator is used to ensure models consistency as artifacts have been created in the development iteration.

Manipulators

To identify the linkages between models, use the three types of View Alignment Manipulators (VAMs). Each of these manipulators corresponds to the process of identifying the linkages (linked elements) in the three different levels detailed in Table 6.1. A manipulator includes a process and a set of techniques that is utilized by the designer to derive a new model by identifying the linked elements from the fully developed models in a workflow. The three VAMs perform different functions as follows:

- A **model elaborator** manipulator is used to elaborate a source model (or its elements) by providing additional information to produce a more detailed, sub-level model. The applications of a model elaborator should normally take place within a workflow (see Figure 6.13). For example, a use case can be elaborated by an activity diagram and a use case description. Hence, a model elaborator can be defined to develop an activity diagram from a use case. Model elaborators provide traceability through the detailed representation of models in different levels of abstraction.
- A **model transitor** manipulator is used to discover the requirements of a target model based on the linked elements identified in the source model. While the target model and the source model focus on different aspects of the system, there are some linked elements that share a common view and exist in both the target and source models. A model transitor is normally used when a workflow has fully been explored (see Figure 6.13).

  Suppose that the development of the requirements workflow is completed and the use case model including the identification of use cases is fully created, each already elaborated by a use case description. Now, you wish to move on to the analysis workflow. At this point, apply a model transitor to develop a system-level sequence diagram from the flow of events of the use case description. Model transitors provide traceability and discovery of requirements through the linked elements.
- A **view aligner** manipulator is used to establish points of connection between different models (see Figure 6.13). The connections between models can help identify the elements that need to be updated in one model when the linked elements of another have changed. The view aligner is normally applied iteratively upon the completion of a new workflow. For example, a view aligner can define the linked elements between a Model/View/Control (MVC)-level sequence diagram and a design class diagram. Changes in the linked elements of the MVC sequence diagram, e.g. the addition of a new incoming message to an object, may trigger changes in the design class diagram. View aligners provide traceability by establishing multiple points of connections of the linked elements between models. They often facilitate discovery of requirements and, more importantly, enable us to ensure models consistency. View aligners also help identify model(s) that need to be revisited when some other models have been updated or changed.

Table 6.1. Applications of model manipulators

Manipulator	Application level in workflow	Function	Linked pattern
Model Elaborator	within	Fully elaborate the workflow with models at different levels of abstraction	High level source model → Lower level target models
Model Transitor	within/between	Discover new requirements from existing models	Linked elements of weak view → Linked elements of strong view
View Aligner	among	Ensure model consistency among workflows	Points of connection → Linked elements among models

The above refinement steps are applicable to the elaboration of a workflow (model elaborator), the navigation between two adjacent workflows (model transitor) and the consistency checking of different workflows (view aligner). By combining these steps with the Unified Process, we have a general architecture of a software method based on the VATs (see Figure 6.13).

Grammar of Model Manipulators

Model manipulators are used to help refine existing models, develop new ones, and maintain the consistency among them. A model manipulator can also be used to perform elaboration, transition and alignment within, between and amongst the workflows respectively. Since we may need to apply model manipulators many times in the whole software development process, there is a need for a precise and concise grammar to represent these linkages of the model elements that exist in various workflows.

Figure 6.13. Three model manipulators for VATs

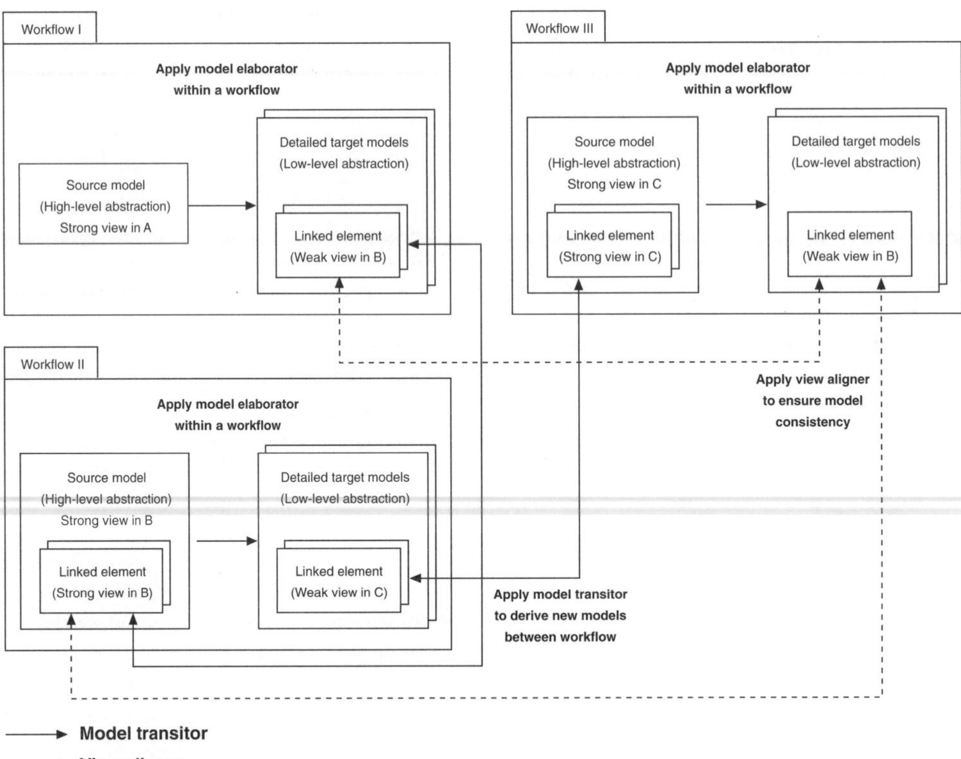

We shall use the Backus-Naur Form (BNF) notation to specify the syntax of the relationships between models. The grammar for the model manipulators is specified as follows:

```
<model relationship> ::= <model manipulator> ‘(’ <parameter list> ‘)’ | <parameter> <operator> <parameter>

<operator> ::= ‘->’, ‘=>’, ‘⇔’

<model manipulator> ::= ‘elaborator’ | ‘transitor’ | ‘aligner’

<parameter list> ::= <parameter> | <parameter> ‘,’ <parameter list>

<parameter> ::= <model> | <model> ‘[’ <version> ‘]’ | <model> ‘.’ <element list> | <model> ‘[’ <version> ‘]’ ‘.’ <element list>

<element list> ::= <element> | ‘{’ <elements> ‘}’
```

<elements> ::= <element> | <element> ',' <elements>

<element> ::= "a part of a model" | <element> '.' <element list>

<model> ::= "a model, a diagram, an entity, or an artifact used for modeling a system"

<version> ::= "the version"

Note: The following symbols are used to represent the three manipulators:

- '->' for model elaborators
- '=>' for model transitors
- '⇔' for view aligners

With this notation, there are two ways to express a model relationship between models: the long form and the short form. The long form is represented by a manipulator followed by a set of source and target models in the relationship. For example, *elaborator(use_case_A, use_case_description_B)* means that the second model, a use case description, is an elaboration of the first model, a use case. The short form is represented by a source model followed by an operator ('->', '=>, or '⇔') and then a target model. The same relationship can be represented by *use_case_A -> use_case_description_B.*

The short form is very useful when we are specifying a series of the manipulators. For example, *use_case_A -> use_case_description_B => activity_diagram_C* means to use an elaborator to develop the use case description and then apply a transitor to develop an activity diagram. The dot notation specifies an element of a model. For example, *use_case_diagram.use_case_A* means *use_case_A* of *use_case_diagram.* We can also specify the version of a model by placing the version in a pair of square bracket next to the model. For example, *use_case_diagram[requirement workflow]* means the version of the use case diagram for the requirements workflow.

Model Elaborator

An elaborator can be considered to be analogous to a sub-diagram that details the main diagram. For example, the DFD is the sub-diagram of the context diagram in the traditional structured approach and a use case can be elaborated by a use case description, an activity diagram, etc. The elaboration relationship is represented by *elaborator(source_model, target_model)* or simply *source_model –> target_model*, which means that the target model is an elaboration of the source model. For example, the following relationship means that *use_case_description_B* is an elaboration of *use_case_A* of *use_case_diagram1*:

elaborator(use_case_diagram1.use_case_A, use_case_description_B) or
use_case_diagram1.use_case_A –> use_case_description_B

Model Transitor

Apply a separate model transitor when connecting one group of linked elements in a model to another group of linked elements in another model. The syntax is similar to the way in which the model elaborator is described. It should be noted that *one linked element in a model may exist in the same form in another*. For example, a message associated with an object in the sequence diagram may appears exactly in the same form in the collaboration diagram. However, *sometimes a linked element may be presented in a similar form in another*. For example, suppose a new object has been identified from a sequence diagram when walking through a scenario of a use case. This new object may be connected as a linked element of a similar form, e.g. a class in the class diagram. Assume that we are applying a transitor to an input model to generate an output model. The transition relationship is represented by *transitor (input_model, output_model)* in the long form or *input_model => output_model* in the short form.

Example: Data Dictionary to a Use Case Diagram. The application of a transitor to generate a use case diagram from a data dictionary is represented as follows:

Transitor(data_dictionary.{use_case_list, actor_list}, use_case_diagram) or
data_dictionary.{use_case_list, actor_list} => use_case_diagram

Example: Textual Analysis. The application of a transitor to generate a list of use cases from a problem statement (use case level) through a textual analysis is represented by

Transitor(problem_statement[use case level], use_case_list) or
problem_statement[use case level] => use_case_list

Example: Specification of Workflow. Apply a model transitor to identify linked elements for a use case description that has been developed in the requirements workflow. Each event in the flow of events of a use case description can be translated using a model transitor as an action state of an activity diagram. The model transitor can be represented by

Transitor(use_case_description[requirement workflow].flow_of_event, activity_diagram) or
use_case_description[requirement workflow].flow_of_event => activity_diagram.action_state_list

View Aligner

A view aligner is used after a model transitor. A view aligner establishes the points of connection that exist between various models residing in different workflows. For simple cases, it often serves as a means to revisit models that were previously developed. A view aligner establishes a binary relationship between two elements and therefore may appear to be very similar to a model transitor. For example, the data dictionary or class diagram has to be revisited on many occasions; new classes are often updated when each of the scenarios (represented by sequence diagrams) of a use case has been walked through. However, *the real significance of a view aligner is its multiple points of linkage (points of connection) that coexist in various models. This implies that if any of these linked elements is changed, all the models linked to that element will be affected*. In other words, these linkages are a many-to-many relationship instead of a binary relationship like the model transitors. The view alignment relationship is represented by *aligner(model_1, ..., model_n)* in the long form or *model_1* <=> ... <=> *model_n* in the short form, indicating that consistency between the models is maintained.

Example: Simple View Aligner

sequence_diagram.object_list <=> class diagram.class_list

Example: Points of Connection for Multiple Models

sequence_diagram.object_list <=> collaboration_diagram.object_list <=> class_diagram.class_list

Architecture of View Alignment Techniques

The overall architecture of the VATs is presented in Figure 6.14. The upper part of this diagram describes the architecture of the Process Roadmap which consists of the development workflows from business modeling, requirements, analysis, design and so on. Each of these workflows contains linked elements that exist in other workflows.

Suppose a new software project has begun. We would begin at the first workflow (business modeling) of the first iteration of the inception phase.

Figure 6.14. Architecture of a software method based on VATs

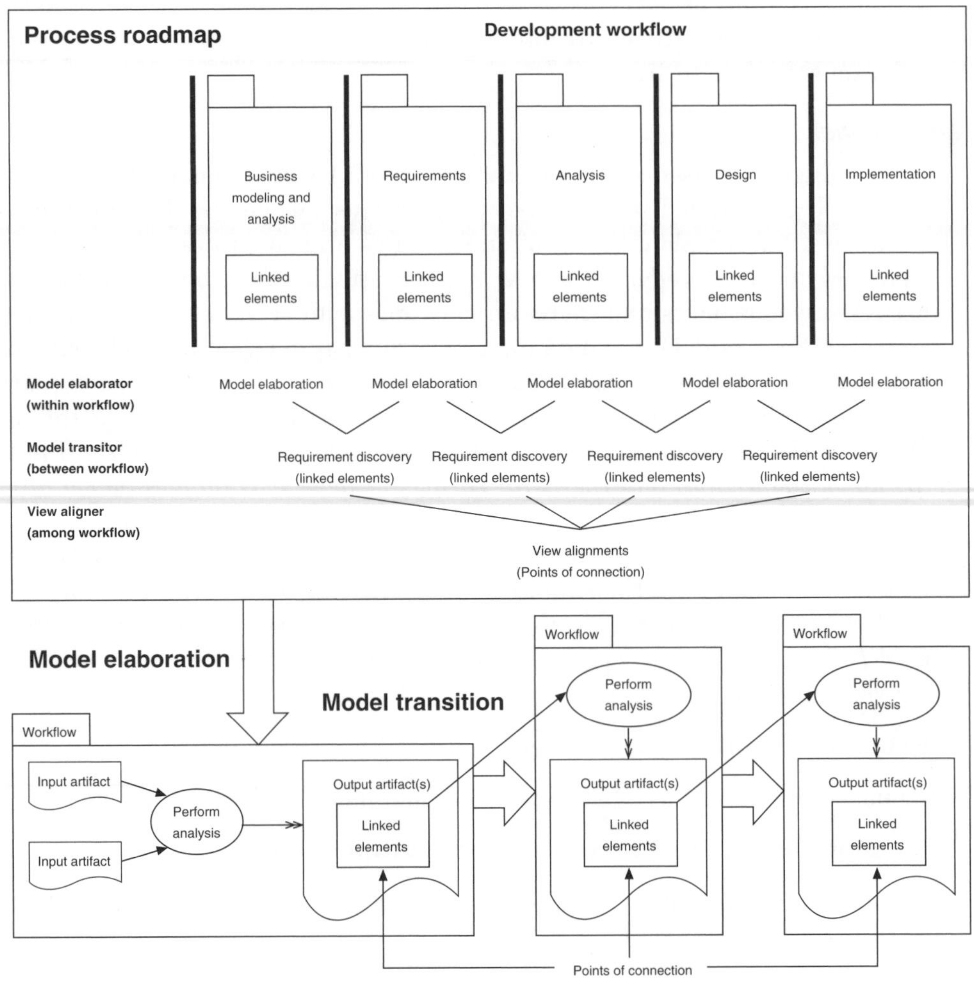

Because of the nature of the workflow, there may only be a limited choice of models to start with. For example, it does not take an experienced designer to know that the activity diagram is a suitable model to represent the business workflow. It is also possible to judge when the workflow has been completely modeled by applying the model elaborator within the workflow. Because when this happens, we should be able to identify some linked elements which can then be used to form a partial (or sometimes even complete) model of the next workflow. This is an important heuristic for applying model elaborators, as one of the major advantages of object-oriented design is the seamless transition from one model to another. Linked elements allow the discovery of the unknown requirements for the next workflow, and as such, new models are derived based on these reference points (linked elements).

To transit from one workflow to the next, we can apply the model transitor by establishing the linked elements between two consecutive workflows. The transition from one workflow to the next should be incremental and seamless. For example, if no linked element exists between the two adjacent workflows, it implies that there is no connection between them. This is considered a big leap between two workflows and is not advisable. Many suggest that a use case diagram can be elaborated to a detailed sequence diagram or collaboration diagram. This transition is neither incremental nor seamless, potentially resulting in serious traceability problems in the models.

Finally, the linked elements, which have been used to derive other models or to transit from one workflow to another, should ultimately be inter-related among different models by establishing their points of connection through the view aligner. This will help ensure consistency among all the models in different workflows.

The lower half of Figure 6.14 shows a detailed view of the Process Roadmap that describes the three manipulators in greater specifics. The model elaborator consists of input artifacts that provide useful information for the analysis to be conducted in the workflow. The resulting artifacts produced by the analysis consist of the linked elements, which in turn using model transistors, become the input artifacts of the analysis stage of the next workflow using model transitors. The more linked elements that are identified, the more requirements will be discovered for developing other models. Thus, connect the linked elements between two adjacent workflows first, and then establish the points of connection for different models residing in different workflows using view aligners.

Applying View Alignment Techniques

The VATs equip designers with the ability to create new or to customize existing software development methods. In the case of method creation, VATs can help the designer to select the suitable models out of the rich set of UML notations for different workflows in the development process. For customizing an existing method to suit the specific needs of an organization, the VATs can provide guidance and hints when the existing method does not seem to work well.

Developing a new software method is in many respects analogous to playing detective. There are no fixed procedures or heuristics to start the investigation as each crime generally has its own unique circumstances; all relevant facts will have to be considered as they are uncovered. Nonetheless, a detective would logically start from a point or area where he/she can quickly gather clues or evidence about the crime. The strategy here is to quickly uncover as many relevant facts as possible. Often, the discovery of one fact may reveal other leads. Sometimes, however, a detective may get stuck on a lead. It would be natural for him to move on to other areas and dig deeper. But as more facts and evidences are unveiled, the detective will try to consolidate these and fit the bits and pieces together to obtain a global perspective of the situation. If the detective previously made certain assumptions and contradictory evidence is later found, he would have to initiate further investigations to ensure all the facts are consistent and logical.

In applying the VATs, do not adhere to a fixed set of procedures, techniques or models. Instead, prepare only a rough plan. The VATs can help design or customize the process as more details of the system are discovered. Typically start with the most suitable or convenient model where there is a lot of information about the system; then develop other models by applying the appropriate manipulators. Ultimately, the VATs will guide us through the necessary and relevant models of the system. The following seven steps describe how the VATs should be applied.

1. Configure the process
   a. Determine the suitability of the development phases, the number of iterations and workflows in the development process.
   b. Determine the artifacts and deliverables associated with each workflow.
2. Select models for the workflow under development
   Find an appropriate starting point for the workflow according to the sequence defined in the configured Unified Process.
      If (you can start with the workflow as defined in each iteration)
         Start with the model you feel most comfortable with in the workflow;
      Else if (you find you don't have much information on the defined workflow)
         You should revisit the configuration of the Unified Process and redo Step 2.
3. Apply model elaborators
   Apply model elaborators to complete the workflow. Normally, if the linked elements for the models of the next workflow can be found, it signifies that the current workflow has been completed.

4. Identify linked elements
   If (you can identify the linked elements (discover new requirements) for the next workflow)
      Identify the linked elements and proceed to the next workflow;
   Else if (you find it difficult to identify the linked elements for the next workflow)
      Go to Step 2.
5. Apply model transitors
   Navigate to the next workflow and select the appropriate models to work with this workflow. Make use of the linked elements identified from the models of the last workflow to derive the new models for the current workflow.
6. Apply view aligners
   Identify points of connection of the linked elements between models in the workflows and make the necessary updates to the models if changes have occurred in the linked elements.
7. Update linked elements for related models
   Repeat Steps 5 and 6 until all the workflows of the iterations have been completed.

This seven-step procedure for applying the VATs is represented in graphical form using an activity diagram (see Figure 6.15). Note that the manipulators may be applied more than once for each workflow. For example, in the requirements workflow, the use case diagram is the main model, but you can apply the elaborator twice. In the first application, the model elaborator elaborates each of the use case in the use case diagram with a use case description. In the second application, a different model elaborator elaborates each base use case together with its <<include>> and <<extend>> use cases using an activity diagram. The first elaborator helps realize a system-level sequence diagram, while the second one facilitates the analysis of the requirements of the scenarios needed for that use case.

Likewise, a model transitor and a view aligner may also be applied more than once when we transit from one workflow to another, as there is possibly more than one group of linked elements for a model transitor to help identify and derive new models for the next workflow. Finally, view aligners are used to establish the points of connection for the relevant models in the workflows.

Step 1: Configure the Unified Process

The predefined workflows in an iteration of the Unified Process are business modeling, requirements, analysis, design, etc. Some problems may involve only

Figure 6.15. Seven steps for applying view alignment techniques

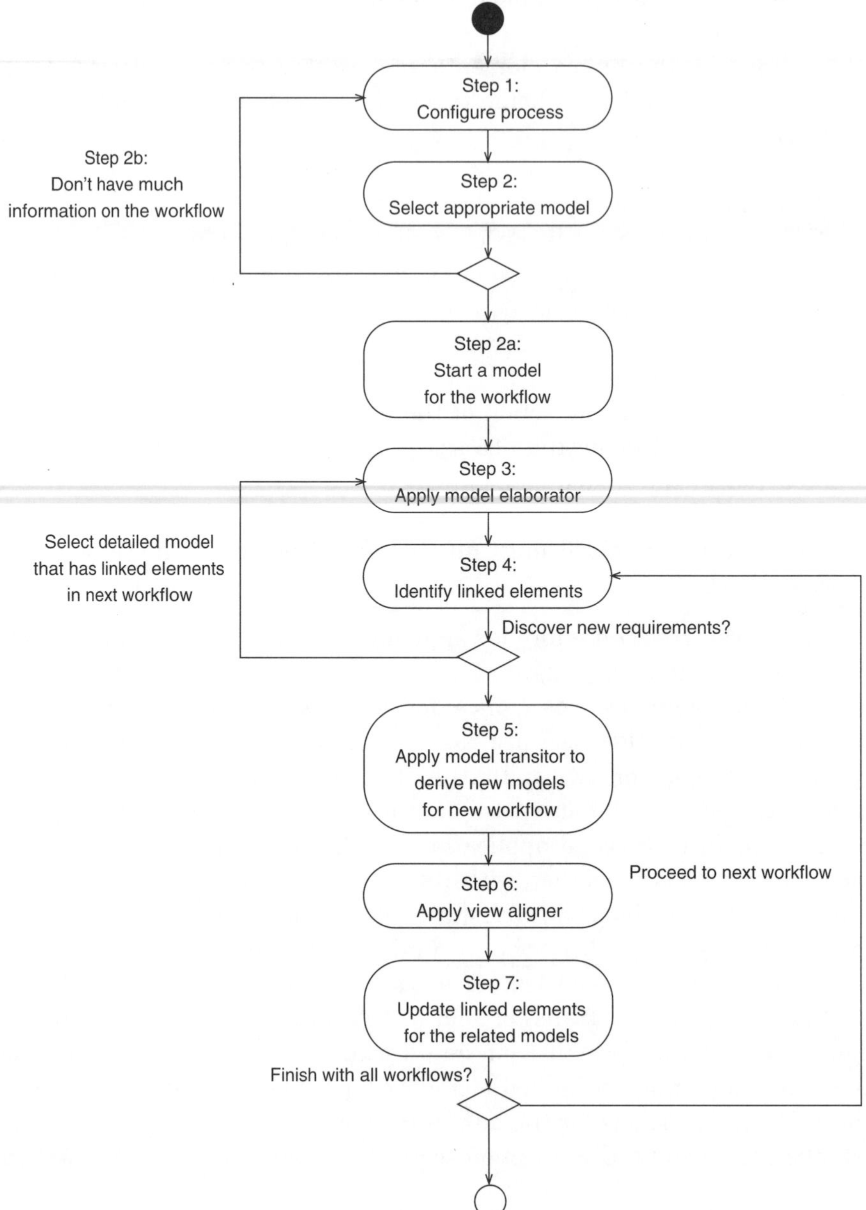

isolated tasks which do not have many connections with the business operations. In such situations, the business modeling workflow may be optionally removed from the development iteration or even the whole process. Some developers feel comfortable to include the workflow up to the design stage, while others may prefer to include implementation, testing and so on.

In this step, configure the standard workflows and the number of iterations involved in each development phase. Do not hesitate to adjust the number of development phases. The procedure for this step is as follows:

- Consider the nature of the problem; include various factors such as the size of the company and the resources available
- Consider also the information at hand: the development team's expertise and knowledge in different modeling techniques
- Configure the process to include the models to be used for each workflow: the input artifacts for analysis, the outputs of the workflow including models, documents, deliverables, test cases, etc.

Step 2: Select Models into Workflows

With the VATs, first consider the amount of information that is readily available and then select the most convenient model for development. For systems handling business activities and interaction-intensive applications, the most readily available information is the business workflow and the description of the business activities. Thus, the predefined workflows are suitable for general business applications, and that is why, for such systems, the business modeling is worked on first and use case modeling is then applied to the requirements workflow.

For systems that involve very little user interaction, the use case approach generally provides little help to designers. For example, a language parser, say, an HTML parser, does not involve much user interaction. The user specifies a HTML file and waits for the system to perform a series of complicated operations before returning the result. The grammar and the translation rules are, therefore, far more important than the use case model for such systems. So first model the grammar of the language using a graphical representation, such as a class diagram. For such an algorithm-intensive application, business workflow modeling or even use case modeling may not be very helpful. Instead, textual analysis or Class-Responsibility-Collaboration (CRC) may help identify objects for the object model. These examples demonstrate that there are multiple points of entry and exit for a particular project. The decision to select an appropriate entry point to come up with a suitable model for a particular workflow should be based on the nature of the project as well as other factors mentioned before. The procedure for this step is as follows:

- Consider the aim and objective of the workflow in the context of how the information at hand can help select the appropriate models to start with
- Determine the strong view of the main model selected, given the nature of the workflow being developed

Step 3: Apply Model Elaborator to Complete Workflow

The strong view is usually determined based on the nature of the workflow being developed. For example, business modeling is often represented by an activity diagram for modeling a business workflow. It is quite obvious that a use case diagram is not a good tool to delineate the business process. Rather, it defines system functionalities, user tasks and the goals associated with it. Once the strong view model has been determined, consider whether the requirements of the next workflow can be derived using this strong view model.

The procedure for this step is as follows:

- Determine the strong view of the next workflow. If the linked elements from the main model can be identified straightaway for the next workflow, then mark them down to discover the requirements for the models of the next workflow.
- Otherwise, try to elaborate the main model with sufficient details, in conjunction with other models in the current workflow. These models should contain the linked elements for the next workflow when the main model has been adequately elaborated.

Step 4: Identify Linked Elements

Having completed a (source) model of the workflow, derive the requirements of the models for the next workflow by identifying the linked elements in the (source) model(s). If you are readily able to do so, it is likely that the transition from this workflow to the next will be both traceable and seamless. However, there are situations where such a transition is not seamless. For example, you cannot seamlessly derive a sequence diagram of the design workflow from a use case. Many textbooks suggest that this is possible but without showing how it can be done. A use case diagram (the main model for the requirements workflow) does not contain enough details for deriving a sequence diagram. Use mainly the flow of events in a use case description (a supplementary model for a use case diagram) to develop a system-level sequence diagram (as mentioned earlier in Chapter 4: Dynamic Modeling and Analysis). If you cannot identify the linked elements in the main model, elaborate it with supplementary model(s) whereby the gap between the two adjacent workflows can be bridged. The procedure for this step is as follows:

- Ask "Does the source model need further clarification or details about its contents?" If so, apply a model elaborator to develop other model(s) within this workflow.
- Ask "Can you identify linked elements straightaway from the main model?" If not, supplement the main model with a number of more detailed models for this workflow, models that contain the linked elements (requirements) for the models of the next workflow.

Step 5: Apply Model Transitor

The designer can apply the transitor to generate new models from existing ones. Not only does this reduce the amount of work, but also improves the consistency between models since the generation of new models from existing ones guarantees that the linked elements of the common views of these models are consistent. The procedure for this step is as follows:

- Ask "Does the weak view(s) of the source model in last workflow provide a set of linked elements to derive models in the next workflow?" If so, apply a model transitor to develop new model(s) by extracting the linked elements from the previous workflow.

Step 6: Apply View Aligner

When one or more workflows are completed, revisit the models in the workflows to check for consistency. For example, the class diagram will be revisited many times, usually each time the sequence diagrams or collaboration diagrams have been developed. The objects that appear in the interaction diagrams (sequence and collaboration) are linked elements corresponding to a number of classes in a class diagram. Through this process, the class diagram will be enriched as other models are completed. These relationships are called points of connection. The procedure for this step is as follows:

- Examine the model elements in both the main and detailed models within the workflows and establish points of connection between the models in the workflows.
- Record the points of connection to prepare for the updates and changes that will take place in the model elements.

Step 7: Update Changes for Related Models in Workflows

As traceability has to be maintained among the models in the workflows, any changes made in one model may potentially need to be updated in other models and perhaps involving other workflows. The procedure for this step is as follows:

- Update the changes made in one model in the other models in other workflows according to the points of connection that have been identified earlier in Step 6.
- Branch to Step 4 if there are still other workflows to be completed.

Method Creation or Customization Using View Alignment Techniques

In the above section, a theoretical treatment of VATs was presented. We shall now apply these techniques to design a new method for software development. Instead of creating a very specialized method for a specific problem, we will provide a *generic* method that enhances the entire development process. More importantly this method can achieve much better model traceability, requirements discovery and models consistency. This *generic* method is not universal (we all know that a universal method does not exist). But it requires little customization for problems of a similar nature. For example, the method being proposed in the next section, which adopts the A^3, is particularly suited for interaction-intensive systems. The A^3 can greatly enhance the use case-driven approach by applying activity analyses at three different levels, hence the name.

To develop a new software development method using the VATs, a *method template* (see Table 6.2) should be used to structure the design process. A software development method is, therefore, specified by an instance of the method template. Once created, the software method can be applied to problems of a similar nature.

The method template consists of two parts: a method roadmap and a workflow roadmap (see Table 6.2). The method roadmap in turn consists of two key components: a general description of the method and a method roadmap diagram. The former describes the overall process of the software development method being designed. The latter is a diagram showing all the workflows within an iteration of the development phase from top to bottom (see Figure 6.16). In the Unified Process, typically these workflows are business modeling, requirements, analysis, design, implementation, etc. Each workflow to be conducted is represented by a UML package containing one or more analyses, enclosed by a rounded rectangle. Each of these rounded rectangles contains an analysis (represented by an ellipse) and an artifact (represented by a document symbol).

Table 6.2. A process template for method creation/customization

Method	[Name of software development method]
Description	[A brief description of the software development method. This may include the aims and objectives of the development method].
Method roadmap diagram	[A description of the high-level diagram that serves as a process roadmap for describing the entire development workflow within an iteration in a particular development phase (e.g. the requirements capturing workflow in the first iteration of the elaboration phase) (see Figure 6.17).]
Workflow	[Name of workflow]
Input artifacts or model elements	[The name of artifacts or model elements required for conducting the analysis]
Other sources of information	[Other sources of information that may be required for conducting the analysis.]
Analysis involved	[Name of the analysis]
Procedure	[The steps involved in conducting the analysis.]
Artifacts produced by the workflow	[The output artifacts produced by the analysis.]
Workflow roadmap diagram	[reference to workflow roadmap diagram]
Revisit from other workflow	[Additional steps required for refining the models that have been developed in the previous workflow.]
Manipulators	[list of manipulators used in the workflow]

Figure 6.16. Generic process for method and workflow roadmap diagrams

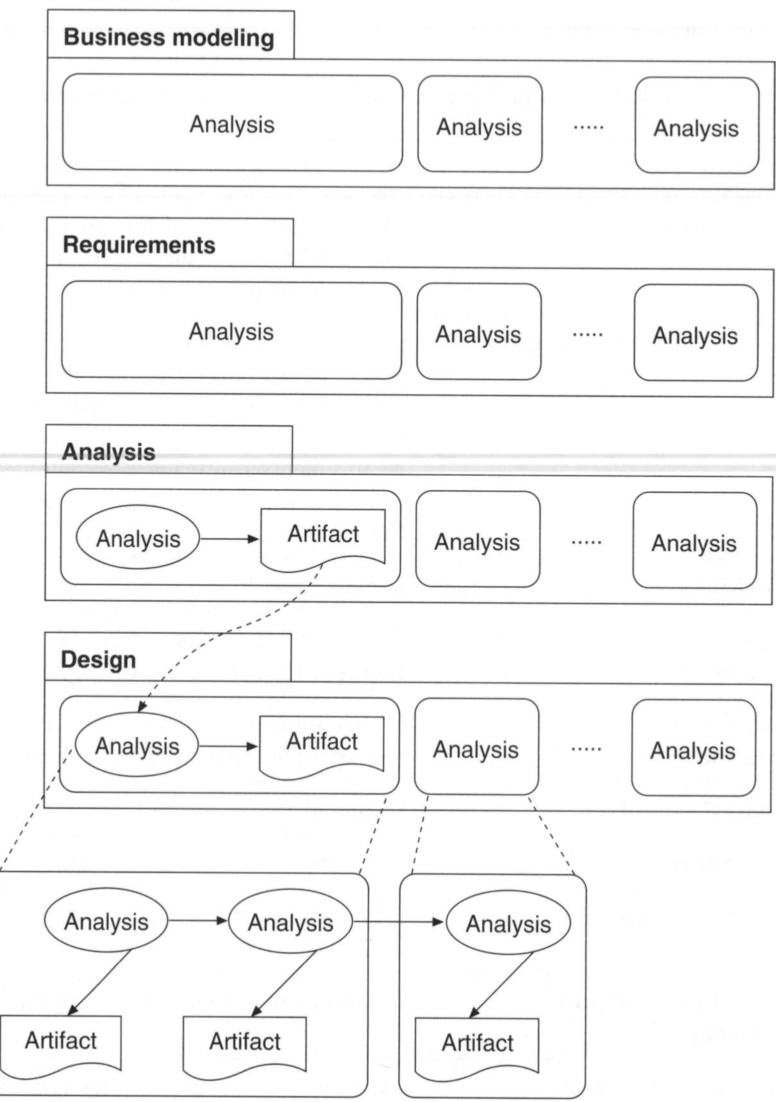

Figure 6.17. Method roadmap diagram for Activity Analysis Approach

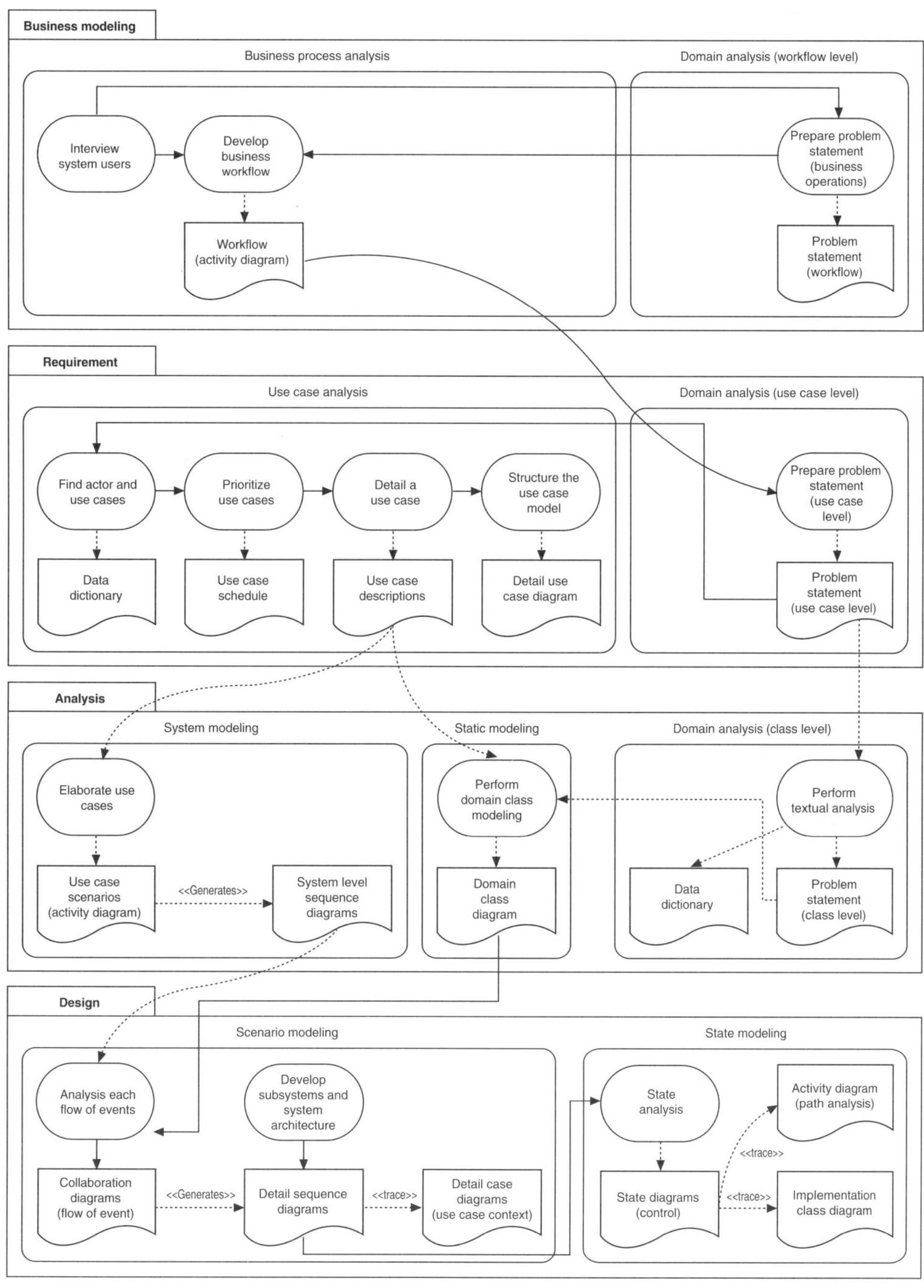

The second part of the method template, the workflow template, has three major components. The first component describes the input artifacts, output artifacts, the analysis involved and the procedure to be conducted within it. The second component is the workflow roadmap diagram which describes detailed activities such as the analysis to be conducted and output artifacts that will be produced by these analyses. A typical workflow roadmap diagram includes two adjacent workflows, which together show the connection of the linked elements between them. As mentioned earlier, a workflow may contain one or more rounded rectangles in it. Finally, the third component consists of a set of manipulators in a tabulated form which describes their application in the current and following workflows.

Method and Workflow Roadmap Diagrams

A high-level method includes all the workflows of a process, from top to bottom of the diagram according to the sequence of the workflow. Each workflow consists of a number of analyses represented by rounded rectangles. The workflow roadmap diagram provides a detailed view of what is inside each analysis.

Manipulator Descriptions

Manipulator descriptions show a list of manipulators that should be applied in the workflow. As each type of manipulator may be applied a number of times in a workflow, specify the link (interface) that takes place in between two model artifacts. For example, a model elaborator may be used in the requirements workflow three times as shown in Table 6.3.

Table 6.3. Manipulator descriptions

Manipulator	Brief description
Elaborator (use case list, use case diagram)	Develop a use case diagram from candidate use cases
Elaborator (use case, use case description)	Elaborate each use case with a use case description
Elaborator (use case, activity diagram)	Elaborate each use case with an activity diagram

Class Diagram for Method Template

Figure 6.18 shows the structure of a method template that can be conveniently represented in a class diagram, showing the artifacts that will be produced during the development process. A method template has its own name and consists of two components. The first is the method roadmap which consists of a description and the method roadmap diagram. The second is the workflow roadmap which contains the analyses to be conducted within this workflow. It contains a number of workflow roadmap diagrams, describing all the workflows included in an iteration within the development process. Each workflow roadmap diagram contains a list of model manipulators that are included in the manipulator description form, and each model manipulator is further described in detail by a model manipulator form.

Figure 6.18. Class diagram for method template

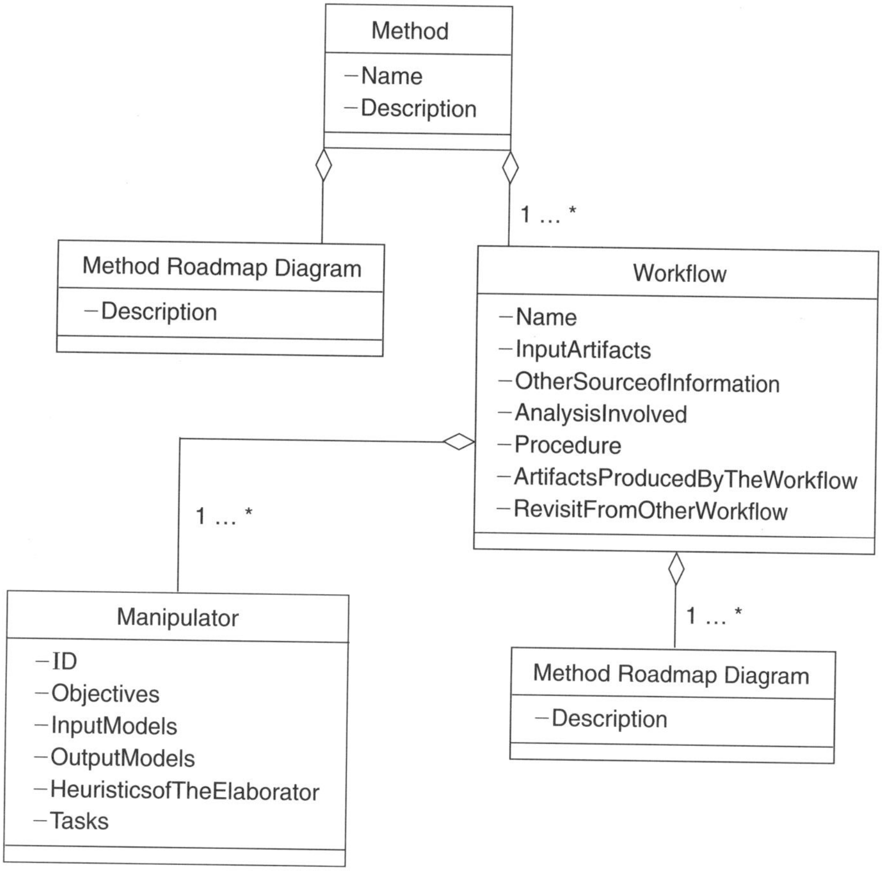

Method Creation: A Case Study

New software methods seem to emerge every ever so often in the industry. Some liken them to the latest apparel in the fashion industry in that software designers and vendors eagerly want to be the first to adopt new methods for fear of lagging behind. Perhaps this explains why some designers blindly follow the steps prescribed by some "universal methods," while not knowing their weaknesses and limitations.

The use case-driven approach has become very popular and so has been widely adopted over the past few years. It has also become a core component of UML. While object-oriented design is much more sophisticated than the traditional structured approach, practitioners often face the following difficulties:

- Use cases are used to specify the requirements of a system. While users can generally describe their business activities and processes, they cannot specifiy which parts should be computerized and which should remain as manual procedures. Obviously, there is a gap between the business activities described by the users and the use case model. It is also necessary to specify how the manual and computerized procedures should be integrated. A high-level (activity or workflow) model is required to fill this gap and to guide designers in identifying the use cases.
- Object identification is not an easy task. This process often frustrates many especially if they are new to the object-oriented approach. Traditionally, a textual analysis is performed on the problem statement or the use case descriptions. The nouns and noun phrases are highlighted and then evaluated by the developer for inclusion as objects. However, nouns or noun phrases only provide a list of candidate objects. To decide whether these candidate objects are objects truly relevant to the systems still requires the experience and good judgment of the design team.
- Realizing a set of sequence diagrams (containing a collaborative set of objects) from a use case is another difficult task. A use case may have many pathways of execution, involving many different scenarios and sequence diagrams to specify the collaborations between objects. In this process, there is also the need to identify certain objects for the user interface and the control flow. However, traditional use case descriptions are not good at specifying logic and multiple pathways of execution. Thus, managing the use case and the associated scenarios and sequence diagrams can be another hard task for the designer.

In this section, we will introduce a new software method that can greatly enhance the use case-driven approach. The A^3 provides effective solutions to all the above problems and fills the gaps between different UML models. The aim of the A^3 is to make it easier to identify use cases through the use of the business workflow analysis. Once the use case diagram is developed, we need to analyze the internal logic and determine the number of scenarios involved in each use case. The A^3 fills these gaps by guiding the designer through the process of object identification seamlessly.

Seven Steps of Method Creation Process

The A^3 uses UML as the notation, the Unified Process as the process and VATs for the techniques part. We have named the approach as the A^3 because activity analyses are performed at three different levels: business workflow, use case and scenario levels (see Figure 6.19):

- Business workflow analysis. The workflows of a company or organization are represented by swimlane activity diagrams at different levels of abstraction. At the top level, the workflows between the company and its business partners are described. At the middle level, activity diagrams for the workflows between the departments of the company are analyzed. At the bottom level, the workflows between individual actors are described. These analyses can help identify the scope of the software system being developed as well as the relationships between the software system, the human system and the computer system.
- Use case analysis. The flow of events of a use case can be elaborated by an activity diagram. An activity diagram is useful for analyzing the control flow of a use case if the use case has complex conditional branching or concurrent flows. The activity diagram can be used to determine the number of possible execution paths of the use case and to generate the necessary use case scenarios.
- Scenario analysis. Each of the action states which describes a use case in the activity diagram is elaborated by a collaboration diagram using the scenario analysis. As each of these action states represents a transaction (or sequence of transactions) of the use case, the transaction may be executed differently according to the way the user interacts with the system; it may be performed fully or not at all. Therefore, a number or collaboration diagrams may be required to describe each of the possible paths of the transaction.

Figure 6.19. The Three Levels of Activity Analysis

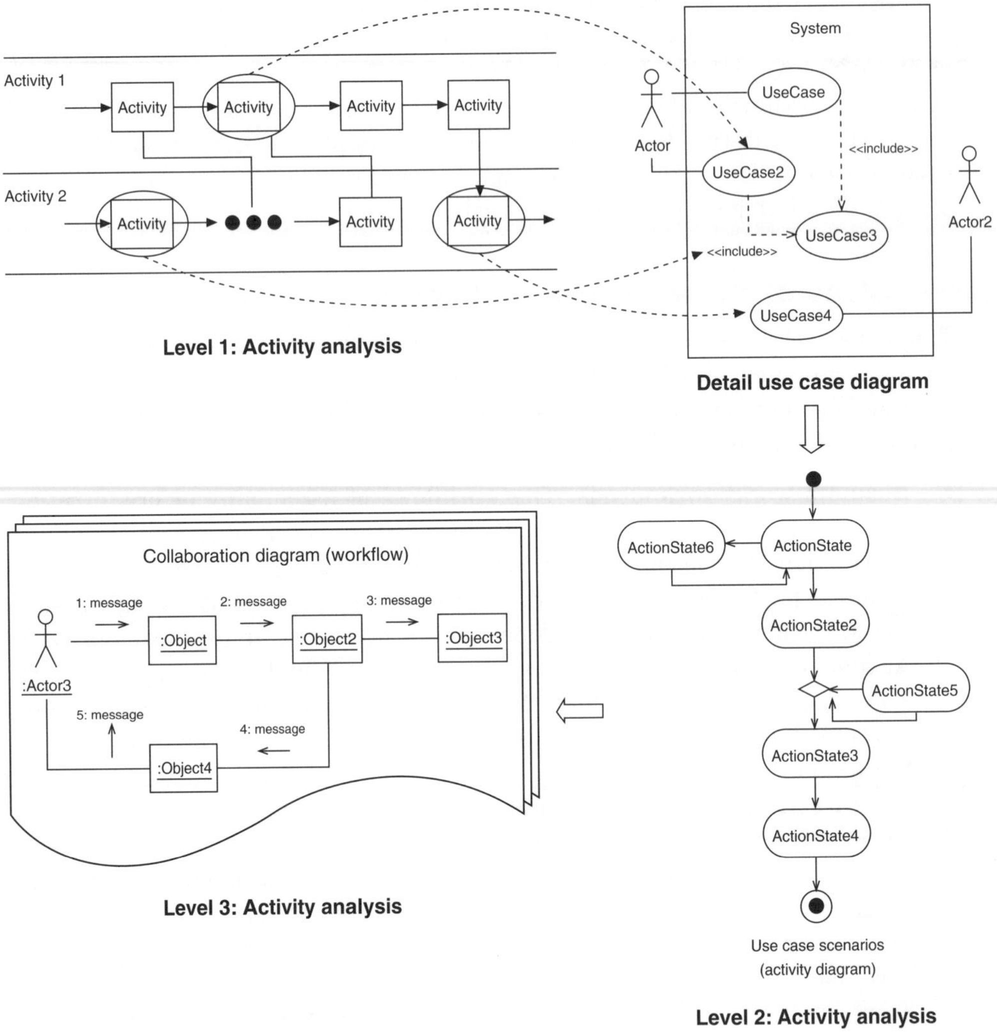

Level 1: Activity analysis

Detail use case diagram

Use case scenarios
(activity diagram)

Level 2: Activity analysis

Level 3: Activity analysis

Step 1: Configure Process

To design a new method, determine what workflows are to be included in an iteration within a phase of the development process (the four phases of the Unified Process are illustrated in Figure 6.4). For the entire development process, consider adopting either a unified process or simply the spiral software development life cycle model (SDLC). In addition to the configuration of workflows, designers may also determine the prototypes and deliverables for different checkpoints or milestones.

a. Determine the suitability of the development phases, the number of iterations and the workflows of the development process

   For the A^3, keep the case study precise and concise, so only *business modeling, requirements, analysis and design* workflows will be included in the case study as shown in Figure 6.20.

b. Determine the artifacts and deliverables for each workflow

   Select the architecturally significant use cases in the use case schedule to be developed first. At the end of each iteration, a prototype should be produced for the selected use case(s) with major subsystems integration for each of the development phases as shown in Figure 6.20.

c. Fill in the initial information for the method being created using the view alignment method design template (Table 6.4).

Figure 6.20. Process and workflow configuration for A^3

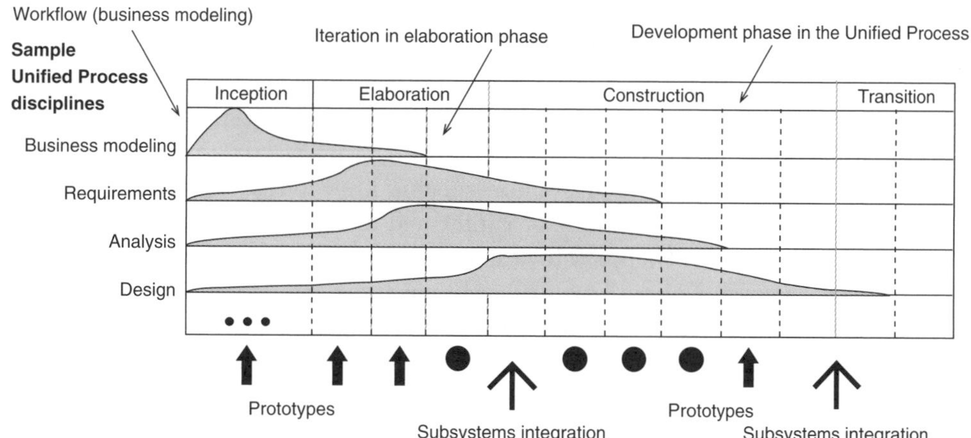

Step 2: Select Models for Workflow under Development

In the previous step, business modeling, requirements, analysis and design workflows were included in each of the development iterations. The first workflow to start with, in the order of the development iteration, is the *business modeling* workflow. Now, we need to select the appropriate models for this workflow.

Table 6.4. View alignment method design template for method creation

Method	Activity analysis approach (A^3)
Description	The Activity Analysis Approach enhances the use case-driven approach in terms of object identification, model traceability, requiremenets discovery and models consistency. It is a general software development process. This approach also supports multiple project development works of a company or organization.
Method roadmap diagram	The first workflow in an iteration of the Unified Process is business model and analysis, followed by requirements capturing, and so on, ending with the design workflow. This process template should be extended to cover testing and possibily other optional workflows. (Figure 6.17)

Select Models for Business Modeling

To understand the business operation and workflows of the company, we need to conduct interviews with the potential users of the system being developed. For problems related to a specific domain, it is necessary to interview domain experts to gain the required domain-specific knowledge. If the system is to be integrated with legacy systems or conformed to certain standards, these legacy systems, together with the relevant documentation, must be reviewed at the very early stages. Thus, there are two objectives the designers need to satisfy. The first objective is to model the business operation and workflows of the company and the second to take various factors into consideration, such as standard terminology, legacy systems, etc., to develop the target solution. If we only consider the views of the users to the conclusion of the standards, terminology and general practice in the industry, the target system will generally be difficult to integrate with other subsystems or to communicate with the outside world.

Thus, we need to have two analysis here in the business modeling workflow. Activity diagrams are an excellent analysis tool, while textual analysis is widely used to reveal static information such as documentation, standards or user guides of legacy systems. These two analyses are complementary to each other: use cases identified from the business workflow analysis activity diagram can be contrasted with those found from the textual analysis. In this case study, we shall choose the business workflow analysis as the main model (one of the entry points) and at the same time, the textual analysis will also be conducted to examine the domain, standard practice and/or legacy systems (as another entry point) for developing more standardized and reusable systems.

Business workflow analysis. The business process (workflow) of a company is analyzed using activity diagrams. The primary goal is to identify the candidate business activities for automation by software systems. Once this information is determined, the scope of the software system can then be set out.

Depending on the nature of the business, it is sometimes necessary to create more than one activity diagram to represent the business workflows of the company. Determine the activities in the workflows that should or should not be computerized. Start by analyzing the most important business processes of the company first. This will help the designers to quickly understand the core business processes of the company and identify which activities should be computerized. Where possible, interview the relevant representatives of the company.

Textual Analysis. The problem statement produced after interviewing end users and domain experts and the documentation describing the standard terminologies that need to be conformed with are excellent artifacts for the designer to prepare the groundwork for use cases identification, fact finding and the preparation of the data dictionary.

Step 3: Apply Model Elaborator

In this step, we apply the model elaborator to complete the workflow. Normally, if the linked elements for models of the next workflow are found, it is a strong signal that analysis of the current workflow is completed. We can then identify use cases from both the business workflow analysis and textual analysis which can be used straightaway for the next workflow – requirements. Use the use case diagram as the main model for the requirements workflow. Thus, the linked elements are a list of candidate use cases identified from the business workflow and textual analysis.

However, for very complex problems involving many activities, it might be necessary to develop a lower-level activity diagram to get a magnified view and a better understanding of the functions that these activities perform. Figure 6.21 shows the high-level business activities of a company. Several business activities (encased in ovals) are identified as needing computerization. For each of these business activities, elaborate it by a lower-level activity diagram and then identify the steps that require computerization.

Figure 6.21. Multi-level activity diagram for business modeling

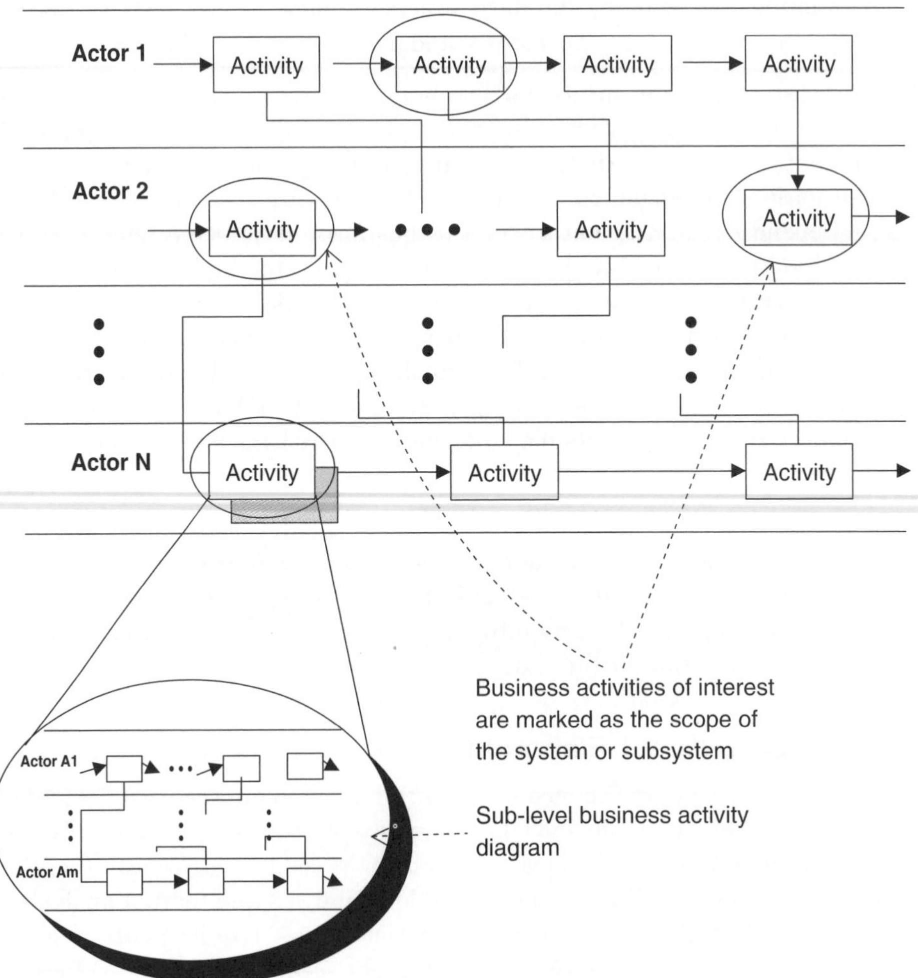

Business Modeling Workflow

Table 6.5 provides the description of the input artifacts, output artifacts and the process of the business modeling and analysis workflow.

Table 6.5. Description of business modeling process

Workflow Business Modeling	
Input artifacts or model elements	Problem statement, business workflow and possible sub-level business workflow diagrams for complex problems
Other sources of information	Legacy systems, domain knowledge of experts, end users, standards and terminologies in the field
Analysis involved	• Domain analysis (workflow) • Business process analysis
Procedure	• Interview users and prepare a problem statement at the business operation level • Model business processes using swimlane activity diagrams • Determine system scope
Artifacts produced by the workflow	Activity diagram (workflow)
Workflow roadmap diagram	See Figure 6.22
Revisit from other workflow	Any changes in business operations should be updated in the business workflow diagram
Manipulators	• Elaborator(Problem_Statement[interview], Swimlane_Activity_Diagram) • Elaborator(Swimlane_Activity_Diagram, Swimline_Activity_Diagram)

Step 4: Identify Linked Elements

At this stage, identify the linked elements (or discover new requirements) for the next workflow and proceed with the following steps.

The candidate use cases have now been identified from the business workflow and possibly from the textual analysis. The terminologies and descriptions used for naming the use cases should be consistent and documented in the data dictionary later on.

Once the linked elements extracted from the model(s) in this workflow have been found, use them to derive the model for the next workflow – requirements. Use case modeling and analysis techniques are widely used for interaction-intensive applications. The business workflow diagram (activity diagram) can often be modeled in a swimlane format, where each swimlane of the diagram may be associated with an actor (or sometimes a department) who is involved in or participates in that part of the business workflow. Basically, all the crucial information that is necessary for developing the use case diagram has been readily extracted from the models within the business modeling workflow. Thus, the transition from business modeling to requirements is expected to be seamless and traceable between each workflow. However, not all problem domains are heavily involved in the business workflow. Thus, we may at times need to develop several business workflow diagrams for operations that are quite independent of each other.

It may be more helpful to start with the domain analysis instead of the business workflow diagram. So, be flexible with the starting point(s) of the process; do not blindly follow the steps that were previously defined. If the business modeling workflow does not help in dealing with the type of problem at hand, reconfigure your workflow in the development process.

Previously, we used the crime-solving analogy to emphasize the importance of being flexible and always working on the available information. We should explore all possible entry points to identify linked elements from other views. In so doing, any missing pieces will become apparent when tracing the relevant link elements extracted from other models.

Step 5: Apply Model Transitor

Navigate to the next workflow and select appropriate models to work with this workflow. Make use of the linked elements extracted from the model of the previous workflow to derive the new models for this workflow.

At the end of the business workflow analysis and the textual analysis, we will have obtained the two artifacts: a list of candidate use cases and a high-level problem statement that describes the business operations and workflows, and the people participating in them.

At this point, the designer can develop the use case diagram for the requirements workflow. He/she can then develop the workflow roadmap diagram for the business modeling workflow (see Figure 6.22).

Step 6: Apply View Aligner

Having completed the first workflow (business modeling), focus on the next one (requirements). Because there is not a lot of completed models, the view aligner is not applied at this point.

Step 7: Develop Next Workflow

Having finished the business modeling workflow, we are ready to proceed to the requirements workflow which is done by repeating Steps 5 to 7 of the process of applying the VATs (see Figure 6.15) until all the workflows have been completed.

Summary of Business Workflow

To sum up the analysis involved in the business modeling workflow, we started off with two models (workflow level activity diagrams and workflow level problem statements) in parallel. Sometimes, the workflow level activity diagram is the main model and the workflow level problem statement the supplementary model. But it is possible it could be the other way round depending on the available information and the nature of the problem. Optionally, sub-level activity diagrams may be necessary for some complex problems. For certain independent business operations, several workflow level activity diagrams may be required, and model elaborators may be applied where necessary to create sub-level activity diagrams.

Transiting to Next Workflow: Requirements

The requirements workflow captures the requirements from the users' perspective. The system requirements are recorded by use case diagrams, use case descriptions, and actor specifications. Start with the list of business activities that have been identified for computerization in the business modeling and analysis workflow and prepare a problem statement (use case level) for the system. The problem statement will then be used to identify actors

Figure 6.22. Business modeling process

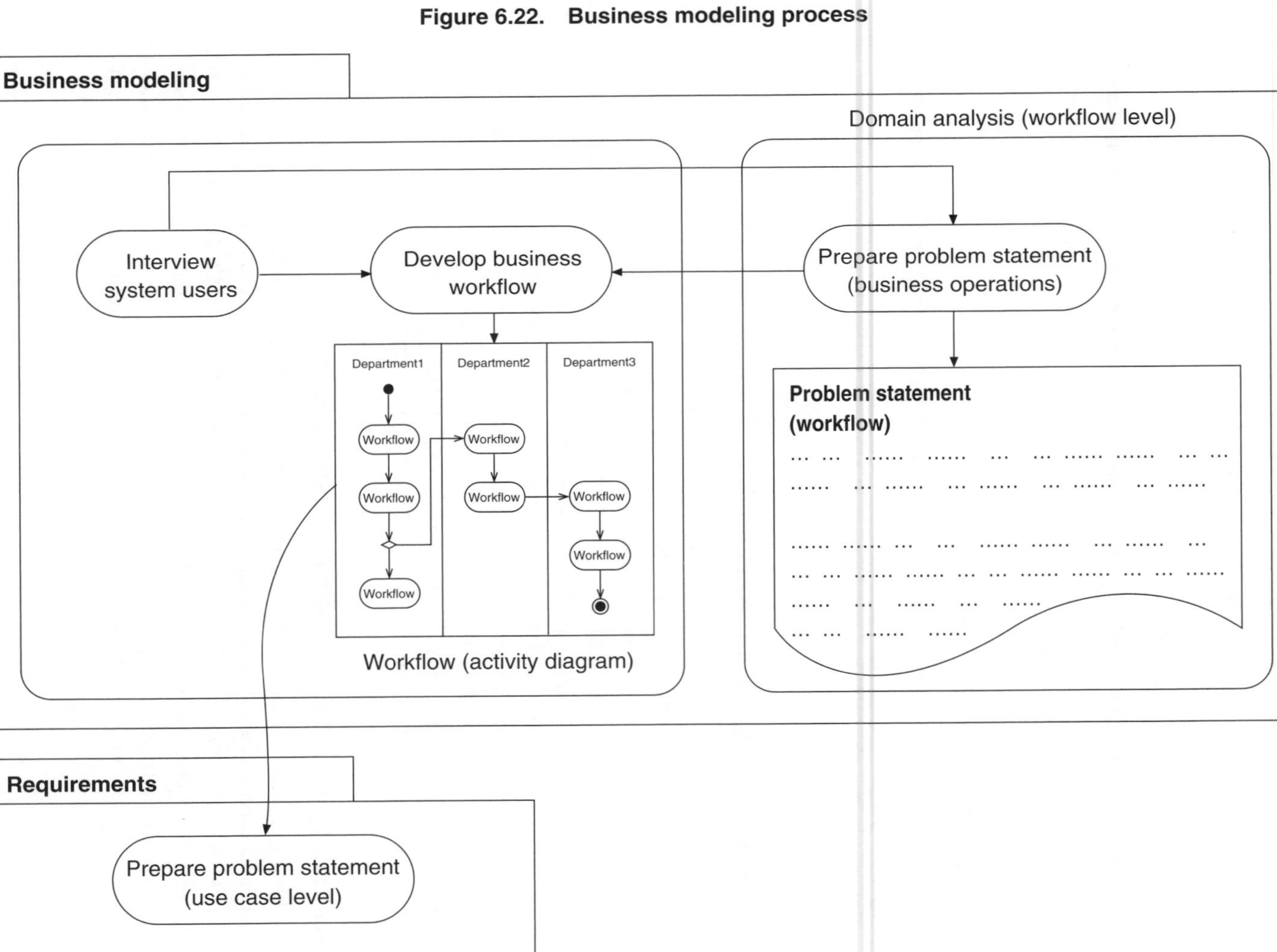

and use cases. Also, the problem statement can be refined to include details at the class level for implementation in the next workflow (analysis).

Two analyses are involved in the requirements workflow. The use case analysis is selected as the main analysis and the domain analysis as the supplementary analysis. This approach is particularly suitable for interaction-intensive systems. The use case analysis focuses on information provided by the end users who will interact with the new system to carry out their tasks. The domain analysis takes into consideration the terminologies and standards adopted by the industry and contrasting those used in the organization to ensure that the system does not deviate too much from the outside world. This will also improve system reusability and extendibility in the future.

Repeating Steps 4 and 6

In applying the model manipulators, there is an analysis pattern that designers can follow. In the first workflow (in this case, business modeling), only the appropriate model for the workflow need to be selected as there is none before it. Thus, a main model will be selected for the workflow, and some supplementary models may be needed if the linked elements are difficult to identify by applying the model elaborator.

When proceeding to the second workflow, use the models created in the previous workflow to generate partial models for the next workflow which contain the linked elements extracted by the model transitors. Then derive supplementary models by using model elaborators which again help bridge the gap between the workflow currently being developed and the one that follows. Through this process, more and more workflows are completed, and the application of view aligners becomes necessary to ensure models consistency. The analysis patterns can be summarized in Table 6.6.

Table 6.6. Application patterns of manipulators

Development status	Workflows	Application of manipulators' patterns
First workflow	Business modeling	Elaborators
Second workflow	Requirements	Transitor → Elaborators
Third workflow and beyond	Analysis, design, etc...	Transitor → Elaborators → Aligners

Workflow for Requirements

We shall skip the details of the steps associated with this (requirements) workflow since they have been described in detail in Chapter 3 (Use Case Modeling and Analysis). By repeating Steps 5 and 6, the requirements of the system are described by use case diagrams and the associated use case descriptions. Figure 6.23 shows the steps and models involved in the workflow. Table 6.7 provides a detailed description of the workflow.

Table 6.7. Description of requirements workflow

Workflow: Requirements	
Input artifacts or model elements	Activity diagram [workflow], problem statement [workflow]
Other sources of information	Legacy systems, domain knowledge of experts, end users, standards and terminologies in the field
Analysis involved	• Domain analysis (use case level) • Use case analysis
Procedure	• Prepare the problem statement at the use case level • Perform textual analysis to identify major actors and use cases • Create use case diagrams • Describe the use cases • Structure the use case diagrams with <<include>>, <<extend>> and generalization relationships • Develop instance scenarios of the use cases • Prioritize the use cases
Artifacts produced by workflow	Use case model (use cases)
Workflow roadmap diagram	See Figure 6.23
Revisit from other workflows	Any changes in business operations should be updated in the problem statement at the use case level

Table 6.7. (Con't)

Manipulators	• Transitor(Activity_Diagram[Business Workflow], Problem_Statement [use case level]) • Transitor(Problem_Statement [use case level], Actor_List) • Transitor(Problem_Statement[use case level], Use_Case_List) • Elaborator(Use_Case_List, Data_Dictionary.Use_Case_List) • Elaborator(Actor_List, Data_Dictionary.Actor_List) • Elaborator(Data_Dictionary.Use_Case_List, Use_Case_Schedule) • Elaborator(Data_Dictionary.{Use_Case_List, Actor_List}, Use_Case_Diagram} • Elaborator(Use_Case, Use_Case_ Description)

Transiting to the Next Workflow: Analysis

The purpose of the analysis workflow is to identify the classes and objects of the system from the models of the requirements workflow and the ways in which the users invoke the use cases. Identify the classes and objects of the system by performing a textual analysis on the problem statement and the use case descriptions. However, it is generally difficult to ascertain sequence information from the use case description. The activity diagrams will enable the designers to do so effectively.

It can be seen that the transition from requirements to analysis is natural, and that the creation of activity diagrams from use case descriptions is also straightforward through the use of the linked elements between them. The flow of events part in the use case description details the external interactions between the system and the actor. The activity diagrams for concrete use cases will also cover the flow of events of the <<include>> and <<extend>> use cases.

Repeating Steps 5 and 6

Figure 6.24 shows the roadmap for the analysis workflow which contains three analyses. The main model is system modeling which realizes each of the use cases using the second level of A^3 (recall that the first level of A^3 is the representation of the business workflow using activity diagrams in the business modeling workflow). The activity diagram provides the graphical representation

Figure 6.23. Requirements workflow process

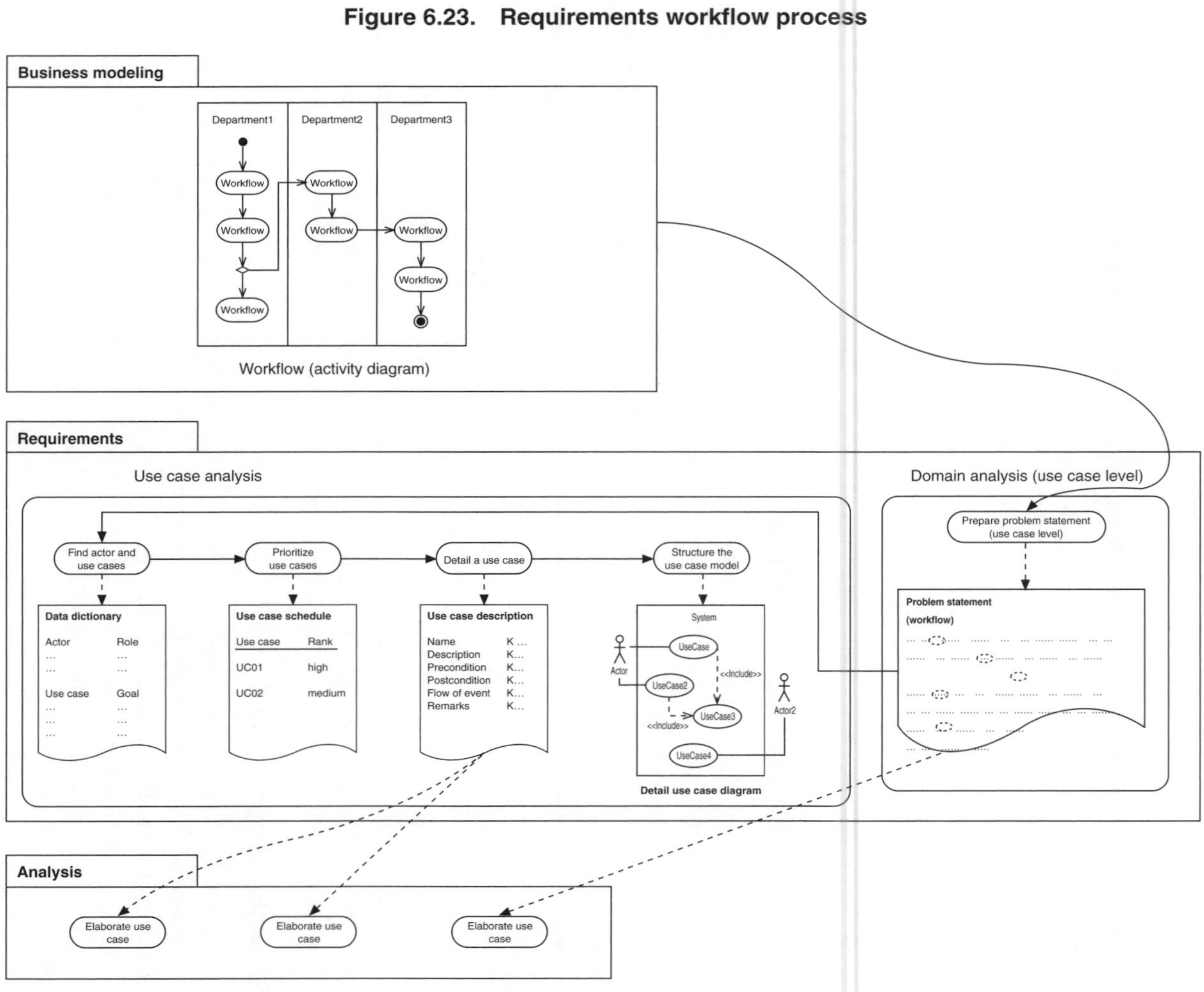

Figure 6.24. Analysis workflow process

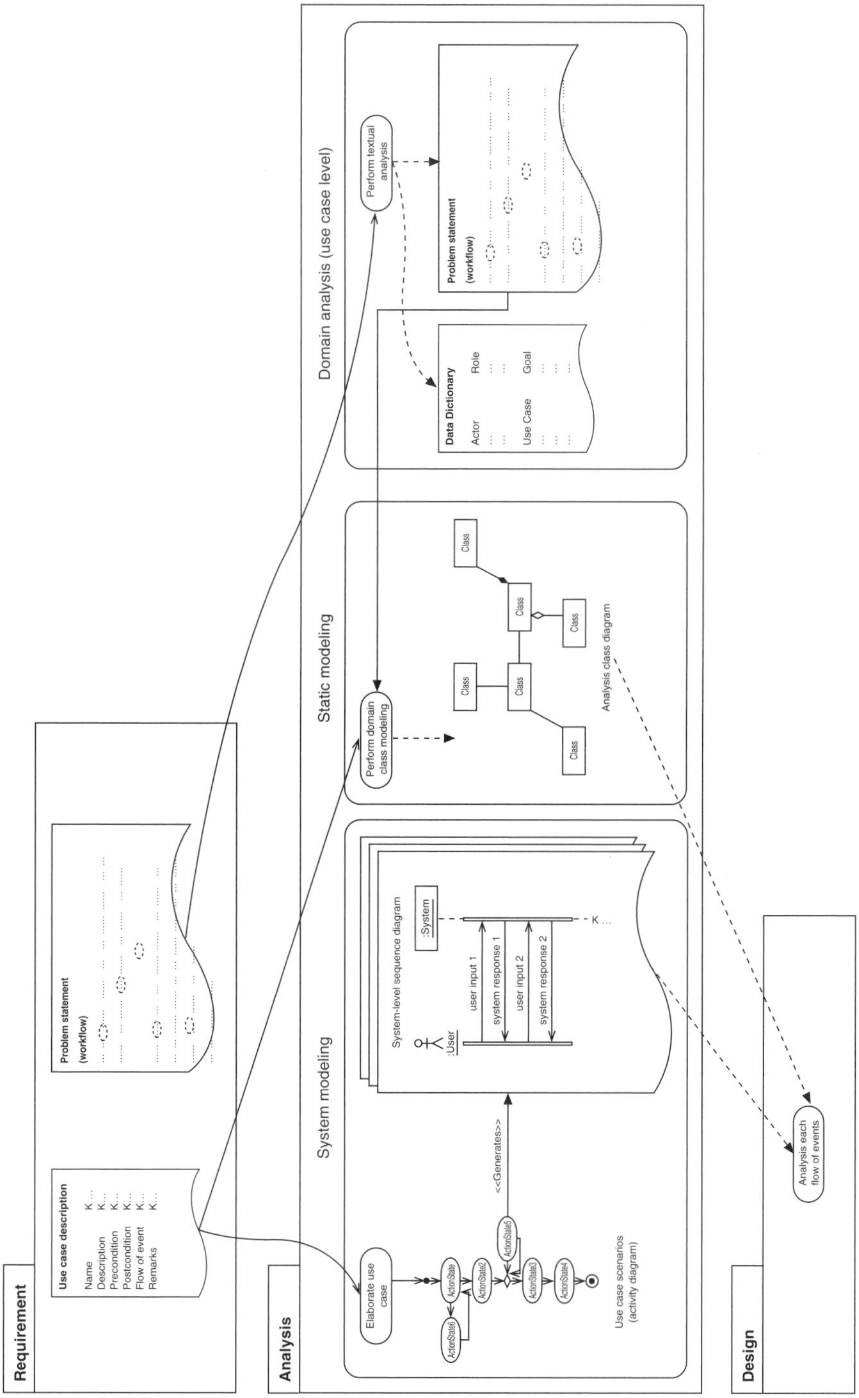

of a use case which is structured into the base use case and its associated abstract use cases. The use case level problem statement is used to perform textual analysis to identify candidate domain classes. These classes will, in turn, be structured into an analysis class diagram through static analysis. The purpose of the analysis class diagram is to provide an alternative way, in addition to the use case approach, to identify important objects for the application. This is because the use case approach is focused on the requirements obtained from end users, and does not consider the overall terminologies and standards currently used in the industry.

The current analysis workflow is third in line. The analysis pattern requires the application of first, the model transitors, then the model elaborators (if necessary) and finally the view aligners. Let us follow this analysis pattern in the application of the model manipulators for the analysis workflow. First apply the model transitor for the use case description by connecting the linked elements (flow of events) with the main model (activity diagram). Each action state in the activity diagram corresponds to an event in the flow of events of the use case description. The main flow of the activity diagram corresponds to a base use case, and each <<extend>> or <<include>> use case is represented by a group of action states in the activity diagram. For the <<extend>> use case, a decision branching is necessary.

Each message in the system-level sequence diagram or flow of events in a use case description corresponds to a collaboration diagram which is the third level of the activity analysis for the A^3 development method. By applying the model transitor, the flow of events in the use case description are turned into an activity diagram. At this point, analyze the number of scenarios there should be for the use case and then develop corresponding system-level sequence diagrams by using the model elaborators. Therefore, the messages in the system-level sequence diagram (linked elements) enable us to discover the requirements for the next workflow – design.

Although the application of the view aligner is optional here, it can be argued that any changes or updates in the data dictionary obtained in the domain analysis should be reflected in the related models using the view aligner. Likewise, the view aligner should be applied to ensure the extension points in the use case diagram are consistent with the corresponding branching in the activity diagram. Table 6.8 provides a detailed description of the analysis workflow.

Table 6.8. Description of analysis workflow

Workflow Analysis	
Input artifacts or model elements	Problem statement[use case level], use case model
Other sources of information	Legacy systems, domain knowledge of experts, end users, standards and terminologies used in the field
Analysis involved	• Domain analysis (class level) • Static modeling • System modeling
Procedure	• Perform domain analysis of the problem statement to develop a domain class model • Perform textual analysis of the use case description to identify system-specific classes and combine the results with the domain class model • Elaborate a use case with system-level sequence diagrams • For use cases with complex control flows, elaborate the use cases with activity diagrams first
Workflow Analysis	
Artifacts produced by workflow	System-level sequence diagrams, analysis class model
Workflow roadmap diagram	See Figure 6.25
Revisit from other workflows	Any changes in the problem statement or use case model should be updated in the analysis class model and the system-level sequence diagrams

Table 6.8. (Con't)

Manipulators	• Transitor(Problem_Statement, Class_Diagram[domain]) • Transitor(Use_Case_Description, Class_Diagram[analysis]) • Aligner(Class_Diagram[domain], Class_Diagram[analysis]) • Transitor(Use_Case_Description. Flow_of_Events, Activity_ Diagram) • Aligner(Activity_Diagram, Use_Case_Diagram.Use_Case.Extension_Point_List) • Elaborator(Activity_Diagram.Path,: System_Level_Sequence_Diagram)

Transiting to Next Workflow: Design

The aim of the design workflow is to conduct behavioral modeling and analysis so that we can progress from the stage of getting a detailed understanding of what the problem is, to the stage of discovering how the problem is going to be solved. For example, up to this point, we have the use case model of the problem under development and each use case may be elaborated by an activity diagram which, in turn, describes the possible scenarios. Each of these scenarios can be represented by a system-level sequence diagram. Remember that these diagrams describe only the external interactions between the users and the system and not anything related to the internal logic of the system.

At this point, proceed from a detailed description of the system's external behavior to the design of the system's internal logic. An effective method should help the designer make gradual progress from one workflow to another. The third level of the A^3 leads the designer through this important transition from the "What to do" stage to the "How to do" stage by applying the scenario analysis in the design workflow.

Repeating Steps 4 to 6

The design workflow contains two analyses: the scenario analysis and the state analysis. The first step of the scenario analysis concerns the design of the realization of each action state in the activity diagram (representing a use case) using a collaboration diagram. The collection of all these collaboration diagrams representing action states forms a detailed Model/View/Control (MVC)-level sequence diagram. The control object or subsystem will, in turn, be represented by a state diagram. To ensure models traceability and

Figure 6.25. Process of design workflow

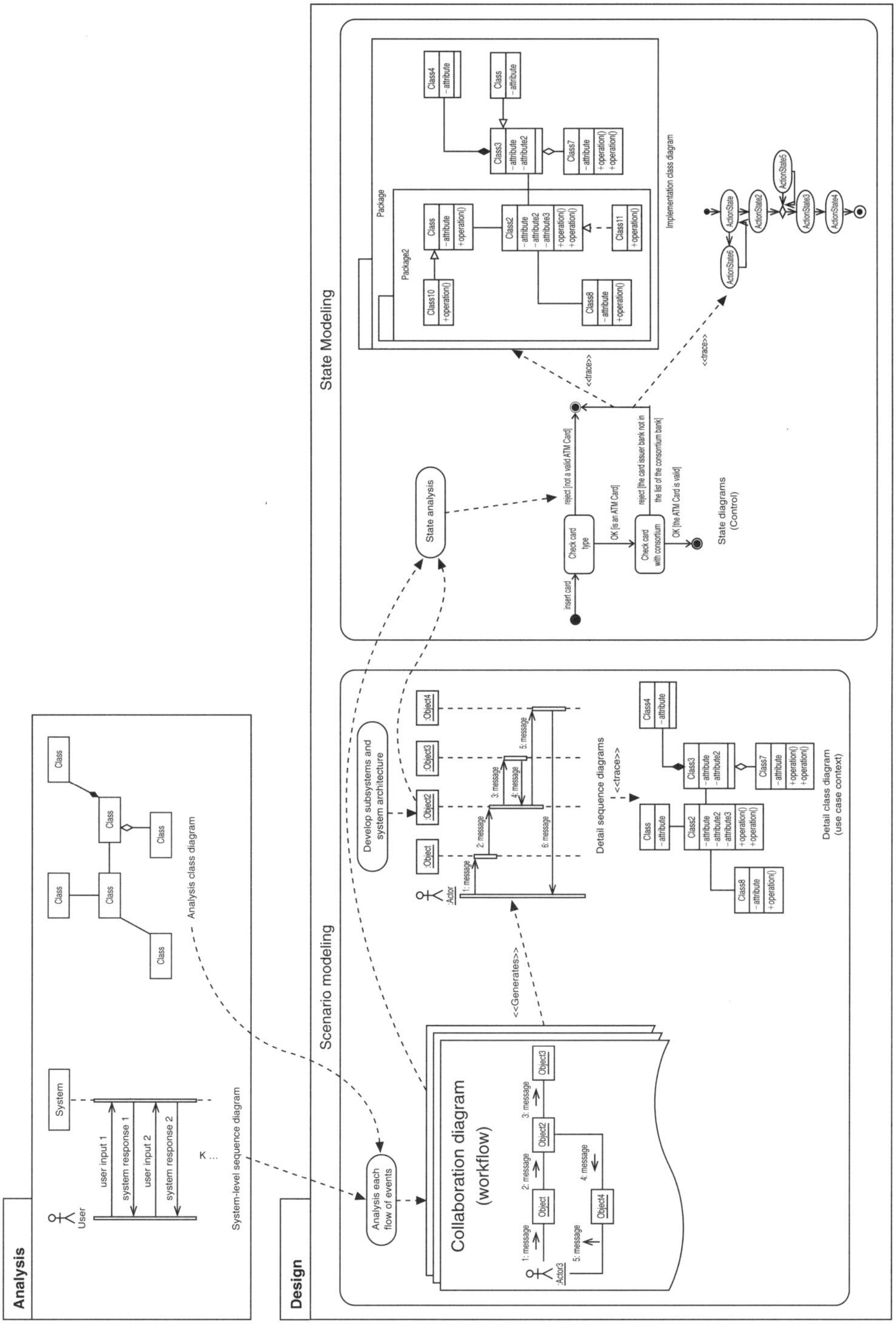

consistency, applications of view aligners are necessary. For example, revisiting the activity diagram (use case level) enables us to refine the precondition, post-condition and use case lifetime invariances after the state diagram of a control object has been created. Updates of the class diagram after the completion of each scenario of a use case also call for the application of view aligners. As the number of classes grows, they can be grouped into packages, while the system architecture should be revised where necessary for ease of management (see Table 6.9).

Table 6.9. Description for design workflow

Workflow Design	
Input artifacts or model elements	System-level sequence diagram, analysis class diagram
Other sources of information	—
Analysis involved	• Flow of events analysis • Development of subsystem or system architecture
Procedure	• Elaborate the flow of events using collaboration diagrams (flow of events) • Generate MVC-level sequence diagrams from the collaboration diagrams (flow of events) • Revise the class diagrams • Perform state analysis on the control objects • Revise activity diagrams through path analysis • Revise the class diagrams
Workflow Design	
Artifacts produced by workflow	Detailed sequence diagrams, design class diagrams, state diagrams
Workflow roadmap diagram	See Figure 6.25
Revisit from other workflows	Whenever changes in analysis workflow require changes in the corresponding models of the design workflow

Table 6.9. (Con't)

Manipulators	• Elaborator(Activity_Diagram, Collaboration_Diagram_List) • Elaborator(Activity_Diagram.Path, Sequence_Diagram[Design]) • Aligner(Sequence_Diagram, Class_Diagram) • Transitor(Sequence_Diagram, State_Diagram) • Aligner(State_Diagram, Class_Diagram) • Aligner(State_Diagram, Activity_Diagram) • Aligner(State_Diagram, Class_Diagram)

Figure 6.24 shows the overview of the process roadmap and description for the design workflow. The high-level architecture for the business operation will be identified after we have analyzed the business workflow. We subsequently identify use cases and group them into appropriate packages. The lower system architectures **will be also fine-tuned in this development workflow** such as the identification of subsystems and their components, and their implementation in the form of software frameworks and design patterns.

In the design workflow, there are two major analysis blocks. The first analysis block is concerned with the realization of use cases through scenario analysis in which each of the events in the flow of events are fully elaborated by a collaboration diagram. These collaboration diagrams are in turn used to form a detailed sequence diagram representing a scenario of a use case. The second analysis block deals with the detailed logic of a control object or a subsystem by performing a state analysis. We also need to revisit the activity diagram to refine the use case's conditional branchings between the scenarios. The following section explains these two analyses in detail.

Manipulators for Scenario Modeling

Scenario modeling is about modeling or analyzing the internal behaviors of a system. A use case can be considered as a sequence of "transactions," where each transaction corresponds to a pair of input and response messages between the primary actor and the system. Each pair of input and response messages is elaborated by an MVC collaboration diagram, providing details about the object collaboration inside the system. The set of collaboration diagrams of a system-level sequence diagram can then be used to generate an MVC-level sequence diagram using a CASE tool.

Manipulators for State Modeling

After the behavioral analysis, the detailed scenarios of the use cases are examined and both the dynamic and static requirements identified. In the implementation workflow, we aim to develop the detailed control logic for the subsystems and control objects, and refine the high-level branching requirements at the use case level (see Chapter 4).

In the MVC software framework, the control objects act as the mediator for communicating between the boundary and entity objects. The subsystems and control objects are usually active objects. They contain more complex dynamic behaviors that need to be modeled. State diagrams are developed to represent the logic of these control components.

In developing the state diagrams for the control object of a use case (or a single transaction of a use case), we also model all the possible execution paths of the use case (or the transaction), including the cases in which the transaction is canceled or incorrectly carried out. Remember that a use case (or a transaction) is performed either fully or not at all. In order to maintain atomicity of a use case, additional branchings may need to be added in the activity diagram of the use case.

We have now completed all the workflows that were configured in the development process including business modeling, requirements, analysis and design. We now have all the information available to develop the method roadmap diagram and to complete the method template.

Method Roadmap Diagram

Figure 6.17 illustrates the A^3 in a single iteration of the Unified Process. In Chapters 2 to 5, we presented the detailed procedure and the tips and tricks in applying the A^3 software development method, a method that is suited for interaction-intensive applications. In the above example, it was demonstrated that the A^3 software development method covers all the important workflows right up to analysis and design. Readers can apply what they have learned in this example for the implementation and testing of workflows as well.

Summary

A software development method consists of three key components: process, representation and techniques. Over the past few years, the Unified Process has emerged as the *de facto* standard and the UML has now become a well-recognized standard for representing software systems. However, it is quite evident that the techniques part is the weakest link of the software development method. We have proposed a framework of VATs to address this problem.

The VATs consist of three manipulators, and their heuristics guide the designer through a customization process which closely follows the Unified Process. The major advantage of these techniques is that they provide the developer with a set of procedures to follow from one model to the next, based on the amount of information available at hand. This allows the developer to create and customize a software method for a particular problem.

As mentioned before, there are no universal software development methods that are applicable to all problems. The heuristics and techniques component of a software development method can only be built up over a long period of time through experience. The VATs is effective in assisting the designer to accelerate the learning curve and acquire the necessary skills and knowledge to perform analysis and design tasks in a structured and systematic way. Designers may adopt these techniques for most business applications with only minor modifications. As they gain more experience with VATs, they will be able to customize or even tailor them to suit the needs of their organizations. The beauty of VATs is that they provide the model manipulators, enabling designers to start the process and select the right models for different workflows. Furthermore, designers can also tell when the workflows are completed and how to proceed on to the next workflow, etc. But more importantly, designers should never blindly follow steps that are prescribed by the methodologists or textbooks.

Based on the framework of VATs, this chapter has presented the process of new software development using the A^3. This method is particularly suited for those user interaction-intensive systems which are typical in many business applications. We will illustrate how this method is applied for a business application in the next chapter.

Exercises

Q1. Briefly explain the uses of the elaborator, transitor and view aligner manipulators in a workflow.

Q2. For each pair of the following models, identify the linked elements between them:

- Sequence diagram and class diagram
- State diagram and sequence diagram
- Use case diagram and activity diagram

- Activity diagram and state diagram
- Collaboration diagram and class diagram

Q3. Briefly explain why the manipulators are usually applied to a workflow in the following sequence: transitor, elaborator, and then view aligner.

Chapter

7

A Case Study: Applying the Activity Analysis Approach

Overview

In the previous chapter, we introduced the Activity Analysis Approach (A^3) as a generic method for developing activity-based systems such as business systems. In this chapter, we will demonstrate the application of the A^3 to a real-life problem: a mail order system. We shall show in detail all the necessary steps involved to perform system analysis and design using the A^3.

What You Will Learn

On completing the study of this chapter, you should be able to:

- understand each step of the A^3
- apply the A^3 to system development

The Case Study

This case study describes the development of a mail order system by applying the Activity Analysis Approach (A^3). Throughout this case study, we will show the main steps and the artifacts produced in the A^3 in one iteration of the development process. Typically, due to the complexity of modern systems, several iterations are necessary to elicit and model all the requirements specified.

It should be noted that the example used in this chapter shows how the A^3 process may be applied to a typical activity-based system in one specific way.

In practice, steps of A^3 workflows are often repeated in iterations of the development process as the target system is being developed incrementally.

This chapter is organized into different sections of A^3 workflows, with each section of workflows further subdivided into smaller subsections.

Business Modeling

Figure 6.17 in Chapter 6 shows a detailed roadmap for the A^3, showing four distinct workflows: business modeling, requirements, analysis and design. In the business modeling workflow, the process begins with a high-level problem statement which enables us to develop the different activity diagrams to model the operation of the organization. In the requirements workflow, these high-level activity diagrams are used to identify the scope of the system and to develop the use case models of the target system. In the analysis workflow, the use case descriptions are analyzed to create domain class diagrams and system-level sequence diagrams. Finally, in the design workflow, low-level collaboration, state and sequence diagrams are developed to model the realization of the use cases.

Domain Analysis (Workflow)

The business modeling starts by gathering information about the business processes of an organization. The goal is to identify those candidate activities that are targets for computerization. The developer can collect the information through the following ways:

- Interviewing users
- Distributing questionnaires to be completed
- Documenting the business procedures
- Interviewing domain experts
- Looking at the standards and terminologies in the business domain

Interviewing staff members of the organization is an effective way of collecting valuable information. Start with the managers of various departments and then the front line staff members within these departments to gain an overview of the business activities and from that, the organizational requirements.

System analysts can use problem statements to document these requirements for later use in the analysis workflow. The following is a preliminary problem statement at the workflow level of a mail order system:

Problem statement 7.1. Problem statement [workflow] for the mail order system

In order to improve the operational efficiency of a mail order company, the chief executive officer is interested in computerizing the company's business process. The major business activities of the company can be briefly described as follows:

- The company aims to provide high quality mail order services to all registered members of the company.
- An individual or a company registers as a member by completing the registration form and sending it to the customer service department.
- A member orders items by filling an order form and sending it to the customer service department. The customer service department verifies the membership and forwards the order to the sales department. If the order can be processed through existing stock, the sales department processes the order and issues delivery notes to the inventory department. Otherwise, the sales department issues a purchase order to the supplier. When all items are available, the inventory department delivers the items to the member, and the accounts department issues an invoice to the member.
- When the accounts department receives an invoice from a supplier, it verifies that the items in the purchase order have been received, and issues payment to the supplier.

Business Process Analysis

After having collected the required information, apply the *Elaborator (Problem_Statement[workflow], Swimlane_Activity_Diagram)* manipulator to develop an activity diagram (see Figure 7.1). The purpose of this manipulator is to model the business workflow by a swimlane activity diagram. The swimlane activity diagram can help visualize the business activities of the company and hence identify the business activities for computerization. The activity diagram can be created by representing the steps of a business procedure as action states and the flow of the business procedure as arrows between action states. For example, the procedure for registering a new customer involves two steps: (1) the *customer fills a registration form* and (2) the customer service department *registers the customer*.

Determining System Scope

By interviewing the manager of the accounts department, it is discovered that the business activities are currently covered by an existing accounting system. Figure 7.1 illustrates the high-level business activities of the company. The developer can then discuss with the stakeholders of the system and decide on the business activities that are required to be computerized. Let us assume that the developer and the stakeholders have agreed to computerize the business activities related to membership, sales, ordering, and inventory control of the mail order company. We can now proceed with the requirements workflow (the next workflow of the A^3).

Figure 7.1. Activity diagram showing business workflow of mail order company

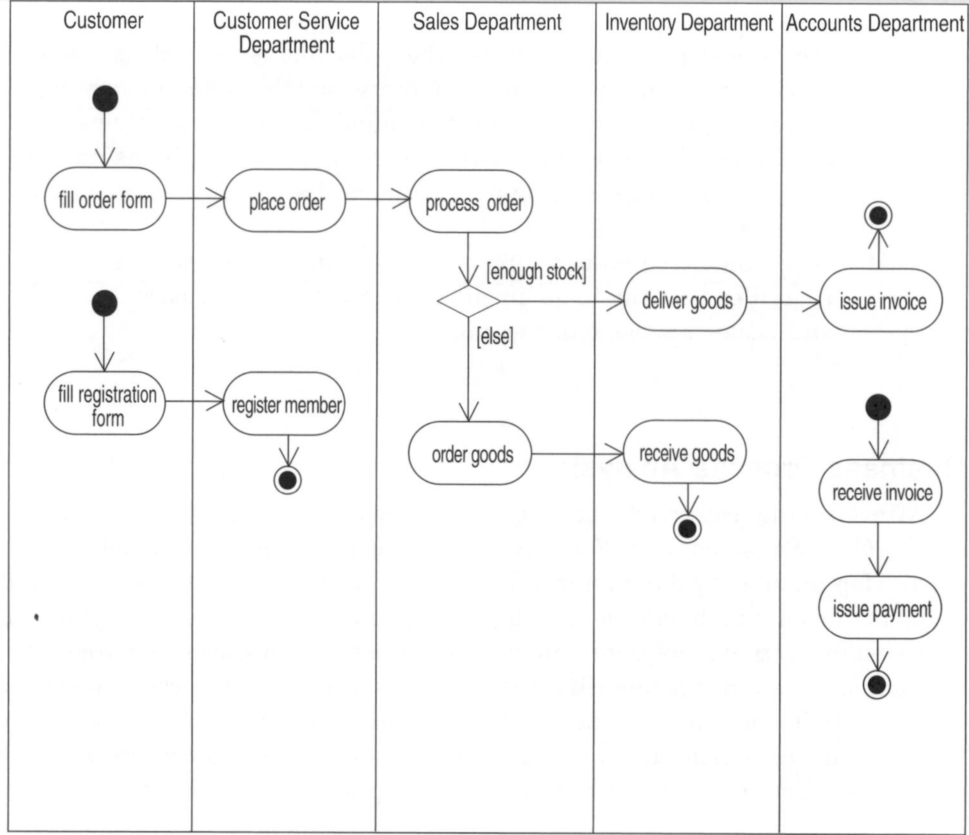

Requirements

In this workflow, start with a set of activities that require computerization and prepare a more detailed (use case level) problem statement. Then conduct a textual analysis on this problem statement to identify the actors and use cases. By elaborating the use cases with more details, the use case descriptions can be used as the input to the analysis workflow.

Domain Analysis (Use Case Level)

After determining the scope of the system, prepare a (use case level) problem statement to describe the required activities. In the previous section, we decided to computerize the activities related to membership maintenance, order processing and inventory control. The problem statement should give enough details to identify the responsibilities of individual users and to describe the procedure to follow in order for them to perform their tasks. The following is a use case-level problem statement of the business activities:

Problem statement 7.2: Problem statement [use case level] for the *Mail Order System*

- A customer registers as a member by completing the membership form and mailing it back to the company. A member who has not been active (i.e. no transactions) for a period of one year will be removed from the membership list and needs to apply for reinstatement of the lapsed membership.
- A member informs the company of any changes in personal details, such as home address, telephone numbers, etc.
- A member makes an order by filling out a sales order form and then faxing it to the company. Alternatively, the Customer Service Assistant handles the order over the phone.
- The Customer Service Assistant always checks the validity of the membership before entering the sales order information into the system.
- The Order Processing Clerk checks the availability of the ordered items and holds them for the order. If all the items are available, the Order Processing Clerk schedules delivery.
- The Inventory Control Clerk controls and maintains an appropriate level of stock and is also responsible for reordering new items.

- If there is a problem with an order, members phone the Customer Service Assistant who takes appropriate action to follow up the sales order.
- Members may return defective goods within 30 days and get their money back.
- Each task carried out by the system has the name and ID of the staff member concerned recorded into the system.

Use Case Analysis

The detailed processes, steps and heuristics of use case analysis are already discussed in Chapter 3. Here, the process of performing the use case analysis will be demonstrated in the A^3.

Finding Actor and Use Cases

Apply the *Transitor(Problem_Statement[use case level] Actor_List)* manipulator to identify all the actors. To identify the actors of the system, consider the business activities that are being computerized. In this case study, the business activities relating to membership, sales, ordering and inventory control are covered by the system. So the following actors can be identified:

- *Customer Service Assistant* (membership registration, placement of order)
- *Order Processing Clerk* (process order)
- *Inventory Control Clerk* (inventory control)

Each actor is then described by an actor specification. Figures 7.2 to 7.4 detail the specification of these actors.

Figure 7.2. Specification of the Customer Service Assistant actor

Actor Name	Customer Service Assistant
Description	The Customer Service Assistant is responsible for the maintenance of membership records, handling of goods returns, creating sales orders, monitoring sales order status and validating membership status

Figure 7.3. Specification of the Order Processing Clerk actor

Actor Name	Order Processing Clerk
Description	The Order Processing Clerk is responsible for processing sales orders, submitting reorder requests, requesting necessary deposits from members and scheduling the delivery of the goods to the member

Figure 7.4. Specification of the Inventory Control Clerk actor

Actor Name	Inventory Control Clerk
Description	The Inventory Control Clerk is responsible for ordering and reordering of goods. The Inventory Control Clerk uses the system to update the stock level when goods are received

Apply the *Transitor(Problem_Statement[use case level], Use_Case_List)* manipulator to identify all use cases. The goals of the actors are described in the (use case level) problem statement. For example, the Customer Service Assistant is responsible for *checking order status*, *placing order*, *registering new member*, *updating membership*, *archiving membership* and *handling goods return*. The following are the use cases of the mail order system:

- *Check Order Status*
- *Place Order*
- *Handle Goods Return*
- *Update Membership Record*
- *Archive Membership*
- *Register New Member*
- *Process Order*
- *Schedule Delivery*
- *Order Goods*
- *Receive Goods*

Then develop the use case diagram by applying the *Elaborator(Data_Dictionary.{Use_Case_List, Actor_List}, Use_Case_Diagram)* manipulator (see Figure 7.5). It should be noted that the mail order system can be naturally partitioned into subsystems, which handle different groups of requirements. These requirements are then partitioned into suitable packages.

Figure 7.5. Initial use case diagram

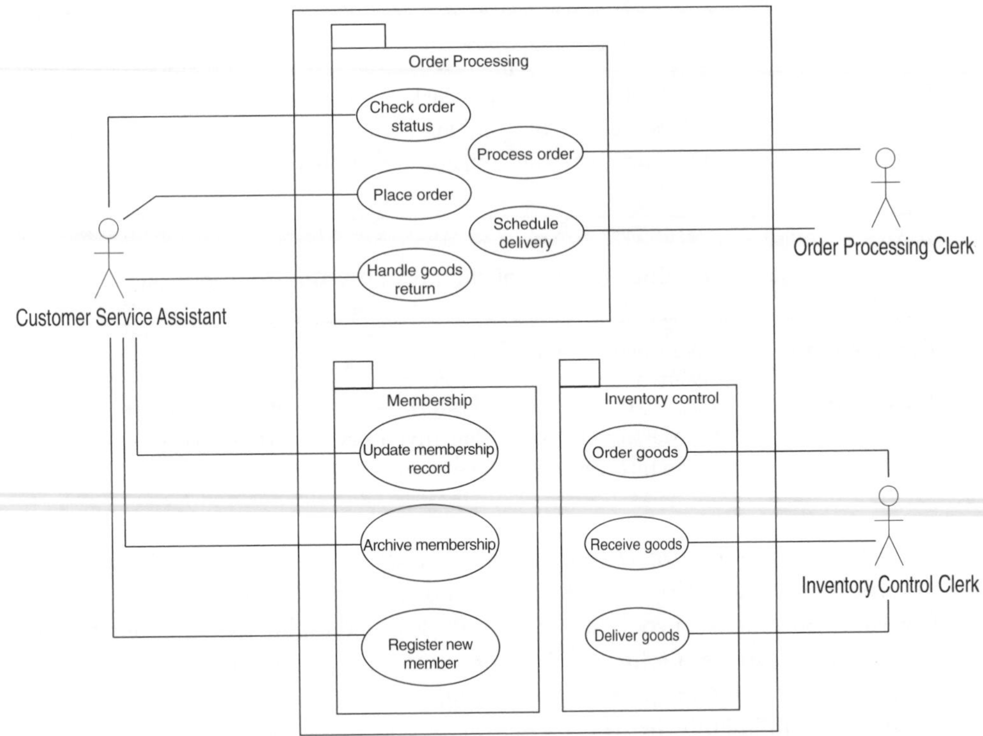

Prioritizing Use Cases

The use cases are prioritized according to their relative importance in the system. The developer evaluates the risks and the significance of the use cases to the stakeholders of the system. The developer and stakeholders of the system meet to decide on the priority of the use cases. Table 7.1 shows the priority of each of the system use cases which, it is assumed, is agreed by the developer and the stakeholders.

Table 7.1. Ranking of use cases

Priority rank	Use case	Reason
High	Process order	Directly improves the efficiency of the business process and affects the system architecture

Table 7.1. (Cont'd)

Priority rank	Use case	Reason
High	Place order	Same as above
High	Check order status	Improve efficiency and quality of customer service
Medium	Order goods	Ordering goods is less often than processing orders but is still one of the major business processes
Medium	Deliver goods	Improve the control of stock level
Medium	Schedule delivery	Improve the efficiency of the goods delivery team
Medium	Receive goods	Improve the control of stock level
Medium	Handle goods return	Improve the control of stock level
Low	Update membership record	Small impact on system architecture
Low	Register new member	Same as above
Low	Archive membership	Same as above

Describing Use Cases

Having captured the requirements of the system by creating the initial use cases, elaborate the use cases to provide further details. Apply the *Elaborator(Use_Case, Use_Case_Description)* manipulator to develop the use case description. The purpose of this manipulator is to give a detailed description of the use cases which can then be used for constructing other diagrams such as the interaction diagrams, state diagrams, class diagrams, etc. Table 7.2 shows the use case description of the *Process Order* use case.

Table 7.2. Use case description for process order use case

Use case name	Process Order
Use case ID	UC-200
Primary actor(s)	Order Processing Clerk
Secondary actor(s)	
Brief description	The order processing clerk selects a sales order from the system. He/she then checks each line item in the sales order for the availability of stock before finding the stock for each line item. The system records the name of the order processing clerk who handles the sales order.
Preconditions	The sales order is stored in the system.
Post-conditions	The sales order status is changed to "filled" and the stock items are held for the sale.
Flow of events	1. The Order Processing Clerk selects a sales order. The system displays the items and quantity of the order. 2. The Order Processing Clerk checks the availability of each item. 3. The Order Processing Clerk holds the stock items for the sales order. The system changes the order status to "filled".
Alternative flows and exceptions	If an item is not available from stock, the sales order status of the item is changed to "hold." If the number of reorder items exceeds the reorder limit of the member, the clerk prints out a "request deposit" letter to the member, and the sales order is marked as "deposit pending." When the deposit is received or if the reorder amount does not exceed the reorder limit of the member, the system then forwards a reorder request to the inventory control clerk. The sales order status is changed to "filled" when the stock items are received, and the system notifies the order processing clerk.
Non-behavioral requirements	The system should be able to handle 2,000 sales orders per day.
Assumptions	
Issues	Can the available items be delivered first?
Source	User Interview Memo 21, 8/9/01

Structuring Use Case Model

After elaborating the use cases, *Place Order*, *Register New Member* and *Archive Membership* share a common behavior in that they all involve finding the member record from the system. Hence, the <<include>> relationship is created with the *Find Member Record* use case. The revised use case diagram is shown in Figure 7.6. Now, move on to the next workflow: analysis.

Figure 7.6. Revised use case diagram

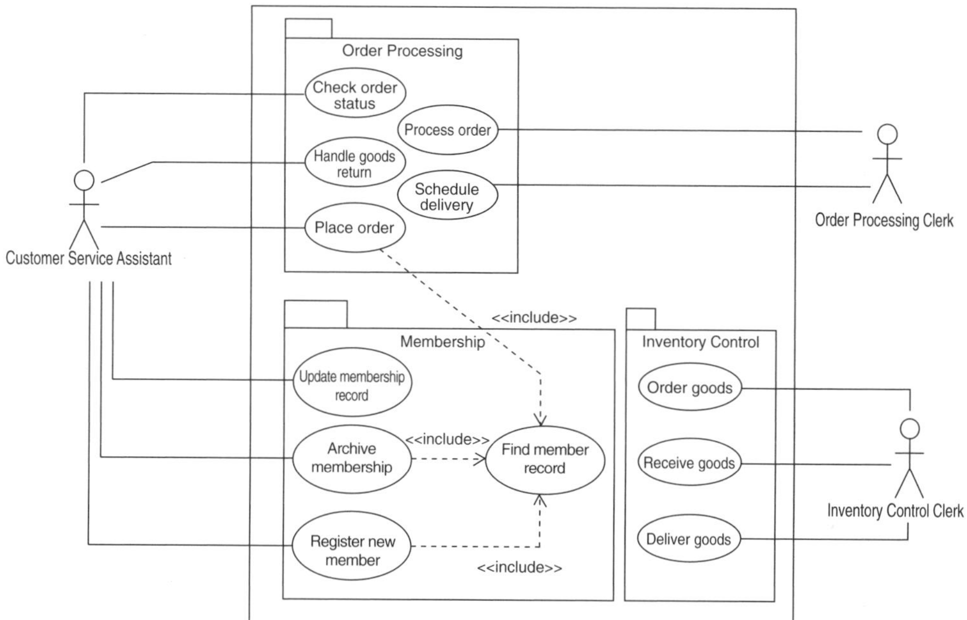

Analysis

The analysis workflow develops the domain class model and starts the dynamic modeling. First, develop the domain class model by applying the *Transitor(problem statement, domain class model)* manipulator. Using this manipulator, it is possible to construct the class model for the system (static modeling) and analyze the dynamic behaviors of the use cases (system modeling).

Domain Analysis (Class Level)

Apply the *Transitor(Problem_Statement[use case level], Class_Diagram [domain])* manipulator to obtain the domain class model (see Figure 7.7).

Figure 7.7. Domain class model

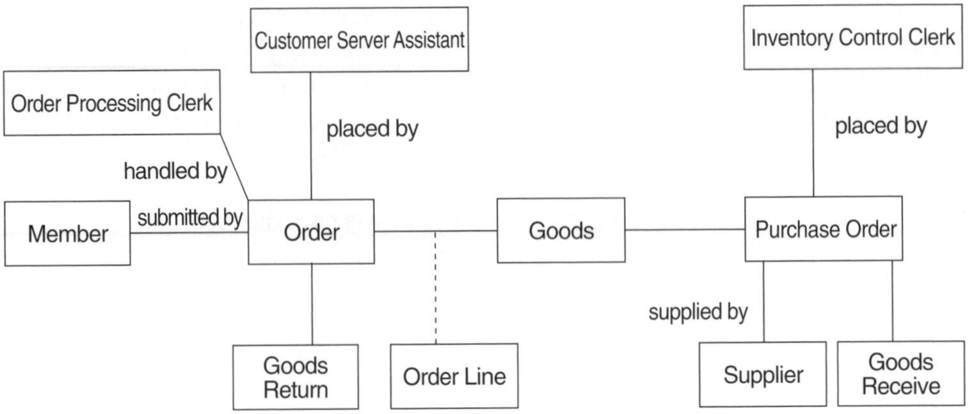

Static Modeling

The domain class model provides us with the classes that are common to most mail order systems. Since the use case descriptions contain the specific requirements of the system, apply the *Transitor(Use_Case_Description, Class_Diagram[analysis])* manipulator to identify the objects of the system. The purpose of this manipulator is to perform a textual analysis on the use case description to identify entity objects and create a class diagram. The resulting class diagram generated is combined with the domain class model to create the analysis class diagram of the system (see Figure 7.8).

System Modeling

System modeling helps us understand the dynamic aspects of the system. First apply the *Elaborator(Use_Case_Description.Flow_of_Events, Activity_Diagram)* manipulator to analyze the dynamic behavior of a use case and then elaborate each action state of the activity diagram by a set of collaboration diagrams for the action state.

Elaborating Use Cases

From the use case description, the *Process Order* use case involves many complex activities. Therefore, the *Elaborator(Use_Case_Description. Flow_of_Events, Activity_Diagram)* manipulator is applied to develop an activity diagram to further analyze the use case (see Figure 7.9). This manipulator creates an activity diagram representing the activities described in the flow of events of the use case description of the *Process Order* use case.

Figure 7.8. Analysis class diagram

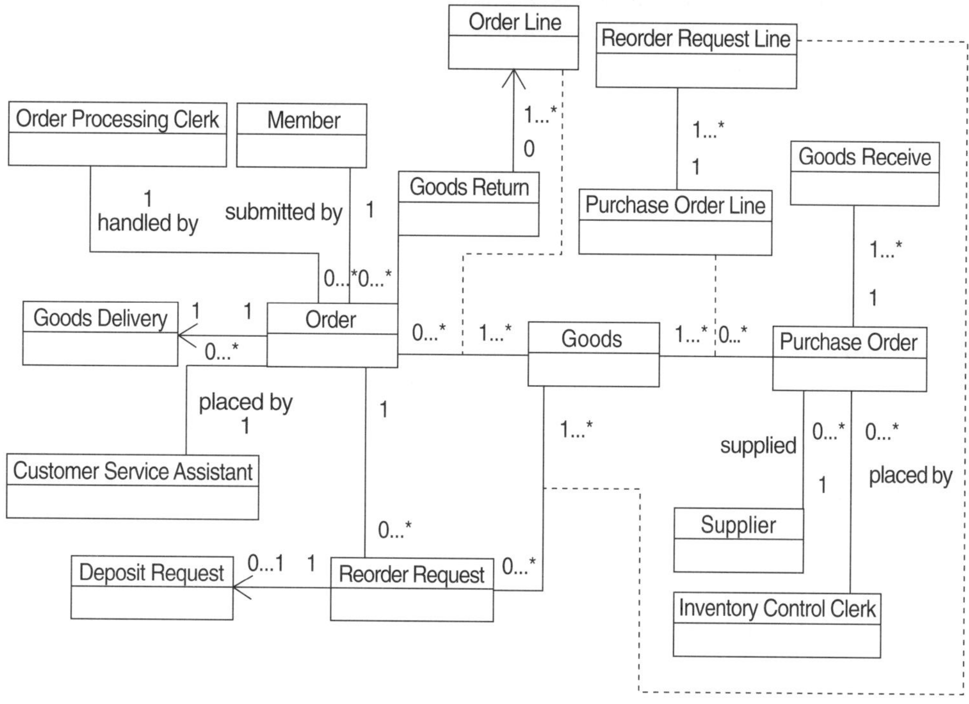

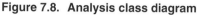

Figure 7.9. Activity diagram for elaborating *Process Order* use case

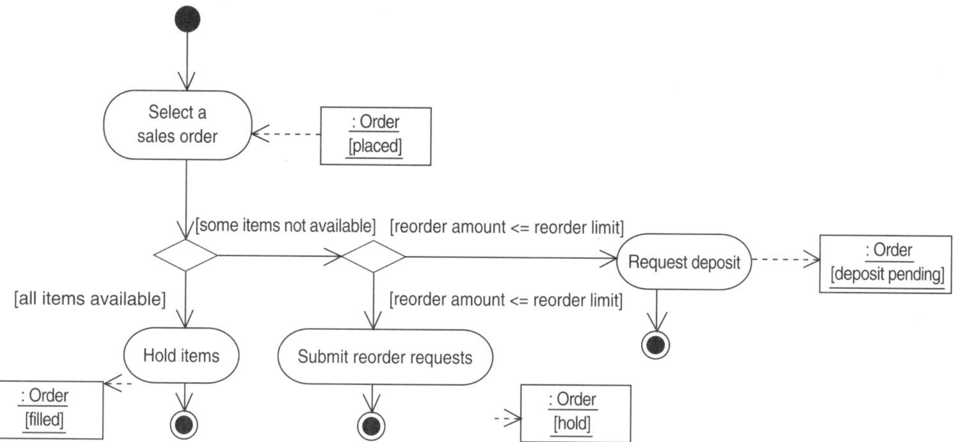

The activity diagram generated can be used to establish all the scenarios of the use case and hence the system-level sequence diagrams. For example, Tables 7.3 to 7.5 contain the normal scenarios of execution, followed by two alternative scenarios of the *Process Order* use case. Note that each scenario corresponds to a different path in the activity diagram.

Table 7.3. Normal scenario of the *Process Order* use case

Parent use case name	Process Order
Parent use case ID	UC-200
Instance name	A deposit is required before the sales order can be processed
Instance ID	UCIS-200-1
Environmental conditions and assumptions	All items of the order are available
Inputs	A sales order of available items
Instance flow description	• The Order Processing Clerk selects a sales order. The system displays the items and quantities of the order • The Order Processing Clerk checks the availability of each item. The system confirms all items are available • The Order Processing Clerk holds all items of the order. The system updates the status of the sales order to "filled"
Outputs	The sales order is filled

Table 7.4. Alternative scenario of *Process Order* use case

Parent use case name	Process Order
Parent use case ID	UC-200
Instance name	An item needs to be reordered

Table 7.4. (Cont'd)

Instance ID	UCIS-200-2
Environmental conditions and assumptions	Some stock items are not available and the value of the items needed to be reordered exceeds the preset reorder limit of the member
Inputs	A sales order of a stock item costs $1,000 and the preset reordering limit of the member is $2,000
Instance flow description	• The Order Processing Clerk selects a sales order. The system displays the items and quantities of the order • The Order Processing Clerk checks the availability of each item • An item which costs $1,000 is not available. The Order Processing Clerk submits a reorder request • The sales order is marked as "deposit pending"
Outputs	The sales order is marked as "hold" and a reorder request is submitted

Table 7.5. Another alternative scenario of *Process Order* use case

Parent use case name	Process Order
Parent use case ID	UC-200
Instance name	A deposit is required before the sales order can be processed
Instance ID	UCIS-200-3
Environmental conditions and assumptions	Some stock items are not available, and the value of the items needed to be reordered exceeds the preset reorder limit of the member
Inputs	A sales order of a stock item costs $5,000 and the preset reordering limit of the member is $2,000

Table 7.5. (Cont'd)

Instance flow description	• The Order Processing Clerk selects a sales order. The system displays the items and quantity of the order • The Order Processing Clerk checks the availability of each item • An item which costs $5,000 is not available. The system prints a deposit request letter to the member • The sales order is marked as "deposit pending"
Outputs	The sales order is marked as "deposit pending" and a request deposit letter is sent to the member

Design

The purpose of the design workflow is to analyze and design how object collaboration is to be achieved for the performance of the use cases. First elaborate each of the action states in the activity diagram (representing a use case) using a collaboration diagram. Since each use case scenario corresponds to a path in the activity diagram, generate the MVC (Model/View/Control)-level sequence diagram for the scenario by translating the collaboration diagrams corresponding to the action states of the path in the activity diagram. The generation of the MVC-level sequence diagram can be achieved using a modern CASE tool that provides traceability and consistency checks among the activity diagrams and automatically maintains MVC-level interaction diagrams synchronization with minimal effort. For objects with complex dynamic behaviors, especially control objects or subsystems, model them by using state diagrams. In the process, apply the view aligners to revise the activity diagram (use case level) and class diagram to maintain consistency among models. As the number of classes in the class diagram grows, consider grouping related classes into packages for ease of management.

Elaborating Flow of Events

For each action state of the activity diagram representing a use case, create MVC-level collaboration diagram. In other words, apply *Elaborator(Activity_Diagram, Collaboration_Diagram_List)* to obtain a list of collaboration diagrams for the action states of an activity diagram. For example, the action states of the activity diagram in Figure 7.9 are realized by the collaboration diagrams in Figures 7.10 to 7.13.

Figure 7.10. Collaboration diagram of select a sales order action state

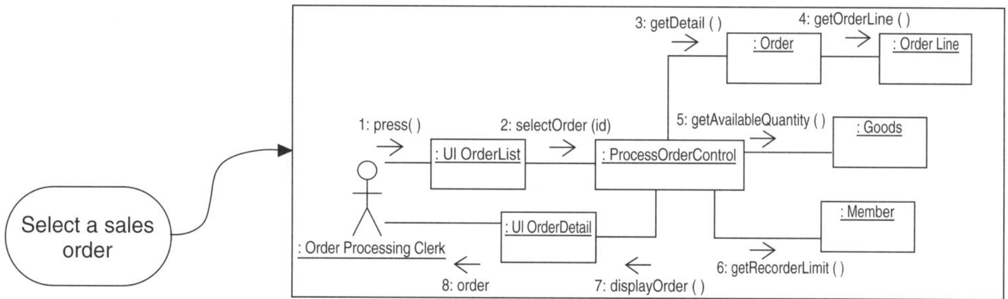

Figure 7.11 Collaboration diagram of hold items action state

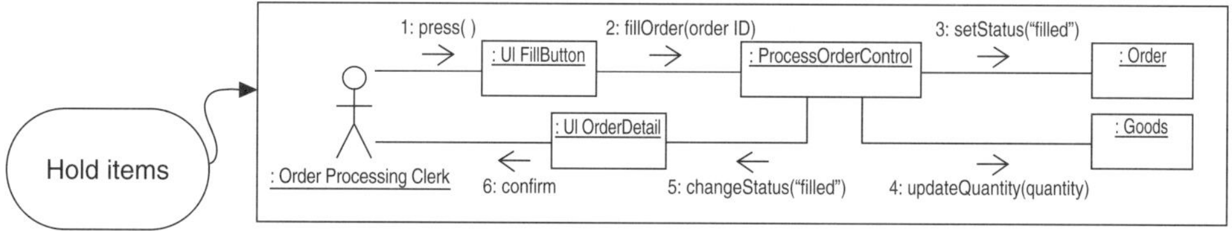

Figure 7.12 Collaboration diagram of submit reorder requests action state

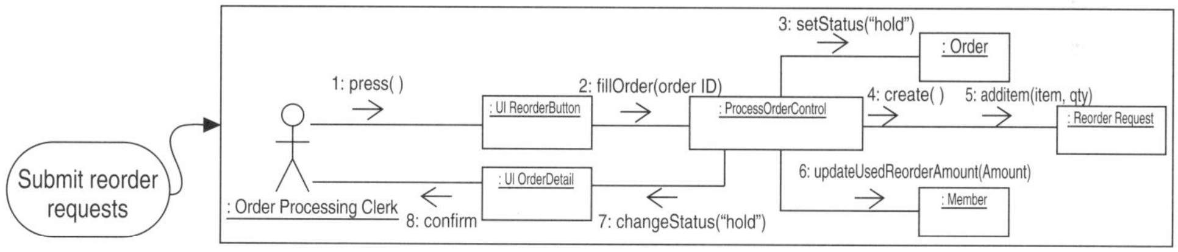

Figure 7.13 Collaboration diagram of request deposit action state

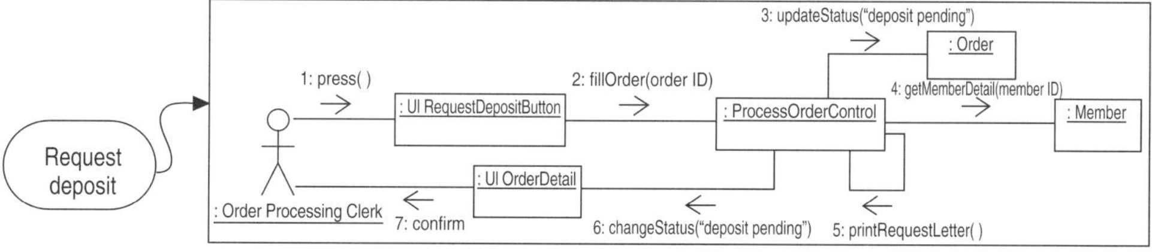

Generating MVC-level Sequence Diagrams

Having created the collaboration diagrams for the action states of the activity diagram, apply *Elaborator(Activity_Diagram.Path, Sequence_Diagram[Design])* to generate MVC-level sequence diagrams by tracing paths in the activity diagram and translating the collaboration diagrams of the action states in the path into an MVC-level sequence diagram. For example, Figure 7.14 shows the paths for the normal, first alternative and alternative scenarios of the *Process Order* use case. Figures 7.15 to 7.17 show the various MVC-level sequence diagrams for the scenarios. For the normal scenario, the action states select a sales order and hold items are executed. As illustrated in Figure 7.15, each action state corresponds to a pair of actor input and system response and a sequence of internal messages between the boundary objects, control objects and entity objects. For other scenarios, we can also find the corresponding sequence of messages between objects for each of the action states involved in individual scenarios.

Figure 7.14. Activity diagram for elaborating *Process Order* use case

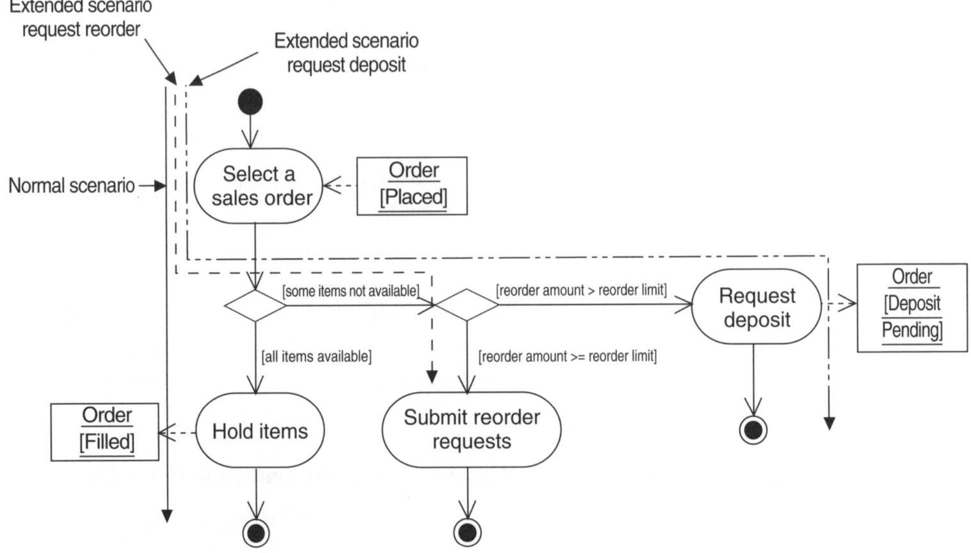

Figure 7.15. MVC-level sequence diagram for normal scenario of process order

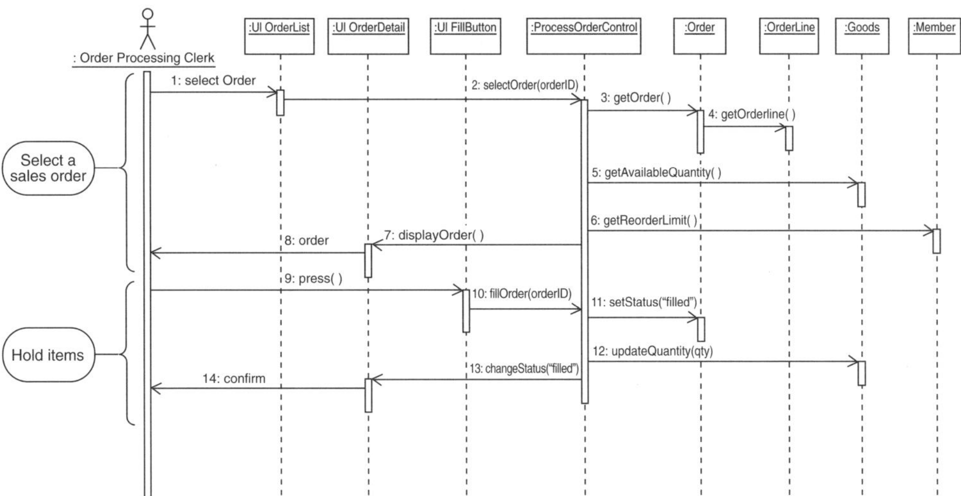

Figure 7.16. MVC-level sequence diagram for alternative scenario

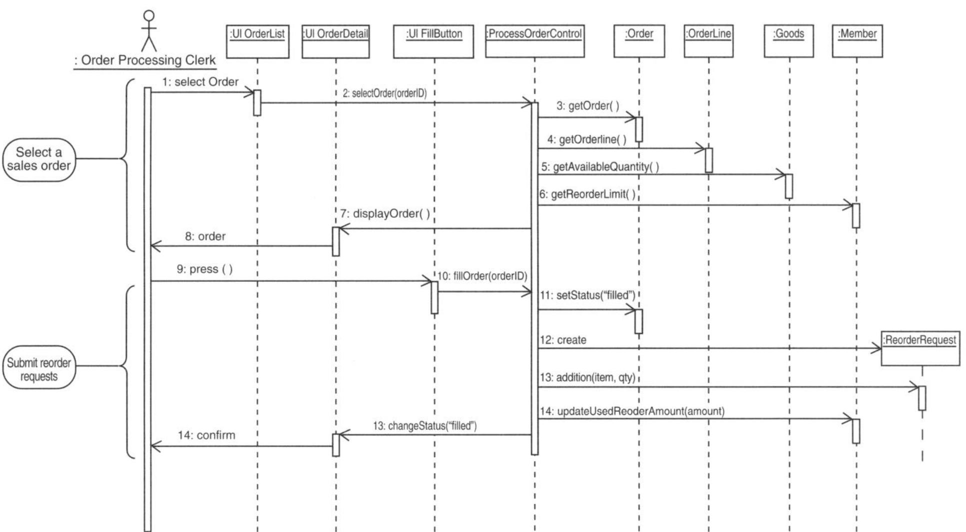

Figure 7.17. MVC-level sequence diagram for another alternative scenario

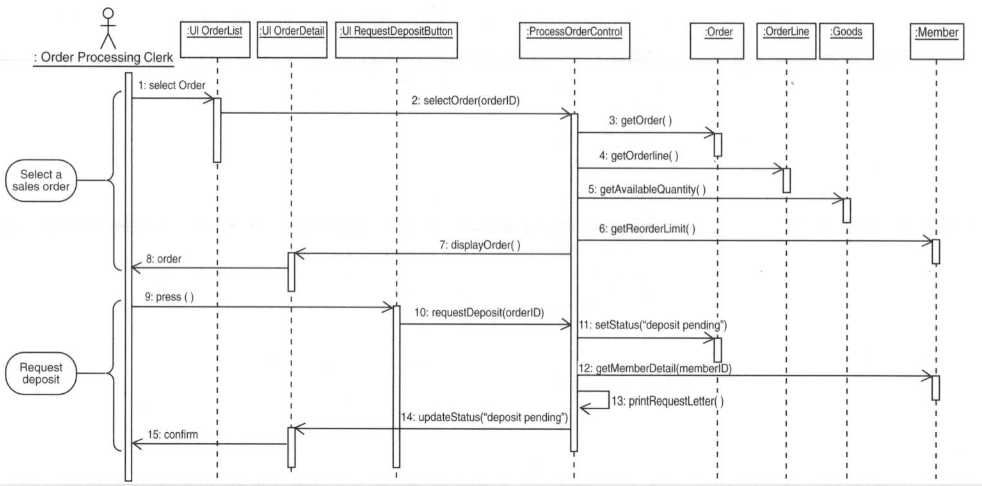

Revising Class Diagrams

After having drawn the sequence diagram for the *Process Order* use case, apply *Aligner(Sequence_Diagram, Class_Diagram)* to refine the class diagram by adding the operations and attributes identified in the sequence diagrams. The revised class diagram (see Figure 7.18) can help us perform the analysis for other use cases.

Performing State Analysis on Control Object(s)

In the MVC-level sequence diagram, the control object glues all other objects together, handles the control flow and deals with all other transaction-related requirements. Consequently, a control object is usually complex enough to be modeled by a state diagram. For example, as the *Process Order* use case has several scenarios, the control object has different paths in its state diagram. As discussed in Chapter 4, we can create the state diagram of the control object by consolidating the required states and transitions from the sequence diagrams of the use case, i.e. apply *Transitor(Sequence_Diagram, State_Diagram)*. Alternatively, we can translate the activity diagram of the use case to obtain a rough state diagram for the control object, because the activity diagram provides information about the control flow of the use case. For example, the activity diagram of the *Process Order* use case (see Figure 7.9), together with the collaboration diagrams, can be used to construct the state diagram for the control object *ProcessOrderControl* (see Figure 7.19).

Figure 7.18. Revised class diagram

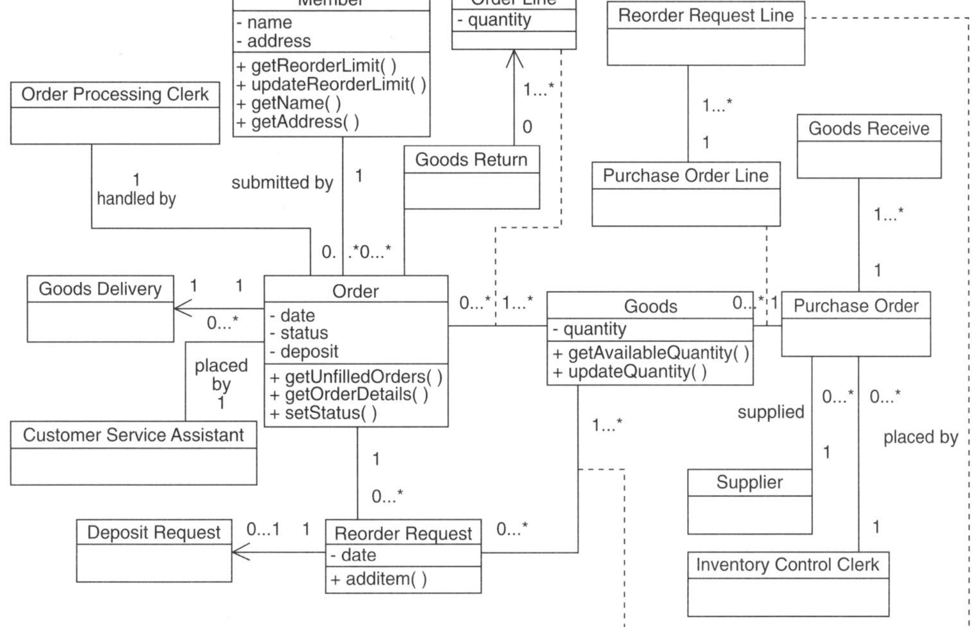

Revising Class Diagram(s)

After developing the state diagram of the control objects, revise the class diagrams according to the operations and attributes identified in the state diagrams (apply *Aligner(State_Diagram, Class_Diagram)*). Figure 7.20 shows the design class diagram. The design class diagram now provides design information for the classes required for the implementation of the *Process Order* use case. Hence, the implementation work for the *Process Order* use case can proceed. For other use cases, the work flows of the A^3 can be repeated to develop the design of the classes required for the implementation of the use cases. The design class diagram will then be incrementally refined by going through the development process iteratively.

Figure 7.19. State diagram for *ProcessOrderControl* class

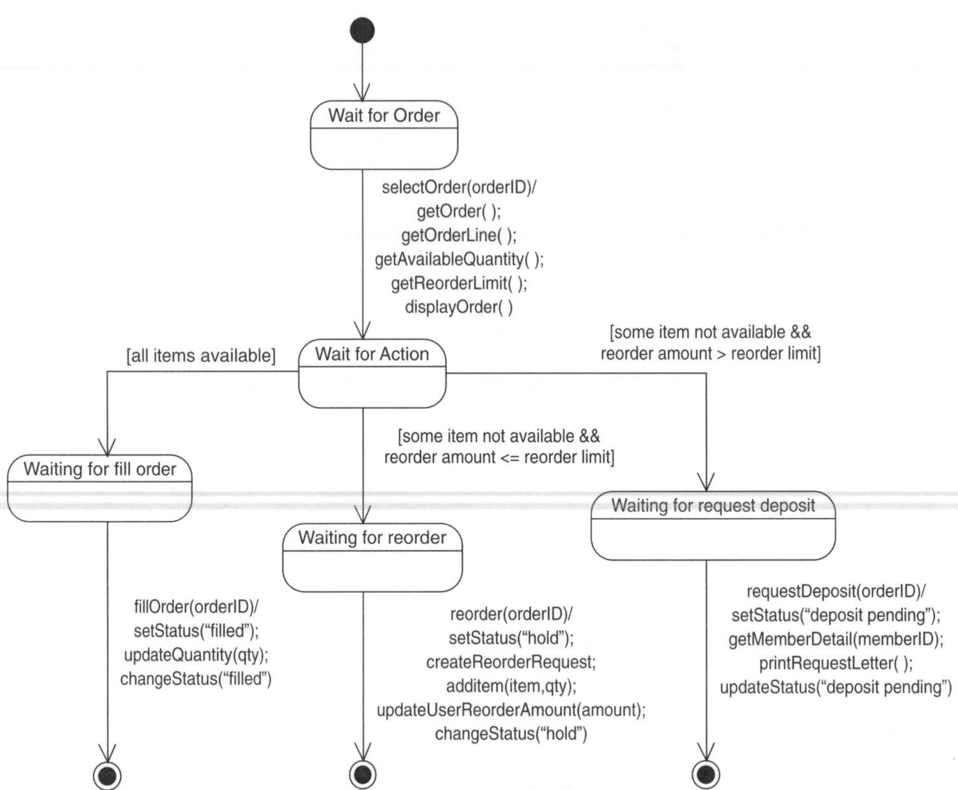

At this point, the A^3 has been applied in a single iteration of the development process, the requirements of the *Process Order* use case analyzed and the relevant design of implementation completed. The implementation of the *Process Order* use case can then be carried out by using the implementation techniques described in Chapter 6. After the prototype implementation of the *Process Order* use case has been demonstrated to the target users for their feedback, another iteration of the development process may be carried out. These steps in the A^3 can then be repeated for other use cases of the system.

Figure 7.20. Revised design class diagram

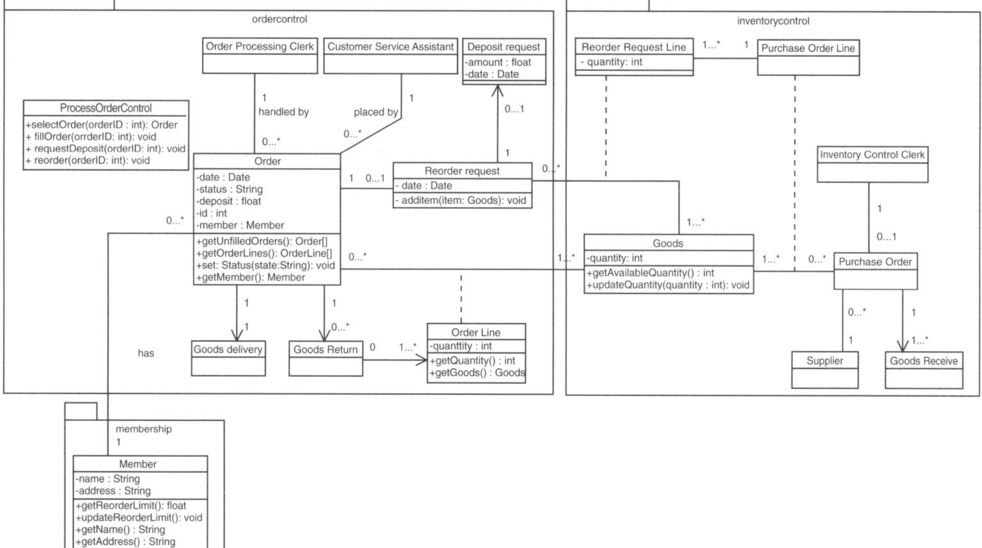

Applying the Activity Analysis Approach with VP-UML

In the remaining part of this chapter, it will be shown that the VP-UML CASE tool can be used to carry out the steps for applying the A^3 in analyzing and designing the *mail order system*. We shall follow closely the A^3 development workflows which have been discussed in detail earlier in this chapter. All the steps associated with the use of the VP-UML CASE tool will be presented in a box.

Business Modeling

The first workflow is concerned with modeling the business operation which consists of three major activities: performing domain analysis (workflow) and business process analysis and determining the system scope.

Domain Analysis (Workflow)

After interviewing the users and collecting the required information about the business process, the business activities of the company are recorded as a workflow-level problem statement. The VP-UML CASE tool can then be used to document this analysis through its textual analysis screen.

- Create a new Textual Analysis to document the workflow-level problem statement (Problem Statement 7.1)
    1. Click the **Create Textual Analysis** button on the toolbar.
    2. Type the problem statement into the textual analysis working area (see Figure 7.21)

Figure 7.21. Problem statement [workflow]

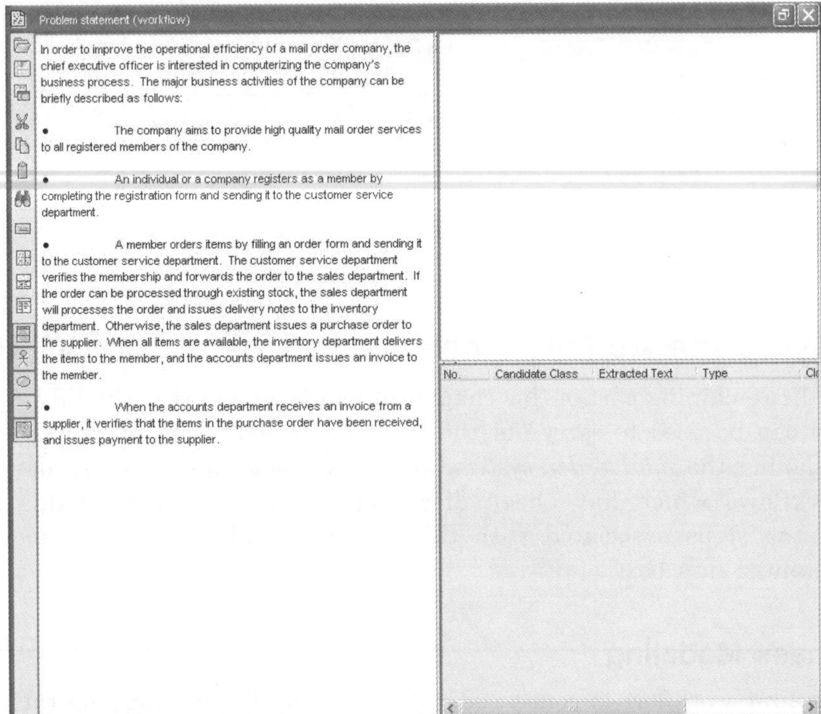

Business Process Analysis

Having created the workflow-level problem statement, perform the business process analysis. Apply the *Elaborator(Problem_Statement[workflow], Swimlane_Activity_Diagram)* manipulator to manually create a swimlane activity diagram, which helps visualize the business activities. The activity diagram as shown in Figure 7.1 can be created as follows:

- Create the activity diagram
  1. Click the **New Activity Diagram** button on the toolbar.
  2. Create the initial states using the **palette** on the left of the **diagram pane**.
  3. Use the resource-centric interface to create the transitions and action states.
- Create swimlanes to partition the activities in the working area (see Figure 7.22).
  1. Click the new **swinlane** button using the **palette** on the left of the **diagram pane**.

Figure 7.22. Business workflow activity diagram

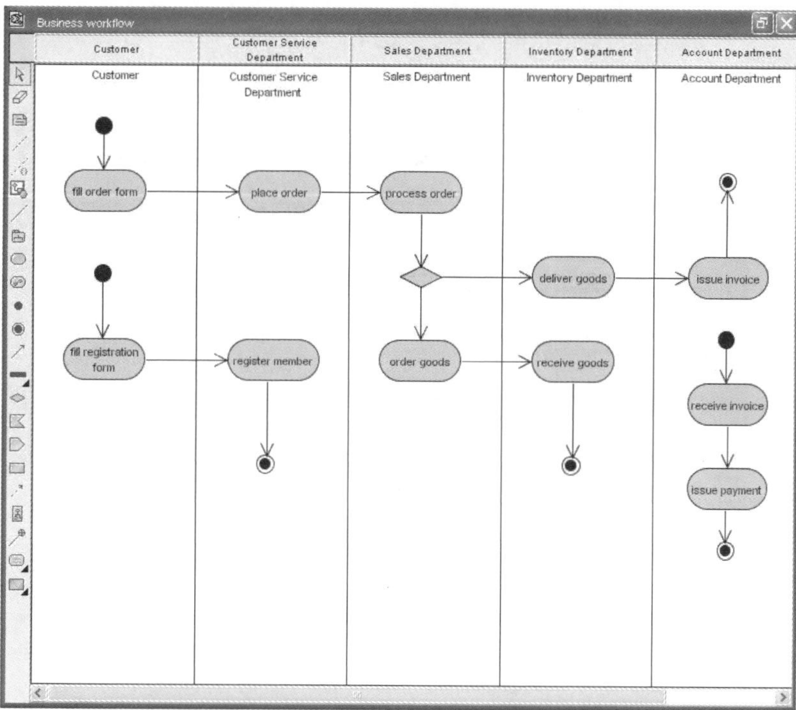

Determining System Scope

This is primarily a manual process because the decision-making process involves the developer and the stakeholders and, therefore, does not involve the use of the CASE tool.

Requirements

The workflow consists of two activities: domain analysis (use case level) and use case analysis, both supported by the VP-UML CASE tool.

Domain Analysis (Use Case Level)

Based on the business workflow, the developer and the stakeholders of the system can then discuss and decide on the scope of the system, i.e. the business activities in Figure 7.22, that require computerization. After determining the scope of the system, a use case level problem statement (Problem Statement 7.2) can be prepared on which a textual analysis will be performed.

- Create a new textual analysis to enter the problem statement in Problem Statement 7.2.
  1. Click the **Create Textual Analysis** button on the toolbar.
  2. Type the use case level problem statement into the textual analysis working area (see Figure 7.23)

Figure 7.23. Problem statement (use case)

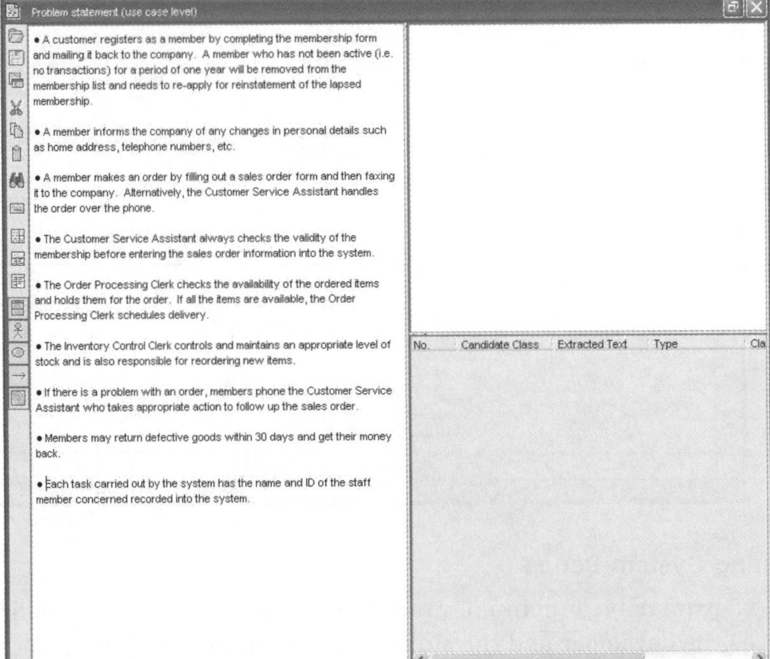

From the problem statement, we know that *Customer Service Assistant*, *Order Processing Clerk* and *Inventory Control Clerk* are the users of the system. Therefore, they will become the actors in the use case diagram.

- Identify use case actors and candidate classes
  1. Select the name of each actor from the use case-level problem statement and drag it to the **candidate class pane** in the top right-hand corner of the display. The candidate class will be created automatically in the **data dictionary pane** in the bottom right-hand corner.
  2. Right click the candidate class and select the type from the pop-up menu.
  3. Repeat the above step for all the use cases (see Figure 7.24).

Figure 7.24. Candidate actors and use cases

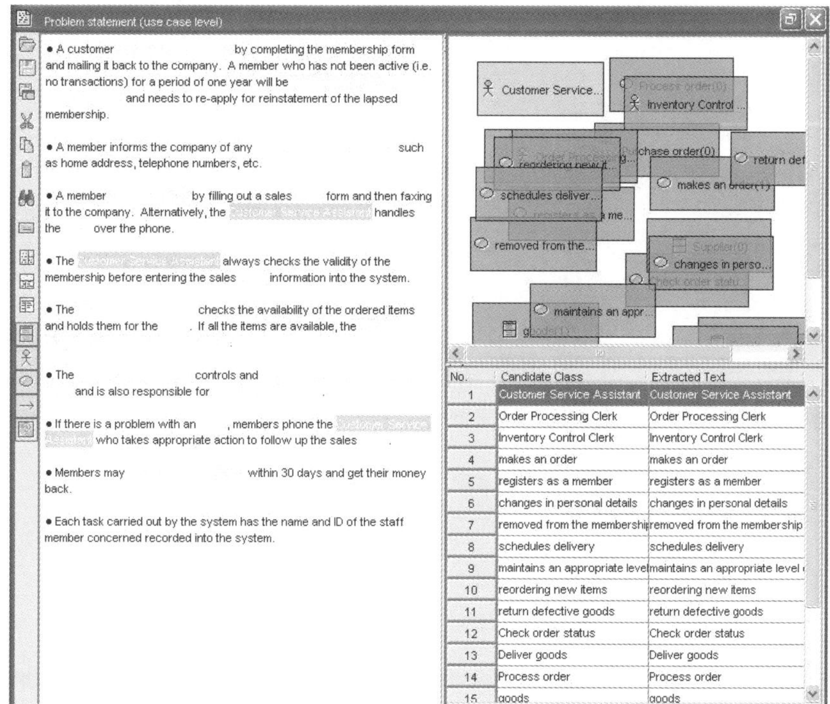

Use Case Analysis

Finding Actors and Use Cases

To complete the data dictionary created, manually fill in the description for each of actor and use case.

- Maximize the working space of the data dictionary situated in the lower right-hand corner of the display
  1. Click the data **dictionary view button** on the textual analysis toolbar to switch to **Data Dictionary View** (see Figure 7.25).

Figure 7.25. Data dictionary view

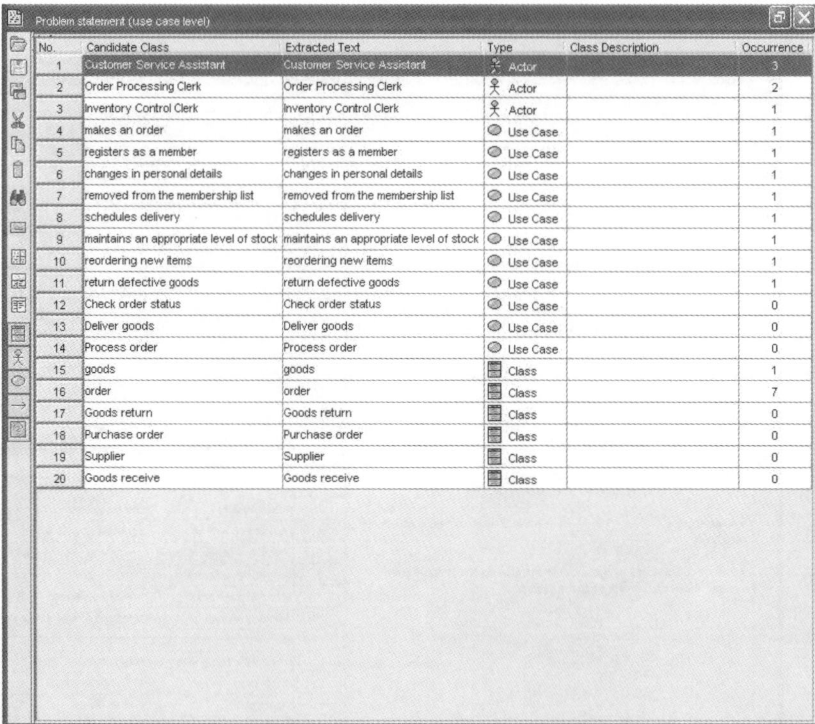

Problem statement (use case level)

No.	Candidate Class	Extracted Text	Type	Class Description	Occurrence
1	Customer Service Assistant	Customer Service Assistant	Actor		3
2	Order Processing Clerk	Order Processing Clerk	Actor		2
3	Inventory Control Clerk	Inventory Control Clerk	Actor		1
4	makes an order	makes an order	Use Case		1
5	registers as a member	registers as a member	Use Case		1
6	changes in personal details	changes in personal details	Use Case		1
7	removed from the membership list	removed from the membership list	Use Case		1
8	schedules delivery	schedules delivery	Use Case		1
9	maintains an appropriate level of stock	maintains an appropriate level of stock	Use Case		1
10	reordering new items	reordering new items	Use Case		1
11	return defective goods	return defective goods	Use Case		1
12	Check order status	Check order status	Use Case		0
13	Deliver goods	Deliver goods	Use Case		0
14	Process order	Process order	Use Case		0
15	goods	goods	Class		1
16	order	order	Class		7
17	Goods return	Goods return	Class		0
18	Purchase order	Purchase order	Class		0
19	Supplier	Supplier	Class		0
20	Goods receive	Goods receive	Class		0

- Fill in the description of the candidate objects
  1. Double click the **class description** column to fill in the description for each of the candidate actors and use cases. The entries in the occurrence column will be automatically generated by the system (see Figure 7.26).

Figure 7.26. Completing the description of candidate actors

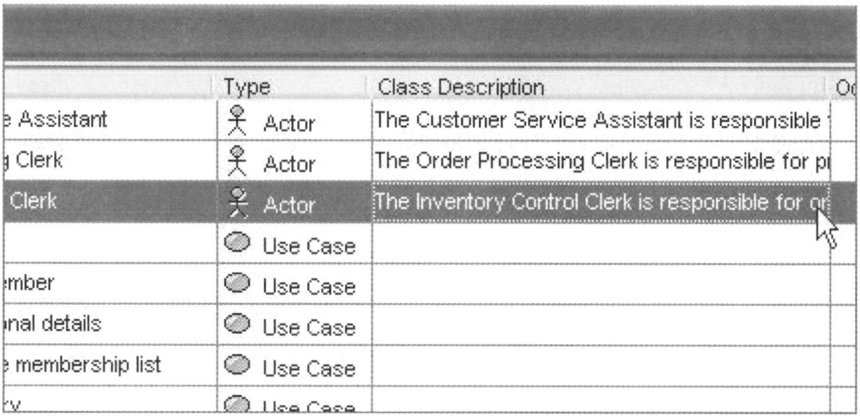

	Type	Class Description	Oc
e Assistant	Actor	The Customer Service Assistant is responsible	
g Clerk	Actor	The Order Processing Clerk is responsible for pi	
Clerk	Actor	The Inventory Control Clerk is responsible for or	
	Use Case		
ember	Use Case		
nal details	Use Case		
e membership list	Use Case		
ry	Use Case		

The name of the candidate object does not need to be identical to the one used in the text of the problem statement. The name of the candidate class can be modified by editing the **Candidate Class** column.

- Create a model from the candidate objects after filling the description for each of the candidate objects
  1. Change the textual analysis working area into **Candidate Class View** by clicking on the button on the palette left of the textual analysis working area.
  2. Create the model from each candidate object by right clicking on the **candidate object**.
  3. Select the model depending on the type specified earlier.

The type of the candidate object will automatically change to *Generated Model* under the **Type** column in the data dictionary, indicating that model has been created (see Figure 7.27).

Figure 7.27. All candidates are created into models

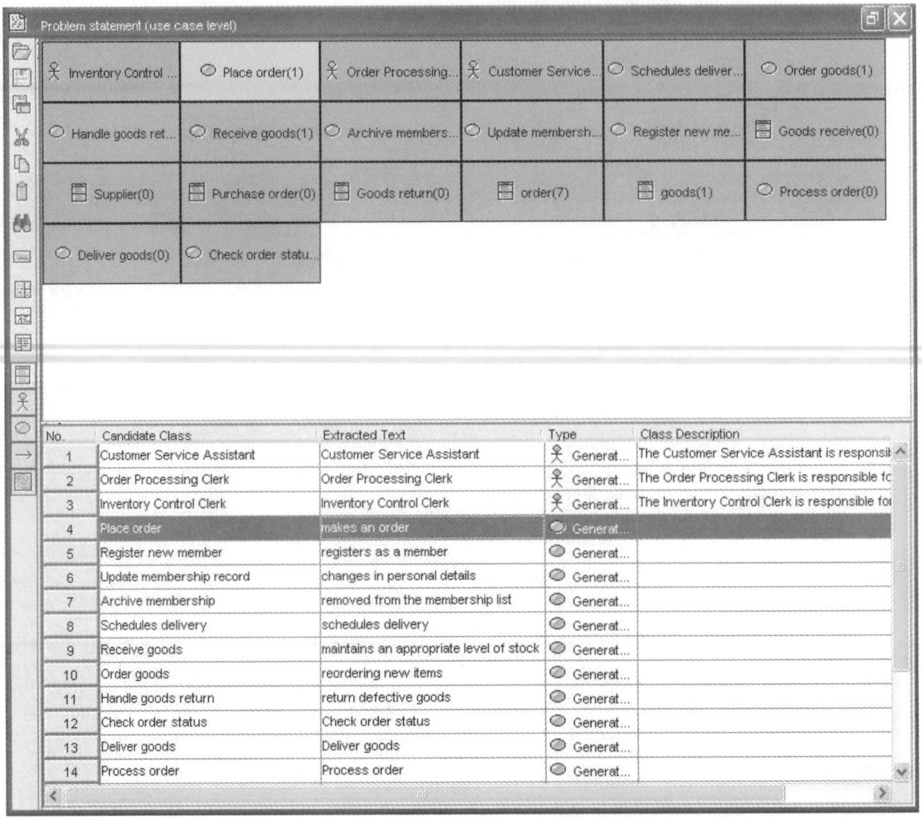

No.	Candidate Class	Extracted Text	Type	Class Description
1	Customer Service Assistant	Customer Service Assistant	Generat...	The Customer Service Assistant is responsit
2	Order Processing Clerk	Order Processing Clerk	Generat...	The Order Processing Clerk is responsible fc
3	Inventory Control Clerk	Inventory Control Clerk	Generat...	The Inventory Control Clerk is responsible foi
4	Place order	makes an order	Generat...	
5	Register new member	registers as a member	Generat...	
6	Update membership record	changes in personal details	Generat...	
7	Archive membership	removed from the membership list	Generat...	
8	Schedules delivery	schedules delivery	Generat...	
9	Receive goods	maintains an appropriate level of stock	Generat...	
10	Order goods	reordering new items	Generat...	
11	Handle goods return	return defective goods	Generat...	
12	Check order status	Check order status	Generat...	
13	Deliver goods	Deliver goods	Generat...	
14	Process order	Process order	Generat...	

We are now ready to create the use case diagram. First start with the system boundary which contains the use cases in that system scope. Rename the boundary to *Mail Order System*.

The mail order system can be partitioned into several systems to handle different areas of requirements. We can use packages to partition the system into more specific components as shown in Figure 7.5. Reuse the model created from textual analysis to draw the use case diagram.

- Create a new use case diagram and the system boundary
  1. Click the **new use case diagram** button in the **toolbar**.
  2. Click the **system boundary** button in the palette and then in the diagram area.
  3. Rename the **system boundary** as *Mail Order System*.
- Change the **Project Explorer** to **model tree view**
  1. Select the **model tree view** tab in the **Project Explorer**.
- Draw the use case diagram by reusing the model created earlier and then group the use cases into packages
  1. Drag the model required from the **Model Tree** to the diagram area.
  2. Repeat the drag-and-drop steps to create all the use cases and actors in the diagram.
  3. Click the **new package** button on the palette and then the diagram area.
  4. Drag the selected use cases into the package. Repeat this step until all the packages are created.
  5. Create the communication link between the actors and use cases by using the resource-centric interface (see Figure 7.28).

Figure 7.28. Complete use case diagram

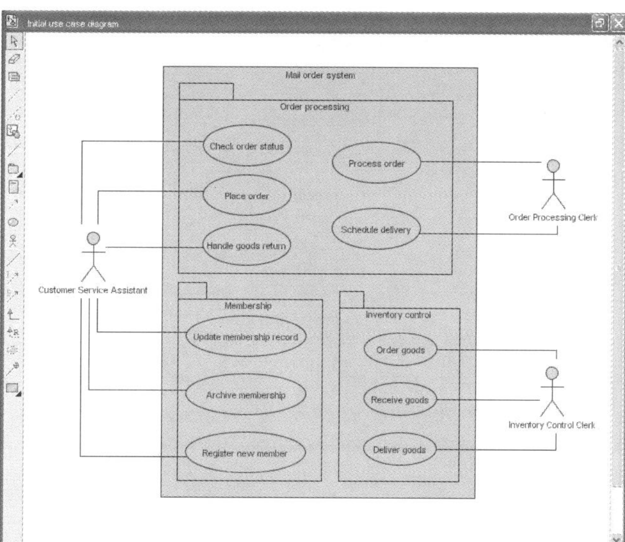

Prioritizing Use Cases

Use the **Use Case Scheduling** feature to prioritize the use cases as detailed in Table 7.1.

- Specify the priority ranking of each use case
  1. Right click the use case diagram and select **Use Case Scheduling** from the pop-up menu (see Figure 7.29).
  2. Double click the **Rank** cell of the use case to open the pull-down menu, and select a rank from the menu.
  3. Double click the **Justification** cell to provide a justification for the rank where necessary.

Figure 7.29. Prioritizing use cases

Rank	Use Case Name	Justification
High	Process order	Directly improves the efficiency of the business process and affects the system architecture
High	Place order	Same as above
High	Check order status	Improve efficiency and quality of customer service
Medium	Schedule delivery	Improve the efficiency of the goods delivery team
Medium	Receive goods	Improve the control of stock level of goods
Medium	Handle goods return	Improve the control of stock level of goods
Medium	Order goods	Ordering goods is less often than processing orders but is still one of the major business processes
Medium	Deliver goods	Improve the control of stock level of goods
Low	Update membership record	Small impact on system architecture
Low	Register new member	Same as above
Low	Archive membership	Same as above

Describing Use Cases

The **use case description** feature is designed to help document the use case.

- Specify the use case description of each use case
  1. Right click a use case in the use case diagram and select **Open Specification** from the menu.
  2. Click the **Use Case Description** tab and fill in the use case description.
  3. Repeat the above steps for all use cases (see Figure 7.30).
  4. Press **OK** when all the use case descriptions have been entered.

Figure 7.30. Full description of a use case

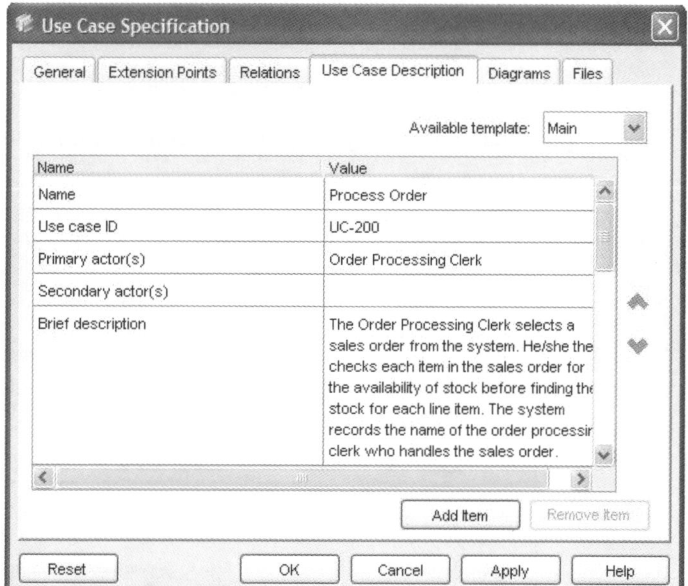

The **Add Item** button allows you to add a new item to the use case description. When this button is activated, a dialog will ask you to enter the name of the new item. The complete use case description is shown in Figure 7.30.

Structuring Use Case Model

After elaborating all the use cases, revise the use case diagram. Copy the diagram elements in the existing diagram and create new ones by modifying them.

- Revise the use case diagram
  1. Press Ctrl-A to select all the elements in the diagram, then right click on the selected elements and choose **Copy → Copy within VP-UML** from the pop-up menu (see Figure 7.31).
  2. Create a new use case diagram.
  3. Paste the selected diagram elements to the new diagram by right clicking the working area and then selecting **Paste** from the pop-up menu (see Figure 7.32).
  4. Draw the <<include>> relationships between the use cases where appropriate, using the resource-centric interface (see Figure 7.33).

Figure 7.31. Copying diagram elements within VP-UML

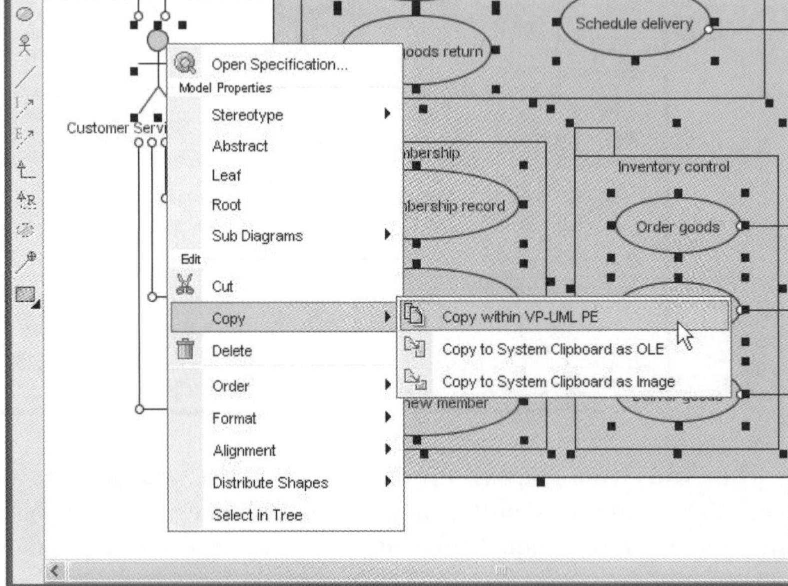

Figure 7.32. Pasting diagram elements to new diagram

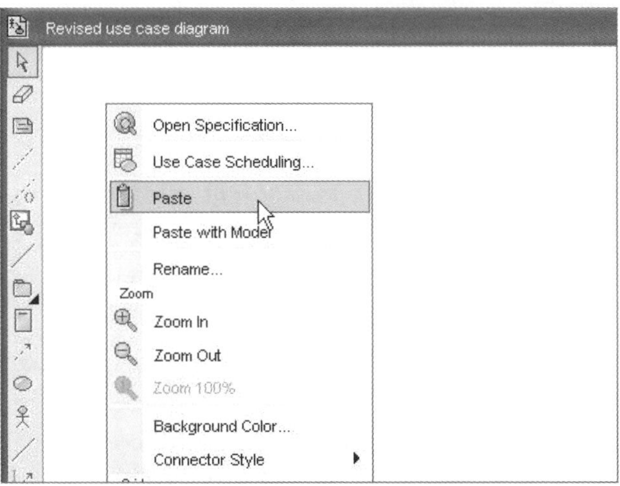

Figure 7.33. Revised use case diagram

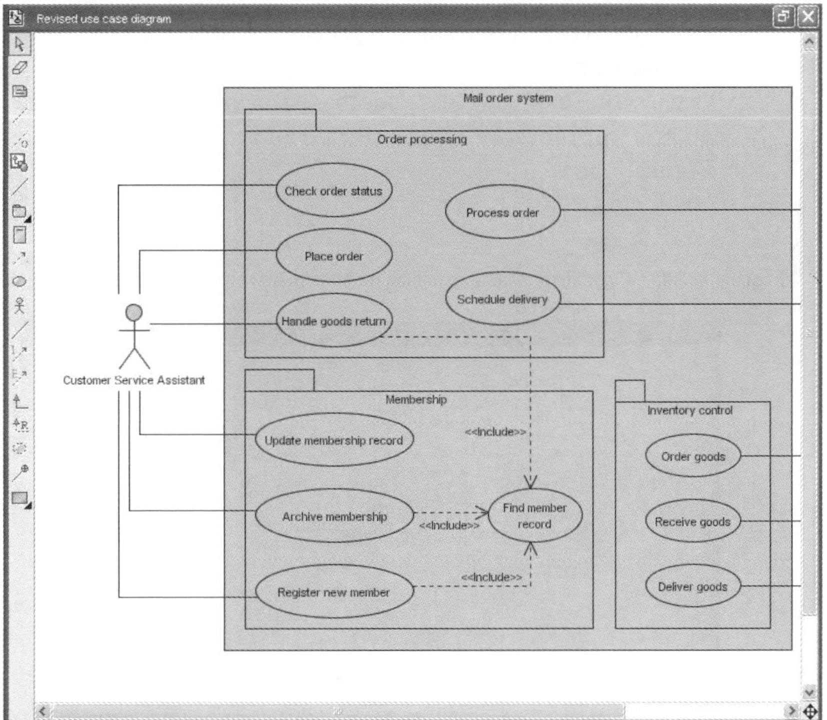

Now that we have completed the requirements workflow, we can proceed on to the next workflow: Analysis.

Analysis

Domain Analysis (Class Level)

By applying the *Transitor(Problem_Statement[use case level], Class_Diagram[domain])* manipulator, construct the domain class model.

- Construct the domain class model
  1. Click the button from the **toolbar** to create a class diagram and rename it *Domain Class Model.*
  2. Click the **Class Repository** tab in the **Project Explorer** and drag the classes from the **class repository** to the diagram area (see Figure 7.34).
  3. Using the resource-centric interface, create the *Order Processing Clerk*, *Customer Service Assistant* and *Inventory Control Clerk* classes explicitly because they are not in the **class repository**.
  4. Create the associations and the association class (*Order Line*) where appropriate using the resource-centric interface (see Figure 7.35).

Figure 7.34. Creating class model in the diagram from class repository

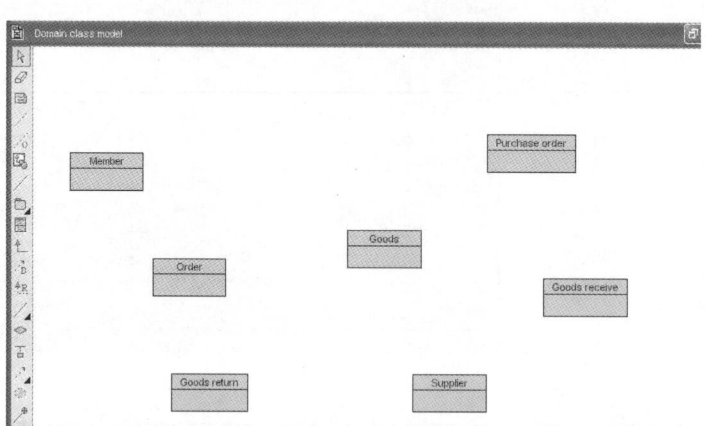

Figure 7.35. Created association class

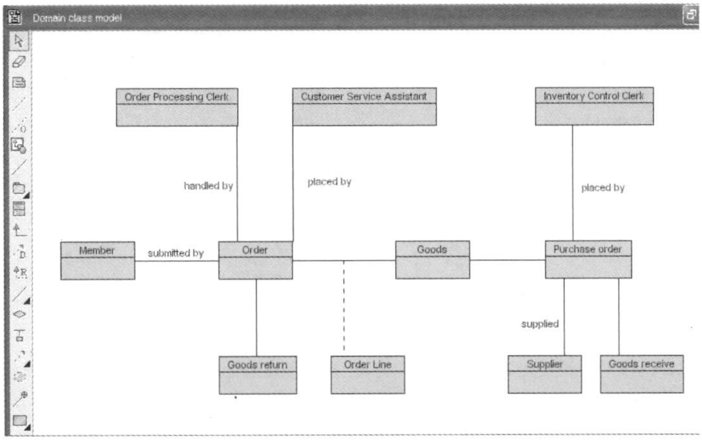

Static Modeling

By applying the *Transitor(Use_Case_Description, Class_Diagram[analysis])* manipulator, create the analysis class diagram.

- Perform textual analysis on the use case descriptions to identify the entity objects
    1. Double click the tree node *Revised Use Case Diagram* in the **diagram tree** to open the diagram.
    2. Right click a use case and select textual analysis from the pop-up menu (see Figure 7.36).
    3. Perform textual analysis to identify objects from the use case description. Create class models for classes that have been added to the **model repository**.
    4. Repeat the above steps for other use cases.
- Create the analysis class diagram from the use case descriptions
    1. Create a new class diagram and rename it *Analysis Class Diagram.*
    2. Copy the models in the domain class diagram to the *Analysis Class Diagram.*
    3. Add classes and related associations identified from the textual analysis to the use case descriptions to complete the analysis diagram (see Figure 7.37).

Figure 7.36. Creating use case-level textual analysis

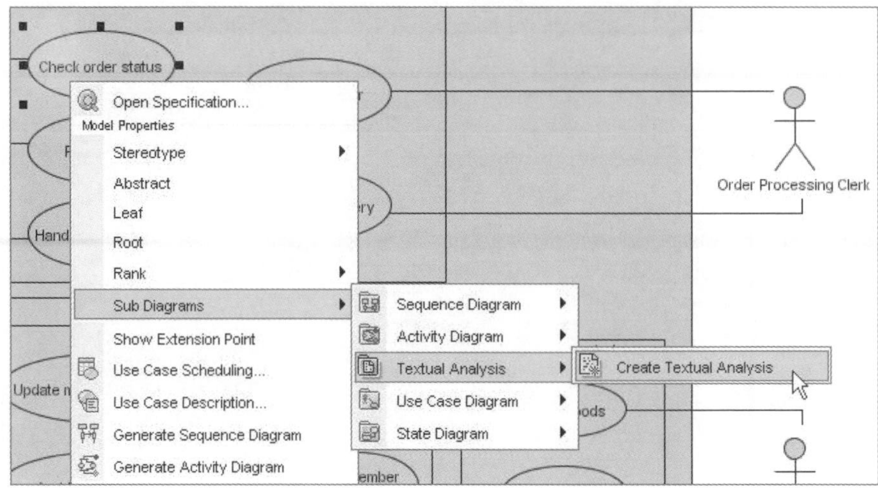

Figure 7.37. Analysis class diagram

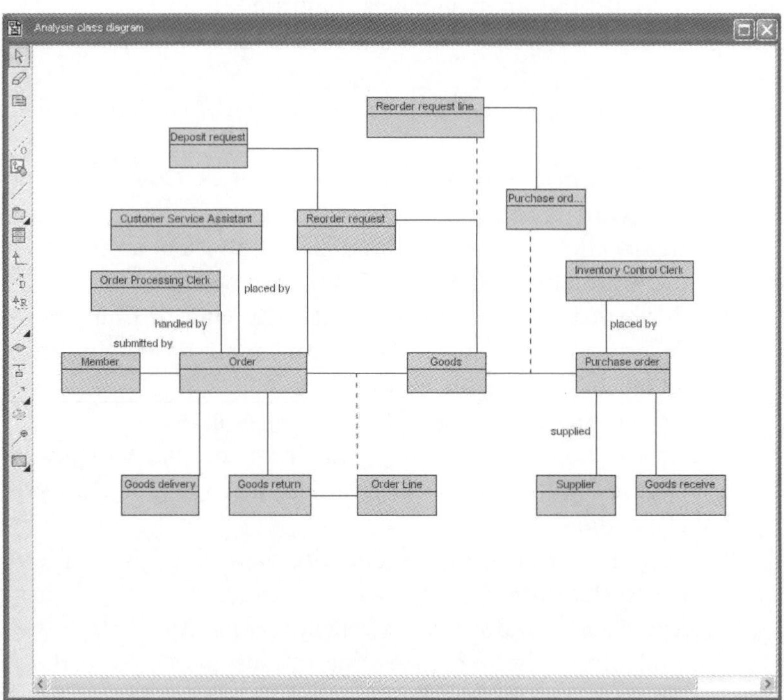

- Define the navigability and multiplicity of the associations where appropriate
  1. Right click an association and select the role and check or uncheck the **navigability button**.
  2. Right click an association, select the role → **Multiplicity** and then choose the appropriate multiplicity value. For multiplicity values not listed in the submenu, click the **Other ...** button and then fill in the multiplicity value in the dialog. Click **OK** when finished (see Figure 7.38).

Figure 7.38. Complete analysis class diagram

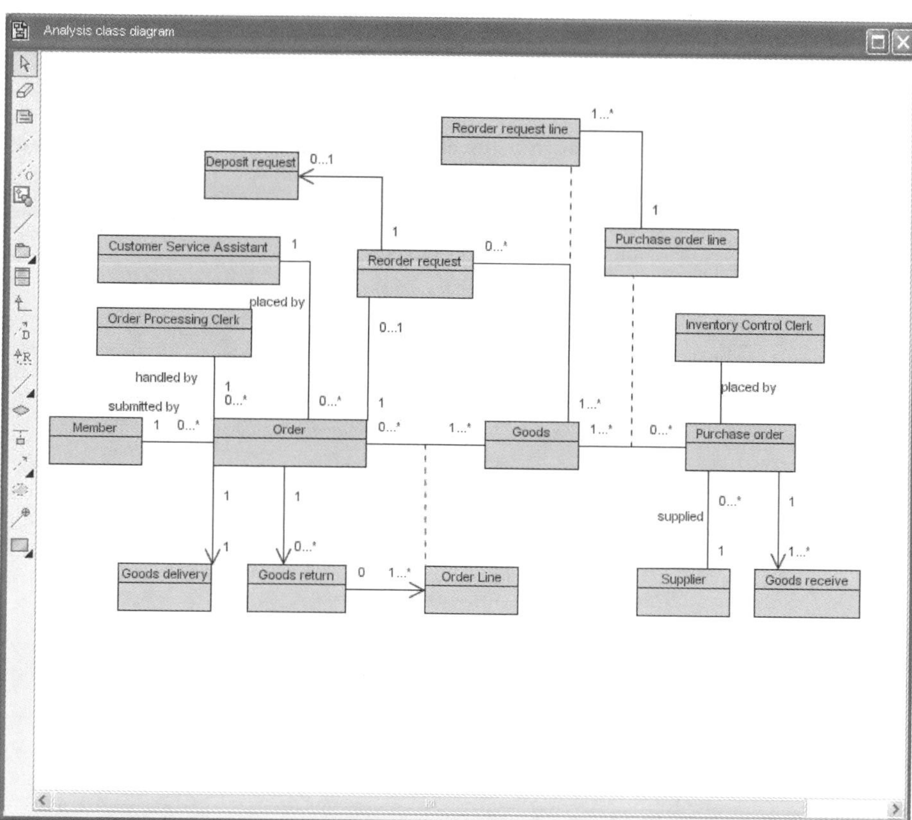

System Modeling

Elaborating Use Cases

We can elaborate the use case from the use case description and then construct an activity diagram. Figure 7.39 shows an example of the completed activity diagram of the *Process Order* use case.

- Create an activity diagram for each use case
  1. Create a new activity diagram by clicking the **new activity diagram** button on the toolbar.
  2. Construct the activity diagram using the resource-centric interface.
  3. Repeat Steps 1 and 2 for all use cases to create the complete activity diagram.

Figure 7.39. Activity diagram for elaborating the *Process Order* use case

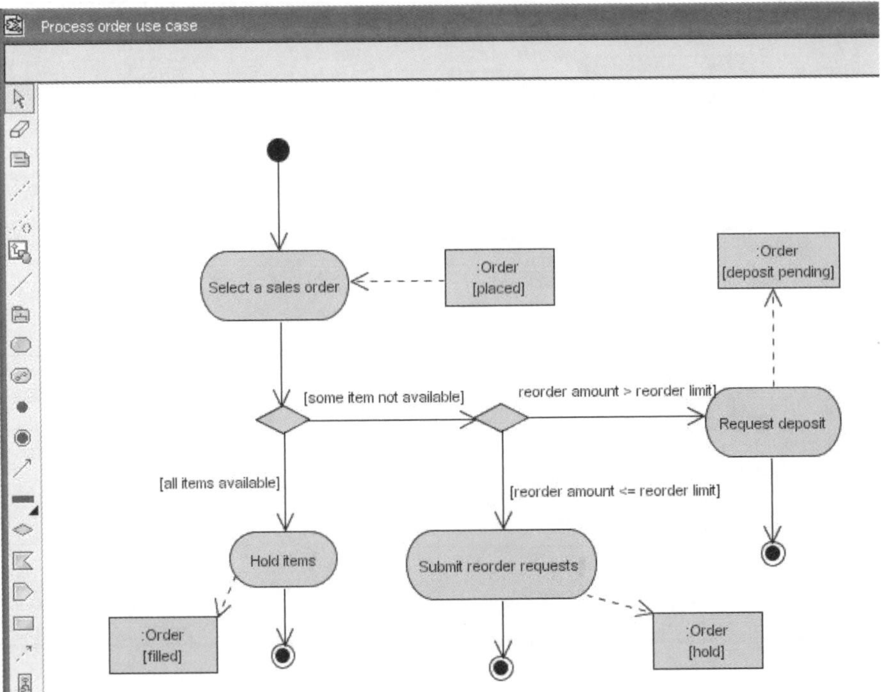

Design

Elaborating Flow of Events

We shall develop an MVC-level collaboration diagram for each of the action states. Figure 7.40 shows an example of the sales order action state.

- Create a collaboration diagram for each action state
1. Right click an action state and select **Subdiagrams →Collaboration Diagram → Create Collaboration Diagram** from the pop-up menu.
2. Construct an MVC-level collaboration diagram using the resource-centric interface.
3. Repeat Steps 1 and 2 for all action states.

Figure 7.40. Collaboration diagram for select a sales order action state

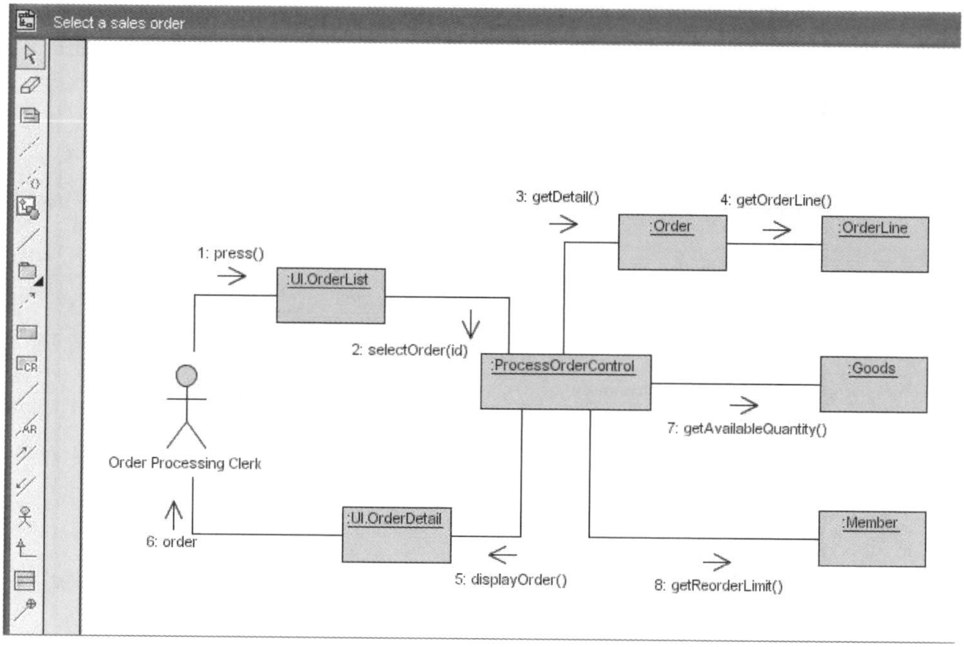

Generating MVC-level Sequence Diagrams

After creating the collaboration diagrams for each action state, generate the MVC-level sequence diagrams with VP-UML. Figures 7.41–7.46 show the sequence diagrams generated by selecting different paths of the activity diagram.

1. Right click on the Activity Diagram and select **Scenario** → **Create New Scenario** from the pop up menu (see Figure 7.41).
2. Fill in the scenario name in the **Create Scenario** dialog box (see Figure 7.42).
3. Select the path to create the sequence diagram from the **Path** combo box (see Figure 7.43).
4. Press **OK**.

Figure 7.41. Creating new scenario

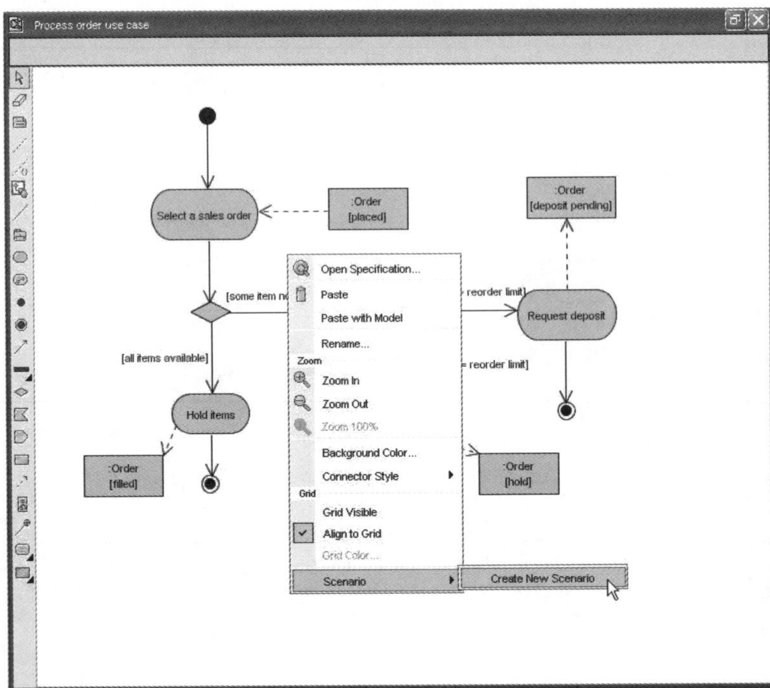

Figure 7.42. Naming the scenario

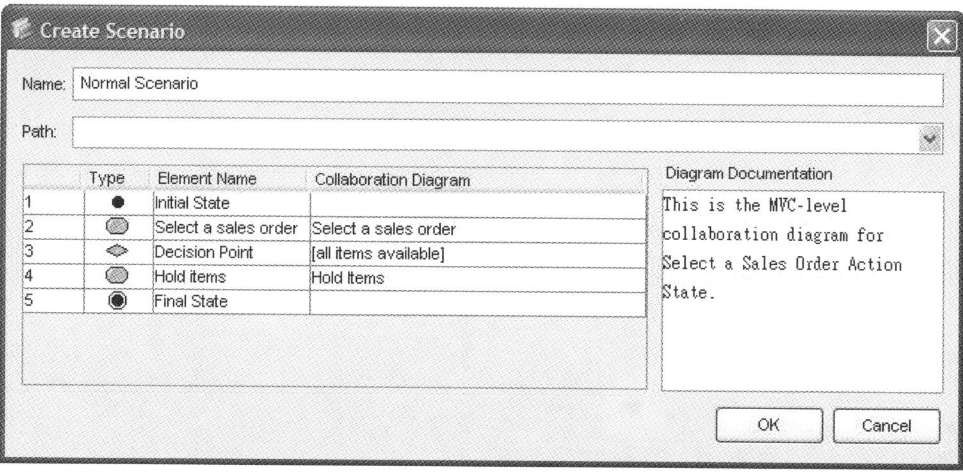

Figure 7.43. Selecting a path in the activity diagram

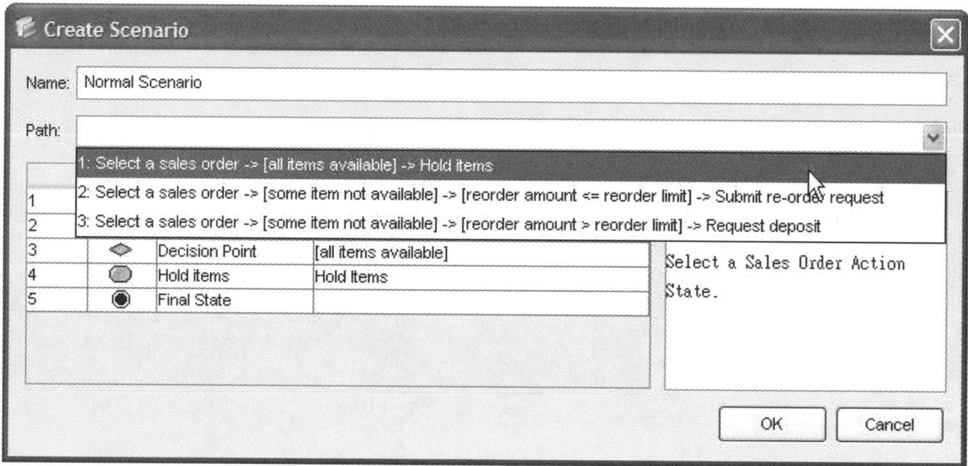

Figure 7.44. Generated sequence diagram for normal scenario

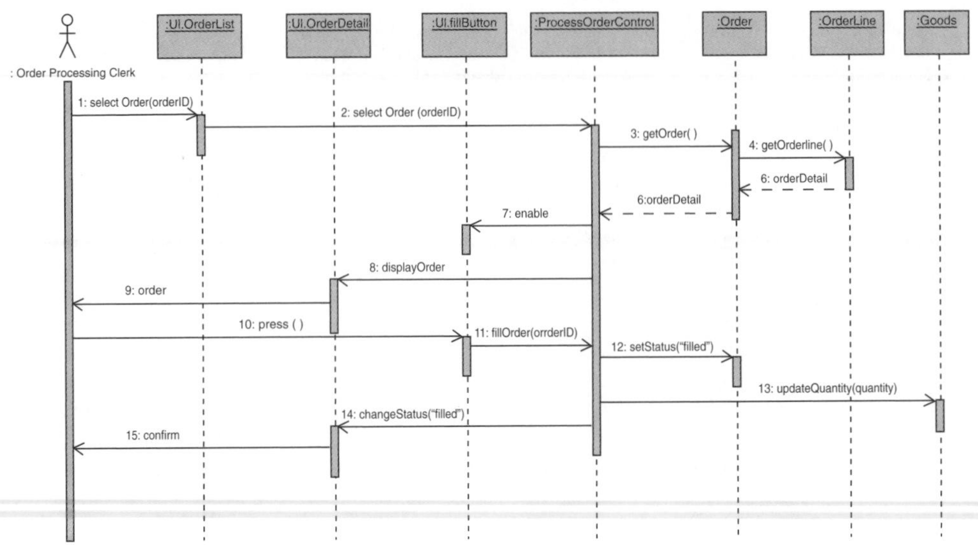

Figure 7.45. Generated sequence diagram for first alternative path

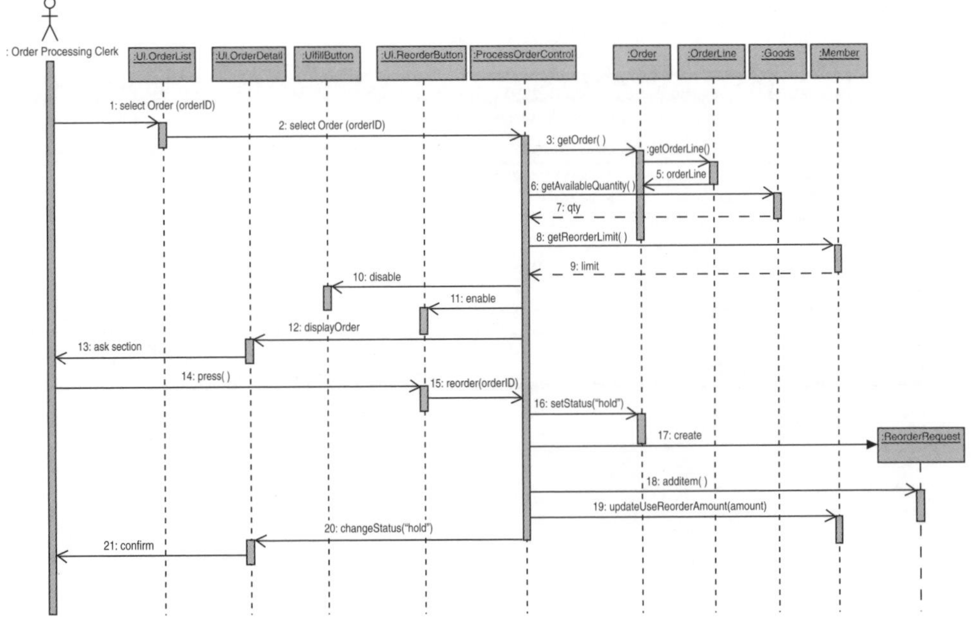

Figure 7.46. Generated sequence diagram for second alternaive path

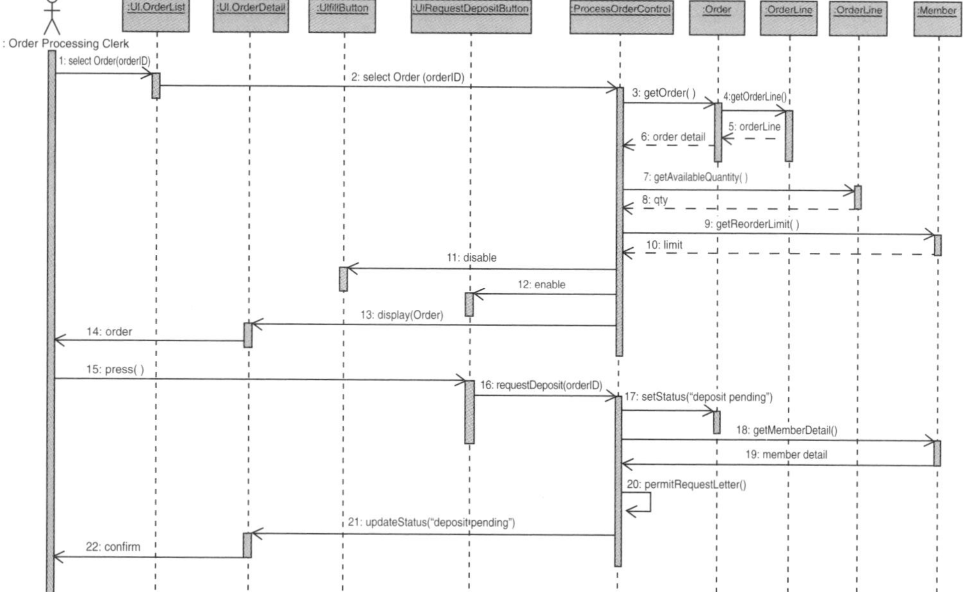

Revising Class Diagrams

Based on the generated sequence diagrams, now revise the class diagrams by adding the necessary attributes and operations. The revised class diagram is shown in Figure 7.47.

- Fill in the attributes and operations for each class

1. Right click on a class in the class diagram and select **New Attribute** button from the pop-up menu.
2. Enter the details of the attribute directly in the label.
3. Right click on a class in the class diagram and select **New Operation** button from the pop-up menu.
4. Enter the details of the operation directly in the label.
5. Repeat Steps 1 to 4 for all the classes (see Figure 7.47).

Figure 7.47. Revised class diagram

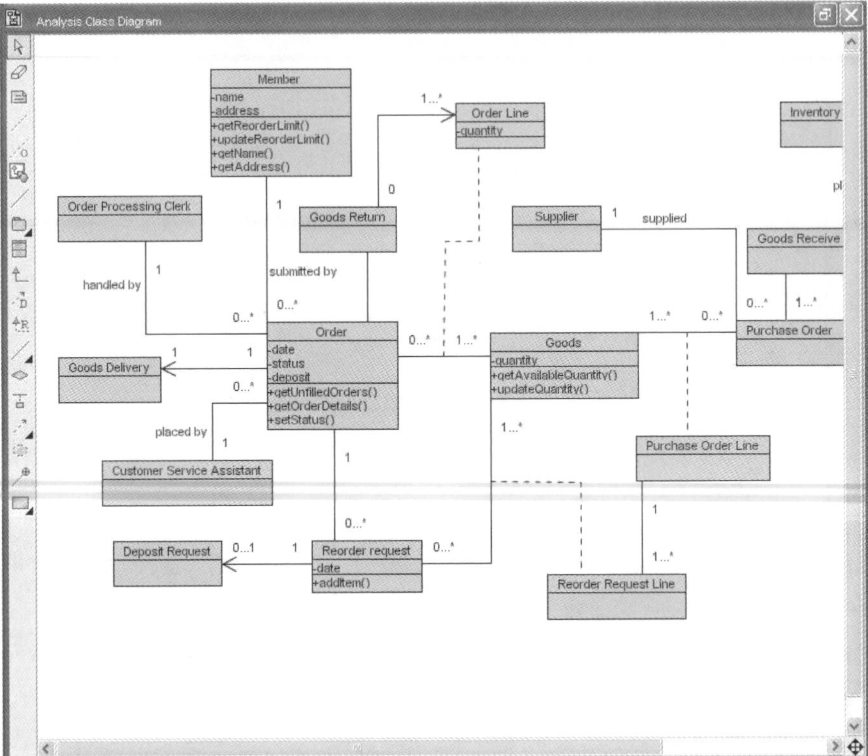

Performing State Analysis on Control Objects

Create a new state diagram to perform state analysis on the control objects.

- Create state diagrams for the control objects
  1. Create a new state diagram by clicking the **New State Diagram** button on the toolbar.
  2. Construct the state diagram for the control object. (see Figure 7.48 for the *Process Order Control* class).
  3. Right click on a transition and select **Open Specification** from the pop-up menu.

4. Click the **edit button** in the **Trigger** block to open the specification dialog of the trigger event and fill in the trigger details. Click **OK** when finished.
5. Click the **edit button** in the **Effect** block to open the specification dialog of the effect action and fill in the effect details. Click **OK** when finished.
6. Click the **edit button** in the **Guard** block to open the specification dialog of the guard and fill in the details. Click **OK** when finished (see Figure 7.49).
7. Repeat Steps 1 to 6 for all the control objects.

Figure 7.48. State diagram of *ProcessOrderControl* class

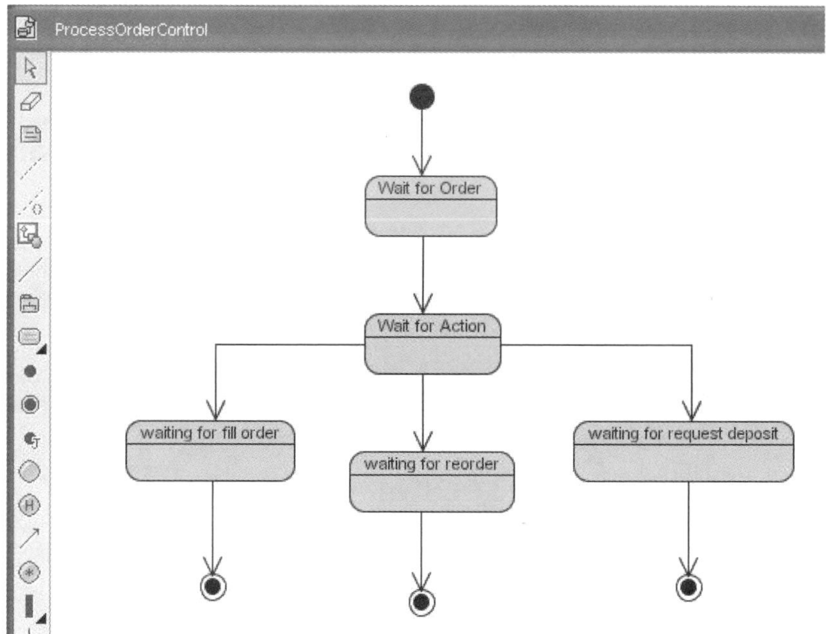

Figure 7.49. Complete state diagram

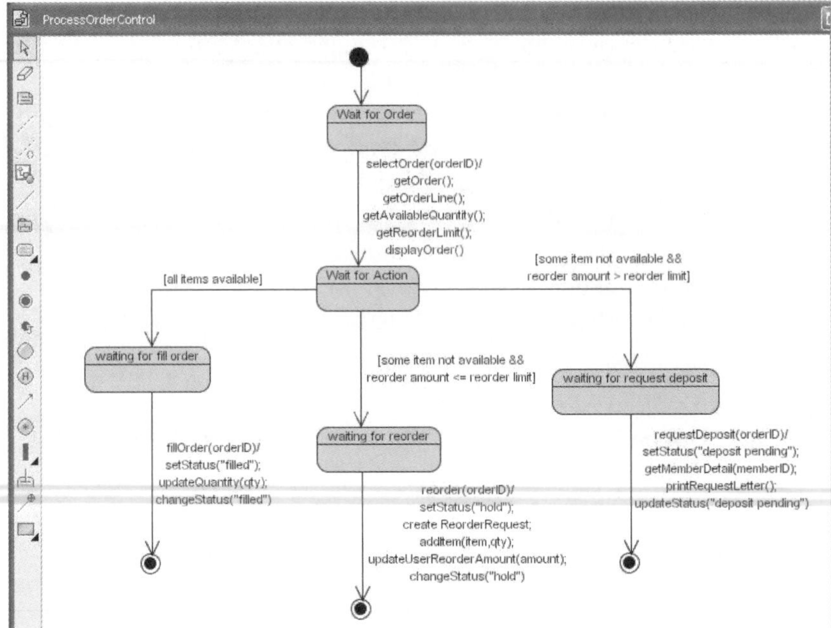

Revising Class Diagram(s)

Now modify the analysis class diagram to obtain the design class diagram (Figure 7.50).

- Create the revised design class diagram
    1. Create a new class diagram and rename it *Revised Design Class Diagram*.
    2. Copy the models in the analysis class diagram to the *Revised Design Class Diagram*.
    3. Click the **new package** button on the palette and then the diagram area.
    4. Drag the selected classes into the package.
    5. Repeat Steps 3 and 4 to create the other packages.

Figure 7.50. Revised design class diagram

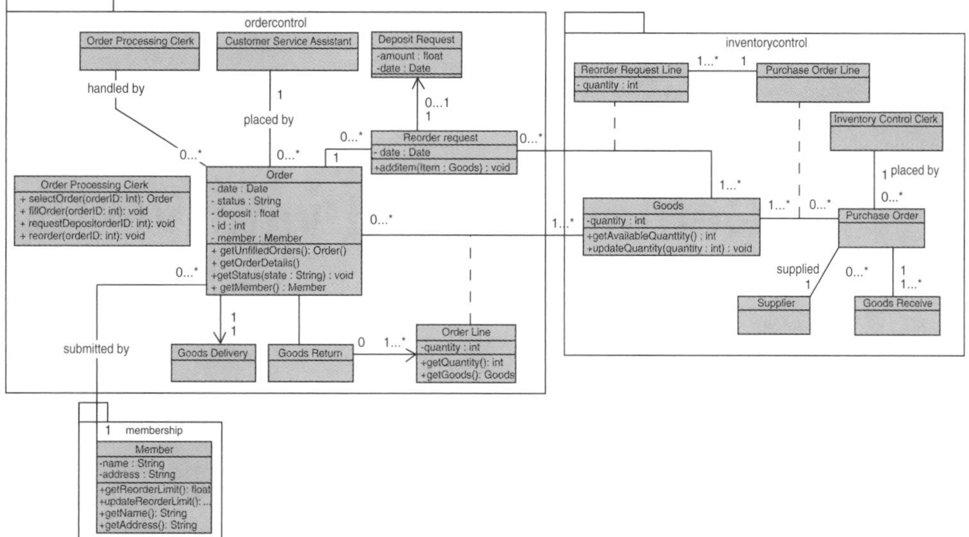

Summary

We have shown how the A^3 can be applied to perform the analysis and design of the mail order system in a single iteration of the development process. We have also demonstrated how these steps can be processed by VP-UML, a powerful UML CASE tool. With VP-UML, new diagrams or models can be created from existing model elements in the model repository or by transforming existing diagrams. VP-UML greatly improves the consistency between UML models and enhances developers' productivity because many manual steps are automated. The reverse engineering capability of this CASE tool provides real-time synchronization between code and models which significantly minimizes errors during the whole development life cycle. The UML, together with the A^3 and a powerful CASE tool like VP-UML, offers an effective and efficient combination for software development.

Appendix

Getting Started with VP-UML

Visual Paradigm for the Unified Modeling Language (VP-UML) is a very powerful CASE tool that has been used extensively in this book to explain various important concepts in object-oriented technology. This appendix serves to provide quick hints and guidance on some of the basic features of VP-UML, enabling you to operate it effectively with little training or effort. Given the complexity of this CASE tool, it is obviously not possible to cover with detailed explanations every aspect of VP-UML in this short appendix. Interested readers can find out more about VP-UML from the online User's Guide of VP-UML, which is included in the accompanying CD-ROM.

VP-UML has the look and feel of many contemporary software packages and, indeed, readers who have used packages like JBuilder and Microsoft products, should have the basic background knowledge in operating VP-UML.

In this appendix, we will first describe the installation process for the VP-UML software, followed by its operating environment and most commonly used features.

Installing VP-UML

System Configuration

Hardware Requirements

In terms of hardware, VP-UML runs on the IBM PC family of computers and their compatibles, with a Pentium III 400 MHz (or higher) processor and 64 MB of RAM. However, 128 MB of RAM is highly recommended, especially when developing complex diagrams where significant improvement in performance is noticeable with an increase in primary storage capacity.

The required free hard disk space to install the product is listed in Table A.1 (the actual required disk space may vary depending on the operating system):

Table A.1. Estimated required disk space to install VP-UML

Edition	Required disk space
VP-UML Community Edition	220 MB
VP-UML Standard Edition	220 MB
VP-UML Professional Edition	300 MB

Software Requirements

In terms of operating systems, VP-UML runs on Windows (98, ME, NT, 2000 or XP) and all other Java-enabled platforms.

System Installation

There are two types of installers available: the Windows installer (see Figure A.1) and the "No Install" installer.

The Windows installer installs VP-UML into the system and also registers VP-UML project files (with file extension "vpp") with the operating system so that it can be opened using VP-UML by double clicking the project file. Optionally shortcuts can be created on the Desktop or Start Menu for quick access to the application.

The "No Install" installer is a zip file containing all the required files for running VP-UML. Just extract the zip file to a directory. A folder will be created and all the files will be extracted into that folder.

Running VP-UML

When installing VP-UML using the Windows installer, just go to the directory where VP-UML has been installed and execute "Visual Paradigm for UML <Edition Name>.exe". If you have chosen to create program shortcuts during installation, just double click or click the shortcut on the Desktop or Start Menu to run VP-UML.

Figure A.1. Windows installer

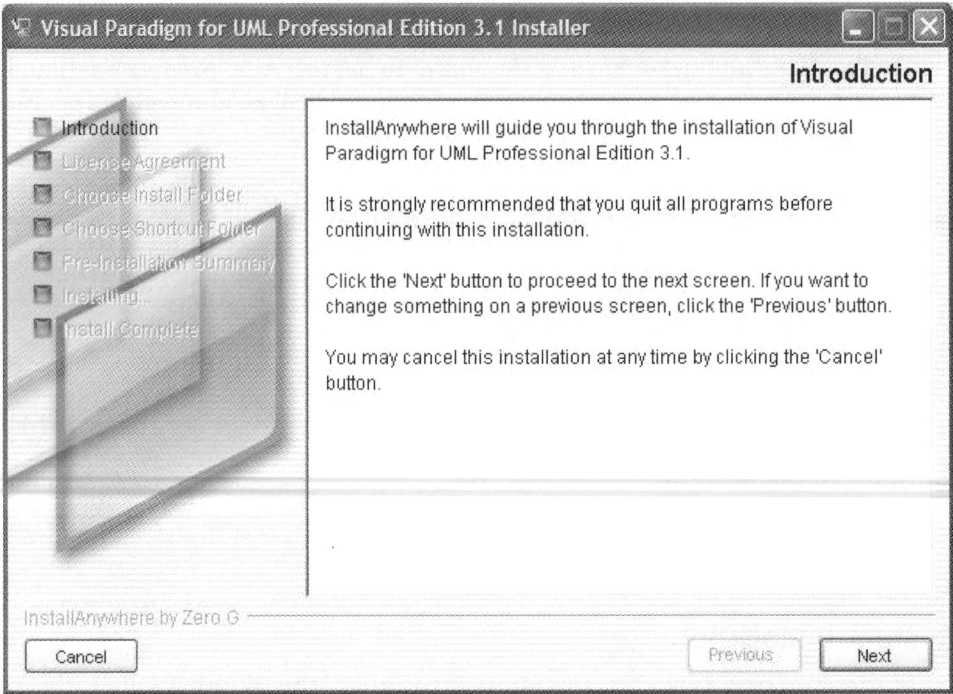

When installing VP-UML using the "No Install" installer, open the folder where the files have been extracted and execute the program executable for the platform in use. For Windows, the executable is named "Visual Paradigm for UML.exe". For Unix or Linux, the executable is named runVPUML.sh; you will have to use the "chmod 711" command to change the access permission of the executable before it can be executed.

VP-UML Environment

The VP-UML environment provides an intuitive means to carry out object-oriented system analysis and design, where UML diagrams can be created through simple drag and drop operations. It consists of a collection of menus, toolbars and windows that make up the development workspace, allowing the creation of different types of diagrams in a totally visual and interactive environment. A description of each of these interface components is presented in Table A.2.

When executing the VP-UML program, a window similar to the one shown in Figure A.2 will appear.

Table A.2. User interface components in VP-UML environment

Component	Description
Menu Bar	The menu bar at the top of the window allows you to select and perform various operations in VP-UML
Toolbar	Below the menu bar, there is a list of buttons presented as groups of icons, which enable the designer to carry out various diagram editing operations
Project explorer	The project explorer contains three views: • **Diagram tree view**: Shows all the diagrams within the project • **Model tree view**: Shows all the model elements within the project • **Class repository view**: Shows all the classes within the project
Properties pane	There are four pages associated with the properties pane: • **Property**: Allows the designer to edit the properties of the current diagram or selected diagram elements • **Preview**: Shows the overall view of the current diagram. Any part of the diagram can be accessed by dragging the rectangle • **Documentation**: Allows the user to enter the description for the current diagram or a selected diagram element • **Element viewer**: Displays a detailed view of a selected diagram element
Diagram pane	This workspace allows the editing of multiple diagrams at the same time. The full view of the active diagram is displayed in the preview pane of the properties pane. The designer can zoom in to get a close-up view of the active diagram or zoom out to get an overall veiw of the diagram.
Diagram toolbar	The diagram toolbar contains the buttons of the diagram elements available for developing the active diagram

Figure A.2. VP-UML Environment

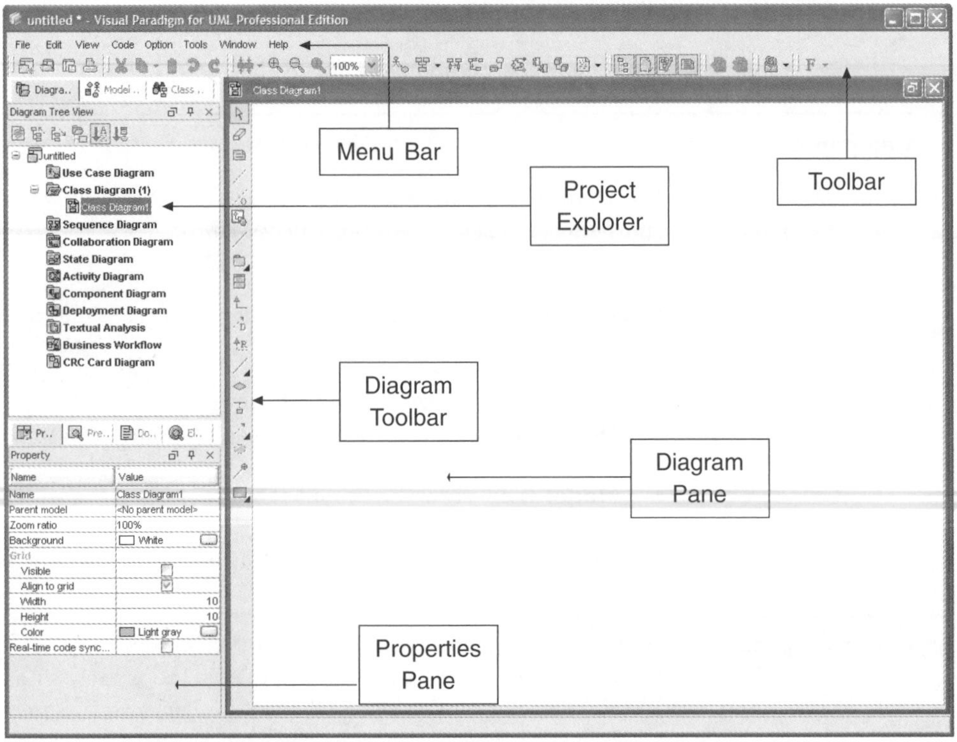

Working with Diagrams

Creating a Diagram

To create a new diagram, click the File button on the menu bar to select New Diagram. A submenu will appear and then select the diagram type to be created from the submenu (see Figure A.3).

Opening a Diagram

To open a diagram, simply double click on the diagram tree node in the project explorer.

Figure A.3. Creating a diagram

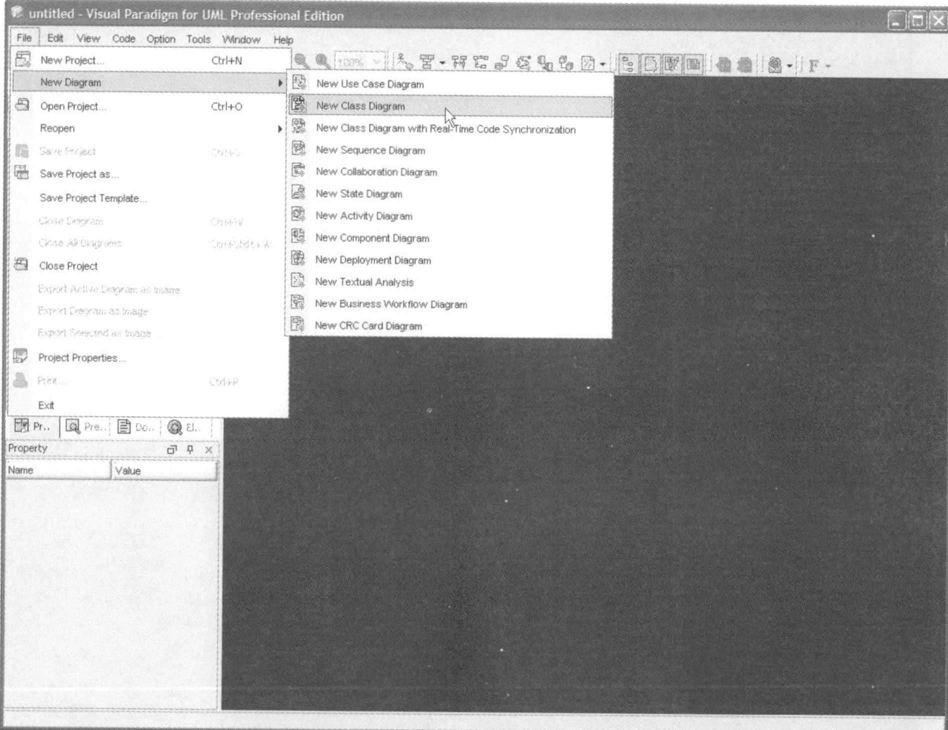

Renaming a Diagram

To rename a diagram, right click on the diagram in the project explorer. A pop-up menu will then appear. Select Rename ... (see Figure A.4) to rename the diagram.

Deleting a Diagram

To delete a diagram, right click on the diagram in the project explorer. A pop-up menu will appear. Then select Delete.

Diagram Properties

To edit the properties of a diagram, either right click on the diagram to set the properties using its pop-up menu, or use the properties table from the properties pane (see Figure A.5).

Figure A.4. Renaming a diagram

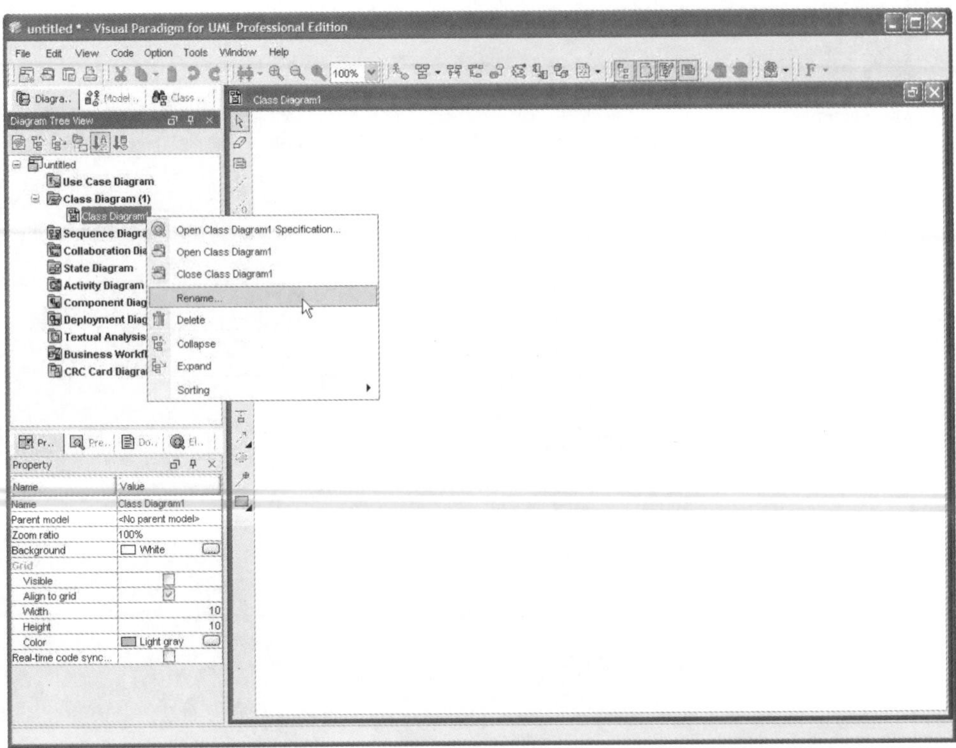

Figure A.5. Editing properties of a diagram using properties table

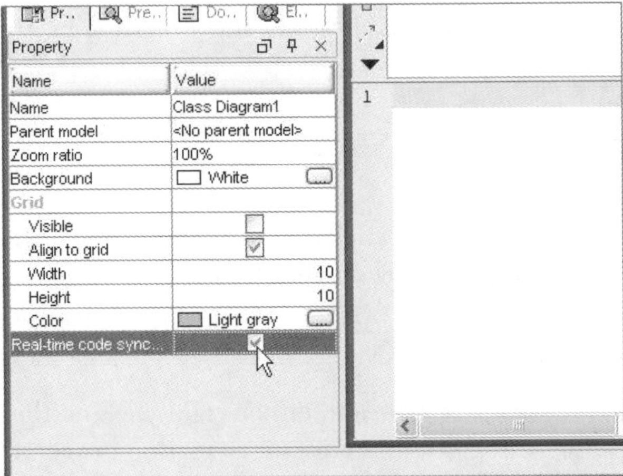

Creating Diagram Elements

Creating Shapes

To create a shape, simply click on the shape button on the diagram toolbar (see Figure A.6), and then click once on the diagram.

Figure A.6. Creating shapes using buttons on diagram toolbar

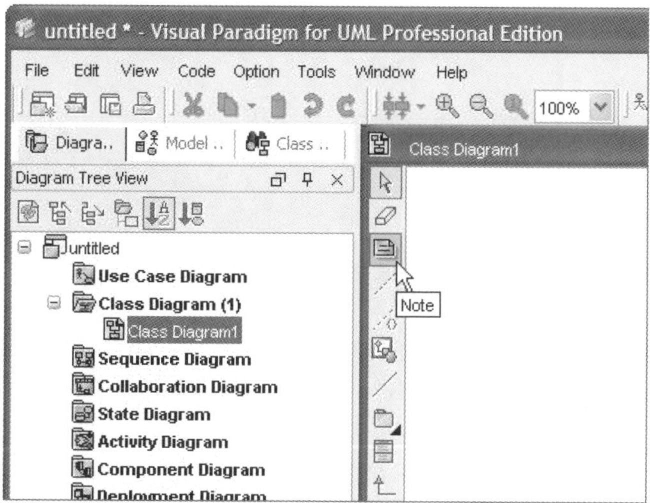

Creating Connectors

To create a connector, click the connector button on the diagram toolbar, then the source shape, and drag the connector to the destination shape. A blue-rounded rectangle surrounding the destination shape will appear when a valid connection can be made (see Figure A.7). Release the mouse button.

Creating Self-connections

Some of the shapes can have a connection to itself, for example, the self-message of a sequence object. To create a self-connection, simply click the self-connector button on the diagram toolbar and then click once on the shape.

Figure A.7. Creating a connector

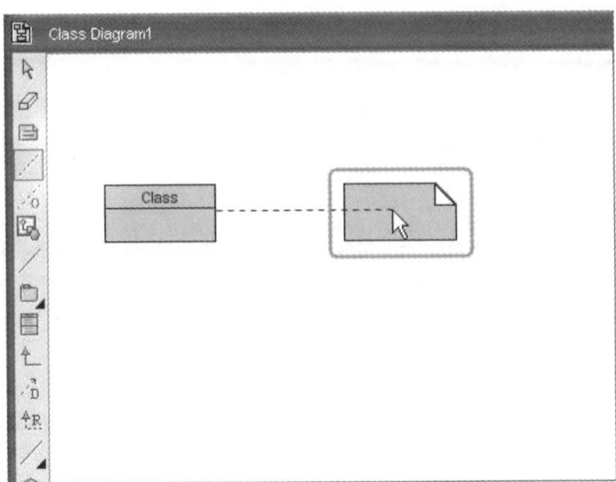

Resource-centric Interface

What is Resource-centric Interface?

A user interface based on the resource-centric approach is adopted in VP-UML to enable UML diagrams to be constructed intuitively with minimal effort. With this novel interface, only valid editing resources are grouped around a graphical entity, totally eliminating invalid operations during diagram construction.

Using Resource-centric Interface

A resource is usually used to create a shape from another shape, and connect them with a connector. For example, if you drag the resource "Association → Use Case" from an actor to the white space in the diagram, a new use case will be created, connecting the actor with an association (see Figure A.8).

Figure A.8. Creating a use case from an actor using resource-centric-interface

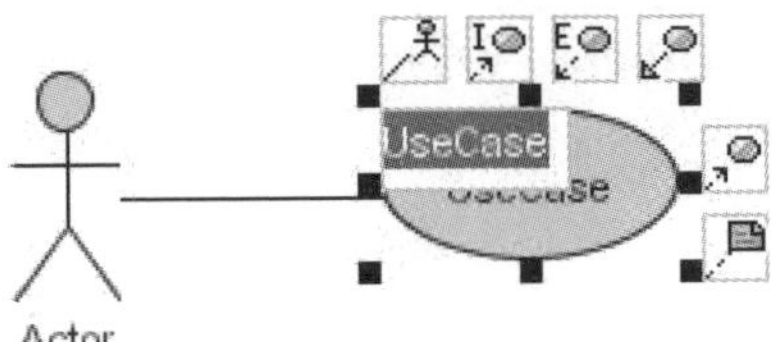

We can also use the resource-centric interface to create a connection between existing shapes. For example, if an actor and a use case have been created, drag the resource "Association → Use Case" from the actor to the use case to connect them with an association relationship (see Figure A.9).

Figure A.9. Using resource-centric interface to connect existing shapes

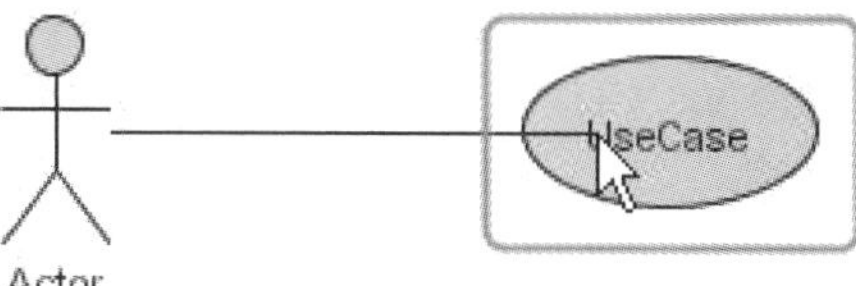

If we try to use the resource-centric interface to perform an invalid connection between shapes, for example, dragging the "Association → Actor" resource from an actor to a use case, a stop sign will be displayed, indicating that the current action is invalid (see Figure A.10).

Figure A.10. Stop sign indicating an invalid action with selected resource

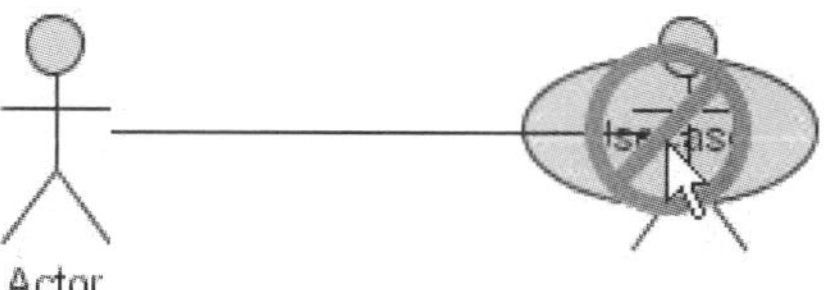

Enabling or Disabling Resource-centric Interface Feature

To enable or disable the resource-centric interface feature, click on the View menu to select or deselect the resource-centric checkbox.

Showing Extra Resources in Resource-centric Interface

By default, the resource-centric interface displays the most commonly used resources of a diagram element. We can choose to view those less commonly used resources by clicking the View menu and select Show Extra Resources. Figure A.11 shows a class element with "Show Extra Resources" turned off and on.

Figure A.11. Class element with "Show Extra Resources" (a) turned off and (b) turned on

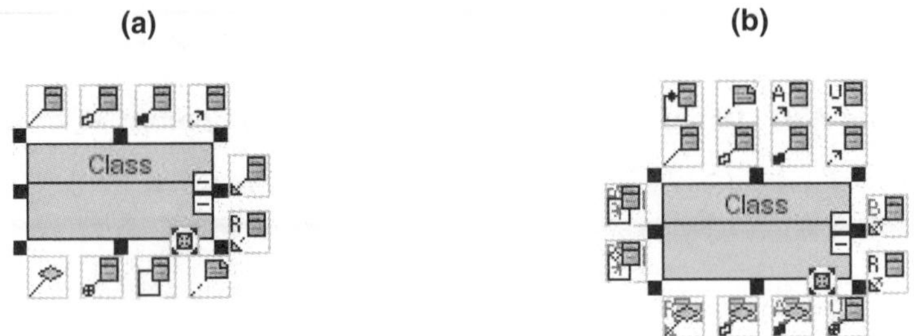

Diagram Element Properties

Diagram Element Pop-up Menu

Set the properties of a diagram element using its pop-up menu. To invoke the pop-up menu, simply right click on the diagram element.

Properties Table

We can also set the properties of a diagram element directly in the properties table (see Figure A.12).

Figure A.12. Setting properties of a diagram element using properties table

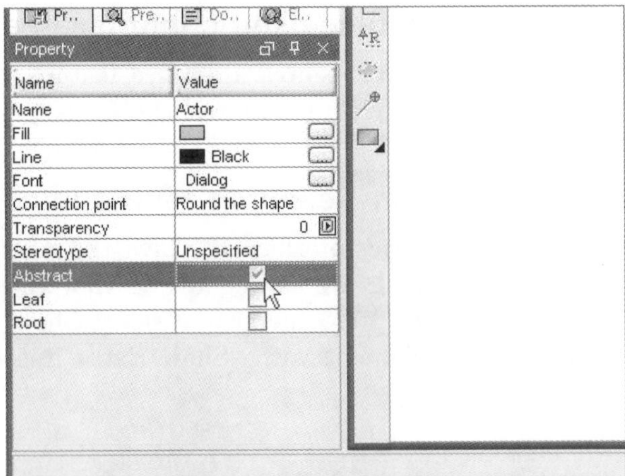

Open Specification Dialog Box

To open the specification dialog box of a diagram element, simply right click on the diagram element and select **Open Specification ...** from the pop-up menu. The open specification dialog box allows the configuration of the detail model data of the diagram element (see Figure A.13).

Figure A.13. Open specification dialog box

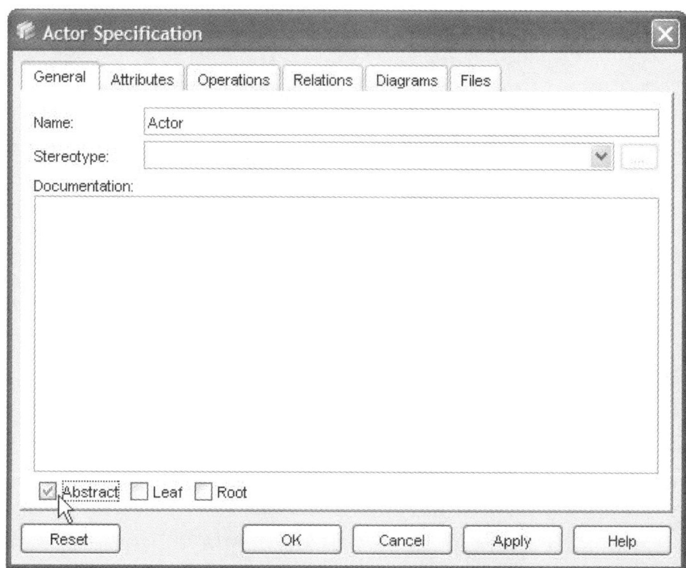

Sub-diagrams

Creating or Removing Sub-diagrams

For diagram elements that allow sub-diagrams, sub-diagrams using its open specification dialog box can be created or removed. Just select the Diagram page and click the Add button to select the sub-diagram to create it (see Figure A.14). Or remove selected sub-diagrams by clicking the Remove button.

Viewing or Opening Sub-diagrams

To view the sub-diagrams owned by a diagram element, right click on the diagram element and select Sub Diagrams from its pop-up menu.

Figure A.14. Creating a sub-diagram

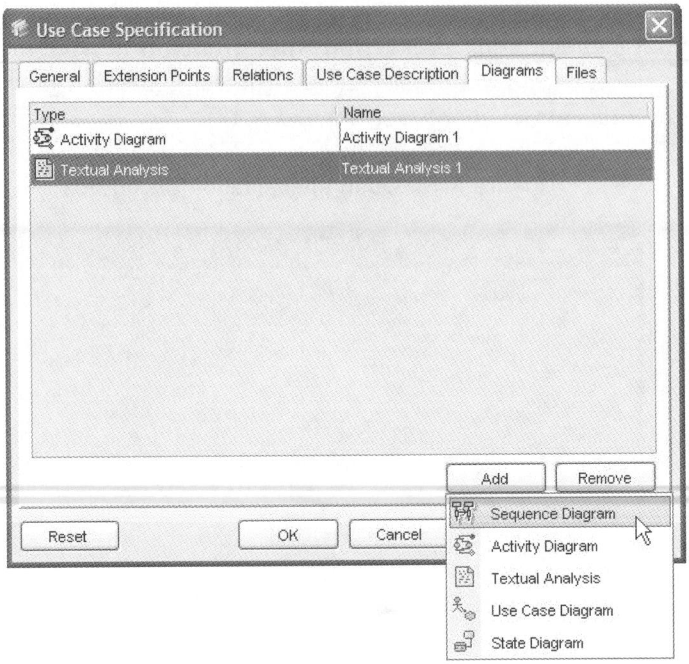

Use Case Specification

General | Extension Points | Relations | Use Case Description | Diagrams | Files

Type	Name
Activity Diagram	Activity Diagram 1
Textual Analysis	Textual Analysis 1

Add Remove

Reset OK Cancel

Sequence Diagram
Activity Diagram
Textual Analysis
Use Case Diagram
State Diagram

Then select the diagram type (for example, Activity Diagram). A list of sub-diagrams (if there is any) will be displayed upon selection.

To open a sub-diagram, simply click on the menu item of the sub-diagram (see Figure A.15).

Code Generation

Real-time Code Generation

Creating Class Diagrams with Real-time Code Generation

To create a class diagram with real-time code generation, simply right click on the **Class Diagram** tree node in the project explorer and select **Create Class Diagram with Real-Time Code Generation** from the pop-up menu (see Figure A.16).

Figure A.15. Opening a sub-diagram

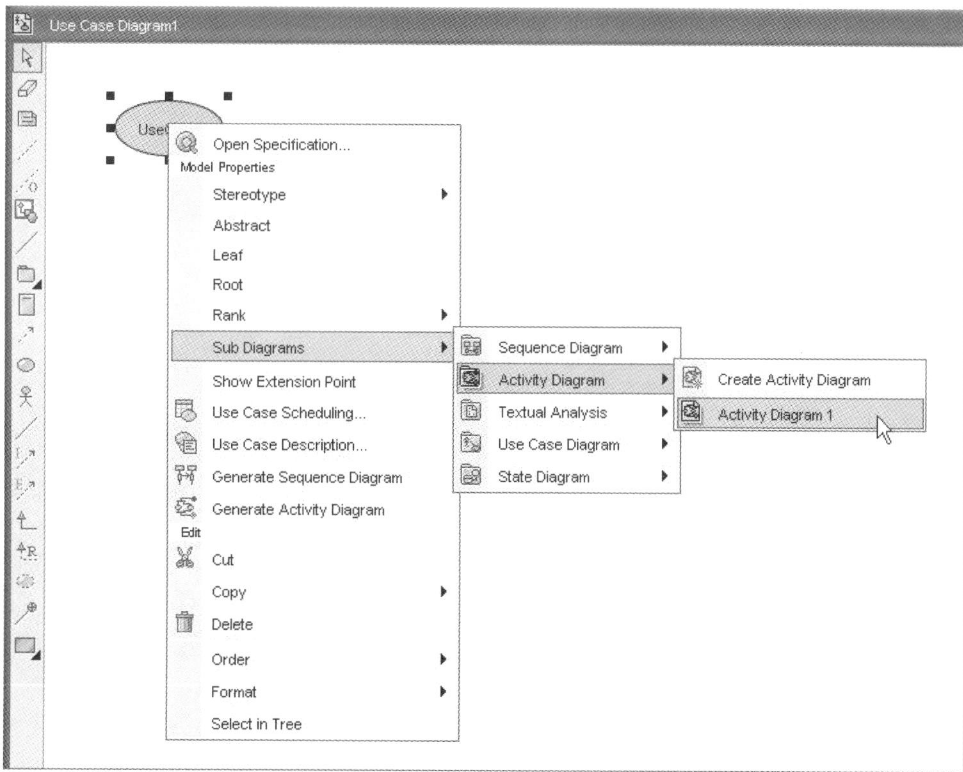

Figure A.16. Creating class diagram with real-time code generation

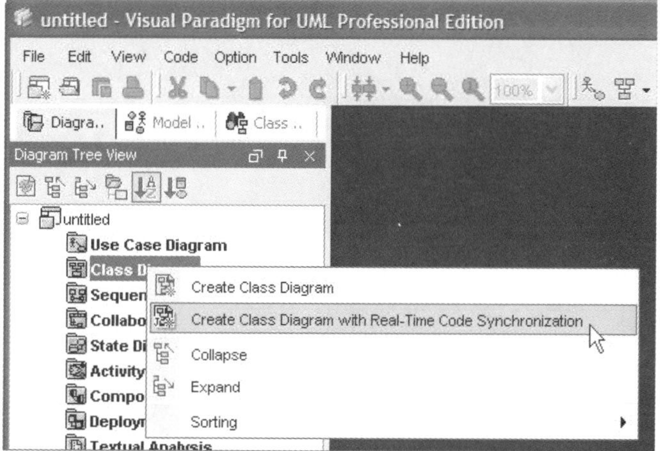

Viewing or Editing Generated Code

The code pane at the bottom of the class diagram shows the generated code (see Figure A.17). You can edit the code directly in the code pane. Any changes made in the code will be automatically reflected in the class diagram.

Figure A.17. Viewing or editing generated code using code pane

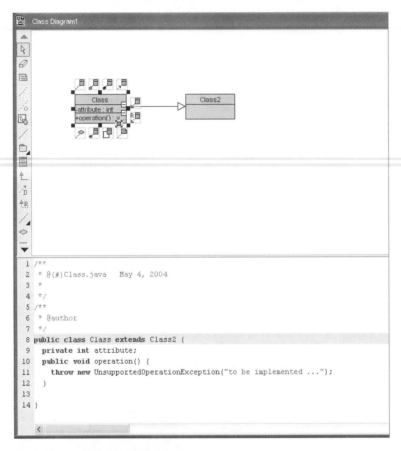

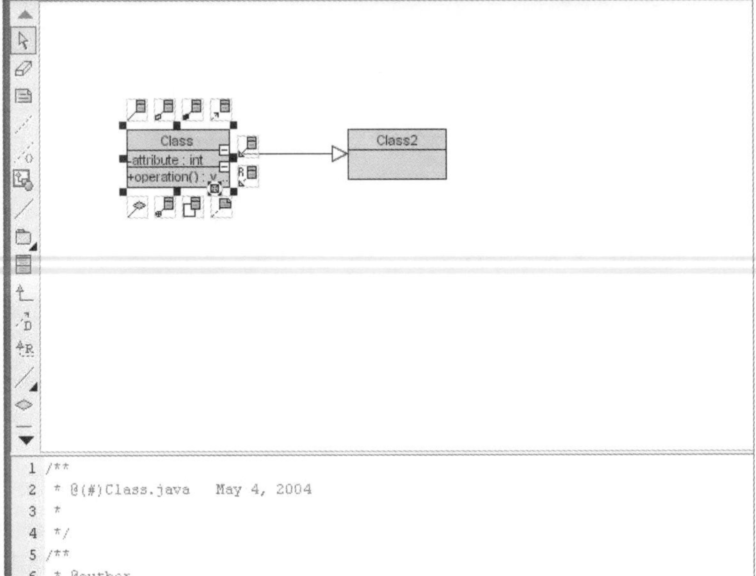

Selecting Classes for Code Generation

Before performing code generation, make sure to select the class for which the code is generated.

To select classes for code generation:

1. Click on **Code** from the menu bar, then the code menu appears.
2. Click on **Java** from the code menu and then select **Option ...** . **The Code Engine Set Configuration** dialog box will be displayed.

3. Select the **Code Generation** page.
4. Select the classes from **Available Classes for Code Engineering** pane and then click the **Add Selected Classes from Available Classes to Classes to Generate** button to select them for code generation (see Figure A.18).

Figure A.18. Selecting classes for code generation

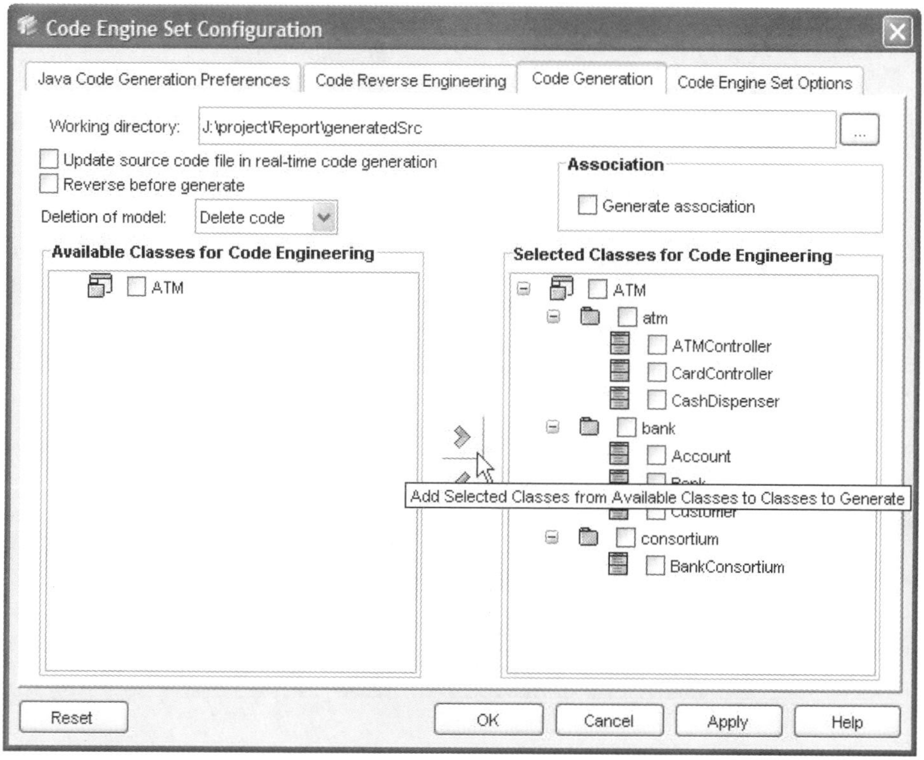

Performing Code Generation

To perform code generation, click on **Code** from the menu bar. When the code menu appears, click on **Java** from the code menu and then select Generate Code (see Figure A.19).

Java Code Syntax Checking

To perform Java code syntax checking, click **Code** from the menu bar. When the code menu appears, click **Java** from the code menu, and then select Code Generation Syntax Check (see Figure A.20).

Figure A.19. Performing code generation

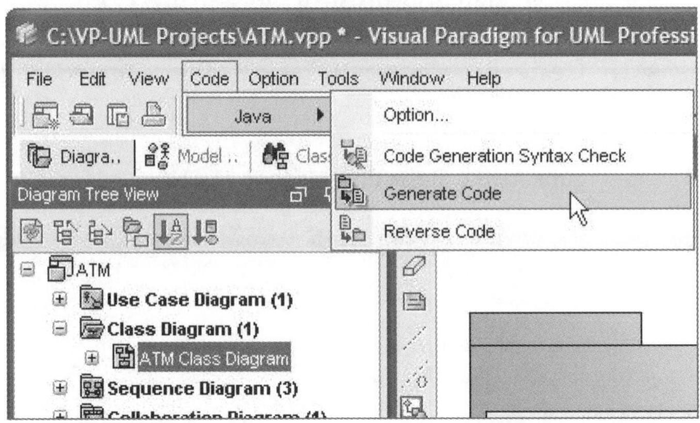

Figure A.20. Performing Java code syntax checking

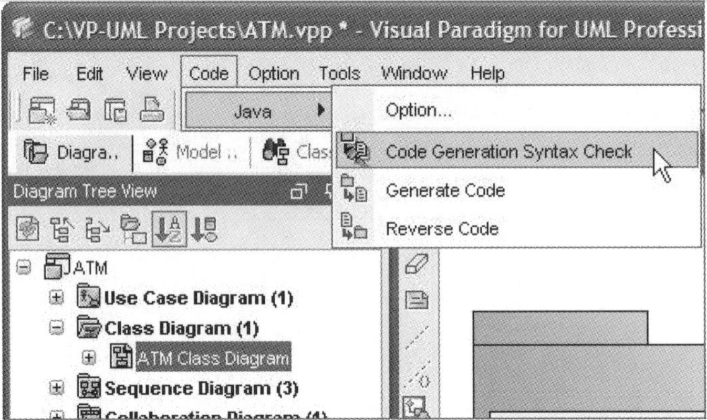

All the classes that are selected for code generation will be checked to determine if they conflict with the Java language syntax, and the appropriate messages will be directed to the message pane (see Figure A.21).

Code Reverse Engineering

VP-UML provides code reverse engineering from source code to model. Simply click **Code** from the menu bar. When the code menu appears, click **Java** from the code menu and then select **Reverse Code** to perform code reverse engineering. The new model elements created in the reverse engineering process will be added to the model repository.

Figure A.21. Result of Java code syntax checking

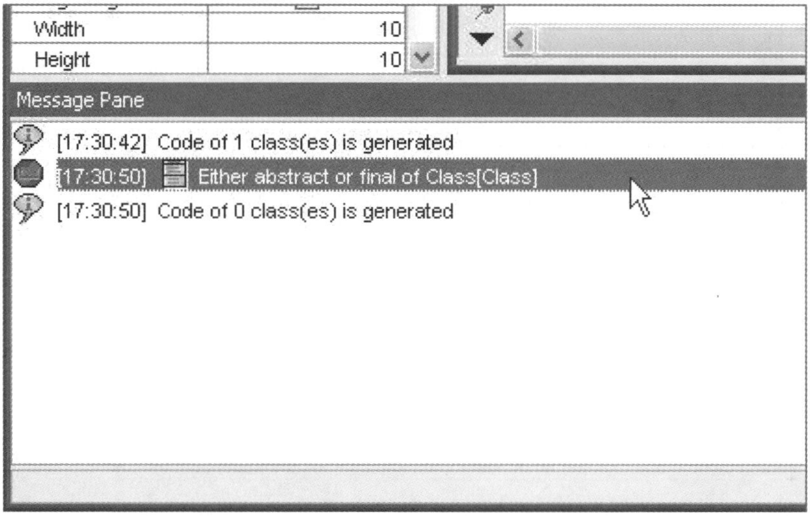

Code Generation Options

To configure code generation options, click **Code** from the menu bar. When the code menu appears, click **Java** from the code menu, and then select **Option ...** . The **Code Engine Set Configuration** dialog box will be displayed (see Figure A.22). Various code generation options, such as output directory and coding style, can be configured here.

Textual Analysis

What Is Textual Analysis?

Textual analysis is a process to analyze the system domain. It facilitates the identification of candidate classes from a problem statement.

Performing Textual Analysis

VP-UML allows us to perform textual analysis to identify candidate classes and add them to the model repository. To create a new textual analysis, click **File** from the menu bar. When the file menu appears, click **New Diagram** from the tools menu, and then select **New Textual Analysis** from the cascading menu (see Figure A.23).

Figure A.22. Code Engine Set Configuration dialog box

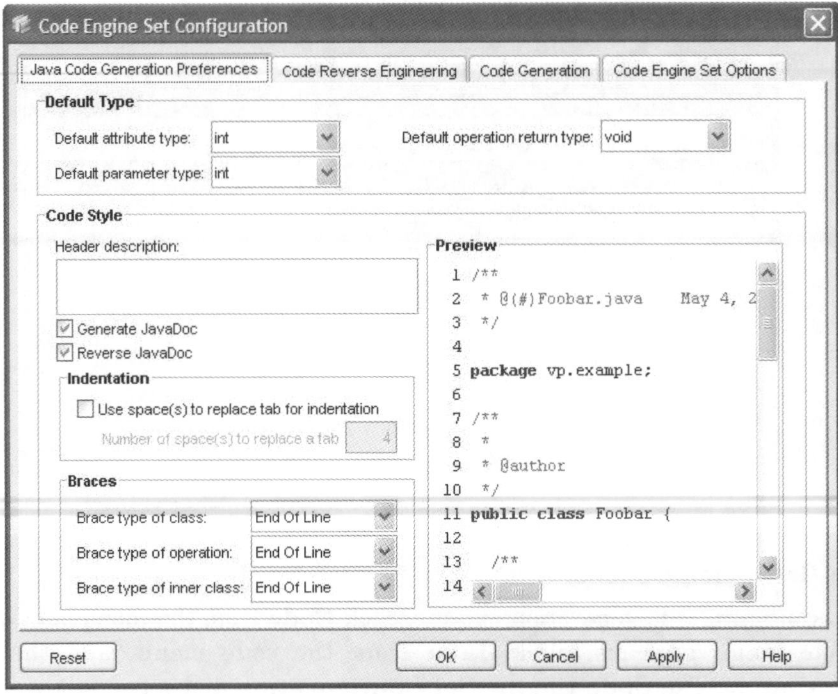

Figure A.23. Creating a new textual analysis

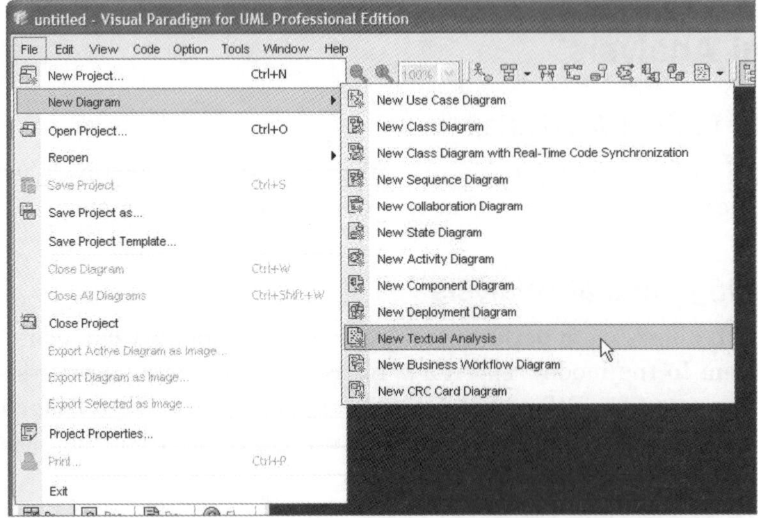

Defining Problem Statement

To define the problem statement, either type the content directly in the text area, or click on the **Import Text File** button to import a text file containing the problem statement (see Figure A.24).

Figure A.24. Importing text file containing problem statement

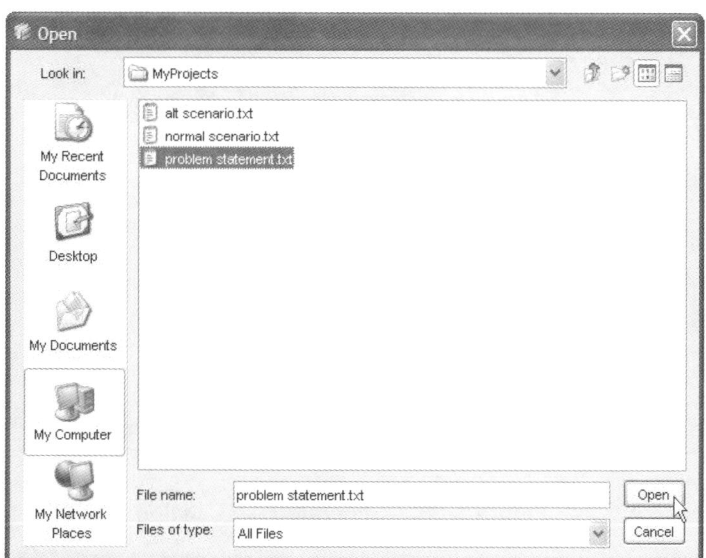

Identifying Candidate Classes

To identify and define candidate classes, either select the keyword from the text area and drag it to the candidate class pane (a class will be created in the model repository), or right click the selected text and select the type of model element that we want to define from the pop-up menu (see Figure A.25).

Report Generation

Professional-looking reports may be generated in HTML or PDF format.

Generating Reports in HTML Format

To generate a report in HTML format, click **Tools** from the menu bar. When the tools menu appears, click **Report** from the tools menu and then select **HTML ...** . The **General HTML** dialog box will appear (see Figure A.26) where various report generation settings can be configured.

Figure A.25. Defining a candidate class

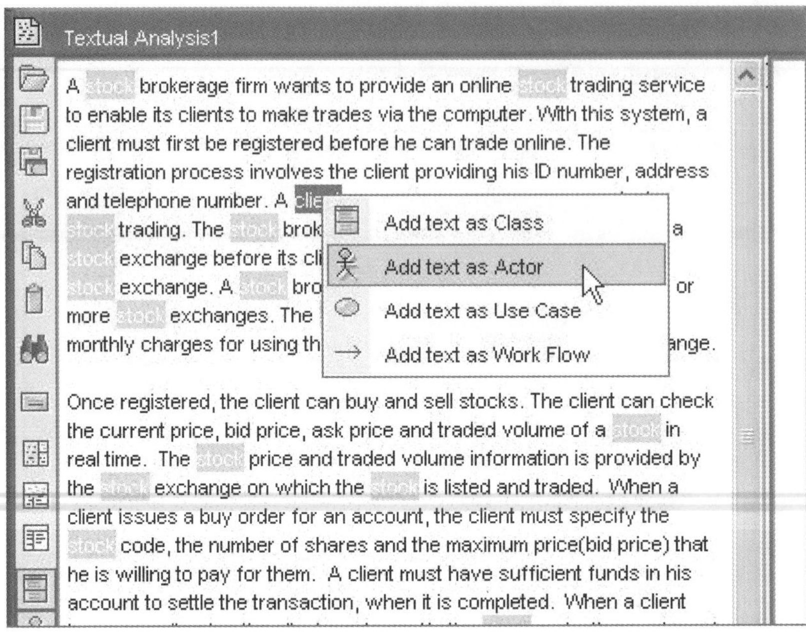

Figure A.26. Generate HTML dialog box

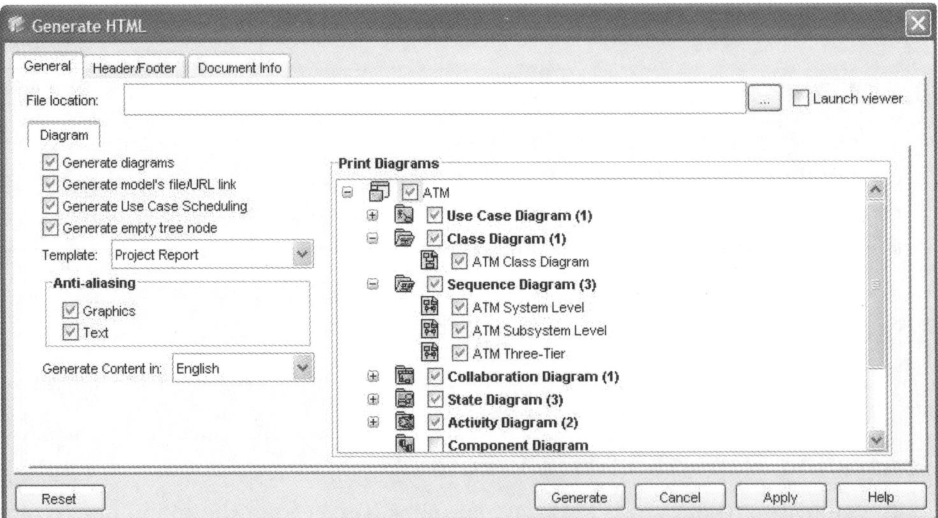

Generating Reports in PDF Format

To generate a report in PDF format, click **Tools** from the menu bar. When the tools menu appears, click **Report** from the tools menu and then select **PDF ...** . The **Generate PDF** dialog box will appear (see Figure A.27) where various report generation settings can be configured. Figure A.28 shows a sample PDF report.

Importing Models or Diagrams

VP-UML supports the importing of models or diagrams from two file formats: Rational Rose project files or XMI files.

Importing Rational Rose Project Files

To import a Rational Rose project file, click **Tools** from the menu bar. When the file menu appears, click the **Import from Rose ...** button. The **Import Rose Option** dialog box will appear (see Figure A.29), where we can select both the Rose file to import as well as the import mode. Figure A.30 shows a Rational Rose diagram and the imported version in VP-UML.

Importing XMI File

To import an XMI file, click **Tools** from the menu bar. When the file menu appears, click the **Import from XMI ...** button. The **Import XMI** dialog box (see Figure A.31) will then appear where the path of the imported XMI file can be specified.

Figure A.32 shows the diagram in Together before exporting to an XMI file, while Figure A.33 shows the same diagram imported into VP-UML.

Figure A.27. Generate PDF dialog box

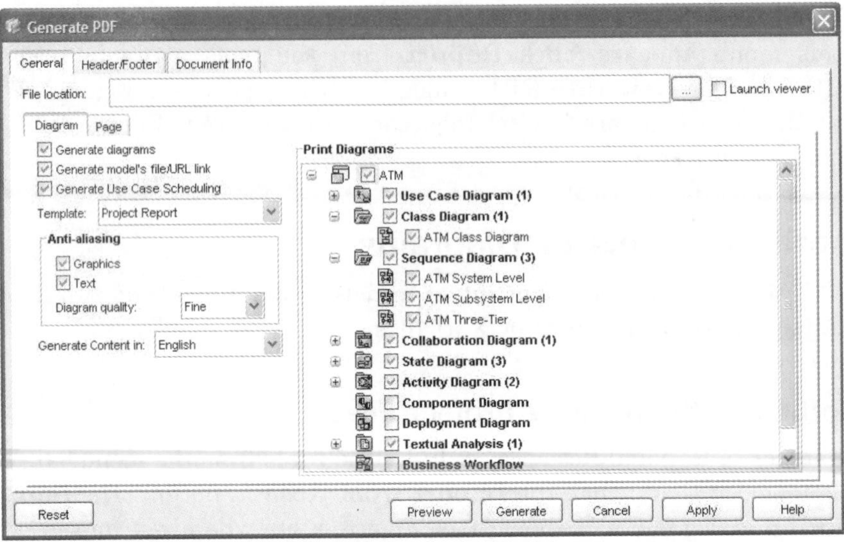

Figure A.28. Sample PDF report generated by VP-UML

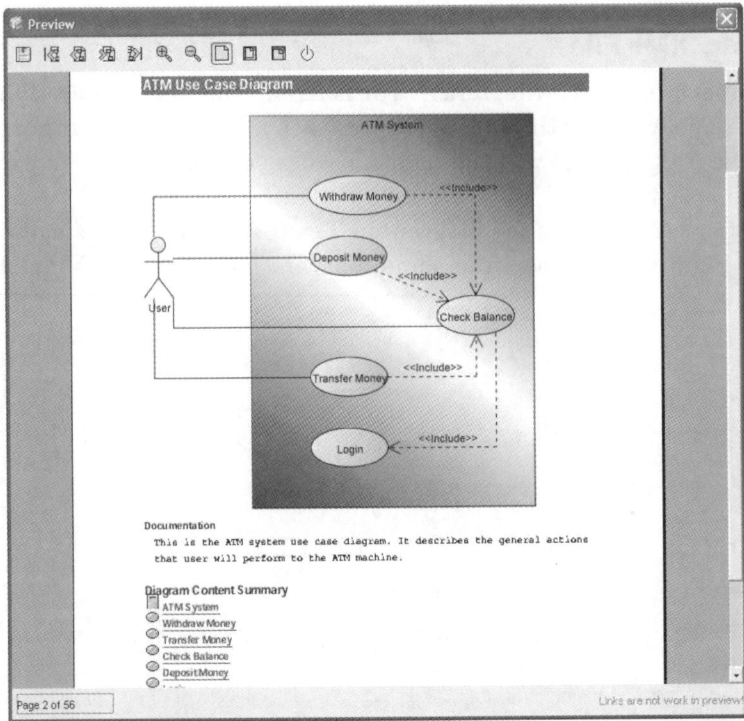

Figure A.29. Import Rose Option dialog box

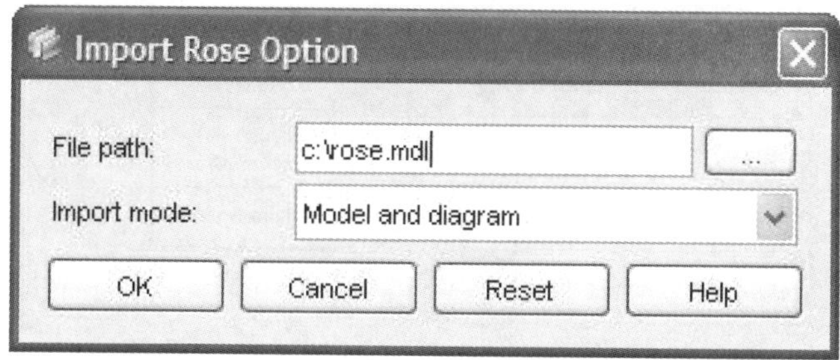

Figure A.30. (a) Rational Rose diagram and (b) the same diagram in VP-UML

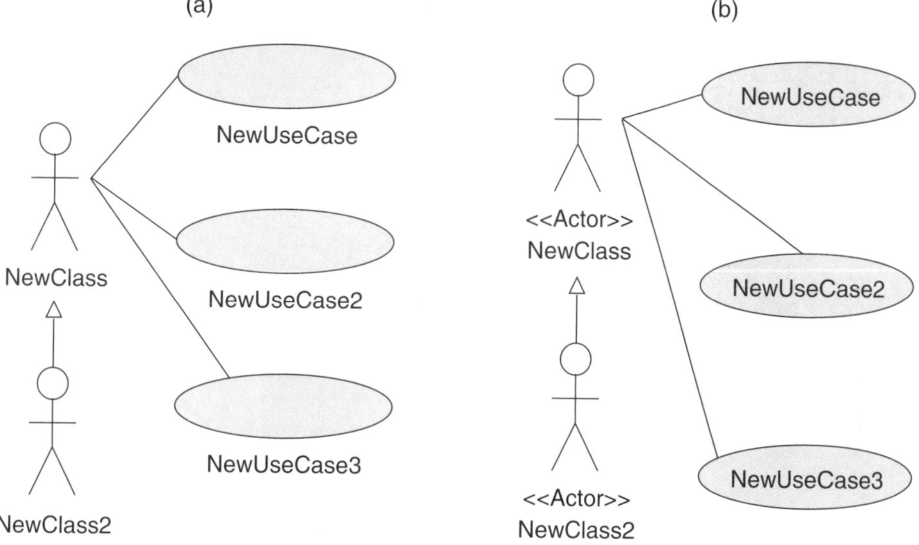

Figure A.31. Import XMI dialog box

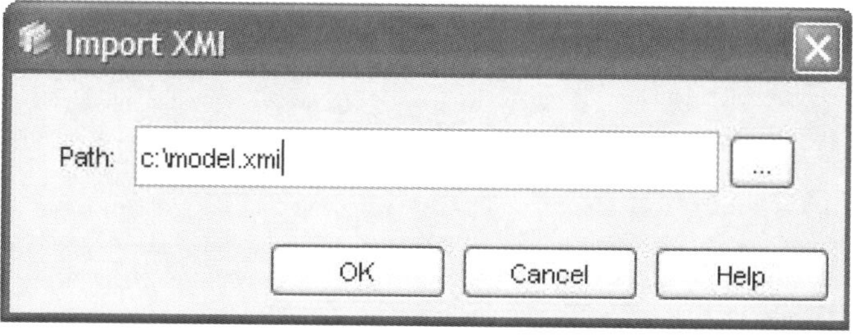

Figure A.32. Diagram in Together before exporting to XMI file

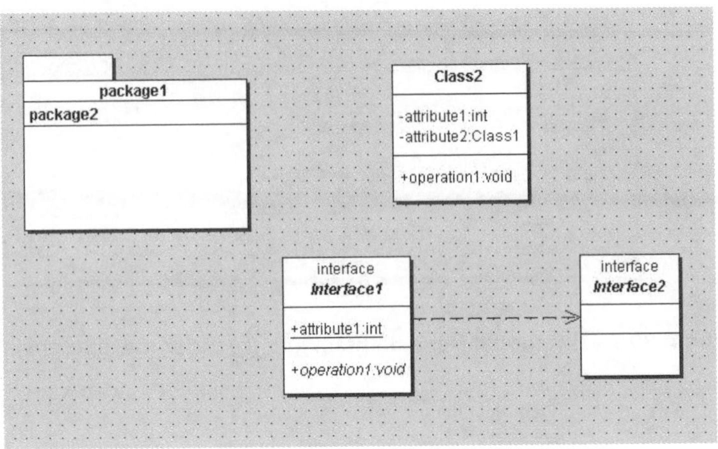

Figure A.33. Diagram in Together as it appears in VP-UML

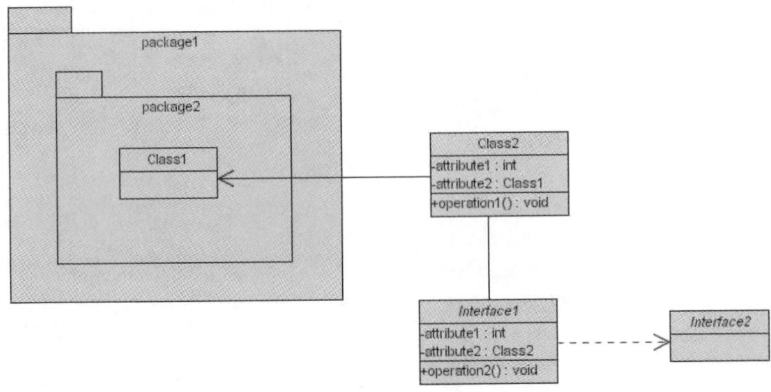

Appendix

B

Basic UML Concepts

As mentioned in earlier sections, a system can be described by three orthogonal views: the functional view, the static view and the dynamic view. In addition to these views, UML provides another view for model management and extension mechanisms for the inclusion of new notation to UML models.

A model usually contains more than one view so that the software engineer can understand the relationships between the entities from different perspectives. A UML model consists of one or more diagrams and related documentations, such as a data dictionary, which provides a detailed description of the entities in the diagrams. A UML diagram contains model elements which are notations used to represent common object-oriented concepts and their relations. UML defines the following model elements:

- Structural elements. These are the basic elements of diagrams. The elements include classes, interfaces, collaborations, use cases, active classes, components and nodes.
- Behavioral elements. These elements are the dynamic parts of UML models. They can be used to describe dynamic behaviors of structural elements. These elements include the interaction and state machine diagrams.
- Grouping elements. These elements are the organizational parts of UML models. They include package and subsystem.
- Relationships. These elements are used to define relationships between model elements. They include dependency, association, generalization and realization.
- General elements. They provide extra comments, information or semantics about a model element.

- Extension elements. UML also defines extensibility mechanisms to adapt or extend the UML to a specific method or process, organization or user by using the extension elements such as stereotypes, tagged values and constraints.

The UML specifies a variety of diagrams to capture the static, dynamic and behavioral aspects of a system:

- Use case diagram. The use case diagram captures the requirements of the system being developed. The diagram describes the visible functions (use cases) as seen from the user's perspective. The user can invoke the use cases to achieve his/her goal. Each use case has a description written in natural language so that both the user and the developer of the system can understand. For example, the four use cases (*Make a Call, Make a Three-party Conference Call, Register New Subscriber* and *Check Bill*) of a telephone billing system are illustrated in Figure B.1.

Figure B.1. Use case diagram of telephone billing system

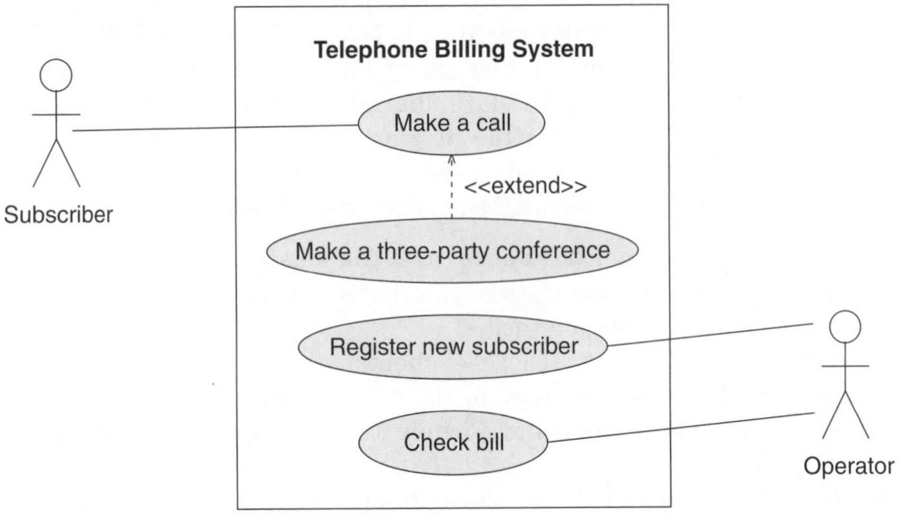

- Class diagram. The class model is used to describe the types of objects and their relationships by providing a static and structural view of a system in terms of its classes and relationships. It is, therefore, the backbone of nearly all object-oriented methods. A class diagram does not express specific relationships between objects, but it describes the potential links from one object to other objects. For example, the types of objects and their relationships of the telephone billing system are illustrated in Figure B.2.

Figure B.2. Class diagram for telephone billing system

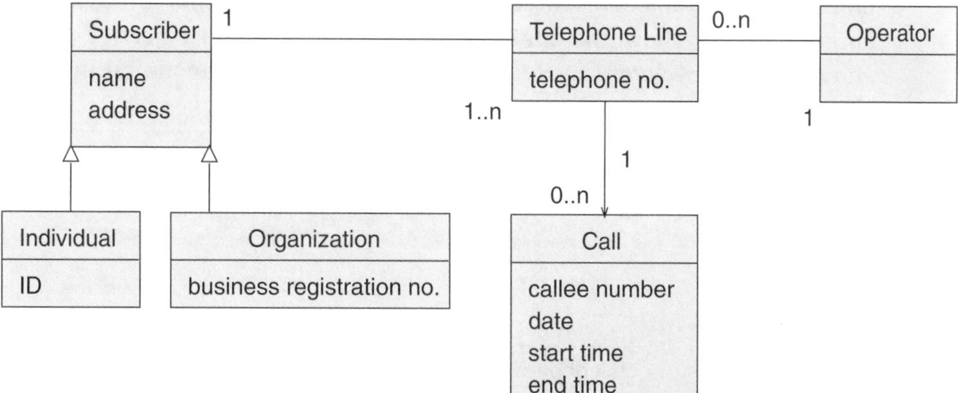

- Interaction diagram. There are two types of interaction diagrams: the sequence diagram and the collaboration diagram. Both diagrams are used to describe the internal behaviors of the system and how the objects collaborate to realize the execution of a use case. The sequence diagram and the collaboration diagram have equivalent expressive power; a sequence diagram can be represented by a collaboration diagram with equivalent semantics and vice versa. The sequence diagram focuses on the temporal order of operations of objects, while the collaboration diagram focuses on the static relationships. Figure B.3 is a sequence diagram showing the sequence of operations of a successful scenario of the *Make a Call* use case of the telephone billing system example. Figure B.4 shows a collaboration diagram with the equivalent semantics.
- Activity diagram. The activity diagram is used to model workflow and computational flow. Activity diagrams are organized according to actions and represent the internal behavior of a method or a use case. They describe the sequencing of activities, supporting both conditional and parallel behaviors. The activity diagram is usually used to elaborate the execution flow of a use case that has complex behaviors. Figure B.5 shows the activity diagram that illustrates the *Make a Call* use case of the telephone billing system example.
- State diagram. State diagrams, sometimes referred to as statechart diagrams, are a common technique to describe the dynamic behavior of a system. They represent state machines from the perspective of states and transitions, describing all the possible states that a particular object can get

into and how the object's state changes as a result of events that affect the object. In most object-oriented techniques, state diagrams are drawn for a single class to show the lifetime behavior of a single object. Figure B.6 shows the life cycle of the *Subscriber* object of the telephone billing system example.

Figure B.3. Sequence diagram for *Make a Call* use case

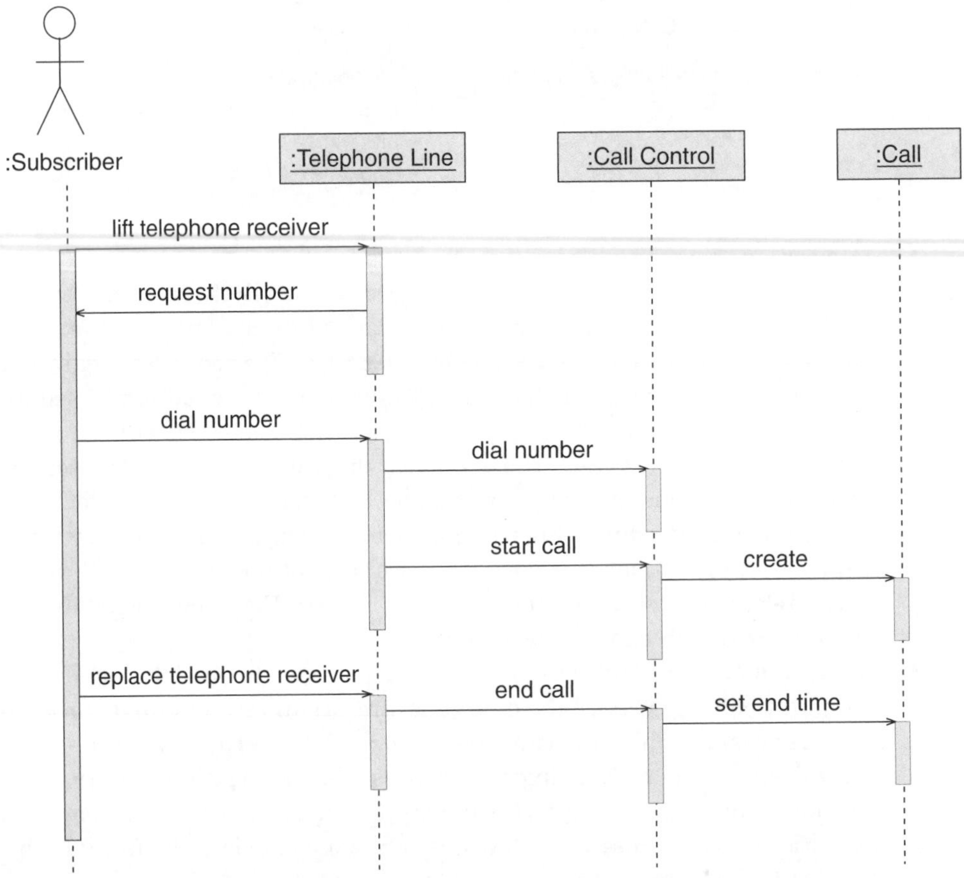

Figure B.4. Collaboration diagram for *Make a Call* use case

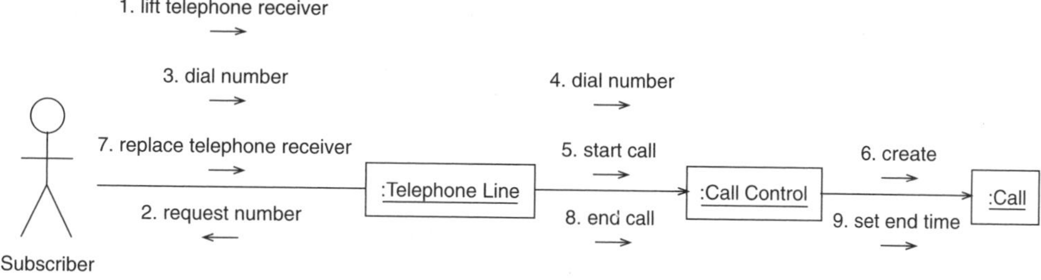

Figure B.5. Activity diagram for elaboration of *Make a Call* use case elaboration

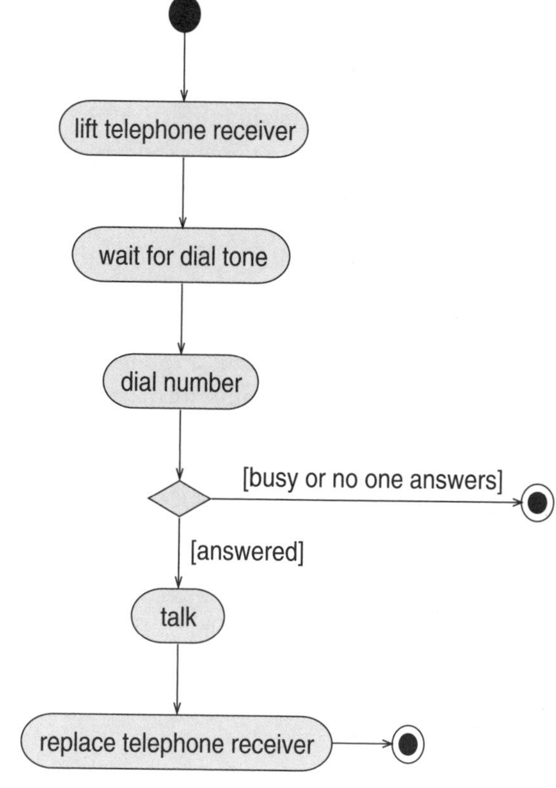

Figure B.6. State diagram for *Subscriber* class

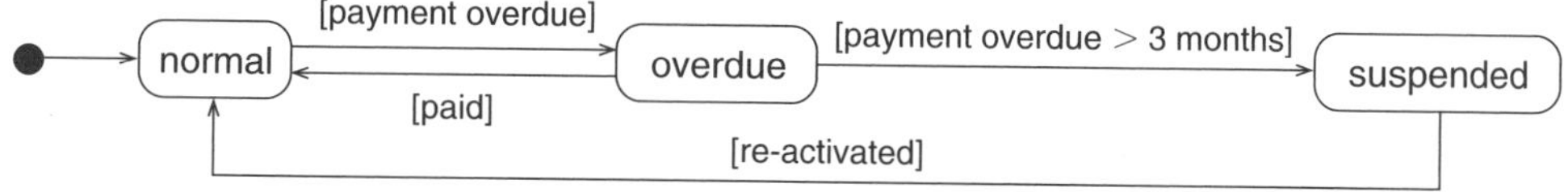

- Package diagram. A package contains UML diagrams and may contain other packages. Related diagrams are usually grouped in a single package. For example, the Java AWT package contains all the first generation GUI implementation of Java. A package diagram describes the relationships between different packages. Figure B.7 shows a package diagram where the *TelephoneBillingApplication* package depends on the *Telephone* and the *Billing* packages.
- Deployment diagram. The deployment diagram is used to describe the runtime mapping of software components to the hardware resources (nodes). A software component is a replaceable part of the system with well-defined interfaces. Figure B.8 shows a deployment diagram illustrating the deployment of various components for the telephone billing system.

The following models are commonly used by software engineers in various stages of the system development life cycle:

- The use case model describes the boundary and interaction between the system and users. It corresponds in some respects to a requirements model. The use case model contains use case diagrams, use case descriptions and, optionally, activity diagrams.
- The behavioral model describes the dynamic aspects of the system. It is often used during the analysis and design stages. A behavioral model can describe the internal behavior of a single object, the sequence of interactions between the user and the system in a use case, and interactions between objects. A behavioral model can contain activity diagrams, state diagrams, interaction diagrams and related documentations.
- The class model describes the static aspects of the system. It is used to specify the classes and objects that make up the system. A class model contains class diagrams and a data dictionary for defining the elements in the model.
- The physical component model describes the software (and sometimes hardware) components that makes up the system. The physical component model contains component diagrams and related documentations.
- The physical deployment model describes the physical architecture and the deployment of components on that hardware architecture. The physical deployment model contains deployment diagrams and related documentations.

Figure B.7. Package diagram

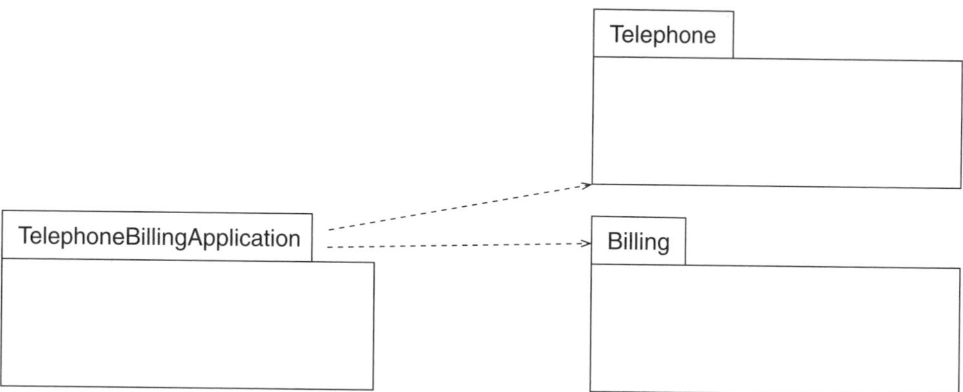

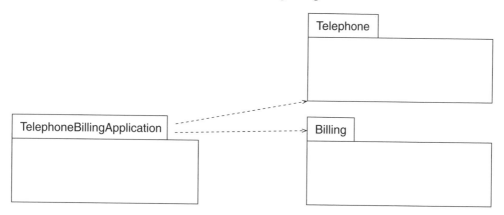

Figure B.8. Deployment diagram

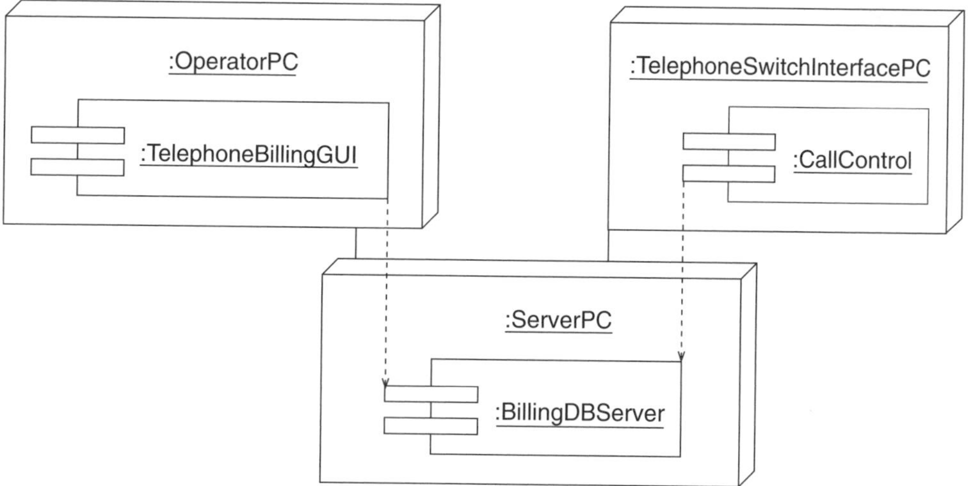

Relationships between UML Diagrams

Software development projects usually start with the modeling of use cases. The software developer interviews users and captures the requirements of the system using use case diagrams. The use case diagram describes the types of users (the actors), the roles and responsibilities of the actors and the visible functions of the systems (use cases). Then the software developer can identify the objects in the system by performing a textual analysis of the use case descriptions, and the identified objects are recorded in a class diagram. The use case can be further elaborated by an activity diagram which shows more detailed workflow and computational flow. The sequence diagram or collaboration diagram is then developed to describe how the objects collaborate to realize the execution of the use case. The operations and attributes identified in the sequence diagrams and collaboration diagrams are summarized in the class diagram. Figure B.9 illustrates the relationships between these UML models.

Figure B.9. Relationships between UML models

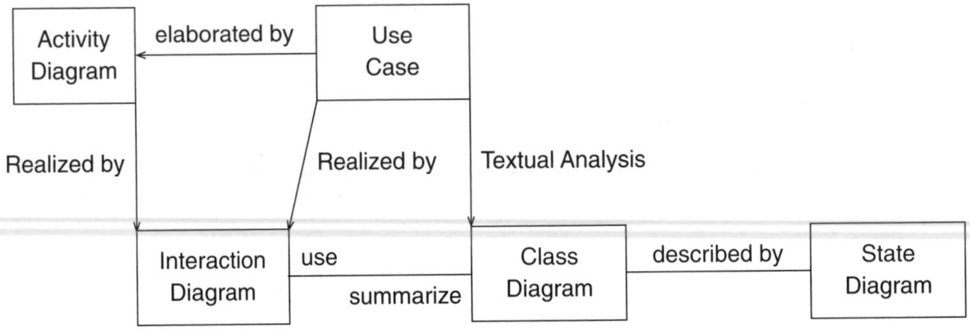

Activity Diagram
elaborated by
Use Case
Realized by
Realized by
Textual Analysis
Interaction Diagram
use
summarize
Class Diagram
described by
State Diagram

Appendix

C

Implementation of the Lift Control System in Chapter 5

The following source code is a solution to the lift control system example described in Chapter 5.

```
// LiftController.java
import javax.swing.*;
import java.awt.*;
import java.awt.event.*;
import java.util.*;

public class LiftController {
  public final int DIRECTION_UP = 0;
  public final int DIRECTION_DOWN = 1;
  final int GROUND_FLOOR = 0;
  final int MOVING_UP = 1;
  final int MOVING_DOWN = 2;
  final int WAITING_FOR_FLOOR_NUMBER = 3;
  final int HOMING = 4;
  final int DOOR_TIME_OUT = 3000;   // the time for timeout
  final int SPEED = 3000; // the speed of the lift
  private int _state;
  private int _currentFloor;   // the current floor of the lift
  private int _nextFloor; // the target floor of the lift
  private Vector _floors; // the vector for keeping the floors pressed by
the passenger in the lift
  private javax.swing.Timer _doorTimer;
  private javax.swing.Timer _motorTimer;
  // the following attributes are required for the implementation of the
associations with other classes
  private Motor _motor;
```

```
private Door _internalDoor;
private Door[] _floorDoors;
private LiftPanelUI _liftPanelUI;
private FloorPanelUI[] _floorPanels;
// for displaying state information
private JLabel _stateDisplay;

// attributes for associations

public LiftController() {
  _currentFloor = 0;
  _state = GROUND_FLOOR;
  _floors = new Vector();
  ActionListener _taskPerformer = new ActionListener() {
    public void actionPerformed(ActionEvent evt) {
      javax.swing.Timer t = (javax.swing.Timer) evt.getSource();
      t.stop();
      timeout();
    }
  };
  _doorTimer = new javax.swing.Timer(DOOR_TIME_OUT, _taskPerformer);
  _taskPerformer = new ActionListener() {
    public void actionPerformed(ActionEvent evt) {
      javax.swing.Timer t = (javax.swing.Timer) evt.getSource();
      t.stop();
      arrive();
    }
  };
  _motorTimer = new javax.swing.Timer(SPEED, _taskPerformer);
}

public void request(int floor, int direction) {
  System.out.println("request: " + floor);
  if (_state == GROUND_FLOOR) {
    if (floor > 0) {
      System.out.println("Close Door");
      _internalDoor.close();
      _floorDoors[_currentFloor].close();
      _state = MOVING_UP;
      System.out.println("Moving Up");
      _motor.moveUp();
      _motorTimer.setDelay(floor * SPEED);
      _motorTimer.restart();
    } else {
      _state = this.WAITING_FOR_FLOOR_NUMBER;
      System.out.println("Open Door");
      _internalDoor.open();
```

```
      _floorDoors[_currentFloor].open();
      _doorTimer.restart();
    }
    _nextFloor = floor;
  }
  showState();
  showCurrentFloor();
}

public void timeout() {
  System.out.println("Door timeout");
  if (_state == this.WAITING_FOR_FLOOR_NUMBER) {
    _nextFloor = getNextFloor();
    while (_nextFloor == _currentFloor)
      _nextFloor = getNextFloor();
    if (_nextFloor == -1) { // go back to ground floor
      if (_currentFloor > 0) {
        System.out.println("Close Door");
        _internalDoor.close();
        _floorDoors[_currentFloor].close();
        _state = HOMING;
        System.out.println("Moving Down");
        _motor.moveDown();
        _motorTimer.setDelay(_currentFloor * SPEED);
        _motorTimer.restart();
      } else {
        System.out.println("Close Door");
        _internalDoor.close();
        _floorDoors[_currentFloor].close();
          _state = GROUND_FLOOR;
      }
    } else if (_nextFloor > _currentFloor) {
      System.out.println("Closing Door");
      _internalDoor.close();
      _floorDoors[_currentFloor].close();
      _state = MOVING_UP;
      System.out.println("Moving Up");
      _motor.moveUp();
      _motorTimer.setDelay((_nextFloor - _currentFloor) * SPEED);
      _motorTimer.restart();
    } else if (_nextFloor < _currentFloor) {
      System.out.println("Closing Door");
      _internalDoor.close();
      _floorDoors[_currentFloor].close();
      _state = MOVING_DOWN;
      System.out.println("Moving Down");
      _motor.moveDown();
```

```
        _motorTimer.setDelay( (_currentFloor - _nextFloor ) * SPEED);
        _motorTimer.restart();
      }
    }
    showState();
    showCurrentFloor();
  }

  public void arrive() {
    if (_state == MOVING_UP || _state == MOVING_DOWN) {
      System.out.println("Stop Motor");
      _motor.stop();
      _currentFloor = _nextFloor;

      _state = this.WAITING_FOR_FLOOR_NUMBER;
      System.out.println("Open Door");
      _internalDoor.open();
      _floorDoors[_currentFloor].open();
      _doorTimer.restart();
    } else if (_state == HOMING) {
      _motor.stop();
      _state = this.GROUND_FLOOR;
      _currentFloor = 0;

    }

    showState();
    showCurrentFloor();
    System.out.println("Lift Arrived at " + _currentFloor + "/F");
  }

  public void gotoFloor(int floor) {
    System.out.println("Pressed " + floor + "/F button");
    if (_state == this.WAITING_FOR_FLOOR_NUMBER) {
      _floors.add(new Integer(floor));
    }
  }

  private int getNextFloor() {
    if (_floors.isEmpty())
      return -1;
    else {
      int nextFloor = ((Integer) _floors.remove(0)).intValue();
      return nextFloor;
    }
  }
```

```
public void setMotor(Motor motor) {
  _motor = motor;
}

public void setInternalDoor(Door door) {
  _internalDoor = door;
}

public void setFloorDoors(Door[] doors) {
  _floorDoors = doors;
}

public void setLiftPanelUI(LiftPanelUI panel) {
  _liftPanelUI = panel;
}

public void setStateDisplay(JLabel display) {
  _stateDisplay = display;
  showState(); // initialize the display
}

public void setFloorPanels(FloorPanelUI[] panels) {
  _floorPanels = panels;
  showCurrentFloor(); // initialize the displays
}

void showState() {
  switch (_state) {
    case GROUND_FLOOR:
      _stateDisplay.setText("Ground Floor");
      break;
    case MOVING_UP:
      _stateDisplay.setText("Moving Up");
      break;
    case MOVING_DOWN:
      _stateDisplay.setText("Moving Down");
      break;
    case WAITING_FOR_FLOOR_NUMBER:
      _stateDisplay.setText("Waiting");
      break;
    case HOMING:
      _stateDisplay.setText("Homing");
  }
}

void showCurrentFloor() {
  _liftPanelUI.showCurrentFloor(_currentFloor);
```

```
    for (int i=0; i < _floorPanels.length; i++) {
      if (_floorPanels[i] != null) {
        if (_state == MOVING_UP || _state == MOVING_DOWN || _state ==
HOMING)
          if (_nextFloor < 0)
            _floorPanels[i].showCurrentFloor("Moving to " + 0 + "/F");
          else
            _floorPanels[i].showCurrentFloor("Moving to " + _nextFloor +
"/F");
        else
          _floorPanels[i].showCurrentFloor(_currentFloor + "/F");
      }
    }
  }
}
// Lift.java
public class Lift {
  private LiftController _liftController;
  private Motor _motor;
  private Door _internalDoor;
  private Door[] _floorDoors;
  private LiftController _control;

  public Lift(int numOfFloor) {
    _motor = new Motor();
    // create the doors
    _internalDoor = new Door();
    _floorDoors = new Door[numOfFloor];
    for (int i=0; i < numOfFloor; i++)
      _floorDoors[i] = new Door();
    // create the lift panel
    _control = new LiftController();
    _control.setMotor(_motor);
    _control.setInternalDoor(_internalDoor);
    _control.setFloorDoors(_floorDoors);
  }

  public LiftController getLiftController() {
    return _control;
  }

  public Door getInternalDoor() {
    return _internalDoor;
  }

  public Door[] getFloorDoors() {
    return _floorDoors;
```

```
  }

  public Motor getMotor() {
    return _motor;
  }

}

// Door.java
import javax.swing.*;
public class Door {
  private JLabel _doorDisplay;
  public Door() {
  }
  public void setDisplay(JLabel display) {
    _doorDisplay = display;
  }
  public void open() {
    if (_doorDisplay != null)
      _doorDisplay.setText("Open");
  }
  public void close() {
    if (_doorDisplay != null)
      _doorDisplay.setText("Close");
  }
}

// Motor.java
import javax.swing.*;
public class Motor {
  private JLabel _motorStatus;
  public Motor() {
  }
  public void setDisplay(JLabel display) {
    _motorStatus = display;
  }
  public void moveUp() {
    if (_motorStatus != null)
      _motorStatus.setText("Moving Up");
  }
  public void moveDown() {
    if (_motorStatus != null)
      _motorStatus.setText("Moving Down");
  }

  public void stop() {
    _motorStatus.setText("Stop");
```

```
  }
}

// LiftButton.java
import java.awt.*;
import java.awt.event.*;
import javax.swing.*;
public class LiftButton {
  protected int _floorNo;
  protected LiftController _control;
  protected JButton _button;
  public LiftButton(int floor) {
    _button = null;
    _control = null;
    _floorNo = floor;
  }
  public void setButton(JButton button) {
    _button = button;
  }
  public void setControl(LiftController control) {
    _control = control;
  }
}
// FloorNumberButton.java
import java.awt.event.*;
import javax.swing.*;
public class FloorNumberButton extends LiftButton {
  public FloorNumberButton(int floor) {
    super(floor);
  }
  public void setButton(JButton button) {
    super.setButton(button);
    _button.addActionListener(new ActionListener() {
      public void actionPerformed(ActionEvent evt) {
        _control.gotoFloor(_floorNo);
      }
    });
  }
}
// DownButton.java
import java.awt.event.*;
import javax.swing.*;
public class DownButton extends LiftButton {
  public DownButton(int floor) {
    super(floor);
  }
  public void setButton(JButton button) {
```

```
    super.setButton(button);
    _button.addActionListener(new ActionListener() {
      public void actionPerformed(ActionEvent evt) {
        _control.request(_floorNo, _control.DIRECTION_DOWN);
      }
    });
  }
}

// UpButton.java
import java.awt.event.*;
import javax.swing.*;
public class UpButton extends LiftButton {
  public UpButton(int floor) {
    super(floor);
  }
  public void setButton(JButton button) {
    super.setButton(button);
    _button.addActionListener(new ActionListener() {
      public void actionPerformed(ActionEvent evt) {
        _control.request(_floorNo, _control.DIRECTION_UP);
      }
    });
  }
}

// LiftPanelUI.java
import javax.swing.*;
public class LiftPanelUI {
  FloorNumberButton _buttons[];
  LiftController _liftController;
  JLabel _currentFloorDisplay;
  public LiftPanelUI(int numOfButtons) {
    _buttons = new FloorNumberButton[numOfButtons];
    for (int i = 0; i < numOfButtons; i++)
      _buttons[i] = new FloorNumberButton(i);
  }
  public FloorNumberButton[] getButtons() {
    return _buttons;
  }
  public void setLiftController(LiftController control) {
    _liftController = control;
    for (int i = 0; i < _buttons.length; i++)
      _buttons[i].setControl(control);
  }
  public void setButtonDisplay(JButton[] buttons) {
    for (int i = 0; i < _buttons.length; i++)
```

```
        _buttons[i].setButton(buttons[i]);
    }
    public void showCurrentFloor(int floor) {
      _currentFloorDisplay.setText(floor+"/F");
    }
    public void setCurrentFloorDisplay(JLabel display) {
      _currentFloorDisplay = display;
      showCurrentFloor(0); // initialize display to "0/F"
    }
  }

  // FloorPanelUI.java
  import javax.swing.*;
  public class FloorPanelUI {
    LiftButton _downButton, _upButton;
    LiftController _liftController;
    JLabel _floorDisplay;
    public FloorPanelUI(int floor) {
        _downButton = new DownButton(floor);
        _upButton = new UpButton(floor);
    }
    public void setLiftController(LiftController control) {
      _liftController = control;
      _downButton.setControl(control);
      _upButton.setControl(control);
    }
    public void setDownButtonDisplay(JButton b) {
      _downButton.setButton(b);
    }
    public void setUpButtonDisplay(JButton b) {
      _upButton.setButton(b);
    }

  // Main.java
  public class Main {
    public static void main(String args[]) throws Exception {
      Lift lift = new Lift(7);
      LiftController liftController = lift.getLiftController();
      LiftPanelUI liftPanel = new LiftPanelUI(7);
      liftController.setLiftPanelUI(liftPanel);
      liftPanel.setLiftController(liftController);
      LiftFrame liftFrame = new LiftFrame();
      // link the Floor Number Button to the actual JButton
      liftPanel.setButtonDisplay(liftFrame.getButtons());
      liftPanel.setLiftController(liftController);
      // link the door to the display
      lift.getInternalDoor().setDisplay(liftFrame.getDoorDisplay());
```

```
    // link the motor to the display
    lift.getMotor().setDisplay(liftFrame.getMotorDisplay());
    liftController.setMotor(lift.getMotor());
    // link the LiftPanelUI to the current floor display
    liftPanel.setCurrentFloorDisplay(liftFrame.getCurrentFloorDisplay());
    // link the liftController to the state display
    liftController.setStateDisplay(liftFrame.getStateDisplay());
    liftFrame.setBounds(0,0,400,400);
    liftFrame.show();
    // create the floor panel for G/F
    FloorFrame floorFrame = new FloorFrame(0);
    FloorPanelUI floorPanel = new FloorPanelUI(0);
    // link the down button to the actual JButton
    floorPanel.setDownButtonDisplay(floorFrame.getDownButton());
    // link the up button to the actual JButton
    floorPanel.setUpButtonDisplay(floorFrame.getUpButton());
    // link the floor current floor display to the actual display
    floorPanel.setFloorDisplay(floorFrame.getFloorDisplay());
    // link the floor door to the actual display
    lift.getFloorDoors()[0].setDisplay(floorFrame.getDoorDisplay());
    // link the floor panel UI to the controller
    floorPanel.setLiftController(liftController);
    floorFrame.setBounds(500, 400, 400, 400);
    // create the floor panel for 6/F
    FloorFrame floorFrame6 = new FloorFrame(6);
    FloorPanelUI floorPanel6 = new FloorPanelUI(6);
    // link the down button to the actual JButton
    floorPanel6.setDownButtonDisplay(floorFrame6.getDownButton());
    // link the up button to the actual JButton
    floorPanel6.setUpButtonDisplay(floorFrame6.getUpButton());
    // link the floor current floor display to the actual display
    floorPanel6.setFloorDisplay(floorFrame6.getFloorDisplay());
    // link the floor door to the actual display
    lift.getFloorDoors()[6].setDisplay(floorFrame6.getDoorDisplay());
    // link the floor panel UI to the controller
    floorPanel6.setLiftController(liftController);
    // link the controller to the floor panels
    FloorPanelUI[] panels = new FloorPanelUI[7];
    panels[0] = floorPanel;
    panels[6] = floorPanel6;
    liftController.setFloorPanels(panels);
    floorFrame6.setBounds(500, 0, 400, 400);
    floorFrame.show();
    floorFrame6.show();
  }
}
```

```
// LiftFrame.java
import javax.swing.*;
import java.awt.*;
import java.awt.event.*;
public class LiftFrame extends JFrame {
  JButton _fifthFloor = new JButton();
  JButton _sixFloor = new JButton();
  JButton _fourthFloor = new JButton();
  JButton _thirdFloor = new JButton();
  JButton _secondFloor = new JButton();
  JButton _firstFloor = new JButton();
  JButton _groundFloor = new JButton();
  JPanel _buttonPanel = new JPanel();
  GridLayout _buttonLayout = new GridLayout();
  JLabel _stateLabel = new JLabel();
  JLabel _currentFloorDisplay = new JLabel();
  JLabel _motorDisplay = new JLabel();
  JLabel _doorLabel = new JLabel();
  JLabel _motorLabel = new JLabel();
  JLabel _stateDisplay = new JLabel();
  JLabel _doorDisplay = new JLabel();
  JLabel _currentFloorLabel = new JLabel();
  JPanel _displayPanel = new JPanel();
  GridLayout _displayLayout = new GridLayout();
  JButton[] _buttons;
  public LiftFrame() throws HeadlessException {
    super("Lift");
    _buttons = new JButton[7];
    _buttons[0] = _groundFloor;
    _buttons[1] = _firstFloor;
    _buttons[2] = _secondFloor;
    _buttons[3] = _thirdFloor;
    _buttons[4] = _fourthFloor;
    _buttons[5] = _fifthFloor;
    _buttons[6] = _sixFloor;

    try {
      initUI ();
    }
    catch(Exception e) {
      e.printStackTrace();
    }
  }
  public JButton[] getButtons() {
    return _buttons;
  }
  public JLabel getMotorDisplay() {
```

```
    return this._motorDisplay;
  }
  public JLabel getDoorDisplay() {
    return this._doorDisplay;
  }
  public JLabel getCurrentFloorDisplay() {
    return _currentFloorDisplay;
  }
  public JLabel getStateDisplay() {
    return _stateDisplay;
  }
  private void initUI() throws Exception {
    this.getContentPane().setLayout(null);
    _sixFloor.setText("6/F");
    _fifthFloor.setText("5/F");
    _fourthFloor.setText("4/F");
    _thirdFloor.setText("3/F");
    _secondFloor.setText("2/F");
    _firstFloor.setText("1/F");
    _groundFloor.setText("G/F");
    _buttonPanel.setBounds(new Rectangle(10, 20, 57, 262));
    _buttonPanel.setLayout(_buttonLayout);
    _buttonLayout.setColumns(1);
    _buttonLayout.setRows(0);
    _stateLabel.setText("State");
    _currentFloorDisplay.setBackground(Color.blue);
    _currentFloorDisplay.setForeground(Color.red);
    _currentFloorDisplay.setText("");
    _motorDisplay.setBackground(Color.blue);
    _motorDisplay.setForeground(Color.red);
    _motorDisplay.setText("Stop");
    _doorLabel.setText("Door");
    _motorLabel.setText("Motor");
    _stateDisplay.setForeground(Color.red);
    _stateDisplay.setAlignmentY((float) 0.5);
    _stateDisplay.setText("");
    _stateDisplay.setBackground(Color.blue);
    _doorDisplay.setText("Close");
    _doorDisplay.setForeground(Color.red);
    _doorDisplay.setBackground(Color.blue);
    _currentFloorLabel.setText("Current Floor");
    _displayPanel.setDebugGraphicsOptions(0);
    _displayPanel.setBounds(new Rectangle(82, 21, 297, 255));
    _displayPanel.setLayout(_displayLayout);
    _displayLayout.setColumns(2);
    _displayLayout.setHgap(0);
    _displayLayout.setRows(4);
```

```
    this.getContentPane().add(_buttonPanel, null);
    _buttonPanel.add(_sixFloor, null);
    _buttonPanel.add(_fifthFloor, null);
    _buttonPanel.add(_fourthFloor, null);
    _buttonPanel.add(_thirdFloor, null);
    _buttonPanel.add(_secondFloor, null);
    _buttonPanel.add(_firstFloor, null);
    _buttonPanel.add(_groundFloor, null);
    this.getContentPane().add(_displayPanel, null);
    _displayPanel.add(_currentFloorLabel, null);
    _displayPanel.add(_currentFloorDisplay, null);
    _displayPanel.add(_stateLabel, null);
    _displayPanel.add(_stateDisplay, null);
    _displayPanel.add(_motorLabel, null);
    _displayPanel.add(_motorDisplay, null);
    _displayPanel.add(_doorLabel, null);
    _displayPanel.add(_doorDisplay, null);
  }
}
```

```
// FloorFrame.java
import javax.swing.*;
import java.awt.*;
public class FloorFrame extends JFrame {
  JPanel _buttonPanel = new JPanel();
  GridLayout _buttonLayout = new GridLayout();
  JButton _upButton = new JButton();
  JButton _downButton = new JButton();
  JPanel _displayPanel = new JPanel();
  GridLayout _displayLayout = new GridLayout();
  JLabel _floorLabel = new JLabel();
  JLabel _floorDisplay = new JLabel();
  JLabel _doorLabel = new JLabel();
  JLabel _doorDisplay = new JLabel();
  public FloorFrame(int floor) throws HeadlessException {
    super(floor + "/F Floor Panel");
    try {
      InitUI();
    }
    catch(Exception e) {
      e.printStackTrace();
    }
  }
  private void initUI() throws Exception {
    this.getContentPane().setLayout(null);
    _buttonPanel.setBounds(new Rectangle(28, 27, 90, 239));
    _buttonPanel.setLayout(_buttonLayout);
```

```
    _buttonLayout.setColumns(1);
    _buttonLayout.setHgap(0);
    _buttonLayout.setRows(2);
    _upButton.setText("Up");
    _downButton.setText("Down");
    _displayPanel.setBounds(new Rectangle(153, 32, 231, 232));
    _displayPanel.setLayout(_displayLayout);
    _displayLayout.setColumns(2);
    _displayLayout.setRows(2);
    _floorLabel.setText("Floor");
    _doorLabel.setText("Floor Door");
    _doorDisplay.setForeground(Color.red);
    _doorDisplay.setText("Close");
    _floorDisplay.setForeground(Color.red);
    _floorDisplay.setText("");
    this.getContentPane().add(_buttonPanel, null);
    _buttonPanel.add(_upButton, null);
    _buttonPanel.add(_downButton, null);
    this.getContentPane().add(_displayPanel, null);
    _displayPanel.add(_floorLabel, null);
    _displayPanel.add(_floorDisplay, null);
    _displayPanel.add(_doorLabel, null);
    _displayPanel.add(_doorDisplay, null);
  }
  public JLabel getDoorDisplay() {
    return _doorDisplay;
  }
  public JLabel getFloorDisplay() {
    return _floorDisplay;
  }
  public JButton getDownButton() {
    return _downButton;
  }
  public JButton getUpButton() {
    return _upButton;
  }
}
```

References

Arlow, J., & Neustadt, I. (2001). *UML and the Unified Process: Practical object-oriented analysis and design*. Boston, MA: Addison-Wesley.

Armour, F., & Miller, G. (2000). *Advanced use case modeling: Software systems*. New York: Addison-Wesley.

Bellin, D., & Simone, S.S. (1997). *The CRC card book*. Boston, MA: Addison-Wesley.

BergstrÖm, S., & Råberg, L. (2003). *Adopting the Rational Unified Process: Success with the RUP*. Boston, MA: Addison-Wesley.

Bernard, E.V. (1998). *Basic object-oriented concepts*. The Object Agency, Inc. from http://www.toa.com/pub/oobasics/oobasics.htm

Bittner, K., & Spence, I. (2003). *Use case modeling*. Boston, MA: Addison-Wesley.

Booch, G. (1993). *Object-oriented analysis and design with Applications* (2nd edition). Redwood City, CA: Addison-Wesley.

Booch, G., Rumbaugh, J., & Jacobson, I. (1998). *The Unified Modeling Language user guide*. Indianapolis, IN: Addison-Wesley.

Budgen, D. (2003). *Software design* (2nd edition). Harlow, Essex, England: Addison-Wesley.

Buschmann, F., Meunier, R., Rohnert, H., Sommerlad, P., & Stal, M. (1996). *Pattern-oriented software architecture: A system of pattern*. New York: John Wiley & Sons.

Coad, P., & Nicola, J. (1993). *Object-oriented programming*. Upper Saddle River, NJ: Prentice Hall PTR.

Coad, P., North, D., & Mayfield, M. (1996). *Object models: Strategies, patterns, and applications* (2nd edition). New York: Prentice Hall PTR.

Coad, P., & Yourdon, E. (1990). *Object oriented analysis* (2nd edition). Upper Saddle River, NJ: Prentice Hall PTR.

Cockburn, A. (1997). *Humans and technology. Structuring use cases with goals*, from http://alistair.cockburn.us/crystal/articles/sucwg/structuringucswithgoals.htm

Cockburn, A. (2000). *Surviving object-oriented projects: A manager's guide*. Boston, MA: Addison-Wesley.

Cockburn, A. (2000). *Writing effective use cases*. New York: Addison-Wesley.

Cook, S., & Daniels, J.D. (1994). *Designing object systems: Object-oriented modeling with syntropy*. Upper Saddle River, NJ: Prentice Hall.

DeMarco, T., & Lister, T. (1999). *Peopleware: Productive projects and teams* (2nd Edition). New York: Dorset House.

Fowler, M. (1996). *Analysis patterns: Reusable object models*. Upper Saddle River, NJ: Addison-Wesley.

Fowler, M., Beck, K., Brant, J., Opdyke, W., & Roberts, D. (1999). *Refactoring: Improving the design of existing code*. Upper Saddle River, NJ: Addison-Wesley.

Fowler, M., & Scott, K. (1999). *UML distilled: A brief guide to the Standard Object Modeling Language* (2nd edition). Boston, MA: Addison-Wesley.

Gamma, E., Helm, R., Johnson, R., & Vlissides, J. (1995). *Design patterns: Elements of reusable object-oriented software*. Upper Saddle River, NJ: Addison-Wesley.

Hofmeister, C., Nord, R., & Soni, D. (1999). *Applied software architecture*. Upper Saddle River, NJ: Addison-Wesley.

Jacobson, I. (1999). IBM Rational. *Applying UML in the Unified Process, Seminar Slide*. http://www.jeckle.de/flies/uniproc.pdf

Jacobson, I., Booch, G., & Rumbaugh, J. (1999). *The Unified Software Development Process*. Indianapolis, IN: Addison-Wesley.

Jacobson, I., Christerson, M., Jonsson, P., & Overgaard, G. (1992). *Object-oriented software engineering: A use case driven approach*. Reading, MA: Addison-Wesley.

Jacobson, I., Griss, M., & Jonsson, P. (1997). *Software reuse: Architecture, process, and organization for business success*. New York: Addison-Wesley.

Kotonya G., & Sommerville, I. (1998). *Requirements engineering: Processes and techniques*. New York: John Wiley & Sons.

Kroll, P., & Kruchten, P. (2003). *The Rational Unified Process made easy: A practitioner's guide to Rational Unified Process*. Boston, MA: Addison-Wesley.

Krutchten, P. (2000). *The Rational Unified Process: An introduction* (2nd edition). Boston, MA: Addison-Wesley.

Larman, C. (2001). *Applying UML and patterns: An introduction to object-oriented analysis and design and the Unified Process* (2nd edition). Upper Saddle River, NJ: Prentice Hall PTR.

Leffingwell, D., & Widrig, D. (1999). *Managing software requirements: A unified approach*. Upper Saddle River, NJ: Addison-Wesley.

Marshall, C. (1999). *Enterprise modeling with UML: Designing successful software through business analysis*. Reading, MA: Addison-Wesley.

Martin, R.C. (1995). *Designing object oriented C++ applications using the Booch Method*. Upper Saddle River, NJ: Prentice Hall.

Martin, R.C. (2002). *Agile software development, principles, patterns, and practices*. Upper Saddle River, NJ: Prentice Hall.

McConnell, S.C. (1997). *Software project survival guide*. Redmond, WA: Microsoft Press.

Meyer, B. (2000). *Object-oriented software construction* (2nd edition). Upper Saddle River, NJ: Prentice Hall PTR.

Oestereich, B. (2002). *Developing software with UML: Object-oriented analysis and design in practice*. Harlow, Essex, England: Addison-Wesley.

OMG. Unified Modeling Language Specification, Version 1.5 (formal/03-03-01). (2003). http://www.omg.org/cgi-bin/doc?formal/03-03-01

Page-Jones, M. (1999). *Fundamentals of object-oriented design in UML*. Boston, MA: Addison-Wesley.

Pollice, G., Augustine, L., Lowe, C., & Madhur, J. (2003). *Software development for small teams: A RUP-centric approach*. Boston, MA: Addison-Wesley.

Quatrani, T. (1999). *Visual modeling with Rational Rose 2000 and UML*. Upper Saddle River, NJ: Addison-Wesley.

Riel, A.J. (1996). *Object-oriented design heuristics*. Boston, MA: Addison-Wesley.

Rosenberg, D., & Kendall, S. (1999). *Use case driven object modeling with UML: A practical approach*. Boston, MA: Addison-Wesley.

Rumbaugh, J. (1997). *OMT Insights: Perspective on modeling from the Journal of Object-Oriented Programming*. New York: Signature Sounds Recording.

Rumbaugh, J., Blaha, M.R., Lorensen, W., Eddy, F., & Premerlani, W. (1991). *Object-oriented modeling and design*. Upper Saddle River, NJ: Prentice Hall.

Rumbaugh, J., Jacobson, I., & Booch, G. (1998). *The Unified Modeling Language reference manual*. Reading, MA: Addison-Wesley.

Schneider, G., & Winters, J.P. (2001). *Applying use cases: A practical guide* (2nd edition). Upper Saddle River, NJ: Addison-Wesley.

Shlaer, S., & Mellor, S.J. (1988). *Object-oriented systems analysis: Modeling the world in data*. Upper Saddle River, NJ: Pearson Education.

Shlaer, S., & Mellor, S.J. (1992). *Object lifecycles: Modeling the world in state*. Englewood Cliffs, NJ: Pearson Education.

Shlaer, S., & Mellor, S.J. (1997). *Recursive design of an application-independent architecture*. IEEE Software.

Sommerville, I., & Sawyer, P. (1997). *Requirements engineering: A good practice guide*. New York: John Wiley & Sons

Spolsky, J. (2001). *Big Macs vs. The Naked Chef*. http://www.joelonsoftware.com/printerFriendly/articles/fog0000000024.html.2001.

Stevens, P., & Pooley, R.J. (2000). *Using UML: Software engineering with objects and components*. Addison-Wesley.

Tkach, D., Fang, W., & So, A. (1996). *Visual modeling technique: Object technology using Visual Programming*. Menlo Park: Addison-Wesley.

Unhelkar, B. (2002). *Process quality assurance for UML-based projects*. Boston, MA: Addison-Wesley.

Vlissides, J.M., Coplien, J.O., & Kerth, N.L. (1996). *Pattern languages of Program Design 2*. Boston, MA: Addison-Wesley.

Walden, K., & Nerson, J-M. (1995). *Seamless object-oriented software architecture: Analysis and design of reliable systems*. Upper Saddle River, NJ: Prentice Hall.

Warmer, J., & Kleppe, A. (1998). *The Object Constraint Language: Precise modeling with UML*. Reading, MA: Addison-Wesley.

Wirfs-Brock, R., & McKean, A. (2002). *Object design: Roles, responsibilities, and collaborations*. Boston, MA: Addison-Wesley.

Wirfs-Brock, R., Wilkerson, B., & Wiener, L. (1990). *Designing object-oriented software*. Upper Saddle River, NJ: Prentice Hall PTR.

Yourdon, E. (1988). *Modern structured analysis*. Englewood Cliffs, NJ: Prentice Hall PTR.

Index